AFRICA
DEVELOPMENT
INDICATORS
2008/09

YOUTH AND EMPLOYMENT IN AFRICA

The Potential, the Problem, the Promise

THE WORLD BANK

To order *Africa Development Indicators 2008/09*, *The Little Data Book on Africa 2008/09*, the *Africa Development Indicators 2008/09-Multiple User CD-ROM*, please visit *www.worldbank.org/publications*. To subscribe to Africa Development Indicators Online please visit: *http://publications.worldbank.org/ADI*

For more information about *Africa Development Indicators* and its companion products, please visit www.worldbank.org/africa. You can email us at ADI@worldbank.org.

Cover design by Word Express, Inc.

Dohatec New Media prepared the navigation structure and interface design of the Africa Development Indicators 2008/09 CD-ROM.

Photo credits: front cover Jonathan Ernst and back cover Arne Hoel/World Bank.
The map of Africa is provided by The Map Design Unit/World Bank.

ISBN: 978-0-8213-7787-1
e-ISBN: 978-0-8213-7795-6
DOI: 10.1596/978-0-8213-7787-1
SKU: 17787

Contents

Part II. Millennium Developing Goals

3. Millennium Developing Goals

Part III. Development outcomes

4. Paris Declaration indicators

5. Private sector development

6. Trade

7. Infrastructure

8. Human development

9. Agriculture, rural development, and environment

10. Labor, migration, and population

Foreword

For centuries, data have been used as an instrument for decision-making. To choose between two public policy options—whether or not to build a bridge, for example—analysts use data to evaluate the costs and benefits of each option and inform the decision-maker accordingly. More recently, data have taken on a new role: as an instrument for holding policymakers accountable. When data are made publicly available, the public can use data to question policymakers' decisions, and hold them accountable, if not immediately then periodically through the ballot box. The publication of citizen report cards in Bangalore, India; the public expenditure tracking surveys in Uganda; and Transparency International's worldwide corruption indices are but three examples where data have empowered citizens to hold public officers to account.

The Africa Development Indicators (ADI) seeks to fulfill both roles. Originally intended as a tool for aiding decision-making by presenting cross-country comparisons of various data (to discern patterns in African development, as well as exceptions to those patterns), ADI has evolved into a tool for transparency as well. Journalists, researchers, students, Civil Society Organizations and other citizens use the comparative data in ADI to ask questions such as: why their country is not performing as well in some dimensions as other, comparable countries; or alternatively, why their country is in fact doing so well but getting very little credit for it.

To effectively serve as a tool for transparency, any data set must meet certain criteria. First, it must be accurate. All data in the ADI are rigorously checked and cross-checked; only those data that pass various statistical tests make it in the document. Second, the data must be accessible to the public. This is why ADI is disseminated worldwide; the new, improved on-line version permits easy access and manipulation of the data to suit individual needs and tastes. Third, the data must be salient—it must be about issues that people care about. This year's version includes new datasets on climate change, conflict, and governance, among others.

Following a two-year-old tradition, the ADI also has an essay: "Youth and Employment in Africa—The Potential, the Problem, the Promise." The choice of this topic is obvious. Finding productive employment for the 200 million Africans between the ages of 15 and 24 is surely one of the continent's greatest challenges. What the essay shows, however, is that the median young person in Africa is a poor, out-of-school female living in a rural area. This finding—based on a careful examination of the data—has important implications for policy design, as well as for the politics of youth-sensitive policies. Once again, data can play the dual role of informing policy choices and empowering citizens to hold politicians accountable.

Obiageli K. Ezekwesili
Vice President, Africa Region

Acknowledgments

Africa Development Indicators (ADI) is a product of the Africa Region of the World Bank.

Jorge Saba Arbache was the manager of this book and its companions—Africa Development Indicators Online 2008/09, Africa Development Indicators 2008/09—Multiple User CD-ROM, and Little Data Book on Africa 2008/09. Rose Mungai led the work on data gathering, consistency checks and compilation. The core team included Mpho Chinyolo, Francoise Genouille, Jane K. Njuguna, and Christophe Rockmore. The overall work was carried out under the guidance and supervision of Shantayanan Devarajan, Chief Economist of the Africa Region.

Pablo Suarez Robles provided research assistance, and Harold Alderman, Mayra Buvinic, Louise Fox, Caterina R. Laderchi, and Paul Moreno-Lopez provided useful comments on an earlier draft of the essay.

Azita Amjadi, Abdolreza Farivari, Richard Fix, Shelley Lai Fu, Shahin Outadi, William Prince, Atsushi Shimo and Malarvizhi Veerappan collaborated in the data production. Maja Bresslauer, Mahyar Eshragh-Tabary, Victor Gabor and Soong Sup Lee collaborated in the update of the Live Data Base. Mehdi Akhlaghi collaborated in the production of the Little Data Book on Africa 2008/09.

The boxes in the book and in the technical notes benefited from contributions from Aziz Bouzaher (climate change), Sebastien Dessus (PPP), John May (demographic transition), Gary Milante (conflicts), Deepak Mishra and Mesfin Girma Bezawagaw (inflation), Pierella Paci and Catalina Gutierrez (unemployment), David Wilson and Elizabeth Lule (HIV prevalence and incidence), Quentin Wodon (food prices, role of faith-inspired organizations, and poverty and migration), and Ali Zafar (franc zone).

Aziz Bouzaher provided guidance for the table on climate change, and Gary Milante for the tables on conflicts and polity.

Ann Karasanyi and Ken Omondi provided administrative and logistical support. Delfin Go and Yutaka Yoshino provided general comments and suggestions.

Several institutions provided data to ADI. Their contribution is very much appreciated.

The Word Express, Inc. provided design direction, editing, and layout. Dohatec New Media prepared the navigation structure and interface design of the Africa Development Indicators 2008/09 CD-ROM.

Staff from External Affairs, including Herbert Boh, Richard Crabbe, Lillian Foo, Gozde Isik, Valentina Kalk, and Malika Khek oversaw publication and dissemination of the book and its companions.

Youth and Employment in Africa – The Potential, the Problem, the Promise

Introduction

Today's world population counts an estimated 1.2 billion people at the ages of 15 to 24 years, an increase of 17% compared to 1995, or 18% of the world population. About 87% of these young people live in countries with developing economies. In Africa, 200 million people are in this age range, comprising more than 20% of the population (United Nations 2007). In 2005, 62% of Africa's overall population fell below the age of 25. The still very high fertility rate along with a demographic transition that is slowly taking place in the region are likely to increase the pressure African countries face for job creation over the coming decades.[1]

Worldwide, and in Africa as well, the ratio of the youth-to-adult unemployment rate equals three (ILO 2006), which clearly points out the substantial difficulties of youth participation in the labor market. Yet, the youth employment elasticity to GDP growth is low and only a fifth of that observed for all workers (Kapsos 2005). As a consequence, youth made up 43.7% of the total unemployed people in the world despite accounting for only 25% of the working population. More than one third of the youth in the world is either seeking but unable to find work, has given up on the job search entirely, or is working but still living below the $2 a day poverty line. In Sub-Saharan Africa, 3 in 5 of the total unemployed are youth (ILO 2006) and on average 72% of the youth population live with less than $2 a day (Table 1).

Young people in Africa are not a homogeneous group and their employment prospects vary according to region, gender, age, educational level, ethnicity, and health status, thus requiring different sets of policy interventions. However, the typical African youth, as given by medians, is easily identifiable: she is an 18.5-year-old female, living in

Table 1	Incidence of poverty among young people (in %) in Sub-Saharan Africa
Country	**Less than US$ 2 per day**
Burundi, 1998	85.7
Côte d'Ivoire, 1998	46.5
Cameroun, 2001	49.1
Ethiopia, 2000	70.7
Ghana, 1998	66.5
Kenya, 1997	54.4
Madagascar, 2001	81.7
Mozambique, 1996	75.4
Malawi, 1997	66.3
Nigeria, 1996	92.9
Sierra Leone, 2003	68.0
Uganda, 1999	93.8
Zambia, 1998	86.3
SSA-13 (mean)	72.1
SSA-13 (median)	70.7

Source: World Bank Survey-Based Harmonized Indicators Program (SHIP).
Note: A person is considered poor if per capita total annual household expenditure divided by 365 falls below the poverty line. The "$2-a-day" poverty line – $2.17 per day in purchasing power parity (PPP) at 1993 prices – is defined as 2.17 times the product of the 1993 consumption PPP exchange rate and the ratio of the average consumer price index for the year of the survey to the average consumer price index for 1993. CPIs and PPP exchange rates were respectively taken from World Development Indicators 2007 and PovCalNet (World Bank).

a rural area, and literate but not attending school (Table 2).[2]

As a way to escape poverty, many youth look for better opportunities by migrating. Indeed, migration to urban areas is unavoidable and even desirable as a way to improve allocation of human resources, especially in land-scarce countries. While youth are more likely than older people to move from rural to urban areas or to move across urban areas,

---

[1] The definition of youth is age 15 to 24 years, and adults 25–64.
[2] Higher death rate of males due to homicides, war-related conflicts, diseases and other causes help explain this pattern.

Table 2	Typical African youth – median								
Country	**Location**		**Sex**		**Age**	**Literate**		**Attending school**	
SHIP data									
Burundi, 1998	Rural	93.9%	Female	54.9%	18	Yes	71.4%	No	25.6%
Côte d'Ivoire, 1998	Urban	46.8%	Female	51.9%	19	Yes	60.7%	No	27.6%
Cameroun, 2001	Rural	56.4%	Female	52.5%	19	Yes	82.4%	No	46.2%
Ghana, 1998	Rural	57.8%	Male	49.7%	18	Yes	65.9%	No	41.3%
Guinea, 1994	Rural	57.2%	Female	50.6%	19	No	30.6%	No	18.4%
Kenya, 1997	Rural	81.0%	Female	51.9%	19	Yes	93.5%	No	42.0%
Mozambique, 1996	Rural	76.9%	Female	52.3%	19	Yes	51.1%	No	19.2%
Mauritania, 2000	Rural	55.5%	Female	52.9%	18	Yes	70.2%	No	27.6%
Malawi, 1997	Rural	87.4%	Female	52.7%	19	Yes	62.9%	No	40.1%
Nigeria, 1996	Rural	56.4%	Female	53.8%	18	Yes	74.3%	No	46.7%
Sierra Leone, 2003	Rural	51.9%	Female	52.4%	18	No	43.2%	No	42.8%
São Tomé and Principe, 2000	Urban	40.9%	Male	49.9%	19	Yes	94.1%	No	25.0%
Uganda, 1999	Rural	82.8%	Female	51.3%	18	Yes	79.0%	No	43.7%
Zambia, 1998	Rural	59.8%	Female	52.8%	19	—	—	No	30.2%
SSA-14 (mean)	—	64.6%	—	52.1%		—	67.6%	—	34.0%
SSA-14 (median)	—	57.5%	—	52.4%		—	70.2%		35.1%
LFS data									
Ethiopia, 2005	Rural	79.6%	Female	53.2%	19	No	49.9%	—	—
Madagascar, 2005	Rural	76.0%	Female	51.7%	19	Yes	75.2%	No	23.0%
Tanzania, 2005	Rural	70.5%	Female	53.1%	19	Yes	83.0%	No	28.7%

Source: World Bank Survey-Based Harmonized Indicators Program (SHIP), Ethiopia LFS 2005, Tanzania ILFS 2005/06 and Madagascar EPM 2005.
Note: — Not available.

this increased youth migration has a wide impact. It increases the strain for jobs without necessarily improving the job conditions of those who are left in rural areas; impacts provision of public goods, education, utilities, housing, and infrastructure; and affects demographic and skills composition in both urban and rural areas. Given that about 70% of the African youth population is still in rural areas, and that urban areas have been very slow to create job opportunities for most new job seekers, there is a need for an integrated, coherent approach in which policies appropriate for the youth in urban areas are closely connected with policies appropriate for the youth in rural areas. This type of approach is essential if governments want to smooth the deleterious impacts of rapid migration while preparing the rural youth for a more rewarding mobility.

While in some countries demographic change is the main factor behind high youth unemployment and underemployment rates, much of the youth employment challenges can also be related to labor market dynamics and labor market opportunities. How easily and how effectively young people find jobs is also dependent on how well the labor market is prepared to receive them, and on how well they are prepared for the labor market.

A large group of young people enter the labor market very early, which affects their progress in the labor market. In the short term, poor families gain from child labor; thus, there are short-term welfare losses for rural families from sanctions on child labor.[3] For long-term development, however, child labor elicits a cost in terms of foregone education and persistence of long- term poverty.

Post-conflict settings pose specific challenges for the youth (e.g., recently disarmed idle men and displaced young men) as these settings have prominently young populations, many of whom have been deprived of education, have grown up in violent societ-

---

[3] Participation rate of children 5–14 years old is about 30% in Sub-Saharan Africa (World Bank 2008).

ies, and often have been combatants themselves. Employment and the creation of jobs for young people should therefore form a key component of any peace building processes.

The energy, skills and aspirations of young people are invaluable assets that no country can afford to squander, and helping them to realize their full potential by gaining access to employment is a precondition for poverty eradication, sustainable development, and lasting peace. Given the immense challenges youth face to get a job, youth employment has obtained growing prominence on development agendas after having been largely neglected in national development strategies in the past.

The youth employment challenge confronts all countries in Africa, regardless of their stage of socio-economic development, but the socio-economic context has an important contribution on the nature and extent of the problem. As they consider measures to help young people make the transition into the labor market and obtain work, policymakers are hampered by a lack of information on what their options are, what works in different situations, and what has been tried and failed.

This essay examines these issues. The first part presents stylized facts of youth and labor markets in Africa. The second part discusses past youth employment interventions in the region. It argues for the need of an integrated approach should governments want to tackle youth employment issues in a sustainable manner. Indeed, in African countries, with large informal sectors and dominance of rural population, solely reforming labor market institutions and implementing active labor market policies are likely to have limited impact. It argues that the most needed and well-rounded approaches are: expanding job and education alternatives in the rural areas – where most youth live; promoting and encouraging mobility; creating a conducive business environment; encouraging the private sector; improving the access and quality of skills formation; taking care of demographic issues that more directly affects the youth; and reducing child labor.

Stylized facts about youth and labor markets in Africa

In 2005, the labor force participation rate of young males was 73.7% (ILO 2006), one of the highest in the world (ILO 2006, United Nations 2007).

Youth make up 36.9% of the working-age population, but 59.5% of the total unemployed, which is much higher than the world's average for 2005 (43.7%), reflecting serious labor demand deficiencies in the region (ILO 2006). The share of unemployed youth among the total unemployed can be as high as 83% in Uganda, 68% in Zimbabwe, and 56% in Burkina.[4]

Unemployment among youth is often higher than among adults (Table 3).

Youth unemployment is more prevalent in urban areas (Table 4) and is higher among those with higher education attainment and those in wealthy households. On average, unemployment among those with secondary education or above is three times higher than among those with no education attainment, and unemployment is twice as high among youth from households in the fifth (or highest) income quintile as compared to those in the first income quintile (Figure 1).[5]

Youth are more likely than adults to be in the informal sector, and less likely to be wage employed or self-employed. In 2005 in Ethiopia, respectively 81.4% and 12.5% of youth

Table 3	Distribution of youth and adults by job status (in %)					
	Employed		Unemployed		Out of the labor force	
	Youth	Adults	Youth	Adults	Youth	Adults
SHIP data						
Burundi, 1998	70.4	95.8	0.3	0.4	29.3	3.8
Côte d'Ivoire, 1998	51.4	81.8	3.0	2.9	45.6	15.3
Cameroun, 2001	42.7	80.9	7.2	4.7	50.1	14.4
Ghana, 1998	17.7	78.4	31.3	8.7	51.0	12.9
Guinea, 1994	69.9	87.8	8.3	5.3	21.8	6.9
Kenya, 1997	20.8	58.2	3.7	1.1	75.5	40.7
Mozambique, 1996	22.0	59.5	2.2	1.4	75.8	39.1
Mauritania, 2000	28.4	50.4	3.1	3.4	68.6	46.2
Malawi, 1997	20.3	58.8	1.3	1.5	78.4	39.7
Nigeria, 1996	23.1	76.7	5.5	1.2	71.4	22.1
Sierra Leone, 2003	40.4	85.4	52.5	10.2	7.1	4.4
São Tomé and Principe, 2000	32.8	68.1	4.1	0.8	63.1	31.1
Uganda, 1999	17.9	66.0	0.7	0.6	81.4	33.4
Zambia, 1998	38.7	77.7	6.7	4.2	54.6	18.1
SSA-14 (mean)	35.5	73.3	9.3	3.3	55.3	23.4
SSA-14 (median)	30.6	77.2	3.9	2.2	58.9	20.1
LFS data						
Ethiopia, 2005	72.8	86.5	2.9	1.9	24.3	11.6
Madagascar, 2005	71.7	93.3	1.7	2.6	26.6	4.1
Tanzania, 2005	74.4	93.5	4.9	1.9	20.7	4.6

Source: World Bank Survey-Based Harmonized Indicators Program (SHIP)), Ethiopia LFS 2005, Madagascar EPM 2005 and Tanzania ILFS 2005/06.

---

[4] Unemployment as defined by ILO is increasingly seen as inadequate to characterize low income countries' labor markets (Cling et al. 2006; Fares et al. 2006; World Bank 2006, inter alia). Youth unemployment does not provide a full and adequate description of the difficulties youth face in the labor market. In fact, in countries with widespread poverty, looking at the unemployment rate may be misleading because most youth cannot afford to be unemployed. The difficulties in the labor market may be better reflected by measures of quality of employment or measures of underemployment. As an illustration, youth unemployment was only 0.8% in Malawi, 2.1% in Burkina, and 0.7% in Rwanda (United Nations 2007). Therefore, unemployment should not be the main component of a youth employment strategy or the main results performance indicator of labor markets in Africa.

[5] Distinguishing between who is rural and urban is increasingly difficult, especially with the expansion of semi-urban areas where large proportions of populations rely on agricultural activities to meet their livelihood needs.

Table 4	Distribution of urban and rural youth by job status (in %)					
	Employed		Unemployed		Out of the labor force	
	Urban	Rural	Urban	Rural	Urban	Rural
SHIP data						
Burundi, 1998	14.9	74.0	5.2	0.0	79.9	26.0
Côte d'Ivoire, 1998	31.5	73.6	5.1	0.6	63.4	25.9
Cameroun, 2001	25.9	55.6	12.5	3.1	61.6	41.3
Ghana, 1998	16.2	18.7	36.7	27.4	47.1	53.9
Guinea, 1994	40.0	92.2	16.2	2.4	43.8	5.4
Kenya, 1997	36.2	17.2	8.4	2.6	55.4	80.2
Mozambique, 1996	20.9	22.4	3.5	1.7	75.6	75.9
Mauritania, 2000	17.6	37.0	5.4	1.2	77.0	61.8
Malawi, 1997	14.5	21.2	2.6	1.1	82.9	77.7
Nigeria, 1996	22.9	23.3	6.4	4.8	70.7	71.9
Sierra Leone, 2003	22.9	56.6	67.9	38.2	9.2	5.2
São Tomé and Principe, 2000	30.5	36.3	3.2	5.4	66.4	58.3
Uganda, 1999	25.6	16.3	2.3	0.4	72.1	83.3
Zambia, 1998	16.6	53.6	11.9	3.2	71.5	43.2
SSA-14 (mean)	24.0	42.7	13.4	6.6	62.6	50.7
SSA-14 (median)	22.9	36.7	5.9	2.5	68.6	56.1
LFS data						
Ethiopia, 2005	40.7	81.1	10.0	1.0	49.3	17.9
Madagascar, 2005	50.5	78.4	4.6	0.7	44.9	20.9
Tanzania, 2005	56.0	82.1	13.4	1.3	30.6	16.6

Source: World Bank Survey-Based Harmonized Indicators Program (SHIP), Ethiopia LFS 2005, Madagascar EPM 2005 and Tanzania ILFS 2005/06.

low productivity and meager earnings. Underemployment is more prevalent among youth than adults, and is more prevalent in rural rather than urban areas (Figures 2 and 3).[6]

Youth are employed primarily in agriculture (Figure 4), in which they account for 65% of total employment (ILO 2007).

In rural areas the youth work longer hours and spend a lot of their time in household work. In rural Ethiopia they work 43 hours a week in contrast to the 31 hours worked in urban areas. Of those 43 hours worked, the rural youth spends 31 hours in household work (fetching water, collecting fire wood, and other domestic activities), in contrast to the 22 spent on these tasks in urban areas.

Rural youth attached to agriculture are disadvantaged in terms of employment status as compared to those engaged in nonfarm activities (Table 5).

Sub-Saharan Africa has the lowest primary education completion rate of any region (60% compared to 91% in MENA, 98% in EAP, 99% in LAC, and 86% in all regions in 2005). More than a third of the youth popu-

were in the informal and self-employment sectors, against 43% and 49.6% of adults.

Young people are more likely to work longer hours under intermittent and insecure work arrangements, characterized by

[6] Underemployment rate refers to total underemployed expressed as a proportion of total employed. A person is classified as underemployed if the total number of hours worked during the week is less than 30. As regards Ethiopia and Tanzania, a person is classified as underemployed if in addition he or she is available for more work. This information is not available for the other countries.

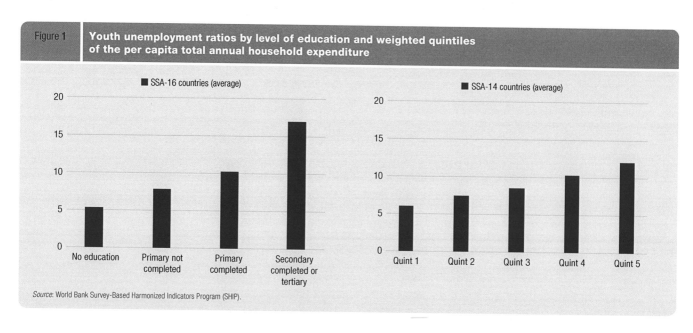

| Figure 1 | Youth unemployment ratios by level of education and weighted quintiles of the per capita total annual household expenditure |

Source: World Bank Survey-Based Harmonized Indicators Program (SHIP).

lation in the region was still illiterate in 2002 (ILO 2006).

Urban youth enjoy greater educational opportunities, stay longer in school and join the labor force later than rural youth. In Burundi 57% of urban youth are in school in contrast to 23% in rural areas; in Cameroon 48% and 24%; in Mozambique 30% and 15% (Garcia and Fares 2008).

Young women are more likely to be underemployed, and more likely to be out of the labor force (Tables 6 and 7).

Women work more hours than males and are more likely to engage in non market activities. In Ethiopia they work 48 hours a week versus 32 for males. Of those hours they spend 36 in household activities in contrast to the 15 males work in these tasks (Ethiopia LFS 2005).

Young women have lower levels of school attainment and school enrollment. In Sierra Leone (2003) 53% of young men and 33% of young women were attending school while in Uganda (1999), the figures were 53% and 35%, respectively (SHIP data). In 2005, the male and female net school enrollment ratios in Africa were 71% and 65% in primary education and 28% and 23% in secondary education, respectively. The male gross school enrollment ratio in tertiary education was 6%, while that of women was 4%.

Africa's youth follow two paths in their transitions to working life: many go to work directly, with little benefit of formal schooling, while others join the work force after a time in the formal school system. The estimated school life expectancy ranges from 2.9 years for Niger (2002) and 4.4 for DRC (1999), to 11.7 for Mauritius (2002) and 12.4 for South Africa (2001).[7] With a few exceptions, the estimated school life expectancy is higher for males.

Those who enter the labor market directly are unprepared, making them more vulnerable to demographic and demand changes. Thus, they are more likely to be stuck in low productivity jobs.

Children and young people start to work early—a quarter of children ages 5–14 are working, and among children ages 10–14, 31% are estimated to be working. In Burundi this number reaches 50% (Garcia and Fares, 2008).

Many youth move from rural to urban areas in search of greater opportunities.

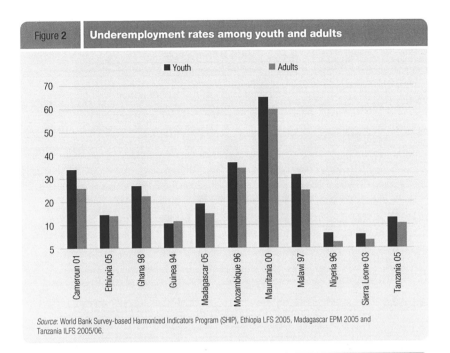

| Figure 2 | Underemployment rates among youth and adults |

Source: World Bank Survey-based Harmonized Indicators Program (SHIP), Ethiopia LFS 2005, Madagascar EPM 2005 and Tanzania ILFS 2005/06.

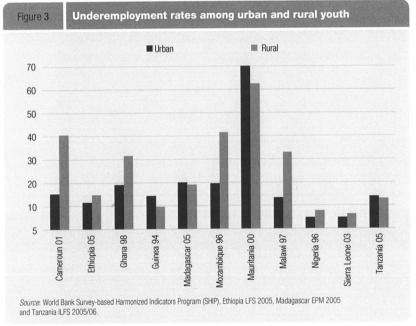

| Figure 3 | Underemployment rates among urban and rural youth |

Source: World Bank Survey-based Harmonized Indicators Program (SHIP), Ethiopia LFS 2005, Madagascar EPM 2005 and Tanzania ILFS 2005/06.

In Ethiopia, 53% of the rural-to-urban migrants are youth, and the main reasons that push them to migrate are access to education (57%) and search for work (22%) (Ethiopia LFS 2005).

---

[7] Definition of School Life Expectancy from UNESCO: "Number of years a child is expected to remain at school, or university, including years spent on repetition. It is the sum of the age-specific enrolment ratios for primary, secondary, post-secondary non-tertiary and tertiary education." (Source: UNESCO Institute for Statistics Database).

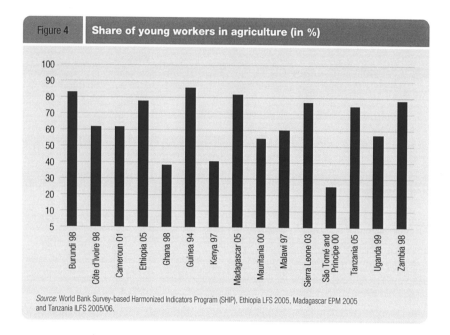

Figure 4 — Share of young workers in agriculture (in %)

Source: World Bank Survey-based Harmonized Indicators Program (SHIP), Ethiopia LFS 2005, Madagascar EPM 2005 and Tanzania ILFS 2005/06.

Table 5 — Distribution of rural young workers in the agricultural and non-agricultural sectors by employment status (in %)

	Wage employment		Self-employment		Unpaid family workers	
	Agric.	Non-agric.	Agric.	Non-agric.	Agric.	Non-agric.
Ethiopia, 2005	2.2	20.2	14.8	45.1	83.0	34.7
Madagascar, 2005	3.6	37.7	10.0	22.7	86.4	39.6
Tanzania, 2005	1.5	19.6	82.5	42.1	16.0	38.3

Source: Ethiopia LFS 2005, Madagascar EPM 2005 and Tanzania ILFS 2005/06.

Table 6 — Underemployment rates among young men and women (in %)

	Men	Women
SHIP data		
Cameroun, 2001	26.3	40.7
Ghana, 1998	22.2	30.0
Guinea, 1994	4.4	16.3
Mozambique, 1996	33.6	42.0
Mauritania, 2000	63.1	66.9
Malawi, 1997	26.5	36.7
Nigeria, 1996	6.1	6.7
Sierra Leone, 2003	2.9	7.4
SSA-8 (mean)	23.1	30.8
SSA-8 (median)	24.3	33.4
LFS data		
Ethiopia, 2005	12.0	16.4
Madagascar, 2005	15.1	23.2
Tanzania, 2005	13.5	12.4

Source: World Bank Survey-Based Harmonized Indicators Program (SHIP), Ethiopia LFS 2005, Madagascar EPM 2005 and Tanzania ILFS 2005/06.
Source: World Bank Survey-Based Harmonized Indicators Program (SHIP).

Young male migrants are more likely to be unemployed and out of the labor force than their non-migrant counterparts (Garcia and Fares 2008).

Urban residents are less likely to be employed than recent rural-to-urban youth migrants. However, recent migrants who are employed are more likely to work in insecure jobs. In Ethiopia they are three times more likely to be engaged in informal activities.

Recent youth rural migrants are more educated than rural residents, but less educated than native urban residents, thus suggesting self-selection. In Ethiopia, 74.9% of recent young migrants were illiterate or had only primary education, compared to 57% of native youth urban residents, and 97.7% of rural youth residents (Ethiopia LFS 2005).

In 1999–2003 the youth employment elasticity of GDP growth in Sub-Saharan Africa was 0.62, down from 0.90 in 1995–1999 (Kapsos 2005).

Before the age of 24, most female youth have already been married, but in many countries they get married even earlier: In Mozambique, 47% of females were already married before the age of 19; in Chad 49%; in Guinea, 46%; in Mali, 50%; in Sierra Leone, 46%; in Niger, 62% (United Nations 2007). In rural areas, the median age of first marriage for women is as low as 15.2 in Niger (1998), 15.8 in Chad (1997), 16.1 in Guinea (1999), 16.3 in Mali (2001), and 16.7 in Ethiopia (2000) and Senegal (1997).[8]

Motherhood starts very early. In 2003 in Mozambique, 58% of females in the range of 15–24 had already given birth at least once, and 18% of males at this age were parents. These figures are respectively 57% and 17% in Malawi (2004), 57% and 7% in Niger (2006), 53% and 10% in Chad (2004), 47% and 15% in Uganda (2006), and 47% and 17% in Gabon (2000). The median age at first birth is 17.9 in Niger (1998), 18.2 in Chad (1997), 18.6 in Guinea (1999), and 18.7 in Gabon (2000), Mali (2001) and Mozambique (1997).[9]

---

[8] For the cohort of women age 25–29 at the time of the survey. (Source: ORC Macro, 2004. Measure DHS STATcompiler).

[9] For the cohort of women age 25–29 at the time of the survey. (Source: ORC Macro, 2004. Measure DHS STATcompiler).

Young women who have given birth have substantially lower education attainment than those who have not given birth (Table 9).

These stylized facts suggest that the youth at large comprise a vulnerable group facing challenges in labor markets, but also indicate that youth attached to agriculture and female youth face particularly stronger challenges.

Table 7	Distribution of young men and women by job status (in %)					
	Employed		**Unemployed**		**Out of the labor force**	
	Men	Women	Men	Women	Men	Women
SHIP data						
Burundi, 1998	67.4	72.8	0.4	0.3	32.2	26.9
Côte d'Ivoire, 1998	53.4	49.4	3.0	3.0	43.6	47.6
Cameroun, 2001	43.6	41.8	8.5	6.0	47.9	52.2
Ghana, 1998	15.7	19.7	29.0	33.7	55.3	46.6
Guinea, 1994	66.3	73.4	6.6	9.9	27.1	16.7
Kenya, 1997	23.5	18.3	4.6	2.8	71.9	78.9
Mozambique, 1996	28.6	16.0	3.7	0.7	67.7	83.2
Mauritania, 2000	36.4	21.2	4.1	2.2	59.5	76.6
Malawi, 1997	21.9	18.9	2.0	0.8	76.1	80.3
Nigeria, 1996	27.1	19.6	7.9	3.4	65.0	77.0
Sierra Leone, 2003	31.5	48.5	60.6	45.2	7.9	6.3
São Tomé and Principe, 2000	47.4	18.2	5.3	2.8	47.3	78.9
Uganda, 1999	22.1	13.9	1.0	0.5	76.9	85.6
Zambia, 1998	38.1	39.3	8.1	5.5	53.8	55.3
SSA-14 (mean)	37.4	33.6	10.3	8.3	52.3	58.0
SSA-14 (median)	34.0	20.5	5.0	2.9	54.6	66.0
LFS data						
Ethiopia, 2005	78.7	67.7	2.2	3.4	19.1	28.9
Madagascar, 2005	72.3	71.1	1.3	2.0	26.4	26.9
Tanzania, 2005	74.9	74.0	4.1	5.5	21.0	20.5

Source: World Bank Survey-Based Harmonized Indicators Program (SHIP), Ethiopia LFS 2005, Madagascar EPM 2005 and Tanzania ILFS 2005/06.

Table 8	School enrollment ratios, 2005	
School enrollment, primary		
Male (% gross)		99
Female (% gross)		87
Male (% net)		71
Female (% net)		65
School enrollment, secondary		
Male (% gross)		35
Female (% gross)		28
Male (% net)		28
Female (% net)		23
School enrollment, tertiary		
Male (% gross)		6
Female (% gross)		4

Source: WDI 2007.
Note: Gross enrollment ratio is the ratio of total enrollment, regardless of age, to the population of the age group that officially corresponds to the level of education shown. Net enrollment ratio is the ratio of children of official school age based on the International Standard Classification of education 1997 who are enrolled in school to the population of the corresponding official school age.

Table 9	Distribution of young women who have given birth or not by highest education level attended (in %)							
	No education		Primary		Secondary		Higher	
	Have given birth	Have not given birth	Have given birth	Have not given birth	Have given birth	Have not given birth	Have given birth	Have not given birth
Benin, 2006	69.2	32.7	20.6	26.0	9.9	39.3	0.3	2.0
Burkina Faso, 2003	82.4	60.9	12.7	19.0	4.8	19.3	0.0	0.8
Cameroun, 2004	24.5	9.4	43.0	32.4	32.2	55.5	0.3	2.7
Chad, 2004	71.8	58.9	21.4	26.3	6.6	14.4	0.2	0.4
Ethiopia, 2005	73.6	36.1	20.4	41.5	5.6	20.7	0.3	1.7
Gabon, 2000	5.6	3.4	37.4	29.7	56.0	64.4	1.0	2.5
Ghana, 2003	26.7	10.9	27.6	19.4	45.3	66.3	0.4	3.4
Guinea, 2005	79.4	47.4	12.3	23.9	8.0	28.3	0.2	0.4
Kenya, 2003	10.3	4.7	70.2	60.8	18.3	29.5	1.2	5.0
Lesotho, 2004	1.4	0.3	62.2	53.1	36.1	45.9	0.3	0.7
Madagascar, 2004	28.1	13.9	54.5	42.8	17.0	40.7	0.3	2.7
Malawi, 2004	12.5	4.0	70.8	66.2	16.5	28.7	0.1	1.1
Mali, 2006	79.9	55.0	12.3	17.1	7.6	26.8	0.2	1.1
Mozambique, 2003	38.1	19.7	56.4	60.3	5.4	19.7	0.1	0.4
Namibia, 2000	9.2	2.9	28.4	31.2	61.7	65.3	0.7	0.6
Niger, 2006	86.9	65.3	10.1	17.1	3.0	17.2	0.0	0.5
Nigeria, 2003	53.7	17.5	21.0	18.6	24.0	57.9	1.3	6.0
Rwanda, 2005	24.4	9.2	69.9	80.9	5.4	9.5	0.3	0.4
Senegal, 2005	70.4	42.4	24.1	33.3	5.3	23.4	0.2	0.9
Swaziland, 2006	6.4	1.7	35.1	32.2	56.6	63.3	1.9	2.8
Tanzania, 2004	27.5	16.7	68.2	66.8	3.8	15.3	0.5	1.2
Uganda, 2006	12.1	2.9	68.0	58.9	18.0	33.2	1.9	5.0
Zambia, 2002	12.8	6.4	61.1	50.4	25.0	41.2	1.1	2.0
23-SSA (average)	**39.4**	**22.7**	**39.5**	**39.5**	**20.5**	**35.9**	**0.6**	**1.9**
23-SSA (median)	**27.5**	**13.9**	**35.1**	**32.4**	**16.5**	**29.5**	**0.3**	**1.2**

Source: Demographic and Health Surveys.

Note: Young women who have already given birth at least once are those young women for whom the total number of children ever born (including children who have died) is at least equal to one.

Policy response requires an integrated, multi-sector approach and close monitoring

Given the challenges faced by the youth in labor markets in Africa, as suggested by the stylized facts, assuring that young people can achieve success in pursuing employment may require long term, concerted actions, that span a wide range of policies and programs. Indeed, success will not be achieved and sustained through fragmented and isolated interventions. Policy response will require working with households and communities across multiple sectors in both rural and urban areas, and creating policies that will evolve over extended and varied time periods. An over- arching, but most essential guideline for addressing the youth employment challenge is the need for an integrated strategy for rural development, growth and job creation. This type of integrated policy would cover both the demand and the supply sides of the labor market and take into account the youth mobility from rural to urban areas. It should, then, be combined with targeted interventions to help young people overcome disadvantages in entering and remaining in the labor market.

Targeted, but coherent interventions should address the gender and age specific challenges of young people; the aspirations of youth which do not match the realities in the labor market; the lack of job experience which makes them less attractive to employers; the difficult access to and low quality of education and training, especially in rural areas; the lack of organization and voice to ensure their needs are addressed in policies and programs; the demographic bulge and migration from rural to urban areas; early motherhood; and the difficult access to the means needed for the youth to engage productively in the economy. These challenges are amplified by conflicts and by discrimination based on sex, ethnicity, race, religious, cultural, health, or family status, which also require decisive action.

Past interventions to support young workers in Sub-Saharan Africa: What do we know?

The World Bank has compiled a world-wide inventory of interventions designed to integrate young people into the labor market (Puerto 2007, Rother 2006). Eleven out of the 29 programs in Sub-Saharan Africa covered in the inventory have a comprehensive, multiple service approach. In most cases, these programs depend almost entirely on external funding from international donor institutions, bilaterals and their national implementation agencies. Such programs included elements targeted at helping young people to start their own businesses, combined with elements of skills development and training. Seven programs focused exclusively at improving chances for young entrepreneurs. They typically encompassed modules such as supporting young people in starting their own business, including providing training on writing project proposals and business plans; conducting feasibility studies; counseling on legal requirements; and improving their access to credit/start-up loans. An example of this category of programs is the *Youth Dairy Farm Project in Uganda,* which supports youth by training them in the management of husbandry and farm products, which the youth then sell. Six programs focused mainly on skills training for young people and four programs adopted the objective of making existing training systems work better for young people. The latter intended to improve highly fragmented, input-orientated training systems by upgrading training facilities; improving the quality of training centers; enhancing the quality of instruction; and upgrading the matching processes between labor demand and supply through better coordination and information systems. Finally, one program was categorized as making the labor market better for young people: The public works program in South Africa covers infrastructure projects, the environmental sector, and the social sector, and seeks to increase the labor intensity of government-funded programs and to create work opportunities in public environmental programs.

Interventions in the poorest countries have generally focused mainly on young entrepreneurs and followed a scheme of multiservice programs. This contrasts with the situation of middle-income countries such as South Africa and Namibia, where multiservice comprehensive approaches were used predominantly to integrate unemployed youth into the labor force, mainly through the provision of skills training programs.

Young workers were the primary focus of most employment interventions included in the inventory. Twenty-two out of the 29 programs (76%) targeted young workers exclusively, while seven programs were open to unemployed workers of all age groups. Most of the programs targeting youth workers aimed at improving employment prospects for young entrepreneurs, skills training, or implementing the multiple service approach. Eight programs focused on urban areas, six on rural areas, and fifteen on both areas.

Eleven out of the 29 programs were directed towards young women, and three programs targeted young workers with disabilities. Moreover, 12 programs were aimed at young people with low-income, and 17 at youths with low levels of formal education. By contrast, ethnicity did not appear to be a selection criterion. In general, significant complementarities can be observed in programs targets. For example, the majority of programs that target low-income youth also target youth with low-levels of education. A similar trend is observable for programs targeting women or disabled youth, which focus at the same time on young people from low-income families with no or only low levels of education.

However, evaluations of the impact of the programs—an invaluable element for guiding policy—have been very low in Sub-Saharan Africa, and lower than in any other developing region. This can be explained partially by the low number of youth employment programs in the region, poor data availability, and the fact that evaluations rarely tracked post-program outcomes.

In general, programs in Sub-Saharan Africa included in the inventory were not evaluated appropriately. For example, while 11 programs included information on gross labor market outcomes, 16 programs lacked any information on results or the level of evaluation was unknown. Only two had enough information to suggest a positive impact. In the case of 10 programs—including three entrepreneurship programs, three skills training programs, one "making training systems work better for young people" program, one public works program, and two multiple service programs—a tentative assessment based on limited available information would suggest a positive impact on labor market outcomes. However, it is not clear whether the benefits exceeded the costs associated with the programs' implementation in all cases.

Two programs (PCY Uganda and the Swiss-South African Co-operation Initiative) that have a comprehensive, multiple service approach, for which an impact analysis was conducted, were awarded the highest rankings for the quality of their intervention. These programs had a positive impact on labor market outcomes and were cost-effective. PCY pursues an integrated, multi-dimensional approach to promoting the needs of children and youth in the areas of social work for and with young people, information and counseling, entrepreneurship and self-employment activities, and local skills development.

According to the inventory, it appears that successful interventions in the region are often associated with a multifaceted, integrated bundle of services such as skills training, promoting entrepreneurship and addressing social elements. Moreover, programs aimed at strengthening entrepreneurship also seem to deliver satisfactory results in many cases.

Accounting for all programs with net impacts evaluations included in the inventory—73 out of 289 programs implemented in 84 countries around the world—it appears that comprehensive, multiple service approaches did better than average. In Latin America, the Jovenes Programs, for example, have been widely analyzed and cited as a successful story in assisting young workers in developing countries (World Bank 2007). They use a demand-driven model that targets economically disadvantaged youth, fosters private sector participation, and promotes competition among training providers. It has been successful in improving job placement and earnings, but has become particularly expensive for some countries where it has been replaced by smaller and more focused interventions.[10] Entrepreneurship programs also performed better than average. Despite its low frequency in interventions and evaluations, this category of program shows improvements in employment and earning of young people. Overall, training-related programs were relatively less successful than average.

As long as youth employment programs in Sub-Saharan Africa countries are relatively rare, more systematic and careful evaluations of program performance are needed to draw strong policy conclusions. To the extent that evaluations exist, they typically fail to analyze the effect of policy interventions.

The particularities of African countries and the lack of more systematic information and evaluation of what works leaves the need to discuss and explore areas for interventions. In what follows, this essay discusses areas that should be included as important elements in development agendas aimed at tackling youth employment in Africa.

Expanding rural job opportunities

Africa's rural population is very high and a substantial share of the labor force is attached to agriculture, making rural activities a major part of the equation of youth employment. Unless urban areas can create a massive number of jobs, which is unlikely because most countries have not yet initiated their transition to industrialization, any development agenda must recognize that in the short term only rural activities, farm or non-farm, can effectively create occupation for most new job seekers.

There are conceptual issues relating to the specificities of African economies and labor markets. Indeed, labor markets in developing countries, and particularly in Sub-Saharan Africa, differ from those in other countries in that most of the labor force is either in informal jobs, self employment, or inactive. Rural wage labor markets are very thin and almost all occupied youth are in subsistence agriculture or unremunerated home production activities, and unemployment there is typically very low. Working conditions in agriculture are particularly unfavorable and can be hazardous. This fact, along with low income and limited perspectives of improving living standards and educational attainment, encourages youth to migrate.

Making well balanced choices for employment-intensive investments in agriculture and other rural non-farm activities can create immediate short term employment opportunities which can be more easily tapped by young people. Combined with appropriate local economic development strategies, this approach can generate more and sustainable jobs. Indeed, an study in Liberia (FAO/ILO/Ministry of Agriculture 2007) demonstrated that modern agriculture has considerable potential for job and wealth creation and may absorb large numbers of would-be youth migrants or youths who currently crowd the cities with underemployment. However, this requires strategies to make agriculture an attractive enough option for youth to engage

---

[10] Estimates on unit cost for the Jovenes Programs range from the upper US$ 600s to about US$2,000 per participant served. Across programs, there is impact evaluation evidence of increased employment probability and earnings of participants upon graduation compared to their control group. Although expensive, they proved to be cost-effective. Early evidence from Peru indicates that the positive earnings effect shall last at least 7 years for PROJoven to yield a positive net gain. A recent longitudinal version of propensity score matching of PROJoven shows a positive internal rate of return, consistently above 4%. In Dominican Republic, the investment on training is recuperated after 2 years. Although the program has yielded positive results in Latin America, it does not mean they will necessarily work in other contexts. Piloting and carefully evaluating results are therefore needed should governments want to replicate them in Africa.

in, including moving away from subsistence agriculture, and introducing commercialization and productivity improvements through technological changes and infrastructure support. Recent changes in the global food market, in science and technology, and in a range of institutions that affect competitiveness are creating new challenges to the competitiveness of smallholders, but are creating income opportunities, too.

In order to create jobs, accelerated progress will be needed to increase agricultural productivity and to connect poor people to markets. Sustained growth that reduces rural poverty will require significant growth in agricultural value-added and multi-sector approaches that solve gaps as well as support agribusiness, and rural diversification. To create jobs that will increase rural income and welfare and, thereby, retain young people, it is necessary to increase investments in irrigation, water resources management, and research and extension; increase rural public services; and increase use of improved seeds, fertilizers and better agricultural practices. It is also necessary to address vulnerability to weather-related shocks and limited farmer capacity, distorted incentives (including Government policies) that keep farmers in subsistence farming, poorly functioning input/output markets, and weak institutional capacity to manage the risk of food insecurity. Increased investment in rural roads, rural electricity, and communications will permit rural areas to become better connected to market opportunities.

Investments in rural education are also necessary to increase rural productivity and enhance the well being of the rural residents. As the rural young workers today may be the urban workers tomorrow, investing in human capital in rural areas is important not only as a way out of poverty in the agriculture sector, but also as a way to create opportunities for people to migrate more successfully and contribute to the economic growth of cities (World Bank 2009). Indeed, better educated migrants are more likely to have a successful migration outcome.

Because young people are the most mobile, they are the most likely to switch sectors to take advantage of new opportunities (see Box 1). So policies to designed to develop the farm and non-farm sectors will likely have a particularly pronounced effect on youth, even if not specifically targeted at them. For example, the promotion of small and medium rural enterprises that use new technologies could have a differential impact on youth, given their advantage in using them.

By creating jobs and educational opportunities, rural areas can increase their attractiveness to young workers, thus eventually delaying the rural-urban migration. This is a very critical issue that governments should attempt to mitigate in order to prevent the growth of urban youth unemployment and underemployment, and the worsening of well being in already congested African cities.

Youth migration can significantly change the composition of the rural population, which poses its own challenges for rural development because migration is often selective. Those who leave are generally younger, better educated, and more skilled. Youth migration can thus diminish entrepreneurship and education level among the remaining population. In addition, migration can change the gender composition of rural populations. But migration has several benefits too, as it diversifies risks, contributes to rural income through remittances, and increases knowledge and opportunities. The challenge, then, is to find the appropriate set of incentives that makes youth migration contribute the most to lift the livelihoods in both rural and urban areas.

Employment opportunities for the rural youth are not only in agriculture but also non-farm. Including rural towns, the rural non-farm sector accounts for about 20% of employment opportunities in Sub-Saharan Africa. The history of economic development has shown that development of the non-farm sector is tied to improved productivity on the farm. As technological innovations raise productivity on the farm, labor is freed up to move to the non-farm sector. The range of opportunities in rural areas is far wider than might be apparent at first glance.

The rural non-farm economy can generate a significant share of rural incomes, shares that have grown in many countries. Earnings are significantly higher in non-farm activities mostly due to skills differences. In some instances, this higher income share is a

In a recent study the International Movement ATD Fourth World tells the life story of Paul, a youth who lived in the streets of Ouagadougou when he left his village about 35 km from the capital in search of opportunities. Like other children from the streets, Paul never accepted to be called a 'Street Child' as this was a pejorative label. After meeting the Fourth World team, it took Paul several years to return to his village in part due to the shame that he had felt from having ended up in the streets. But he did manage to stabilize his life by going back to his village, and he is now back in the city and doing well.

Paul's story highlights how employment conditions for youths in poverty are often made up of a stream of activities in a process of trial and errors in search of a decent livelihood. During four years spent in his village after coming back from Ouagadougou, Paul engaged did seasonal gardening in his uncle's garden. Then this uncle gave Paul the opportunity to grow and sell vegetables on his own and he made a small profit from it. He later helped another uncle to work with a tractor and was paid for this work. Still with another uncle he sold clothes at a local market, and another relative introduced him to buying chickens and selling them to merchants who came from the city. With friends and relatives he made bricks of clay to sell as building material. He also raised chickens, goats, and pigs. Basically every activity that Paul participated in involved a relative or a member of his community, suggesting that the quality of social links between community members is essential for access to work and training for youths.

After four years in his village, Paul left again for Ouagadougou. As he explained it, "*In the village you can't earn a living by farming without trading. I came to Ouagadougou in search of money to start trading. I want to sell new clothes in the village: hats, caps, and Nike sportswear. I expect to work in my village and I want to help my parents and my brothers.*" Shortly after his arrival in the city, Paul found a job in a restaurant. He also found accommodation in a yard in the same area. Paul's job consists in selling roasted chicken. He is in charge of the cash register, which is a sign that the owner of the restaurant trusts him. Paul still goes back to the village every third Sunday, which is a market day. He visits his parents and grandmother. He leaves them some money. He leaves his savings with an uncle in the village. Thus, even though Paul went back to live in the city as it did provide better job opportunities, he still identifies himself as a member of his family and as a villager. He describes his future project as follows: "*I will begin trading during the holiday season. Once I begin trading, I will stop working at the restaurant. I will look after my relatives during the rainy season and provide them with food. My young brothers can learn trading with me. They can come and help me, take things to sell and go around the market.*"

Can it be concluded from Paul's life story that he and his family moved out of poverty and that migration and employment in the capital ultimately played a positive role in this process? Probably yes, at least to some extent. Nowadays, Paul is in a better economic situation than before, even if he still has an informal and potentially unstable job, as most other youngsters in Burkina Faso. Today, Paul keeps as one of his key objectives the ability for him to support his family. He actually measures the success of his activities in part by his ability to support his parents and brothers. As Paul said as a conclusion to his experiences, "*I have a job, that's good. If you don't have a job, you don't know what you are going to do to earn money. What is also good is that I am not far from my village: I can go see my family and come back. I am lucky because if I go back to live in the village, I will always find work and the people will always show me what to do.*" At the same time, the story shows that migration for the sake of better employment is often an iterative process, especially when the migrant stays within his/her country, and that it may entail substantial costs, as evidenced by the period during which Paul was forced to live in the streets of Ouagadougou, lost contacts with his family, and thereby lacked the support that such contacts may bring.

Source: Wodon (2008).

result of crop failures or other adverse shocks to the farm sector. In most cases, however, rising productivity growth in the agriculture sector raises farm income and hence the demand for goods and services produced outside agriculture. International evidence shows that labor productivity is higher there as measured by value added per worker.

Although agriculture is still the largest source of rural income in Africa, the shares of incomes from non-farm rural activities in total income are already relatively high and increasing. The small participation of the non-agricultural sector in employment suggests that it has the potential to contribute substantially to job creation and income. In Latin America, for example, about half the youth population in rural areas, and more than 65% of those ages 25–34, work in nonagricultural activities (World Bank 2007).

The demand for youth labor will not increase without a dynamic rural economy in both the agriculture and non-farm sectors. An appropriate investment climate along with adequate infrastructures that prepare towns and cities for business and urbanization is therefore critical. Indeed, rural Investment Climate Assessments reveal substantial constraints on rural investment, including access to credit, land titling, inadequate supply of energy, poor quality of roads and infrastructure, lack of well-functioning legal structures, and weak governance.

Improving the investment and macroeconomic environments

Though improving the investment climate is not youth specific, it can have a significant impact on youth by creating more and better jobs. Indeed, economic growth and job creation benefit most participants in the labor market, youth included. When labor demand is strong, youth employment and labor force participation for both males and females increases while the unemployment rate for youth tends to go down.[11]

Governments should create a better investment climate by tackling unjustified costs, risks, and barriers to competition. They can do this by ensuring political stability and security, improving the regulatory and tax climate for investment, and providing needed infrastructure. Trade facilitation and adequate industrial policies can also play a key role in the business environment in the region. In the case of Africa, which is a high risk and high cost place for doing business, improvements in the investment climate can rapidly be accompanied by creation of jobs.

Expanding world trade has shifted production around the world. Because the young are the most able to respond to the growing demand for labor, these shifts can favor them. The young may also be particularly attractive to firms in new and growing sectors of the economy because they are more adaptable than older workers to new production methods.

Industrial growth led by foreign direct investment can be stimulated partly by the availability of cheaper young labor. However, as the dynamic growth process occurs, the demand for a more educated labor force able to adapt to new technology with appropriate knowledge, skills, and behavior will increase. Indeed, opportunities in more dynamic sectors can provide incentives for youth to acquire more skills. Among 48 developing countries, increases in apparel and shoe exports as a share of GDP were found to be positively associated with subsequent upturns in both male and female secondary school enrollment. For the average country, a doubling of apparel and footwear exports as a share of GDP raises female secondary school attendance by 20–25% (Gruben and McLeod, 2006).

The poor job creation observed in virtually all Sub-Saharan African economies, whatever their geographic and demographic characteristics, income level, and whether or not reforms were undertaken, suggests that the supply side explanation may be incomplete. Yet small domestic and regional market sizes and low purchase power of consumers trap firms in low scale production and low productivity and help explain the limited labor demand and the types of jobs created. Limited economic activity is therefore an important determinant of youth unemployment and underemployment. Resolving these problems requires growth of employment at a sustained level. Well-designed macroeconomic policies that balance objectives of macroeconomic stability with employment generation are of primary importance. Given that youth employment is highly dependent on the general employment situation, policies to boost and sustain job-rich economic growth are fundamental for young peoples' successful integration in the labor market.

During recent decades, growth in Sub-Saharan Africa has been both low and highly volatile, which helps explain the poor investment climate and gloomy job creation (Arbache and Page, 2008). Indeed, volatility reduces the time horizon and incentives for long- term investments, and increases risks. Africa's poor long-term growth was a product of good and bad times for its economies that featured surprisingly high rates of growth and decline that occurred with almost equal frequency (Arbache and Page, 2007). There is now sufficient evidence that economic, social, governance, and institutional variables are significantly different during growth acceleration and deceleration episodes, and that reducing growth volatility and preventing growth collapses turns out to be critical for sustainable growth and job creation.

---

[11] In poor countries where few can afford to be unemployed, increasing labor demand is likely to impact primarily quality than quantity of jobs.

Encouraging and supporting entrepreneurship

A main factor behind the high rate of youth underemployment in Africa is the lack of productive jobs to meet the supply of youth. An alternative to reducing the underemployment is encouraging entrepreneurship, a driving force for initiating business ideas, mobilizing human, financial and physical resources, and for establishing and expanding enterprises. Entrepreneurship is not youth specific, but can unleash the economic potential of young people and provide living alternatives for them. An enterprise and entrepreneurial culture is of primary importance. Societies that appreciate entrepreneurship and promote its values and norms can create a dynamic and vibrant class of young entrepreneurs. Empirical evidence shows that educating young minds in enterprising behavior, thus boosting confidence for calculated risk taking, increases incidence of adopting entrepreneurship as a career option.

Young people, and in particular young women in rural areas, face particular challenges. They have less capital in the form of skills, knowledge and experience, savings and credit, and more difficult access to business networks and sources of information. Weak representation of young people in policy and decision-making is another issue. They lack the influence and the connection with representative business associations and networks that generally work with the government on relevant policies. Enhancing their capacity for participation in association building and policy advocacy can address this disadvantaged position. Young women entrepreneurs face additional hurdles, as in many cultures their roles in the family and society keep them from tapping opportunities in business development. Because of this, they are more likely to be in the informal economy, in self- employment activities, and are less likely to be entrepreneurs employing others.

Youth entrepreneurship can be maximized through programs and strategies that address the barriers to doing business, identify youth with entrepreneurial drive and talent to be nurtured, build the appropriate skills, and help new entrepreneurs develop their businesses. Successful development of youth business hinges upon good access to well integrated services such as management training, business mentoring programs, financial services, support in gaining access markets, and networking opportunities (see Box 2).

In most countries, the fastest growing form of employment is the non-agricultural household enterprise. This sector already accounts for 24% of the labor force in Uganda, and 30% in Senegal. This employment is mostly urban, although there is an important rural non-farm sector as well. Informal economy agents should be strengthened to improve the quality of employment and increase productivity. The service sector offers immense possibilities in both rural and urban areas. By encouraging informal sector enterprises to grow and succeed, without encouraging illegal activities and tax evasion, several productive jobs can be created for the youth.

Improving access to education and skills

A young person's employment prospects are closely related to the education received. Access to basic education is widely recognized as an effective means of combating child labor and eradicating poverty. Indeed, education and skills development generate important economic as well as social benefits. Unskilled youth workers are more vulnerable to economic shocks, less likely to find work, more likely to get stuck in low quality jobs with few opportunities to develop their human capital, and are also more vulnerable to demographic changes. In Ethiopia, young-age cohorts have a much larger impact on the probability of unskilled youth in urban areas to find jobs than those more educated (Garcia and Fares, 2008).

Education and skills are central to increasing productivity and income. Boosting productivity requires technological change, which in turn is only possible if new and higher skills are available at large. Investment climate surveys show that more than a fifth of all firms in developing countries as diverse as Algeria and Zambia rate inadequate skills and education of workers as a major or severe obstacle to their operations (World Bank, 2007). It is important to take these factors into account in policy planning. Capital investment and introduction of new technologies without having a locally skilled and educated workforce available means that local youth will be ill-equipped to take up emerging jobs. On the other hand, having highly-skilled and educated persons available without job opportunities will lead to outward migration, or trigger frustrations with negative consequences.

There have been significant improvements in primary school enrollment in most parts of the region, but access to and quality of education are still major issues, especially in rural areas. Lack of access to education has been shown to be among the most important reasons for youth migration; it was cited by 57% of Ethiopian youth who recently migrated from rural to urban areas (Ethiopia LFS 2005). Although the enterprise surveys in Africa suggest that skills of workers is low on their list of complaints, a finer look reveals that the better companies, such as the large foreign owned companies in demanding sectors (export industries as opposed to retail), do complain quite a bit about skills.

Reaction to improved access to education can be significant as suggested by the result of the elimination of school fees for primary education in Kenya and Uganda. This action produced large increases in school enrollment and had large impacts on completion rates for fourth and fifth graders from poor households. Other costs, however, can still hinder the chances of the poor to attend school. For example, in some countries, distance to school was found to be a major correlate of program uptake (World Bank 2008).

Providing specific technical skills in high demand by the private sector (e.g. English proficiency, plumbers, mechanics and accountants) and in rural areas are also important for successful youth employment policies. It is necessary to expand public training opportunities to provide better access to disadvantaged urban and rural youth, the less educated, and girls.[12] Indeed, to the extent that women engaged in the labor market have lower fertility, higher bargaining power and improved allocation of resources at the household level, targeted job opportunity programs for girls may have far-reaching beneficial consequences.

Policies should include the introduction of new fundamentals into the skills development systems such as: national occupational standards; curriculum development which emphasizes both the acquisition of knowledge and understanding and the demonstration of occupational performance; skills assessment based on demonstration of competencies; additional skills for employability along with occupational training; funding focused on performance and outcomes of the Technical and Vocational Education and Training (TVET) institutions (see Box 2); and skills recognition and certification to help youth to seek jobs in the formal economy. The provision of public technical and vocational training has, however, been less than adequate as it often offers insufficient opportunities for practice and is biased toward white collar jobs in the urban wage sector; provides courses that are often rigid and too standardized to meet the multi-skill needs of the workplace; and often includes little accountability and few incentives to monitor and adjust to changes in the demand for skills of formal and informal sectors (Adams 2008).

Informal apprenticeship is a major provider of skills in the informal economy, mostly for the poorer and less educated youth. Governments and social partners need to review informal apprenticeship systems and provide guidance and support to this system through introduction of regulations (such as the maximum duration of training per trade in order to prevent exploitation of apprentices); improvement of the learning processes through training of master craftsmen and provision of incentives to these craftsmen; assistance with the testing and certification of graduate apprentices; inclusion of evening literacy or theoretical classes to apprentices in the public education/training institutions; and offering a fiscal allowance to apprentices, giving many more youth a chance pay for their training.

Developing second chance education programs for dropouts should also be an important element of an effective program. Examples of such are in Uganda and Malawi,

---

[12] Low rural educational levels, poor learning outcomes, scattered populations, limited demand, and low cost-recovery are challenges in providing quality training services in rural areas (Bennell 2007).

One of the best known programs under this heading is Kenya's Jua Kali voucher program, established in 1997 as a pilot program, under the auspices of the Micro and Small Enterprise Training and Technology Project. Under this type of program, vouchers are issued to unemployed youth, who can personally select a training provider based on their needs and objectives, rather than having them chosen by a bureaucratic institution. The voucher program intends to empower recipients with the capacity to buy training on the open market and thereby promote competition between private and public suppliers. The approach should improve the quality of training and bring down the costs, while at the same time ensuring a better match between the participant and the training course. Under the Jua Kali pilot program, anyone eligible for training is given a voucher which can be cashed in at the chosen training provider. Participants pay only 10% of the cost of the voucher with the government subsidizing the remaining 90%. Master craftsmen were the major providers of training, responding to demand from clients. Although the Jua Kali voucher scheme did not focus entirely on youth, the majority of those trained were young and disadvantaged. Under this program, 37,606 vouchers were issued to entrepreneurs and employees in enterprises with fifty workers or less over the 1997–2001 period. There is evidence that the scheme has had a positive impact on those who were trained and that it has boosted employment, assets, and business for enterprises which participated (in comparison with a control group). These findings relate to a small population served by the pilot program; there is no evidence of outcomes/impact in a large (national) sample. The scheme was complex and costly to establish, and it has proven to be difficult to phase out the subsidization of the vouchers. Lessons learned from the experience include the following: such schemes should be administered through the private sector rather than (as in Kenya) through a government ministry; the scheme should include provision for upgrading of training providers, especially those from small enterprises; and it should promote the willingness of clients to pay for training. An exit strategy is needed unless subsidies are to last forever. But, overall, the Jua Kali experience suggests that there is scope for the use of vouchers in a system more precisely targeted at the most vulnerable.

Source: Johanson and Adams (2004).

where social funds projects are providing training to local youth at community owned training centers. This training could have a rapid, strong effect on key sensitive populations (including pregnant girls and young mothers). Half of the 19-year-olds in school are at the primary level in Malawi (World Bank, 2007). It is important, however, to carefully evaluate the cost/benefit ratios of these programs, which tend to be expensive.

To make optimal use of investments in education and training systems, policies related to education and skills need to be fully synchronized with other policies and programs for productivity, income growth, and job creation. These policies must also consider the flow of capital investments in the economy. Therefore, inter-ministerial coordination and collaboration among different stakeholders becomes crucial.

Addressing demographic issues

Africa's population is growing fast and is experiencing a slow demographic transition. The projections are that this will not stabilize before 2050. This transition has fiscal, political, and social implications, ranging from increased education and health costs to risks of social unrest. The demographic transition makes youth the most abundant asset that the region can claim, thus making it a window of opportunity. Indeed, East Asia put the right policies and institutions in place and was able to reap the demographic dividend from a large work force with fewer dependents, and part of the Asian Miracle is often attributed to the demographic dividend.

The demographic pressure from a large youth cohort entering the labor market can adversely affect youth employment prospects. In Ethiopia, the size of the youth cohort has already reduced the probability of their employment. In Tanzania, the increase in the size of the youth cohort has increased the incidence of unemployment among urban youth, particularly among urban females, and increased inactivity among urban males (Garcia and Fares 2008). Given the large and increasing size of the youth population, African countries will have to recognize that finding proper jobs for most new job seekers, especially in cities, will be a challenge, and that it is likely that the informal sector will continue to play a key role as a means of job opportunities for a long time to come (Fox and Gaal, 2008).

Although crude birth rates have been declining, especially among young women,

The World Bank's Adolescent Girl Initiative began as a US$3 million public-private sector partnership between the Government of Liberia, the World Bank Group and the Nike Foundation. In a pilot-phase, it will expand to at least six other low-income or post-conflict countries, adding the participation of new donors, governments, foundations and corporations. This initiative promotes the economic empowerment of young women by smoothing their path to productive employment. A new model of skills training matched to market needs for women aged 15–24 in Liberia has been developed with incentive structures in place to maximize access to wage jobs or successful self-employment. This model will be brought to the other pilot countries and, if successful there, to many more. In addition, depending on the economic environment, interventions such as business development skills training, job placement incentives and assistance, access to micro finance, and mentoring and apprenticeship programs will be added.

Source: Gender Equality as Smart Economics Newsletter, World Bank Group Action Plan, September 2008.

they are still quite high as compared to other regions—39 per 1,000 in Sub-Saharan Africa compared to 14 in East Asia and Pacific, 20 in Latin America and the Caribbean, 24 in Middle East and North Africa and South Asia, and 20 in all regions in 2006.[13] This has labor market repercussions for the mother, the father and the children. Indeed, early motherhood, a serious issue in Africa, has substantial impact on skills development and labor market and career development, thus compromising the likelihood of young mothers to invest in education and find good jobs (see Box 3). Evidence shows that high fertility traps young mothers, especially from rural areas, into household and low productivity activities. Easily accessible and effective sexual and reproductive health programs targeted to young women can play a key role in addressing this issue.

Addressing youth in violent and post conflict settings

Sub-Saharan Africa has been the site of numerous armed conflicts in which young people have been both the victims and the perpetrators of violence. The period 1990–2000 alone saw 19 major armed conflicts in Africa, ranging from civil wars to the 1998–2000 war between Eritrea and Ethiopia. Children and youth are increasingly participating in armed conflicts as active soldiers. Many

young people do so because of poverty. The region has thousands of ex-young combatants—100,000 in Sudan alone. In one study, crippling poverty and hopelessness were unanimously identified as key motivators for the 60 combatants interviewed (Human Rights Watch, 2005).

It is becoming increasingly recognized that non-economic aspects of poverty, such as the absence or inadequacy of essential services, the lack of livelihood and educational opportunities, and the non-participation of youth in decision- and policy-making are conditions that promote the involvement of young people in conflict. Conflict prevents children from obtaining a decent education and learning useful skills. Lacking any real social capital, many feel excluded from mainstream society and seek to become part of an armed militia, where they feel accepted (Integrated Regional Information Networks, 2007). Whatever the cause, conflict creates heavy losses in resources, thereby deepening poverty. Combined with poverty, conflict exacerbates the alienation of young people from society and hampers their ability to participate fully in development, even after the conflict is over.

There is a need for programs specifically designed to meet the needs of youth in conflict-affected countries. Such programs should include the recognition of prior skills through certification (e.g. Eritrea); and vocational training of ex-combatants with disabilities, such as in Sierra Leone. These programs should be more gender balanced and should not ignore the huge employment needs of young women.

Improving the labor market conditions

Active labor market policies and programs have increasingly been used in several countries to raise demand for young workers and enhance their employability. Their function is to mediate between labor supply and demand, to mitigate education and labor market failures, and to promote efficiency, equity, and growth. If properly targeted and implemented, these programs

---

[13] Crude birth rate indicates the number of live births occurring during the year, per 1,000 midyear population. (WDI 2007).

can effectively benefit disadvantaged youth. They can also assist rural workers in finding better employment opportunities by linking them to jobs in semi-urban and urban areas, thus helping households transition out of poverty. These programs are useful, however, in countries where mismatch between job-seekers and existing vacant jobs is a significant problem, which is not the case of most African countries. In spite of this, active labor market policies can play a role in improving labor market conditions in the rapidly growing urban areas of the region and where demand for skilled people is on the rise.

One barrier to matching the supply of young labor to demand is the lack of both labor market information and job search skills. Regardless of a country's stage of development, labor market information, job-search techniques, and career guidance play an important role in helping young people in their career choices and can bring about better labor market outcomes should jobs become available. Labor market information improves the quantity and quality of job matches between employers and jobseekers, reduces unemployment spells, and increases labor market efficiency. The collection, analysis and dissemination of labor market information have a pivotal role in informing young jobseekers about employment opportunities and in providing indications for policy and program design. Furthermore, the availability of reliable and up-to-date labor market information is essential for the design and monitoring of youth employment interventions. Youth should also be given access to vocational and labor market guidance in order to understand labor markets and select the right occupation for which to train. This will reduce the time required for the job search and permit the utilization of knowledge and skills acquired through train-

ing in the job. To be effective, employment services have to keep up with the changing requirements of the labor market and offer targeted packages of services that meet both the young people's and the employers' needs.

Labor market regulations are also an important element of policies to promote efficiency and equity in the labor market. However, youth wages and employment protection legislation continue to attract controversy in the debate on youth employment. In countries where labor law compliance is weak and wage jobs are very limited, as is the case of many African countries, this is less than a problem. Labor codes have, nevertheless, often been considered a potential cause of high youth unemployment. The question for developing countries is not whether to regulate or not, but what kind and what level of regulations are appropriate to get the best forms of protection for young people, who are usually vulnerable and insecure, without inhibiting formal firms from hiring.

Good and effective public governance are critical for the successful design, implementation and impact of labor regulations, policies and programs. Key aspects of good governance include the rule of law, and institutions for the representation of all interests and for social dialogue. Social dialogue is a central element in the development of effective and credible interventions to promote employment for young people. It requires strong, independent and well informed partners. Participation of young people in membership-based organizations and their engagement in decision-making processes affecting their employment and working conditions are also important to fostering social inclusion and advancing democratization.

Conclusions

Successfully addressing the youth employment challenge requires a coherent and integrated response that recognizes the particularities of Africa, especially the very large share of rural youth population, gender and demographic traits, and tiny labor markets. In many countries interventions have focused on programs that are narrow in scope, limited in time, and biased toward urban areas. Increasingly, the political priority attached to youth employment has brought policy-makers to recognize that achieving productive employment and work for young people entails long-term action covering a range of economic and social policies focusing on labor demand and supply, and addressing both quantitative and qualitative dimensions of youth employment. Such policies and programs need to be integrated in broader development frameworks, and be made up of two key elements: an integrated strategy for growth and job-creation in both rural and urban areas, as well as targeted interventions to help young people overcome the specific barriers they face in entering and remaining in the labor market.

Job creation can be supported through employment rich growth, with specific focus on sector attractive to youth, and choices for employment intensive investment. The potential of entrepreneurship is high, but to be well tapped, specific support measures are needed. Training is a key intervention area, but it is not a panacea. Planning of training interventions needs to be well synchronized with other economic policies, and challenges must be well understood so that interventions are effective, in particular as many countries are about to reforming their training systems. Specific attention has to be given to training needs in the informal economy.

There is also heightened recognition of the need to work in partnership. Clearly the primary responsibility for promoting youth employment lies with governments. Therefore, coherence, coordination and cooperation are needed across different government institutions and agencies, at central and local levels. The challenge at stake, however, is daunting and the responsibility reaches beyond the national level. This calls for renewed efforts to work together in a concerted and effective way. Governments, the social partners, civil society, the international community, as well as young people themselves, all have an important contribution to make to this process.

Finally, as seen above, youth employment is not an isolated issue; it reflects economic, geographic, demographic, and other conditions, and the particularities of each country. Youth specific policies will be more effective when they are aligned with other policies and priorities and when they take into account the economic and social contexts. The main challenge for governments, however, is to determine how to bridge the short to the long term perspective, and to identify the appropriate policies to absorb the youth in the economy.

Essay references

Adams, Arvil V. 2008. "A Framework for the Study of Skills Development in the Informal Sector of Sub-Saharan Africa." World Bank.

Arbache, J.S. and J. Page (2007), More Growth or Fewer Collapses? An Investigation of the Growth Challenges of Sub-Saharan African Countries, World Bank Policy Research Working Paper # 4384.

Arbache, J.S. and J. Page (2008), Patterns of Long Term Growth in Sub-Saharan Africa, in D. Go and J. Page (eds.), Africa at a Turning Point? Growth, Aid and External Shocks, Washington, DC: The World Bank.

Bennell, Paul. 2007. "Promoting Livelihoods Opportunities for Rural Youth." International Fund for Agricultural Development.

Cling, Jean-Pierre Gubert, Flore Nordman, J. Christophe, and Anne-Sophie Robilliard. 2007. "Youth and Labour Markets in Africa: A Critical Review of Literature." Document de Travail No. 49. Agence Française de Développement, Paris.

FAO/ILO/Ministry of Agriculture. 2007. "Comparative Study of the Job-Creating Capacity and Efficiency of Crops and Related Activities in Liberia." Report submitted by ITTAS Consultancy Ltd, Accra, Ghana.

Fares, Jean Montenegro, E. Claudio, and Peter F. Orazem. 2006. "How are Youth Faring in the Labor Market? Evidence from Around the World." Policy Research Working Paper Series 4071. The World Bank.

Fox, Louise and Melissa S. Gaal. 2008. "Working Out of Poverty." Washington, DC: The World Bank.

Garcia, Marito and Jean Fares. 2008. "Youth in Africa's Labor market." Washington, DC: The World Bank.

Gruben, William C., and Darryl McLeod. 2006. "Apparel Exports and Education: How Developing Nations Encourage Women's Schooling." Economic Letter – Insights from the Federal Reserve Bank of Dallas Vol. 1, No. 3.

ILO. 2007. "African Employment Trends." Geneva.

ILO. 2006. "Global Employment Trends for Youth 2006." Geneva.

Human Rights Watch. 2005. "Youth, Poverty and Blood: The Lethal Legacy of West Africa's Regional Warriors." Vol. 17, No. 5.

Integrated Regional Information Networks. 2007. "IRIN In-Depth – Youth in Crisis: Coming of Age in the 21st Century." Special Series, February.

Johanson, Richard K., and Avril V. Adams. 2004. "Skills Development in Sub-Saharan Africa." Washington, DC: The World Bank.

Kapsos, Steven. 2005. "The Employment Intensity of Growth: Trends and Macroeconomic Determinants", Employment Strategy Papers, ILO.

Puerto, Olga S. 2007. "International Experience on Youth Employment Interventions: The Youth Employment Inventory." Background paper for the Sierra Leone Youth and Employment ESW, Washington, DC: The World Bank.

Rother, Friederike. 2006., "Interventions to Support Young Workers in Sub Saharan Africa." Washington, DC: The World Bank.

United Nations. 2007. "World Youth Report 2007: Young People's Transition to Adulthood: Progress and Challenges." New York.

United Nations. 2005. "World Youth Report 2005: Young People Today, and in 2015." New York.

Wodon, Quentin. 2008. Understanding Youth Migration and Employment: Insights from a Faith-Based Organization in Burkina Faso." Development Dialogue on Values and Ethics Note. World Bank, Washington DC.

World Bank. 2009. "World Development Report 2009: Reshaping Economic Geography" Washington, DC.

World Bank. 2008. "World Development Report 2008: Agriculture for Development." Washington, DC.

World Bank. 2007. "World Development Report 2007: Development and the Next Generation." Washington, DC.

World Bank. 2006. "Labor Diagnostics for Sub-Saharan Africa: Assessing Indicators and Data Available". Washington, DC.

Data references

Demographic and Health Surveys. http://www.measuredhs.com

Ethiopia Labour Force Survey 2005. Central Statistical Agency, Addis Ababa.

Madagascar Enquête Auprès des Ménages 2005. Institut National de la Statistique, Antananarivo.

Survey-Based harmonized Indicators Program (SHIP). The World Bank, Washington, DC.

Tanzania Integrated Labour Force Survey 2005/2006. National Bureau of Statistics, Dar es Salaam.

World Development Indicators 2007. The World Bank, Washin

Indicator tables

Table 1.1 Basic Indicators

	Population (millions) 2006	Land area (thousands of sq km) 2006	GDP per capita Constant 2000 prices		Life expectancy at birth (years) 2006	Under-five mortality rate (per 1,000) 2006	Gini index 2000–06[a]	Adult literacy rate (% ages 15 and older)		Net ODA aid per capita (current $) 2006
			Dollars 2006	Average annual growth (%) 2000–06				Male 2000–06[a]	Female 2000–06[a]	
SUB-SAHARAN AFRICA	**782.5**	**23,629**	**580**	**2.3**	**50.5**	**157**	..	..	..	**48.5**
Excl. South Africa	**735.1**	**22,414**	**388**	**2.7**	**50.5**	**160**	..	..	..	**50.7**
Excl. South Africa & Nigeria	**590.3**	**21,504**	**371**	**2.3**	**51.4**	**152**	..	..	..	**43.7**
Angola	16.6	1,247	1,070	8.3	42.4	260	..	82.9	54.2	10.3
Benin	8.8	111	323	0.5	56.2	148	36.5	47.9	23.3	42.8
Botswana	1.9	567	4,511	4.2	49.8	124	..	80.4	81.8	35.0
Burkina Faso	14.4	274	258	2.7	51.9	204	39.5	31.4	16.6	60.6
Burundi	8.2	26	102	–1.0	49.0	181	..	67.3	52.2	50.8
Cameroon	18.2	465	687	1.3	50.3	149	44.6	77.0	59.8	92.7
Cape Verde	0.5	4	1,384	2.2	71.0	34	50.5	87.8	75.5	266.6
Central African Republic	4.3	623	223	–2.3	44.4	175	..	64.8	33.5	31.4
Chad	10.5	1,259	266	10.1	50.6	209	..	40.8	12.8	27.1
Comoros	0.6	2	382	0.3	63.2	68	..	..	..	49.5
Congo, Dem. Rep.	60.6	2,267	91	1.6	46.1	205	..	80.9	54.1	33.9
Congo, Rep.	3.7	342	1,145	2.0	54.8	127	..	90.5	79.0	69.0
Côte d'Ivoire	18.9	318	549	–1.7	48.1	127	44.6	60.8	38.6	13.3
Djibouti	0.8	23	817	1.3	54.5	130	..	..	..	143.2
Equatorial Guinea	0.5	28	7,470	16.6	51.1	206	..	93.4	80.5	54.1
Eritrea	4.7	101	160	–1.4	57.3	74	..	..	..	27.5
Ethiopia	77.2	1,000	161	3.9	52.5	123	..	50.0	22.8	25.2
Gabon	1.3	258	4,263	–0.1	56.7	91	..	88.5	79.7	23.7
Gambia, The	1.7	10	326	1.0	59.1	113	47.4	..	..	44.5
Ghana	23.0	228	294	3.0	59.7	120	..	66.4	49.8	51.1
Guinea	9.2	246	406	1.1	55.5	161	38.6	42.6	18.1	17.8
Guinea-Bissau	1.6	28	131	–3.2	46.2	200	..	..	..	50.0
Kenya	36.6	569	440	1.3	53.4	121	..	77.7	70.2	25.8
Lesotho	2.0	30	528	2.5	42.9	132	..	73.7	90.3	36.0
Liberia	3.6	96	134	–6.9	45.3	235	..	58.3	45.7	75.1
Madagascar	19.2	582	238	–0.2	59.0	115	47.5	76.5	65.3	39.4
Malawi	13.6	94	145	–0.2	47.6	120	39.0	..	..	49.3
Mali	12.0	1,220	290	2.6	53.8	217	40.1	32.7	15.9	69.0
Mauritania	3.0	1,031	483	2.0	63.7	125	39.0	59.5	43.4	61.6
Mauritius	1.3	2	4,522	3.0	73.2	14	..	88.2	80.5	14.8
Mozambique	21.0	786	330	5.6	42.5	138	47.3	..	..	76.8
Namibia	2.0	823	2,166	3.3	52.5	61	..	86.8	83.5	71.0
Niger	13.7	1,267	169	0.3	56.4	253	..	42.9	15.1	29.2
Nigeria	144.7	911	454	4.1	46.8	191	43.7	78.2	60.1	79.0
Rwanda	9.5	25	263	3.5	45.6	160	46.8	71.4	59.8	61.8
São Tomé and Principe	0.2	1	..	..	65.2	96	..	92.2	77.9	138.9
Senegal	12.1	193	499	1.9	62.8	116	41.3	51.1	29.2	68.3
Seychelles	0.1	0	7,005	–1.7	72.2	13	..	91.4	92.3	164.9
Sierra Leone	5.7	72	225	7.7	42.2	270	37.0	46.7	24.2	63.4
Somalia	8.4	627	..	..	47.7	146	..	..	..	46.4
South Africa	47.4	1,214	3,562	2.8	50.7	69	57.8	..	..	15.1
Sudan	37.7	2,376	489	4.4	58.1	89	..	71.1	51.8	54.6
Swaziland	1.1	17	1,297	0.2	40.8	164	50.4	80.9	78.3	30.3
Tanzania	39.5	886	339	4.0	51.9	118	34.6	77.5	62.2	46.3
Togo	6.4	54	240	–0.3	58.2	108	..	68.7	38.5	12.3
Uganda	29.9	197	274	2.3	50.7	134	40.8	76.8	57.7	51.9
Zambia	11.7	743	371	3.0	41.7	182	50.8	..	..	121.8
Zimbabwe	13.2	387	..	–6.4	42.7	105	..	92.7	86.2	21.2
NORTH AFRICA	**154.2**	**5,738**	**2,060**	**2.7**	**71.5**	**35**	..	..	..	**16.8**
Algeria	33.4	2,382	2,123	3.3	72.0	38	..	79.6	60.1	6.3
Egypt, Arab Rep.	74.2	995	1,724	2.2	71.0	35	34.4	83.0	59.4	11.8
Libya	6.0	1,760	7,040	1.1	74.0	18	..	92.8	74.8	6.2
Morocco	30.5	446	1,667	3.9	70.7	37	..	65.7	39.6	34.3
Tunisia	10.1	155	2,518	3.6	73.6	23	39.8	83.4	65.3	42.7
AFRICA	**936.6**	**29,367**	**823**	**2.2**	**53.9**	**144**	..	..	..	**43.3**

a. Data are for the most recent year available during the period specified.

Table 2.1

Gross domestic product, nominal

	Current prices ($ millions)									Average annual growth (%)		
	1980	1990	2000	2001	2002	2003	2004	2005	2006[a]	1980–89	1990–99	2000–06
SUB-SAHARAN AFRICA	276,319	297,064	342,099	335,631	363,915	446,080	550,041	645,195	744,731	0.6	1.7	15.6
Excl. South Africa	197,202	185,167	209,287	217,294	253,313	279,554	333,682	403,314	490,318	3.0	1.4	15.6
Excl. South Africa & Nigeria	129,406	156,754	163,234	169,222	194,086	211,757	245,610	290,742	342,847	2.1	1.1	13.5
Angola	..	10,260	9,129	8,936	11,432	13,956	19,775	30,632	45,163	..	–3.8	32.2
Benin	1,405	1,845	2,255	2,372	2,807	3,558	4,047	4,287	4,623	2.3	3.5	14.1
Botswana	1,061	3,792	6,177	6,033	5,933	8,278	9,827	10,513	11,006	12.6	4.4	12.7
Burkina Faso	1,929	3,101	2,611	2,813	3,290	4,270	5,109	5,427	5,771	4.8	0.0	15.9
Burundi	920	1,132	709	662	628	595	664	796	903	2.2	–3.3	4.2
Cameroon	6,741	11,152	10,075	9,598	10,880	13,622	15,775	16,588	17,953	7.3	–2.5	12.1
Cape Verde	..	339	531	550	616	797	925	1,006	1,182	..	6.4	15.4
Central African Republic	797	1,488	959	968	1,042	1,195	1,307	1,350	1,477	8.1	–4.3	8.1
Chad	1,033	1,739	1,385	1,709	1,988	2,737	4,415	5,873	6,300	5.7	–1.3	32.2
Comoros	124	250	202	220	251	324	362	387	403	8.0	–2.0	13.6
Congo, Dem. Rep.	14,395	9,350	4,306	4,692	5,548	5,673	6,570	7,104	8,545	–6.2	–7.1	11.5
Congo, Rep.	1,706	2,799	3,220	2,794	3,020	3,564	4,343	6,087	7,731	2.3	–2.4	17.6
Côte d'Ivoire	10,175	10,796	10,417	10,545	11,487	13,737	15,481	16,345	17,268	2.0	2.2	10.1
Djibouti	..	452	551	572	591	622	666	709	769	..	1.7	5.7
Equatorial Guinea	..	132	1,254	1,737	2,166	2,966	4,899	7,528	8,565	..	22.5	40.5
Eritrea	..	..	634	671	631	584	635	970	1,085	..	7.2	8.8
Ethiopia	..	12,083	8,180	8,169	7,791	8,558	10,054	12,305	15,166	5.8	–5.7	11.0
Gabon	4,279	5,952	5,068	4,713	4,932	6,055	7,178	8,666	9,546	0.6	–1.7	13.3
Gambia, The	241	317	421	418	370	367	401	461	511	1.7	3.6	3.1
Ghana	4,445	5,886	4,977	5,309	6,160	7,624	8,872	10,720	12,715	3.2	2.6	17.8
Guinea	6,684	2,667	3,112	3,039	3,208	3,619	3,938	3,261	3,204	–15.6	3.0	1.6
Guinea-Bissau	111	244	215	199	201	235	270	301	308	4.3	–0.6	8.0
Kenya	7,265	8,591	12,604	12,983	13,152	14,986	16,199	18,730	22,779	2.5	7.6	10.5
Lesotho	431	615	853	752	687	1,039	1,319	1,425	1,494	1.3	4.2	13.2
Liberia	954	384	561	543	559	410	460	530	614	–0.5	1.8	0.7
Madagascar	4,042	3,081	3,878	4,529	4,397	5,474	4,364	5,040	5,499	–5.2	3.9	4.6
Malawi	1,238	1,881	1,744	1,717	2,665	2,425	2,625	2,855	3,164	1.7	–0.1	10.5
Mali	1,787	2,421	2,422	2,630	3,343	4,362	4,874	5,305	5,866	3.4	0.1	17.2
Mauritania	709	1,020	1,081	1,122	1,150	1,285	1,548	1,837	2,663	3.7	1.4	15.3
Mauritius	1,153	2,383	4,469	4,539	4,549	5,248	6,064	6,290	6,347	9.2	6.7	7.4
Mozambique	3,526	2,463	4,249	4,075	4,201	4,666	5,698	6,579	6,833	–5.7	8.3	10.1
Namibia	2,169	2,350	3,414	3,216	3,122	4,473	5,649	6,230	6,566	1.5	4.6	14.9
Niger	2,509	2,481	1,798	1,945	2,170	2,639	2,897	3,330	3,597	1.8	–1.8	13.1
Nigeria	64,202	28,472	45,984	48,000	59,117	67,656	87,845	112,249	146,867	–12.0	3.2	22.0
Rwanda	1,163	2,584	1,735	1,675	1,641	1,777	1,971	2,379	2,869	8.6	–1.5	11.8
São Tomé and Principe	..	..	..	76	91	98	107	114	123	..	..	9.4
Senegal	3,503	5,717	4,692	4,878	5,334	6,858	8,030	8,688	9,269	6.2	–1.4	14.8
Seychelles	147	369	615	622	698	706	700	723	775	10.0	6.1	3.6
Sierra Leone	1,101	650	634	806	936	991	1,073	1,215	1,420	–4.3	0.1	12.8
Somalia	604	917	..	..	..	..	..	..	..	6.4	..	..
South Africa	80,710	112,014	132,878	118,479	110,874	166,654	216,443	242,059	254,993	4.8	2.1	14.8
Sudan	7,617	9,016	12,366	13,362	14,976	17,780	21,684	27,386	36,402	7.6	7.8	19.7
Swaziland	543	882	1,389	1,317	1,188	1,821	2,377	2,613	2,784	1.9	5.9	16.0
Tanzania	..	4,259	9,079	9,441	9,758	10,283	11,351	14,142	14,178	..	8.9	8.8
Togo	1,136	1,628	1,329	1,328	1,476	1,759	2,061	2,154	2,218	4.5	–0.1	10.3
Uganda	1,245	4,304	5,927	5,681	5,836	6,250	6,817	8,738	9,495	20.7	8.5	9.5
Zambia	3,884	3,288	3,238	3,637	3,716	4,374	5,525	7,349	10,886	–3.1	0.2	21.4
Zimbabwe	6,679	8,784	7,399	10,256	21,897	7,397	4,712	3,418	..	–0.1	–2.9	–18.8
NORTH AFRICA	131,760	172,192	245,626	240,561	225,619	249,576	278,878	321,692	370,017	2.7	4.2	7.5
Algeria	42,345	62,045	54,790	55,181	57,053	68,019	85,014	102,339	116,459	4.5	–1.2	14.9
Egypt, Arab Rep.	22,912	43,130	99,839	97,632	87,851	82,924	78,845	89,686	107,484	6.8	10.8	–0.2
Libya	35,545	28,905	34,495	29,994	19,195	23,822	30,498	41,743	49,711	–6.2	–0.9	8.3
Morocco	18,821	25,821	37,059	37,766	40,472	49,819	56,392	58,956	65,401	6.1	5.2	11.0
Tunisia	8,743	12,291	19,443	19,988	21,047	24,992	28,129	28,968	30,962	2.3	6.0	9.1
AFRICA	407,093	469,167	587,721	576,188	589,450	695,491	828,652	966,561	1,114,365	1.4	2.6	12.5

a. Provisional

Table 2.2

Gross domestic product, real

	Constant prices (2000 $ millions)									Average annual growth (%)		
	1980	1990	2000	2001	2002	2003	2004	2005	2006ª	1980–89	1990–99	2000–06
SUB-SAHARAN AFRICA	**227,238**	**273,268**	**342,099**	**354,758**	**366,789**	**382,293**	**405,831**	**428,769**	**453,537**	**1.8**	**2.4**	**4.8**
Excl. South Africa	**131,915**	**162,335**	**209,287**	**218,323**	**225,347**	**236,450**	**252,945**	**268,099**	**284,894**	**2.1**	**2.7**	**5.3**
Excl. South Africa & Nigeria	**99,157**	**127,317**	**163,234**	**170,846**	**177,140**	**183,259**	**194,103**	**206,081**	**219,033**	**2.6**	**2.8**	**4.9**
Angola	..	8,464	9,129	9,416	10,780	11,137	12,383	14,935	17,707	..	1	11.5
Benin	1,084	1,412	2,255	2,368	2,474	2,571	2,650	2,727	2,831	2.7	4.7	3.8
Botswana	1,209	3,395	6,177	6,499	6,867	7,281	7,730	8,105	8,382	10.9	5.6	5.4
Burkina Faso	1,101	1,556	2,611	2,785	2,915	3,150	3,296	3,505	3,698	4	5.5	6
Burundi	559	865	709	724	756	747	783	790	830	4.5	–3.2	2.5
Cameroon	6,339	8,793	10,075	10,530	10,952	11,393	11,815	12,087	12,476	4.5	1.3	3.6
Cape Verde	..	303	531	552	577	613	608	648	717	..	5.9	4.7
Central African Republic	735	815	959	962	956	883	895	914	950	1.6	1.8	–0.7
Chad	665	1,106	1,385	1,547	1,678	1,925	2,572	2,776	2,780	6.7	2.3	14.1
Comoros	136	181	202	209	217	223	222	232	234	2.9	1.2	2.5
Congo, Dem. Rep.	7,016	7,659	4,306	4,215	4,362	4,614	4,921	5,239	5,505	2.1	–5	4.7
Congo, Rep.	1,746	2,796	3,220	3,342	3,503	3,563	3,691	3,975	4,223	3.8	0.8	4.4
Côte d'Ivoire	7,727	8,298	10,417	10,415	10,266	10,106	10,287	10,409	10,382	0.7	3.5	0
Djibouti	..	660	551	563	577	596	619	638	669	..	–2.3	3.3
Equatorial Guinea	..	207	1,254	2,036	2,454	2,775	3,668	3,920	3,702	..	20.7	19.4
Eritrea	..	..	634	692	697	739	753	757	749	..	7.9	2.7
Ethiopia	..	6,234	8,180	8,859	8,993	8,798	9,993	11,174	12,387	2.1	3.7	6.7
Gabon	3,594	4,298	5,068	5,176	5,162	5,290	5,361	5,523	5,588	0.5	2.9	1.7
Gambia, The	213	305	421	445	431	461	484	509	542	3.5	2.7	4.1
Ghana	2,640	3,267	4,977	5,177	5,410	5,691	6,010	6,364	6,771	2.6	4.3	5.3
Guinea	1,539	2,088	3,112	3,236	3,372	3,440	3,534	3,651	3,730	3	4.4	3
Guinea-Bissau	115	186	215	216	201	199	204	211	215	3.8	1.4	–0.2
Kenya	7,060	10,518	12,604	13,168	13,240	13,628	14,321	15,140	16,065	4.1	2.2	4
Lesotho	392	602	853	868	893	917	954	982	1,053	4.1	4.3	3.4
Liberia	1,391	433	561	577	599	411	422	444	479	–3.3	0.2	–4.7
Madagascar	3,099	3,266	3,878	4,111	3,590	3,941	4,149	4,339	4,551	0.8	1.7	2.7
Malawi	1,000	1,243	1,744	1,657	1,584	1,683	1,779	1,819	1,963	2.4	3.8	2.4
Mali	1,536	1,630	2,422	2,716	2,828	3,039	3,105	3,294	3,469	0.5	3.9	5.7
Mauritania	693	816	1,081	1,112	1,125	1,188	1,249	1,317	1,471	1.9	2.9	5
Mauritius	1,518	2,679	4,469	4,718	4,846	5,000	5,235	5,475	5,668	5.9	5.3	4
Mozambique	2,581	2,620	4,249	4,754	5,173	5,485	5,918	6,414	6,925	–0.9	5.5	8.2
Namibia	2,002	2,263	3,414	3,495	3,729	3,858	4,114	4,308	4,433	1.1	4	4.8
Niger	1,523	1,507	1,798	1,926	1,984	2,071	2,054	2,206	2,320	–0.4	2.4	3.9
Nigeria	31,452	34,978	45,984	47,409	48,143	53,102	58,731	61,902	65,740	0.8	2.4	6.7
Rwanda	1,368	1,673	1,735	1,882	2,089	2,096	2,207	2,363	2,492	2.5	–1.6	5.9
São Tomé and Principe	..	..	..	..	..	..	..	..	..	..	..	..
Senegal	2,683	3,463	4,692	4,907	4,939	5,268	5,579	5,893	6,029	2.7	2.8	4.5
Seychelles	292	395	615	601	608	572	556	563	593	3.1	4.5	–1.2
Sierra Leone	935	1,022	634	749	955	1,043	1,120	1,202	1,290	0.5	–5.4	12.3
Somalia	..	..	..	..	..	..	..	..	..	..	..	..
South Africa	95,503	110,945	132,878	136,512	141,520	145,935	152,996	160,793	168,809	1.4	2	4.1
Sudan	5,523	7,059	12,366	13,133	13,842	14,825	15,581	16,562	18,434	2.4	5.4	6.6
Swaziland	490	1,033	1,389	1,289	1,317	1,367	1,402	1,435	1,476	7.2	3.1	1.6
Tanzania	..	6,801	9,079	9,646	10,345	10,931	11,667	12,526	13,370	..	2.7	6.7
Togo	964	1,071	1,329	1,327	1,382	1,419	1,461	1,480	1,541	1.5	3.6	2.6
Uganda	..	3,077	5,927	6,220	6,618	6,930	7,306	7,794	8,190	2.3	7.2	5.6
Zambia	2,730	3,028	3,238	3,396	3,488	3,686	3,886	4,088	4,341	1	0.2	5
Zimbabwe	4,376	6,734	7,399	7,199	6,883	6,167	5,933	5,618		3.3	2.7	–5.7
NORTH AFRICA	**128,670**	**179,235**	**245,626**	**255,900**	**264,663**	**274,772**	**288,005**	**300,872**	**317,549**	**3.4**	**3.2**	**4.3**
Algeria	35,291	46,367	54,790	56,215	58,857	62,918	66,190	69,565	70,817	2.9	1.7	4.8
Egypt, Arab Rep.	38,519	65,600	99,839	103,357	106,649	110,055	114,611	119,681	127,872	5.5	4.3	4
Libya	14,354		..	34,495	36,053	37,228	36,204	38,014	40,409	42,511	–7	..	3.2
Morocco	20,068	29,286	37,059	39,875	41,191	43,704	45,976	47,080	50,846	4.2	2.4	5.1
Tunisia	8,622	12,237	19,443	20,401	20,738	21,891	23,213	24,136	25,503	3.2	4.6	4.6
AFRICA	**357,720**	**453,974**	**587,721**	**610,657**	**631,452**	**657,062**	**693,824**	**729,620**	**771,057**	**2.4**	**2.7**	**4.6**

a. Provisional

Table 2.3

Gross domestic product growth

	Annual growth (%)									Annual average		
	1980	1990	2000	2001	2002	2003	2004	2005	2006ᵃ	1980–89	1990–99	2000–06
SUB-SAHARAN AFRICA	**4.2**	**1.1**	**3.5**	**3.7**	**3.4**	**4.2**	**6.2**	**5.7**	**5.8**	**2.2**	**2.0**	**4.6**
Excl. South Africa	**2.0**	**2.1**	**3.1**	**4.3**	**3.2**	**4.9**	**7.0**	**6.0**	**6.3**	**2.1**	**2.5**	**5.0**
Excl. South Africa & Nigeria	**1.1**	**0.6**	**2.5**	**4.7**	**3.7**	**3.5**	**5.9**	**6.2**	**6.3**	**2.6**	**2.3**	**4.7**
Angola	..	–0.3	3.0	3.1	14.5	3.3	11.2	20.6	18.6	4.2	1.0	10.6
Benin	6.8	3.2	5.8	5.0	4.5	3.9	3.1	2.9	3.8	3.1	4.5	4.1
Botswana	12.0	6.8	8.2	5.2	5.7	6.0	6.2	4.9	3.4	11.5	6.1	5.7
Burkina Faso	0.8	–0.6	1.8	6.6	4.7	8.0	4.6	6.4	5.5	3.7	5.1	5.4
Burundi	1.0	3.5	–0.9	2.1	4.4	–1.2	4.8	0.9	5.1	4.3	–1.4	2.2
Cameroon	–2.0	–6.1	4.2	4.5	4.0	4.0	3.7	2.3	3.2	4.0	0.4	3.7
Cape Verde	..	0.7	6.6	3.8	4.6	6.2	–0.7	6.5	10.7	4.8	5.2	5.4
Central African Republic	–4.5	–2.1	2.3	0.3	–0.6	–7.6	1.3	2.1	4.0	0.9	1.3	0.3
Chad	–6.0	–4.2	–0.9	11.7	8.5	14.7	33.6	7.9	0.2	5.4	2.2	10.8
Comoros	..	5.1	0.9	3.3	4.1	2.5	–0.2	4.2	1.2	2.7	1.6	2.3
Congo, Dem. Rep.	2.2	–6.6	–6.9	–2.1	3.5	5.8	6.6	6.5	5.1	1.8	–5.5	2.6
Congo, Rep.	17.6	1.0	7.6	3.8	4.8	1.7	3.6	7.7	6.2	6.8	0.8	5.1
Côte d'Ivoire	–11.0	–1.1	–3.7	0.0	–1.4	–1.6	1.8	1.2	–0.3	–0.2	2.6	–0.6
Djibouti	..	..	0.4	2.0	2.6	3.2	3.8	3.2	4.8	..	–2.0	2.9
Equatorial Guinea	..	3.3	13.5	62.3	20.6	13.1	32.2	6.9	–5.6	0.9	20.2	20.4
Eritrea	..	..	–13.1	9.2	0.7	6.1	1.9	0.5	–1.0	..	8.1	0.6
Ethiopia	..	2.7	6.1	8.3	1.5	–2.2	13.6	11.8	10.9	2.4	2.7	7.1
Gabon	2.6	5.2	–1.9	2.1	–0.3	2.5	1.3	3.0	1.2	1.9	2.5	1.1
Gambia, The	6.3	3.6	5.5	5.8	–3.2	7.0	5.1	5.0	6.5	3.9	3.1	4.5
Ghana	0.5	3.3	3.7	4.0	4.5	5.2	5.6	5.9	6.4	2.0	4.3	5.0
Guinea	..	4.3	1.9	4.0	4.2	2.0	2.7	3.3	2.2	3.0	4.3	2.9
Guinea-Bissau	–16.0	6.1	7.5	0.2	–7.1	–0.6	2.2	3.5	1.8	2.9	2.0	1.1
Kenya	5.6	4.2	0.5	4.5	0.5	2.9	5.1	5.7	6.1	4.2	2.2	3.6
Lesotho	–2.7	6.4	2.6	1.8	2.9	2.7	4.0	2.9	7.2	3.6	4.0	3.4
Liberia	–4.1	–51.0	25.7	2.9	3.7	–31.3	2.6	5.3	7.8	–4.5	1.2	2.4
Madagascar	0.8	3.1	4.8	6.0	–12.7	9.8	5.3	4.6	4.9	0.4	1.6	3.2
Malawi	0.4	5.7	1.6	–5.0	–4.4	7.4	5.7	2.3	7.9	1.7	4.1	2.0
Mali	–4.3	–1.9	3.2	12.1	4.2	7.4	2.2	6.1	5.3	0.6	3.6	5.8
Mauritania	3.4	–1.8	1.9	2.9	1.1	5.6	5.2	5.4	11.7	2.2	2.6	4.8
Mauritius	..	5.8	4.0	5.6	2.7	3.2	4.7	4.6	3.5	5.9	5.4	4.0
Mozambique	..	1.0	1.1	11.9	8.8	6.0	7.9	8.4	8.0	0.4	5.1	7.4
Namibia	..	2.5	3.5	2.4	6.7	3.5	6.6	4.7	2.9	1.1	4.1	4.3
Niger	–2.2	–1.3	–1.4	7.1	3.0	4.4	–0.8	7.4	5.2	0.0	1.9	3.6
Nigeria	4.2	8.2	5.4	3.1	1.5	10.3	10.6	5.4	6.2	0.9	3.1	6.1
Rwanda	9.0	–2.4	8.1	8.5	11.0	0.3	5.3	7.1	5.5	3.2	2.1	6.5
São Tomé and Principe	..	..	..	..	..	..	..	..	..	..	..	..
Senegal	–3.3	–0.7	3.2	4.6	0.7	6.7	5.9	5.6	2.3	2.4	2.7	4.1
Seychelles	–4.2	7.0	4.3	–2.3	1.2	–5.9	–2.9	1.2	5.3	2.1	4.9	0.1
Sierra Leone	4.8	3.4	3.8	18.2	27.5	9.3	7.4	7.3	7.4	1.1	–4.3	11.5
Somalia	..	..	..	..	..	..	..	..	..	..	..	..
South Africa	6.6	–0.3	4.2	2.7	3.7	3.1	4.8	5.1	5.0	2.2	1.4	4.1
Sudan	1.5	–5.5	8.4	6.2	5.4	7.1	5.1	6.3	11.3	3.4	4.4	7.1
Swaziland	12.4	8.9	2.6	–7.1	2.2	3.8	2.6	2.4	2.8	8.2	3.6	1.3
Tanzania	..	7.0	5.1	6.2	7.2	5.7	6.7	7.4	6.7	3.8	3.1	6.4
Togo	14.6	–0.2	–0.8	–0.2	4.1	2.7	3.0	1.3	4.1	2.6	2.6	2.0
Uganda	..	6.5	5.6	4.9	6.4	4.7	5.4	6.7	5.1	3.0	6.9	5.6
Zambia	3.0	–0.5	3.6	4.9	2.7	5.7	5.4	5.2	6.2	1.4	0.4	4.8
Zimbabwe	14.4	7.0	–7.9	–2.7	–4.4	–10.4	–3.8	–5.3	..	5.2	2.6	–5.8
NORTH AFRICA	**4.6**	**4.0**	**3.5**	**4.2**	**3.4**	**3.8**	**4.8**	**4.5**	**5.5**	**3.4**	**3.3**	**4.2**
Algeria	0.8	0.8	2.2	2.6	4.7	6.9	5.2	5.1	1.8	2.8	1.6	4.1
Egypt, Arab Rep.	10.0	5.7	5.4	3.5	3.2	3.2	4.1	4.4	6.8	5.9	4.3	4.4
Libya	0.6	..	1.1	4.5	3.3	–2.7	5.0	6.3	5.2	–6.4	..	3.2
Morocco	3.6	4.0	1.8	7.6	3.3	6.1	5.2	2.4	8.0	3.9	2.8	4.9
Tunisia	7.4	7.9	4.7	4.9	1.7	5.6	6.0	4.0	5.7	3.6	5.1	4.6
AFRICA	**4.4**	**2.1**	**3.5**	**3.9**	**3.4**	**4.1**	**5.6**	**5.2**	**5.7**	**2.6**	**2.5**	**4.5**

a. Provisional

Table 2.4

Gross domestic product per capita, real

	1980	1990	2000	2001	2002	2003	2004	2005	2006[a]	1980–89	1990–99	2000–06
										Average annual growth (%)		
SUB-SAHARAN AFRICA	**593**	**532**	**508**	**513**	**517**	**526**	**545**	**562**	**580**	**–1.0**	**–0.6**	**2.2**
Excl. South Africa	**371**	**339**	**332**	**338**	**340**	**347**	**362**	**374**	**388**	**–0.9**	**–0.3**	**2.6**
Excl. South Africa & Nigeria	**348**	**331**	**323**	**329**	**333**	**335**	**346**	**358**	**371**	**–0.3**	**–0.2**	**2.3**
Angola	..	804	655	658	732	734	792	928	1,070	..	–2.3	8.2
Benin	292	273	312	317	321	323	322	321	323	–0.7	1.2	0.6
Botswana	1,214	2,483	3,573	3,707	3,869	4,056	4,259	4,415	4,511	7.6	3.3	3.9
Burkina Faso	161	175	220	227	230	241	244	252	258	1.3	2.6	2.6
Burundi	135	152	106	106	107	102	103	101	102	1.2	–3.7	–0.8
Cameroon	698	718	635	648	659	670	679	679	687	1.3	–1.6	1.3
Cape Verde	..	852	1,179	1,196	1,221	1,267	1,229	1,279	1,384	..	3.2	2.7
Central African Republic	316	271	248	245	239	218	217	218	223	–1.2	–1.0	–1.8
Chad	144	181	164	176	184	203	262	274	266	3.3	–0.6	8.1
Comoros	405	416	374	378	386	387	378	386	382	0.0	–1.0	0.4
Congo, Dem. Rep.	250	202	85	81	82	84	87	89	91	–1.2	–8.6	1.1
Congo, Rep.	969	1,154	1,005	1,017	1,040	1,033	1,046	1,101	1,145	2.2	–2.1	2.2
Côte d'Ivoire	926	649	611	599	580	562	563	560	549	–3.4	0.0	–1.8
Djibouti	..	1,177	755	753	757	767	783	794	817	..	–4.7	1.3
Equatorial Guinea	..	611	2,913	4,618	5,438	6,008	7,756	8,098	7,470	..	16.2	15.7
Eritrea	..	..	172	181	174	177	173	167	160	..	..	–1.2
Ethiopia	..	130	124	131	129	123	137	149	161	..	–0.8	4.3
Gabon	5,271	4,683	4,287	4,294	4,205	4,235	4,221	4,279	4,263	–1.5	–0.5	–0.1
Gambia, The	318	316	304	311	292	302	308	315	326	0.0	–0.7	1.1
Ghana	232	210	247	251	257	264	273	282	294	–1.2	1.7	2.9
Guinea	336	346	379	387	396	397	400	406	406	0.2	1.0	1.1
Guinea-Bissau	144	183	157	153	138	133	132	132	131	2.3	–2.2	–3.1
Kenya	434	449	403	411	402	403	413	425	440	0.3	–0.9	1.4
Lesotho	302	376	452	454	462	470	485	496	528	1.9	2.0	2.6
Liberia	745	203	183	181	184	125	126	129	134	–6.6	–3.1	–5.2
Madagascar	342	271	240	247	209	224	229	233	238	–2.6	–1.6	–0.1
Malawi	161	132	150	139	129	134	138	138	145	–2.4	1.6	–0.6
Mali	253	213	242	264	267	278	276	284	290	–1.5	1.4	3.0
Mauritania	461	419	421	421	413	424	433	445	483	–0.6	0.2	2.3
Mauritius	1,572	2,535	3,766	3,932	4,004	4,089	4,245	4,404	4,522	4.8	4.1	3.1
Mozambique	213	193	234	255	270	280	295	312	330	–1.0	2.3	5.8
Namibia	2,017	1,596	1,816	1,827	1,920	1,960	2,064	2,133	2,166	–2.4	1.3	2.9
Niger	263	193	162	167	166	168	160	166	169	–3.0	–1.4	0.7
Nigeria	443	370	369	370	367	394	426	438	454	–2.5	–0.3	3.5
Rwanda	263	229	212	221	239	235	244	256	263	–1.3	–1.0	3.6
São Tomé and Principe	..	..	..	..	..	..	..	..	..	..	..	..
Senegal	457	439	454	463	454	471	486	501	499	–0.1	0.3	1.6
Seychelles	4,532	5,645	7,579	7,400	7,267	6,913	6,740	6,789	7,005	1.8	2.9	–1.3
Sierra Leone	289	250	140	159	194	202	208	215	225	–1.8	–6.5	7.9
Somalia	..	..	..	..	..	..	..	..	..	..	..	..
South Africa	3,463	3,152	3,020	3,046	3,128	3,186	3,301	3,429	3,562	–0.8	–0.7	2.8
Sudan	281	272	371	386	398	418	431	449	489	0.5	2.8	4.6
Swaziland	867	1,342	1,329	1,207	1,210	1,236	1,252	1,269	1,297	4.3	–0.1	–0.4
Tanzania	..	267	268	278	291	299	311	326	339	..	–0.2	3.9
Togo	346	270	246	238	241	240	241	237	240	–2.4	–0.6	–0.4
Uganda	..	173	240	244	252	255	261	269	274	..	3.4	2.2
Zambia	459	373	310	318	321	333	345	356	371	–1.9	–2.2	3.0
Zimbabwe	601	642	585	564	535	477	456	428		0.3	0.0	..
NORTH AFRICA	**1,409**	**1,531**	**1,749**	**1,794**	**1,826**	**1,867**	**1,927**	**1,982**	**2,060**	**0.7**	**1.3**	**2.7**
Algeria	1,876	1,834	1,796	1,816	1,874	1,973	2,045	2,117	2,123	–0.1	–0.3	2.8
Egypt, Arab Rep.	882	1,190	1,501	1,525	1,546	1,566	1,602	1,643	1,724	2.9	2.2	2.3
Libya	4,686	..	6,453	6,608	6,686	6,371	6,555	6,828	7,040	..	..	1.5
Morocco	1,036	1,212	1,302	1,383	1,411	1,481	1,541	1,562	1,667	1.5	0.7	4.1
Tunisia	1,351	1,501	2,033	2,109	2,120	2,225	2,337	2,407	2,518	0.6	3.0	3.6
AFRICA	**753**	**719**	**722**	**732**	**739**	**752**	**776**	**797**	**823**	**–0.5**	**–0.1**	**2.2**

Constant prices (2000 $)

a. Provisional.

Table 2.5 Gross domestic product per capita growth

	Annual growth (%)									Annual average		
	1980	1990	2000	2001	2002	2003	2004	2005	2006ª	1980–89	1990–99	2000–06
SUB-SAHARAN AFRICA	**1.1**	**–1.7**	**0.8**	**1.1**	**0.8**	**1.7**	**3.6**	**3.1**	**3.2**	**–0.8**	**–0.7**	**2.0**
Excl. South Africa	**–1.0**	**–0.8**	**0.4**	**1.6**	**0.6**	**2.3**	**4.3**	**3.3**	**3.6**	**–0.9**	**–0.3**	**2.3**
Excl. South Africa & Nigeria	**–1.9**	**–2.3**	**–0.2**	**1.9**	**1.0**	**0.8**	**3.2**	**3.5**	**3.6**	**–0.5**	**–0.4**	**2.0**
Angola	..	–3.0	0.4	0.3	11.2	0.3	7.9	17.2	15.3	1.6	–1.8	7.5
Benin	3.5	–0.3	2.6	1.7	1.2	0.6	–0.2	–0.3	0.6	–0.2	1.1	0.9
Botswana	8.0	3.7	6.5	3.7	4.4	4.8	5.0	3.7	2.2	7.9	3.5	4.3
Burkina Faso	–1.5	–3.4	–1.2	3.3	1.4	4.6	1.3	3.1	2.4	1.1	2.1	2.1
Burundi	–1.9	0.8	–2.8	–0.5	1.3	–4.5	1.1	–2.9	1.1	1.0	–3.1	–1.0
Cameroon	–4.8	–8.9	1.8	2.1	1.6	1.6	1.4	0.1	1.1	0.9	–2.2	1.4
Cape Verde	..	–1.6	4.1	1.4	2.2	3.7	–3.0	4.1	8.2	2.6	2.8	3.0
Central African Republic	–7.0	–4.5	0.3	–1.5	–2.2	–9.0	–0.2	0.4	2.2	–1.6	–1.3	–1.4
Chad	–8.1	–7.2	–4.3	7.6	4.5	10.5	28.9	4.4	–2.9	2.5	–1.0	7.0
Comoros	..	2.4	–1.2	1.2	2.0	0.3	–2.3	2.1	–0.9	0.1	–0.6	0.2
Congo, Dem. Rep.	–0.9	–9.7	–9.1	–4.6	0.6	2.7	3.4	3.2	1.8	–1.2	–8.2	–0.3
Congo, Rep.	14.1	–1.9	4.8	1.2	2.2	–0.7	1.2	5.3	3.9	3.7	–2.0	2.6
Côte d'Ivoire	–15.1	–4.6	–5.8	–2.0	–3.1	–3.1	0.2	–0.5	–2.0	–4.5	–0.4	–2.3
Djibouti	..	..	–2.4	–0.4	0.5	1.3	2.0	1.4	3.0	..	–4.5	0.8
Equatorial Guinea	..	1.5	10.8	58.5	17.8	10.5	29.1	4.4	–7.8	–1.4	17.5	17.6
Eritrea	..	..	–16.2	5.0	–3.5	1.6	–2.3	–3.3	–4.5	..	6.5	–3.3
Ethiopia	..	–0.5	2.9	5.2	–1.2	–4.7	10.8	8.9	8.0	–0.9	–0.5	4.3
Gabon	–0.2	2.1	–3.9	0.2	–2.1	0.7	–0.3	1.4	–0.4	–1.1	–0.2	–0.6
Gambia, The	2.9	–0.3	2.0	2.4	–6.3	3.7	2.0	2.0	3.5	0.3	–0.6	1.3
Ghana	–2.0	0.5	1.3	1.6	2.1	2.9	3.3	3.7	4.2	–1.1	1.6	2.7
Guinea	..	0.7	–0.1	2.0	2.3	0.2	0.8	1.4	0.2	0.3	1.0	1.0
Guinea-Bissau	–18.8	3.1	4.5	–2.7	–9.9	–3.6	–0.9	0.4	–1.2	0.3	–1.0	–1.9
Kenya	1.7	0.8	–2.1	1.8	–2.0	0.3	2.4	3.0	3.3	0.5	–0.8	1.0
Lesotho	–5.2	4.9	1.0	0.4	1.7	1.7	3.2	2.2	6.4	1.3	2.3	2.4
Liberia	–7.2	–50.5	18.9	–0.7	1.6	–32.2	0.9	2.4	3.7	–6.2	–3.1	–0.8
Madagascar	–2.0	0.2	1.7	3.0	–15.1	6.7	2.4	1.7	2.1	–2.4	–1.3	0.4
Malawi	–2.6	1.8	–1.4	–7.5	–6.9	3.6	3.1	–0.3	5.2	–2.4	1.9	–0.6
Mali	–6.4	–4.3	0.3	8.9	1.1	4.3	–0.9	2.9	2.2	–1.7	0.9	2.7
Mauritania	0.6	–4.3	–1.1	–0.1	–1.8	2.6	2.2	2.6	8.7	–0.4	–0.2	1.9
Mauritius	..	5.0	3.0	4.4	1.8	2.1	3.8	3.7	2.7	4.9	4.2	3.1
Mozambique	..	–0.3	–1.4	9.1	6.1	3.5	5.4	6.0	5.7	–0.6	2.2	4.9
Namibia	..	–1.7	1.4	0.6	5.1	2.1	5.3	3.4	1.6	–2.4	1.0	2.8
Niger	–5.2	–4.4	–4.9	3.4	–0.6	0.8	–4.2	3.7	1.5	–2.9	–1.6	0.0
Nigeria	1.2	5.1	2.7	0.5	–1.0	7.6	7.9	2.9	3.7	–1.9	0.2	3.5
Rwanda	5.4	–2.3	1.3	4.0	8.1	–1.4	3.7	5.0	2.9	–0.5	1.2	3.4
São Tomé and Principe	..	..	..	..	..	..	..	..	..	..	..	..
Senegal	–6.0	–3.5	0.5	1.9	–2.0	3.9	3.2	3.0	–0.2	–0.6	0.0	1.5
Seychelles	–5.4	6.1	3.3	–2.4	–1.8	–4.9	–2.5	0.7	3.2	1.2	3.3	–0.6
Sierra Leone	2.9	1.6	0.6	13.6	21.7	4.2	2.8	3.5	4.4	–1.2	–5.2	7.3
Somalia	..	..	..	..	..	..	..	..	..	..	..	..
South Africa	4.2	–2.3	1.6	0.9	2.7	1.9	3.6	3.9	3.9	–0.3	–0.8	2.6
Sudan	–1.7	–7.7	6.0	4.0	3.3	5.0	3.0	4.1	8.9	0.5	1.8	4.9
Swaziland	9.0	5.6	0.1	–9.1	0.3	2.1	1.3	1.3	2.2	4.9	0.4	–0.3
Tanzania	..	3.7	2.6	3.6	4.5	3.0	4.0	4.7	4.1	0.6	0.2	3.8
Togo	11.1	–3.1	–4.1	–3.3	1.1	–0.1	0.2	–1.4	1.3	–0.9	–0.5	–0.9
Uganda	..	2.6	2.5	1.7	3.1	1.4	2.1	3.3	1.7	–0.5	3.4	2.3
Zambia	–0.3	–3.3	1.3	2.8	0.8	3.8	3.5	3.3	4.2	–1.7	–2.2	2.8
Zimbabwe	10.4	3.8	–8.9	–3.5	–5.1	–11.0	–4.4	–6.0	..	1.4	0.5	–6.5
NORTH AFRICA	**1.9**	**1.8**	**1.8**	**2.5**	**1.8**	**2.2**	**3.2**	**2.9**	**3.9**	**0.9**	**1.4**	**2.6**
Algeria	–2.5	–1.7	0.7	1.1	3.2	5.3	3.6	3.5	0.3	–0.3	–0.4	2.5
Egypt, Arab Rep.	7.6	3.5	3.5	1.6	1.3	1.3	2.3	2.6	4.9	3.5	2.4	2.5
Libya	–4.0	..	–0.9	2.4	1.2	–4.7	2.9	4.2	3.1	–10.2	..	1.2
Morocco	1.1	2.0	0.4	6.2	2.1	4.9	4.1	1.4	6.7	1.6	1.1	3.7
Tunisia	4.6	5.4	3.5	3.7	0.5	4.9	5.1	3.0	4.6	1.0	3.3	3.6
AFRICA	**1.4**	**–0.6**	**1.0**	**1.4**	**1.0**	**1.7**	**3.2**	**2.8**	**3.3**	**–0.3**	**–0.1**	**2.0**

a. Provisional

Table 2.6

2.6 Gross national income, nominal

	Current prices ($ millions)									Average annual growth (%)		
	1980	1990	2000	2001	2002	2003	2004	2005	2006ᵃ	1980–89	1990–99	2000–06
SUB-SAHARAN AFRICA	**261,181**	**281,251**	**323,815**	**319,118**	**345,348**	**423,590**	**521,464**	**607,922**	**706,165**	**0.8**	**1.8**	**15.5**
Excl. South Africa	**185,642**	**173,533**	**194,148**	**204,504**	**237,516**	**261,645**	**309,373**	**370,913**	**456,982**	**−1.1**	**1.7**	**15.5**
Excl. South Africa & Nigeria	**120,565**	**148,013**	**153,848**	**160,336**	**184,716**	**201,540**	**231,074**	**271,216**	**320,956**	**2.6**	**1.3**	**13.2**
Angola	..	8,214	7,449	7,375	9,791	12,230	17,295	26,601	39,660	..	−2.4	33.8
Benin	1,402	1,806	2,243	2,351	2,781	3,515	4,006	4,259	4,623	2.1	3.7	14.2
Botswana	1,028	3,686	5,826	5,896	5,235	7,562	8,801	9,702	10,234	10.8	3.9	12.1
Burkina Faso	1,924	3,094	2,606	2,807	3,288	4,269	5,102	5,411	5,756	4.8	0.0	15.9
Burundi	922	1,117	723	650	614	577	646	776	870	1.9	−3.3	3.5
Cameroon	5,618	10,674	9,464	9,177	10,207	13,097	15,374	16,126	17,702	9.0	−2.4	13.0
Cape Verde	..	340	520	544	605	781	907	972	1,137	..	6.2	15.0
Central African Republic	800	1,465	947	960	1,033	1,193	1,306	1,379	1,554	7.8	−4.3	9.1
Chad	1,038	1,721	1,368	1,687	1,928	2,279	3,720	4,847	4,942	5.5	−1.2	26.7
Comoros	124	249	202	221	250	323	360	385	404	7.9	−2.0	13.5
Congo, Dem. Rep.	14,102	8,579	3,918	4,280	5,250	5,485	6,276	6,760	8,145	−6.8	−7.0	12.5
Congo, Rep.	1,544	2,324	2,275	1,960	2,201	2,679	3,247	4,509	5,979	1.9	−5.2	19.4
Côte d'Ivoire	9,680	9,209	9,715	9,912	10,807	13,018	14,763	15,625	16,473	1.3	3.3	10.5
Djibouti	..	..	567	585	606	673	731	776	854	..	1.3	7.3
Equatorial Guinea	..	124	884	864	1,181	1,406	1,970	3,483	5,241	..	16.9	36.1
Eritrea	..	..	634	668	625	574	620	962	1,079	..	..	8.6
Ethiopia	..	12,016	8,119	8,117	7,751	8,492	9,990	12,269	15,127	5.8	−5.8	11.1
Gabon	3,856	5,336	4,289	4,081	4,450	5,299	5,971	6,678	7,511	−0.1	−1.9	11.1
Gambia, The	237	291	400	395	347	348	381	446	460	1.6	3.7	2.7
Ghana	4,426	5,774	4,831	5,201	6,030	7,459	8,674	10,533	12,596	2.9	2.6	18.1
Guinea	..	2,518	3,035	2,947	3,170	3,580	3,879	3,212	3,257	..	3.3	2.1
Guinea-Bissau	105	233	203	183	193	225	258	289	298	3.4	−0.7	8.8
Kenya	7,043	8,224	12,474	12,836	13,031	14,820	16,069	18,766	22,850	2.6	8.2	10.5
Lesotho	695	1,022	1,072	927	848	1,287	1,620	1,729	1,874	1.3	1.2	13.6
Liberia	930	..	389	403	453	350	373	417	477	−3.2	..	1.8
Madagascar	4,024	2,958	3,807	4,470	4,326	5,394	4,285	4,962	5,419	−6.0	3.8	4.6
Malawi	1,138	1,837	1,707	1,683	2,621	2,385	2,582	2,813	3,125	2.2	0.2	10.6
Mali	1,768	2,405	2,392	2,464	3,103	4,203	4,679	5,099	5,524	2.8	0.1	16.9
Mauritania	672	1,076	1,092	1,089	1,276	1,343	1,613	1,901	2,769	4.7	1.8	15.9
Mauritius	1,130	2,363	4,434	4,551	4,541	5,246	6,028	6,285	6,391	7.7	6.6	7.5
Mozambique	3,550	2,320	4,017	3,771	4,028	4,469	5,358	6,095	6,141	−5.6	8.6	9.4
Namibia	1,818	2,388	3,447	3,215	3,156	4,702	5,733	6,118	6,494	0.2	4.5	14.5
Niger	2,476	2,423	1,782	1,930	2,146	2,718	3,039	3,397	3,707	0.1	−1.7	14.0
Nigeria	61,079	25,585	40,256	44,107	52,716	59,996	78,110	99,421	135,425	−12.5	3.7	22.4
Rwanda	1,165	2,572	1,720	1,652	1,622	1,746	1,936	2,354	2,850	8.5	−2.0	9.0
São Tomé and Principe	..	..	..	..	..	..	..	111	120	..	..	..
Senegal	3,403	5,520	4,601	4,800	5,232	6,753	7,938	8,532	9,107	6.1	−1.6	13.8
Seychelles	142	355	583	605	630	663	666	683	731	8.9	5.9	3.6
Sierra Leone	1,071	580	614	780	906	964	1,041	1,177	1,385	−4.8	1.4	12.9
Somalia	603	835	..	..	..	..	..	..	..	5.5	..	..
South Africa	77,425	107,918	129,702	114,739	108,079	162,044	212,125	237,120	249,710	4.3	2.2	15.7
Sudan	7,508	8,245	10,479	11,919	13,749	16,446	19,990	25,397	33,503	7.2	8.4	21.2
Swaziland	548	941	1,423	1,419	1,186	1,862	2,396	2,633	2,799	1.9	5.9	15.2
Tanzania	..	4,072	8,959	9,356	9,579	10,135	11,153	14,002	14,097	..	9.3	8.6
Togo	1,096	1,598	1,300	1,298	1,454	1,736	2,033	2,118	2,180	4.6	−0.1	10.8
Uganda	1,237	4,227	5,819	5,571	5,719	6,127	6,694	8,504	9,257	20.7	9.1	8.9
Zambia	3,594	3,008	3,082	3,472	3,565	4,231	5,128	6,740	9,885	−4.1	0.7	20.4
Zimbabwe	6,610	8,494	7,145	9,919	21,651	7,207	4,503	3,220	..	−0.2	−2.6	−19.2
NORTH AFRICA	**122,344**	**159,989**	**239,394**	**239,753**	**234,377**	**254,995**	**283,367**	**326,056**	**378,147**	**2.8**	**5.4**	**8.1**
Algeria	41,147	59,955	52,080	53,491	54,823	65,319	81,414	97,259	111,939	4.5	−1.3	14.9
Egypt, Arab Rep.	21,453	42,025	100,838	98,496	88,763	83,006	78,758	89,474	107,219	7.5	11.2	−0.5
Libya	35,480		..	..	..	24,357	30,253	41,462	50,765	−6.0	..	28.6
Morocco	18,402	24,835	36,091	36,784	39,504	48,779	55,404	58,307	64,469	3.3	5.3	11.3
Tunisia	8,450	11,882	18,526	19,077	20,096	23,957	26,895	27,309	29,553	2.0	6.0	9.0
AFRICA	**384,584**	**444,713**	**562,782**	**558,146**	**580,935**	**682,652**	**810,310**	**940,432**	**1,091,816**	**1.6**	**3.0**	**12.8**

a. Provisional

2.7 Gross national income, real

						Constant prices (2000 $ millions)				Average annual growth (%)		
	1980	1990	2000	2001	2002	2003	2004	2005	2006ᵃ	1980–89	1990–99	2000–06
SUB-SAHARAN AFRICA	**227,238**	**273,268**	**342,099**	**354,758**	**366,789**	**382,293**	**405,831**	**428,769**	**453,537**	**1.8**	**2.4**	**4.8**
Excl. South Africa	**131,915**	**162,335**	**209,287**	**218,323**	**225,347**	**236,450**	**252,945**	**268,099**	**284,894**	**2.1**	**2.7**	**5.3**
Excl. South Africa & Nigeria	**99,157**	**127,317**	**163,234**	**170,846**	**177,140**	**183,259**	**194,103**	**206,081**	**219,033**	**2.6**	**2.8**	**4.9**
Angola	..	8,464	9,129	9,416	10,780	11,137	12,383	14,935	17,707	..	1	11.5
Benin	1,084	1,412	2,255	2,368	2,474	2,571	2,650	2,727	2,831	2.7	4.7	3.8
Botswana	1,209	3,395	6,177	6,499	6,867	7,281	7,730	8,105	8,382	10.9	5.6	5.4
Burkina Faso	1,101	1,556	2,611	2,785	2,915	3,150	3,296	3,505	3,698	4	5.5	6
Burundi	559	865	709	724	756	747	783	790	830	4.5	–3.2	2.5
Cameroon	6,339	8,793	10,075	10,530	10,952	11,393	11,815	12,087	12,476	4.5	1.3	3.6
Cape Verde	..	303	531	552	577	613	608	648	717	..	5.9	4.7
Central African Republic	735	815	959	962	956	883	895	914	950	1.6	1.8	–0.7
Chad	665	1,106	1,385	1,547	1,678	1,925	2,572	2,776	2,780	6.7	2.3	14.1
Comoros	136	181	202	209	217	223	222	232	234	2.9	1.2	2.5
Congo, Dem. Rep.	7,016	7,659	4,306	4,215	4,362	4,614	4,921	5,239	5,505	2.1	–5	4.7
Congo, Rep.	1,746	2,796	3,220	3,342	3,503	3,563	3,691	3,975	4,223	3.8	0.8	4.4
Côte d'Ivoire	7,727	8,298	10,417	10,415	10,266	10,106	10,287	10,409	10,382	0.7	3.5	0
Djibouti	..	660	551	563	577	596	619	638	669	..	–2.3	3.3
Equatorial Guinea	..	207	1,254	2,036	2,454	2,775	3,668	3,920	3,702	..	20.7	19.4
Eritrea	..	..	634	692	697	739	753	757	749	..	7.9	2.7
Ethiopia	..	6,234	8,180	8,859	8,993	8,798	9,993	11,174	12,387	2.1	3.7	6.7
Gabon	3,594	4,298	5,068	5,176	5,162	5,290	5,361	5,523	5,588	0.5	2.9	1.7
Gambia, The	213	305	421	445	431	461	484	509	542	3.5	2.7	4.1
Ghana	2,640	3,267	4,977	5,177	5,410	5,691	6,010	6,364	6,771	2.6	4.3	5.3
Guinea	1,539	2,088	3,112	3,236	3,372	3,440	3,534	3,651	3,730	3	4.4	3
Guinea-Bissau	115	186	215	216	201	199	204	211	215	3.8	1.4	–0.2
Kenya	7,060	10,518	12,604	13,168	13,240	13,628	14,321	15,140	16,065	4.1	2.2	4
Lesotho	392	602	853	868	893	917	954	982	1,053	4.1	4.3	3.4
Liberia	1,391	433	561	577	599	411	422	444	479	–3.3	0.2	–4.7
Madagascar	3,099	3,266	3,878	4,111	3,590	3,941	4,149	4,339	4,551	0.8	1.7	2.7
Malawi	1,000	1,243	1,744	1,657	1,584	1,683	1,779	1,819	1,963	2.4	3.8	2.4
Mali	1,536	1,630	2,422	2,716	2,828	3,039	3,105	3,294	3,469	0.5	3.9	5.7
Mauritania	693	816	1,081	1,112	1,125	1,188	1,249	1,317	1,471	1.9	2.9	5
Mauritius	1,518	2,679	4,469	4,718	4,846	5,000	5,235	5,475	5,668	5.9	5.3	4
Mozambique	2,581	2,620	4,249	4,754	5,173	5,485	5,918	6,414	6,925	–0.9	5.5	8.2
Namibia	2,002	2,263	3,414	3,495	3,729	3,858	4,114	4,308	4,433	1.1	4	4.8
Niger	1,523	1,507	1,798	1,926	1,984	2,071	2,054	2,206	2,320	–0.4	2.4	3.9
Nigeria	31,452	34,978	45,984	47,409	48,143	53,102	58,731	61,902	65,740	0.8	2.4	6.7
Rwanda	1,368	1,673	1,735	1,882	2,089	2,096	2,207	2,363	2,492	2.5	–1.6	5.9
São Tomé and Principe	..	..	..	..	..	..	..	..	..	..	..	..
Senegal	2,683	3,463	4,692	4,907	4,939	5,268	5,579	5,893	6,029	2.7	2.8	4.5
Seychelles	292	395	615	601	608	572	556	563	593	3.1	4.5	–1.2
Sierra Leone	935	1,022	634	749	955	1,043	1,120	1,202	1,290	0.5	–5.4	12.3
Somalia	..	..	..	..	..	..	..	..	..	..	..	..
South Africa	95,503	110,945	132,878	136,512	141,520	145,935	152,996	160,793	168,809	1.4	2	4.1
Sudan	5,523	7,059	12,366	13,133	13,842	14,825	15,581	16,562	18,434	2.4	5.4	6.6
Swaziland	490	1,033	1,389	1,289	1,317	1,367	1,402	1,435	1,476	7.2	3.1	1.6
Tanzania	..	6,801	9,079	9,646	10,345	10,931	11,667	12,526	13,370	..	2.7	6.7
Togo	964	1,071	1,329	1,327	1,382	1,419	1,461	1,480	1,541	1.5	3.6	2.6
Uganda	..	3,077	5,927	6,220	6,618	6,930	7,306	7,794	8,190	2.3	7.2	5.6
Zambia	2,730	3,028	3,238	3,396	3,488	3,686	3,886	4,088	4,341	1	0.2	5
Zimbabwe	4,376	6,734	7,399	7,199	6,883	6,167	5,933	5,618	..	3.3	2.7	–5.7
NORTH AFRICA	**128,670**	**179,235**	**245,626**	**255,900**	**264,663**	**274,772**	**288,005**	**300,872**	**317,549**	**3.4**	**3.2**	**4.3**
Algeria	35,291	46,367	54,790	56,215	58,857	62,918	66,190	69,565	70,817	2.9	1.7	4.8
Egypt, Arab Rep.	38,519	65,600	99,839	103,357	106,649	110,055	114,611	119,681	127,872	5.5	4.3	4
Libya	14,354	..	34,495	36,053	37,228	36,204	38,014	40,409	42,511	–7	..	3.2
Morocco	20,068	29,286	37,059	39,875	41,191	43,704	45,976	47,080	50,846	4.2	2.4	5.1
Tunisia	8,622	12,237	19,443	20,401	20,738	21,891	23,213	24,136	25,503	3.2	4.6	4.6
AFRICA	**357,720**	**453,974**	**587,721**	**610,657**	**631,452**	**657,062**	**693,824**	**729,620**	**771,057**	**2.4**	**2.7**	**4.6**

a. Provisional

Table 2.8

Gross national income per capita

			Dollars[a]							Annual average		
	1980	1990	2000	2001	2002	2003	2004	2005	2006[b]	1980–89	1990–99	2000–06
SUB-SAHARAN AFRICA	**669**	**578**	**482**	**474**	**469**	**516**	**621**	**753**	**861**	**590**	**534**	**597**
Excl. South Africa	**541**	**371**	**303**	**310**	**321**	**358**	**422**	**488**	**569**	**426**	**324**	**396**
Excl. South Africa & Nigeria	**463**	**396**	**311**	**309**	**315**	**344**	**394**	**454**	**514**	**406**	**340**	**377**
Angola	..	730	420	460	620	700	940	1,360	1,970	740	452	924
Benin	390	330	340	320	330	370	450	510	530	319	328	407
Botswana	1,020	2,560	3,310	3,500	3,130	3,640	4,320	5,360	5,680	1,263	3,019	4,134
Burkina Faso	300	330	240	240	240	280	340	400	420	270	269	309
Burundi	220	210	120	100	90	90	90	90	100	231	165	97
Cameroon	600	910	620	610	590	670	810	920	980	848	753	743
Cape Verde	..	940	1,280	1,240	1,210	1,400	1,630	1,920	2,190	910	1,122	1,553
Central African Republic	340	460	270	250	240	250	300	340	370	345	362	289
Chad	240	260	180	180	190	210	330	410	440	218	235	277
Comoros	..	540	400	400	400	470	550	650	670	383	501	506
Congo, Dem. Rep.	610	220	80	80	90	100	110	120	130	350	151	101
Congo, Rep.	820	900	550	610	670	710	830	1,050	1,370	998	684	827
Côte d'Ivoire	1,120	720	630	590	560	620	750	840	860	808	703	693
Djibouti	..	..	760	760	780	870	950	1,000	1,060	..	790	883
Equatorial Guinea	..	360	1,540	1,990	2,660	2,690	3,540	5,500	8,510	353	570	3,776
Eritrea	..	..	170	170	160	160	150	170	190	..	202	167
Ethiopia	..	250	130	130	120	110	140	160	190	233	186	140
Gabon	4,890	4,990	3,220	3,460	3,580	3,750	4,210	4,700	5,360	4,541	4,450	4,040
Gambia, The	360	300	310	290	250	250	260	270	270	295	322	271
Ghana	410	380	320	280	260	300	370	440	510	365	376	354
Guinea	..	430	410	380	370	390	430	430	410	538	476	403
Guinea-Bissau	150	220	160	140	130	130	150	180	180	178	202	153
Kenya	460	380	420	400	390	420	470	530	580	381	345	459
Lesotho	460	640	590	540	490	530	660	840	980	517	708	661
Liberia	530	..	130	130	140	100	110	120	130	399	120	123
Madagascar	440	230	240	250	220	280	290	290	280	320	233	264
Malawi	190	180	150	140	150	180	220	220	230	168	186	184
Mali	290	300	260	250	250	320	390	450	460	236	293	340
Mauritania	480	570	470	420	460	470	530	600	760	483	593	530
Mauritius	..	2,300	3,740	3,860	3,820	4,090	4,670	5,250	5,430	1,390	3,202	4,409
Mozambique	..	170	230	230	230	230	260	290	310	250	170	254
Namibia	..	1,710	1,880	1,780	1,750	2,010	2,410	2,950	3,210	1,449	1,981	2,284
Niger	420	300	170	170	170	200	220	250	270	314	230	207
Nigeria	780	270	270	310	350	410	530	620	790	478	258	469
Rwanda	250	350	240	220	210	200	210	250	280	284	274	230
São Tomé and Principe	..	..	..	..	..	..	..	760	800	..	..	780
Senegal	590	680	490	470	450	530	640	740	760	548	591	583
Seychelles	2,080	5,020	7,420	7,380	6,850	7,490	8,240	8,610	8,870	2,764	6,420	7,837
Sierra Leone	380	200	140	160	190	200	210	220	230	280	177	193
Somalia	100	140	..	..	..	..	..	..	..	127	..	..
South Africa	2,510	3,390	3,050	2,830	2,640	2,870	3,630	4,810	5,390	2,805	3,473	3,603
Sudan	460	400	310	340	370	430	510	620	780	511	255	480
Swaziland	960	1,200	1,380	1,310	1,160	1,360	1,650	2,180	2,450	948	1,404	1,641
Tanzania	..	190	260	270	270	290	310	350	370	..	189	303
Togo	410	380	270	240	240	260	310	340	350	306	326	287
Uganda	..	320	260	240	230	230	250	270	300	283	243	254
Zambia	610	430	300	310	320	360	410	500	640	443	356	406
Zimbabwe	930	860	450	530	780	760	560	340	..	862	661	570
NORTH AFRICA	**1,277**	**1,379**	**1,680**	**1,710**	**1,679**	**1,740**	**1,877**	**2,093**	**2,333**	**1,307**	**1,385**	**1,873**
Algeria	2,060	2,420	1,610	1,680	1,750	1,950	2,290	2,720	3,110	2,462	1,759	2,159
Egypt, Arab Rep.	500	770	1,460	1,480	1,420	1,330	1,270	1,270	1,360	636	962	1,370
Libya	10,390	..	..	..	..	4,270	4,420	5,870	7,390	7,730	..	5,488
Morocco	970	1,030	1,340	1,350	1,330	1,500	1,780	1,990	2,160	801	1,174	1,636
Tunisia	1,360	1,430	2,090	2,060	2,000	2,260	2,650	2,870	3,040	1,264	1,808	2,424
AFRICA	**785**	**733**	**689**	**684**	**674**	**723**	**834**	**979**	**1,107**	**728**	**692**	**813**

a. Calculated using the World Bank Atlas method.
b. Provisional.

Table 2.9

Gross domestic product deflator (local currency series)

	1980	1990	2000	2001	2002	2003	2004	2005	2006[a]	1980–89	1990–99	2000–06
										Annual average		
				Index (2000=100)								
SUB-SAHARAN AFRICA	**13**	**38**	**100**	**105**	**111**	**117**	**123**	**131**	**140**	**22.0**	**66.0**	**118.0**
Excl. South Africa	**14**	**39**	**100**	**105**	**110**	**117**	**122**	**130**	**139**	**23.0**	**66.0**	**118.0**
Excl. South Africa & Nigeria	**15**	**39**	**100**	**105**	**110**	**117**	**121**	**130**	**139**	**24.0**	**66.0**	**117.0**
Angola	..	..	100	208	460	931	1,329	1,780	2,041	..	3.0	979.0
Benin	38	50	100	103	111	113	113	116	120	47.0	73.0	111.0
Botswana	13	41	100	106	107	110	117	130	150	22.0	62.0	117.0
Burkina Faso	52	76	100	104	110	111	115	115	115	67.0	84.0	110.0
Burundi	21	31	100	105	107	120	130	151	155	24.0	51.0	124.0
Cameroon	34	58	100	102	105	106	107	110	115	50.0	79.0	107.0
Cape Verde	..	66	100	103	105	106	113	115	121	60.0	81.0	109.0
Central African Republic	32	70	100	104	107	110	108	109	114	54.0	83.0	108.0
Chad	46	60	100	114	116	116	127	157	166	55.0	78.0	128.0
Comoros	36	70	100	109	113	119	121	124	126	54.0	82.0	116.0
Congo, Dem. Rep.	..	..	..	..	..	..	..	..	..	..	..	..
Congo, Rep.	29	38	100	86	84	82	87	113	134	39.0	50.0	98.0
Côte d'Ivoire	39	50	100	105	110	111	112	117	122	50.0	75.0	111.0
Djibouti	..	69	100	102	102	104	108	111	115	..	85.0	106.0
Equatorial Guinea	..	24	100	88	86	87	99	142	170	26.0	41.0	110.0
Eritrea	..	..	100	114	131	147	180	206	231	..	66.0	158.0
Ethiopia	..	49	100	94	91	102	106	117	130	42.0	79.0	106.0
Gabon	35	53	100	94	94	93	99	116	125	44.0	63.0	103.0
Gambia, The	15	64	100	115	134	170	194	203	207	31.0	82.0	160.0
Ghana	..	11	100	135	166	213	244	280	316	3.0	37.0	208.0
Guinea	5	48	100	105	108	120	145	186	256	17.0	77.0	145.0
Guinea-Bissau	..	6	100	95	98	96	98	106	105	1.0	47.0	100.0
Kenya	10	24	100	102	103	109	117	123	134	16.0	57.0	112.0
Lesotho	12	38	100	107	117	124	129	133	139	21.0	65.0	121.0
Liberia	2	2	100	112	141	145	146	166	182	2.0	22.0	142.0
Madagascar	4	21	100	107	124	127	145	172	191	10.0	54.0	138.0
Malawi	2	7	100	126	217	236	270	312	368	3.0	29.0	233.0
Mali	35	57	100	100	116	117	116	119	124	50.0	79.0	113.0
Mauritania	20	42	100	108	116	119	133	157	203	29.0	75.0	134.0
Mauritius	21	54	100	104	111	117	124	130	136	33.0	74.0	118.0
Mozambique	..	6	100	115	124	131	141	153	162	1.0	45.0	132.0
Namibia	12	39	100	114	127	126	128	133	145	21.0	63.0	125.0
Niger	49	63	100	104	107	104	105	112	114	63.0	78.0	106.0
Nigeria	2	7	100	111	146	162	195	234	280	3.0	41.0	175.0
Rwanda	20	33	100	101	96	117	132	144	163	25.0	70.0	122.0
São Tomé and Principe	..	..	..	..	..	..	..	..	..	..	..	..
Senegal	39	63	100	103	106	107	107	110	113	55.0	81.0	106.0
Seychelles	56	87	100	106	110	117	121	124	126	70.0	92.0	115.0
Sierra Leone	..	5	100	102	98	106	123	139	155	1.0	41.0	118.0
Somalia	..	..	..	..	..	..	..	..	..	..	..	..
South Africa	9	38	100	108	119	124	132	138	147	18.0	65.0	124.0
Sudan	..	..	..	..	..	..	..	..	..	..	..	..
Swaziland	12	32	100	127	137	145	158	167	184	19.0	57.0	145.0
Tanzania	..	15	100	107	114	122	132	159	166	11.0	49.0	129.0
Togo	35	58	100	103	105	101	105	108	106	49.0	78.0	104.0
Uganda	..	30	100	107	102	112	119	129	140	4.0	72.0	116.0
Zambia	..	1	100	124	151	181	218	258	290	0.0	32.0	189.0
Zimbabwe	2	7	100	177	394	1,883	9,064	30,632	..	4.0	24.0	7042.0
NORTH AFRICA	**30**	**54**	**100**	**101**	**104**	**111**	**123**	**132**	**142**	**44.0**	**77.0**	**116.0**
Algeria	6	16	100	101	103	111	123	143	159	9.0	50.0	120.0
Egypt, Arab Rep.	13	43	100	102	104	111	124	132	142	20.0	73.0	117.0
Libya	143	..	100	98	128	166	204	264	300	153.0	81.0	180.0
Morocco	35	68	100	101	102	103	102	104	106	50.0	84.0	103.0
Tunisia	30	64	100	103	105	107	110	114	118	46.0	82.0	108.0
AFRICA	**14**	**39**	**100**	**104**	**110**	**116**	**123**	**132**	**141**	**23.0**	**67.0**	**118.0**

a. Provisional

Table 2.10 Gross domestic product deflator (U.S. dollar series)

	1980	1990	2000	2001	2002	2003	2004	2005	2006[a]	Annual average		
										1980–89	1990–99	2000–06
SUB-SAHARAN AFRICA	**122**	**109**	**100**	**95**	**99**	**117**	**136**	**150**	**164**	**108**	**108**	**123**
Excl. South Africa	**149**	**114**	**100**	**100**	**112**	**118**	**132**	**150**	**172**	**123**	**103**	**126**
Excl. South Africa & Nigeria	**131**	**123**	**100**	**99**	**110**	**116**	**127**	**141**	**157**	**120**	**111**	**121**
Angola	..	121	100	95	106	125	160	205	255	95	91	149
Benin	130	131	100	100	113	138	153	157	163	103	116	132
Botswana	88	112	100	93	86	114	127	130	131	77	108	112
Burkina Faso	175	199	100	101	113	136	155	155	156	147	135	131
Burundi	164	131	100	92	83	80	85	101	109	153	123	93
Cameroon	106	127	100	91	99	120	134	137	144	102	125	118
Cape Verde	..	112	100	100	107	130	152	155	165	95	117	130
Central African Republic	108	183	100	101	109	135	146	148	155	117	143	128
Chad	155	157	100	111	118	142	172	212	227	121	129	154
Comoros	91	138	100	106	116	146	163	167	172	89	125	138
Congo, Dem. Rep.	205	122	100	111	127	123	134	136	155	133	126	127
Congo, Rep.	98	100	100	84	86	100	118	153	183	84	81	118
Côte d'Ivoire	132	130	100	101	112	136	150	157	166	108	123	132
Djibouti	..	69	100	102	102	104	108	111	115	..	85	106
Equatorial Guinea	..	64	100	85	88	107	134	192	231	54	65	134
Eritrea	..	..	100	97	91	79	84	128	145	..	99	103
Ethiopia	..	194	100	92	87	97	101	110	122	167	151	101
Gabon	119	138	100	91	96	114	134	157	171	96	104	123
Gambia, The	113	104	100	94	86	80	83	91	94	91	109	90
Ghana	168	180	100	103	114	134	148	168	188	177	166	136
Guinea	434	128	100	94	95	105	111	89	86	420	136	97
Guinea-Bissau	97	131	100	92	100	118	132	143	143	105	116	118
Kenya	103	82	100	99	99	110	113	124	142	86	86	112
Lesotho	110	102	100	87	77	113	138	145	142	92	115	115
Liberia	69	89	100	94	93	100	109	119	128	76	101	106
Madagascar	130	94	100	110	122	139	105	116	121	108	101	116
Malawi	124	151	100	104	168	144	148	157	161	118	132	140
Mali	116	149	100	97	118	144	157	161	169	108	132	135
Mauritania	102	125	100	101	102	108	124	139	181	108	140	122
Mauritius	76	89	100	96	94	105	116	115	112	71	104	105
Mozambique	137	94	100	86	81	85	96	103	99	150	92	93
Namibia	108	104	100	92	84	116	137	145	148	90	111	117
Niger	165	165	100	101	109	127	141	151	155	137	127	126
Nigeria	204	81	100	101	123	127	150	181	223	127	76	144
Rwanda	85	154	100	89	79	85	89	101	115	112	123	94
São Tomé and Principe	..	..	..	..	..	..	..	..	..	..	..	..
Senegal	131	165	100	99	108	130	144	147	154	120	136	126
Seychelles	50	93	100	104	115	123	126	128	131	65	103	118
Sierra Leone	118	64	100	108	98	95	96	101	110	97	98	101
Somalia	..	..	..	..	..	..	..	..	..	..	..	..
South Africa	85	101	100	87	78	114	141	151	151	88	115	117
Sudan	138	128	100	102	108	120	139	165	197	186	89	133
Swaziland	111	85	100	102	90	133	170	182	189	84	100	138
Tanzania	..	63	100	98	94	94	97	113	106	76	77	100
Togo	118	152	100	100	107	124	141	145	144	106	131	123
Uganda	..	140	100	91	88	90	93	112	116	164	114	99
Zambia	142	109	100	107	107	119	142	180	251	111	111	144
Zimbabwe	153	130	100	142	318	120	79	61	..	136	101	137
NORTH AFRICA	**102**	**96**	**100**	**94**	**85**	**91**	**97**	**107**	**117**	**95**	**92**	**99**
Algeria	120	134	100	98	97	108	128	147	164	128	101	120
Egypt, Arab Rep.	59	66	100	94	82	75	69	75	84	62	76	83
Libya	248	..	100	83	52	66	80	103	117	263	89	86
Morocco	94	88	100	95	98	114	123	125	129	73	99	112
Tunisia	101	100	100	98	101	114	121	120	121	89	111	111
AFRICA	**114**	**103**	**100**	**94**	**93**	**106**	**119**	**132**	**145**	**102**	**101**	**113**

a. Provisional

Table 2.11

2.11 Consumer price index*

	Annual (% change)									Annual average		
	1980	1990	2000	2001	2002	2003	2004	2005	2006ª	1980–89	1990–99	2000–06
SUB-SAHARAN AFRICA												
Excl. South Africa												
Excl. South Africa & Nigeria												
Angola	..	..	325.0	169.7	95.6	98.2	43.5	24.8	11.7	..	1,122.5	109.8
Benin	..	..	4.2	4.0	2.5	1.5	0.9	5.4	3.8	..	9.7	3.2
Botswana	13.6	11.4	8.6	6.6	8.0	9.2	6.9	8.6	11.6	10.8	10.8	8.5
Burkina Faso	12.2	–0.8	–0.3	5.0	2.2	2.0	–0.4	6.4	2.3	5.0	4.5	2.5
Burundi	2.5	7.0	24.3	9.2	–1.3	7.9	10.7	13.5	2.8	7.2	13.5	9.6
Cameroon	9.6	1.1	1.2	4.4	2.8	0.6	0.2	2.0	5.1	9.1	5.6	2.4
Cape Verde	..	10.7	–2.5	3.3	1.9	1.2	–1.9	0.4	5.4	6.7	6.4	1.1
Central African Republic	..	–0.4	3.2	3.8	2.3	4.1	–2.1	2.9	..	3.7	3.9	2.4
Chad	..	–0.7	3.8	12.4	5.2	–1.8	–5.4	7.9	8.0	3.0	5.5	4.3
Comoros	..	..	..	..	..	..	..	..	..	..	..	..
Congo, Dem. Rep.	46.6	81.3	550.0	313.7	38.1	12.9	4.0	21.3	..	57.0	3,367.2	156.7
Congo, Rep.	..	2.9	–0.8	0.0	3.7	2.3	1.0	5.3	3.4	1.0	8.5	2.1
Côte d'Ivoire	14.7	–0.8	2.5	4.3	3.1	3.3	1.4	3.9	2.5	6.7	6.0	3.0
Djibouti	12.1	..	..	..	..	..	..	..	..	5.3	..	..
Equatorial Guinea	..	0.9	4.8	8.8	7.6	7.3	4.2	..	..	–5.5	6.6	6.6
Eritrea	..	..	..	..	..	..	..	..	..	..	..	..
Ethiopia	4.5	5.2	0.7	–8.2	1.7	17.8	3.3	11.6	12.3	4.6	8.0	5.6
Gabon	12.3	7.7	0.5	2.1	0.0	2.2	0.4	1.2	–1.4	6.5	3.7	0.7
Gambia, The	6.8	12.2	0.2	4.4	8.6	17.0	14.2	3.2	..	17.5	5.5	7.9
Ghana	50.1	37.3	25.2	32.9	14.8	26.7	12.6	15.1	10.9	48.3	27.6	19.7
Guinea	..	..	..	..	..	..	..	..	..	..	..	..
Guinea-Bissau	..	33.0	8.6	3.3	3.3	–3.5	0.9	3.3	2.0	70.5	37.4	2.6
Kenya	13.9	17.8	10.0	5.7	2.0	9.8	11.6	10.3	14.5	11.8	17.4	9.1
Lesotho	16.3	11.6	6.1	–9.6	33.8	6.7	5.0	3.4	6.0	13.9	12.4	7.4
Liberia	14.7	..	..	..	..	..	..	..	..	5.9	..	..
Madagascar	18.2	11.8	12.0	6.9	15.9	–1.2	13.8	18.5	10.8	18.6	17.3	11.0
Malawi	..	11.8	29.6	22.7	14.7	9.6	11.4	15.4	14.0	16.8	31.0	16.8
Mali	..	0.6	–0.7	5.2	5.0	–1.3	–3.1	6.4	1.5	–0.1	4.2	1.9
Mauritania	..	6.6	3.3	4.7	3.9	5.2	10.4	12.1	6.2	7.5	6.4	6.5
Mauritius	42.0	13.5	4.2	5.4	6.5	3.9	4.8	4.9	8.9	11.2	7.6	5.5
Mozambique	..	47.0	12.7	9.0	16.8	13.4	12.7	7.2	13.2	45.1	34.5	12.2
Namibia	..	..	..	..	..	7.2	4.1	2.3	5.1	..	..	4.7
Niger	10.3	–0.8	2.9	4.0	2.6	–1.6	0.3	7.8	0.0	3.6	4.3	2.3
Nigeria	10.0	7.4	6.9	18.9	12.9	14.0	15.0	17.9	8.2	20.9	30.6	13.4
Rwanda	7.2	4.2	4.3	3.0	2.3	7.1	12.3	9.0	8.9	4.7	8.6	6.7
São Tomé and Principe	..	..	..	..	..	..	..	..	..	..	..	..
Senegal	8.7	0.3	0.7	3.1	2.2	0.0	0.5	1.7	2.1	6.9	4.4	1.5
Seychelles	13.6	3.9	6.3	6.0	0.2	3.3	3.8	0.9	–0.3	4.0	2.0	2.9
Sierra Leone	12.9	110.9	–0.8	2.1	–3.3	7.6	14.2	12.1	9.5	63.0	45.9	5.9
Somalia	..	..	..	..	..	..	..	..	..	..	..	..
South Africa	13.7	14.3	5.3	5.7	9.2	5.9	1.4	3.4	4.6	14.6	9.9	5.1
Sudan	25.4	65.2	6.9	5.8	9.8	6.5	8.3	8.5	7.2	36.2	80.4	7.6
Swaziland	18.7	13.1	12.2	5.9	12.0	7.3	3.4	4.8	5.3	15.0	9.5	7.3
Tanzania	30.2	35.8	5.9	5.1	1.0	3.5	0.0	8.6	6.4	30.1	23.1	4.4
Togo	12.3	1.0	1.9	3.9	3.1	–1.0	0.4	6.8	2.2	5.0	7.1	2.5
Uganda	..	33.1	2.8	2.0	–0.3	7.8	3.3	8.2	6.8	111.2	15.9	4.4
Zambia	..	107.0	26.0	21.4	22.2	21.4	18.0	18.3	9.0	69.3	76.2	19.5
Zimbabwe	5.4	17.4	55.9	76.7	140.1	431.7	282.4	302.1	1,096.7	12.8	28.6	340.8
NORTH AFRICA												
Algeria	9.5	16.6	0.3	4.2	1.4	2.6	3.6	1.6	2.5	9.0	18.6	2.3
Egypt, Arab Rep.	20.8	16.8	2.7	2.3	2.7	4.5	11.3	4.9	7.6	17.4	10.5	5.1
Libya	12.4	8.5	–2.9	–8.8	–9.9	–2.1	–2.2	2.0	3.4	8.1	6.7	–2.9
Morocco	9.4	6.9	1.9	0.6	2.8	1.2	1.5	1.0	3.3	7.6	4.5	1.7
Tunisia	..	6.5	2.9	2.0	2.7	2.7	3.6	2.0	4.5	7.6	4.9	2.9
AFRICA												

a. Provisional

* For a discussion on the impacts of the recent food prices acceleration, see Box 3 in the technical notes.

Table 2.12 Price indices*

	Inflation, GDP deflator (annual %)		Consumer price index (2000 = 100)		Exports price index (goods and services, 2000 = 100)		Imports price index (goods and services, 2000 = 100)	
	2005	2006	2005	2006	2005	2006	2005	2006
SUB-SAHARAN AFRICA	**8.8**	**7.4**	**128.1**	**139.5**	..	..	**139.8**	**147.5**
Excl. South Africa	**8.8**	**7.9**	**128.1**	**140.9**	..	..	**137.0**	**146.0**
Excl. South Africa & Nigeria	**8.8**	**7.2**	**127.4**	**139.5**	..	..	**137.0**	**146.0**
Angola	34.0	14.7	1,872.8	2,091.5	..	..	..	..
Benin	2.8	3.0	115.0	119.3	145.5	..	158.5	..
Botswana	11.1	15.6	146.0	162.9	144.5	139.2	146.2	141.7
Burkina Faso	−0.3	−0.1	116.0	118.7	160.1	158.0	158.2	164.4
Burundi	16.6	2.6	146.1	150.2	..	..	..	..
Cameroon	2.6	3.9	110.5	116.1	133.6	160.5	144.0	148.7
Cape Verde	2.0	5.2	105.0	110.6	63.0	63.5	107.4	108.3
Central African Republic	1.0	4.3	111.5	..	120.2	127.8	161.8	177.6
Chad	23.1	6.2	118.7	128.2	211.6	226.6	211.6	226.6
Comoros	2.3	2.0	..	..	167.2	172.0	167.2	172.0
Congo, Dem. Rep.	21.6	13.1	813.6	..	161.2	176.6	106.3	126.5
Congo, Rep.	29.9	18.5	112.8	116.7	..	..	..	..
Côte d'Ivoire	4.2	5.0	117.1	120.0	126.9	139.0	171.9	169.2
Djibouti	3.2	3.5	..	..	111.0	115.0	111.0	115.0
Equatorial Guinea	43.5	19.4	..	..	186.3	232.6	129.1	138.6
Eritrea	14.9	12.0	..	..	106.5	110.0	126.0	127.8
Ethiopia	9.9	11.6	126.6	142.2	97.6	110.4	129.5	139.2
Gabon	17.0	7.9	106.1	104.6	179.8	212.5	134.2	141.3
Gambia, The	4.3	2.1	156.4	..	84.5	..	114.8	..
Ghana	15.0	12.7	250.6	278.0	142.3	168.9	143.4	163.9
Guinea	28.6	37.4	..	..	115.1	135.2	129.2	145.5
Guinea-Bissau	7.6	−0.5	107.4	109.5	136.1	146.6	157.1	151.3
Kenya	4.4	9.4	145.8	166.9	125.7	131.6	134.9	151.2
Lesotho	3.4	4.2	140.2	148.6	174.5	172.3	146.0	148.1
Liberia	13.8	9.2	..	..	..	..	..	..
Madagascar	18.4	11.3	165.2	183.0	140.6	137.0	101.1	106.0
Malawi	15.6	18.0	198.4	226.1	216.8	216.6	115.6	117.2
Mali	2.4	4.1	112.4	114.1	138.1	172.0	155.9	178.5
Mauritania	18.0	29.8	141.6	150.4	140.4	142.0	107.2	..
Mauritius	4.8	4.1	128.1	139.5	109.9	109.0	121.7	124.1
Mozambique	8.8	6.0	174.4	197.5	101.1	122.5	145.9	151.1
Namibia	3.7	9.1	114.1	119.9	151.2	159.8	150.9	153.4
Niger	6.8	1.8	113.5	113.5	..	..	..	..
Nigeria	19.8	19.6	207.4	224.5	..	..	..	..
Rwanda	8.9	13.1	138.1	150.3	77.0	80.7	116.2	108.3
São Tomé and Principe	7.6	19.9	..	..	..	..	..	..
Senegal	2.3	3.4	107.7	110.0	155.5	170.9	165.5	180.2
Seychelles	2.0	2.2	114.9	114.5	128.4	130.7	128.4	130.7
Sierra Leone	12.9	11.6	135.9	148.9	..	..	..	..
Somalia	..	..	..	..	..	..	..	..
South Africa	4.8	6.8	128.1	134.0	156.2	169.3	143.5	149.3
Sudan	12.2	6.5	145.5	155.9	161.8	194.0	161.8	194.1
Swaziland	5.7	10.3	138.0	145.3	106.5	95.2	112.8	98.8
Tanzania	20.2	4.2	119.4	127.1	103.7	108.9	142.3	139.6
Togo	3.0	−1.9	113.7	116.3	132.1	..	131.6	..
Uganda	7.9	8.6	122.5	130.8	114.2	133.5	103.8	105.1
Zambia	18.1	12.6	251.4	274.1	100.3	137.6	91.2	97.8
Zimbabwe	237.9	..	34,682.2	415,034.4	102.9	..	111.7	..
NORTH AFRICA	**6.3**	**7.4**	**113.8**	**117.0**	..	..	**121.0**	**122.2**
Algeria	16.5	10.8	114.1	117.0	178.6	..	134.3	..
Egypt, Arab Rep.	6.3	7.4	128.1	137.9	103.0	100.5	93.9	89.5
Libya	29.1	13.7	80.3	83.0	..	..	..	..
Morocco	2.1	1.9	107.2	110.8	139.1	145.7	132.1	139.7
Tunisia	3.1	3.8	113.8	118.9	133.0	153.2	136.1	152.0
AFRICA	**8.3**	**7.4**	**126.6**	**132.4**	..	..	**132.5**	**138.8**

*For a discussion on the perception of the public about inflation, see Box 4 in the technical notes.

Table 2.13

2.13 Gross domestic savings

	Share of GDP (%)									Annual average		
	1980	1990	2000	2001	2002	2003	2004	2005	2006[a]	1980–89	1990–99	2000–06
SUB-SAHARAN AFRICA	**35.4**	**16.2**	**20.5**	**19.9**	**21.9**	**21.7**	**22.6**	**25.1**	**29.0**	**22.3**	**14.6**	**23.0**
Excl. South Africa	**31.5**	**9.9**	**20.9**	**18.5**	**20.1**	**22.5**	**26.3**	**29.8**	**34.8**	**16.3**	**10.7**	**24.7**
Excl. South Africa & Nigeria	**14.4**	**12.8**	**16.9**	**14.2**	**14.5**	**16.1**	**17.9**	**20.2**	**23.5**	**13.3**	**12.5**	**17.6**
Angola	..	29.7	41.8	15.1	23.9	19.2	25.1	37.9	49.5	24.0	22.0	30.4
Benin	–6.3	2.2	6.0	6.5	3.7	6.0	5.5	6.9	..	–2.4	3.8	5.8
Botswana	26.7	42.6	53.9	55.9	52.2	50.4	50.7	52.4	52.4	35.3	39.7	52.6
Burkina Faso	–7.2	5.4	0.6	–0.1	3.7	4.5	1.8	4.8	2.8	–1.6	9.0	2.6
Burundi	–0.6	–5.4	–6.0	–7.8	–9.7	–8.7	–11.0	–23.1	–20.2	3.1	–5.2	–12.4
Cameroon	21.7	20.7	20.3	19.0	19.0	17.8	18.5	18.1	18.9	24.2	18.5	18.8
Cape Verde	..	–8.1	–14.2	–15.1	–15.7	–15.8	–1.5	4.4	4.7	–2.2	–5.6	–7.6
Central African Republic	–8.9	–0.6	5.2	3.9	4.3	1.7	0.1	0.2	1.1	–1.1	3.7	2.4
Chad	..	–7.7	5.5	5.3	–40.8	18.5	24.5	35.5	39.8	–8.1	–0.5	12.6
Comoros	–10.1	–3.2	–5.7	–5.2	–4.0	–5.8	–10.6	–12.9	–14.0	–4.5	–4.5	–8.3
Congo, Dem. Rep.	10.1	9.3	4.5	3.2	4.0	5.0	4.0	6.5	4.7	10.9	8.8	4.5
Congo, Rep.	35.7	23.8	59.3	50.5	51.0	51.3	51.3	57.6	65.7	31.9	28.8	55.2
Côte d'Ivoire	20.4	11.3	17.9	19.5	26.7	21.0	20.0	17.2	20.4	19.6	17.8	20.4
Djibouti	..	–10.4	–6.5	–0.6	4.9	5.3	4.3	8.6	12.1	..	–6.4	4.0
Equatorial Guinea	..	–20.1	74.5	81.2	79.0	79.8	83.5	87.3	86.0	..	13.7	81.6
Eritrea	..	..	–34.7	–27.0	–33.7	–59.7	–61.4	–26.8	–23.3	..	–30.9	–38.1
Ethiopia	..	9.6	8.3	9.7	9.9	7.7	8.8	2.6	1.5	10.5	9.7	7.0
Gabon	60.6	36.9	58.3	51.7	43.7	48.2	53.9	67.2	64.7	44.3	43.6	55.4
Gambia, The	5.8	10.7	8.5	12.0	12.9	11.1	10.5	4.4	..	6.5	7.4	9.9
Ghana	4.9	5.5	5.6	7.0	7.4	7.0	7.3	3.4	7.9	4.8	7.5	6.5
Guinea	..	22.2	15.4	14.1	9.5	7.8	7.4	11.3	10.5	15.1	18.3	10.9
Guinea-Bissau	–1.0	2.8	–8.5	–19.3	–12.1	1.2	–3.0	1.5	6.3	–0.9	1.5	–4.8
Kenya	18.1	18.5	9.4	7.0	8.4	10.4	9.3	6.1	9.5	18.3	15.5	8.6
Lesotho	–52.0	–52.9	–20.6	–16.6	–19.8	–17.3	–12.4	–16.2	–15.0	–65.5	–38.3	–16.8
Liberia	14.8	..	..	–3.4	–3.3	–3.2	–0.7	2.4	..	2.2	..	–1.6
Madagascar	–1.4	5.5	7.7	15.3	7.7	8.9	9.4	8.4	13.6	2.9	4.2	10.2
Malawi	10.8	13.4	3.8	3.8	..	–3.4	2.0	7.7	11.2	12.7	3.4	4.2
Mali	1.1	6.4	12.0	14.0	11.3	13.3	8.6	11.0	14.8	–0.4	7.6	12.1
Mauritania	–3.5	4.9	–8.6	3.1	–1.9	–5.0	–3.1	–15.0	18.8	3.1	2.4	–1.7
Mauritius	14.5	23.5	23.9	26.0	25.2	24.8	23.4	18.9	17.5	20.0	24.1	22.8
Mozambique	–8.9	–5.8	11.5	3.7	11.6	6.1	10.0	9.3	13.3	–6.2	–2.9	9.4
Namibia	38.4	18.2	14.0	17.0	17.8	26.2	20.0	24.2	28.4	10.8	12.7	21.1
Niger	14.6	1.2	3.5	4.4	5.3	5.2	4.1	13.7	..	7.3	2.7	6.0
Nigeria[b]	..	..	..	..	..	..	..	..	..	..	..	..
Rwanda	4.2	6.2	1.3	2.9	–0.5	0.4	3.5	3.3	3.2	5.0	–5.5	2.0
São Tomé and Principe	..	..	..	..	..	..	..	..	..	..	..	..
Senegal	2.1	2.4	11.2	9.4	6.8	8.8	7.9	14.1	10.5	4.3	5.4	9.8
Seychelles	27.1	20.3	21.9	19.2	24.4	21.5	14.7	3.8	10.2	24.1	21.7	16.5
Sierra Leone	0.9	8.7	–14.4	–11.6	–9.4	–7.4	–1.7	–0.6	1.7	9.1	2.8	–6.2
Somalia	–12.9	–12.5	..	..	..	..	..	..	..	–6.3	..	..
South Africa	37.9	23.2	18.9	19.3	19.9	19.2	17.2	17.3	17.1	28.5	19.4	18.4
Sudan	2.1	3.1	15.9	9.8	13.3	15.7	18.7	14.2	14.4	4.0	7.6	14.6
Swaziland	1.2	6.6	3.0	2.9	19.6	20.8	15.9	9.0	8.1	3.7	2.0	11.3
Tanzania	..	1.3	10.2	8.8	11.8	12.0	11.2	9.7	10.8	..	2.0	10.7
Togo	23.2	14.7	–2.2	1.0	0.6	5.3	4.5	6.9	..	12.3	6.7	2.7
Uganda	–0.4	0.6	8.1	6.5	4.7	6.3	8.4	7.6	8.1	2.3	4.3	7.1
Zambia	19.3	16.6	3.0	2.8	7.9	13.0	19.6	21.2	30.9	14.0	9.0	14.0
Zimbabwe	13.8	17.5	13.3	11.6	7.1	6.2	4.1	0.6	..	16.5	16.9	7.2
NORTH AFRICA	**41.3**	**22.8**	**24.8**	**23.6**	**24.3**	**27.5**	**31.1**	**35.5**	**37.0**	**29.4**	**20.2**	**29.1**
Algeria	43.1	27.1	44.8	42.0	40.9	44.9	47.7	54.1	..	31.5	30.1	45.7
Egypt, Arab Rep.	15.2	16.1	12.9	13.4	13.9	14.3	15.6	15.7	17.1	15.5	14.2	14.7
Libya	56.9	27.2	32.9	23.5	26.4	..	..	..	..	46.9	17.6	27.6
Morocco	14.9	19.9	20.1	23.5	23.7	24.5	23.5	24.1	26.2	16.7	17.8	23.7
Tunisia	24.0	20.0	23.7	23.3	21.4	21.2	21.2	20.5	23.6	22.7	22.3	22.1
AFRICA	**37.7**	**19.3**	**22.4**	**21.6**	**23.2**	**24.3**	**26.0**	**29.1**	**32.2**	**25.4**	**17.3**	**25.5**

a. Provisional

b. For 1994–2000 Nigeria's values were distorted because the official exchange rate used by the Government for oil exports and oil value added was significantly overvalued.

Table 2.14

Gross national savings

	Share of GDP (%)									Annual average		
	1980	1990	2000	2001	2002	2003	2004	2005	2006[a]	1980–89	1990–99	2000–06
SUB-SAHARAN AFRICA	**13.3**	**12.9**	**12.9**	**11.4**	**10.9**	**12.3**	**11.8**	**9.8**	**9.0**	**13.1**	**12.1**	**11.1**
Excl. South Africa	**4.7**	**9.0**	**11.0**	**9.2**	**8.2**	**10.1**	**10.1**	**7.2**	**6.4**	**7.1**	**8.8**	**8.9**
Excl. South Africa & Nigeria	**7.1**	**10.7**	**14.1**	**11.8**	**10.7**	**13.4**	**13.8**	**10.0**	**9.2**	**8.9**	**10.5**	**11.9**
Angola	..	9.0	23.8	−1.4	9.8	7.6	12.6	24.8	37.0	13.7	−3.7	16.3
Benin	1.1	9.9	10.9	12.5	9.3	10.5	10.3	10.6	..	2.1	7.7	10.7
Botswana	28.7	43.3	51.7	56.9	44.1	45.3	45.6	51.3	53.3	33.7	41.6	49.7
Burkina Faso	−1.6	13.7	5.1	4.1	7.5	9.1	5.1	7.9	6.3	4.7	15.8	6.4
Burundi	..	..	0.5	1.6	2.9	6.0	5.2	1.3	..	..	1.4	2.9
Cameroon	6.3	16.1	16.1	16.7	15.1	15.5	16.9	16.6	18.9	19.8	13.6	16.5
Cape Verde	..	17.6	9.1	8.0	9.4	8.4	21.8	28.8	26.8	24.2	21.3	16.0
Central African Republic	1.6	−0.4	8.2	6.7	7.4	3.9	4.4	4.6	11.7	5.6	4.1	6.7
Chad	..	−2.7	7.9	6.6	−40.2	5.4	12.6	20.3	20.4	−3.3	2.8	4.7
Comoros	..	−1.3	9.9	12.5	9.6	7.2	6.5	6.0	4.9	..	3.8	8.1
Congo, Dem. Rep.	9.3	0.8	−3.5	−1.7	5.3	9.9	6.1	6.7	8.9	7.4	0.3	4.5
Congo, Rep.	..	6.6	30.1	20.9	24.2	26.7	26.0	31.7	43.0	18.0	4.9	28.9
Côte d'Ivoire	..	−4.3	10.0	12.4	19.3	14.5	14.2	11.7	14.7	9.2	7.0	13.8
Djibouti	..	..	5.4	11.6	15.6	17.6	16.2	20.1	20.7	..	11.4	15.3
Equatorial Guinea	..	−22.0	45.7	30.8	33.0	26.3	22.8	32.7	46.2	..	6.0	33.9
Eritrea	..	..	20.4	28.7	26.3	−6.5	−20.9	10.3	8.7	..	11.7	9.6
Ethiopia	..	11.9	16.3	18.7	19.5	20.6	21.5	16.8	15.1	11.8	15.7	18.3
Gabon	..	24.2	41.7	36.6	31.3	32.7	34.7	42.1	41.3	21.8	29.3	37.2
Gambia, The	..	5.3	13.6	13.8	18.4	18.4	21.1	15.0	10.0	..	11.6	15.8
Ghana	4.5	7.0	15.7	21.2	20.0	20.5	25.7	21.4	27.4	4.7	12.5	21.7
Guinea	..	14.6	13.3	12.7	9.2	6.8	5.7	9.3	11.8	8.8	14.2	9.8
Guinea-Bissau	−6.3	15.3	−2.7	−15.7	−8.0	5.1	16.2	11.2	22.7	−0.3	5.5	4.1
Kenya	15.4	18.6	15.2	11.4	11.9	13.4	10.2	9.7	12.5	16.2	16.0	12.0
Lesotho	49.6	59.5	21.4	24.6	21.3	22.7	29.6	25.3	27.3	41.8	41.1	24.6
Liberia	..	..	..	−21.4	−11.1	−6.4	33.1	39.8	..	..	..	6.8
Madagascar	−2.4	9.2	9.4	17.2	10.0	13.0	15.2	11.7	16.0	2.1	4.9	13.2
Malawi	..	13.6	2.2	2.4	..	0.7	4.8	13.0	15.5	..	2.3	6.4
Mali	1.9	15.1	16.0	12.8	9.0	14.4	8.6	11.4	13.0	2.6	14.4	12.1
Mauritania	3.9	17.6	0.8	11.4	16.8	9.9	8.4	−5.4	28.7	17.1	9.0	10.1
Mauritius	14.0	26.3	25.3	27.6	26.6	26.3	23.8	19.7	19.0	19.7	26.5	24.0
Mozambique	−6.9	2.1	6.0	−3.7	7.5	1.8	4.0	1.9	3.1	−3.8	0.1	3.0
Namibia	26.9	34.8	26.2	26.6	26.6	40.2	33.3	33.5	42.2	18.5	27.0	32.7
Niger	17.1	−2.1	2.8	4.4	4.7	10.8	11.7	..	..	9.9	0.3	6.9
Nigeria[b]	..	..	..	..	..	..	..	..	..	..	..	..
Rwanda	13.3	11.3	12.9	13.0	10.3	11.3	17.6	18.9	13.8	10.9	8.1	14.0
São Tomé and Principe	..	..	..	..	..	..	..	..	..	..	..	..
Senegal	0.1	−0.5	14.6	13.9	11.8	15.9	14.9	21.2	18.3	0.5	5.3	15.8
Seychelles	..	21.7	17.2	16.9	16.4	16.7	12.4	2.6	9.4	..	21.5	13.1
Sierra Leone	0.5	2.6	−9.1	−3.2	5.3	6.3	5.2	9.1	9.5	7.2	0.2	3.3
Somalia	−5.8	..	..	..	..	..	..	..	..	3.2	..	..
South Africa	34.1	19.6	15.8	15.6	16.9	15.8	14.4	14.2	13.9	25.0	16.7	15.2
Sudan	7.0	−4.4	3.5	1.7	9.5	12.3	16.0	13.2	10.3	6.8	−2.5	9.5
Swaziland	16.7	24.8	13.2	13.3	24.7	25.6	20.6	14.7	14.5	20.2	19.6	18.1
Tanzania	..	7.7	8.5	7.6	9.7	10.6	9.6	8.8	10.7	..	4.2	9.4
Togo	..	20.4	0.3	4.1	5.0	10.8	9.9	12.0	..	11.7	9.1	7.0
Uganda	−1.0	1.2	9.3	7.6	6.0	7.3	9.5	7.2	12.9	2.9	6.7	8.5
Zambia	7.3	6.9	−1.3	−0.7	5.9	10.7	12.7	14.4	23.3	2.2	0.6	9.3
Zimbabwe	..	15.7	9.6	9.4	7.0	5.9	4.0	−0.4	..	17.3	16.0	5.9
NORTH AFRICA	**17.5**	**14.2**	**12.9**	**14.2**	**15.0**	**14.6**	**14.4**	**13.8**	**14.6**	**15.6**	**11.7**	**14.2**
Algeria	40.8	26.2	41.3	40.1	38.8	43.5	46.3	51.0	..	30.3	28.1	43.5
Egypt, Arab Rep.	..	21.4	18.7	18.4	20.0	19.5	20.5	21.3	22.0	20.4	22.6	20.1
Libya	53.5	..	..	..	..	..	..	..	..	40.5	..	..
Morocco	18.6	25.1	24.2	30.4	29.6	30.6	30.4	32.2	34.5	20.4	21.6	30.3
Tunisia	..	21.7	23.2	23.7	22.3	22.3	22.3	20.0	25.4	22.2	21.8	22.7
AFRICA	**14.7**	**13.4**	**12.9**	**12.6**	**12.4**	**13.1**	**12.7**	**11.1**	**10.8**	**13.9**	**12.0**	**12.2**

a. Provisional

b. For 1994–2000 Nigeria's values were distorted because the official exchange rate used by the Government for oil exports and oil value added was significantly overvalued.

Table 2.15 General government final consumption expenditure

	Share of GDP (%)									Annual average		
	1980	1990	2000	2001	2002	2003	2004	2005	2006ª	1980–89	1990–99	2000–06
SUB-SAHARAN AFRICA	**12.4**	**17.4**	**14.6**	**14.4**	**13.8**	**15.0**	**15.2**	**14.6**	**13.7**	**15.2**	**16.8**	**14.5**
Excl. South Africa	**11.7**	**15.5**	**11.9**	**12.0**	**11.8**	**12.0**	**11.7**	**11.0**	**10.3**	**13.7**	**14.2**	**11.5**
Excl. South Africa & Nigeria	**14.6**	**15.0**	**12.5**	**12.6**	**12.6**	**13.0**	**13.0**	**12.5**	**12.1**	**14.2**	**13.9**	**12.6**
Angola	..	34.5	..	..	..	..	..	..	..	31.5	40.7	..
Benin	8.6	11.0	11.6	11.6	12.5	13.3	13.6	15.0	..	12.7	10.5	12.9
Botswana	21.3	24.1	22.9	20.4	20.9	21.5	21.3	20.6	19.2	24.3	26.7	20.9
Burkina Faso	9.2	21.1	20.8	21.7	25.2	22.2	21.6	22.3	22.0	15.6	22.5	22.3
Burundi	9.2	10.8	17.5	19.9	19.1	22.7	26.1	26.5	29.3	9.3	17.0	23.0
Cameroon	9.7	12.8	9.5	10.2	10.2	10.0	10.2	10.0	9.6	10.0	10.6	9.9
Cape Verde	..	14.7	21.3	11.3	11.7	14.7	20.6	20.3	20.7	13.1	17.0	17.2
Central African Republic	15.1	14.9	14.0	11.9	12.9	10.5	10.2	13.3	10.6	15.6	13.9	11.9
Chad	..	10.0	7.7	7.5	7.7	7.6	4.9	4.5	5.9	11.3	8.1	6.5
Comoros	30.9	24.5	11.7	16.2	17.4	14.7	14.3	13.5	12.6	28.6	20.3	14.3
Congo, Dem. Rep.	8.4	11.5	7.5	6.0	5.5	6.3	8.2	8.3	7.3	9.0	9.9	7.0
Congo, Rep.	17.6	13.8	11.6	14.1	18.4	17.0	16.0	13.0	13.2	17.7	18.1	14.8
Côte d'Ivoire	16.9	16.8	7.2	7.5	7.8	8.2	8.3	8.3	8.4	16.5	11.9	8.0
Djibouti	..	31.5	29.7	26.9	28.3	29.5	29.7	27.1	28.0	..	31.8	28.5
Equatorial Guinea	..	39.7	4.6	3.3	5.1	3.8	3.1	3.0	2.9	27.4	25.1	3.7
Eritrea	..	..	63.8	51.5	44.0	51.5	52.6	44.6	42.4	..	39.7	50.0
Ethiopia	..	13.2	17.9	14.6	14.8	13.4	13.1	12.3	12.1	11.2	9.8	14.0
Gabon	13.2	13.4	9.6	11.5	11.0	10.1	9.3	8.3	8.4	18.3	13.2	9.7
Gambia, The	31.2	13.7	13.7	14.4	12.9	11.0	11.1	..	..	29.1	13.8	12.6
Ghana	11.2	9.3	10.2	9.7	9.9	11.5	12.2	11.7	13.4	9.0	11.7	11.2
Guinea	..	11.0	6.8	6.9	7.5	7.8	6.3	5.7	5.6	11.8	8.2	6.7
Guinea-Bissau	27.6	10.3	14.0	12.6	13.0	12.8	14.5	18.2	17.7	18.9	8.4	14.7
Kenya	19.8	18.6	15.3	16.0	17.1	18.0	17.6	17.1	16.3	18.3	16.0	16.8
Lesotho	21.8	14.1	19.2	18.0	17.7	17.9	17.2	18.1	18.1	19.2	16.8	18.0
Liberia	19.1	..	..	14.4	13.7	8.5	10.4	11.1	..	22.0	..	11.6
Madagascar	12.1	8.0	9.0	9.1	8.1	9.2	9.8	8.4	8.8	9.8	7.9	8.9
Malawi	19.3	15.1	14.6	15.8	10.7	11.9	12.2	12.1	11.8	17.5	16.6	12.7
Mali	11.6	13.8	8.6	9.2	8.7	8.4	10.0	9.9	9.9	12.3	12.7	9.3
Mauritania	45.3	25.9	25.8	23.7	22.3	30.1	21.9	22.7	19.9	30.6	14.5	23.8
Mauritius	14.4	12.8	13.1	12.9	12.8	14.1	14.2	14.4	14.5	13.5	13.0	13.7
Mozambique	12.2	13.5	9.0	9.1	9.4	10.6	10.8	10.4	11.1	13.8	9.7	10.1
Namibia	17.4	30.6	28.8	28.4	26.4	26.5	24.7	24.6	23.7	27.9	31.0	26.2
Niger	10.4	15.0	13.0	12.4	12.2	11.7	13.2	11.7	..	11.9	14.6	12.4
Nigeria	..	..	..	..	..	..	..	..	..	..	..	..
Rwanda	12.5	10.1	11.0	11.9	12.5	14.4	12.0	12.0	11.7	13.0	11.5	12.2
São Tomé and Principe	..	..	..	..	..	..	..	..	..	..	..	..
Senegal	24.8	18.4	12.8	12.6	13.3	13.3	13.7	9.6	9.6	19.3	15.0	12.1
Seychelles	28.7	27.7	24.2	24.6	22.7	25.5	28.3	26.0	24.7	33.1	29.0	25.1
Sierra Leone	8.4	7.8	14.3	17.6	16.4	15.6	13.5	13.4	13.1	7.7	10.6	14.9
Somalia	15.6	..	..	..	..	..	..	..	..	17.6	..	..
South Africa	14.3	19.7	18.1	18.3	18.4	19.3	19.6	19.6	19.5	17.4	19.4	19.0
Sudan	16.0	7.3	7.6	8.6	4.5	10.8	11.8	17.1	16.7	11.1	6.7	11.0
Swaziland	27.0	18.1	24.5	17.0	18.6	19.5	22.3	20.8	19.5	21.5	22.6	20.3
Tanzania	..	17.8	10.6	11.5	12.4	14.8	15.9	15.2	16.3	..	14.0	13.8
Togo	22.4	14.2	10.2	10.0	8.4	9.8	9.7	9.8	..	16.9	12.8	9.7
Uganda	..	7.5	13.7	13.8	15.3	14.8	14.7	14.4	14.7	9.9	11.1	14.5
Zambia	25.5	19.0	9.5	10.2	11.8	14.4	17.7	9.4	10.0	23.0	17.7	11.9
Zimbabwe	18.5	19.4	13.9	17.7	17.9	16.6	23.3	27.2	..	20.1	17.2	19.4
NORTH AFRICA	**14.0**	**16.2**	**14.5**	**14.9**	**14.9**	**14.8**	**14.6**	**13.6**	**..**	**17.4**	**16.1**	**14.5**
Algeria	15.2	16.1	13.6	14.7	15.4	14.8	13.8	12.1	..	17.2	16.6	14.1
Egypt, Arab Rep.	15.7	11.3	11.2	11.3	12.5	12.7	12.8	12.7	12.3	16.2	10.9	12.2
Libya	21.8	24.4	20.5	21.6	16.7	..	..	..	..	30.0	24.3	19.6
Morocco	18.3	15.5	18.4	18.6	18.3	18.0	18.8	19.2	18.3	16.6	17.0	18.5
Tunisia	14.5	16.4	15.6	15.6	15.9	15.7	15.4	15.4	13.4	16.5	16.0	15.3
AFRICA	**12.5**	**16.8**	**14.5**	**14.6**	**14.2**	**14.9**	**14.9**	**14.2**	**13.3**	**15.7**	**16.4**	**14.4**

a. Provisional

Table 2.16 Household final consumption expenditure

	Share of GDP (%)									Annual average		
	1980	1990	2000	2001	2002	2003	2004	2005	2006[a]	1980–89	1990–99	2000–06
SUB-SAHARAN AFRICA	**58.9**	**65.5**	**68.5**	**68.6**	**68.1**	**67.4**	**67.8**	**68.0**	**66.9**	**63.3**	**68.1**	**67.9**
Excl. South Africa	..	**72.8**	**73.6**	**74.3**	**74.1**	**72.7**	**72.0**	**72.3**	**70.3**	**72.5**	**74.3**	**72.8**
Excl. South Africa & Nigeria	**71.4**	**72.8**	**73.6**	**74.3**	**74.1**	**72.7**	**72.0**	**72.3**	**70.3**	**72.4**	**74.3**	**72.8**
Angola	..	35.8	..	..	..	..	..	..	..	44.5	42.6	..
Benin	97.7	86.8	82.4	81.9	83.8	80.7	80.9	78.1		89.7	85.7	81.3
Botswana	52.0	33.2	23.2	23.7	26.9	28.1	28.0	27.0	28.4	40.4	33.6	26.5
Burkina Faso	98.0	73.5	78.5	78.4	71.2	73.3	76.6	72.8	75.2	86.0	68.5	75.2
Burundi	91.4	94.5	88.5	88.0	90.6	85.9	84.9	96.6	90.9	87.5	88.3	89.4
Cameroon	68.6	66.6	70.2	70.7	70.8	72.2	71.4	72.0	71.5	65.8	70.2	71.3
Cape Verde	..	93.4	92.9	103.8	104.0	101.1	80.9	75.3	74.6	89.1	88.6	90.4
Central African Republic	93.7	85.7	80.8	84.2	82.8	87.8	89.6	86.5	88.3	85.5	82.4	85.7
Chad	..	97.6	86.8	87.3	133.1	74.4	70.6	59.8	50.5	96.8	92.5	80.3
Comoros	79.2	78.7	94.0	89.0	86.6	91.1	96.2	99.5	101.4	75.9	84.2	94.0
Congo, Dem. Rep.	81.5	79.1	88.0	90.8	90.4	88.7	87.8	85.2	88.1	80.0	81.3	88.4
Congo, Rep.	46.8	62.4	29.1	35.4	30.7	31.7	32.7	29.4	21.1	50.3	53.1	30.0
Côte d'Ivoire	62.8	71.9	74.9	72.9	65.5	70.8	71.7	74.5	71.2	63.9	70.3	71.7
Djibouti	..	78.9	76.8	73.7	66.8	65.2	66.0	64.2	59.9	..	73.8	67.5
Equatorial Guinea	..	80.3	20.9	15.6	15.9	16.5	13.3	9.7	11.1	..	61.2	14.7
Eritrea	..	..	70.9	75.6	89.6	108.2	108.8	82.2	80.9	..	91.2	88.0
Ethiopia	..	77.2	73.8	75.6	75.2	78.8	78.2	85.1	86.4	78.4	80.5	79.0
Gabon	26.1	49.7	32.2	36.8	45.3	41.7	36.8	24.4	26.9	37.4	43.2	34.9
Gambia, The	63.0	75.6	77.8	73.6	74.3	78.0	78.5	..	..	64.4	78.8	76.4
Ghana	83.9	85.2	84.3	83.3	82.7	81.5	80.5	84.9	78.7	86.2	80.8	82.2
Guinea	..	66.9	77.7	79.1	83.0	84.4	86.3	82.9	83.8	73.1	73.5	82.5
Guinea-Bissau	73.3	86.9	94.6	106.7	99.1	86.0	88.5	80.3	76.0	82.0	90.1	90.2
Kenya	62.1	62.8	75.2	77.1	74.5	71.6	73.1	76.8	74.3	63.3	68.5	74.6
Lesotho	130.2	138.8	101.3	98.5	102.1	99.4	95.2	98.1	96.9	146.4	121.5	98.8
Liberia	66.1	..	..	89.1	89.7	94.7	90.3	86.4	..	75.8	..	90.0
Madagascar	89.3	86.4	83.2	75.6	84.2	81.9	80.8	83.2	77.6	87.2	87.9	80.9
Malawi	69.9	71.5	81.6	80.4	..	91.6	85.8	80.1	77.0	69.8	80.0	82.8
Mali	87.4	79.8	79.4	76.7	80.0	78.3	81.4	79.1	75.3	88.1	79.7	78.6
Mauritania	58.2	69.2	82.8	73.2	79.7	74.9	81.2	92.3	61.3	66.3	83.0	77.9
Mauritius	71.0	63.7	63.0	61.1	62.0	61.1	62.4	66.7	68.1	66.5	62.9	63.5
Mozambique	96.7	92.3	79.5	87.2	78.9	83.3	79.2	80.4	75.6	92.3	93.2	80.6
Namibia	44.2	51.2	57.1	54.6	55.8	47.3	55.2	51.3	47.9	61.3	56.3	52.8
Niger	75.1	83.8	83.4	83.2	82.5	83.1	82.7	74.6	..	80.8	82.7	81.6
Nigeria	..	..	..	..	..	..	..	..	..	..	..	..
Rwanda	83.3	83.7	87.7	85.2	88.0	85.3	84.6	84.7	85.1	82.0	94.0	85.8
São Tomé and Principe	..	..	..	..	..	..	..	..	..	..	..	..
Senegal	73.1	79.2	76.0	78.0	80.0	77.9	78.4	76.3	79.9	76.4	79.6	78.1
Seychelles	44.2	52.0	53.9	56.5	52.9	52.9	57.0	70.2	65.2	42.7	49.3	58.3
Sierra Leone	90.7	83.5	100.1	94.0	93.0	91.8	88.2	87.1	85.3	83.2	86.6	91.4
Somalia	97.3	..	..	..	..	..	..	..	..	100.6	..	..
South Africa	47.8	57.1	63.0	62.4	61.7	61.5	63.2	63.2	63.5	54.2	61.2	62.6
Sudan	81.9	89.6	76.5	81.7	82.2	73.5	69.5	68.7	68.9	84.9	85.7	74.4
Swaziland	71.8	75.2	72.4	80.1	61.8	59.7	61.9	70.2	72.3	74.7	75.4	68.3
Tanzania	..	80.9	79.2	79.7	75.8	73.1	72.9	75.1	72.8	..	84.0	75.5
Togo	54.5	71.1	92.0	89.0	91.0	84.8	85.8	83.3	..	70.8	80.5	87.6
Uganda	..	91.9	78.2	79.7	80.1	78.8	76.9	78.0	77.2	87.2	84.6	78.4
Zambia	55.2	64.4	87.4	87.1	80.3	72.6	62.7	69.4	59.1	62.9	73.3	74.1
Zimbabwe	67.7	63.1	72.8	70.7	75.0	77.2	72.6	72.2	..	63.4	65.9	73.4
NORTH AFRICA	**56.0**	**64.1**	**61.3**	**62.0**	**61.8**	**61.4**	**60.3**	**59.0**	**..**	**61.1**	**65.6**	**61.0**
Algeria	41.7	56.8	41.6	43.4	43.7	40.4	38.5	33.8	..	51.3	53.3	40.2
Egypt, Arab Rep.	69.2	72.6	75.9	75.3	73.6	73.0	71.7	71.6	70.6	68.3	75.0	73.1
Libya	21.3	48.4	46.6	54.9	56.9	..	..	..	..	23.1	58.1	52.8
Morocco	66.8	64.6	61.5	57.8	57.9	57.5	57.6	56.6	55.5	66.7	65.3	57.8
Tunisia	61.5	63.6	60.7	61.1	62.7	63.1	63.4	64.1	63.0	60.8	61.7	62.6
AFRICA	**57.5**	**64.8**	**65.2**	**65.6**	**65.3**	**64.9**	**64.7**	**64.2**	**66.6**	**62.3**	**67.0**	**65.2**

a. Provisional

Table 2.17

Final consumption expenditure plus discrepancy

	Share of GDP (%)									Annual average		
	1980	1990	2000	2001	2002	2003	2004	2005	2006ª	1980–89	1990–99	2000–06
SUB-SAHARAN AFRICA	**64.6**	**83.8**	**79.5**	**80.1**	**78.1**	**78.3**	**77.4**	**74.9**	**71.0**	**77.7**	**85.4**	**77.0**
Excl. South Africa	**68.5**	**90.1**	**79.1**	**81.5**	**79.9**	**77.5**	**73.7**	**70.2**	**65.2**	**83.7**	**89.3**	**75.3**
Excl. South Africa & Nigeria	**85.6**	**87.2**	**83.1**	**85.8**	**85.5**	**83.9**	**82.1**	**79.8**	**76.5**	**86.7**	**87.5**	**82.4**
Angola	..	70.3	58.2	84.9	76.1	80.8	74.9	62.1	50.5	76.0	78.0	69.6
Benin	106.3	97.8	94.0	93.5	96.3	94.0	94.5	93.1	..	102.4	96.2	94.2
Botswana	73.3	57.4	46.1	44.1	47.8	49.6	49.3	47.6	47.6	64.7	60.3	47.4
Burkina Faso	107.2	94.6	99.4	100.1	96.3	95.5	98.2	95.2	97.2	101.6	91.0	97.4
Burundi	100.6	105.4	106.0	107.8	109.7	108.7	111.0	123.1	120.2	96.9	105.2	112.4
Cameroon	78.3	79.3	79.7	81.0	81.0	82.2	81.5	81.9	81.1	75.8	81.5	81.2
Cape Verde	..	108.1	114.2	115.1	115.7	115.8	101.5	95.6	95.3	102.2	105.6	107.6
Central African Republic	108.9	100.6	94.8	96.1	95.7	98.3	99.9	99.8	98.9	101.1	96.3	97.6
Chad	..	107.7	94.5	94.7	140.8	81.5	75.5	64.5	60.2	108.1	100.5	87.4
Comoros	110.1	103.2	105.7	105.2	104.0	105.8	110.6	112.9	114.0	104.5	104.5	108.3
Congo, Dem. Rep.	89.9	90.7	95.5	96.8	96.0	95.0	96.0	93.5	95.3	89.1	91.2	95.5
Congo, Rep.	64.3	76.2	40.7	49.5	49.0	48.7	48.7	42.4	34.3	68.1	71.2	44.8
Côte d'Ivoire	79.6	88.7	82.1	80.5	73.3	79.0	80.0	82.8	79.6	80.4	82.2	79.6
Djibouti	..	110.4	106.5	100.6	95.1	94.7	95.7	91.4	87.9	..	106.4	96.0
Equatorial Guinea	..	120.1	25.5	18.8	21.0	20.2	16.5	12.7	14.0	..	86.3	18.4
Eritrea	..	..	134.7	127.0	133.7	159.7	161.4	126.8	123.3	..	130.9	138.1
Ethiopia	..	90.4	91.7	90.3	90.1	92.3	91.2	97.4	98.5	89.5	90.3	93.0
Gabon	39.4	63.1	41.7	48.3	56.3	51.8	46.1	32.8	35.3	55.7	56.4	44.6
Gambia, The	94.2	89.3	91.5	88.0	87.1	88.9	89.5	95.6	..	93.5	92.6	90.1
Ghana	95.1	94.5	94.4	93.0	92.6	93.0	92.7	96.6	92.1	95.2	92.5	93.5
Guinea	..	77.8	84.6	85.9	90.5	92.2	92.6	88.7	89.5	84.9	81.7	89.1
Guinea-Bissau	101.0	97.2	108.5	119.3	112.1	98.8	103.0	98.5	93.7	100.9	98.5	104.8
Kenya	81.9	81.5	90.6	93.0	91.6	89.6	90.7	93.9	90.5	81.7	84.5	91.4
Lesotho	152.0	152.9	120.6	116.6	119.8	117.3	112.4	116.2	115.0	165.5	138.3	116.8
Liberia	85.2	..	..	103.4	103.3	103.2	100.7	97.6	..	97.8	..	101.6
Madagascar	101.4	94.5	92.3	84.7	92.3	91.1	90.6	91.6	86.4	97.1	95.8	89.8
Malawi	89.2	86.6	96.2	96.2	..	103.4	98.0	92.3	88.8	87.3	96.6	95.8
Mali	98.9	93.6	88.0	86.0	88.7	86.7	91.4	89.0	85.2	100.4	92.4	87.9
Mauritania	103.5	95.1	108.6	96.9	101.9	105.0	103.1	115.0	81.2	96.9	97.6	101.7
Mauritius	85.5	76.5	76.1	74.0	74.8	75.2	76.6	81.1	82.5	80.0	75.9	77.2
Mozambique	108.9	105.8	88.5	96.3	88.4	93.9	90.0	90.7	86.7	106.2	102.9	90.6
Namibia	61.6	81.8	86.0	83.0	82.2	73.8	80.0	75.8	71.6	89.2	87.3	78.9
Niger	85.4	98.8	96.5	95.6	94.7	94.8	95.9	86.3	..	92.7	97.3	94.0
Nigeria	..	..	..	..	..	..	..	..	..	..	..	..
Rwanda	95.8	93.8	98.7	97.1	100.5	99.6	96.5	96.7	96.8	95.0	105.5	98.0
São Tomé and Principe	..	..	..	..	..	..	..	..	..	..	..	..
Senegal	97.9	97.6	88.8	90.6	93.2	91.2	92.1	85.9	89.5	95.7	94.6	90.2
Seychelles	72.9	79.7	78.1	80.8	75.6	78.5	85.3	96.2	89.8	75.9	78.3	83.5
Sierra Leone	99.1	91.3	114.4	111.6	109.4	107.4	101.7	100.6	98.3	90.9	97.2	106.2
Somalia	112.9	112.5	..	..	..	..	..	..	..	106.3	..	..
South Africa	62.1	76.8	81.1	80.7	80.1	80.8	82.8	82.7	82.9	71.5	80.6	81.6
Sudan	97.9	96.9	84.1	90.2	86.7	84.3	81.3	85.8	85.6	96.0	92.4	85.4
Swaziland	98.8	93.4	97.0	97.1	80.4	79.2	84.1	91.0	91.9	96.3	98.0	88.7
Tanzania	..	98.7	89.8	91.2	88.2	88.0	88.8	90.3	89.2	..	98.0	89.3
Togo	76.8	85.3	102.2	99.0	99.4	94.7	95.5	93.1	..	87.7	93.3	97.3
Uganda	100.4	99.4	91.9	93.5	95.3	93.7	91.6	92.4	91.9	97.7	95.7	92.9
Zambia	80.7	83.4	97.0	97.2	92.1	87.0	80.4	78.8	69.1	86.0	91.0	86.0
Zimbabwe	86.2	82.5	86.7	88.4	92.9	93.8	95.9	99.4	..	83.5	83.1	92.8
NORTH AFRICA	**58.7**	**77.2**	**75.2**	**76.4**	**75.7**	**72.5**	**68.9**	**64.5**	**63.0**	**70.6**	**79.8**	**70.9**
Algeria	56.9	72.9	55.2	58.0	59.1	55.1	52.3	45.9	..	68.5	69.9	54.3
Egypt, Arab Rep.	84.8	83.9	87.1	86.6	86.1	85.7	84.4	84.3	82.9	84.5	85.8	85.3
Libya	43.1	72.8	67.1	76.5	73.6	..	..	..	..	53.1	82.4	72.4
Morocco	85.1	80.1	79.9	76.5	76.3	75.5	76.5	75.9	73.8	83.3	82.2	76.3
Tunisia	76.0	80.0	76.3	76.7	78.6	78.8	78.8	79.5	76.4	77.3	77.7	77.9
AFRICA	**62.3**	**80.7**	**77.6**	**78.4**	**76.8**	**75.7**	**74.0**	**70.9**	**67.8**	**74.6**	**82.7**	**74.5**

a. Provisional

Table 2.18

Final consumption expenditure plus discrepancy per capita

						Dollars				Annual average		
	1980	1990	2000	2001	2002	2003	2004	2005	2006[a]	1980–89	1990–99	2000–06
SUB-SAHARAN AFRICA	**465**	**485**	**404**	**389**	**401**	**480**	**572**	**633**	**676**	**462**	**464**	**508**
Excl. South Africa	**380**	**348**	**263**	**274**	**305**	**318**	**352**	**395**	**435**	**349**	**300**	**335**
Excl. South Africa & Nigeria	**389**	**356**	**269**	**280**	**312**	**325**	**360**	**404**	**444**	**357**	**306**	**342**
Angola	..	685	381	530	590	743	948	1,182	1,376	586	477	821
Benin	403	349	293	297	351	420	465	470	..	313	317	383
Botswana	781	1,591	1,647	1,517	1,597	2,287	2,668	2,724	2,817	821	1,789	2,180
Burkina Faso	303	331	218	230	250	312	371	371	391	260	235	306
Burundi	224	210	113	104	98	89	98	125	133	215	169	108
Cameroon	581	723	506	479	530	658	739	764	802	663	631	640
Cape Verde	..	1,030	1,347	1,373	1,509	1,910	1,895	1,898	2,172	807	1,189	1,729
Central African Republic	373	497	236	237	249	289	317	321	343	352	341	285
Chad	..	306	155	184	307	236	340	373	362	221	232	280
Comoros	406	593	395	420	464	596	682	728	749	394	507	576
Congo, Dem. Rep.	461	223	81	87	99	98	111	113	134	287	153	103
Congo, Rep.	609	881	409	421	440	503	600	715	719	688	617	544
Côte d'Ivoire	971	750	502	488	476	603	678	728	727	680	628	600
Djibouti	..	891	805	771	737	759	806	805	826	..	833	787
Equatorial Guinea	..	467	742	742	1,008	1,300	1,705	1,969	2,413	..	482	1,411
Eritrea	..	..	232	222	211	223	235	272	285	..	241	240
Ethiopia	..	227	114	109	101	111	125	159	194	201	161	130
Gabon	2,471	4,095	1,789	1,889	2,260	2,511	2,603	2,199	2,573	2,582	2,784	2,261
Gambia, The	338	294	278	257	218	214	229	273	..	268	303	245
Ghana	371	357	233	239	270	329	373	459	509	337	345	345
Guinea	..	344	321	312	341	385	413	321	312	1,173	390	344
Guinea-Bissau	141	233	171	168	155	155	180	186	175	177	205	170
Kenya	365	299	365	377	366	398	424	494	564	299	310	427
Lesotho	506	588	545	459	426	625	754	836	861	471	674	644
Liberia	435	..	..	177	178	129	138	150	..	446	..	154
Madagascar	453	242	221	230	237	283	218	248	248	301	231	241
Malawi	178	172	144	138	..	200	200	199	207	150	180	181
Mali	291	296	213	220	280	346	396	407	418	238	267	326
Mauritania	489	499	458	411	431	482	554	713	711	459	571	537
Mauritius	1,020	1,725	2,865	2,800	2,813	3,226	3,766	4,103	4,180	1,078	2,412	3,393
Mozambique	316	193	207	210	194	224	255	291	283	275	187	238
Namibia	1,346	1,357	1,562	1,396	1,322	1,677	2,266	2,339	2,299	1,459	1,659	1,837
Niger	371	314	156	161	172	202	217	217	..	279	217	188
Nigeria	..	..	..	..	..	..	..	..	..	..	..	..
Rwanda	214	332	209	191	188	199	210	249	294	268	275	220
São Tomé and Principe	..	..	..	..	..	..	..	..	..	..	..	..
Senegal	584	707	403	417	457	560	645	634	687	527	555	543
Seychelles	1,667	4,196	5,919	6,193	6,301	6,688	7,234	8,386	8,228	2,170	5,142	6,993
Sierra Leone	337	145	160	191	208	206	203	219	243	250	181	204
Somalia	105	154	..	..	..	..	..	..	..	136	..	..
South Africa	1,818	2,444	2,450	2,133	1,963	2,941	3,865	4,270	4,463	2,094	2,782	3,155
Sudan	380	337	312	354	374	423	488	637	826	493	257	488
Swaziland	949	1,070	1,288	1,197	878	1,304	1,786	2,102	2,248	812	1,300	1,543
Tanzania	..	165	241	248	242	248	269	332	320	..	194	271
Togo	314	351	251	236	256	282	324	321	..	270	303	278
Uganda	99	240	221	209	212	216	223	279	292	231	217	236
Zambia	527	338	300	332	315	344	394	505	644	406	334	405
Zimbabwe	791	691	507	710	1,582	536	347	259	..	703	532	657
NORTH AFRICA	**847**	**1,136**	**1,316**	**1,288**	**1,179**	**1,228**	**1,286**	**1,367**	**1,511**	**973**	**1,165**	**1,311**
Algeria	1,281	1,789	991	1,034	1,074	1,176	1,374	1,430	..	1,697	1,217	1,180
Egypt, Arab Rep.	445	656	1,307	1,248	1,096	1,011	930	1,038	1,201	545	851	1,119
Libya	5,007	4,824	4,328	4,206	2,537	..	..	..	..	4,992	5,113	3,691
Morocco	827	856	1,040	1,001	1,057	1,274	1,445	1,484	1,582	654	1,006	1,269
Tunisia	1,041	1,206	1,551	1,584	1,691	2,001	2,231	2,296	2,337	961	1,467	1,956
AFRICA	**534**	**600**	**560**	**542**	**530**	**602**	**686**	**749**	**806**	**554**	**585**	**639**

a. Provisional

Table 2.19

Agriculture value added

	Share of GDP (%)									Annual average (%)		
	1980	1990	2000	2001	2002	2003	2004	2005	2006[a]	1980–89	1990–99	2000–06
SUB-SAHARAN AFRICA	**17.4**	**21.6**	**17.1**	**18.2**	**18.1**	**16.0**	**14.0**	**13.9**	**14.5**	**19.8**	**20.0**	**15.9**
Excl. South Africa	**21.8**	**32.1**	**26.0**	**26.4**	**24.3**	**23.6**	**21.3**	**20.8**	**20.7**	**27.4**	**31.9**	**23.3**
Excl. South Africa & Nigeria	**25.9**	**29.7**	**26.1**	**26.5**	**24.8**	**25.2**	**23.7**	**23.1**	**22.8**	**27.0**	**29.8**	**24.6**
Angola	..	17.9	5.7	8.2	7.9	8.3	8.6	7.7	8.9	15.2	11.3	7.9
Benin	35.4	36.1	36.5	35.5	33.8	32.1	32.1	32.2	..	33.8	36.1	33.7
Botswana	12.7	4.5	2.3	2.2	2.2	2.2	2.0	1.8	1.7	7.8	3.9	2.1
Burkina Faso	28.4	28.0	27.5	34.5	32.6	33.4	30.6	33.0	32.8	28.9	32.0	32.1
Burundi	57.6	51.1	36.0	35.6	36.5	36.1	36.1	31.6	..	53.1	46.0	35.3
Cameroon	28.7	24.0	20.5	20.4	20.4	20.1	19.0	19.0	19.3	24.4	22.9	19.8
Cape Verde	..	14.4	12.0	7.8	7.1	6.8	9.7	9.2	8.8	16.6	12.9	8.8
Central African Republic	37.6	43.8	50.0	51.5	51.0	54.2	53.9	53.7	53.4	41.4	45.6	52.5
Chad	45.7	27.9	40.7	40.3	37.9	32.3	22.9	20.9	20.9	36.3	35.4	30.8
Comoros	34.0	41.4	48.6	50.0	50.2	50.5	50.9	51.0	45.2	36.3	40.2	49.5
Congo, Dem. Rep.	25.3	30.1	49.4	58.7	50.1	50.1	46.3	44.7	43.3	29.0	46.5	48.9
Congo, Rep.	11.7	12.9	5.3	5.8	6.3	6.4	5.9	4.6	4.0	10.0	10.5	5.5
Côte d'Ivoire	25.9	32.5	24.2	24.7	25.7	25.6	23.2	22.8	23.1	27.1	27.2	24.2
Djibouti	..	2.7	3.1	3.1	3.1	3.1	3.1	3.1	3.1	2.8	3.0	3.1
Equatorial Guinea	..	58.9	9.6	6.7	6.2	5.6	4.0	2.8	2.7	62.4	40.3	5.4
Eritrea	..	..	14.0	16.6	11.5	13.2	12.4	20.7	16.0	..	20.6	14.9
Ethiopia	..	51.7	46.6	44.2	40.4	38.9	40.4	43.0	44.4	53.3	55.4	42.6
Gabon	6.8	7.3	6.2	6.4	6.1	6.1	5.6	4.9	4.9	7.7	7.7	5.7
Gambia, The	27.0	24.3	31.5	32.5	24.9	28.2	30.0	29.6	..	29.2	24.6	29.4
Ghana	57.9	44.8	35.3	35.2	35.1	36.5	38.0	37.5	38.0	51.9	39.5	36.5
Guinea	..	24.7	19.0	19.7	18.7	21.5	15.0	19.0	12.7	24.2	19.5	17.9
Guinea-Bissau	42.2	56.9	52.1	50.1	55.7	61.3	58.9	59.3	60.3	47.0	53.7	56.8
Kenya	27.8	25.3	29.4	27.9	25.9	25.7	24.8	24.6	24.0	28.0	27.0	26.0
Lesotho	22.4	19.6	16.2	15.5	14.8	15.5	15.0	15.0	14.4	20.6	15.4	15.2
Liberia	32.2	54.4	72.0	73.3	75.5	71.6	68.2	65.8	..	33.5	67.2	71.1
Madagascar	26.7	26.1	26.5	25.7	29.8	26.8	26.2	25.8	25.1	30.5	26.4	26.6
Malawi	39.2	38.5	35.7	35.3	34.6	33.8	32.8	29.3	30.5	39.2	33.5	33.1
Mali	43.6	44.1	38.7	35.0	32.3	35.8	33.4	33.7	34.1	41.1	42.9	34.7
Mauritania	28.5	26.6	25.6	24.6	23.6	25.1	23.1	21.4	12.1	27.5	31.0	22.2
Mauritius	14.0	11.0	5.2	6.0	6.3	5.4	5.4	5.3	4.9	12.9	9.1	5.5
Mozambique	33.9	34.1	20.9	20.0	25.4	25.4	24.8	24.5	25.6	37.8	32.3	23.8
Namibia	10.5	10.6	9.9	9.3	10.0	10.6	9.4	10.9	9.9	10.4	10.1	10.0
Niger	43.1	35.3	37.8	40.0	39.6	41.3	..	..	..	38.6	39.4	39.7
Nigeria	..	..	..	..	47.1	41.5	33.4	32.4	31.7	..	..	37.2
Rwanda	45.8	32.5	37.2	37.3	35.5	38.5	38.8	38.9	41.3	40.2	40.6	38.2
São Tomé and Principe	..	..	..	19.7	19.9	21.1	22.6	16.8	..	..	..	20.0
Senegal	17.9	17.9	16.9	16.3	13.6	15.4	13.9	14.5	13.6	19.6	17.7	14.9
Seychelles	6.8	4.8	3.0	3.0	3.0	3.0	3.0	3.0	3.0	6.1	3.9	3.0
Sierra Leone	30.4	44.0	55.0	44.0	44.9	44.2	43.5	43.5	45.1	37.4	45.6	45.7
Somalia	64.4	62.7	..	..	..	..	..	..	..	62.7	..	..
South Africa	5.8	4.2	3.0	3.2	3.8	3.2	2.8	2.4	2.4	5.0	3.8	3.0
Sudan	29.9	..	40.1	41.0	40.2	36.9	33.1	32.3	31.3	31.8	43.8	36.4
Swaziland	19.5	10.8	10.8	8.8	8.8	7.8	7.1	6.9	6.1	16.4	12.2	8.0
Tanzania	..	42.0	41.6	41.2	41.2	41.4	42.3	37.7	37.9	..	43.0	40.5
Togo	27.5	33.8	34.2	37.7	38.1	40.8	41.2	42.7	..	31.8	37.4	39.1
Uganda	71.8	53.3	34.0	33.5	28.5	29.9	29.6	30.3	28.7	54.8	44.3	30.6
Zambia	14.0	18.2	19.9	19.7	19.9	20.5	21.1	20.5	19.9	14.3	18.8	20.2
Zimbabwe	15.1	14.8	15.9	15.7	12.7	15.0	14.1	13.4	..	14.8	15.0	14.5
NORTH AFRICA	**9.6**	**12.8**	**11.8**	**12.4**	**12.6**	**12.7**	**11.8**	**10.2**	**10.3**	**11.1**	**12.6**	**11.7**
Algeria	7.9	10.4	8.4	9.7	9.2	9.7	9.4	7.9	..	9.1	10.3	9.0
Egypt, Arab Rep.	17.4	18.4	15.5	15.4	15.4	15.3	14.3	14.0	13.2	18.9	16.2	14.7
Libya	1.6	..	..	..	..	..	..	..	..	3.3	..	..
Morocco	18.4	17.7	13.3	14.7	14.7	15.5	14.7	12.0	14.0	16.2	16.9	14.1
Tunisia	14.1	15.7	12.3	11.6	10.3	12.1	12.7	11.5	11.1	13.8	14.0	11.7
AFRICA	**14.5**	**18.0**	**14.9**	**15.7**	**15.9**	**14.7**	**13.2**	**12.7**	**13.1**	**16.3**	**17.0**	**14.3**

a. Provisional

2.20 Industry value added

	Share of GDP (%)									Annual growth (%)		
	1980	1990	2000	2001	2002	2003	2004	2005	2006[a]	1980–89	1990–99	2000–06
SUB-SAHARAN AFRICA	**29.5**	**32.7**	**29.9**	**28.9**	**28.5**	**29.6**	**31.3**	**33.2**	**34.0**	**30.7**	**30.9**	**30.8**
Excl. South Africa	**21.1**	**29.6**	**30.7**	**29.1**	**28.8**	**31.3**	**35.0**	**38.2**	**39.1**	**24.0**	**28.8**	**33.2**
Excl. South Africa & Nigeria	**22.4**	**24.3**	**27.4**	**26.0**	**26.2**	**27.3**	**29.8**	**32.9**	**34.5**	**21.2**	**24.0**	**29.2**
Angola	..	40.8	72.1	64.9	68.2	67.4	66.1	72.6	69.7	39.4	56.9	68.7
Benin	12.3	13.2	13.9	14.4	13.7	13.7	13.3	13.4	..	14.0	13.7	13.7
Botswana	43.9	56.9	55.1	55.0	50.7	47.6	48.2	49.3	50.9	52.4	50.5	51.0
Burkina Faso	19.8	20.4	23.1	18.1	19.8	20.3	21.6	21.9	22.0	20.4	20.0	21.0
Burundi	11.7	17.3	16.8	17.1	16.7	17.0	17.0	18.2	..	13.7	16.9	17.1
Cameroon	23.5	28.8	33.3	30.1	29.6	28.4	28.4	29.7	31.5	30.2	28.6	30.1
Cape Verde	..	21.4	17.9	14.7	16.1	19.7	15.2	16.7	16.3	19.0	19.7	16.7
Central African Republic	18.9	18.1	14.9	14.8	14.3	14.2	14.2	14.8	14.8	15.2	19.1	14.6
Chad	9.0	16.9	10.9	13.1	14.3	23.4	46.0	52.8	55.7	13.2	13.3	30.9
Comoros	13.2	8.3	11.5	11.7	11.6	12.7	12.2	11.0	11.8	12.5	11.4	11.8
Congo, Dem. Rep.	33.1	28.2	20.1	19.8	21.1	21.1	24.0	26.4	26.3	28.7	20.4	22.7
Congo, Rep.	46.6	40.6	72.2	65.5	63.3	61.5	63.6	68.6	70.2	45.1	45.4	66.4
Côte d'Ivoire	19.7	23.2	24.9	24.1	22.9	21.6	23.1	25.8	26.8	20.8	22.2	24.2
Djibouti	..	19.2	13.4	13.8	14.0	14.0	14.5	14.8	14.6	17.6	14.6	14.2
Equatorial Guinea	..	10.2	84.1	87.5	87.3	87.5	91.1	93.4	93.6	8.5	37.9	89.2
Eritrea	..	..	21.4	20.8	22.2	22.8	23.0	20.8	21.1	..	16.5	21.7
Ethiopia	..	10.6	11.5	12.1	12.9	13.1	12.8	11.9	11.7	11.0	9.6	12.3
Gabon	60.4	43.0	56.3	51.3	51.7	52.0	55.3	61.4	61.2	53.7	48.2	55.6
Gambia, The	13.0	11.0	11.5	11.6	13.1	12.7	12.1	11.9	..	11.8	11.7	12.1
Ghana	11.9	16.8	25.4	25.2	25.3	25.2	24.7	25.1	25.8	12.8	22.5	25.2
Guinea	..	34.6	30.6	30.9	30.4	28.9	29.5	33.1	36.7	33.8	29.2	31.4
Guinea-Bissau	18.7	17.4	12.0	12.5	12.8	13.1	11.7	11.5	11.2	15.2	12.0	12.1
Kenya	17.8	16.3	15.5	15.3	15.5	15.6	16.0	16.9	16.7	16.8	15.6	15.9
Lesotho	24.2	27.0	37.5	38.4	38.3	36.8	35.5	37.2	38.3	23.1	33.9	37.4
Liberia	25.2	16.8	11.6	9.6	8.0	10.6	13.4	15.7	..	25.8	11.0	11.5
Madagascar	14.3	11.7	12.9	13.5	13.6	14.1	14.5	14.2	13.9	12.3	11.2	13.8
Malawi	20.2	24.7	16.2	15.2	15.6	16.8	16.7	18.2	17.6	20.2	20.4	16.6
Mali	11.9	15.4	19.1	24.4	25.4	21.8	21.9	22.3	22.2	13.7	15.6	22.4
Mauritania	24.4	25.8	27.6	24.1	25.0	21.5	25.4	26.4	44.0	24.4	24.3	27.7
Mauritius	22.3	27.7	27.0	27.4	27.5	26.6	25.7	24.5	23.5	24.1	28.0	26.0
Mozambique	31.5	16.9	21.3	23.0	21.2	23.6	24.8	23.0	23.4	23.4	15.8	22.9
Namibia	52.7	34.3	25.6	27.7	28.7	26.2	26.8	25.3	27.6	41.4	27.4	26.9
Niger	22.9	16.2	17.8	17.0	17.0	17.4	..	..	..	19.8	17.4	17.3
Nigeria	..	..	..	..	29.6	35.7	41.1	43.0	41.6	..	..	38.2
Rwanda	21.5	24.6	13.6	14.2	13.9	12.8	13.7	14.0	13.3	21.0	19.5	13.6
São Tomé and Principe	..	..	..	16.9	17.1	17.8	21.0	20.5	..	..	..	18.7
Senegal	17.9	19.9	20.5	21.7	22.3	21.3	21.8	20.7	19.7	18.4	21.1	21.1
Seychelles	15.6	16.3	29.0	28.1	30.3	27.4	28.2	26.8	25.5	16.5	21.5	27.9
Sierra Leone	20.2	18.0	26.8	24.0	23.2	23.3	23.5	23.5	24.3	14.8	30.8	24.1
Somalia	7.5	..	..	..	..	..	..	..	..	7.5	..	..
South Africa	45.5	36.4	28.9	29.4	30.1	28.6	27.6	27.3	27.3	40.4	31.9	28.5
Sudan	12.9	..	20.7	18.3	19.7	20.9	24.2	26.7	27.7	14.4	14.7	22.6
Swaziland	25.9	34.3	31.1	38.3	38.0	39.0	36.8	34.8	34.9	27.2	33.8	36.1
Tanzania	..	16.1	14.5	14.7	14.9	15.2	15.2	13.8	14.5	..	14.3	14.7
Togo	24.8	22.5	17.8	17.2	18.5	22.2	22.8	23.5	..	22.0	21.0	20.3
Uganda	4.5	10.4	18.5	18.6	19.8	19.6	19.5	16.8	16.7	8.9	13.8	18.5
Zambia	39.1	45.3	22.5	22.7	23.4	24.1	25.5	27.8	31.3	40.9	34.8	25.3
Zimbabwe	27.9	29.8	21.4	20.2	18.8	19.2	18.0	16.8	..	27.6	27.1	19.1
NORTH AFRICA	**47.9**	**35.4**	**37.0**	**36.0**	**38.3**	**39.1**	**40.2**	**41.9**	**..**	**40.1**	**34.8**	**38.8**
Algeria	53.8	44.0	55.4	49.7	48.7	50.6	52.3	57.4	..	47.9	45.5	52.3
Egypt, Arab Rep.	35.1	27.3	30.8	30.9	32.6	33.4	34.7	34.1	36.2	29.2	29.9	33.2
Libya	74.2	..	..	..	..	..	..	..	..	59.7	..	..
Morocco	30.9	32.4	25.8	24.5	24.3	25.0	25.0	26.1	24.8	32.9	30.5	25.1
Tunisia	31.1	29.8	28.6	28.8	29.6	28.3	28.2	28.4	27.8	31.5	28.8	28.5
AFRICA	**35.7**	**33.6**	**32.9**	**31.9**	**32.2**	**33.1**	**34.6**	**36.4**	**37.4**	**34.0**	**32.2**	**34.1**

a. Provisional

Table 2.21

Services plus discrepancy value added

	Share of GDP (%)									Average annual growth (%)		
	1980	1990	2000	2001	2002	2003	2004	2005	2006[a]	1980–89	1990–99	2000–06
SUB-SAHARAN AFRICA	**30.6**	**43.6**	**45.5**	**44.8**	**43.4**	**44.7**	**45.1**	**43.5**	**42.6**	**37.1**	**47.0**	**44.2**
Excl. South Africa	**26.2**	**40.9**	**36.8**	**37.9**	**38.5**	**37.3**	**36.9**	**35.1**	**35.2**	**32.9**	**40.7**	**36.8**
Excl. South Africa & Nigeria	**34.1**	**41.2**	**40.2**	**41.5**	**42.8**	**41.7**	**40.5**	**38.4**	**37.8**	**35.3**	**41.5**	**40.4**
Angola	..	41.2	22.2	27.0	24.0	24.3	25.3	19.8	21.4	45.4	31.8	23.4
Benin	52.3	50.7	49.6	50.0	52.6	54.2	54.6	54.4	..	52.2	50.2	52.6
Botswana	29.9	31.8	36.1	36.8	39.9	41.8	41.2	40.5	39.6	30.6	37.5	39.4
Burkina Faso	48.5	48.8	44.1	41.6	41.1	40.2	41.0	41.8	43.7	24.5	27.7	41.9
Burundi	23.2	23.0	36.4	37.4	36.8	36.9	36.9	41.0	..	24.5	27.7	37.6
Cameroon	39.6	44.9	38.7	41.7	42.4	44.1	45.3	48.7	46.6	40.4	42.9	43.9
Cape Verde	..	64.3	70.2	77.4	76.9	73.4	75.1	74.1	74.9	64.4	67.4	74.6
Central African Republic	37.6	30.2	29.2	28.5	28.6	27.0	27.2	28.0	27.4	37.0	29.6	28.0
Chad	46.7	50.5	44.6	43.0	43.9	40.4	28.7	24.4	25.1	48.6	47.9	35.7
Comoros	52.8	50.3	39.9	38.3	38.3	36.7	36.9	38.0	..	51.2	48.4	38.0
Congo, Dem. Rep.	36.1	39.0	29.4	19.8	27.0	27.0	27.7	27.0	25.3	37.8	32.0	26.2
Congo, Rep.	41.7	46.5	22.5	28.7	30.4	32.0	30.5	26.8	25.8	44.9	44.1	28.1
Côte d'Ivoire	54.4	44.3	50.9	51.2	51.4	52.8	53.7	51.4	50.2	52.0	50.6	51.7
Djibouti	..	65.4	70.8	71.3	70.4	69.5	69.4	71.0	71.4	65.1	70.1	70.6
Equatorial Guinea	..	26.6	4.2	4.2	5.0	5.0	3.7	2.9	2.9	23.9	19.4	4.0
Eritrea	..	..	57.6	55.1	55.2	53.9	53.4	50.2	54.5	..	52.7	54.3
Ethiopia	..	32.8	35.3	36.4	39.5	40.9	38.2	37.1	36.5	30.1	29.7	37.7
Gabon	32.8	49.7	37.5	42.3	42.2	41.9	39.1	33.8	33.9	38.6	44.0	38.7
Gambia, The	47.6	48.6	45.0	45.5	52.2	49.8	48.6	49.2	..	45.1	49.1	48.4
Ghana	30.2	38.4	39.3	39.5	39.6	38.2	37.3	37.4	36.3	35.3	38.0	38.2
Guinea	..	44.5	44.4	43.4	43.9	43.0	49.4	41.8	45.0	42.7	48.4	44.4
Guinea-Bissau	34.4	19.3	28.2	34.8	31.9	24.9	27.8	27.6	26.2	34.8	29.7	28.8
Kenya	39.7	44.1	43.8	45.7	47.4	47.7	48.3	49.7	48.0	41.7	44.3	47.2
Lesotho	44.5	35.8	36.8	37.0	36.6	37.9	37.3	35.7	35.8	42.2	37.0	36.7
Liberia	32.3	28.8	16.4	17.1	16.4	17.7	18.4	18.4	..	34.0	21.8	17.4
Madagascar	47.8	53.5	51.2	53.1	50.8	50.8	50.4	51.6	52.2	46.2	54.9	51.4
Malawi	30.3	22.3	38.4	40.5	41.4	39.2	39.7	41.4	41.2	29.5	36.1	40.2
Mali	34.7	37.4	35.3	33.1	34.5	34.7	36.5	36.2	36.0	37.6	33.5	35.2
Mauritania	41.0	37.3	39.5	42.5	42.9	44.5	41.8	42.5	35.9	38.5	36.0	41.4
Mauritius	48.5	45.0	54.4	54.9	55.2	55.6	56.0	57.2	59.0	47.2	49.7	56.0
Mozambique	26.0	40.9	49.0	48.9	45.0	41.8	41.2	43.4	41.4	34.0	43.8	44.4
Namibia	31.2	45.3	54.7	52.9	51.7	55.4	54.0	53.9	52.9	41.7	51.9	53.6
Niger	34.0	48.6	44.4	43.0	43.4	41.4	..	..	..	41.6	43.2	43.1
Nigeria	..	..	..	..	20.3	19.9	23.2	23.5	25.9	..	..	22.5
Rwanda	32.6	42.8	39.8	38.6	39.3	48.8	47.5	47.2	45.4	38.8	39.9	43.8
São Tomé and Principe	..	..	..	63.5	63.0	61.2	56.4	62.7	..	..	..	61.3
Senegal	53.3	52.0	50.8	50.3	51.8	51.1	51.9	51.7	53.1	51.0	50.9	51.5
Seychelles	77.5	78.9	68.0	68.9	66.7	69.6	68.8	70.2	71.5	77.4	74.6	69.1
Sierra Leone	41.4	31.8	12.5	25.4	25.8	27.0	27.8	28.0	25.8	41.3	18.7	24.6
Somalia	22.2	..	..	..	..	..	..	..	..	23.5	..	..
South Africa	42.7	50.2	59.0	58.4	57.1	58.8	59.3	59.2	58.9	46.8	55.6	58.7
Sudan	48.3	..	35.4	36.4	35.7	37.4	36.5	37.1	38.0	47.0	37.7	36.7
Swaziland	40.5	36.4	27.6	35.1	35.5	35.2	35.1	35.4	34.2	40.4	33.6	34.0
Tanzania	..	33.3	36.2	36.3	36.1	35.3	34.1	30.3	31.2	..	34.8	34.2
Togo	47.7	43.7	47.9	45.0	43.3	37.1	36.0	31.7	..	46.2	41.7	40.2
Uganda	23.4	30.5	38.6	39.9	43.6	42.9	42.9	45.1	46.7	31.2	34.3	42.8
Zambia	39.7	24.8	46.7	46.5	46.8	46.2	45.0	44.6	43.9	34.8	35.2	45.7
Zimbabwe	53.1	45.4	48.5	54.4	58.1	55.0	52.2	40.0	..	49.0	46.3	51.4
NORTH AFRICA	**33.4**	**41.9**	**43.4**	**45.0**	**46.8**	**45.1**	**43.8**	**41.9**	**40.9**	**39.0**	**43.3**	**43.8**
Algeria	31.6	37.0	30.7	33.6	33.8	32.0	31.0	28.1	..	34.9	35.8	31.6
Egypt, Arab Rep.	42.9	49.5	46.5	46.5	45.6	44.9	45.1	45.9	44.7	47.5	47.8	45.6
Libya	21.4	..	..	..	..	..	..	..	..	34.8	..	..
Morocco	50.3	46.8	49.8	49.7	50.0	49.1	50.1	51.8	50.4	49.9	47.8	50.1
Tunisia	54.8	54.5	59.1	59.6	60.2	59.7	59.1	60.1	61.1	54.8	57.3	59.8
AFRICA	**31.5**	**43.1**	**44.6**	**44.9**	**44.7**	**45.1**	**45.1**	**43.5**	**42.5**	**37.8**	**45.8**	**44.3**

a. Provisional

Table 2.22

Gross fixed capital formation

	Share of GDP (%)									Annual average		
	1980	1990	2000	2001	2002	2003	2004	2005	2006[a]	1980–89	1990–99	2000–06
SUB-SAHARAN AFRICA	17.7	18.1	16.0	16.2	15.5	16.6	16.6	16.8	17.6	18.5	17.4	16.5
Excl. South Africa	14.0	17.6	16.8	17.3	16.2	17.3	17.2	16.9	17.4	16.0	18.4	17.0
Excl. South Africa & Nigeria	17.5	17.0	17.7	18.2	17.4	18.7	19.1	19.2	20.4	16.6	18.0	18.7
Angola	..	11.1	15.1	13.4	12.6	12.7	9.1	8.1	13.7	14.2	23.2	12.1
Benin	..	13.4	18.9	19.2	18.1	18.1	17.5	18.9	..	14.8	15.7	18.5
Botswana	34.5	32.4	21.7	20.8	21.9	21.5	20.2	19.0	17.9	29.0	27.2	20.4
Burkina Faso	14.1	17.7	18.7	14.7	17.1	17.5	19.3	19.4	20.8	17.4	21.2	18.2
Burundi	13.9	15.2	6.1	6.2	6.1	10.6	13.0	10.5	16.7	16.1	9.0	9.9
Cameroon	20.0	17.3	16.0	20.3	19.8	18.1	18.3	17.7	16.7	21.1	14.5	18.1
Cape Verde	..	22.9	19.7	18.3	20.9	18.7	37.4	37.1	38.1	26.9	29.6	27.2
Central African Republic	6.9	11.4	9.5	8.4	9.0	6.0	6.1	9.0	8.9	10.2	11.2	8.1
Chad	..	4.8	20.9	36.6	59.7	48.6	22.7	19.1	21.2	4.4	11.0	32.7
Comoros	28.5	11.9	10.1	10.1	11.0	10.3	9.4	9.3	9.8	24.3	14.6	10.0
Congo, Dem. Rep.	8.8	12.8	3.5	5.2	9.0	12.2	12.8	..	..	11.4	8.0	8.5
Congo, Rep.	35.8	17.2	20.9	26.3	22.5	25.1	23.6	21.5	22.4	32.5	24.9	23.2
Côte d'Ivoire	24.4	8.5	11.2	9.9	10.9	9.7	9.8	9.7	9.9	15.8	11.4	10.2
Djibouti	..	14.1	8.8	7.9	10.0	14.4	21.5	19.0	29.6	..	11.1	15.9
Equatorial Guinea	..	17.4	61.3	71.9	32.1	59.4	45.1	38.2	41.6	..	59.5	49.9
Eritrea	..	..	31.9	28.7	26.0	25.4	22.8	20.1	18.7	..	25.0	24.8
Ethiopia	..	12.9	20.3	21.5	23.9	21.8	25.5	23.0	24.2	15.7	16.5	22.9
Gabon	26.7	21.4	21.9	25.7	24.5	24.0	24.5	22.7	23.1	33.8	25.4	23.8
Gambia, The	..	22.3	17.4	17.4	21.2	19.2	24.8	..	..	18.9	20.1	20.0
Ghana	6.1	14.4	23.1	27.1	18.8	22.9	28.4	29.0	32.9	7.9	19.7	26.0
Guinea	..	22.9	18.9	14.5	13.2	10.1	11.3	14.0	13.3	16.4	20.0	13.6
Guinea-Bissau	28.2	29.9	11.3	15.0	9.6	12.6	13.2	14.6	17.2	32.0	25.9	13.4
Kenya	18.3	20.6	16.8	18.2	17.2	15.8	16.1	18.6	18.8	18.8	17.6	17.4
Lesotho	35.6	52.8	44.9	43.4	43.5	40.5	35.7	34.4	33.3	39.5	57.0	39.4
Liberia	..	..	..	4.9	4.7	9.4	13.2	16.4	..	..	..	9.7
Madagascar	14.4	14.8	15.0	18.5	14.3	17.9	24.3	22.5	24.8	10.8	12.4	19.6
Malawi	22.2	20.1	12.3	13.8	..	16.2	18.2	21.5	21.8	15.8	15.2	17.3
Mali	15.5	23.0	24.6	31.0	18.6	24.2	21.0	22.6	22.9	17.2	22.5	23.6
Mauritania	..	20.0	19.4	22.0	21.1	25.9	46.4	44.8	23.3	26.6	13.6	29.0
Mauritius	24.2	28.3	25.3	23.1	22.3	22.2	22.1	21.3	22.9	21.1	27.1	22.8
Mozambique	7.6	22.1	31.0	20.0	30.0	22.3	18.6	18.7	19.3	12.2	20.7	22.8
Namibia	27.2	21.2	18.8	21.9	21.2	29.2	25.7	26.3	28.2	18.6	21.0	24.5
Niger	25.5	11.4	11.2	11.9	14.0	14.5	16.6	18.9	..	14.2	9.0	14.5
Nigeria	..	..	..	..	..	..	..	..	..	..	..	..
Rwanda	12.2	14.6	18.3	19.0	17.7	18.6	20.4	21.6	20.3	14.4	14.5	19.4
São Tomé and Principe	..	..	..	..	..	..	..	..	..	..	..	..
Senegal	14.6	18.0	22.4	22.7	24.8	21.2	22.7	29.7	28.9	17.4	19.9	24.6
Seychelles	36.5	23.0	25.2	40.7	25.6	10.4	12.7	30.2	32.7	25.6	29.2	25.3
Sierra Leone	14.9	9.6	6.9	6.7	10.1	13.9	10.7	17.4	15.5	11.4	7.2	11.6
Somalia	43.1	14.9	..	..	..	..	..	..	..	26.9	..	..
South Africa	25.9	19.1	15.1	15.1	15.0	15.9	16.1	17.0	18.7	23.1	16.3	16.1
Sudan	10.8	8.2	12.1	11.1	13.2	14.1	17.2	19.2	21.0	12.6	10.8	15.4
Swaziland	35.0	18.4	18.6	17.6	19.9	18.8	18.4	18.0	15.8	25.4	20.5	18.2
Tanzania	..	25.8	17.4	16.8	19.0	18.5	18.2	16.1	16.6	..	21.0	17.5
Togo	28.2	25.3	17.8	21.3	18.8	20.9	21.2	21.8	..	19.0	15.6	20.3
Uganda	..	12.7	19.6	18.2	18.9	20.1	22.1	21.3	23.0	9.3	15.9	20.5
Zambia	18.2	13.5	16.0	17.7	20.6	24.1	22.6	22.3	22.7	12.4	12.4	20.8
Zimbabwe	14.1	18.2	11.8	12.1	10.2	13.8	17.1	21.0	..	16.0	20.1	14.3
NORTH AFRICA	23.4	24.1	20.1	20.0	21.2	20.5	20.9	21.0	21.3	25.6	21.4	20.7
Algeria	33.8	27.0	20.7	22.7	24.4	24.0	24.1	23.8	..	31.9	26.2	23.3
Egypt, Arab Rep.	24.6	26.9	18.9	17.7	17.8	16.3	16.4	17.9	18.7	27.8	20.4	17.7
Libya	21.2	13.9	12.9	11.9	14.4	..	..	..	..	25.8	12.7	13.1
Morocco	22.2	24.0	26.0	24.8	25.2	25.2	26.7	28.5	28.7	23.1	22.2	26.4
Tunisia	28.3	24.4	26.0	26.2	25.4	23.4	22.6	22.4	22.7	27.5	25.3	24.1
AFRICA	19.3	20.4	17.8	17.8	17.7	18.0	18.1	18.2	18.9	21.0	18.9	18.1

a. Provisional

Table 2.23

2.23 Gross general government fixed capital formation

	Share of GDP (%)									Annual average		
	1980	1990	2000	2001	2002	2003	2004	2005	2006ª	1980–89	1990–99	2000–06
SUB-SAHARAN AFRICA	..	**5.0**	**4.2**	**4.4**	**4.3**	**4.4**	**4.4**	**4.4**	**5.2**	**5.4**	**4.5**	**4.5**
Excl. South Africa	..	**5.9**	**5.5**	**5.7**	**5.4**	**5.8**	**6.0**	**5.7**	**6.8**	**6.4**	**6.1**	**5.8**
Excl. South Africa & Nigeria	..	**5.8**	**5.7**	**6.0**	**5.8**	**6.2**	**6.6**	**6.5**	**7.9**	**6.0**	**6.0**	**6.4**
Angola	..	..	6.1	6.4	6.8	7.6	4.9	5.0	11.3	..	7.8	6.9
Benin	..	7.4	7.6	7.8	6.6	6.1	5.4	6.7	..	9.1	7.5	6.7
Botswana	..	8.6	10.0	10.2	10.6	10.2	8.7	7.7	8.3	9.7	11.7	9.4
Burkina Faso	..	9.7	7.7	6.1	6.4	6.3	7.2	7.4	8.0	10.4	10.5	7.0
Burundi	12.8	12.5	5.4	3.7	4.6	8.3	10.7	8.8	..	13.8	9.3	6.9
Cameroon	4.4	5.5	2.1	2.2	2.3	2.3	2.6	2.5	2.4	6.9	2.9	2.3
Cape Verde	..	10.3	12.5	10.8	13.0	9.8	7.7	8.9	8.7	19.3	20.3	10.2
Central African Republic	3.7	4.7	4.7	3.5	4.8	2.1	2.0	4.0	3.3	5.5	6.2	3.5
Chad	..	..	10.5	8.8	10.1	12.5	7.8	7.0	8.0	3.8	7.4	9.2
Comoros	23.2	5.2	3.9	4.4	5.8	5.4	4.4	4.5	5.0	18.7	7.0	4.8
Congo, Dem. Rep.	5.1	4.0	0.5	0.1	1.0	2.7	2.8	..	..	4.4	1.7	1.4
Congo, Rep.	..	5.6	7.0	10.0	8.7	6.5	7.0	5.3	8.6	11.1	6.4	7.6
Côte d'Ivoire	11.4	3.6	2.8	1.9	3.2	2.7	2.8	2.7	3.1	7.1	5.6	2.7
Djibouti	..	9.1	2.7	2.5	4.5	6.7	7.7	9.3	7.5	..	6.1	5.8
Equatorial Guinea	..	10.5	5.1	7.4	8.4	9.8	14.0	10.1	15.1	..	6.9	10.0
Eritrea	..	..	26.8	23.5	21.7	17.7	17.2	15.4	14.0	..	16.4	19.5
Ethiopia	..	4.0	12.2	13.1	14.0	12.8	15.7	14.7	16.7	4.9	6.6	14.2
Gabon	5.3	3.9	2.9	4.7	4.0	3.7	4.2	4.2	4.8	6.7	6.5	4.1
Gambia, The	..	7.4	4.6	11.2	7.9	5.7	10.9	9.0	7.9	10.4	7.8	8.2
Ghana	..	7.5	10.4	10.4	9.6	8.9	12.4	12.0	14.6	6.3	11.1	11.2
Guinea	..	9.7	4.9	4.9	4.0	4.4	4.0	3.4	3.2	7.5	6.1	4.1
Guinea-Bissau	..	27.4	10.0	13.7	9.0	11.1	11.1	14.1	10.8	33.3	20.2	11.4
Kenya	..	9.7	4.6	4.4	4.3	4.2	4.2	3.8	3.6	0.8	7.1	4.2
Lesotho	9.9	23.0	8.0	10.5	11.2	8.7	7.4	7.5	7.2	15.4	16.2	8.6
Liberia	..	..	..	..	..	..	..	..	..	..	..	..
Madagascar	..	7.9	6.7	7.3	4.8	7.8	12.5	10.3	10.3	6.9	6.9	8.5
Malawi	17.5	7.7	10.0	10.3	..	2.4	2.0	7.0	7.4	9.5	9.2	6.5
Mali	..	10.5	8.6	7.0	7.0	6.9	7.5	7.7	8.6	10.2	10.1	7.6
Mauritania	..	6.2	..	7.2	9.1	12.0	9.1	8.1	5.6	7.6	5.0	8.5
Mauritius	9.1	4.6	7.8	6.8	7.0	7.9	7.7	6.6	7.0	6.0	3.7	7.3
Mozambique	7.6	12.0	9.2	14.0	12.2	12.0	9.7	8.6	12.3	9.5	12.1	11.1
Namibia	15.7	8.2	6.1	8.7	6.2	7.0	7.3	7.4	8.2	10.7	8.2	7.3
Niger	20.4	7.4	6.6	7.1	8.8	8.6	5.4	6.4	..	11.2	5.6	7.1
Nigeria	..	..	..	..	..	..	..	..	..	..	..	..
Rwanda	12.2	5.9	6.2	6.7	5.2	5.4	7.9	9.1	7.5	12.1	7.2	6.9
São Tomé and Principe	..	..	..	..	..	..	..	..	..	..	..	..
Senegal	4.7	4.1	4.5	5.1	5.7	6.2	6.7	10.0	9.8	3.7	4.5	6.8
Seychelles	..	8.2	11.4	25.0	7.4	1.7	3.1	5.6	10.1	12.0	9.9	9.2
Sierra Leone	5.3	3.9	5.2	4.4	4.4	4.8	4.6	5.8	5.1	4.0	3.8	4.9
Somalia	..	..	..	..	..	..	..	..	..	..	..	..
South Africa	6.4	3.9	2.7	2.5	2.5	2.6	2.6	2.7	2.9	5.7	2.8	2.6
Sudan	6.9	..	2.3	2.3	3.0	2.9	5.0	5.5	6.4	4.3	0.8	3.9
Swaziland	11.9	5.7	6.3	10.0	12.4	12.9	10.2	9.5	8.4	8.0	6.6	9.9
Tanzania	..	10.5	6.0	5.6	7.6	7.4	7.3	6.4	6.7	..	5.8	6.7
Togo	20.2	7.3	3.0	2.3	1.4	3.7	5.3	4.1	..	11.2	3.7	3.3
Uganda	..	6.2	6.4	5.8	5.3	4.7	5.2	4.7	4.9	4.4	5.6	5.3
Zambia	..	6.2	10.0	11.9	11.8	11.4	8.6	6.9	3.9	..	6.8	9.2
Zimbabwe	1.8	3.4	0.7	2.1	2.1	2.1	5.1	1.5	..	2.9	2.9	2.3
NORTH AFRICA	..	**9.2**	**8.6**	**8.2**	**9.1**	**8.7**	**8.6**	**8.3**	**..**	**11.8**	**8.5**	**8.6**
Algeria	11.0	8.2	7.8	8.4	10.0	10.8	10.5	9.7	..	13.8	7.2	9.5
Egypt, Arab Rep.	..	14.7	9.9	8.7	9.4	8.5	8.7	8.8	7.3	16.9	12.0	8.8
Libya	19.4	..	..	..	..	..	..	..	..	19.4	..	..
Morocco	..	4.8	4.7	4.7	3.9	3.8	3.9	3.8	3.8	7.1	4.2	4.1
Tunisia	15.0	8.7	12.3	..	..	..	..	..	..	14.1	11.5	12.3
AFRICA	..	**6.5**	**6.0**	**6.0**	**6.2**	**6.0**	**5.9**	**5.8**	**6.3**	**7.9**	**6.0**	**6.0**

a. Provisional

Table 2.24

Private sector fixed capital formation

	Share of GDP (%)									Annual average		
	1980	1990	2000	2001	2002	2003	2004	2005	2006[a]	1980–89	1990–99	2000–06
SUB-SAHARAN AFRICA	**11.2**	**12.5**	**11.7**	**11.8**	**11.1**	**12.2**	**12.2**	**12.4**	**12.5**	**12.1**	**12.6**	**12.0**
Excl. South Africa	..	**10.4**	**11.3**	**11.5**	**10.8**	**11.5**	**11.2**	**11.2**	**10.6**	**9.4**	**11.8**	**11.2**
Excl. South Africa & Nigeria	..	**10.1**	**11.9**	**12.1**	**11.6**	**12.5**	**12.5**	**12.7**	**12.4**	**8.9**	**11.6**	**12.2**
Angola	..	1.7	8.9	7.1	5.8	5.1	4.2	3.0	2.4	9.2	16.5	5.2
Benin	..	6.0	11.3	11.4	11.6	12.0	12.1	12.2	..	4.5	8.3	11.8
Botswana	34.5	23.8	11.6	10.6	11.3	11.3	11.5	11.3	9.6	19.4	15.5	11.0
Burkina Faso	..	8.0	11.0	8.6	10.8	11.1	..	..	..	8.8	10.8	10.4
Burundi	1.1	2.7	0.8	2.5	1.5	2.3	2.3	1.7	..	2.3	–0.3	1.9
Cameroon	15.6	11.9	13.9	18.1	17.5	15.8	15.7	15.2	14.3	14.2	11.7	15.8
Cape Verde	..	12.6	7.2	7.5	7.9	8.9	29.7	28.2	29.4	7.6	9.3	17.0
Central African Republic	3.2	6.7	4.8	4.9	4.2	3.9	4.1	4.9	5.6	4.7	5.0	4.7
Chad	..	..	10.5	27.8	49.6	36.1	14.9	12.0	13.2	0.6	4.3	23.5
Comoros	5.3	6.7	6.2	5.6	5.2	4.9	5.0	4.8	4.9	5.5	7.7	5.2
Congo, Dem. Rep.	3.7	8.9	3.0	5.1	8.0	9.5	10.0	..	..	7.1	6.3	7.1
Congo, Rep.	..	11.6	14.0	16.2	13.8	18.6	16.6	16.2	13.8	11.4	18.5	15.6
Côte d'Ivoire	13.0	4.9	8.4	8.0	7.7	7.0	7.1	7.0	6.8	8.7	6.2	7.4
Djibouti	..	5.1	6.1	5.4	5.6	7.7	13.8	9.7	22.0	..	5.8	10.0
Equatorial Guinea	..	6.9	56.2	64.5	23.7	49.6	31.0	28.1	26.6	..	52.6	40.0
Eritrea	..	..	5.1	5.2	4.3	7.7	5.6	4.7	4.2	..	8.6	5.3
Ethiopia	..	8.9	8.1	8.3	9.9	9.0	9.7	8.3	7.6	12.8	9.9	8.7
Gabon	21.4	17.6	19.0	21.0	20.5	20.2	20.3	18.5	18.3	27.2	18.9	19.7
Gambia, The	..	14.9	12.8	6.2	13.3	13.5	13.9	18.5	14.9	8.6	12.3	13.3
Ghana	..	6.9	12.7	16.7	9.2	14.0	16.0	17.0	18.3	3.8	8.6	14.8
Guinea	..	8.8	14.0	9.6	9.2	5.7	7.4	10.7	10.2	8.9	11.7	9.5
Guinea-Bissau	..	8.4	1.3	1.3	0.6	1.5	2.1	0.5	6.4	10.0	7.7	2.0
Kenya	8.2	10.9	12.2	13.7	12.9	11.5	11.9	14.7	15.2	10.7	10.6	13.2
Lesotho	25.7	29.7	36.9	32.9	32.3	31.8	28.4	26.9	26.1	24.0	40.8	30.8
Liberia	..	..	..	2.0	2.2	4.8	4.2	4.3	..	..	..	3.5
Madagascar	..	6.9	8.3	11.2	9.5	10.1	11.8	12.3	14.5	3.6	5.5	11.1
Malawi	4.7	12.4	2.3	3.5	..	13.8	16.2	14.5	14.4	6.3	6.0	10.8
Mali	..	12.4	15.9	24.0	11.6	17.3	13.5	15.0	14.3	9.9	12.4	15.9
Mauritania	..	13.7	..	14.8	11.9	13.9	37.3	36.7	17.7	19.0	13.9	22.1
Mauritius	15.1	23.7	17.5	16.3	15.3	14.3	14.5	14.8	15.9	15.1	23.4	15.5
Mozambique	..	10.1	21.7	6.0	17.7	10.2	8.9	10.1	7.1	2.7	8.6	11.7
Namibia	11.4	13.0	12.7	13.2	14.9	22.1	18.3	18.9	20.0	7.8	12.8	17.2
Niger	5.1	4.0	4.6	4.8	5.2	5.9	11.3	12.5	..	3.0	3.4	7.4
Nigeria	..	..	..	..	..	..	..	..	..	..	..	..
Rwanda	..	8.7	12.1	12.3	12.5	13.3	12.5	12.5	12.8	7.8	7.2	12.6
São Tomé and Principe	..	..	..	..	..	..	..	..	..	..	..	..
Senegal	9.9	13.9	17.9	17.7	19.2	15.0	16.0	19.7	19.1	13.7	15.4	17.8
Seychelles	..	14.8	13.8	15.7	18.2	8.7	9.7	24.6	22.6	10.1	19.3	16.2
Sierra Leone	9.5	5.7	1.7	2.2	5.7	9.0	6.1	11.6	10.4	7.3	3.3	6.7
Somalia	..	..	..	..	..	..	..	..	..	..	..	..
South Africa	19.5	15.3	12.4	12.5	12.5	13.3	13.5	14.3	15.8	17.4	13.5	13.5
Sudan	3.8	..	9.7	8.8	10.1	11.2	12.2	13.7	14.5	8.9	10.2	11.5
Swaziland	23.1	12.7	12.3	7.7	7.5	5.9	8.2	8.5	7.5	17.3	13.8	8.2
Tanzania	..	15.3	11.4	11.2	11.4	11.1	10.9	9.6	9.9	..	15.2	10.8
Togo	8.0	18.0	14.8	19.0	17.4	17.2	15.9	17.7	..	7.8	11.8	17.0
Uganda	..	6.5	13.3	12.4	13.7	15.4	16.9	16.6	18.2	5.4	10.3	15.2
Zambia	..	7.2	6.0	5.8	8.8	12.7	14.1	15.3	18.8	4.9	5.7	11.6
Zimbabwe	12.3	14.8	11.1	10.1	8.1	11.7	20.0	19.5	..	13.1	17.2	12.1
NORTH AFRICA	..	**16.0**	**12.5**	**12.9**	**13.8**	**13.4**	**14.0**	**14.8**	..	**13.4**	**13.8**	**13.6**
Algeria	22.8	18.8	12.9	14.3	14.5	13.2	13.6	14.1	..	18.1	19.0	13.7
Egypt, Arab Rep.	..	12.3	9.1	9.0	8.4	7.9	7.7	9.1	11.4	9.3	8.3	8.9
Libya	1.8	..	..	..	..	..	..	..	..	1.8	..	..
Morocco	16.7	19.2	21.3	20.1	21.2	21.4	22.8	24.7	24.9	16.1	18.0	22.4
Tunisia	13.3	15.6	13.7	..	..	..	..	..	..	13.5	13.8	13.7
AFRICA	**12.1**	**13.8**	**12.1**	**12.2**	**12.1**	**12.7**	**12.9**	**13.3**	**13.7**	**12.6**	**13.1**	**12.7**

a. Provisional

2.25 Resource balance (exports minus imports)

	Share of GDP (%)									Annual average		
	1980	1990	2000	2001	2002	2003	2004	2005	2006ᵃ	1980–89	1990–99	2000–06
SUB-SAHARAN AFRICA	**2.4**	**1.7**	**3.1**	**0.3**	**–1.1**	**–0.9**	**0.6**	**2.1**	**2.6**	**–0.5**	**–0.9**	**1.0**
Excl. South Africa	**–0.1**	**–0.8**	**3.1**	**–1.7**	**–3.2**	**–2.8**	**1.2**	**3.9**	**5.8**	**–3.7**	**–3.7**	**0.9**
Excl. South Africa & Nigeria	**–5.4**	**–3.2**	**–2.2**	**–5.2**	**–4.0**	**–4.4**	**–2.9**	**–0.6**	**1.9**	**–4.6**	**–5.0**	**–2.5**
Angola	..	18.0	26.8	1.7	11.3	6.6	16.0	29.8	35.8	9.1	2.2	18.3
Benin	–21.5	–12.0	–12.9	–12.7	–13.9	–12.8	–12.7	–12.6	..	–17.5	–12.5	–13.0
Botswana	–13.4	5.3	18.9	16.2	11.5	8.7	9.9	17.2	22.5	5.3	9.7	15.0
Burkina Faso	–22.3	–13.5	–16.1	–13.9	–12.4	–12.9	–13.5	–15.6	–15.3	–19.6	–13.5	–14.2
Burundi	–14.5	–19.9	–12.2	–14.0	–16.2	–19.3	–24.3	–33.9	–36.9	–13.5	–14.4	–22.4
Cameroon	0.8	2.9	3.6	–1.3	–0.8	0.3	–0.4	–1.0	2.1	0.4	3.7	0.3
Cape Verde	..	–31.0	–33.9	–33.4	–36.3	–34.5	–38.9	–32.7	–33.4	–29.0	–35.2	–34.8
Central African Republic	–15.9	–12.9	–4.3	–4.5	–4.6	–4.3	–6.0	–8.8	–7.9	–12.1	–7.7	–5.8
Chad	–11.9	–14.4	–17.8	–35.0	–101.0	–34.1	0.2	15.5	21.3	–13.5	–13.6	–21.5
Comoros	–43.2	–22.9	–15.8	–15.3	–15.0	–16.1	–19.9	–22.2	–23.8	–33.3	–22.6	–18.3
Congo, Dem. Rep.	0.1	0.3	1.0	–2.0	–4.9	–7.2	–8.8	–7.7	–11.5	–0.8	1.2	–5.9
Congo, Rep.	–0.1	7.9	36.7	24.1	27.6	25.6	27.0	35.6	42.9	–0.5	2.9	31.4
Côte d'Ivoire	–6.2	4.6	7.1	8.4	16.6	10.9	9.2	7.5	10.5	3.2	6.5	10.0
Djibouti	..	–24.6	–15.3	–8.5	–5.2	–9.2	–17.2	–10.3	–17.4	..	–17.5	–11.9
Equatorial Guinea	..	–37.4	13.2	9.3	46.9	20.3	38.5	49.2	44.4	–28.6	–45.8	31.7
Eritrea	..	..	–66.6	–55.7	–59.7	–85.1	–84.2	–46.9	–42.0	..	–55.8	–62.9
Ethiopia	..	–3.3	–11.9	–11.7	–14.0	–14.1	–16.7	–20.4	–22.7	–5.3	–6.8	–15.9
Gabon	33.1	15.2	36.4	26.0	19.2	24.3	29.5	44.5	41.6	9.7	17.7	31.6
Gambia, The	–20.9	–11.7	–8.9	–5.4	–8.3	–9.2	–17.6	–20.6	..	–13.2	–12.6	–11.7
Ghana	–0.7	–9.0	–18.4	–19.6	–12.3	–15.9	–21.1	–25.6	–24.9	–3.1	–12.4	–19.7
Guinea	3.1	–2.4	–4.3	–1.3	–4.0	–2.4	–4.0	–2.7	–2.8	0.8	–3.0	–3.1
Guinea-Bissau	–29.2	–27.1	–19.8	–34.3	–21.7	–11.4	–16.2	–13.1	–10.9	–32.9	–24.5	–18.2
Kenya	–6.4	–5.6	–8.1	–11.8	–6.7	–6.0	–7.6	–10.7	–12.4	–4.9	–2.8	–9.1
Lesotho	–89.1	–105.6	–63.1	–57.3	–61.4	–58.4	–48.3	–50.3	–48.0	–105.4	–94.8	–55.3
Liberia	–0.1	..	–4.5	–8.4	–8.1	–12.6	–13.9	–14.0	–45.3	2.9	–39.6	–15.2
Madagascar	–16.4	–11.4	–7.3	–3.2	–6.6	–9.0	–14.9	–14.1	–11.2	–7.7	–8.2	–9.5
Malawi	–14.0	–9.6	–9.7	–11.1	–24.9	–21.8	–18.2	–15.7	–12.5	–6.7	–14.3	–16.3
Mali	–14.4	–16.6	–12.6	–17.0	–7.3	–10.9	–12.4	–11.7	–8.1	–17.6	–14.9	–11.4
Mauritania	–29.8	–15.1	–28.0	–18.9	–23.0	–30.9	–49.4	–59.8	–4.5	–24.4	–11.2	–30.6
Mauritius	–10.9	–7.2	–1.9	2.7	3.8	2.1	–0.6	–4.4	–7.1	–3.5	–4.3	–0.8
Mozambique	–16.5	–27.9	–19.5	–16.2	–18.3	–16.2	–8.6	–9.4	–6.1	–18.4	–23.6	–13.5
Namibia	7.8	–15.5	–5.5	–6.4	–2.0	–3.6	–6.1	–3.5	–1.0	–7.6	–10.0	–4.0
Niger	–13.5	–6.9	–7.9	–7.7	–8.9	–9.5	–10.5	–9.4	..	–8.0	–6.2	–9.0
Nigeriaᵇ	10.2	14.6	21.9	10.7	–0.7	2.3	12.9	15.5	14.9	1.1	4.1	11.1
Rwanda	–11.9	–8.5	–17.0	–16.1	–18.2	–18.3	–16.9	–18.4	–17.1	–10.3	–19.9	–17.4
São Tomé and Principe	..	..	..	..	..	..	..	..	..	..	..	..
Senegal	–14.5	–6.8	–9.3	–9.0	–10.4	–12.1	–12.9	–15.6	–18.5	–12.1	–7.1	–12.5
Seychelles	–11.2	–4.3	–3.3	–21.5	–1.2	11.2	2.0	–26.4	–22.5	–2.3	–8.6	–8.8
Sierra Leone	–15.4	–1.3	–21.3	–18.2	–19.5	–21.3	–12.4	–18.0	–13.8	–3.1	–4.5	–17.8
Somalia	–55.3	–28.0	..	..	..	..	..	..	..	–35.1	..	..
South Africa	8.0	5.5	3.0	4.0	3.8	2.3	–0.4	–0.9	–3.4	5.1	2.8	1.2
Sudan	–12.6	–4.2	–2.4	–7.8	–6.2	–4.2	–3.8	–9.9	–10.9	–8.5	–9.4	–6.5
Swaziland	–39.4	–12.5	–15.6	–14.7	–0.3	2.0	–2.6	–8.9	–7.7	–23.5	–19.1	–6.8
Tanzania	..	–24.8	–7.4	–8.2	–7.4	–6.6	–7.1	–6.5	–5.9	..	–19.3	–7.0
Togo	–5.3	–11.9	–20.0	–19.4	–18.0	–13.6	–13.5	–13.2	..	–7.2	–9.6	–16.3
Uganda	–6.6	–12.1	–11.9	–12.1	–14.7	–14.2	–13.9	–13.9	–15.3	–6.2	–11.7	–13.7
Zambia	–4.0	–0.7	–14.4	–16.3	–14.0	–12.4	–4.3	–2.0	8.3	–2.1	–5.6	–7.9
Zimbabwe	–3.2	0.1	–0.3	1.3	–0.9	–5.2	–10.1	–16.2	..	–0.8	–2.6	–5.2
NORTH AFRICA	**5.0**	**–3.6**	**3.4**	**2.0**	**0.9**	**3.4**	**4.2**	**7.6**	**..**	**–3.2**	**–2.4**	**3.6**
Algeria	4.0	–1.5	19.8	14.6	9.7	14.4	14.4	24.1	..	–2.5	1.6	16.2
Egypt, Arab Rep.	–12.4	–12.7	–6.6	–4.9	–4.4	–2.6	–1.4	–2.3	–1.6	–13.2	–6.7	–3.4
Libya	34.8	8.6	19.8	11.3	11.4	..	..	..	..	20.4	3.6	14.1
Morocco	–9.4	–5.4	–5.4	–2.6	–2.2	–3.0	–5.2	–6.1	–5.4	–7.4	–4.9	–4.3
Tunisia	–5.4	–7.0	–3.6	–4.6	–4.3	–3.9	–2.9	–2.6	0.1	–6.1	–4.3	–3.1
AFRICA	**3.0**	**–0.2**	**3.2**	**1.0**	**–0.3**	**0.6**	**1.8**	**3.9**	**4.6**	**–1.6**	**–1.4**	**2.1**

a. Provisional

b. For 1994–2000 Nigeria's values were distorted because the official exchange rate used by the government for oil exports and oil value added was significantly overvalued.

Table 2.26

Exports of goods and services, nominal

	Current prices ($ millions)									Annual average		
	1980	1990	2000	2001	2002	2003	2004	2005	2006a	1980–89	1990–99	2000–06
SUB-SAHARAN AFRICA	**83,550**	**79,605**	**116,864**	**109,587**	**113,346**	**144,936**	**184,890**	**231,798**	**276,758**	**66,400**	**87,538**	**168,311**
Excl. South Africa	**54,743**	**52,178**	**79,830**	**73,890**	**76,767**	**98,175**	**127,193**	**165,291**	**200,761**	**39,893**	**55,790**	**117,415**
Excl. South Africa & Nigeria	**34,970**	**40,246**	**55,014**	**53,265**	**57,948**	**69,295**	**88,593**	**113,059**	**137,379**	**32,457**	**43,560**	**82,079**
Angola	..	3,993	8,182	6,847	8,406	9,716	13,780	24,286	33,317	2,613	4,265	14,934
Benin	222	264	342	360	380	487	539	577	..	214	327	448
Botswana	563	2,087	3,248	2,933	2,811	3,697	4,357	5,120	5,581	999	2,350	3,964
Burkina Faso	173	340	237	260	290	376	549	542	665	189	286	417
Burundi	81	89	55	45	39	50	64	91	99	111	89	63
Cameroon	1,880	2,251	2,343	2,104	2,169	2,757	3,061	3,393	4,130	2,240	2,198	2,851
Cape Verde	..	43	146	167	194	253	138	171	229	41	79	185
Central African Republic	201	220	190	160	162	154	168	170	207	181	185	173
Chad	175	234	234	251	252	674	2,252	3,234	3,852	153	254	1,536
Comoros	11	36	34	34	40	51	46	48	47	22	40	43
Congo, Dem. Rep.	2,372	2,759	964	875	1,174	1,483	1,994	2,242	2,517	2,016	1,595	1,607
Congo, Rep.	1,024	1,502	2,585	2,163	2,462	2,825	3,662	5,160	6,717	1,092	1,393	3,654
Côte d'Ivoire	3,561	3,421	4,211	4,412	5,747	6,297	7,517	8,354	9,004	3,142	4,129	6,506
Djibouti	..	244	193	213	228	248	246	288	307	..	210	246
Equatorial Guinea	..	42	1,236	1,760	2,139	2,859	4,766	7,285	8,096	32	160	4,020
Eritrea	..	..	96	133	128	80	82	85	87	..	132	99
Ethiopia	..	672	984	980	982	1,140	1,498	1,858	2,097	608	715	1,363
Gabon	2,770	2,740	3,498	2,782	2,642	3,350	4,412	5,844	6,238	1,964	2,728	4,110
Gambia, The	103	190	202	150	157	158	185	207	..	108	195	176
Ghana	376	993	2,429	2,401	2,625	3,101	3,487	3,869	5,063	554	1,684	3,282
Guinea	2,084	829	735	809	785	806	829	925	1,073	2,021	798	852
Guinea-Bissau	14	24	68	57	61	77	84	114	129	15	32	84
Kenya	2,144	2,207	2,817	2,866	3,105	3,557	4,248	5,004	5,720	1,805	2,599	3,902
Lesotho	91	104	256	319	390	520	763	708	755	70	187	530
Liberia	613	..	120	126	111	133	171	201	175	519	43	148
Madagascar	539	512	1,190	1,317	704	1,264	1,425	1,355	1,635	414	673	1,270
Malawi	307	447	446	480	907	723	655	610	537	295	465	623
Mali	263	415	649	876	1,066	1,153	1,237	1,359	1,884	255	514	1,175
Mauritania	261	465	500	379	382	356	473	659	1,453	387	465	600
Mauritius	539	1,529	2,801	2,978	2,757	3,099	3,350	3,556	3,809	764	2,191	3,193
Mozambique	383	201	744	1,004	1,188	1,353	1,828	2,164	2,831	215	373	1,587
Namibia	1,712	1,220	1,558	1,446	1,548	2,300	2,594	2,967	3,577	1,139	1,543	2,284
Niger	617	372	320	329	330	438	491	512	..	420	325	403
Nigeria	18,859	12,366	24,821	20,637	18,839	28,891	38,609	52,238	63,391	7,725	12,563	35,347
Rwanda	168	145	151	157	133	139	189	229	296	173	107	185
São Tomé and Principe	..	..	..	..	..	..	..	..	..	..	..	..
Senegal	837	1,453	1,310	1,401	1,523	1,826	2,123	2,340	2,351	989	1,347	1,839
Seychelles	100	230	481	508	586	671	684	717	860	123	298	644
Sierra Leone	252	146	115	129	153	197	233	268	333	187	155	204
Somalia	200	90	..	..	..	..	..	..	..	119	..	..
South Africa	28,555	27,149	37,034	35,695	36,578	46,760	57,700	66,523	76,106	26,088	31,523	50,914
Sudan	806	499	1,892	1,714	1,996	2,613	3,822	4,992	6,014	841	579	3,292
Swaziland	405	658	1,133	1,156	1,131	1,580	2,056	1,897	1,774	394	886	1,532
Tanzania	..	538	1,527	1,505	1,631	2,022	2,538	2,964	3,106	..	962	2,185
Togo	580	545	409	421	498	595	691	743	..	464	441	559
Uganda	242	312	663	690	697	778	933	1,154	1,403	371	500	903
Zambia	1,608	1,180	878	1,021	1,030	1,256	2,079	2,482	4,120	1,060	1,099	1,838
Zimbabwe	1,561	2,009	2,660	2,369	2,019	1,854	2,002	1,941	..	1,530	2,469	2,141
NORTH AFRICA	**45,633**	**46,844**	**69,807**	**66,721**	**66,896**	**80,121**	**99,631**	**125,521**	**..**	**35,544**	**48,909**	**84,783**
Algeria	14,541	14,546	22,560	20,002	20,012	26,028	34,067	48,690	..	12,221	12,420	28,560
Egypt, Arab Rep.	6,992	8,647	16,175	17,066	16,091	18,074	22,258	27,214	32,191	6,654	12,435	21,296
Libya	23,523	11,468	12,078	9,054	9,164	..	..	..	..	17,320	8,527	10,099
Morocco	3,273	6,830	10,333	11,069	12,109	14,092	16,458	18,656	21,592	3,790	8,360	14,901
Tunisia	3,518	5,353	8,661	9,530	9,520	10,950	13,199	13,766	16,477	3,312	7,168	11,729
AFRICA	**127,967**	**126,562**	**186,675**	**176,313**	**180,245**	**225,548**	**285,379**	**358,340**	**426,668**	**102,286**	**136,482**	**262,738**

a. Provisional

Table 2.27

2.27 Imports of goods and services, nominal

	Current prices ($ millions)									Annual average		
	1980	1990	2000	2001	2002	2003	2004	2005	2006ᵃ	1980–89	1990–99	2000–05
SUB-SAHARAN AFRICA	**76,888**	**74,423**	**106,369**	**108,470**	**117,220**	**148,888**	**181,663**	**218,410**	**257,218**	**67,756**	**90,329**	**162,606**
Excl. South Africa	**54,934**	**53,569**	**73,286**	**77,610**	**84,950**	**105,971**	**123,151**	**149,702**	**172,411**	**46,247**	**62,444**	**112,440**
Excl. South Africa & Nigeria	**41,909**	**45,298**	**58,543**	**62,096**	**65,676**	**78,554**	**95,829**	**114,795**	**130,745**	**38,672**	**51,150**	**86,605**
Angola	..	2,147	5,736	6,697	7,110	8,801	10,621	15,144	17,129	1,895	4,032	10,177
Benin	524	486	634	662	772	944	1,055	1,119	..	447	579	864
Botswana	705	1,888	2,079	1,958	2,130	2,979	3,380	3,308	3,109	842	1,896	2,706
Burkina Faso	603	758	658	650	697	928	1,240	1,390	1,547	567	640	1,016
Burundi	214	314	141	138	140	165	225	360	432	254	234	229
Cameroon	1,829	1,931	1,981	2,228	2,254	2,712	3,128	3,562	3,762	2,219	1,816	2,804
Cape Verde	..	148	326	351	419	529	497	500	624	118	237	464
Central African Republic	327	411	231	203	210	205	246	289	324	292	282	244
Chad	298	485	480	849	2,259	1,608	2,241	2,324	2,509	305	469	1,753
Comoros	64	93	66	68	77	103	118	134	143	67	93	101
Congo, Dem. Rep.	2,354	2,731	920	971	1,447	1,892	2,573	2,792	3,499	2,107	1,537	2,013
Congo, Rep.	1,026	1,282	1,404	1,490	1,629	1,913	2,488	2,994	3,398	1,093	1,309	2,188
Côte d'Ivoire	4,190	2,927	3,471	3,529	3,837	4,796	6,093	7,132	7,189	2,906	3,406	5,150
Djibouti	..	355	278	262	259	305	361	361	441	..	295	324
Equatorial Guinea	..	92	1,071	1,599	1,124	2,256	2,882	3,583	4,295	61	270	2,401
Eritrea	..	..	518	507	505	577	617	540	543	..	482	544
Ethiopia	..	1,069	1,961	1,938	2,073	2,346	3,175	4,366	5,539	1,093	1,330	3,057
Gabon	1,354	1,837	1,656	1,557	1,694	1,882	2,298	1,983	2,267	1,586	1,823	1,905
Gambia, The	153	227	239	173	188	192	255	302	..	137	242	225
Ghana	407	1,522	3,347	3,441	3,380	4,316	5,356	6,610	8,234	709	2,509	4,955
Guinea	1,878	892	867	849	912	892	986	1,013	1,163	1,953	905	955
Guinea-Bissau	46	90	111	125	105	104	127	153	162	67	91	127
Kenya	2,608	2,691	3,840	4,403	3,986	4,456	5,485	7,012	8,534	2,154	2,963	5,388
Lesotho	475	753	794	750	812	1,127	1,400	1,426	1,472	503	977	1,112
Liberia	614	..	146	171	156	184	235	275	453	491	180	232
Madagascar	1,202	864	1,474	1,463	993	1,756	2,073	2,067	2,252	668	942	1,725
Malawi	480	629	616	672	1,570	1,251	1,134	1,058	932	384	716	1,033
Mali	520	817	954	1,322	1,311	1,630	1,841	1,979	2,360	536	882	1,628
Mauritania	473	619	803	591	647	753	1,239	1,758	1,573	576	607	1,052
Mauritius	665	1,701	2,888	2,854	2,584	2,988	3,389	3,830	4,257	809	2,334	3,256
Mozambique	965	888	1,571	1,665	1,958	2,108	2,320	2,783	3,245	773	1,001	2,236
Namibia	1,542	1,584	1,746	1,652	1,610	2,461	2,940	3,186	3,644	1,284	1,844	2,463
Niger	957	545	462	479	523	688	795	825	..	583	448	629
Nigeria	12,324	8,203	14,728	15,499	19,245	27,360	27,282	34,849	41,518	7,362	11,214	25,783
Rwanda	307	364	445	427	430	464	522	666	787	354	405	534
São Tomé and Principe	..	..	..	..	..	..	..	..	..	..	..	..
Senegal	1,344	1,840	1,746	1,842	2,078	2,657	3,162	3,694	4,062	1,408	1,719	2,749
Seychelles	117	246	501	641	594	593	671	908	1,034	123	344	706
Sierra Leone	421	154	250	276	336	408	366	487	529	225	191	379
Somalia	534	346	..	..	..	..	..	..	..	403	..	..
South Africa	22,073	21,016	33,107	30,897	32,316	42,967	58,544	68,754	84,692	21,441	27,961	50,183
Sudan	1,763	877	2,189	2,760	2,924	3,367	4,650	7,701	9,995	1,744	1,289	4,798
Swaziland	619	768	1,349	1,350	1,134	1,543	2,117	2,130	1,988	515	1,116	1,659
Tanzania	..	1,595	2,200	2,283	2,353	2,703	3,344	3,881	3,941	..	2,000	2,958
Togo	640	738	674	678	763	833	969	1,026	..	542	586	824
Uganda	324	834	1,366	1,378	1,554	1,662	1,879	2,369	2,854	619	1,042	1,866
Zambia	1,764	1,203	1,343	1,612	1,552	1,796	2,319	2,631	3,221	1,148	1,283	2,068
Zimbabwe	1,771	2,002	2,680	2,232	2,218	2,238	2,477	2,495	..	1,598	2,661	2,390
NORTH AFRICA	**39,100**	**53,024**	**61,430**	**61,875**	**64,800**	**71,674**	**88,038**	**100,933**	**115,394**	**40,426**	**53,419**	**80,592**
Algeria	12,847	15,472	11,700	11,920	14,491	16,239	21,808	24,020	..	13,875	11,636	16,696
Egypt, Arab Rep.	9,822	14,109	22,780	21,802	19,917	20,219	23,330	29,246	33,931	10,787	16,572	24,461
Libya	11,167	8,996	5,252	5,674	6,979	..	..	..	..	10,722	7,464	5,968
Morocco	5,033	8,227	12,329	12,033	12,992	15,579	19,393	22,272	25,125	4,955	9,905	17,103
Tunisia	3,987	6,220	9,369	10,446	10,421	11,918	14,026	14,525	16,449	3,834	7,842	12,450
AFRICA	**115,856**	**127,727**	**167,801**	**170,345**	**182,017**	**221,305**	**270,566**	**320,728**	**375,095**	**108,542**	**143,841**	**243,980**

a. Provisional

Table 2.28

2.28 Exports of goods and services

	Share of GDP (%)									Annual average		
	1980	1990	2000	2001	2002	2003	2004	2005	2006a	1980–89	1990–99	2000–06
SUB-SAHARAN AFRICA	**30.2**	**26.8**	**34.2**	**32.7**	**31.1**	**32.5**	**33.6**	**35.9**	**37.2**	**25.3**	**27.6**	**33.9**
Excl. South Africa	**27.8**	**28.2**	**38.1**	**34.0**	**30.3**	**35.1**	**38.1**	**41.0**	**40.9**	**23.2**	**30.7**	**36.8**
Excl. South Africa & Nigeria	**27.0**	**25.7**	**33.7**	**31.5**	**29.9**	**32.7**	**36.1**	**38.9**	**40.1**	**24.2**	**28.7**	**34.7**
Angola	..	38.9	89.6	76.6	73.5	69.6	69.7	79.3	73.8	34.8	63.4	76.0
Benin	15.8	14.3	15.2	15.2	13.5	13.7	13.3	13.5	..	16.6	16.4	14.1
Botswana	53.1	55.1	52.6	48.6	47.4	44.7	44.3	48.7	50.7	62.0	51.2	48.1
Burkina Faso	9.0	11.0	9.1	9.2	8.8	8.8	10.7	10.0	11.5	9.5	11.1	9.7
Burundi	8.8	7.9	7.8	6.9	6.2	8.4	9.6	11.4	10.9	10.4	9.0	8.7
Cameroon	27.9	20.2	23.3	21.9	19.9	20.2	19.4	20.5	23.0	25.7	20.9	21.2
Cape Verde	..	12.7	27.5	30.3	31.5	31.7	14.9	17.0	19.4	15.5	16.9	24.6
Central African Republic	25.2	14.8	19.8	16.5	15.5	12.9	12.8	12.6	14.0	20.5	16.2	14.9
Chad	16.9	13.5	16.9	14.7	12.7	24.6	51.0	55.1	61.1	14.3	16.1	33.7
Comoros	8.7	14.3	16.7	15.5	15.7	15.8	12.7	12.5	11.7	14.7	17.4	14.4
Congo, Dem. Rep.	16.5	29.5	22.4	18.6	21.2	26.1	30.4	31.6	29.5	21.4	23.1	25.7
Congo, Rep.	60.0	53.7	80.3	77.4	81.5	79.3	84.3	84.8	86.9	52.0	60.2	82.1
Côte d'Ivoire	35.0	31.7	40.4	41.8	50.0	45.8	48.6	51.1	52.1	37.1	36.8	47.1
Djibouti	..	53.8	35.1	37.3	38.6	39.9	37.0	40.6	39.9	..	43.2	38.3
Equatorial Guinea	..	32.2	98.6	101.3	98.7	96.4	97.3	96.8	94.5	35.9	52.9	97.7
Eritrea	..	..	15.1	19.9	20.3	13.6	12.9	8.8	8.0	..	22.0	14.1
Ethiopia	..	5.6	12.0	12.0	12.6	13.3	14.9	15.1	13.8	6.6	8.1	13.4
Gabon	64.7	46.0	69.0	59.0	53.6	55.3	61.5	67.4	65.4	53.3	54.0	61.6
Gambia, The	42.7	59.9	48.0	35.9	42.5	43.1	46.0	44.8	..	47.8	52.6	43.4
Ghana	8.5	16.9	48.8	45.2	42.6	40.7	39.3	36.1	39.8	11.2	25.2	41.8
Guinea	31.2	31.1	23.6	26.6	24.5	22.3	21.0	28.4	33.5	29.6	23.8	25.7
Guinea-Bissau	12.7	9.9	31.8	28.6	30.2	32.9	31.0	37.7	41.8	9.9	13.3	33.4
Kenya	29.5	25.7	22.3	22.1	23.6	23.7	26.2	26.7	25.1	25.7	27.7	24.3
Lesotho	21.0	16.8	30.0	42.4	56.8	50.0	57.9	49.7	50.5	16.7	21.7	48.2
Liberia	64.3	..	21.5	23.2	19.9	32.4	37.3	37.9	28.6	55.3	11.4	28.7
Madagascar	13.3	16.6	30.7	29.1	16.0	23.1	32.6	26.9	29.7	13.6	20.1	26.9
Malawi	24.8	23.8	25.6	28.0	34.0	29.8	25.0	21.4	17.0	23.7	25.1	25.8
Mali	14.7	17.1	26.8	33.3	31.9	26.4	25.4	25.6	32.1	15.8	20.8	28.8
Mauritania	36.8	45.6	46.2	33.8	33.3	27.7	30.6	35.9	54.6	47.9	36.7	37.4
Mauritius	46.8	64.2	62.7	65.6	60.6	59.1	55.2	56.5	60.0	53.1	61.5	60.0
Mozambique	10.9	8.2	17.5	24.6	28.3	29.0	32.1	32.9	41.4	6.8	12.8	29.4
Namibia	78.9	51.9	45.6	45.0	49.6	51.4	45.9	47.6	54.5	61.2	49.7	48.5
Niger	24.6	15.0	17.8	16.9	15.2	16.6	16.9	15.4	..	21.0	16.2	16.5
Nigeria	29.4	43.4	54.0	43.0	31.9	42.7	44.0	46.5	43.2	21.4	42.0	43.6
Rwanda	14.4	5.6	8.7	9.4	8.1	7.9	9.6	9.6	10.3	10.4	6.0	9.1
São Tomé and Principe	..	..	..	..	..	..	..	..	..	..	..	..
Senegal	23.9	25.4	27.9	28.7	28.5	26.6	26.4	26.9	25.4	27.4	26.4	27.2
Seychelles	68.0	62.5	78.2	81.6	84.0	95.1	97.8	99.2	111.0	62.1	59.9	92.4
Sierra Leone	22.9	22.4	18.1	16.0	16.4	19.9	21.7	22.1	23.4	19.5	19.8	19.7
Somalia	33.2	9.8	..	..	..	..	..	..	..	15.5	9.8	..
South Africa	35.4	24.2	27.9	30.1	33.0	28.1	26.7	27.5	29.8	28.8	23.5	29.0
Sudan	10.6	5.5	15.3	12.8	13.3	14.7	17.6	18.2	16.5	7.7	7.4	15.5
Swaziland	74.6	74.6	81.6	87.8	95.2	86.8	86.5	72.6	63.7	70.2	74.8	82.0
Tanzania	..	12.6	16.8	15.9	16.7	19.7	22.4	21.0	21.9	..	16.4	19.2
Togo	51.1	33.5	30.7	31.7	33.8	33.8	33.5	34.5	..	46.1	30.2	33.0
Uganda	19.4	7.2	11.2	12.1	11.9	12.4	13.7	13.2	14.8	11.6	9.8	12.8
Zambia	41.4	35.9	27.1	28.1	27.7	28.7	37.6	33.8	37.8	34.4	32.8	31.5
Zimbabwe	23.4	22.9	35.9	23.1	9.2	25.1	42.5	56.8	..	21.4	34.1	32.1
NORTH AFRICA	**34.6**	**27.2**	**28.4**	**27.7**	**29.7**	**32.1**	**35.7**	**39.0**	**..**	**25.5**	**26.4**	**32.1**
Algeria	34.3	23.4	41.2	36.2	35.1	38.3	40.1	47.6	..	23.8	25.8	39.7
Egypt, Arab Rep.	30.5	20.0	16.2	17.5	18.3	21.8	28.2	30.3	29.9	22.2	21.8	23.2
Libya	66.2	39.7	35.0	30.2	47.7	..	..	..	..	54.7	28.7	37.6
Morocco	17.4	26.5	27.9	29.3	29.9	28.3	29.2	31.6	33.0	22.2	25.9	29.9
Tunisia	40.2	43.6	44.5	47.7	45.2	43.8	46.9	47.5	53.2	36.9	42.5	47.0
AFRICA	**31.4**	**27.0**	**31.8**	**30.6**	**30.6**	**32.4**	**34.4**	**37.1**	**38.3**	**25.4**	**27.1**	**33.6**

a. Provisional

 Table 2.29 Imports of goods and services

	Share of GDP (%)									Annual average		
	1980	1990	2000	2001	2002	2003	2004	2005	2006ᵃ	1980–89	1990–99	2000–06
SUB-SAHARAN AFRICA	**27.8**	**25.1**	**31.1**	**32.3**	**32.2**	**33.4**	**33.0**	**33.9**	**34.5**	**25.9**	**28.5**	**32.9**
Excl. South Africa	**27.9**	**28.9**	**35.0**	**35.7**	**33.5**	**37.9**	**36.9**	**37.1**	**35.2**	**26.9**	**34.4**	**35.9**
Excl. South Africa & Nigeria	**32.4**	**28.9**	**35.9**	**36.7**	**33.8**	**37.1**	**39.0**	**39.5**	**38.1**	**28.9**	**33.7**	**37.2**
Angola	..	20.9	62.8	74.9	62.2	63.1	53.7	49.4	37.9	25.6	61.3	57.7
Benin	37.3	26.3	28.1	27.9	27.5	26.5	26.1	26.1	..	34.1	28.9	27.0
Botswana	66.4	49.8	33.7	32.5	35.9	36.0	34.4	31.5	28.2	56.7	41.5	33.2
Burkina Faso	31.3	24.5	25.2	23.1	21.2	21.7	24.3	25.6	26.8	29.2	24.6	24.0
Burundi	23.3	27.8	19.9	20.9	22.3	27.7	33.9	45.3	47.8	23.8	23.4	31.1
Cameroon	27.1	17.3	19.7	23.2	20.7	19.9	19.8	21.5	21.0	25.3	17.2	20.8
Cape Verde	..	43.7	61.4	63.7	68.1	66.3	53.8	49.7	52.8	44.6	52.1	59.4
Central African Republic	41.1	27.6	24.1	21.0	20.1	17.2	18.8	21.4	21.9	32.5	24.0	20.7
Chad	28.9	27.9	34.7	49.7	113.7	58.7	50.8	39.6	39.8	27.7	29.7	55.3
Comoros	51.9	37.1	32.5	30.8	30.8	31.8	32.6	34.7	35.5	47.9	40.0	32.7
Congo, Dem. Rep.	16.4	29.2	21.4	20.7	26.1	33.3	39.2	39.3	41.0	22.2	21.9	31.6
Congo, Rep.	60.1	45.8	43.6	53.3	53.9	53.7	57.3	49.2	43.9	52.6	57.3	50.7
Côte d'Ivoire	41.2	27.1	33.3	33.5	33.4	34.9	39.4	43.6	41.6	33.9	30.3	37.1
Djibouti	..	78.4	50.4	45.8	43.7	49.1	54.2	50.9	57.3	..	60.7	50.2
Equatorial Guinea	..	69.6	85.4	92.0	51.9	76.1	58.8	47.6	50.1	64.5	98.6	66.0
Eritrea	..	..	81.8	75.6	80.0	98.7	97.1	55.7	50.0	..	77.8	77.0
Ethiopia	..	8.8	24.0	23.7	26.6	27.4	31.6	35.5	36.5	11.9	14.9	29.3
Gabon	31.6	30.9	32.7	33.0	34.3	31.1	32.0	22.9	23.7	43.6	36.3	30.0
Gambia, The	63.6	71.6	56.8	41.3	50.8	52.3	63.7	65.4	..	61.0	65.3	55.1
Ghana	9.2	25.9	67.2	64.8	54.9	56.6	60.4	61.7	64.8	14.3	37.6	61.5
Guinea	28.1	33.4	27.9	27.9	28.4	24.6	25.0	31.1	36.3	28.8	26.9	28.8
Guinea-Bissau	41.8	37.0	51.6	63.0	51.9	44.3	47.2	50.8	52.7	42.8	37.7	51.6
Kenya	35.9	31.3	30.5	33.9	30.3	29.7	33.9	37.4	37.5	30.6	30.6	33.3
Lesotho	110.1	122.4	93.1	99.7	118.2	108.4	106.2	100.0	98.5	122.1	116.5	103.5
Liberia	64.4	..	26.0	31.6	27.9	44.9	51.2	51.9	73.8	52.4	51.0	43.9
Madagascar	29.7	28.0	38.0	32.3	22.6	32.1	47.5	41.0	40.9	21.3	28.3	36.3
Malawi	38.8	33.4	35.3	39.1	58.9	51.6	43.2	37.1	29.4	30.4	39.4	42.1
Mali	29.1	33.7	39.4	50.3	39.2	37.4	37.8	37.3	40.2	33.4	35.7	40.2
Mauritania	66.7	60.7	74.2	52.7	56.2	58.6	80.0	95.7	59.1	72.2	47.9	68.1
Mauritius	57.6	71.4	64.6	62.9	56.8	56.9	55.9	60.9	67.1	56.6	65.8	60.7
Mozambique	27.4	36.1	37.0	40.9	46.6	45.2	40.7	42.3	47.5	25.1	36.4	42.9
Namibia	71.1	67.4	51.2	51.4	51.6	55.0	52.0	51.1	55.5	68.7	59.7	52.5
Niger	38.1	22.0	25.7	24.6	24.1	26.1	27.4	24.8	..	29.0	22.4	25.4
Nigeria	19.2	28.8	32.0	32.3	32.6	40.4	31.1	31.0	28.3	20.3	38.5	32.5
Rwanda	26.4	14.1	25.7	25.5	26.2	26.1	26.5	28.0	27.4	20.7	26.0	26.5
São Tomé and Principe	..	..	..	..	..	..	..	..	..	..	..	..
Senegal	38.4	32.2	37.2	37.8	39.0	38.7	39.4	42.5	43.8	39.6	33.5	39.8
Seychelles	79.1	66.7	81.4	103.0	85.2	84.0	95.8	125.7	133.5	64.4	68.4	101.2
Sierra Leone	38.2	23.8	39.4	34.3	35.9	41.2	34.1	40.1	37.2	22.5	24.3	37.5
Somalia	88.5	37.7	..	..	..	..	..	..	..	50.6	37.7	..
South Africa	27.3	18.8	24.9	26.1	29.1	25.8	27.0	28.4	33.2	23.8	20.7	27.8
Sudan	23.1	9.7	17.7	20.7	19.5	18.9	21.4	28.1	27.5	16.2	16.8	22.0
Swaziland	114.0	87.1	97.2	102.5	95.5	84.7	89.1	81.5	71.4	93.7	93.9	88.8
Tanzania	..	37.5	24.2	24.2	24.1	26.3	29.5	27.4	27.8	..	35.6	26.2
Togo	56.4	45.3	50.7	51.1	51.7	47.4	47.0	47.6	..	53.3	39.8	49.3
Uganda	26.0	19.4	23.0	24.3	26.6	26.6	27.6	27.1	30.1	17.8	21.6	26.5
Zambia	45.4	36.6	41.5	44.3	41.8	41.1	42.0	35.8	29.6	36.5	38.4	39.4
Zimbabwe	26.5	22.8	36.2	21.8	10.1	30.3	52.6	73.0	..	22.2	36.7	37.3
NORTH AFRICA	**29.7**	**30.8**	**25.0**	**25.7**	**28.7**	**28.7**	**31.6**	**31.4**	**31.2**	**28.7**	**28.8**	**28.9**
Algeria	30.3	24.9	21.4	21.6	25.4	23.9	25.7	23.5	..	26.3	24.2	23.6
Egypt, Arab Rep.	42.9	32.7	22.8	22.3	22.7	24.4	29.6	32.6	31.6	35.4	28.5	26.6
Libya	31.4	31.1	15.2	18.9	36.4	..	..	..	..	34.3	25.1	23.5
Morocco	26.7	31.9	33.3	31.9	32.1	31.3	34.4	37.8	38.4	29.6	30.9	34.2
Tunisia	45.6	50.6	48.2	52.3	49.5	47.7	49.9	50.1	53.1	43.0	46.8	50.1
AFRICA	**28.5**	**27.2**	**28.6**	**29.6**	**30.9**	**31.8**	**32.7**	**33.2**	**33.7**	**27.0**	**28.6**	**31.5**

a. Provisional

Table 2.30 Balance of payment and current account

	Exports of goods and services		Imports of goods and services		Net income		Net current transfers		Current account balance		Total reserves including gold	
Current prices ($ millions)	2005	2006ᵃ	2005	2006ᵃ	2005	2006ᵃ	2005	2006ᵃ	2005	2006ᵃ	2005	2006ᵃ
SUB-SAHARAN AFRICA	231,798	276,758	218,410	257,218	..	..	..	..	11,361	−14,234	83,557	113,863
Excl. South Africa	165,291	200,761	149,702	172,411	−30,902	−32,092	..	..	21,084	2,253	62,928	88,250
Excl. South Africa & Nigeria	113,059	137,379	114,795	130,745	−18,075	−20,792	..	..	−3,118	2,253	34,296	45,515
Angola	24,286	33,317	15,144	17,129	−4,031	−6,178	27	−190	5,138	10,690	3,197	8,599
Benin	577	..	1,119	..	−18	..	164	..	−226	..	529	496
Botswana	5,120	5,581	3,308	3,109	−836	−772	678	871	1,597	1,940	6,309	7,992
Burkina Faso	542	665	1,390	1,547	..	..	..	..	..	..	..	..
Burundi	91	99	360	432	−18	−9	239	229	−11	−135	101	131
Cameroon	3,393	4,130	3,562	3,762	..	..	..	..	..	..	801	1,026
Cape Verde	171	229	500	624	−33	−45	279	295	−35	−40	181	..
Central African Republic	170	207	289	324	..	..	..	..	..	..	145	132
Chad	3,234	3,852	2,324	2,509	..	..	..	..	..	..	371	459
Comoros	48	47	134	143	..	..	..	..	..	..	86	94
Congo, Dem. Rep.	2,242	2,517	2,792	3,499	..	..	..	..	..	..	360	470
Congo, Rep.	5,160	6,717	2,994	3,398	−1,122	..	−22	..	903	..	740	1,998
Côte d'Ivoire	8,354	9,004	7,132	7,189	−653	−710	−462	−531	40	479	1,322	1,798
Djibouti	288	307	361	441	21	23	73	79	20	−17	88	117
Equatorial Guinea	7,285	8,096	3,583	4,295	..	..	..	..	..	..	2,102	3,067
Eritrea	85	87	540	543	..	..	..	..	..	..	16	16
Ethiopia	1,858	2,097	4,366	5,539	−5	18	1,402	1,274	−1,568	−1,786	1,555	1,158
Gabon	5,844	6,238	1,983	2,267	..	..	..	..	..	..	675	1,122
Gambia, The	207	..	302	..	−32	−38	69	87	−44	−66	85	95
Ghana	3,869	5,063	6,610	8,234	−187	−127	1,794	2,248	−1,105	−1,040	1,951	2,084
Guinea	925	1,073	1,013	1,163	..	..	..	..	..	..	125	232
Guinea-Bissau	114	129	153	162	..	..	..	..	..	..	213	210
Kenya	5,004	5,720	7,012	8,534	−108	−70	1,253	1,781	−261	−526	2,043	2,654
Lesotho	708	755	1,426	1,472	305	379	301	390	−98	67	447	455
Liberia	201	175	275	453	−113	−131	318	307	7	−138	10	..
Madagascar	1,355	1,635	2,067	2,252	−80	..	236	..	−554	..	498	532
Malawi	610	537	1,058	932	..	..	..	..	..	..	..	..
Mali	1,359	1,884	1,979	2,360	−207	−269	228	325	−438	−231	929	977
Mauritania	659	1,453	1,758	1,573	..	..	..	..	..	..	70	..
Mauritius	3,556	3,809	3,830	4,257	−8	50	61	71	−324	−611	1,487	1,391
Mozambique	2,164	2,831	2,783	3,245	−360	−496	403	501	−761	−634	1,103	1,241
Namibia	2,967	3,577	3,186	3,644	−127	−85	673	946	334	1,064	316	513
Niger	512	..	825	..	−10	..	182	..	−312	..	250	371
Nigeria	52,238	63,391	34,849	41,518	−6,732	..	3,310	..	24,202	..	28,632	42,735
Rwanda	229	296	666	787	−16	−21	366	296	−52	−180	406	440
São Tomé and Principe	..	..	..	..	−3	3	3	0	−36	−58	27	35
Senegal	2,340	2,351	3,694	4,062	..	..	..	..	..	..	1,261	897
Seychelles	717	860	908	1,034	−40	−44	31	48	−195	−164	56	111
Sierra Leone	268	333	487	529	−51	−41	137	62	−104	−101	112	142
Somalia	..	..	..	..	..	..	..	..	..	..	..	..
South Africa	66,523	76,106	68,754	84,692	−4,929	−5,293	−2,801	−2,817	−9,723	−16,487	20,629	25,613
Sudan	4,992	6,014	7,701	9,995	−1,362	−2,014	1,446	1,324	−2,768	−4,722	554	..
Swaziland	1,897	1,774	2,130	1,988	62	1	131	168	86	98	230	209
Tanzania	2,964	3,106	3,881	3,941	−117	−85	496	550	−881	−1,442	2,049	2,259
Togo	743	..	1,026	..	−35	..	188	..	−461	..	..	..
Uganda	1,154	1,403	2,369	2,854	−249	−226	833	1,429	−414	−323	1,168	1,398
Zambia	2,482	4,120	2,631	3,221	−595	−1,168	107	362	−600	128	331	595
Zimbabwe	1,941	..	2,495	..	..	..	..	..	..	..	..	..
NORTH AFRICA	125,521	..	100,933	115,394	−7,141	−9,572	..	..	17,854	26,023	99,382	133,559
Algeria	48,690	..	24,020	..	..	..	..	..	..	..	59,167	81,463
Egypt, Arab Rep.	27,214	32,191	29,246	33,931	−35	738	5,748	5,770	2,103	2,635	19,322	26,660
Libya	..	..	..	..	−281	−595	−634	586	14,945	22,170	..	..
Morocco	18,656	21,592	22,272	25,125	−314	−421	5,375	6,333	1,110	1,851	17,936	18,613
Tunisia	13,766	16,477	14,525	16,449	−1,668	−1,586	1,502	1,639	−304	−634	2,957	6,824
AFRICA	358,340	426,668	320,728	375,095	−42,983	−46,947	..	..	29,215	11,789	182,939	247,423

a. Provisional

Table 2.31 Structure of demand

	Household final consumption expenditure			General government final consumption expenditure			Gross fixed capital formation			Exports of goods and services			Imports of goods and services			Gross national savings		
Share of GDP %	1990	2000	2006a	1990	2000	2006a	1990	2000	2006a	1990	2000	2006a	1990	2000	2006a	1990	2000	2006a
SUB-SAHARAN AFRICA	**65.5**	**68.5**	**66.9**	**17.4**	**14.6**	**13.7**	**18.1**	**16.0**	**17.6**	**26.8**	**34.2**	**37.2**	**25.1**	**31.1**	**34.5**	**12.9**	**12.9**	**9.0**
Excl. South Africa	**72.8**	**73.6**	**70.3**	**15.5**	**11.9**	**10.3**	**17.6**	**16.8**	**17.4**	**28.2**	**38.1**	**40.9**	**28.9**	**35.0**	**35.2**	**9.0**	**11.0**	**6.4**
Excl. South Africa & Nigeria	**72.8**	**73.6**	**70.3**	**15.0**	**12.5**	**12.1**	**17.0**	**17.7**	**20.4**	**25.7**	**33.7**	**40.1**	**28.9**	**35.9**	**38.1**	**10.7**	**14.1**	**9.2**
Angola	35.8	..	..	34.5	..	..	11.1	15.1	13.7	38.9	89.6	73.8	20.9	62.8	37.9	9.0	23.8	37.0
Benin	86.8	82.4	..	11.0	11.6	..	13.4	18.9	..	14.3	15.2	..	26.3	28.1	..	9.9	10.9	..
Botswana	33.2	23.2	28.4	24.1	22.9	19.2	32.4	21.7	17.9	55.1	52.6	50.7	49.8	33.7	28.2	43.3	51.7	53.3
Burkina Faso	73.5	78.5	75.2	21.1	20.8	22.0	17.7	18.7	20.8	11.0	9.1	11.5	24.5	25.2	26.8	13.7	5.1	6.3
Burundi	94.5	88.5	90.9	10.8	17.5	29.3	15.2	6.1	16.7	7.9	7.8	10.9	27.8	19.9	47.8	..	0.5	..
Cameroon	66.6	70.2	71.5	12.8	9.5	9.6	17.3	16.0	16.7	20.2	23.3	23.0	17.3	19.7	21.0	16.1	16.1	18.9
Cape Verde	93.4	92.9	74.6	14.7	21.3	20.7	22.9	19.7	38.1	12.7	27.5	19.4	43.7	61.4	52.8	17.6	9.1	26.8
Central African Republic	85.7	80.8	88.3	14.9	14.0	10.6	11.4	9.5	8.9	14.8	19.8	14.0	27.6	24.1	21.9	-0.4	8.2	11.7
Chad	97.6	86.8	50.5	10.0	7.7	5.9	4.8	20.9	21.2	13.5	16.9	61.1	27.9	34.7	39.8	-2.7	7.9	20.4
Comoros	78.7	94.0	101.4	24.5	11.7	12.6	11.9	10.1	9.8	14.3	16.7	11.7	37.1	32.5	35.5	-1.3	9.9	4.9
Congo, Dem. Rep.	79.1	88.0	88.1	11.5	7.5	7.3	12.8	3.5	..	29.5	22.4	29.5	29.2	21.4	41.0	0.8	-3.5	8.9
Congo, Rep.	62.4	29.1	21.1	13.8	11.6	13.2	17.2	20.9	22.4	53.7	80.3	86.9	45.8	43.6	43.9	6.6	30.1	43.0
Côte d'Ivoire	71.9	74.9	71.2	16.8	7.2	8.4	8.5	11.2	9.9	31.7	40.4	52.1	27.1	33.3	41.6	-4.3	10.0	14.7
Djibouti	78.9	76.8	59.9	31.5	29.7	28.0	14.1	8.8	29.6	53.8	35.1	39.9	78.4	50.4	57.3	..	5.4	20.7
Equatorial Guinea	80.3	20.9	11.1	39.7	4.6	2.9	17.4	61.3	41.6	32.2	98.6	94.5	69.6	85.4	50.1	-22.0	45.7	46.2
Eritrea	..	70.9	80.9	..	63.8	42.4	..	31.9	18.7	..	15.1	8.0	..	81.8	50.0	..	20.4	8.7
Ethiopia	77.2	73.8	86.4	13.2	17.9	12.1	12.9	20.3	24.2	5.6	12.0	13.8	8.8	24.0	36.5	11.9	16.3	15.1
Gabon	49.7	32.2	26.9	13.4	9.6	8.4	21.4	21.9	23.1	46.0	69.0	65.4	30.9	32.7	23.7	24.2	41.7	41.3
Gambia, The	75.6	77.8	..	13.7	13.7	..	22.3	17.4	..	59.9	48.0	..	71.6	56.8	..	5.3	13.6	10.0
Ghana	85.2	84.3	78.7	9.3	10.2	13.4	14.4	23.1	32.9	16.9	48.8	39.8	25.9	67.2	64.8	7.0	15.7	27.4
Guinea	66.9	77.7	83.8	11.0	6.8	5.6	22.9	18.9	13.3	31.1	23.6	33.5	33.4	27.9	36.3	14.6	13.3	11.8
Guinea-Bissau	86.9	94.6	76.0	10.3	14.0	17.7	29.9	11.3	17.2	9.9	31.8	41.8	37.0	51.6	52.7	15.3	-2.7	22.7
Kenya	62.8	75.2	74.3	18.6	15.3	16.3	20.6	16.8	18.8	25.7	22.3	25.1	31.3	30.5	37.5	18.6	15.2	12.5
Lesotho	138.8	101.3	96.9	14.1	19.2	18.1	52.8	44.9	33.3	16.8	30.0	50.5	122.4	93.1	98.5	59.5	21.4	27.3
Liberia	..	..	..	..	..	..	..	..	..	..	21.5	28.6	..	26.0	73.8	..	..	..
Madagascar	86.4	83.2	77.6	8.0	9.0	8.8	14.8	15.0	24.8	16.6	30.7	29.7	28.0	38.0	40.9	9.2	9.4	16.0
Malawi	71.5	81.6	77.0	15.1	14.6	11.8	20.1	12.3	21.8	23.8	25.6	17.0	33.4	35.3	29.4	13.6	2.2	15.5
Mali	79.8	79.4	75.3	13.8	8.6	9.9	23.0	24.6	22.9	17.1	26.8	32.1	33.7	39.4	40.2	15.1	16.0	13.0
Mauritania	69.2	82.8	61.3	25.9	25.8	19.9	20.0	19.4	23.3	45.6	46.2	54.6	60.7	74.2	59.1	17.6	0.8	28.7
Mauritius	63.7	63.0	68.1	12.8	13.1	14.5	28.3	25.3	22.9	64.2	62.7	60.0	71.4	64.6	67.1	26.3	25.3	19.0
Mozambique	92.3	79.5	75.6	13.5	9.0	11.1	22.1	31.0	19.3	8.2	17.5	41.4	36.1	37.0	47.5	2.1	6.0	3.1
Namibia	51.2	57.1	47.9	30.6	28.8	23.7	21.2	18.8	28.2	51.9	46.5	54.5	67.4	51.2	55.5	34.8	26.2	42.2
Niger	83.8	83.4	..	15.0	13.0	..	11.4	11.2	..	15.0	17.8	..	22.0	25.7	..	-2.1	2.8	..
Nigeria	..	..	..	..	..	..	..	..	..	43.4	54.0	43.2	28.8	32.0	28.3	..	..	..
Rwanda	83.7	87.7	85.1	10.1	11.0	11.7	14.6	18.3	20.3	5.6	8.7	10.3	14.1	25.7	27.4	11.3	12.9	13.8
São Tomé and Principe	..	..	..	..	..	..	..	..	..	..	..	..	..	..	..	..	..	..
Senegal	79.2	76.0	79.9	18.4	12.8	9.6	18.0	22.4	28.9	25.4	27.9	25.4	32.2	37.2	43.8	-0.5	14.6	18.3
Seychelles	52.0	53.9	65.2	27.7	24.2	24.7	23.0	25.2	32.7	62.5	78.2	111.0	66.7	81.4	133.5	21.7	17.2	9.4
Sierra Leone	83.5	100.1	85.3	7.8	14.3	13.1	9.6	6.9	15.5	22.4	18.1	23.4	23.8	39.4	37.2	2.6	-9.1	9.5
Somalia	..	..	..	..	..	..	14.9	..	..	9.8	..	..	37.7	..	..	..	..	..
South Africa	57.1	63.0	63.5	19.7	18.1	19.5	19.1	15.1	18.7	24.2	27.9	29.8	18.8	24.9	33.2	19.6	15.8	13.9
Sudan	89.6	76.5	68.9	7.3	7.6	16.7	8.2	12.1	21.0	5.5	15.3	16.5	9.7	17.7	27.5	-4.4	3.5	10.3
Swaziland	75.2	72.4	72.3	18.1	24.5	19.5	18.4	18.6	15.8	74.6	81.6	63.7	87.1	97.2	71.4	24.8	13.2	14.5
Tanzania	80.9	79.2	72.8	17.8	10.6	16.3	25.8	17.4	16.6	12.6	16.8	21.9	37.5	24.2	27.8	7.7	8.5	10.7
Togo	71.1	92.0	..	14.2	10.2	..	25.3	17.8	..	33.5	30.7	..	45.3	50.7	..	20.4	0.3	..
Uganda	91.9	78.2	77.2	7.5	13.7	14.7	12.7	19.6	23.0	7.2	11.2	14.8	19.4	23.0	30.1	1.2	9.3	12.9
Zambia	64.4	87.4	59.1	19.0	9.5	10.0	13.5	16.0	22.7	35.9	27.1	37.8	36.6	41.5	29.6	6.9	-1.3	23.3
Zimbabwe	63.1	72.8	..	19.4	13.9	..	18.2	11.8	..	22.9	35.9	..	22.8	36.2	..	15.7	9.6	..
NORTH AFRICA	**64.1**	**61.3**	**..**	**16.2**	**14.5**	**..**	**24.1**	**20.1**	**21.3**	**27.2**	**28.4**	**..**	**30.8**	**25.0**	**31.2**	**14.2**	**12.9**	**14.6**
Algeria	56.8	41.6	..	16.1	13.6	..	27.0	20.7	..	23.4	41.2	..	24.9	21.4	..	26.2	41.3	..
Egypt, Arab Rep.	72.6	75.9	70.6	11.3	11.2	12.3	26.9	18.9	18.7	20.0	16.2	29.9	32.7	22.8	31.6	21.4	18.7	22.0
Libya	48.4	46.6	..	24.4	20.5	..	13.9	12.9	..	39.7	35.0	..	31.1	15.2	..	..	..	..
Morocco	64.6	61.5	55.5	15.5	18.4	18.3	24.0	26.0	28.7	26.5	27.9	33.0	31.9	33.3	38.4	25.1	24.2	34.5
Tunisia	63.6	60.7	63.0	16.4	15.6	13.4	24.4	26.0	22.7	43.6	44.5	53.2	50.6	48.2	53.1	21.7	23.2	25.4
AFRICA	**64.8**	**65.2**	**66.6**	**16.8**	**14.5**	**13.3**	**20.4**	**17.8**	**18.9**	**27.0**	**31.8**	**38.3**	**27.2**	**28.6**	**33.7**	**13.4**	**12.9**	**10.8**

a. Provisional

2.32 Exchange rates and Purchasing Power Parity*

	Official exchange rate		Purchasing power parity (PPP) conversion factor		Ratio of PPP conversion factor to market exchange rate	
	local currency units to US$		local currency units to international $			
	2005	2006	2005	2006	2005	2006
SUB-SAHARAN AFRICA						
Excl. South Africa						
Excl. South Africa & Nigeria						
Angola	44.5	49.4	87.2	80.4	0.5	0.6
Benin	219.6	219.2	527.5	522.9	0.4	0.4
Botswana	2.4	2.7	5.1	5.8	0.5	0.5
Burkina Faso	200.2	193.9	527.5	522.9	0.4	0.4
Burundi	343.0	341.2	1,081.6	1,028.7	0.3	0.3
Cameroon	251.0	252.9	527.5	522.9	0.5	0.5
Cape Verde	69.4	70.7	88.7	87.9	0.8	0.8
Central African Republic	263.7	266.5	527.5	522.9	0.5	0.5
Chad	208.0	214.0	527.5	522.9	0.4	0.4
Comoros	226.2	223.6	395.6	392.2	0.6	0.6
Congo, Dem. Rep.	214.3	234.9	473.9	468.3	0.5	0.5
Congo, Rep.	268.8	308.7	527.5	522.9	0.5	0.6
Côte d'Ivoire	287.5	292.6	527.5	522.9	0.5	0.6
Djibouti	84.7	84.9	177.7	177.7	0.5	0.5
Equatorial Guinea	287.4	332.9	527.5	522.9	0.5	0.6
Eritrea	6.1	6.6	15.4	15.4	0.4	0.4
Ethiopia	2.3	2.4	8.7	8.7	0.3	0.3
Gabon	256.2	268.0	527.5	522.9	0.5	0.5
Gambia, The	7.6	7.5	28.6	28.1	0.3	0.3
Ghana	3,720.6	4,064.5	0.9	0.9	0.4	0.4
Guinea	1,219.3	1,623.6	3,644.3	..	0.3	0.3
Guinea-Bissau	217.3	209.4	527.5	522.9	0.4	0.4
Kenya	29.5	31.3	75.6	72.1	0.4	0.4
Lesotho	3.5	3.5	6.4	6.8	0.5	0.5
Liberia	28.1	29.7	57.1	58.0	0.5	0.5
Madagascar	649.6	700.4	2,003.0	2,142.3	0.3	0.3
Malawi	39.5	45.1	118.4	136.0	0.3	0.3
Mali	240.1	242.2	527.5	522.9	0.5	0.5
Mauritania	98.8	124.3	265.5	..	0.4	0.5
Mauritius	14.7	14.8	29.5	31.7	0.5	0.5
Mozambique	10,909.4	11,203.4	23.1	25.4	0.5	0.4
Namibia	4.3	4.5	6.4	6.8	0.7	0.7
Niger	226.7	223.7	527.5	522.9	0.4	0.4
Nigeria	60.2	69.8	131.3	128.7	0.5	0.5
Rwanda	186.2	204.1	557.8	551.7	0.3	0.4
São Tomé and Principe	5,558.1	6,456.4	10,558.0	12,448.6	0.5	0.5
Senegal	251.7	252.1	527.5	522.9	0.5	0.5
Seychelles	3.8	3.8	5.5	5.5	0.7	0.7
Sierra Leone	1,074.1	1,161.9	2,889.6	2,961.9	0.4	0.4
Somalia	..	..	..	..	..	..
South Africa	3.9	4.0	6.4	6.8	0.6	0.6
Sudan	107.7	111.1	2.4	2.2	0.4	0.5
Swaziland	3.3	3.5	6.4	6.8	0.5	0.5
Tanzania	395.6	399.4	1,128.9	1,251.9	0.4	0.3
Togo	240.4	228.5	527.5	522.9	0.5	0.4
Uganda	619.6	652.4	1,780.7	1,831.5	0.4	0.4
Zambia	2,414.8	2,635.0	4,463.5	3,603.1	0.5	0.7
Zimbabwe	..	..	22.4	164.4	..	..
NORTH AFRICA						
Algeria	31.0	33.3	73.3	72.6	0.4	0.5
Egypt, Arab Rep.	1.6	1.7	5.8	5.7	0.3	0.3
Libya	0.7	0.8	1.3	1.3	0.5	0.6
Morocco	4.9	4.8	8.9	8.8	0.6	0.5
Tunisia	0.6	0.6	1.3	1.3	0.4	0.4
AFRICA						

* For a discussion on the new purchase power parity data, and on the exchange rate in Franc Zone countries, see Boxes 5 and 6 in the technical notes.

| Real effective exchange rate | | Gross domestic product | | | |
| Index 2000=100 | | PPP $ billions | | Per capita PPP $ | |
2005	2006	2005	2006	2005	2006
		1,329	**1,455**	**1,741**	**1,860**
		938	1,031	1,309	1,403
		690	**759**	**1,199**	**1,286**
..	..	60	73	3,729	4,435
..	..	10	11	1,213	1,259
..	..	22	24	12,088	12,744
..	..	14	16	1,026	1,084
71.0	73.2	3	3	319	333
109.7	113.2	35	37	1,959	2,043
..	..	1	1	2,538	2,833
122.3	129.3	3	3	644	679
119.8	126.7	15	15	1,468	1,470
..	..	1	1	1,127	1,152
29.4	32.8	16	17	268	281
..	..	12	13	3,309	3,550
116.4	115.9	30	31	1,614	1,632
..	..	1	2	1,850	1,965
147.7	150.8	14	13	28,536	27,161
..	..	2	3	544	536
91.2	99.6	47	54	628	700
103.8	100.5	18	19	13,821	14,209
54.5	54.3	2	2	1,078	1,152
109.7	115.3	26	29	1,160	1,247
..	..	10	10	1,081	1,118
..	..	1	1	458	467
..	..	48	52	1,346	1,436
132.8	129.4	3	3	1,311	1,440
..	..	1	1	313	335
..	..	16	17	834	878
75.2	73.3	9	10	648	703
..	..	12	13	1,004	1,058
..	..	5	6	1,684	1,890
..	..	12	13	9,975	10,571
..	..	14	15	677	739
..	..	9	10	4,599	4,820
..	..	8	8	584	612
124.2	133.1	245	268	1,731	1,853
..	..	7	8	772	820
..	..	0	0	1,417	1,534
..	..	18	19	1,547	1,592
..	..	1	1	12,459	13,265
70.9	73.5	3	4	585	631
..	..	..	..	..	..
108.5	104.2	398	431	8,478	9,087
..	..	62	71	1,679	1,887
..	..	5	5	4,462	4,705
..	..	40	44	1,049	1,126
113.7	112.5	5	5	758	792
88.7	87.8	24	27	846	888
134.7	176.6	14	15	1,183	1,273
..	..	..	..	..	..
		823	**894**	**5,424**	**5,800**
83.2	83.2	242	254	7,370	7,626
..	..	333	367	4,574	4,953
..	..	76	83	12,866	13,688
91.8	92.9	107	119	3,554	3,915
85.3	84.6	65	70	6,445	6,958
		2,151	**2,347**	**2,350**	**2,506**

Table 3.1

Millennium Development Goal 1: eradicate extreme poverty and hunger*

National poverty line

	Share of population below national poverty line[a] (poverty headcount ratio)				Share of urban population below national poverty line[a] (poverty headcount ratio)				Share of rural population below national poverty line[a] (poverty headcount ratio)			
	Surveys 1990–99		Surveys 2000–06		Surveys 1990–99		Surveys 2000–06		Surveys 1990–99		Surveys 2000–06	
	Year[b]	Percent	Year[b]	Percent	Year[b]	Percent	Year[b]	Percent	Year[b]	Percent	Year[b]	Percent
SUB-SAHARAN AFRICA												
Angola	..	..	..	..	..	..	..	..	..	..	..	..
Benin	1999	29.0	..	..	1999	23.3	..	..	1999	33.0	..	..
Botswana	..	..	..	..	..	..	..	..	..	..	..	..
Burkina Faso	1998	54.6	2003	46.4	1998	22.4	2003	19.2	1998	61.1	2003	52.4
Burundi	1998	68.0	..	..	1998	66.5	..	..	1998	64.6	..	..
Cameroon	1996	53.3	2001	40.2	1996	41.4	2001	22.1	1996	59.6	2001	49.9
Cape Verde	..	..	..	..	..	..	..	..	..	..	..	..
Central African Republic	..	..	..	..	..	..	..	..	..	..	..	..
Chad	1996	64.0	..	..	1996	63.0	..	..	1996	67.0	..	..
Comoros	..	..	..	..	..	..	..	..	..	..	..	..
Congo, Dem. Rep.	..	..	..	..	..	..	..	..	..	..	..	..
Congo, Rep.	..	..	2005	50.7	..	..	2005	35.2	..	..	2005	64.8
Côte d'Ivoire	..	..	..	..	..	..	..	..	..	..	..	..
Djibouti	..	..	..	..	..	..	..	..	..	..	..	..
Equatorial Guinea	..	..	..	..	..	..	..	..	..	..	..	..
Eritrea	1994	53.0	..	..	..	..	..	..	..	..	..	..
Ethiopia	1996	45.5	2000	44.2	1996	33.3	2000	37.0	1996	47.0	2000	45.0
Gabon	..	..	..	..	..	..	..	..	..	..	..	..
Gambia, The	1998	57.6	2003	61.3	1998	48.0	..	..	1998	61.0	2003	63.0
Ghana	1997	39.5	2005	28.5	1997	19.4	2005	10.8	1997	49.6	2005	39.2
Guinea	1994	40.0	..	..	..	..	..	..	..	..	..	..
Guinea-Bissau	..	..	2002	65.7	..	..	..	..	..	..	..	..
Kenya	1997	52.3	2005	45.9	1997	49.2	2005	33.7	1997	52.9	2005	49.1
Lesotho	1999	68.0	..	..	1993	27.8	..	..	1993	53.9	..	..
Liberia	..	..	..	..	..	..	..	..	..	..	..	..
Madagascar	1999	71.3	..	..	1999	52.1	..	..	1999	76.7	..	..
Malawi	1998	65.3	..	..	1998	54.9	..	..	1998	66.5	..	..
Mali	1998	63.8	..	..	1998	30.1	..	..	1998	75.9	..	..
Mauritania	1996	50.0	2000	46.3	1996	30.1	2000	25.4	1996	65.5	2000	61.2
Mauritius	..	..	..	..	..	..	..	..	..	..	..	..
Mozambique	1996	69.4	2002	54.1	1996	62.0	2002	51.5	1996	71.3	2002	55.3
Namibia	..	..	..	..	..	..	..	..	..	..	..	..
Niger	1993	63.0	..	..	1993	52.0	..	..	1993	66.0	..	..
Nigeria	1992	34.1	2003	54.7	1992	30.4	2003	43.1	1992	36.4	2003	63.8
Rwanda	1993	51.2	2000	60.3	..	..	2000	14.3	..	..	2000	65.7
São Tomé and Principe	..	..	..	..	..	..	..	..	..	..	..	..
Senegal	1992	33.4	..	..	1992	23.7	..	..	1992	40.4	..	..
Seychelles	..	..	..	..	..	..	..	..	..	..	..	..
Sierra Leone	..	..	2003	65.9	..	..	2003	56.4	..	..	2003	78.5
Somalia	..	..	..	..	..	..	..	..	..	..	..	..
South Africa	..	..	..	..	..	..	..	..	..	..	..	..
Sudan	..	..	..	..	..	..	..	..	..	..	..	..
Swaziland	..	..	2001	69.2	..	..	..	..	..	..	2001	75.0
Tanzania	1991	38.6	2001	35.7	1991	31.2	2001	29.5	1991	40.8	2001	38.7
Togo	..	..	..	..	..	..	..	..	..	..	..	..
Uganda	1999	33.8	2005	31.1	1999	9.6	2005	13.4	1999	37.4	2005	34.2
Zambia	1998	72.9	2006	64.0	1998	56.0	2004	53.0	1998	83.1	2004	78.0
Zimbabwe	1996	34.9	..	..	1996	7.9	..	..	1996	48.0	..	..
NORTH AFRICA												
Algeria	1995	22.6	..	..	1995	14.7	..	..	1995	30.3	..	..
Egypt, Arab Rep.	1996	22.9	2000	16.7	1996	22.5	..	..	1996	23.3	..	..
Libya	..	..	..	..	..	..	..	..	..	..	..	..
Morocco	1999	19.0	..	..	1999	12.0	..	..	1999	27.2	..	..
Tunisia	1995	7.6	..	..	1995	3.6	..	..	1995	13.9	..	..

a. Data are based on expenditure shares, except for Namibia and Swaziland, where data are based on income shares.
b. Data are for most recent year available during the period specified.
* For a discussion on service delivery in Africa, see Box 7 in the technical notes.

Share of poorest quintile in national consumption or income[a]				Prevalence of child malnutrition, underweight (% of children under age 5)				Population below minimum dietary energy consumption	
Surveys 1990–99		Surveys 2000–06		Surveys 1990–99		Surveys 2000–06		Share (%)	Millions
Year[b]	Percent	Year[b]	Percent	Year[b]	Percent	Year[b]	Percent	2004	2004
..	..	..	..	1996	37.0	2001	27.5	35	4.8
..	..	2003	7.4	..	..	2001	21.5	12	0.8
1993	3.2	..	..	..	..	2000	10.7	32	0.6
1998	5.9	2003	6.9	..	..	2003	35.2	15	2.0
1998	5.1	..	..	..	..	2000	38.9	66	4.5
1996	5.7	2001	5.6	1998	17.8	2004	15.1	26	4.2
..	..	2001	4.4	..	..	..	..	..	..
1993	2.0	..	..	1995	23.3	2000	21.8	44	1.7
..	..	..	..	1997	34.3	2004	33.9	35	3.0
..	..	..	..	1996	22.3	2000	25.0	60	0.5
..	..	..	..	..	..	2001	33.6	74	39.0
..	..	..	..	..	..	2005	11.8	33	1.2
1998	5.8	2002	5.2	1999	18.2	2006	20.2	13	2.2
..	..	..	..	..	..	2006	25.6	24	0.2
..	..	..	..	..	..	2000	15.7	..	..
..	..	..	..	1996	38.3	2002	34.5	75	3.1
1999	9.1	..	..	..	..	2005	34.6	46	32.7
..	..	..	..	..	..	2001	8.8	5	0.1
1998	4.0	2003	4.8	..	..	2000	15.4	29	0.4
1998	5.6	..	..	1999	20.3	2003	18.8	11	2.3
..	..	2003	7.0	1999	21.2	2005	22.5	24	2.0
1993	5.2	..	..	..	..	2000	21.9	39	0.6
1997	6.0	..	..	1998	17.6	2003	16.5	31	9.9
1995	1.5	..	..	..	..	2005	16.6	13	0.2
..	..	..	..	..	..	2000	22.8	50	1.7
1999	5.9	2001	4.9	1997	35.5	2004	36.8	38	6.6
..	..	2004	7.0	1992	24.4	2005	18.4	35	4.2
1994	4.6	2001	6.1	1996	38.2	2001	30.1	29	3.8
1996	6.3	2000	6.2	..	..	2001	30.4	10	0.3
..	..	..	..	..	..	..	..	5	0.1
1997	5.6	2002	5.4	1997	28.1	2003	21.2	44	8.3
1993	1.4	..	..	1992	21.5	2000	20.3	24	0.5
1995	2.6	..	..	1998	45.0	2006	39.9	32	3.9
1996	5.0	2003	5.0	1990	35.1	2003	27.2	9	11.4
..	..	2000	5.3	1992	24.3	2005	18.0	33	2.8
..	..	..	..	..	..	2000	10.1	10	..
1995	6.5	2001	6.6	1993	21.9	2005	14.5	20	2.1
..	..	..	..	..	..	..	..	9	..
1990	1.1	2003	6.5	..	..	2000	24.7	51	2.5
..	..	..	..	..	..	2006	32.8	..	..
1995	3.6	2000	3.5	..	..	..	..	3	..
..	..	..	..	..	..	2000	38.4	26	8.7
1995	2.7	2000	4.3	..	..	2000	9.1	22	0.2
1991	7.4	2000	7.3	1999	25.3	2005	16.7	44	16.4
..	..	..	..	1998	23.2	..	..	24	1.2
1999	6.0	2002	5.7	1995	21.5	2001	19.0	19	4.8
1998	3.4	2004	3.6	1997	19.6	2002	23.3	46	5.0
1995	4.6	..	..	1999	11.5	2006	14.0	47	6.0
1995	7.0	..	..	1995	11.3	2002	10.2	4	1.4
1995	8.8	2004	8.9	..	..	2005	5.4	4	2.6
..	..	..	..	1995	4.3	..	..	3	..
1998	6.5	..	..	1992	8.1	2004	9.9	6	1.8
1995	5.6	2000	6.0	..	..	..	..	3	..

Table 3.2

Millennium Development Goal 2: achieve universal primary education

	Net primary enrollment ratio (% of relevant age group)			Primary completion rate (% of relevant age group)			Share of cohort reaching grade 5 (% of grade 1 students)			Youth literacy rate (% of ages 15–24)		
	1991	2000	2006	1991	2000	2006	1991	2000	2006a	1991	2000	2000–06b
SUB-SAHARAN AFRICA												
Angola	50.3	..	..	34.7	..	..	..	..	..	..	..	72.2
Benin	41.1	51.8	80.2	20.7	34.9	64.4	54.8	84.0	71.5	..	..	45.3
Botswana	88.3	81.6	..	89.5	89.9	..	84.0	89.5	..	89.3	..	94.0
Burkina Faso	27.0	35.4	46.9	19.5	25.0	31.3	69.7	69.1	72.5	20.2	..	33.0
Burundi	53.0	42.6	74.6	45.9	24.9	36.3	61.7	56.1	87.9	..	73.3	73.3
Cameroon	69.4	..	..	53.0	49.9	51.8	..	..	..	..	..	..
Cape Verde	91.1	97.7	87.8	..	101.8	92.3	..	..	91.9	..	..	96.3
Central African Republic	51.8	..	45.6	26.7	..	24.4	23.0	..	49.8	..	58.5	58.5
Chad	33.9	53.1	..	17.9	22.3	..	50.5	53.9	..	..	37.6	37.6
Comoros	56.7	55.1	..	..	..	..	..	..	..	..	..	..
Congo, Dem. Rep.	53.9	..	..	45.9	..	..	54.7	..	..	..	..	70.4
Congo, Rep.	81.9	..	54.7	54.3	..	73.2	60.1	..	..	..	..	97.4
Côte d'Ivoire	44.6	52.2	..	43.4	39.1	42.8	72.5	87.6	..	..	60.7	60.7
Djibouti	28.5	26.9	37.8	26.9	28.0	35.5	87.3	..	89.9	..	..	..
Equatorial Guinea	96.2	90.7	..	..	..	..	..	..	..	..	94.9	94.9
Eritrea	14.7	37.8	46.5	..	36.4	48.9	..	60.5	73.7	..	..	..
Ethiopia	21.9	38.4	65.2	..	21.6	43.0	18.3	64.6	65.3	..	..	49.9
Gabon	93.9	..	..	..	..	..	..	..	..	..	..	96.2
Gambia, The	46.4	64.0	61.8	..	..	63.0	..	..	..	..	..	..
Ghana	53.6	60.2	63.6	61.2	..	..	80.5	66.2	..	..	70.7	70.7
Guinea	27.4	47.9	71.6	17.4	32.8	63.7	58.6	..	80.9	..	..	46.6
Guinea-Bissau	37.9	45.2	..	..	26.9	..	..	..	..	..	..	..
Kenya	75.6	66.2	75.5	..	..	..	76.7	..	..	..	80.3	80.3
Lesotho	72.0	77.7	72.4	58.9	60.1	78.3	65.9	66.7	73.7	..	..	..
Liberia	..	66.2	39.5	..	..	63.4	..	..	..	..	..	67.4
Madagascar	64.3	64.6	95.9	33.3	35.5	56.9	21.1	..	35.8	..	70.2	70.2
Malawi	48.5	..	91.1	28.7	65.7	55.1	64.4	51.9	44.2	..	..	..
Mali	24.6	..	60.5	12.6	32.8	49.4	69.7	91.7	81.2	..	..	..
Mauritania	36.4	64.5	79.5	34.1	52.6	47.1	75.3	59.6	57.4	..	61.3	61.3
Mauritius	91.3	92.9	95.0	106.6	104.6	92.3	97.4	99.3	98.9	..	94.5	94.5
Mozambique	42.1	56.1	76.0	26.4	16.1	41.8	34.2	51.9	57.6	..	..	..
Namibia	85.9	75.4	76.4	..	81.6	76.4	62.3	94.2	86.8	88.1	..	92.3
Niger	24.1	27.2	43.5	17.6	18.4	32.8	62.4	74.0	56.5	..	..	36.5
Nigeria	55.2	59.7	..	..	..	..	89.1	..	..	71.2	..	84.2
Rwanda	66.9	..	..	35.4	20.7	..	59.9	39.1	..	74.9	77.6	77.6
São Tomé and Principe	95.6	..	96.2	..	..	73.9	..	..	..	93.8	..	95.4
Senegal	45.3	56.5	70.7	..	37.7	48.7	84.5	72.3	65.0	..	..	49.1
Seychelles	..	..	..	..	112.9	..	92.7	91.0	..	..	..	99.1
Sierra Leone	43.1	..	..	..	..	..	..	..	..	..	..	47.9
Somalia	8.9	..	23.0	..	..	..	..	..	..	..	..	..
South Africa	90.2	91.7	..	75.8	90.1	..	..	..	..	..	..	..
Sudan	40.4	41.2	53.7	42.0	37.5	..	93.8	..	..	..	77.2	77.2
Swaziland	74.8	75.4	..	59.9	64.3	..	77.0	73.9	..	..	88.4	88.4
Tanzania	50.5	53.4	97.8	62.4	..	74.3	81.3	81.4	85.0	..	..	78.4
Togo	64.0	76.5	80.1	34.9	61.0	67.2	48.0	73.8	..	..	74.4	74.4
Uganda	51.1	..	..	..	..	..	36.0	56.7	..	69.8	..	76.6
Zambia	78.0	67.2	92.0	..	60.1	84.0	..	..	89.3	..	..	..
Zimbabwe	84.1	83.5	87.8	97.2	..	..	76.1	..	..	..	..	97.7
NORTH AFRICA												
Algeria	88.9	91.6	95.2	79.5	82.6	85.2	94.5	97.2	95.2	..	..	90.1
Egypt, Arab Rep.	86.2	93.4	93.9	..	98.1	93.8	..	99.0	96.2	..	..	84.9
Libya	93.2	..	..	..	..	..	..	..	..	..	..	98.0
Morocco	56.1	75.8	88.1	48.1	56.7	84.0	75.1	80.1	80.3	..	..	70.5
Tunisia	93.5	93.8	96.1	74.2	86.7	119.6	86.4	93.1	96.7	..	..	94.3

a. Provisional

b. Data are for most recent year available during the period specified.

Table 3.3

Millennium Development Goal 3: promote gender equity and empower women

	Ratio of girls to boys in primary and secondary school (%)			Ratio of young literate females to males (% ages 15–24)		Women in national parliament (% of total seats)			Share of women employed in the nonagricultural sector (%)		
	1991	2000	2006ᵃ	1990	2006ᵃ	1990	2000	2006	1990	2000	2004
SUB-SAHARAN AFRICA											
Angola	..	..	..	..	75.4	15.0	16.0	15.0	..	..	..
Benin	49.5	64.2	..	..	56.1	3.0	6.0	7.2	46.0	..	..
Botswana	108.7	101.6	..	..	103.8	5.0	..	11.1	33.5	..	39.5
Burkina Faso	62.3	70.0	79.9	..	65.6	..	8.0	11.7	12.5	..	..
Burundi	81.8	..	88.6	80.7	91.6	..	6.0	30.5	13.3	..	..
Cameroon	83.0	..	82.8	..	..	14.0	6.0	8.9	20.7	..	..
Cape Verde	..	..	103.1	96.1	101.0	12.0	11.0	15.3	..	38.9	..
Central African Republic	59.8	..	..	..	66.6	4.0	7.0	10.5	30.4	..	..
Chad	41.6	55.9	..	..	41.7	..	2.0	6.5	3.8	..	..
Comoros	71.1	84.1	..	..	..	..	..	3.0	..	..	..
Congo, Dem. Rep.	..	..	..	..	80.9	5.0	..	8.4	26.1	..	..
Congo, Rep.	85.1	84.5	..	..	98.1	14.0	12.0	8.5	26.1	..	..
Côte d'Ivoire	65.3	69.1	..	..	73.6	6.0	..	8.5	..	..	..
Djibouti	70.5	71.0	75.8	..	..	..	..	10.8	..	..	..
Equatorial Guinea	..	86.3	..	..	100.2	13.0	5.0	18.0	10.5	..	..
Eritrea	..	77.4	72.0	..	..	..	15.0	22.0	..	..	..
Ethiopia	68.4	65.1	80.5	..	61.9	..	2.0	21.9	..	..	40.6
Gabon	..	95.8	..	..	97.7	13.0	8.0	9.2	37.7	..	..
Gambia, The	65.6	81.7	101.8	..	..	8.0	2.0	13.2	20.9	..	..
Ghana	78.5	89.4	93.9	..	86.2	..	9.0	10.9	56.5	..	..
Guinea	44.9	61.3	74.4	..	57.4	..	9.0	19.3	30.3	..	..
Guinea-Bissau	..	65.0	..	..	..	20.0	..	14.0	10.8	..	..
Kenya	93.6	97.6	96.1	..	101.1	1.0	4.0	7.3	21.4	..	..
Lesotho	123.5	107.2	103.9	..	..	..	4.0	11.7	..	..	..
Liberia	..	72.7	..	..	106.4	..	..	12.5	..	..	..
Madagascar	97.5	..	96.0	..	93.9	7.0	8.0	6.9	..	43.7	..
Malawi	81.3	92.6	100.0	..	..	10.0	8.0	13.6	10.5	..	..
Mali	57.1	68.5	74.4	..	..	..	12.0	10.2	..	..	49.7
Mauritania	71.3	95.0	101.5	..	81.9	..	4.0	..	..	35.8	..
Mauritius	101.6	98.2	..	101.1	101.7	7.0	8.0	17.1	36.7	38.6	37.5
Mozambique	71.5	74.9	84.7	..	..	16.0	..	34.8	11.4	..	..
Namibia	106.4	103.3	103.8	..	102.6	7.0	22.0	26.9	..	47.5	..
Niger	53.3	65.8	70.5	..	44.2	5.0	1.0	12.4	11.0	..	..
Nigeria	77.2	..	..	..	93.5	..	..	6.4	..	18.6	21.0
Rwanda	92.1	96.1	..	..	97.9	17.0	17.0	48.8	..	33.0	..
São Tomé and Principe	..	..	99.0	..	98.8	12.0	9.0	7.3	..	34.8	36.8
Senegal	68.8	82.0	92.4	..	70.0	13.0	12.0	19.2	..	..	..
Seychelles	..	101.4	..	..	100.6	16.0	24.0	29.4	..	..	..
Sierra Leone	66.8	..	..	..	62.7	..	9.0	14.5	..	..	23.2
Somalia	..	55.0	..	..	..	4.0	..	7.8	21.7	..	..
South Africa	103.9	100.4	..	..	..	3.0	30.0	32.8	..	..	42.7
Sudan	77.5	..	89.3	..	84.4	..	..	14.7	22.2	..	..
Swaziland	97.7	95.4	..	..	103.2	4.0	3.0	10.8	..	..	..
Tanzania	96.7	..	..	..	94.2	..	16.0	30.4	..	..	..
Togo	58.9	68.8	..	..	76.0	5.0	..	8.6	41.0	..	..
Uganda	81.7	92.8	..	..	86.1	12.0	18.0	29.8	..	..	..
Zambia	..	91.3	..	97.4	..	7.0	10.0	14.6	29.4	..	..
Zimbabwe	92.1	94.5	97.2	..	100.5	11.0	14.0	16.0	15.4	20.4	..
NORTH AFRICA											
Algeria	82.9	..	..	..	91.6	2.0	3.0	6.2	..	13.0	14.4
Egypt, Arab Rep.	81.4	92.4	..	..	87.6	4.0	2.0	2.0	20.5	19.0	..
Libya	..	..	105.4	..	96.9	..	..	7.7	..	..	..
Morocco	69.6	82.4	..	..	74.9	..	1.0	10.8	24.8	21.7	22.3
Tunisia	86.1	100.0	103.7	..	95.7	4.0	12.0	22.8	..	24.6	..

a. Provisional

Table 3.4

Millennium Development Goal 4: reduce child mortality

	Under–five mortality rate (per 1,000)			Infant mortality rate (per 1,000 live births)			Child immunization rate, measles (% of children ages 12–23 months)		
	1990	2000	2006	1990	2000	2006	1990	2000	2006
SUB-SAHARAN AFRICA									
Angola	260	260	260	154	154	154	38	41	48
Benin	185	160	148	111	95	88	79	68	89
Botswana	58	101	124	45	74	90	87	90	90
Burkina Faso	206	194	204	123	116	122	79	59	88
Burundi	190	181	181	114	109	109	74	75	75
Cameroon	139	151	149	85	88	87	56	49	73
Cape Verde	60	42	34	45	31	25	79	80	65
Central African Republic	173	186	175	114	120	115	83	36	35
Chad	201	205	209	120	122	124	32	28	23
Comoros	120	84	68	88	62	51	87	70	66
Congo, Dem. Rep.	205	205	205	129	129	129	38	46	73
Congo, Rep.	103	117	126	67	74	79	75	34	66
Côte d'Ivoire	153	136	127	105	95	90	56	73	73
Djibouti	175	147	130	116	97	86	85	50	67
Equatorial Guinea	170	200	206	103	120	124	88	51	51
Eritrea	147	97	74	88	61	48	..	86	95
Ethiopia	204	151	123	122	92	77	38	52	63
Gabon	92	91	91	60	60	60	76	55	55
Gambia, The	153	132	113	103	94	84	86	85	95
Ghana	120	113	120	76	72	76	61	84	85
Guinea	235	184	161	139	111	98	35	42	67
Guinea-Bissau	240	218	200	142	129	119	53	59	60
Kenya	97	117	121	64	77	79	78	75	77
Lesotho	101	108	132	81	86	102	80	74	85
Liberia	235	235	235	157	157	157	..	52	94
Madagascar	168	137	115	103	84	72	47	56	59
Malawi	221	155	120	131	95	76	81	73	85
Mali	250	224	217	140	124	119	43	49	86
Mauritania	133	125	125	85	79	78	38	62	62
Mauritius	23	18	14	20	16	13	76	84	99
Mozambique	235	178	138	158	122	96	59	71	77
Namibia	86	69	61	60	50	45	57	69	63
Niger	320	270	253	191	159	148	25	34	47
Nigeria	230	207	191	120	107	99	54	35	62
Rwanda	176	183	160	106	110	98	83	74	95
São Tomé and Principe	100	97	96	65	64	63	71	69	85
Senegal	149	133	116	72	66	60	51	48	80
Seychelles	19	15	13	17	13	12	86	97	99
Sierra Leone	290	277	270	169	162	159	..	37	67
Somalia	203	165	145	121	100	90	30	38	35
South Africa	60	63	69	45	50	56	79	77	85
Sudan	120	97	89	74	65	61	57	58	73
Swaziland	110	142	164	78	98	112	85	72	57
Tanzania	161	141	118	102	88	74	80	78	93
Togo	149	124	108	88	78	69	73	58	83
Uganda	160	145	134	93	85	78	52	61	89
Zambia	180	182	182	101	102	102	90	85	84
Zimbabwe	76	105	105	52	68	68	87	70	90
NORTH AFRICA									
Algeria	69	44	38	54	37	33	83	80	91
Egypt, Arab Rep.	91	51	35	67	40	29	86	98	98
Libya	41	22	18	35	20	17	89	92	98
Morocco	89	54	37	69	45	34	79	93	95
Tunisia	52	31	23	41	25	19	93	95	98

Millennium Development Goal 5: improve maternal health

Table 3.5

	Maternal mortality ratio, modeled estimate (per 100,000 live births)	Maternal mortality ratio (national estimate, per 100,000 live births)	Births attended by skilled health staff (% of total)			
			Surveys 1990–99		Surveys 2000–06	
	2005	2000–06[a]	Year[a]	Percent	Year[a]	Percent
SUB-SAHARAN AFRICA						
Angola	1,400	..	1996	23	2001	45
Benin	840	..	1996	60	2006	79
Botswana	380	..	1996	87	2000	94
Burkina Faso	700	..	1999	31	2005	54
Burundi	1,100	615	..	..	2005	34
Cameroon	1,000	669	1998	55	2006	63
Cape Verde	210	76	1998	89	..	..
Central African Republic	980	543	1995	46	2006	53
Chad	1,500	1,099	1997	15	2004	14
Comoros	400	380	1996	52	2000	62
Congo, Dem. Rep.	1,100	1,289	..	..	2001	61
Congo, Rep.	740	781	..	..	2005	86
Côte d'Ivoire	810	543	1999	47	2006	57
Djibouti	650	..	..	..	2006	93
Equatorial Guinea	680	..	1994	5	2000	65
Eritrea	450	..	1995	21	2002	28
Ethiopia	720	673	..	..	2005	6
Gabon	520	519	..	..	2000	86
Gambia, The	690	730	1990	44	2006	57
Ghana	560	..	1998	44	2006	50
Guinea	910	980	1999	35	2005	38
Guinea-Bissau	1,100	405	1995	25	2006	39
Kenya	560	414	1998	44	2003	42
Lesotho	960	762	1993	50	2004	55
Liberia	1,200	..	..	..	2000	51
Madagascar	510	469	1997	47	2004	51
Malawi	1,100	984	1992	55	2006	54
Mali	970	582	1996	40	2001	41
Mauritania	820	747	1991	40	2001	57
Mauritius	15	22	1999	99	2005	99
Mozambique	520	408	1997	44	2003	48
Namibia	210	271	1992	68	2000	76
Niger	1,800	648	1998	18	2006	18
Nigeria	1,100	..	1999	42	2003	36
Rwanda	1,300	750	1992	26	2005	39
São Tomé and Principe	..	148	..	..	2006	81
Senegal	980	434	1999	48	2005	52
Seychelles	..	57	..	..	..	..
Sierra Leone	2,100	1,800	..	..	2005	43
Somalia	1,400	1,044	1999	32	2006	33
South Africa	400	..	1998	84	2003	92
Sudan	450	..	1999	57	2006	49
Swaziland	390	..	1994	56	2002	74
Tanzania	950	578	1999	44	2005	43
Togo	510	..	1998	51	2006	62
Uganda	550	505	1995	38	2006	42
Zambia	830	729	1999	47	2002	43
Zimbabwe	880	555	1999	73	2006	80
NORTH AFRICA						
Algeria	180	..	1992	77	2006	95
Egypt, Arab Rep.	130	84	1998	55	2005	74
Libya	97	..	1999	99	..	..
Morocco	240	227	1995	40	2004	63
Tunisia	100	..	1995	81	2000	90

a. Data are for most recent year available during the period specified.

Table 3.6

Millennium Development Goal 6: combat HIV/AIDS, malaria, and other diseases

	Prevalence of HIV (% of ages 15–49)	Contraceptive prevalence (% of women ages 15–49)				Deaths due to malaria (per 100,000 people)	
		Surveys 1990–99		Surveys 2000–06		Surveys 2000–06	
	2007	Year[a]	Percent	Year[a]	Percent	Year[a]	Number
SUB-SAHARAN AFRICA							
Angola	2.1	1996	8.1	2001	6.2	2000	354
Benin	1.2	1996	16.4	2006	17.2	2000	177
Botswana	23.9	..	..	2000	44.4	2000	15
Burkina Faso	1.6	1999	11.9	2006	17.4	2000	292
Burundi	2.0	..	..	2005	9.1	2000	143
Cameroon	5.1	1998	19.3	2006	29.2	2000	108
Cape Verde	..	1998	52.9	..	..	2000	22
Central African Republic	6.3	1995	14.8	2006	19.0	2000	137
Chad	3.5	1997	4.2	2004	2.8	2000	207
Comoros	<0.1	1996	21.0	2000	25.7	2000	80
Congo, Dem. Rep.	..	1991	7.7	2001	31.4	2000	224
Congo, Rep.	3.5	..	..	2005	44.3	2000	78
Côte d'Ivoire	3.9	1999	15.0	2006	12.9	2000	76
Djibouti	3.1	..	..	2006	17.8	..	..
Equatorial Guinea	3.4	..	..	..	..	2000	152
Eritrea	1.3	1995	8.0	2002	8.0	2000	74
Ethiopia	2.1	1990	4.3	2005	14.7	2000	198
Gabon	5.9	..	..	2000	32.7	2000	80
Gambia, The	0.9	1990	11.8	2001	17.5	2000	52
Ghana	1.9	1999	22.0	2006	16.7	2000	70
Guinea	1.6	1999	6.2	2005	9.1	2000	200
Guinea-Bissau	1.8	..	..	2006	10.3	2000	150
Kenya	..	1998	39.0	2003	39.3	2000	63
Lesotho	23.2	1992	23.2	2004	37.3	2000	84
Liberia	1.7	..	..	2000	10.0	2000	201
Madagascar	0.1	1997	19.3	2004	27.1	2000	184
Malawi	11.9	1996	21.9	2006	41.7	2000	275
Mali	1.5	1996	6.7	2001	8.1	2000	454
Mauritania	0.8	1991	3.3	2001	8.0	2000	108
Mauritius	1.7	1999	26.0	2002	75.9	..	..
Mozambique	12.5	1997	5.6	2004	16.5	2000	232
Namibia	15.3	1992	28.9	2000	43.7	2000	52
Niger	0.8	1998	8.2	2006	11.2	2000	469
Nigeria	3.1	1999	15.3	2003	12.6	2000	141
Rwanda	2.8	1996	13.7	2005	17.4	2000	200
São Tomé and Principe	..	..	..	2006	30.3	2000	80
Senegal	1.0	1999	10.5	2005	11.8	2000	72
Seychelles	..	..	..	..	..	..	..
Sierra Leone	1.7	..	..	2005	5.3	2000	312
Somalia	0.5	1999	7.9	2006	14.6	2000	81
South Africa	18.1	1998	56.3	2003	60.3	2000	..
Sudan	1.4	1993	9.9	2006	7.6	2000	70
Swaziland	26.1	..	..	2002	48.1	2000	..
Tanzania	6.2	1999	25.4	2005	26.4	2000	130
Togo	3.3	1999	23.5	2006	16.8	2000	47
Uganda	5.4	1995	14.8	2006	23.7	2000	152
Zambia	15.2	1999	22.0	2002	34.2	2000	141
Zimbabwe	15.3	1999	53.5	2006	60.2	2000	1
NORTH AFRICA							
Algeria	0.1	1995	52.0	2006	61.4	..	..
Egypt, Arab Rep.	..	1998	51.7	2005	59.2	..	..
Libya	..	1995	45.2	..	..	..	..
Morocco	0.1	1997	58.8	2004	63.0	..	..
Tunisia	0.1	1995	60.0	2001	62.6	..	..

a. Data are for most recent year available during the period specified.

Children sleeping under insecticide–treated bednets (% of children under age 5) Surveys 2000–06		Incidence of tuberculosis (per 100,000 people) Surveys 1990–99		Surveys 2000–06		Tuberculosis cases detected under DOTS (% of estimated cases) Surveys 1990–99		Surveys 2000–06	
Year[a]	Percent	Year[a]	Number	Year[a]	Number	Year[a]	Percent	Year[a]	Percent
2001	2.3	1999	245.8	2006	285.3	1999	49.7	2006	75.8
2006	20.1	1999	83.8	2006	89.9	1999	85.5	2006	85.9
..	..	1999	573.1	2006	550.5	1999	70.8	2006	80.2
2006	9.6	1999	177.6	2006	248.5	1999	16.0	2006	17.2
2005	8.3	1999	293.7	2006	366.9	1999	34.8	2006	23.5
2006	13.1	1999	153.4	2006	191.6	1999	19.4	2006	91.2
..	..	1999	165.5	2006	168.4	..	..	2006	33.3
2006	15.1	1999	276.1	2006	345.0	1996	58.4	2006	68.6
2000	0.6	1999	239.0	2006	298.6	1999	33.9	2005	18.6
2000	9.3	1999	58.7	2006	43.8	1998	54.4	2006	41.6
2001	0.7	1999	313.4	2006	391.6	1999	51.0	2006	60.6
..	..	1999	322.6	2006	403.0	1998	51.7	2006	51.2
2006	5.9	1999	336.5	2006	420.4	1999	41.4	2006	37.1
2006	1.3	1999	697.0	2006	809.0	1999	71.6	2006	39.6
2000	0.7	1999	204.8	2006	255.8	1998	82.8	2004	74.4
2002	4.2	1999	83.6	2006	93.8	1999	39.8	2006	34.7
2005	1.5	1999	302.6	2006	378.1	1999	23.9	2006	27.0
..	..	1999	210.1	2006	353.6	..	..	2006	57.5
2006	49.0	1999	221.7	2006	257.3	1998	72.2	2006	63.9
2006	21.8	1999	211.8	2006	202.9	1999	30.3	2006	37.6
2005	0.3	1999	188.7	2006	264.9	1999	52.5	2006	54.6
2006	39.0	1999	188.6	2006	218.9	..	..	2006	64.3
2003	4.6	1999	396.5	2006	384.5	1999	58.2	2006	70.0
..	..	1999	519.1	2006	635.1	1998	72.8	2006	79.1
2005	2.6	1999	265.2	2006	331.3	1998	40.2	2006	55.1
2004	0.2	1999	213.4	2006	247.8	1998	67.2	2006	73.2
2006	23.0	1999	417.3	2006	377.1	1999	45.5	2006	42.0
2003	8.4	1999	289.4	2006	279.6	1999	18.9	2006	25.5
2004	2.1	1999	272.5	2006	316.3	..	..	2006	34.5
..	..	1999	24.2	2006	22.7	1999	95.5	2006	67.1
..	..	1999	354.3	2006	442.7	1999	47.6	2006	46.9
2000	3.4	1999	613.6	2006	766.6	1999	79.5	2006	82.9
2006	7.4	1999	149.6	2006	173.6	1999	36.6	2006	49.5
2003	1.2	1999	248.6	2006	310.6	1999	11.9	2006	20.2
2000	5.0	1999	317.7	2006	396.9	1999	44.5	2006	27.4
2006	41.7	1999	115.9	2006	102.8	..	..	..	..
2005	7.1	1999	232.9	2006	270.4	1999	47.6	2005	48.2
..	..	1999	37.1	2006	32.9	1998	67.1	2005	62.1
2005	5.3	1999	351.6	2006	517.0	1998	35.5	2006	35.0
2006	9.2	1999	262.0	2006	218.4	1999	42.9	2006	83.0
..	..	1999	478.8	2006	940.2	1999	61.3	2006	71.2
2006	27.6	1999	208.7	2006	242.2	1999	26.9	2006	30.0
2000	0.1	1999	690.5	2006	1155.3	..	..	2006	48.9
2005	16.0	1999	326.5	2006	312.1	1999	52.0	2006	46.4
2006	38.4	1999	360.5	2006	388.8	1999	10.9	2006	19.4
2006	9.7	1999	324.1	2006	354.7	1999	55.7	2006	44.3
2006	22.8	1999	603.3	2006	552.6	..	..	2006	52.5
2006	2.9	1999	613.1	2006	557.3	1999	47.5	2006	42.4
..	..	1999	46.8	2006	56.1	1997	132.5	2006	101.6
..	..	1999	31.7	2006	24.0	1999	31.7	2006	59.3
..	..	1999	23.2	2006	17.5	1999	146.8	2006	156.3
..	..	1999	114.4	2006	93.3	1999	91.6	2006	94.9
..	..	1999	26.8	2006	24.7	1999	93.5	2006	81.4

Table 3.7

Millennium Development Goal 7: ensure environmental sustainability

	Forest area (% of total land area)			Nationally protected areas (% of total land area)	GDP per unit of energy use (constant 2000 PPP $ per kg of oil equivalent)		
	1990	2000	2005	2004	1990	2000	2005
SUB-SAHARAN AFRICA							
Angola	48.9	47.9	47.4	10.1	5.4	4.6	6.1
Benin	30.0	24.2	21.3	23.9	3.2	4.2	4.0
Botswana	24.2	22.1	21.1	30.9	7.3	9.2	11.7
Burkina Faso	26.1	25.3	24.8	15.4	..	..	..
Burundi	11.3	7.7	5.9	5.7	..	..	..
Cameroon	52.7	48.0	45.6	8.0	5.0	4.6	5.0
Cape Verde	14.3	20.4	20.7	0.2	..	..	..
Central African Republic	37.2	36.8	36.5	16.6	..	..	..
Chad	10.4	9.8	9.5	9.5	..	..	..
Comoros	6.4	4.3	3.0	21.7	..	..	..
Congo, Dem. Rep.	62.0	59.6	58.9	8.6	1.9	0.9	0.9
Congo, Rep.	66.5	66.1	65.8	18.0	8.0	11.4	10.0
Côte d'Ivoire	32.1	32.5	32.7	17.1	5.4	4.4	3.8
Djibouti	0.2	0.2	0.2	0.4	..	..	..
Equatorial Guinea	66.3	60.9	58.2	16.2	..	..	..
Eritrea	..	15.6	15.4	5.0	..	..	..
Ethiopia	15.2	13.7	13.0	18.6	1.7	1.8	2.2
Gabon	85.1	84.7	84.5	3.4	11.2	10.6	10.4
Gambia, The	44.2	46.1	47.1	3.5	..	..	..
Ghana	32.7	26.8	24.2	16.2	2.5	2.6	2.9
Guinea	30.1	28.1	27.4	6.4	..	..	..
Guinea-Bissau	78.8	75.4	73.7	..	..	..	..
Kenya	6.5	6.3	6.2	12.6	2.7	2.7	2.8
Lesotho	0.2	0.2	0.3	0.2	..	..	..
Liberia	42.1	35.9	32.7	15.8	..	..	..
Madagascar	23.5	22.4	22.1	3.1	..	..	..
Malawi	41.4	37.9	36.2	20.6	..	..	..
Mali	11.5	10.7	10.3	3.8	..	..	..
Mauritania	0.4	0.3	0.3	0.2	..	..	..
Mauritius	19.2	18.7	18.2	3.3	..	..	..
Mozambique	25.4	24.8	24.5	5.8	0.8	1.1	1.4
Namibia	10.6	9.8	9.3	5.6	..	7.1	6.7
Niger	1.5	1.0	1.0	7.7	..	..	..
Nigeria	18.9	14.4	12.2	6.0	1.9	2.0	2.4
Rwanda	12.9	13.9	19.5	7.9	..	..	..
São Tomé and Principe	28.5	28.5	28.5	..	..	..	..
Senegal	48.6	46.2	45.0	11.2	4.8	5.5	6.0
Seychelles	87.0	87.0	87.0	8.3	..	..	..
Sierra Leone	42.5	39.8	38.5	4.5	..	..	..
Somalia	13.2	12.0	11.4	0.3	..	..	..
South Africa	7.6	7.6	7.6	6.1	3.0	3.0	3.1
Sudan	32.1	29.7	28.4	5.2	2.5	3.4	3.4
Swaziland	27.4	30.1	31.5	3.5	..	..	..
Tanzania	46.8	42.1	39.8	42.3	2.2	2.2	2.0
Togo	12.6	8.9	7.1	11.9	2.4	2.4	2.4
Uganda	25.0	20.6	18.4	32.6	..	..	..
Zambia	66.1	60.1	57.1	42.0	1.8	1.7	1.9
Zimbabwe	57.5	49.4	45.3	14.9	..	..	..
NORTH AFRICA							
Algeria	0.8	0.9	1.0	5.0	6.8	6.5	7.0
Egypt, Arab Rep.	0.0	0.1	0.1	5.6	5.7	6.1	5.4
Libya	0.1	0.1	0.1	0.1	..	3.8	4.0
Morocco	9.6	9.7	9.8	1.1	9.9	8.5	7.8
Tunisia	4.1	6.2	6.8	1.5	5.9	6.9	7.6

a. Data are for most recent year available during the period specified.

Carbon dioxide emissions (metric tons per capita)			Solid fuels use (% of population)	Population with sustainable access to improved water source (%)			Population with sustainable access to improved sanitation (%)		
1990	2000	2004	2000–06[a]	1990	2000	2006	1990	2000	2006
0.4	0.5	0.5	..	39.0	44.0	51.0	26.0	40.0	50.0
0.1	0.2	0.3	95.6	63.0	64.0	65.0	12.0	24.0	30.0
1.6	2.5	2.4	..	93.0	95.0	96.0	38.0	45.0	47.0
0.1	0.1	0.1	97.5	34.0	56.0	72.0	5.0	9.0	13.0
0.0	0.0	0.0	..	70.0	71.0	71.0	44.0	42.0	41.0
0.1	0.2	0.2	82.6	49.0	63.0	70.0	39.0	47.0	51.0
0.2	0.4	0.6	..	..	80.0	..	..	41.0	..
0.1	0.1	0.1	..	58.0	63.0	66.0	11.0	22.0	31.0
0.0	0.0	0.0	..	..	34.0	48.0	5.0	7.0	9.0
0.2	0.2	0.1	..	93.0	88.0	85.0	18.0	29.0	35.0
0.1	0.0	0.0	..	43.0	45.0	46.0	15.0	25.0	31.0
0.5	0.7	1.0	83.2	..	70.0	71.0	..	20.0	20.0
0.4	0.3	0.3	..	67.0	75.0	81.0	20.0	22.0	24.0
0.6	0.5	0.5	..	76.0	83.0	92.0	..	65.0	67.0
0.3	0.6	11.5	..	43.0	43.0	43.0	51.0	51.0	51.0
..	0.2	0.2	..	43.0	54.0	60.0	3.0	4.0	5.0
0.1	0.1	0.1	89.0	13.0	29.0	42.0	4.0	7.0	11.0
6.5	1.2	1.1	34.1	..	85.0	87.0	..	36.0	36.0
0.2	0.2	0.2	..	..	86.0	86.0	..	49.0	52.0
0.2	0.3	0.3	91.8	56.0	72.0	80.0	6.0	9.0	10.0
0.2	0.2	0.2	79.8	45.0	61.0	70.0	13.0	16.0	19.0
0.2	0.2	0.2	..	..	58.0	57.0	..	30.0	33.0
0.2	0.3	0.3	87.1	41.0	51.0	57.0	39.0	41.0	42.0
..	..	..	62.1	..	77.0	78.0	..	34.0	36.0
0.2	0.1	0.1	..	57.0	63.0	64.0	40.0	32.0	32.0
0.1	0.1	0.2	98.3	39.0	45.0	47.0	8.0	11.0	12.0
0.1	0.1	0.1	97.8	41.0	63.0	76.0	46.0	55.0	60.0
0.1	0.1	0.1	95.9	33.0	51.0	60.0	35.0	42.0	45.0
1.4	1.0	0.9	70.5	37.0	50.0	60.0	20.0	22.0	24.0
1.4	2.3	2.6	..	100.0	100.0	100.0	94.0	94.0	94.0
0.1	0.1	0.1	96.9	..	41.0	42.0	..	27.0	31.0
0.0	0.9	1.2	65.9	57.0	81.0	93.0	26.0	32.0	35.0
0.1	0.1	0.1	..	41.0	41.0	42.0	3.0	5.0	7.0
0.5	0.7	0.8	76.6	50.0	49.0	47.0	26.0	28.0	30.0
0.1	0.1	0.1	99.4	65.0	65.0	65.0	29.0	25.0	23.0
0.6	0.6	0.6	..	..	82.0	86.0	..	22.0	24.0
0.4	0.4	0.4	58.7	67.0	72.0	77.0	26.0	27.0	28.0
1.6	7.0	6.6	..	..	87.0	..	..	..	..
0.1	0.1	0.2	..	..	57.0	53.0	..	12.0	11.0
0.0	..	..	..	..	23.0	29.0	..	21.0	23.0
9.4	9.0	9.4	..	81.0	89.0	93.0	55.0	57.0	59.0
0.2	0.2	0.3	..	64.0	69.0	70.0	33.0	34.0	35.0
0.6	1.0	0.9	..	..	59.0	60.0	..	50.0	50.0
0.1	0.1	0.1	98.1	49.0	53.0	55.0	35.0	34.0	33.0
0.2	0.3	0.4	..	49.0	55.0	59.0	13.0	12.0	12.0
0.0	0.1	0.1	97.4	43.0	56.0	64.0	29.0	32.0	33.0
0.3	0.2	0.2	83.6	50.0	54.0	58.0	42.0	49.0	52.0
1.6	1.2	0.8	..	78.0	80.0	81.0	44.0	45.0	46.0
3.0	6.4	6.0	..	94.0	89.0	85.0	88.0	92.0	94.0
1.4	2.1	2.2	..	94.0	97.0	98.0	50.0	61.0	66.0
8.7	10.3	10.3	..	71.0	71.0	..	97.0	97.0	97.0
1.0	1.2	1.4	..	75.0	80.0	83.0	52.0	65.0	72.0
1.6	2.1	2.3	..	82.0	90.0	94.0	74.0	81.0	85.0

Table 3.8

Millennium Development Goal 8: develop a global partnership for development

	Debt sustainability					
	Heavily indebted Poor Country (HIPC) Debt Initiative		Debt service relief committed ($ millions)	Public and publicly guaranteed debt service (% of exports)		
	Decision point 2006	Completion point 2006	2006	1990	2000	2004–06[a]
SUB-SAHARAN AFRICA						
Angola	..	..	..	7.1	20.4	12.6
Benin	Jul. 2000	Mar. 2003	460	8.6	10.9	7.5
Botswana	..	..	..	4.3	2.0	0.9
Burkina Faso	Jul. 2000	Apr. 2002	930	7.7	15.1	10.1
Burundi	Oct. 2000	..	1,472	40.7	25.1	40.0
Cameroon	Oct. 2000	Apr. 2006	4,917	12.4	13.9	12.7
Cape Verde	Sep. 2008	..	..	8.9	10.5	5.5
Central African Republic	..	..	..	7.5	..	..
Chad	May 2001	..	260	2.4	..	..
Comoros	..	..	..	2.5	..	..
Congo, Dem. Rep.	Jul. 2003	Floating	10,389	..	..	..
Congo, Rep.	Mar. 2006	Floating	2,881	31.6	0.5	2.0
Côte d'Ivoire	Mar. 1998	..	..	14.7	14.9	0.2
Djibouti	..	..	..	..	4.8	5.9
Equatorial Guinea	..	..	..	2.5	..	..
Eritrea	..	..	..	..	2.8	2.8
Ethiopia	Nov. 2001	Apr. 2004	3,275	33.1	12.2	7.1
Gabon	..	..	..	3.8	8.8	4.6
Gambia, The	Dec. 2000	Dec. 2008	90	17.9	..	13.7
Ghana	Feb. 2002	Jul. 2004	3,500	19.9	12.0	4.5
Guinea	Dec. 2000	Floating	800	17.7	17.3	18.1
Guinea-Bissau	Dec. 2000	Floating	790	22.0	..	46.4
Kenya	..	..	..	22.7	15.7	6.5
Lesotho	..	..	..	4.1	10.3	4.0
Liberia	..	..	..	..	..	0.0
Madagascar	Dec. 2000	Oct. 2004	1,900	31.9	8.4	4.9
Malawi	Dec. 2000	Aug.2006	1,000	22.4	10.8	5.8
Mali	Sep. 2000	Mar.2003	895	9.7	10.2	4.2
Mauritania	Feb. 2000	Jun. 2002	1,100	24.8	..	..
Mauritius	..	..	..	4.5	16.3	5.4
Mozambique	Apr. 2000	Sep. 2001	4,300	17.2	7.0	1.8
Namibia	..	..	..	..	..	..
Niger	Dec. 2000	Apr. 2004	1,190	3.2	6.0	4.0
Nigeria	..	..	..	22.3	8.2	16.7
Rwanda	Dec. 2000	Apr. 2005	1,316	9.4	14.8	10.0
São Tomé and Principe	Dec. 2000	Mar. 2008	200	28.6	21.0	39.2
Senegal	Jun. 2000	Apr. 2004	850	13.7	13.2	12.0
Seychelles	..	..	..	7.6	3.3	18.2
Sierra Leone	Mar. 2002	Dec. 2006	950	7.8	29.6	8.4
Somalia	..	..	..	..	..	..
South Africa	..	..	..	..	5.5	3.2
Sudan	..	..	..	4.5	10.1	4.5
Swaziland	..	..	..	5.6	2.3	1.7
Tanzania	Apr. 2000	Nov. 2001	3,000	25.1	10.8	3.0
Togo	..	..	..	8.6	3.2	0.5
Uganda	Feb. 2000	May. 2000	1,950	47.1	6.5	6.4
Zambia	Dec. 2000	Apr. 2005	3,900	12.6	17.4	2.1
Zimbabwe	..	..	..	18.2	..	..
NORTH AFRICA						
Algeria	..	..	..	63.3	..	..
Egypt, Arab Rep.	..	..	..	23.2	8.5	5.3
Libya	..	..	..	..	..	..
Morocco	..	..	..	23.1	23.0	9.0
Tunisia	..	..	..	23.9	20.5	14.6

a. Data are for most recent year available during the period specified.

| Youth unemployment rate (ages 15–24) | | | | | | Information and communications | | | | | | | | |
| Total Share of total labor force | | Male Share of male labor force | | Female Share of female labor force | | Fixed line and mobile phone subscribers (per 100 people) | | | Personal computers (per 100 people) | | | Internet users (per 100 people) | | |
Year	Percent	Year	Percent	Year	Percent	1990	2000	2006	1990	2000	2005–06	1995	2000	2006
..	..	..	..	..	..	0.7	0.7	14.3	..	0.1	0.7	..	0.1	0.6
..	..	..	..	..	..	0.3	1.5	12.9	..	0.1	0.6	..	0.2	1.4
2001	39.6	2001	33.9	2001	46.1	1.9	20.7	51.4	..	3.5	4.8	0.1	2.9	4.3
..	..	..	..	..	..	0.2	0.7	7.7	0.0	0.1	0.6	..	0.1	0.6
..	..	..	..	..	..	0.1	0.5	2.9	..	0.1	0.8	..	0.1	0.7
..	..	..	..	..	..	0.3	1.3	18.0	..	0.3	1.1	..	0.3	2.0
..	..	..	..	..	..	2.3	16.5	34.8	..	5.5	12.0	..	1.8	6.4
..	..	..	..	..	..	0.2	0.4	2.9	..	0.2	0.3	..	0.1	0.3
..	..	..	..	..	..	0.1	0.2	4.6	..	0.1	0.2	..	0.0	0.6
..	..	..	..	..	..	0.8	1.3	9.1	0.0	0.6	0.9	..	0.3	3.4
..	..	..	..	..	..	0.1	0.0	7.3	..	..	0.0	..	0.0	0.3
..	..	..	..	..	..	0.7	2.9	..	..	0.3	0.5	..	0.0	1.9
..	..	..	..	..	..	0.6	4.3	22.9	..	0.5	1.7	0.0	0.2	1.6
..	..	..	..	..	..	1.0	1.4	..	0.2	0.9	2.4	0.0	0.2	1.3
..	..	..	..	..	..	0.4	2.6	..	..	0.5	1.9	..	0.2	1.6
..	..	..	..	..	..	..	0.8	2.1	..	0.2	0.6	..	0.1	2.1
2005	7.7	2005	4.1	2005	11.2	0.3	0.4	2.1	..	0.1	0.6	0.0	0.0	0.3
..	..	..	..	..	..	2.3	13.4	71.3	..	1.0	3.6	..	1.3	6.2
..	..	..	..	..	..	0.6	2.8	27.1	..	1.1	1.9	0.0	0.9	4.9
..	..	..	..	..	..	0.3	1.7	24.2	0.0	0.3	0.6	0.0	0.1	2.7
..	..	..	..	..	..	0.2	0.8	..	..	0.4	0.5	0.0	0.1	0.5
..	..	..	..	..	..	0.6	0.8	10.0	..	..	0.2	..	0.2	2.2
..	..	..	..	..	..	0.7	1.3	20.9	0.0	0.5	1.4	0.0	0.3	7.6
..	..	..	..	..	..	0.8	2.3	20.6	..	..	0.3	..	0.2	3.0
..	..	..	..	..	..	0.4	0.3	..	..	..	..	..	0.0	0.0
2003	7	2003	6.7	2003	7.3	0.3	0.7	6.1	..	0.2	0.5	..	0.2	0.6
..	..	..	..	..	..	0.3	0.8	6.1	..	0.1	0.2	..	0.1	0.4
..	..	..	..	..	..	0.1	0.5	13.3	..	0.1	0.4	..	0.1	0.7
..	..	..	..	..	..	0.3	1.3	36.0	..	1.0	4.6	..	0.2	1.0
2005	25.9	2005	20.5	2005	34.3	5.5	38.8	90.1	0.4	10.1	17.6	..	7.3	25.5
..	..	..	..	..	..	0.4	0.8	11.5	..	0.3	1.4	..	0.1	0.9
2001	44.8	2001	40.4	2001	49.3	3.7	10.2	36.4	..	4.0	19.5	0.0	1.6	4.4
..	..	..	..	..	..	0.1	0.2	..	..	0.0	0.1	..	0.0	0.3
..	..	..	..	..	..	0.3	0.5	23.5	..	0.6	0.8	..	0.1	5.5
..	..	..	..	..	..	0.1	0.7	3.5	..	..	0.3	..	0.1	1.1
..	..	..	..	..	..	1.9	3.3	16.8	..	..	3.9	..	4.6	14.2
..	..	..	..	..	..	0.6	4.4	27.0	0.2	1.5	2.1	0.0	0.4	5.4
..	..	..	..	..	..	12.4	57.4	107.6	..	13.6	20.1	..	7.4	34.3
..	..	..	..	..	..	0.3	0.7	..	..	..	..	..	0.1	0.2
..	..	..	..	..	..	0.2	1.5	7.7	..	..	0.9	..	0.2	1.1
2003	60.1	2003	55.8	2003	64.7	9.4	30.2	93.6	0.7	6.6	8.5	0.7	5.5	7.8
..	..	..	..	..	..	0.2	1.2	13.4	..	0.3	11.2	..	0.0	8.5
..	..	..	..	..	..	1.8	6.2	25.8	..	1.1	3.7	0.0	1.0	3.7
..	..	..	..	..	..	0.3	0.8	15.0	..	0.3	0.9	..	0.1	1.0
..	..	..	..	..	..	0.3	1.7	12.3	..	1.9	3.0	..	1.9	5.0
..	..	..	..	..	..	0.2	0.8	7.1	..	0.2	1.7	0.0	0.2	5.0
..	..	..	..	..	..	0.8	1.7	15.0	..	0.7	1.1	0.0	0.2	4.3
2002	24.9	2002	28.2	2002	21.4	1.2	4.1	9.0	0.0	1.5	6.5	0.0	0.4	9.2
2004	43.4	2004	42.8	2004	46.3	3.2	6.1	71.5	0.1	0.7	1.1	0.0	0.5	7.4
2002	27.1	2002	21.4	2002	40.0	2.9	10.3	38.8	..	1.2	4.3	0.0	0.7	8.1
..	..	..	..	..	..	5.0	12.1	..	..	..	2.2	..	0.2	4.3
2006	16.6	2006	17.5	2006	14.1	1.7	13.2	56.6	..	1.2	3.0	0.0	0.7	20.0
2005	30.7	2005	31.4	2005	29.3	3.7	11.2	85.0	0.3	2.2	6.3	0.0	2.7	12.8

Table 4.1 Status of Paris Declaration Indicators

| | PDI-1 | PDI-2 | | PDI-3 | PDI-4 | PDI-5 | |
	Country with operational national development strategies (rating) 2007	Reliable public financial management (rating) 2007	Reliable country procurement systems (rating) 2007	Government budget estimates comprehensive and realistic (%) 2007	Technical assistance aligned and co-ordinated with country programmes (%) 2007	Aid for government sectors uses country public financial management systems (%) 2007	Aid for government sectors uses of country procurement systems (%) 2007
SUB-SAHARAN AFRICA							
Angola	..	..	..	..	..	..	..
Benin	C	3.5	..	28.5	53.9	47.5	63.3
Botswana	..	..	..	..	..	..	..
Burkina Faso	B	4.0	..	92.2	56.4	43.2	53.8
Burundi	C	3.0	..	53.9	41.0	32.7	34.6
Cameroon	C	3.5	B	85.7	29.9	53.1	63.1
Cape Verde	C	4.0	..	90.2	39.3	22.5	22.1
Central African Republic	D	2.0	..	36.4	36.5	23.8	10.2
Chad	C	..	..	..	..	..	..
Comoros	..	..	..	..	..	..	..
Congo, Dem. Rep.	D	2.5	..	58.3	38.1	..	0.8
Congo, Rep.	..	..	..	..	..	..	..
Côte d'Ivoire	E	2.0	..	64.4	30.9	..	9.3
Djibouti	..	..	..	..	..	..	..
Equatorial Guinea	..	..	..	..	..	..	..
Eritrea	..	..	..	..	..	..	..
Ethiopia	B	4.0	..	61.7	66.8	46.7	41.4
Gabon	N/A	6.0	..	22.4	70.4	4.7	32.3
Gambia, The	..	..	..	..	..	..	..
Ghana	B	4.0	C	94.3	74.7	50.9	56.2
Guinea	..	..	..	..	..	..	..
Guinea-Bissau	..	..	..	..	..	..	..
Kenya	C	3.5	..	67.4	58.1	53.1	35.7
Lesotho	..	..	..	..	..	..	..
Liberia	D	6.0	..	..	35.3	32.0	..
Madagascar	C	3.5	..	87.0	70.9	21.5	25.9
Malawi	C	3.0	C	63.7	52.3	49.9	35.4
Mali	C	3.5	..	72.6	75.4	34.4	34.8
Mauritania	C	2.5	..	57.4	53.4	8.3	22.2
Mauritius	..	..	..	..	..	..	..
Mozambique	C	3.5	..	82.5	27.1	43.5	53.8
Namibia	..	..	..	..	..	..	..
Niger	C	3.5	B	90.7	50.2	25.5	36.5
Nigeria	C	3.0	..	6.3	70.6	..	..
Rwanda	B	4.0	B	51.0	83.6	42.0	42.9
São Tomé and Principe	..	..	..	..	..	..	..
Senegal	C	3.5	B	87.7	54.1	19.0	41.3
Seychelles	..	..	..	..	..	..	..
Sierra Leone	C	3.5	B	53.6	22.5	20.1	38.3
Somalia	..	..	..	..	..	..	..
South Africa	..	..	..	..	..	..	..
Sudan	D	2.0	..	84.6	53.2	3.1	0.4
Swaziland	..	..	..	..	..	..	..
Tanzania	B	4.0	B	83.6	60.5	71.5	68.5
Togo	N/A	2.0	..	68.9	28.9	4.4	15.5
Uganda	B	4.0	B	98.4	58.1	57.0	36.9
Zambia	B	3.5	C	73.5	34.5	59.4	71.0
Zimbabwe	..	..	..	..	..	..	..
NORTH AFRICA							
Algeria	..	..	..	..	..	..	..
Egypt, Arab Rep.	N/A	6.0	..	57.4	86.2	12.0	22.7
Libya	..	..	..	..	..	..	..
Morocco	N/A	6.0	..	80.0	82.0	79.0	81.0
Tunisia	..	..	..	..	..	..	..

Note: See technical notes for further details. PDI is a Paris Declaration Indicator.
PDI-1, PDI-11 and PDI-12. Ratings from A (the highest) to E (lowest)
PDI-2a. Rating rating scale ranges from 1 (low) to 6 (high).
PDI-2b. Ratings from A (the highest) to D (lowest)

PDI-6 Project implementation units parallel to country structures (number) 2007	PDI-7 Aid disbursements on schedule and recorded by government (%) 2007	PDI-8 Bilateral aid that is untied (%) 2007	PDI-9 Aid provided in the framework of programme-based approaches (%) 2007	PDI-10 Donor missions co-ordinated (%) 2007	PDI-10 Country-analysis co-ordinated (%) 2007	PDI-11 Existence of a monitorable performance assessment framework (rating) 2007	PDI-12 Existence of a mutual accountability review (rating) 2007
..	..	..	..	..	..	..	..
58	31.6	98.8	49.0	25.1	44.0	C	B
..	..	..	..	..	..	..	..
102	91.6	91.8	57.2	12.8	39.0	C	B
29	44.4	90.6	35.5	13.5	73.8	D	A
38	50.8	98.5	39.6	25.8	49.2	D	B
18	96.4	60.3	30.9	43.4	64.5	C	B
11	45.2	86.7	34.3	9.8	23.2	D	B
..	..	..	..	..	..	D	..
..	..	..	..	..	..	..	..
146	19.5	93.9	20.8	21.3	22.9	D	B
..	..	..	..	..	..	D	..
29	67.0	91.7	2.6	65.0	75.0	E	B
..	..	..	..	..	..	..	..
..	..	..	..	..	..	..	..
56	73.4	82.2	65.6	19.1	52.1	C	A
5	16.8	99.7	..	4.7	36.8	N/A	B
..	..	..	..	..	..	..	..
16	83.2	91.8	68.9	39.0	59.8	C	A
..	..	..	..	..	..	..	..
21	49.2	84.5	27.5	17.8	63.8	C	B
..	..	..	..	..	..	..	..
16	..	82.4	21.3	11.0	65.6	D	B
48	79.5	83.9	43.5	23.8	41.6	C	B
51	58.1	90.5	42.0	22.3	60.8	C	A
60	68.2	93.4	40.6	15.2	39.3	D	B
27	52.1	67.0	35.1	11.4	25.4	C	B
..	..	..	..	..	..	..	..
26	73.7	90.8	46.4	16.8	31.7	B	A
..	..	..	..	..	..	..	..
47	77.5	84.3	49.0	15.4	31.8	D	B
23	7.1	99.2	3.9	19.1	32.8	C	B
41	66.8	95.1	38.4	13.5	31.5	C	B
..	..	..	..	..	..	..	..
55	60.8	93.0	38.9	16.6	28.1	C	B
..	..	..	..	..	..	..	..
2	29.7	91.6	26.9	27.1	56.3	D	B
..	..	..	..	..	..	..	..
..	..	..	..	..	..	..	..
105	51.6	79.9	19.2	14.9	44.7	D	B
..	..	..	..	..	..	..	..
28	60.8	98.9	60.8	15.8	64.9	B	A
13	14.3	56.1	38.9	15.1	20.7	N/A	B
55	74.4	85.4	65.7	21.0	54.0	B	B
34	85.1	99.6	46.8	10.4	34.8	C	B
..	..	..	..	..	..	..	..
..	..	..	..	..	..	..	B
32	78.9	75.0	48.9	14.1	42.0	N/A	B
..	..	..	..	..	..	..	..
47	68.0	90.0	70.0	12.0	25.0	N/A	B
..	..	..	..	..	..	..	..

Table 5.1 Business environment

	Starting a business				Registering property			Enforcing contracts		
	Number of procedures to register a business 2008	Average time spent for each procedure (days) 2008	Cost (% of GNI per capita) 2008	Minimum capital (% of income per capita) 2008	Number of procedures 2008	Time (days) 2008	Cost (% of property value) 2008	Number of procedures 2008	Time required (days) 2008	Cost (% of debt) 2008
SUB-SAHARAN AFRICA	**11**	**56**	**160.3**	**196.1**	**7**	**103**	**11.3**	**39**	**673**	**48.6**
Angola	12	119	343.7	50.5	7	334	11.1	46	1,011	44.4
Benin	7	31	195.0	354.2	4	120	11.9	42	825	64.7
Botswana	11	108	9.9	-	4	11	5.0	29	987	28.1
Burkina Faso	6	18	82.1	415.7	8	182	12.2	37	446	107.4
Burundi	11	43	251.0	-	5	94	11.5	44	558	38.6
Cameroon	13	37	129.2	177.1	5	93	17.8	43	800	46.6
Cape Verde	12	52	40.1	53.4	6	83	7.8	37	425	21.8
Central African Republic	10	14	205.4	531.2	5	75	18.6	43	660	82.0
Chad	19	75	188.8	398.4	6	44	21.2	41	743	77.4
Comoros	11	23	188.4	280.3	5	24	20.8	43	506	89.4
Congo, Dem. Rep.	13	155	487.2	-	8	57	9.4	43	685	151.8
Congo, Rep.	10	37	150.1	206.3	7	137	27.3	44	560	53.2
Côte d'Ivoire	10	40	135.8	219.8	6	62	13.9	33	770	41.7
Djibouti	11	37	206.6	530.8	7	40	13.2	40	1,225	34.0
Equatorial Guinea	20	136	105.1	23.2	6	23	6.3	40	553	18.5
Eritrea	13	84	125.8	488.0	12	101	5.3	39	405	22.6
Ethiopia	7	16	41.3	960.0	13	43	7.5	39	690	15.2
Gabon	9	58	25.6	38.2	8	60	10.5	38	1,070	34.3
Gambia, The	9	32	279.0	-	5	371	4.6	32	434	37.9
Ghana	11	42	41.4	20.9	5	34	1.3	36	487	23.0
Guinea	13	41	138.3	466.5	6	104	13.9	50	276	45.0
Guinea-Bissau	17	233	255.5	1,006.6	9	211	5.4	41	1,140	25.0
Kenya	12	44	46.1	-	8	64	4.2	44	465	26.7
Lesotho	8	73	37.4	14.3	6	101	8.2	41	695	19.5
Liberia	12	99	493.3	-	13	50	14.9	41	1,280	35.0
Madagascar	5	7	22.7	333.4	8	134	11.6	38	871	42.4
Malawi	10	37	188.7	-	6	88	3.3	42	432	142.4
Mali	11	26	132.1	434.6	5	29	21.2	39	860	52.0
Mauritania	11	65	56.2	503.1	4	49	5.2	46	400	23.2
Mauritius	6	7	5.3	-	6	210	10.8	37	750	17.4
Mozambique	10	29	21.6	115.8	8	42	12.3	31	1,010	142.5
Namibia	10	99	22.3	-	9	23	9.9	33	270	29.9
Niger	11	23	174.8	735.6	4	35	11.1	39	545	59.6
Nigeria	9	34	56.6	-	14	82	22.2	39	457	32.0
Rwanda	9	16	171.5	-	5	371	9.4	24	310	78.7
São Tomé and Principe	10	144	94.5	-	7	62	12.6	43	1,185	34.8
Senegal	10	58	107.0	255.0	6	145	19.5	44	780	26.5
Seychelles	9	38	8.7	-	4	33	7.0	38	720	14.3
Sierra Leone	9	26	1,075.2	-	8	235	14.9	40	515	149.5
Somalia	..	..	..	..	..	..	..	..	..	..
South Africa	8	31	7.1	-	6	24	8.8	30	600	33.2
Sudan	10	39	57.9	-	6	9	3.2	53	810	19.8
Swaziland	13	61	38.7	0.6	11	46	7.1	40	972	23.1
Tanzania	12	29	47.1	-	9	73	4.4	38	462	14.3
Togo	13	53	245.7	546.4	5	295	13.9	41	588	47.5
Uganda	18	28	92.0	-	13	227	4.6	38	535	44.9
Zambia	6	33	30.5	2.2	6	70	9.6	35	471	38.7
Zimbabwe	10	96	676.2	54.6	4	30	25.0	38	410	32.0
NORTH AFRICA	**9.3**	**14**	**15.4**	**35.8**	**8**	**83**	**4.9**	**42**	**705**	**23.8**
Algeria	14	24	13.2	45.2	14	51	7.5	47	630	21.9
Egypt, Arab Rep.	7	9	28.6	12.9	7	193	1.0	42	1,010	26.2
Libya	..	..	..	..	..	..	..	..	..	..
Morocco	6	12	11.5	59.8	8	47	4.9	40	615	25.2
Tunisia	10	11	8.3	25.3	4	39	6.1	39	565	21.8

a. Indexes run from 0 (least desirable) to 10 (most desirable).
b. Average of the disclosure, director liability and shareholder suits indexes.
c. This index is the average of three subindexes: a difficulty of hiring index, a rigidity of hours index, and a difficulty of firing index.

Dealing with construction permits			Protecting investors[a]				Employing workers				
Number of procedures 2008	Time (days) 2008	Cost (% of income per capita) 2008	Disclosure index 2008	Director liability index 2008	Shareholder suits index 2008	Investor protection index[b] 2008	Rigidity of hours index 2008	Difficulty of hiring index 2008	Difficulty of firing index 2008	Firing costs (weeks of wages) 2008	Rigidity of employment index (0 least rigid to 100 most rigid)[c] 2008
18	261	2,676.6	5	3	5	4.2	43	41	41	68	42
14	337	1,109.7	5	6	6	5.7	60	78	70	58	69
15	332	316.6	6	1	3	3.3	40	39	40	36	40
24	167	322.3	8	2	3	4.3	20	0	40	90	20
32	226	701.2	6	1	4	3.7	40	83	30	34	51
20	384	9,939.0	4	1	5	3.3	60	0	30	26	30
15	426	1,202.9	6	1	6	4.3	40	28	70	33	46
18	120	718.3	1	5	6	4.0	40	33	60	91	44
21	239	288.3	6	1	5	4.0	60	72	50	22	61
9	181	1,063.8	6	1	5	4.0	60	39	40	36	46
18	164	77.8	6	1	5	4.0	60	39	40	100	46
14	322	2,112.6	3	3	4	3.3	80	72	70	31	74
14	169	565.9	6	1	3	3.3	60	78	70	33	69
21	628	247.7	6	1	3	3.3	60	33	20	49	38
14	195	1,010.6	5	2	0	2.3	40	67	30	56	46
18	201	239.9	6	1	4	3.7	60	67	70	133	66
..	..	..	4	5	5	4.7	40	0	20	69	20
12	128	1,094.4	4	4	5	4.3	40	33	30	40	34
16	210	49.8	6	1	3	3.3	60	17	80	43	52
17	146	363.7	2	1	5	2.7	40	0	40	9	27
18	220	1,498.3	7	5	6	6.0	40	22	50	178	37
32	255	237.7	6	1	1	2.7	60	33	40	26	44
15	167	2,607.0	6	1	5	4.0	60	67	70	87	66
10	100	58.8	3	2	10	5.0	0	33	30	47	21
15	601	805.3	2	1	8	3.7	40	22	0	44	21
25	398	65,845.6	4	1	6	3.7	20	33	40	84	31
16	268	880.0	5	6	6	5.7	60	89	40	30	63
21	213	1,978.0	4	7	5	5.3	0	56	20	84	25
14	208	1,320.7	6	1	3	3.3	40	33	40	31	38
25	201	565.5	5	3	3	3.7	40	56	40	31	45
18	107	43.3	6	8	9	7.7	20	0	50	35	23
17	361	705.0	5	4	9	6.0	60	83	20	143	54
12	139	188.3	5	5	6	5.3	40	0	20	24	20
17	265	2,822.5	6	1	3	3.3	60	100	50	35	70
18	350	1,016.0	5	7	5	5.7	0	0	20	50	7
16	227	822.1	2	5	1	2.7	40	56	30	26	42
13	255	825.9	3	1	6	3.3	80	50	60	91	63
16	220	570.8	6	1	2	3.0	60	72	50	38	61
19	144	46.5	4	8	5	5.7	20	33	50	39	34
49	235	581.4	3	6	8	5.7	60	44	50	189	51
..	..	..	..	..	..	..	..	..	..	..	..
17	174	30.4	8	8	8	8.0	40	56	30	24	42
19	271	296.0	0	6	4	3.3	20	39	50	118	36
13	93	94.0	0	1	5	2.0	20	11	20	53	17
21	308	2,365.5	3	4	8	5.0	40	89	50	18	60
15	277	1,366.3	6	1	4	3.7	60	61	40	36	54
16	143	811.8	2	5	5	4.0	0	0	10	13	3
17	254	1,518.0	3	6	7	5.3	60	33	20	178	38
19	952	11,799.0	8	1	4	4.3	40	0	60	446	33
22	186	447.4	5	4	4	4.2	40	43	58	63	47
22	240	57.8	6	6	4	5.3	60	44	40	17	48
28	249	474.9	7	3	5	5.0	20	0	60	132	27
..	..	..	..	..	..	..	..	..	..	..	..
19	163	334.7	6	2	1	3.0	40	100	50	85	63
20	93	922.1	0	4	6	3.3	40	28	80	17	49

Investment climate

	Private investment (% of GDP) 2006[a]	Net foreign direct investment ($ millions) 2006	Domestic credit to private sector (% of GDP) 2006	Viewed by firms as a major constraint (% of firms)									
				Corruption 2006–07[b]	Court system is fair, impartial and uncorrupted 2006–07[b]	Crime, theft and disorder 2006–07[b]	Tax rates 2006–07[b]	Finance 2006–07[b]	Electricity 2006–07[b]	Labor regulations 2006–07[b]	Labor skills 2006–07[b]	Trans-portation 2006–07[b]	Trade identifying customs & trade regulations 2006–07[b]
SUB-SAHARAN AFRICA	**12.5**		**65.1**										
Angola	2.4	−228.3	7.5	36.1	31.9	36.6	23.0	55.3	45.8	12.3	21.2	27.3	21.4
Benin	..	..	17.2	..	..	..	..	..	..	..	..	..	..
Botswana	9.6	536.1	18.8	22.6	69.6	24.1	24.6	41.4	6.8	9.0	19.5	13.4	10.9
Burkina Faso	..	..	17.9	54.0	39.1	18.0	75.2	79.9	48.9	12.2	13.0	55.8	31.7
Burundi	..	0.0	24.6	19.7	40.7	19.7	36.1	50.9	72.3	3.9	11.8	21.1	20.9
Cameroon	14.3	..	9.2	52.1	25.6	33.1	75.6	68.0	61.1	9.9	8.1	33.1	34.8
Cape Verde	29.4	122.6	48.4	16.3	61.8	27.6	50.0	38.8	65.3	15.3	16.3	18.6	24.5
Central African Republic	5.6	..	6.6	..	..	..	..	..	..	..	..	..	..
Chad	13.2	..	2.6	..	..	..	..	..	..	..	..	..	..
Comoros	4.9	..	7.9	..	..	..	..	..	..	..	..	..	..
Congo, Dem. Rep.	..	..	2.9	20.0	19.8	22.6	52.4	60.4	70.3	9.0	13.1	30.0	15.1
Congo, Rep.	13.8	..	2.1	..	..	..	..	..	..	..	..	..	..
Côte d'Ivoire	6.8	318.9	14.3	..	..	..	..	..	..	..	..	..	..
Djibouti	22.0	108.3	20.2	..	..	..	..	..	..	..	..	..	..
Equatorial Guinea	26.6	..	2.8	..	..	..	..	..	..	..	..	..	..
Eritrea	4.2	..	29.0	..	..	..	..	..	..	..	..	..	..
Ethiopia	7.6	545.3	23.8	23.1	24.2	11.6	40.0	44.2	21.5	4.0	23.0	11.8	17.0
Gabon	18.3	..	9.3	..	..	..	..	..	..	..	..	..	..
Gambia, The	14.9	82.1	15.6	9.8	62.8	12.3	30.7	40.3	78.1	3.5	11.7	11.1	12.8
Ghana	18.3	434.5	17.8	9.9	59.8	11.4	30.6	66.2	86.2	1.7	4.6	17.6	9.8
Guinea	10.2	..	..	47.7	25.7	30.4	39.4	58.3	83.6	2.5	11.7	51.5	12.4
Guinea-Bissau	6.4	..	3.9	44.0	12.1	29.6	44.0	71.6	74.1	3.5	12.3	24.8	25.6
Kenya	15.2	26.7	25.8	..	..	..	..	..	..	..	..	..	..
Lesotho	26.1	77.8	8.9	..	..	..	..	..	..	..	..	..	..
Liberia	..	..	8.6	..	..	..	..	..	..	..	..	..	..
Madagascar	14.5	..	10.2	..	..	..	..	..	..	..	..	..	..
Malawi	14.4	..	8.7	46.8	59.2	47.2	56.3	42.8	60.4	12.6	49.7	39.0	24.2
Mali	14.3	82.1	17.2	15.7	49.6	4.7	54.0	60.4	55.7	1.9	8.0	20.1	8.2
Mauritania	17.7	..	..	17.1	48.5	1.4	35.2	43.6	28.9	2.8	23.0	16.2	25.9
Mauritius	15.9	97.2	78.0	..	..	..	..	..	..	..	..	..	..
Mozambique	7.1	153.3	13.8	..	..	..	..	..	..	..	..	..	..
Namibia	20.0	342.4	61.7	19.1	66.1	27.6	20.4	18.4	6.5	6.8	19.6	7.9	7.1
Niger	..	..	8.5	58.5	35.7	6.4	69.4	55.7	21.6	6.4	18.4	40.0	31.2
Nigeria	..	..	13.2	..	..	..	..	..	..	..	..	..	..
Rwanda	12.8	25.6	..	4.4	67.1	4.1	44.7	36.0	55.0	2.8	11.7	27.4	13.5
São Tomé and Principe	..	34.4	33.1	..	..	..	..	..	..	..	..	..	..
Senegal	19.1	..	22.9	23.8	55.4	11.6	40.5	49.2	57.7	4.8	9.5	27.4	15.1
Seychelles	22.6	137.8	36.9	..	..	..	..	..	..	..	..	..	..
Sierra Leone	10.4	58.6	4.5	..	..	..	..	..	..	..	..	..	..
Somalia	..	..	..	..	..	..	..	..	..	..	..	..	..
South Africa	15.8	−6,719.3	160.8	..	..	..	..	..	..	..	..	..	..
Sudan	14.5	3,534.1	0.1	..	..	..	..	..	..	..	..	..	..
Swaziland	7.5	34.0	22.5	24.9	40.3	34.4	28.5	32.9	12.4	9.9	12.7	14.2	16.5
Tanzania	9.9	474.5	11.0	19.7	46.7	16.4	36.7	40.6	88.4	4.8	19.7	14.1	11.6
Togo	..	..	16.8	..	..	..	..	..	..	..	..	..	..
Uganda	18.2	393.2	7.9	23.6	43.5	13.4	62.7	47.8	84.2	1.3	10.2	22.2	9.8
Zambia	18.8	615.8	9.6	12.6	54.7	10.1	25.6	20.8	11.9	5.8	7.9	10.6	9.8
Zimbabwe	..	..	..	..	..	..	..	..	..	..	..	..	..
NORTH AFRICA		**17,079.9**	**37.7**										
Algeria	..	..	12.4	64.3	..	20.7	46.7	50.1	48.1	13.8	36.8	24.7	36.1
Egypt, Arab Rep.	11.4	9,894.4	55.3	..	..	..	..	..	..	..	..	..	..
Libya	..	1,590.0	15.7	..	..	..	..	..	..	..	..	..	..
Morocco	24.9	2,355.6	58.1	27.3	43.5	3.4	55.7	31.6	37.0	15.8	31.0	8.2	14.3
Tunisia		3,239.9	63.7	..	..	..	..	..	..	..	..	..	..

a. Provisional
b. Data are for the most recent year available during the period specified.

CAPABLE STATES AND PARTNERSHIP

			Regulation and tax administration								
Number of tax payments 2007	Time to, prepare, file and pay taxes (hours) 2007	Total tax rate (% of profit) 2007	Highest marginal tax rate, corporate rate (%) 2006	Time dealing with officials (% of management time) 2006–07[b]	Average time to clear direct exports through customs (days) 2006–07[b]	Average time to clear imports through customs (days) 2006–07[b]	Interest rate spread (lending rate minus deposit rate) 2006	Listed domestic companies 2006–07[b]	Market capitalization of listed companies (% of GDP) 2006[a]	Turnover ratio for traded stocks (%) 2006–07[b]
38	325	67.3	..	..	7.8	7.8	9.6	..	..	..
31	272	53.2	..	7.1	16.5	28.3	15.0	..	..	..
58	270	75.8	38.0	..	6.3	12.2	..	..	..	..
19	140	17.2	15.0	5.0	1.4	3.1	7.6	18.0	35.9	2.2
45	270	47.6	..	9.5	2.8	5.3	..	..	..	..
32	140	278.7	..	5.7	..	10.8	..	..	..	..
41	1,400	51.9	..	12.8	4.3	11.7	11.0	..	..	..
57	100	54.0	..	12.2	..	10.6	..	..	..	..
54	504	203.8	..	..	..	..	11.0	..	..	..
54	122	63.7	..	..	..	..	11.0	..	..	..
20	100	48.8	..	..	..	..	8.0	..	..	..
32	308	228.1	40.0	6.3	3.6	13.1	..	..	..	..
61	606	65.4	..	..	..	..	11.0	..	..	..
66	270	48.4	35.0	..	..	..	..	38.0	24.1	2.5
35	114	38.7	..	..	..	..	..	..	..	..
46	296	59.5	..	..	..	..	11.0	..	..	..
18	216	84.5	..	..	..	..	..	..	..	..
20	212	31.1	30.0	3.8	4.3	14.1	3.4	..	..	..
26	272	44.7	..	..	..	..	11.0	..	..	..
50	376	292.4	..	7.3	5.0	3.0	17.1	..	..	..
37	304	36.1	25.0	4.0	7.8	6.8	..	32.0	25.4	3.9
56	416	49.9	..	2.7	4.3	10.4	..	..	..	..
46	208	45.9	..	2.9	5.6	11.0	..	..	..	..
42	432	51.4	..	..	4.7	8.9	8.5	51.0	49.9	10.6
21	564	26.2	..	..	2.3	3.5	7.6	..	..	..
32	158	35.8	..	..	..	..	..	..	..	..
26	304	46.5	..	..	3.5	7.0	7.2	..	..	..
19	370	32.6	..	5.8	3.5	6.4	21.3	9.0	18.6	3.5
58	270	51.4	..	2.4	8.1	9.1	..	..	..	..
38	696	107.5	..	5.8	3.9	6.8	..	40.0	..	..
7	161	23.4	25.0	..	4.4	5.1	11.5	90.0	56.7	8.0
37	230	34.3	32.0	..	..	..	8.2	..	..	..
37	375	26.5	35.0	2.9	1.5	3.3	4.9	9.0	8.3	3.7
41	270	42.3	..	11.5	7.4	6.9	..	..	..	..
35	1,120	32.2	..	..	..	..	7.2	212.0	22.3	28.2
34	168	37.2	..	5.9	6.7	12.7	..	..	..	..
42	424	48.7	..	..	..	..	..	..	..	..
59	696	46.0	..	2.9	6.6	8.9	..	..	..	..
16	76	48.4	..	..	..	..	7.4	..	..	..
28	399	270.4	..	..	..	..	13.6	..	..	..
..	..	..	..	..	..	..	..	..	..	..
12	350	37.6	29.0	..	4.5	6.5	4.0	422.0	280.4	55.0
42	180	31.6	..	..	..	..	..	..	..	..
33	104	36.6	30.0	4.4	4.0	2.2	6.2	6.0	7.2	0.0
47	172	43.8	30.0	4.0	5.7	14.9	8.8	7.0	3.8	2.1
53	270	48.0	..	..	..	..	..	..	..	..
33	237	35.8	30.0	5.2	4.7	7.4	9.6	5.0	1.2	5.2
37	132	16.5	..	4.6	2.3	6.6	12.8	15.0	10.9	4.1
53	216	33.6	..	..	..	..	293.1	82.0	..	5.1
34.3	418	57.6	..	..	3.5	10.3	6.3	..	..	..
46	451	76.9	..	25.1	8.6	16.8	6.3	..	..	..
41	596	49.1	..	..	4.8	10.0	6.6	435.0	87.0	45.6
..	..	..	..	..	..	..	3.8	..	..	..
28	358	43.4	..	11.4	2.2	3.8	..	74.0	75.5	42.1
22	268	61.0	..	..	..	..	..	50.0	14.4	13.3

6.1 International trade and tariff barriers

				Trade				
	Merchandise trade (% of GDP) 2006[a]	Exports ($ millions) 2006[a]	Imports ($ millions) 2006[a]	Exports (% of GDP) 2006[a]	Imports (% of GDP) 2006[a]	Annual growth (%)		Terms of trade index (2000=100) 2006[a]
						Exports 2006[a]	Imports 2006[a]	
SUB-SAHARAN AFRICA	**71.7**	**276,758**	**257,218**	**37.2**	**34.5**	**..**	**12.3**	
Angola	111.7	33,317	17,129	73.8	37.9	..	..	..
Benin	..	..	..	..	..	..	..	..
Botswana	78.9	5,581	3,109	50.7	28.2	13.2	1.0	98.3
Burkina Faso	38.3	665	1,547	11.5	26.8	24.4	1.1	96.1
Burundi	58.7	99	432	10.9	47.8	..	..	..
Cameroon	44	4,130	3,762	23	21	1.3	1.0	108.0
Cape Verde	72.2	229	624	19.4	52.8	32.8	1.2	58.6
Central African Republic	36	207	324	14	21.9	14.4	1.0	72.0
Chad	101	3,852	2,509	61.1	39.8	11.2	1.0	100.0
Comoros	47.3	47	143	11.7	35.5	−4.9	1.0	100.0
Congo, Dem. Rep.	70.4	2,517	3,499	29.5	41	2.4	1.1	139.6
Congo, Rep.	130.8	6,717	3,398	86.9	43.9	..	..	..
Côte d'Ivoire	93.8	9,004	7,189	52.1	41.6	−1.6	1.0	82.1
Djibouti	97.2	307	441	39.9	57.3	2.8	1.2	100.0
Equatorial Guinea	144.7	8,096	4,295	94.5	50.1	−11.0	1.1	167.8
Eritrea	58.1	87	543	8	50	−1.1	1.0	86.0
Ethiopia	50.4	2,097	5,539	13.8	36.5	−0.2	1.2	79.3
Gabon	89.1	6,238	2,267	65.4	23.7	−9.7	1.1	150.4
Gambia, The	..	..	..	..	..	..	..	..
Ghana	104.6	5,063	8,234	39.8	64.8	10.3	1.1	103.0
Guinea	69.8	1,073	1,163	33.5	36.3	−1.2	1.0	92.9
Guinea-Bissau	94.5	129	162	41.8	52.7	5.1	1.1	96.9
Kenya	62.6	5,720	8,534	25.1	37.5	9.2	1.1	87.0
Lesotho	149	755	1,472	50.5	98.5	7.9	1.0	116.4
Liberia	102.4	175	453	28.6	73.8	..	..	..
Madagascar	70.7	1,635	2,252	29.7	40.9	23.8	1.0	129.2
Malawi	46.4	537	932	17	29.4	−11.8	0.9	184.9
Mali	72.3	1,884	2,360	32.1	40.2	11.3	1.0	96.3
Mauritania	113.7	1,453	1,573	54.6	59.1	117.9	..	..
Mauritius	127.1	3,809	4,257	60	67.1	8.0	1.1	87.9
Mozambique	88.9	2,831	3,245	41.4	47.5	8.0	1.1	81.1
Namibia	110	3,577	3,644	54.5	55.5	14.1	1.1	104.2
Niger	..	..	..	..	..	..	..	..
Nigeria	71.4	63,391	41,518	43.2	28.3	..	..	..
Rwanda	37.8	296	787	10.3	27.4	23.6	1.3	74.5
São Tomé and Principe	..	..	..	..	..	..	..	..
Senegal	69.2	2,351	4,062	25.4	43.8	−8.6	1.0	94.9
Seychelles	244.5	860	1,034	111	133.5	17.8	1.1	100.0
Sierra Leone	60.7	333	529	23.4	37.2	..	..	..
Somalia	..	..	..	..	..	..	..	..
South Africa	63.1	76,106	84,692	29.8	33.2	5.5	1.2	113.4
Sudan	44	6,014	9,995	16.5	27.5	0.4	1.1	100.0
Swaziland	135.1	1,774	1,988	63.7	71.4	4.6	1.1	96.4
Tanzania	49.7	3,106	3,941	21.9	27.8	−0.2	1.0	78.0
Togo	..	..	..	..	..	..	..	..
Uganda	44.8	1,403	2,854	14.8	30.1	4.0	1.2	127.0
Zambia	67.4	4,120	3,221	37.8	29.6	21.0	1.1	140.8
Zimbabwe	..	..	..	..	..	..	..	..
NORTH AFRICA	**..**	**..**	**115,394**	**..**	**31.2**	**..**	**13.7**	
Algeria	..	..	..	..	..	..	..	..
Egypt, Arab Rep.	61.5	32,191	33,931	29.9	31.6	21.3	1.2	112.3
Libya	..	..	..	..	..	..	..	..
Morocco	71.4	21,592	25,125	33	38.4	10.5	1.1	104.4
Tunisia	106.3	16,477	16,449	53.2	53.1	3.9	1.0	100.8

a. Provisional
b. Data are for most recent year available during the period specified.

| Structure of merchandise exports (% of total) | | | | | Structure of merchandise imports (% of total) | | | | | Export diversification index (0 low to 100 high) |
Food 2000–06[b]	Agricultural raw materials 2000–06[b]	Fuel 2000–06[b]	Ores and metals 2000–06[b]	Manufactures 2000–06[b]	Food 2000–06[b]	Agricultural raw materials 2000–06[b]	Fuel 2000–06[b]	Ores and metals 2000–06[b]	Manufactures 2000–06[b]	2006
15.5	**5.8**	**35.6**	**9.9**	**33.3**	**10.0**	**1.2**	**14.6**	**2.8**	**65.4**	
..	..	..	..	..	..	..	..	..	..	1.1
25.8	64.3	0.2	0.5	9.1	29.8	4.2	20.4	0.9	43.9	5.3
2.4	0.1	0.0	10.7	86.4	13.9	0.8	4.4	1.1	75.1	1.6
16.4	72.3	2.8	0.6	8.0	12.0	0.6	24.4	0.6	62.5	1.5
86.8	4.2	0.1	2.5	6.2	6.5	1.4	8.5	0.8	82.3	3.0
12.0	16.3	61.6	4.9	3.0	18.0	1.7	30.8	1.0	48.4	2.9
62.1	0.0	..	0.3	37.6	29.2	1.4	8.9	0.6	59.9	8.6
0.8	41.2	0.4	16.9	36.1	17.1	27.2	16.9	1.5	36.7	3.9
..	..	..	..	..	..	..	..	..	..	1.2
88.7	0.0	..	0.0	8.2	21.9	0.4	4.1	0.2	72.5	5.5
..	..	..	..	..	..	..	..	..	..	6.3
..	..	..	..	..	..	..	..	..	..	1.3
35.2	8.0	37.0	0.2	15.2	17.3	0.6	31.8	1.1	43.2	6.9
..	..	..	..	..	..	..	..	..	..	22.9
..	..	..	..	..	..	..	..	..	..	1.2
42.0	26.0	0.0	1.8	30.3	45.6	0.9	0.8	0.9	51.7	17.1
62.0	25.9	0.0	0.7	11.4	21.5	0.7	12.0	1.5	64.0	4.6
0.8	6.7	85.6	3.1	3.7	16.6	0.4	4.0	1.1	77.4	1.9
81.1	3.9	0.8	0.9	14.1	31.2	2.1	17.4	0.6	48.7	4.1
61.0	4.0	0.7	3.1	30.9	13.4	1.2	13.8	1.3	70.0	4.3
2.0	0.8	0.1	71.6	25.3	23.1	1.2	21.7	0.8	53.0	4.3
..	..	..	..	..	..	..	..	..	..	1.3
52.0	15.9	0.9	5.5	25.7	10.4	2.1	24.3	1.6	61.3	18.5
7.1	5.1	0.0	0.1	87.4	23.1	0.8	7.4	0.7	62.8	7.5
..	..	..	..	..	..	..	..	..	..	3.2
34.7	4.4	5.5	3.6	41.2	14.5	1.0	18.7	0.7	64.6	19.3
82.9	3.3	0.1	0.1	12.9	15.1	1.0	11.4	0.7	71.1	2.7
13.9	73.5	0.8	0.1	10.4	13.7	0.6	21.1	0.6	63.7	1.7
24.8	0.0	..	68.6	0.0	25.0	0.6	26.9	0.3	47.1	3.9
28.6	0.5	0.1	0.8	68.8	16.5	2.1	16.8	1.0	63.5	12.1
15.8	3.5	14.7	59.9	5.0	13.9	1.0	16.9	0.4	48.2	2.3
25.9	0.7	0.5	26.0	46.5	16.2	0.6	3.2	0.9	78.2	5.0
23.9	3.8	1.9	54.3	14.5	34.2	4.0	14.7	1.4	45.6	1.4
0.0	0.0	97.9	0.0	2.1	15.5	0.6	16.0	1.6	66.3	1.2
52.3	7.3	6.8	23.3	10.3	11.7	4.0	15.6	2.0	66.7	3.0
94.5	0.6	0.0	0.1	4.9	30.6	0.8	20.2	1.4	46.9	4.4
43.8	5.3	0.0	6.9	44.0	23.4	1.6	25.9	1.0	48.1	26.0
93.2	0.0	..	0.0	6.8	24.0	1.3	26.7	0.5	40.5	3.6
91.6	0.8	..	0.1	7.5	22.5	7.6	39.7	0.8	29.3	4.7
..	..	..	..	..	..	..	..	..	..	8.6
7.1	1.8	9.4	28.7	53.0	4.4	1.0	18.4	2.4	66.2	38.4
6.8	4.8	87.3	0.4	0.1	13.0	0.7	1.2	1.0	83.2	1.3
17.2	7.7	0.6	0.5	73.8	18.0	1.1	11.5	0.7	65.8	19.5
53.2	10.7	0.2	17.5	18.4	12.2	0.8	24.2	1.2	61.5	26.4
21.5	8.9	1.2	10.3	58.1	15.5	0.8	29.0	2.1	52.6	7.7
62.3	8.9	5.0	2.4	21.3	13.6	1.4	21.1	1.1	62.5	5.6
6.0	2.8	0.6	84.8	5.8	7.6	0.8	15.1	2.5	74.0	2.2
30.1	8.2	0.3	23.2	38.1	9.6	2.4	15.1	40.4	32.4	14.9
6.6	**0.7**	**62.3**	**2.4**	**26.7**	**15.8**	**3.1**	**14.1**	**3.0**	**58.3**	
0.2	0.0	97.9	0.7	1.2	19.2	2.1	1.1	1.8	75.8	2.3
6.6	1.5	56.4	2.3	21.2	18.9	3.9	16.3	3.3	43.3	13.2
..	..	..	..	..	16.8	0.6	0.7	0.9	81.1	1.3
19.3	1.7	1.9	9.3	67.8	9.3	2.9	21.7	3.5	62.7	69.3
10.4	0.6	13.0	1.2	74.9	8.5	2.6	13.7	3.1	72.0	43.0

International trade and tariff barriers (continued)

	Competitiveness Indicator (%)		Tariff barriers, all products (%)					
	Sectoral effect 2002–06	Global effect 2002–06	Binding coverage 2006	Simple mean bound rate 2006	Simple mean tariff 2006	Weighted mean tariff 2006	Share of lines with international peaks 2006	Share of lines with specific rates 2006
SUB-SAHARAN AFRICA								
Angola	15.4	35.7	100.0	59.2	7.6	6.5	10.4	0.8
Benin	−10.5	−1.2	39.1	28.6	13.4	11.3	53.4	..
Botswana	−19.6	14.9	96.3	19.0	8.7	10.5	20.9	1.3
Burkina Faso	13.5	12.4	38.9	42.2	12.2	9.8	43.5	..
Burundi	−6.4	−5.2	21.2	66.7	14.7	13.5	27.9	..
Cameroon	4.2	5.6	..	..	..	..	..	..
Cape Verde	−13.4	24.9	..	..	..	..	..	..
Central African Republic	−21.4	−13.1	..	..	..	..	..	..
Chad	−14.7	919.7	..	..	..	..	..	..
Comoros	−49.4	20.3	..	..	..	..	..	..
Congo, Dem. Rep.	−7.6	−16.1	100.0	96.2	13.1	11.4	43.3	0.2
Congo, Rep.	14.8	41.5	..	..	..	..	..	..
Côte d'Ivoire	−9.2	−8.4	33.0	11.1	13.5	7.3	49.9	..
Djibouti	1.3	30.0	100.0	41.0	30.2	29.1	87.9	6.3
Equatorial Guinea	4.2	54.8	..	..	..	..	..	..
Eritrea	−14.4	18.2	..	..	..	..	..	..
Ethiopia	−6.1	27.5	..	..	16.4	10.7	49.2	0.1
Gabon	7.3	−18.4	..	..	..	..	..	..
Gambia, The	−20.3	−0.1	..	..	..	..	..	..
Ghana	−9.4	−0.6	..	..	..	..	..	..
Guinea	−2.2	−5.1	..	..	..	..	..	..
Guinea-Bissau	−22.1	−11.4	97.7	48.7	12.7	9.1	50.1	..
Kenya	−2.7	−3.5	14.0	95.1	11.9	6.6	36.2	0.4
Lesotho	−21.0	2.9	100.0	78.4	9.9	16.5	24.2	1.9
Liberia	158.2	−193.1	..	..	..	..	..	..
Madagascar	−21.4	5.8	29.7	27.4	13.3	8.7	43.5	..
Malawi	−20.6	1.9	30.2	74.9	12.9	8.1	40.3	..
Mali	−9.2	−1.6	40.7	29.3	12.6	8.5	46.3	..
Mauritania	2.1	20.2	39.4	19.6	11.6	7.2	44.3	3.9
Mauritius	−6.0	−14.9	18.0	94.0	4.2	1.6	8.5	8.1
Mozambique	−7.8	20.1	12.9	97.4	12.7	8.3	38.2	..
Namibia	−5.3	45.8	96.3	19.4	5.8	0.8	15.7	2.6
Niger	7.1	15.7	96.8	44.6	13.1	9.8	50.3	..
Nigeria	23.5	21.1	18.1	118.5	11.7	11.6	41.5	..
Rwanda	−0.5	−25.3	100.0	89.4	19.7	14.4	52.2	0.1
São Tomé and Principe	18.8	9.9	..	..	..	..	..	..
Senegal	−10.0	−18.3	100.0	30.0	13.5	9.4	51.3	..
Seychelles	−12.9	−7.3	..	..	6.3	30.7	12.2	1.6
Sierra Leone	−6.9	0.1	..	..	..	..	..	..
Somalia	−11.3	5.7	..	..	..	..	..	..
South Africa	2.1	−6.8	96.3	19.4	8.3	5.1	19.3	2.1
Sudan	8.2	14.6	..	..	17.1	15.3	38.1	..
Swaziland	−6.1	−0.9	96.3	19.4	10.3	9.2	25.0	2.4
Tanzania	−0.3	0.1	13.4	120.0	12.5	7.2	37.6	0.4
Togo	−0.7	−15.3	13.2	80.0	14.0	9.7	52.3	..
Uganda	−7.7	−7.0	14.9	73.5	12.0	7.4	37.1	0.5
Zambia	23.1	23.2	..	..	..	..	..	..
Zimbabwe	−5.7	−12.6	..	..	..	..	..	..
NORTH AFRICA								
Algeria	24.2	−3.4	..	..	15.8	10.7	38.7	..
Egypt, Arab Rep.	5.2	32.0	..	..	..	..	..	..
Libya	17.6	20.9	..	..	..	..	..	..
Morocco	−5.3	−3.7	100.0	41.3	15.5	11.0	45.3	2.0
Tunisia	−7.9	2.4	57.9	57.7	22.9	18.5	55.5	..

a. Provisional

b. Data are for most recent year available during the period specified.

Tariff barriers, primary products (%)		Tariff barriers, manufactured products (%)		Average cost to ship 20 ft container from port to final destination ($)		Average time to clear customs (days)	
Simple mean tariff 2006	Weighted mean tariff 2006	Simple mean tariff 2006	Weighted mean tariff 2006	Export 2006	Import 2006	Direct exports 2006	Imports 2006
				1,750	**2,181**	**5.0**	**9.6**
11.5	13.1	6.9	5.0	1,850	2,325	16.5	28.3
13.2	10.9	13.4	11.7	1,167	1,202	6.3	12.2
3.6	0.8	9.2	12.4	2,328	2,595	1.4	3.1
11.3	7.8	12.4	11.0	2,096	3,522	2.8	5.3
15.1	11.7	14.6	13.8	2,147	3,705	..	10.8
..	..	..	..	524	1,360	4.3	11.7
..	..	..	..	..	..	..	10.6
..	..	..	..	4,581	4,534	..	..
..	..	..	..	4,867	5,520	..	..
..	..	..	..	..	..	..	..
14.2	11.3	12.8	11.5	3,120	3,308	3.6	13.1
..	..	..	..	2,201	2,201	..	..
15.4	4.2	13.1	9.5	1,653	2,457		
23.1	23.2	31.3	31.0	..	..	..	..
..	..	..	..	935	1,185	..	..
18.1	12.6	16.3	10.4	1,617	2,793	4.3	14.1
..	..	..	..	..	..	..	..
..	..	..	..	..	..	5.0	3.0
..	..	..	..	822	842	..	..
..	..	..	..	570	995	4.3	10.4
14.3	9.0	12.4	9.2	..	..	5.6	11.0
14.8	6.4	11.6	6.6	1,980	2,325	4.7	8.9
7.5	3.2	10.0	17.3	1,188	1,210	2.3	3.5
..	..	..	..	..	..	..	..
14.2	3.0	13.2	12.2	982	1,282	3.5	7.0
12.8	6.1	12.9	8.9	1,623	2,500	3.5	6.4
11.5	8.6	12.7	8.5	1,752	2,680	8.1	10.0
11.5	9.3	11.6	6.6	3,733	3,733	3.9	6.8
6.1	1.5	3.9	1.7	683	683	4.4	5.1
15.4	8.9	12.3	8.0	1,155	1,185	..	..
3.5	0.6	6.2	0.9	1,539	1,550	1.5	3.3
13.1	10.0	13.1	9.7	2,945	2,946	7.4	6.9
14.8	15.1	11.4	10.2	798	1,460	..	..
17.4	14.0	20.0	14.5	3,840	4,080	6.7	12.7
..	..	..	..	690	577	..	..
14.4	8.5	13.4	10.3	828	1,720	6.6	7.0
12.8	49.6	4.9	6.7	..	..	..	..
..	..	..	..	1,282	1,242	..	..
..	..	..	..	..	..	..	..
5.5	1.7	8.6	6.4	1,087	1,195	4.5	6.5
22.9	19.7	16.6	14.6	1,870	1,970	..	..
8.0	3.8	10.5	9.6	..	..	4.0	2.2
16.9	7.7	12.0	7.0	822	917	5.7	14.9
13.9	8.7	14.0	10.7	463	695	..	..
14.6	7.0	11.7	7.6	1,050	2,945	4.7	7.4
..	..	..	..	2,098	2,840	2.3	4.8
..	..	..	..	1,879	2,420	..	..
				1,023	**1,259**	**3.5**	**6.4**
15.5	9.3	15.8	11.1	1,606	1,886	8.6	23.2
..	..	..	..	1,014	1,049	4.8	10.0
..	15.1	..	..	..	..	..	..
21.9	11.7	14.9	10.6	700	1,500	2.2	2.8
33.1	14.7	22.0	20.0	770	600	..	..

Top three exports and share in total exports, 2006

	First	
	Product	Share of total exports (%)
SUB-SAHARAN AFRICA		
Angola	Petroleum oils and oils obtained from bituminous minerals, crude	96.0
Benin	Cotton, not carded, combed	35.1
Botswana	Diamonds non-industrial unworked or simply sawn, cleaved or bruted	78.6
Burkina Faso	Cotton, not carded, combed	82.7
Burundi	Coffee, not roasted, not decaffeinated	56.3
Cameroon	Petroleum oils and oils obtained from bituminous minerals, crude	57.0
Cape Verde	Tunas, yellowfin, frozen excluding heading No 03.04, livers and roes	24.6
Central African Republic	Logs, tropical hardwoods not elsewhere specified	37.1
Chad	Petroleum oils and oils obtained from bituminous minerals, crude	90.9
Comoros	Electrostatic photo-copying apparatus, indirect process type	25.4
Congo, Dem. Rep.	Diamonds non-industrial unworked or simply sawn, cleaved or bruted	31.2
Congo, Rep.	Petroleum oils and oils obtained from bituminous minerals, crude	88.7
Côte d'Ivoire	Cocoa beans, whole or broken, raw or roasted	31.4
Djibouti	Coffee, not roasted, not decaffeinated	13.1
Equatorial Guinea	Petroleum oils and oils obtained from bituminous minerals, crude	91.7
Eritrea	Medicaments not elsewhere specified, in dosage	12.8
Ethiopia	Coffee, not roasted, not decaffeinated	42.2
Gabon	Petroleum oils and oils obtained from bituminous minerals, crude	72.3
Gambia, The	Cashew nuts, in shell, fresh or dried	46.7
Ghana	Cocoa beans, whole or broken, raw or roasted	46.9
Guinea	Aluminium ores and concentrates	40.0
Guinea-Bissau	Cashew nuts, in shell, fresh or dried	86.9
Kenya	Black tea (fermented) and partly fermented tea in packages exceeding 3 kg	14.5
Lesotho	Pullovers, cardigans and similar articles of cotton, knitted	22.2
Liberia	Cargo vessles not elsewhere specified and other vessels for the transport of both persons and goods	31.4
Madagascar	Pullovers, cardigans and similar articles of wool or fine animal hair, knitted	12.5
Malawi	Tobacco, unmanufactured, partly or wholly stemmed or stripped	59.1
Mali	Cotton, not carded or combed	56.2
Mauritania	Petroleum oils and oils obtained from bituminous minerals, crude	35.8
Mauritius	Raw sugar, cane	17.9
Mozambique	Aluminium unwrought, not alloyed	65.9
Namibia	Diamonds non-industrial unworked or simply sawn, cleaved or bruted	39.5
Niger	Natural uranium & its compounds. Mixtures containing natural uranium & its compounds	58.9
Nigeria	Petroleum oils and oils obtained from bituminous minerals, crude	89.6
Rwanda	Coffee, not roasted, not decaffeinated	53.7
São Tomé and Principe	Cocoa beans, whole or broken, raw or roasted	39.5
Senegal	Ground-nut oil, crude	8.8
Seychelles	Tunas, skipjack & Atl bonito, prepared/preserved, whole/in pieces, excluding minced	49.2
Sierra Leone	Diamonds non-industrial unworked or simply sawn, cleaved or bruted	42.9
Somalia	Goats, live	27.3
South Africa	Platinium unwrought or in powder form	9.4
Sudan	Petroleum oils and oils obtained from bituminous minerals, crude	89.3
Swaziland	Raw sugar, cane	14.3
Tanzania	Tobacco, unmanufactured, partly or wholly stemmed or stripped	7.6
Togo	Cocoa beans, whole or broken, raw or roasted	29.6
Uganda	Coffee, not roasted, not decaffeinated	33.3
Zambia	Copper cathodes and sections of cathodes unwrought	66.2
Zimbabwe	Nickel unwrought, not alloyed	16.8
NORTH AFRICA		
Algeria	Petroleum oils and oils obtained from bituminous minerals, crude	64.7
Egypt, Arab Rep.	Natural gas, liquefied	19.7
Libya	Petroleum oils and oils obtained from bituminous minerals, crude	87.2
Morocco	Phosphoric acid and polyphosphoric acids	5.4
Tunisia	Petroleum oils and oils obtained from bituminous minerals, crude	8.7
AFRICA[a]	**Petroleum oils and oils obtained from bituminous minerals, crude**	**51.9 [19.3]**

Note: Products are reported when accounting for more than 4 percent of total exports.
a. Values in parentheses are Africa's share of total world exports.

Product	Second Share of total exports (%)
Waste and scrap, copper or copper alloy	18.0
Nickel mattes	11.4
Black tea (fermented) and partly fermented tea in packages exceeding 3 kg	10.5
Lumber, tropical hardwood not elsewhere specified, sawn lengthwise >6mm	7.4
Skipjack or stripe-bellid bonito, frozen excluding heading No 03.04, livers and roes	13.7
Diamonds unsorted whether or not worked	32.3
Cloves (whole fruit, cloves and stems)	22.7
Cobalt ores and concentrates	18.2
Petroleum oils and oils obtained from bituminous minerals, crude	17.4
Raw sugar, cane	8.3
Parts of boring or sinking machinery, whether or not self-propelled	11.8
Sesanum seeds, whether or not broken	18.6
Manganese ores and concentrates and the like	8.0
Ground-nut oil, crude	11.8
Manganese ores and concentrates and the like	4.7
Petroleum oils and oils obtained from bituminous minerals, crude	21.9
Cut flowers and flower buds for bouquets or ornamemtal purposes, fresh	14.0
Mens/boys trousers and shorts, of cotton, not knitted	18.2
Tankers	26.4
Shrimps and prawns, frozen, in shell or not, including boiled in shell	12.3
Raw sugar, cane	8.2
Tankers	13.9
Iron ores & concentrates, other than roasted iron pyrites, nonagglomerated	34.0
T-shirts, singlets and other vests, of cotton, knitted	17.7
Aluminium unwrought, alloyed	5.1
Zinc not alloyed unwrought containing by weight 99.99% or more of zinc	15.3
Petroleum oils and oils obtained from bituminous minerals, other than crude and the like	30.9
Natural gas, liquefied	5.0
Niobium, tantalum and vanadium ores and concentrates	18.2
Motorcycles with reciprocating piston engine displacg > 50 cc to 250 cc	20.0
Phosphoric acid and polyphosphoric acids (8.8%)	8.8
Tunas, yellowfin, frozen excluding heading No 03.04, livers and roes	12.2
Aluminium ores and concentrates	11.6
Bovine, live, pure-bred breeding	12.9
Diamonds non-industrial unworked or simply sawn, cleaved or bruted	5.9
Gas turbines not elsewhere specified of a power exceeding 5000 KW	9.2
Fish fillets and other fish meat, minced or not, fresh or chilled	6.9
Natural calcium phosphates, aluminium calcium phosphates and the like ground	11.6
Fish fillets and other fish meat, minced or not, fresh or chilled	23.4
Copper ores and concentrates	5.8
Tobacco, unmanufactured, partly or wholly stemmed or stripped	10.0
Natural gas, liquefied	11.0
Petroleum oils and oils obtained from bituminous minerals, other than crude and the like	13.2
Petroleum oils and oils obtained from bituminous minerals, other than crude and the like	8.1
Mens/boys trousers and shorts, of cotton, not knitted	6.2
Petroleum oils and oils obtained from bituminous minerals, other than crude and the like	**4.1 [4.5]**

Table 6.2 Top three exports and share in total exports, 2006 (continued)

		Third	
	Product	Share of total exports (%)	Number of exports accounting for 75% of total exports
SUB-SAHARAN AFRICA			
Angola			1
Benin	Cashew nuts, in shell, fresh or dried	14.5	4
Botswana	Diamonds industrial unworked or simply sawn, cleaved or bruted	4.1	1
Burkina Faso			1
Burundi	Filtering or purifying machinery and apparatus for liquids not elsewhere specified	4.3	4
Cameroon	Bananas including plantains, fresh or dried	6.1	5
Cape Verde	Turbo-jets of a thrust exceeding 25 KN	10.9	7
Central African Republic	Lumber, tropical hardwood not elsewhere specified, sawn lengthwise >6mm	8.7	3
Chad			
Comoros	Tugs and pusher craft	19.2	4
Congo, Dem. Rep.	Copper ores and concentrates	9.7	5
Congo, Rep.			1
Côte d'Ivoire	Cocoa paste not defatted	6.1	8
Djibouti	Dump trucks designed for off-highway use	6.1	24
Equatorial Guinea			1
Eritrea	Bovine leather, otherwise pre-tanned, not elsehwere specified	9.1	14
Ethiopia			8
Gabon	Logs, tropical hardwoods not elsewhere specified	7.6	2
Gambia, The	Ground-nuts shelled, whether or not broken, not roast or otherwise cooked	8.8	5
Ghana	Aluminium unwrought, not alloyed	3.6	10
Guinea	Aluminium oxide not elsewhere specified	11.6	4
Guinea-Bissau			1
Kenya	Petroleum oils and oils obtained from bituminous minerals, other than crude and the like	5.5	37
Lesotho	Diamonds non-industrial unworked or simply sawn, cleaved or bruted	18.0	6
Liberia	Petroleum oils and oils obtained from bituminous minerals, crude	13.6	4
Madagascar	Womens/girls trousers and shorts, of cotton, not knitted	80.0	25
Malawi	Black tea (fermented) & partly fermented tea in packages exceeding 3 kg	7.5	4
Mali	Cargo vessels nes&oth vessels for the transport of both persons and goods	13.5	7
Mauritania	Octopus, frozen, dried, salted or in brine	9.6	3
Mauritius	Tunas,skipjack & Atl bonito, prepared/preserved,whole/in pieces, excluding minced	9.7	19
Mozambique	Tobacco, unmanufactured, partly or wholly stemmed or stripped	4.6	3
Namibia	Natural uranium and its compounds mixtures containing natural uranium/its compounds	9.8	5
Niger			2
Nigeria			1
Rwanda	Black tea (fermented) & partly fermented tea in packages exceeding 3 kg	9.2	3
São Tomé and Principe	Motorcycles with reciprocatg piston engine displacg > 500 cc to 800 cc	13.1	4
Senegal	Fish not elsewhere specififed, fresh or chilled excluding heading No 03.04, livers and roes	7.4	23
Seychelles	Petroleum oils and oils obtained from bituminous minerals, other than crude and the like	11.0	4
Sierra Leone	Cocoa beans, whole or broken, raw or roasted	8.0	6
Somalia	Wood charcoal (including shell or nut charcoal)	9.3	9
South Africa	Gold in unwrought forms non-monetary	5.7	74
Sudan			1
Swaziland	Mixtures of odoriferous substances for the food or drink industries	8.6	25
Tanzania	Cotton, not carded or combed	6.7	21
Togo	Cement climkers	9.8	8
Uganda	Fish fillets frozen	5.8	6
Zambia	Wire of refined copper of which the maximum cross sectional dimension >6mm	4.7	3
Zimbabwe	Ferro-chronium containing by weight more than 4% of carbon	9.1	17
NORTH AFRICA			
Algeria	Petroleum oils and oils obtained from bituminous minerals, other than crude and the like	9.3	2
Egypt, Arab Rep.	Petroleum oils and oils obtained from bituminous minerals, crude	13.0	48
Libya			1
Morocco			71
Tunisia	Olive oil, virgin	5.4	77
AFRICA[a]	**Natural gas, liquefied**	**3.6 [35.2]**	**24**

Note: Products are reported when accounting for more than 4 percent of total exports.

a. Values in parentheses are Africa's share of total world exports.

Table 6.3 Regional integration, trade blocs

	Year established	Year of entry into force of the most recent agreement	Type of the most recent agreement[a]	Merchandise exports within bloc ($ millions)						
				1990	1995	2000	2003	2004	2005	2006
Economic and Monetary Community of Central African States (CEMAC)	1994	1999	CU	139	127	96	146	174	198	245
Common Market for Eastern and Southern Africa (COMESA)	1994	1994	FTA	1,164	1,390	1,448	2,041	2,427	2,869	3,546
East African Community (EAC)	1996	2000	CU	230	530	595	706	750	857	1059
Economic Community of Central African States (ECCAS)	1983	2004[b]	NNA	163	163	191	198	240	271	334
Economic Community of West African States (ECOWAS)	1975	1993	PS	1,532	1,875	2,715	3,037	4,366	5,497	5,957
Indian Ocean Commission (IOC)	1984	2005[b]	NNA	73	127	106	179	155	159	172
Southern African Development Community (SADC)	1992	2000	FTA	677	1,015	4,383	5,609	6,590	7,668	8,571
West African Economic and Monetary Union (UEMOA)	1994	2000	CU	621	560	741	1,076	1,233	1,390	1,545
				Merchandise exports within bloc (% of total bloc exports)						
Economic and Monetary Community of Central African States (CEMAC)	1994	1999	CU	2.3	2.1	1.0	1.4	1.2	0.9	0.9
Common Market for Eastern and Southern Africa (COMESA)	1994	1994	FTA	4.2	5.4	3.7	4.4	4.1	3.4	3.2
East African Community (EAC)	1996	2000	CU	13.4	17.4	20.5	18.3	16.7	15.1	16.5
Economic Community of Central African States (ECCAS)	1983	2004[b]	NNA	1.4	1.5	1.1	1.0	0.9	0.6	0.6
Economic Community of West African States (ECOWAS)	1975	1993	PS	8.0	9.0	7.6	8.5	9.3	9.3	8.3
Indian Ocean Commission (IOC)	1984	2005[b]	NNA	4.1	6.0	4.4	6.2	4.3	4.6	4.7
Southern African Development Community (SADC)	1992	2000	FTA	6.8	9.2	9.4	10.1	9.7	9.2	9.1
West African Economic and Monetary Union (UEMOA)	1994	2000	CU	13.0	10.3	13.1	13.3	12.9	13.4	13.1

a. FTA is free trade agreement, CU is customs union, EIA is economic integration agreement, PS is partial scope agreement and NNA is not notified agreement, which refers to prefentrial tarde agreements established among member ocuntries that are not notified to the World Trade Organization (these agreements may be functionally equivalent to any of th eother agreements).

b. Years of the most recent agreement are collected from official trade bloc website

Note: Economic and Monetary Community of Central Africa (CEMAC), Cameroon, the Central African Republic, Chad, the Republic of Congo, Equatorial Guinea, Gabon, and São Tomé and Principe; Common Market for Eastern and Southern Africa (COMESA), Angola, Burundi, Comoros, the Democratic Republic of Congo, Djibouti, the Arab Republic of Egypt, Eritrea, Ethiopia, Kenya, Madagascar, Malawi, Mauritius, Namibia, Rwanda, Seychelles, Sudan, Swaziland, Uganda, Tanzania, Zambia, and Zimbabwe; East African Community (EAC), Kenya, Tanzania, and Uganda; Economic Community of Central African States (ECCAS), Angola, Burundi, Cameroon, the Central African Republic, Chad, the Democratic Republic of Congo, the Republic of Congo, Equatorial Guinea, Gabon, Rwanda, and São Tomé and Principe; Economic Community of West African States (ECOWAS), Benin, Burkina Faso, Cape Verde, Côte d'Ivoire, the Gambia, Ghana, Guinea, Guinea-Bissau, Liberia, Mali, Mauritania, Niger, Nigeria, Senegal, Sierra Leone, and Togo; Indian Ocean Commission, Comoros, Madagascar, Mauritius, Réunion, and Seychelles; Southern African Development Community (SADC; formerly Southern African Development Coordination Conference), Angola, Botswana, the Democratic Republic of Congo, Lesotho, Malawi, Mauritius, Mozambique, Namibia, Seychelles, South Africa, Swaziland, Tanzania, Zambia, and Zimbabwe; West African Economic and Monetary Union (UEMOA), Benin, Burkina Faso, Côte d'Ivoire, Guinea-Bissau, Mali, Niger, Senegal, and Togo.

Table 7.1 Water and sanitation

	Access, supply side	Access, demand side					
	Internal freshwater resources per capita (cubic meters) 2000–06[a]	Population with sustainable access to improved water source (%)			Population with sustainable access to improved sanitation (%)		
		Total 2006	Urban 2006	Rural 2006	Total 2006	Urban 2006	Rural 2006
SUB-SAHARAN AFRICA	**5,088**	**58**	**81**	**46**	**31**	**42**	**24**
Angola	9,195	51	62	39	50	79	16
Benin	1,213	65	78	57	30	59	11
Botswana	1,307	96	100	90	47	60	30
Burkina Faso	897	72	97	66	13	41	6
Burundi	1,285	71	84	70	41	44	41
Cameroon	15,341	70	88	47	51	58	42
Cape Verde	592	..	..	..	..	..	..
Central African Republic	33,640	66	90	51	31	40	25
Chad	1,479	48	71	40	9	23	4
Comoros	1,998	85	91	81	35	49	26
Congo, Dem. Rep.	15,322	46	82	29	31	42	25
Congo, Rep.	61,498	71	95	35	20	19	21
Côte d'Ivoire	4,132	81	98	66	24	38	12
Djibouti	373	92	98	54	67	76	11
Equatorial Guinea	53,708	43	45	42	51	60	46
Eritrea	619	60	74	57	5	14	3
Ethiopia	1,623	42	96	31	11	27	8
Gabon	127,064	87	95	47	36	37	30
Gambia, The	1,855	86	91	81	52	50	55
Ghana	1,345	80	90	71	10	15	6
Guinea	25,104	70	91	59	19	33	12
Guinea-Bissau	10,019	57	82	47	33	48	26
Kenya	582	57	85	49	42	19	48
Lesotho	2,625	78	93	74	36	43	34
Liberia	58,109	64	72	52	32	49	7
Madagascar	18,077	47	76	36	12	18	10
Malawi	1,217	76	96	72	60	51	62
Mali	5,168	60	86	48	45	59	39
Mauritania	135	60	70	54	24	44	10
Mauritius	2,252	100	100	100	94	95	94
Mozambique	4,885	42	71	26	31	53	19
Namibia	3,070	93	99	90	35	66	18
Niger	264	42	91	32	7	27	3
Nigeria	1,563	47	65	30	30	35	25
Rwanda	1,029	65	82	61	23	34	20
São Tomé and Principe	14,415	86	88	83	24	29	18
Senegal	2,192	77	93	65	28	54	9
Seychelles	..	..	100	..	..	..	100
Sierra Leone	28,641	53	83	32	11	20	5
Somalia	732	29	63	10	23	51	7
South Africa	955	93	100	82	59	66	49
Sudan	813	70	78	64	35	50	24
Swaziland	2,299	60	87	51	50	64	46
Tanzania	2,183	55	81	46	33	31	34
Togo	1,843	59	86	40	12	24	3
Uganda	1,347	64	90	60	33	29	34
Zambia	6,987	58	90	41	52	55	51
Zimbabwe	938	81	98	72	46	63	37
NORTH AFRICA	**308**	**92**	**96**	**87**	**76**	**90**	**60**
Algeria	341	85	87	81	94	98	87
Egypt, Arab Rep.	25	98	99	98	66	85	52
Libya	101	..	..	..	97	97	96
Morocco	962	83	100	58	72	85	54
Tunisia	419	94	99	84	85	96	64

a. Data are for most recent year available during the period specified.

Quality of supply	Financing	
Water supply failure for firms receiving water (average days per year) 2000–06[a]	Committed nominal investment in water projects with private participation ($ millions) 2000–06[a]	ODA gross aid disbursements for water supply and sanitation sector ($ millions) 2006
		739.2
83.5	..	5.4
19.2	..	32.3
0.0	..	0.1
11.8	..	40.7
94.1	..	2.7
6.8	..	2.5
12.8	..	2.0
..	..	0.9
..	..	13.8
..	..	0.5
81.8	..	0.0
..	0.0	9.3
..	..	1.0
..	..	0.0
..	..	2.9
79.2	..	6.9
0.0	..	30.2
..	..	0.0
..	..	2.9
..	0.0	62.0
..	..	14.4
43.2	..	1.3
85.2	..	30.3
19.2	..	3.9
..	..	0.5
5.2	..	4.6
21.3	..	4.8
2.1	..	27.1
92.5	..	6.3
16.7	..	27.8
..	..	24.4
10.2	0.0	3.8
0.1	3.4	19.8
..	..	15.4
..	..	18.7
..	..	0.3
5.6	0.0	20.5
..	..	..
..	..	0.9
..	..	3.6
4.8	0.0	81.0
..	..	16.8
18.1	..	0.6
105.0	8.5	43.4
..	..	1.0
2.7	0.0	47.6
13.6	0.0	35.6
..	..	1.7
		345.0
31.0	510.0	4.9
5.2	..	55.6
..	..	0.0
1.3	..	170.4
..	..	107.9

Table 7.2 Transportation

	Access, supply side				Access, demand side
			Road density		
	Road network (km) 2000–06[a]	Rail lines (km) 2000–06[a]	Ratio to arable land (road km/1000 ha arable land) 2000–06[a]	Ratio to total land (road km/1000 sq. km of land area) 2000–06[a]	Rural access (% of rural population within 2 km of an all-season road) 2000–06[a]
SUB-SAHARAN AFRICA					
Angola	51,429	2,761	17.1	4.1	..
Benin	19,000	578	6.9	17.2	32.0
Botswana	24,455	888	64.9	4.3	..
Burkina Faso	92,495	622	19.1	33.8	25.0
Burundi	12,322	..	12.6	48.0	..
Cameroon	50,000	1,016	8.4	10.7	22.0
Cape Verde	1,350	..	30.7	33.5	..
Central African Republic	24,307	..	12.6	3.9	..
Chad	33,400	..	9.5	2.7	..
Comoros	880	..	11.0	47.3	..
Congo, Dem. Rep.	153,497	3,641	22.9	6.8	26.0
Congo, Rep.	17,289	795	34.9	5.1	..
Côte d'Ivoire	80,000	639	22.9	25.2	..
Djibouti	3,065	781	3,065.0	13.2	..
Equatorial Guinea	2,880	..	22.2	10.3	..
Eritrea	4,010	306	7.2	4.0	..
Ethiopia	39,477	781	2.8	3.9	30.2
Gabon	9,170	810	28.2	3.6	..
Gambia, The	3,742	..	10.7	37.4	..
Ghana	57,613	977	13.8	25.3	..
Guinea	44,348	1,115	40.3	18.0	37.0
Guinea-Bissau	3,455	..	11.5	12.3	..
Kenya	63,265	1,917	12.0	11.1	..
Lesotho	5,940	..	18.0	19.6	..
Liberia	10,600	490	27.9	11.0	..
Madagascar	49,827	732	17.2	8.6	..
Malawi	15,451	710	6.3	16.4	..
Mali	18,709	733	3.9	1.5	..
Mauritania	7,660	717	15.7	0.7	..
Mauritius	2,015	..	20.2	99.3	..
Mozambique	30,400	3,070	7.8	3.9	11.0
Namibia	42,237	..	51.8	5.1	..
Niger	18,423	..	1.3	1.5	17.0
Nigeria	193,200	3,528	6.2	21.2	..
Rwanda	14,008	..	11.7	56.8	..
São Tomé and Principe	320	..	53.3	33.3	..
Senegal	13,576	906	5.5	7.1	..
Seychelles	458	..	458.0	99.6	..
Sierra Leone	11,300	..	21.1	15.8	22.0
Somalia	22,100	..	21.2	3.5	..
South Africa	364,131	20,247	24.7	30.0	..
Sudan	11,900	5,478	0.7	0.5	..
Swaziland	3,594	301	20.2	20.9	..
Tanzania	78,891	4,582	8.6	8.9	16.0
Togo	7,520	568	3.0	13.8	..
Uganda	70,746	259	13.6	35.9	..
Zambia	91,440	1,273	17.4	12.3	51.0
Zimbabwe	97,267	..	30.2	25.1	..
NORTH AFRICA					
Algeria	108,302	3,572	14.5	4.5	..
Egypt, Arab Rep.	92,370	5,150	31.2	9.3	..
Libya	83,200	2,757	45.8	4.7	..
Morocco	57,626	1,907	6.8	12.9	..
Tunisia	19,232	1,909	6.9	12.4	..

a. Data are for most recent year available during the period specified.

| Access, demand side | | Quality | | Pricing | | Financing | |
| Vehicles fleet (per 1000 people) | | Roads | | | | | |
Commercial vehicles 2000–06[a]	Passenger vehicles 2000–06[a]	Road network in good or fair condition (%) 2000–06[a]	Ratio of paved to total roads (%) 2000–06[a]	Price of diesel fuel (US$ per liter) 2006	Price of gasoline (US$ per liter) 2006	Committed nominal investment in transport projects with private participation ($ millions) 2000–06[a]	ODA gross aid disbursements for transport and storage ($ millions) 2006
..	..	..	..	**0.98**	**1.03**	..	**976.9**
..	8.0	..	10.4	0.36	0.50	..	2.2
..	13.0	82.9	9.5	0.81	0.81	..	13.1
113.0	47.0	..	33.2	0.74	0.78	..	..
7.0	5.0	69.3	4.2	1.12	1.15	..	39.6
..	1.0	..	10.4	1.22	1.20	..	2.2
11.0	11.0	52.0	10.0	1.07	1.14	..	39.9
..	..	..	69.0	0.39	0.59	..	26.0
..	1.0	..	..	1.27	1.37	..	5.2
..	..	72.8	0.8	1.20	1.31	..	20.9
1.0	1.0	..	76.5	..	..	0.5	1.4
..	..	23.2	1.8	1.00	0.94	..	7.1
..	8.0	..	5.0	0.67	0.96	..	25.9
..	7.0	..	8.1	1.06	1.20	..	0.1
..	..	..	45.0	0.54	0.98	300.0	0.5
..	..	..	..	..	..	72.0	..
..	..	..	21.8	0.81	1.90	..	3.6
2.0	1.0	69.0	12.7	0.62	0.93	..	134.7
..	..	..	10.2	0.39	0.64	91.8	10.0
7.0	5.0	94.6	19.3	1.01	1.08	..	2.1
21.0	5.0	73.0	17.9	0.84	0.86	..	78.4
14.0	8.0	44.2	9.8	0.82	0.79	..	5.7
1.0	..	..	27.9	..	..	..	18.4
18.0	9.0	67.2	14.1	0.98	1.12	404.0	46.5
..	..	..	18.3	0.88	0.89	..	2.2
..	6.0	..	6.2	0.85	0.79	..	0.0
..	..	..	11.6	1.00	1.15	12.5	82.4
..	..	..	45.0	1.12	1.17	..	6.5
..	..	62.0	18.0	1.04	1.22	55.4	45.3
..	..	..	11.3	0.84	0.97	..	10.0
130.0	96.0	..	100.0	0.56	0.74	..	0.1
..	..	64.0	18.7	1.06	1.15	186.9	80.8
85.0	42.0	..	12.8	0.87	0.87	..	4.7
5.0	4.0	63.1	20.6	1.11	1.14	..	6.2
..	17.0	..	15.0	0.66	0.51	262.1	0.1
3.0	1.0	..	19.0	1.08	1.11	..	12.7
..	..	..	68.1	0.71	0.90	..	4.4
14.0	10.0	..	29.3	1.09	1.31	55.4	32.7
121.0	74.0	..	96.0	..	..	..	0.1
4.0	2.0	..	8.0	0.98	0.98	..	12.0
..	..	..	11.8	0.67	0.74	..	0.3
143.0	98.0	..	17.3	0.84	0.85	3,483.0	0.0
..	..	..	36.3	0.49	0.72	30.0	9.3
84.0	40.0	..	30.0	0.85	0.80	..	9.6
..	1.0	..	8.6	0.99	1.04	27.7	80.6
..	10.0	..	31.6	1.01	1.03	..	5.7
5.0	2.0	31.0	23.0	1.01	1.17	404.0	20.7
..	..	37.0	22.0	1.22	1.31	15.6	59.8
..	45.0	60.0	19.0	0.65	0.61	..	0.0
..	..	..	..	**0.19**	**0.32**	..	**213.7**
91.0	58.0	..	70.2	0.19	0.32	..	42.3
..	27.0	..	81.0	0.12	0.30	86.2	5.8
257.0	232.0	..	57.2	0.13	0.13	..	..
59.0	46.0	..	61.9	0.87	1.22	140.0	98.3
95.0	83.0	..	65.8	0.57	0.83	..	62.9

Table 7.3 Information and communication technology

	Access, supply side			Access, demand side					Quality	
	Telephone subscribers (per 100 people)			Households with own telephone			Average delay for firm of obtaining a mainline phone connection (days) 2006[a]	Internet users (per 100 people) 2006[a]	Duration of phone outages (hours) 2000–06[a]	Telephone faults (per 100 mainlines) 2000–06[a]
	Total 2006[a]	Mainline telephone 2006[a]	Mobile phone 2006[a]	Total (% of households) 2000–06[a]	Urban (% of urban households) 2000–06[a]	Rural (% of rural households) 2000–06[a]				
SUB-SAHARAN AFRICA	**19.4**	**1.6**	**17.5**					**3.4**		
Angola	14.3	0.6	13.7	..	..	..	41.8	0.6	..	..
Benin	12.9	0.9	12.1	4.4	10.3	1.0	..	1.4	6.1	7.0
Botswana	51.4	7.1	44.3	..	..	..	22.8	4.3	..	..
Burkina Faso	7.7	0.7	7.1	3.7	19.8	0.3	44.8	0.6	..	18.4
Burundi	2.9	0.4	2.5	..	..	..	36.6	0.7	..	6.0
Cameroon	18.0	0.7	17.3	2.3	4.8	0.0	105.2	2.0	..	..
Cape Verde	34.8	13.8	21.0	..	..	..	8.4	6.4	..	3.0
Central African Republic	2.9	0.3	2.6	..	..	..	..	0.3	..	56.0
Chad	4.6	0.1	4.5	0.9	4.3	0.0	..	0.6	..	60.8
Comoros	9.1	3.1	6.0	..	..	..	..	3.4	..	55.8
Congo, Dem. Rep.	7.3	0.0	7.3	..	..	..	29.2	0.3	..	..
Congo, Rep.	..	..	21.7	1.3	2.2	0.2	..	1.9	..	..
Cote d'Ivoire	22.9	1.4	21.5	..	..	..	..	1.6	..	81.0
Djibouti	..	..	5.4	..	..	..	..	1.3	..	136.0
Equatorial Guinea	..	..	28.3	..	..	..	..	1.6	..	..
Eritrea	2.1	0.8	1.3	..	..	..	..	2.1	..	63.8
Ethiopia	2.1	0.9	1.1	4.4	35.4	0.2	58.5	0.3	..	100.0
Gabon	71.3	2.8	68.5	15.3	20.0	1.8	..	6.2	..	13.4
Gambia, The	27.1	2.8	24.3	..	..	..	24.8	5.0	..	..
Ghana	24.2	1.6	22.6	7.5	17.0	0.7	..	2.7	..	3.2
Guinea	..	..	..	7.2	23.7	0.3	59.2	0.5	..	1.6
Guinea-Bissau	10.0	0.4	9.6	..	..	..	27.6	2.3	..	70.5
Kenya	20.9	0.8	20.1	12.3	37.4	6.0	..	7.6	27.2	70.1
Lesotho	20.6	2.7	17.9	16.9	45.8	10.6	..	3.0	26.4	60.0
Liberia	..	..	7.8	..	..	..	..	0.0	..	..
Madagascar	6.1	0.7	5.5	4.9	11.9	3.0	..	0.6	21.3	36.0
Malawi	6.1	1.0	5.2	6.0	26.7	2.1	107.7	0.4	28.0	..
Mali	13.3	0.7	12.6	3.5	12.8	0.1	..	0.7	10.3	177.6
Mauritania	36.0	1.2	34.8	3.6	8.0	0.2	14.5	1.0	..	5.5
Mauritius	90.1	28.5	61.6	..	..	..	..	25.5	5.3	23.0
Mozambique	11.5	0.3	11.2	2.1	6.1	0.1	..	0.9	..	46.0
Namibia	36.4	6.7	29.8	17.4	43.5	4.5	7.3	4.4	..	35.0
Niger	..	..	3.5	..	..	..	60.1	0.3	..	71.4
Nigeria	23.5	1.2	22.3	5.1	11.7	1.8	..	5.5	..	20.6
Rwanda	3.5	0.2	3.3	1.1	6.1	0.2	61.7	1.1	..	18.2
Sao Tome and Principe	16.8	4.9	11.9	..	..	..	..	14.2	..	14.0
Senegal	27.1	2.3	24.7	19.8	35.9	7.5	..	5.4	11.4	2.0
Seychelles	107.6	24.4	83.1	..	..	..	..	34.3	..	6.0
Sierra Leone	..	..	..	..	..	..	..	0.2	..	..
Somalia	7.7	1.2	6.5	..	..	..	..	1.1	..	..
South Africa	93.6	9.9	83.7	..	..	..	..	7.8	3.9	48.2
Sudan	13.4	2.0	11.4	..	..	..	..	8.5	..	5.0
Swaziland	25.8	3.9	22.0	..	..	..	36.9	3.7	..	0.7
Tanzania	15.0	0.4	14.6	9.7	31.4	3.0	23.3	1.0	10.8	26.0
Togo	12.3	1.3	11.0	..	..	..	..	5.0	..	6.2
Uganda	7.1	0.4	6.7	3.1	18.5	0.9	12.8	5.0	16.9	..
Zambia	15.0	0.8	14.2	4.3	11.2	0.6	..	4.3	11.7	108.0
Zimbabwe	9.0	2.5	6.4	..	..	..	..	9.2	..	57.0
NORTH AFRICA	**53.0**	**10.9**	**43.0**	..	..	..	..	**10.5**		
Algeria	71.5	8.5	63.0	..	..	..	..	7.4	..	0.8
Egypt, Arab Rep.	38.8	14.6	24.3	..	..	..	..	8.1	..	0.1
Libya	..	..	65.0	..	..	..	..	4.3	..	..
Morocco	56.6	4.2	52.5	..	..	..	..	20.0	15.0	25.0
Tunisia	85.0	12.5	72.5	..	..	..	..	12.8	..	20.0

a. Data are for most recent year available during the period specified.

| | Pricing | | | | | Financing | | | | |
| | Price of 3-minute telephone calls during peak hours | | | Connection charge | | Annual investment ($ millions) | | | Committed nominal investment in telecommunication projects with private participation ($ millions) 2000–06[a] | ODA gross aid disbursements for communication ($ millions) 2006 |
Price basket for Internet ($ per month) 2006	Fixed telephone local call ($) 2000–06[a]	Cellular local call ($) 2000–06[a]	International call to US ($) 2000–06[a]	Residential telephone ($) 2000–06[a]	Mobile cellular ($) 2000–06[a]	Telephone service 2000–06[a]	Mobile communication 2000–06[a]	Telecommunications 2000–06[a]		
42.1	**0.14**	**0.77**	**0.13**	**45.0**	**18.3**					**65.6**
29.6	0.09	0.74	0.09	46.0	49.2	..	..	157.0	250.0	0.8
20.9	0.16	0.96	0.11	112.6	9.6	..	3.6	3.9	17.0	0.8
18.2	0.13	1.06	0.13	39.4	3.4	..	..	404.0	18.0	0.3
91.4	0.19	0.77	0.19	47.4	28.4	..	66.6	202.6	290.0	0.1
52.0	0.07	0.58	0.07	9.3	9.3	..	..	..	..	1.4
44.0	0.11	1.32	0.29	75.8	9.6	..	110.4	211.4	63.0	0.6
40.7	0.05	1.18	0.05	33.8	45.6	12.4	1.8	15.9	..	1.5
144.6	0.57	0.57	0.57	67.1	37.9	..	..	0.1	..	..
105.0	0.14	1.05	0.14	100.7	7.7	..	..	..	26.4	..
38.1	0.19	0.70	0.13	102.4	63.8	..	..	4.2	..	..
109.5	0.15	..	0.15	118.6	..	..	..	..	74.0	0.2
82.7	..	..	..	..	..	..	..	..	10.0	0.3
67.7	0.29	2.26	0.29	19.1	19.1	32.2	266.2	382.5	13.0	0.2
41.0	0.08	0.51	0.08	56.3	56.3	..	..	12.4	..	0.1
32.2	..	..	..	..	..	..	..	..	..	..
28.6	0.04	0.33	0.04	65.1	91.1	..	7.3	16.5	40.0	0.0
22.8	0.02	0.25	0.02	35.1	52.9	14.5	5.2	60.3	..	1.8
39.2	0.28	0.56	0.29	103.2	23.7	..	..	18.2	..	0.1
17.8	0.03	0.67	0.03	41.2	15.1	..	..	3.7	..	0.0
22.6	0.17	0.20	0.16	101.4	8.3	..	..	59.4	215.0	0.5
17.8	0.07	0.54	0.07	98.0	33.3	..	..	0.8	48.0	0.1
75.0	..	..	..	67.4	..	..	..	..	..	0.1
79.2	0.11	0.64	0.13	30.4	33.1	..	511.8	792.9	619.0	0.9
36.2	0.26	0.46	0.25	53.0	6.3	..	1.5	1.7	5.5	..
..	..	..	..	..	..	..	..	..	10.5	..
43.3	0.20	0.45	0.20	23.2	4.7	..	..	50.8	..	0.1
39.0	0.10	0.60	0.09	10.1	4.2	..	..	..	30.5	0.7
28.7	0.10	0.85	0.10	38.0	56.8	..	..	93.9	..	1.7
52.9	0.11	0.51	0.11	18.8	7.5	..	..	30.2	..	0.0
16.2	0.07	0.11	0.06	33.9	17.7	..	18.4	36.4	..	0.1
29.0	0.15	0.38	0.13	19.3	0.3	..	4.5	21.4	15.6	9.5
45.3	0.06	1.18	0.06	39.4	14.4	..	..	20.4	8.8	0.5
102.4	0.14	0.92	0.14	28.7	40.9	..	..	..	..	0.1
50.3	0.14	0.89	0.14	68.6	3.8	..	..	386.9	2,535.1	0.3
29.4	0.08	0.79	0.18	25.6	2.2	..	..	..	10.0	0.3
62.6	0.14	..	0.12	44.0	..	..	..	1.1	..	0.1
25.8	0.22	0.57	0.23	44.4	40.2	..	100.5	183.6	212.0	9.1
31.9	0.13	1.63	0.13	95.3	9.1	..	..	12.8	..	..
10.7	0.03	0.90	0.03	46.7	13.4	..	..	..	40.0	0.1
..	0.10	0.04	0.10	..	..	..	..	..	..	..
59.4	0.19	1.27	0.19	39.6	23.4	..	360.3	870.6	1,357.0	2.2
70.9	0.06	0.26	0.06	20.5	82.1	..	229.4	128.5	706.3	0.4
48.7	0.09	1.23	0.08	33.5	10.2	..	..	27.6	..	0.1
93.6	0.16	0.69	0.14	35.4	18.1	..	..	9.4	70.0	2.1
45.1	0.22	0.72	0.23	111.9	17.2	26.4	26.3	67.4	..	0.1
95.8	0.28	0.67	0.28	65.5	11.2	..	..	69.0	..	0.8
81.2	0.13	0.62	0.17	11.2	3.1	..	36.9	42.5	238.0	0.6
24.6	0.00	7.62	0.05	0.0	166.7	..	0.7	115.9	20.0	0.8
12.0	**0.05**	**0.34**	**0.02**	**38.1**	**3.8**	**..**				**48.2**
9.3	0.08	0.22	0.08	41.3	16.5	..	..	96.5	702.0	3.5
5.0	0.01	0.16	0.02	86.5	4.3	..	543.5	2,669.8	3,751.0	29.8
22.1	..	0.34	..	38.1	3.8	..	212.4	..	..	..
26.9	0.15	1.14	0.17	67.7	3.4	..	..	463.5	575.6	3.9
12.0	0.02	0.34	0.02	15.0	7.7	..	216.4	311.8	2,343.0	3.3

Table 7.4 Energy

	Electric power consumption (kWh per capita) 2000–06[a]	GDP per unit of energy use (constant 2000 PPP $ per kg of oil equivalent) 2000–06[a]	Access, demand side					
			Access to electricity			Solid fuels use		
			Total (% of total population) 2000–06[a]	Urban (% of urban population) 2000–06[a]	Rural (% of rural population) 2000–06[a]	Total (% of total population) 2000–06[a]	Urban (% of urban population) 2000–06[a]	Rural (% of rural population) 2000–06[a]
SUB-SAHARAN AFRICA								
Angola	141.0	6.1	..	..	..	..	..	..
Benin	69.4	4.0	22.0	50.9	5.6	95.6	89.5	99.1
Botswana	1,405.8	11.7	..	..	..	..	..	..
Burkina Faso	..	..	10.2	53.5	0.8	97.5	88.5	99.4
Burundi	..	..	..	..	..	..	..	..
Cameroon	196.1	5.0	45.8	76.7	16.3	82.6	67.1	97.3
Cape Verde	..	..	..	..	..	..	..	..
Central African Republic	..	..	..	..	..	..	..	..
Chad	..	..	4.3	19.9	0.3	..	..	..
Comoros	..	..	..	..	..	..	..	..
Congo, Dem. Rep.	91.1	0.9	..	..	..	..	..	..
Congo, Rep.	159.6	10.0	34.9	51.3	16.4	83.2	71.3	96.5
Côte d'Ivoire	170.3	3.8	..	..	..	..	..	..
Djibouti	..	..	..	..	..	..	..	..
Equatorial Guinea	..	..	..	..	..	..	..	..
Eritrea	..	..	..	..	..	..	..	..
Ethiopia	34.4	2.2	12.0	85.9	2.0	89.0	69.7	91.6
Gabon	999.5	10.4	75.2	90.6	31.4	34.1	16.4	84.4
Gambia, The	..	..	..	..	..	..	..	..
Ghana	265.8	2.9	44.3	77.0	20.9	91.8	82.7	98.3
Guinea	..	..	20.9	63.5	3.2	79.8	39.3	96.8
Guinea-Bissau	..	..	..	..	..	..	..	..
Kenya	138.4	2.8	13.1	51.4	3.6	87.1	46.0	97.3
Lesotho	..	..	5.7	28.1	0.8	62.1	9.5	73.5
Liberia	..	..	..	..	..	..	..	..
Madagascar	..	..	18.8	52.0	9.7	98.3	96.3	98.9
Malawi	..	..	7.5	34.0	2.5	97.8	88.7	99.5
Mali	..	..	12.8	41.3	2.7	95.9	97.6	95.3
Mauritania	..	..	23.4	50.7	2.7	70.5	51.9	84.4
Mauritius	..	..	..	..	..	..	..	..
Mozambique	450.2	1.4	11.0	29.8	1.5	96.9	91.9	99.5
Namibia	1,428.0	6.7	31.7	74.6	10.4	65.9	18.7	89.3
Niger	..	..	..	..	..	..	..	..
Nigeria	126.6	2.4	51.3	84.0	34.6	76.6	52.0	89.0
Rwanda	..	..	5.4	27.2	1.5	99.4	98.3	99.6
São Tomé and Principe	..	..	..	..	..	..	..	..
Senegal	151.0	6.0	46.4	82.1	19.0	58.7	24.3	85.2
Seychelles	..	..	..	..	..	..	..	..
Sierra Leone	..	..	..	..	..	..	..	..
Somalia	..	..	..	..	..	..	..	..
South Africa	4,847.2	3.1	..	..	..	..	..	..
Sudan	94.3	3.4	..	..	..	..	..	..
Swaziland	..	..	..	..	..	..	..	..
Tanzania	61.2	2.0	10.6	38.9	1.8	98.1	93.4	99.5
Togo	94.1	2.4	..	..	..	..	..	..
Uganda	..	..	8.4	47.5	2.6	97.4	87.8	98.8
Zambia	721.2	1.9	20.1	50.0	3.5	83.6	58.5	97.6
Zimbabwe	953.1	..	..	..	..	..	5.1	..
NORTH AFRICA			..	..	..	..	..	..
Algeria	898.6	7.0	..	..	..	..	..	..
Egypt, Arab Rep.	1,245.4	5.4	..	..	..	..	..	..
Libya	3,299.5	4.0	..	..	..	..	..	..
Morocco	643.5	7.8	..	..	..	..	..	..
Tunisia	1,193.9	7.6	..	..	..	..	..	..

a. Data are for most recent year available during the period specified.

CAPABLE STATES AND PARTNERSHIP

Quality					Financing	
Average delay for firm in obtaining electrical connection (days) 2000–06[a]	Electric power transmission and distribution losses (% of output) 2000–06[a]	Electric power outages in a typical month (number) 2000–06[a]	Firms that share or own their own generator (%) 2000–06[a]	Firms identifying electricity as major or very severe obstacle to business operation and growth (%) 2000–06[a]	Committed nominal investment in energy projects with private participation ($ millions) 2000–06[a]	ODA gross aid disbursements for energy ($ millions) 2006
						156.4
60.2	14.5	7.8	67.7	45.8	9.4	0.3
71.7	..	..	26.9	69.2	590.0	0.0
25.5	14.8	1.7	15.7	6.8	..	1.2
19.6	..	10.1	24.0	48.9	..	13.8
24.1	..	12.0	41.9	72.3	..	0.1
78.9	15.8	12.7	61.3	61.1	440.0	0.1
7.8	..	12.5	34.0	65.3	..	0.0
..	..	..	..	..	..	0.0
..	..	..	..	..	..	0.9
..	..	..	..	..	..	0.1
20.5	3.7	17.8	41.0	70.3	..	0.0
..	55.6	..	..	..	..	0.2
..	18.1	..	..	..	..	0.1
..	..	..	..	..	..	0.0
..	..	..	..	..	..	0.2
..	..	..	..	..	..	0.6
44.2	10.0	5.1	25.6	21.5	..	0.6
..	17.8	..	..	..	..	0.0
63.9	..	23.8	63.9	78.1	..	0.2
..	14.4	..	..	..	590.0	1.7
16.1	..	33.9	59.9	83.6	..	0.0
20.5	..	9.2	68.4	74.1	..	0.0
51.3	17.8	..	70.9	48.2	116.7	20.9
51.4	..	..	26.1	35.6	..	0.1
..	..	..	..	..	..	0.0
58.0	..	..	21.5	41.3	..	2.9
98.5	..	76.9	49.1	60.4	..	0.2
35.6	..	..	45.3	24.2	..	4.1
7.5	..	3.7	28.6	28.9	..	0.4
23.2	..	..	39.5	12.7	..	0.0
..	12.3	..	..	..	5.8	35.4
9.2	18.4	1.7	12.8	6.5	1.0	1.0
20.6	..	20.7	24.8	21.6	..	1.6
..	24.0	..	..	..	1129.0	2.6
18.2	..	13.7	58.0	55.0	1.6	0.2
..	..	..	..	..	50.0	0.1
13.2	30.1	..	62.5	30.7	93.3	2.7
..	..	..	..	..	..	0.4
..	..	..	..	..	..	0.1
7.3	6.3	..	9.5	9.0	9.9	11.3
..	15.7	..	..	..	..	0.5
16.9	..	2.5	36.8	12.4	..	0.0
44.3	26.9	12.0	45.7	88.4	28.4	13.3
..	46.0	..	..	..	590.0	0.0
33.0	..	11.0	28.9	84.2	11.8	10.3
142.4	4.7	..	38.2	39.6	3.0	2.3
..	7.2	..	..	..	..	0.2
						306.1
124.9	13.2	..	29.5	11.5	2320.0	0.3
167.4	15.8	..	26.7	27.4	678.0	181.4
..	13.2	..	..	..	..	..
7.5	17.9	..	18.1	9.3	360.0	121.7
..	12.3	..	..	..	30.0	0.9

Table 7.5 Financial sector infrastructure

	International Foreign currency sovereign ratings		Macroeconomy Gross national savings (% of GDP) 2006[a]	Money and quasi money (M2) (% of GDP) 2006[a]	Real interest rate (%) 2006[a]
	Long-term 2008	Short-term 2008			
SUB-SAHARAN AFRICA			**9.0**	**35.6**	
Angola	..	..	37.0	13.9	4.2
Benin	B	B	..	28.2	..
Botswana	..	..	53.3	30.5	0.7
Burkina Faso	..	..	6.3	19.4	..
Burundi	..	..	..	33.6	14.1
Cameroon	B	B	18.9	17.0	11.0
Cape Verde	B+	B	26.8	76.0	4.4
Central African Republic	..	..	11.7	16.3	10.6
Chad	..	..	20.4	9.5	8.6
Comoros	..	..	4.9	20.8	8.3
Congo, Dem. Rep.	..	..	8.9	8.7	..
Congo, Rep.	..	..	43.0	13.9	-2.7
Côte d'Ivoire	..	..	14.7	24.2	..
Djibouti	..	..	20.7	75.5	..
Equatorial Guinea	..	..	46.2	6.7	-3.4
Eritrea	..	..	8.7	134.6	..
Ethiopia	..	..	15.1	39.2	-4.1
Gabon	BB–	B	41.3	18.2	6.9
Gambia, The	..	..	10.0	48.5	27.1
Ghana	B+	B	27.4	29.2	..
Guinea	BB–	B	11.8	..	..
Guinea-Bissau	..	..	22.7	33.6	..
Kenya	..	..	12.5	36.3	3.9
Lesotho	B–	B	27.3	30.1	7.7
Liberia	B–	B	..	21.0	5.8
Madagascar	..	..	16.0	19.5	16.4
Malawi	..	..	15.5	13.6	12.1
Mali	B	B	13.0	28.3	..
Mauritania	BBB–	F3	28.7	..	-4.5
Mauritius	..	..	19.0	100.3	16.3
Mozambique	BB–	B	3.1	27.0	11.9
Namibia	B–	B	42.2	44.8	1.9
Niger	..	..	..	14.2	..
Nigeria	..	..	..	16.9	-2.2
Rwanda	..	..	13.8	..	2.6
São Tomé and Principe	..	..	..	45.5	7.9
Senegal	..	..	18.3	34.0	..
Seychelles	BBB+	F2	9.4	116.1	7.7
Sierra Leone	..	..	9.5	19.1	11.1
Somalia	..	..	..	..	..
South Africa	..	..	13.9	60.0	4.0
Sudan	..	..	10.3	20.0	..
Swaziland	B	B	14.5	20.7	0.7
Tanzania	..	..	10.7	24.2	10.8
Togo	..	..	..	30.1	..
Uganda	..	..	12.9	19.7	9.2
Zambia	..	..	23.3	17.9	9.4
Zimbabwe	BB+	B	..	..	..
NORTH AFRICA			**14.6**	**66.3**	
Algeria	BBB–	F3	..	49.5	-2.5
Egypt, Arab Rep.	..	..	22.0	91.0	4.9
Libya	..	..	..	27.0	-6.5
Morocco	..	..	34.5	89.5	..
Tunisia	..	..	25.4	57.5	..

a. Data are consolidated for regional security markets where they exist.

Domestic credit to private sector (% of GDP) 2006[a]	Intermediation		Capital markets[a]		
	Interest rate spread (lending rate minus deposit rate) 2006[a]	Ratio of bank non-performing loans to total gross loans (%) 2006[a]	Listed domestic companies, total 2006[a]	Market capitalization of listed companies (% of GDP) 2006[a]	Turnover ratio for traded stocks (%) 2006[a]
65.1					
7.5	15.0	..	..	..	..
17.2	..	..	..	..	..
18.8	7.6	..	18.0	35.9	2.3
17.9	..	..	..	..	..
24.6	..	..	..	..	..
9.2	11.0	..	..	..	..
48.4	..	..	..	..	..
6.6	11.0	..	..	..	..
2.6	11.0	..	..	..	..
7.9	8.0	..	..	..	..
2.9	..	..	..	..	..
2.1	11.0	..	..	..	..
14.3	..	..	40.0	24.1	3.3
20.2	..	..	..	..	..
2.8	11.0	..	..	..	..
29.0	..	..	..	..	..
23.8	3.4	..	..	..	..
9.3	11.0	11.1	..	..	..
15.6	17.1	..	..	..	..
17.8	..	7.9	32.0	25.4	2.1
..	..	..	..	..	..
3.9	..	..	..	..	..
25.8	8.5	..	51.0	49.9	14.6
8.9	7.6	1.0	..	..	..
8.6	..	..	..	..	..
10.2	7.2	..	..	..	..
8.7	21.3	..	10.0	18.6	3.5
17.2	..	..	..	..	..
..	..	..	..	..	..
78.0	11.5	..	41.0	56.7	4.4
13.8	8.2	3.7	..	..	..
61.7	4.9	2.9	9.0	8.3	3.8
8.5	..	..	..	..	..
13.2	7.2	..	202.0	22.3	13.6
..	..	..	..	..	..
33.1	..	..	..	..	..
22.9	..	16.0	..	..	..
36.9	7.4	..	..	..	..
4.5	13.6	..	..	..	..
..	..	..	..	..	..
160.8	4.0	1.2	401.0	280.4	48.8
0.1	..	..	..	..	..
22.5	6.2	2.0	6.0	7.2	0.0
11.0	8.8	..	6.0	3.8	2.1
16.8	..	..	..	..	..
7.9	9.6	2.8	5.0	1.2	5.2
9.6	12.8	..	14.0	10.9	2.1
..	293.1	..	80.0	..	6.2
37.7					
12.4	6.3	..	..	..	..
55.3	6.6	24.7	603.0	87.0	54.8
15.7	3.8	..	..	..	..
58.1	..	10.9	65.0	75.5	35.3
63.7	..	19.2	48.0	14.4	14.3

Table 8.1 Education

| | Literacy rate % | | | | | | Primary education | | | | | | |
| | Youth (ages 15–24) | | | Adult (ages 15 and older) | | | Gross enrollment ratio (% of relevant age group) | | | Net enrollment ratio (% of relevant age group) | | | |
	Total 2000–06[a]	Male 2000–06[a]	Female 2000–06[a]	Total 2000–06[a]	Male 2000–06[a]	Female 2000–06[a]	Total 2006	Male 2006	Female 2006	Total 2006	Male 2006	Female 2006	Student-teacher ratio 2006
SUB-SAHARAN AFRICA													
Angola	72	84	63	67	83	54	..	..	..	..	..	..	..
Benin	45	59	33	35	48	23	96	105	87	80	87	73	44
Botswana	94	92	96	81	80	82	..	..	..	..	..	..	..
Burkina Faso	33	40	26	24	31	17	60	66	54	47	52	42	46
Burundi	73	77	70	59	67	52	103	108	98	75	76	73	54
Cameroon	..	..	..	68	77	60	107	117	98	..	..	..	45
Cape Verde	96	96	97	81	88	76	106	108	103	88	88	87	25
Central African Republic	59	70	47	49	65	33	61	72	49	46	53	38	..
Chad	38	56	23	26	41	13	..	..	..	..	..	..	..
Comoros	..	..	..	..	..	..	..	..	..	..	..	..	..
Congo, Dem. Rep.	70	78	63	67	81	54	..	..	..	..	..	..	..
Congo, Rep.	97	98	97	85	91	79	108	113	102	55	58	52	55
Côte d'Ivoire	61	71	52	49	61	39	71	79	62	..	..	..	46
Djibouti	..	..	..	..	..	..	44	49	39	38	42	34	34
Equatorial Guinea	95	95	95	87	93	80	..	..	..	..	..	..	..
Eritrea	..	..	..	..	..	..	62	69	56	47	50	43	47
Ethiopia	50	62	39	36	50	23	83	90	77	65	68	62	59
Gabon	96	97	95	84	88	80	..	..	..	..	..	..	..
Gambia, The	..	..	..	..	..	..	74	71	77	62	59	64	35
Ghana	71	76	65	58	66	50	92	92	91	64	63	64	35
Guinea	47	59	34	29	43	18	88	96	81	72	77	66	44
Guinea-Bissau	..	..	..	..	..	..	..	..	..	..	..	..	..
Kenya	80	80	81	74	78	70	106	107	104	75	75	76	..
Lesotho	..	..	..	82	74	90	114	115	114	72	71	74	40
Liberia	67	65	69	52	58	46	91	96	87	39	40	39	19
Madagascar	70	73	68	71	77	65	139	142	137	96	96	96	48
Malawi	..	..	..	..	..	..	119	117	121	91	88	94	..
Mali	..	..	..	24	33	16	80	90	71	61	67	54	56
Mauritania	61	68	55	51	60	43	102	99	104	79	78	82	41
Mauritius	95	94	95	84	88	81	102	102	102	95	94	96	22
Mozambique	..	..	..	..	..	..	105	113	97	76	79	73	67
Namibia	92	91	93	85	87	83	107	107	107	76	74	79	31
Niger	37	52	23	29	43	15	51	58	43	43	50	37	40
Nigeria	84	87	81	69	78	60	..	..	..	..	..	..	..
Rwanda	78	79	77	65	71	60	140	137	142	..	..	..	66
São Tomé and Principe	95	96	95	85	92	78	128	130	126	96	97	95	31
Senegal	49	58	41	39	51	29	80	81	79	71	71	70	39
Seychelles	99	99	99	92	91	92	..	..	..	..	..	..	..
Sierra Leone	48	60	37	35	47	24	..	..	..	..	..	..	..
Somalia	..	..	..	..	..	..	..	..	..	23	..	..	..
South Africa	..	..	..	..	..	..	..	..	..	..	..	..	..
Sudan	77	85	71	61	71	52	66	71	61	54	..	..	34
Swaziland	88	87	90	80	81	78	..	..	..	..	..	..	..
Tanzania	78	81	76	69	78	62	110	112	109	98	98	97	52
Togo	74	84	64	53	69	38	102	110	95	80	86	75	38
Uganda	77	83	71	67	77	58	117	116	117	..	..	..	49
Zambia	..	..	..	..	..	..	117	118	116	92	90	94	51
Zimbabwe	98	97	98	89	93	86	101	102	101	88	87	88	38
NORTH AFRICA													
Algeria	90	94	86	70	80	60	110	114	106	95	96	94	24
Egypt, Arab Rep.	85	90	79	71	83	59	103	107	100	94	96	92	26
Libya	98	100	96	84	93	75	110	113	108	..	..	..	..
Morocco	70	81	60	52	66	40	106	112	100	88	91	85	27
Tunisia	94	96	92	74	83	65	108	110	107	96	96	97	19

a. Data are for most recent year available during the period specified.

CAPABLE STATES AND PARTNERSHIP

| Secondary education | | | | | | | Tertiary education | | | Public spending on education (%) | |
| Gross enrollment ratio (% of relevant age group) | | | Net enrollment ratio (% of relevant age group) | | | Student-teacher ratio | Gross enrollment ratio (% of relevant age group) | | | Share of government expenditure | Share of GDP |
Total 2006	Male 2006	Female 2006	Total 2006	Male 2006	Female 2006	2006	Total 2005	Male 2005	Female 2005	2000–06[a]	2000–06[a]
..	..	..	..	..	..	..	..	..	..	..	3.0
..	..	..	..	..	..	..	5	..	..	17.0	3.0
..	..	..	..	..	..	..	..	..	..	22.0	11.0
15	17	12	12	14	10	30	2	3	1	15.0	5.0
14	16	12	..	..	..	..	2	3	1	18.0	5.0
24	26	21	..	..	..	16	7	8	6	17.0	2.0
80	75	86	59	56	63	19	8	8	8	16.0	7.0
..	..	..	..	..	..	..	1	2	0	..	..
..	..	..	..	..	..	..	..	..	..	10.0	2.0
..	..	..	..	..	..	..	..	..	..	24.0	4.0
..	..	..	..	..	..	..	..	..	..	..	..
..	..	..	..	..	..	..	..	..	..	8.0	2.0
..	..	..	..	..	..	..	..	..	..	22.0	5.0
22	27	18	..	..	..	31	2	3	2	22.0	8.0
..	..	..	..	..	..	..	..	..	..	4.0	1.0
31	39	23	25	30	20	54	..	..	..	..	5.0
27	34	21	24	29	19	..	2	4	1	18.0	6.0
..	..	..	..	..	..	..	..	..	..	..	4.0
45	47	43	38	40	37	24	..	..	..	9.0	2.0
46	50	42	38	39	36	20	5	6	3	..	5.0
35	45	24	28	35	20	..	5	8	2	26.0	2.0
..	..	..	..	..	..	..	..	..	..	..	..
50	52	49	42	43	42	..	..	..	..	18.0	7.0
37	33	41	24	19	29	25	4	3	4	30.0	13.0
..	..	..	..	..	..	..	..	..	..	..	..
24	24	23	17	17	18	24	3	3	3	25.0	3.0
29	32	27	24	25	23	..	..	..	..	..	6.0
28	35	21	..	..	..	..	..	..	..	17.0	4.0
25	27	23	16	16	15	26	4	5	2	10.0	2.0
..	..	..	..	..	..	..	17	16	18	13.0	4.0
16	18	13	4	4	4	36	..	..	..	23.0	4.0
57	53	61	35	30	40	25	6	6	5	21.0	7.0
11	14	9	9	12	7	30	1	2	1	18.0	2.0
..	..	..	..	..	..	..	..	..	..	..	..
..	..	..	..	..	..	..	..	..	..	12.0	4.0
46	44	47	..	..	..	22	..	..	..	..	..
24	27	20	20	23	18	..	..	..	..	26.0	5.0
..	..	..	..	..	..	..	..	..	..	13.0	5.0
..	..	..	..	..	..	..	..	..	..	..	5.0
..	..	..	..	..	..	..	..	..	..	..	..
..	..	..	..	..	..	..	15	14	17	18.0	5.0
34	34	33	19	..	..	22	..	..	..	..	..
..	..	..	..	..	..	..	4	4	4	..	6.0
..	..	..	..	..	..	..	..	..	..	..	..
..	..	..	..	..	..	..	..	..	..	14.0	3.0
..	..	..	16	17	15	..	..	..	..	18.0	5.0
..	..	..	..	..	..	..	..	..	..	15.0	2.0
40	41	38	37	38	36	..	..	..	..	..	5.0
..	..	..	..	..	..	..	22	19	24	..	..
..	..	..	..	..	..	..	..	..	..	12.0	..
94	86	101	..	..	..	..	..	..	..	..	..
52	..	..	..	..	..	..	12	13	11	27.0	7.0
85	81	89	..	..	..	19	31	26	37	21.0	7.0

Table 8.2 Health

	Mortality								Diseases	
	Life expectancy at birth (years)			Under-five mortality rate (per 1,000)			Infant mortality rate (per 1,000 live births)	Maternal mortality ratio, modeled estimate (per 100,000 live births)	Prevalence of HIV (% of ages 15–49)	Incidence of tuberculosis (per 100,000 people)	Deaths due to malaria (per 100,000 people)
	Total 2006	Male 2006	Female 2006	Total 2000–06[b]	Male 2000–06[b]	Female 2000–06[b]	2006	2000–06[b]	2007	2006	2000–06[b]
SUB-SAHARAN AFRICA	**50.5**	**49.5**	**51.5**	**157**			**94**	**902**	**5.0**	**368**	
Angola	42.4	40.8	44.0	260	276	243	154	1,400	2.1	285	354
Benin	56.2	55.1	57.4	148	152	153	88	840	1.2	90	177
Botswana	49.8	49.5	50.0	124	123	109	90	380	23.9	551	15
Burkina Faso	51.9	50.4	53.5	204	193	191	122	700	1.6	249	292
Burundi	49.0	47.7	50.5	181	196	184	109	1,100	2.0	367	143
Cameroon	50.3	49.9	50.7	149	156	143	87	1,000	5.1	192	108
Cape Verde	71.0	68.0	74.2	34	38	35	25	210	..	168	22
Central African Republic	44.4	43.0	45.8	175	201	185	115	980	6.3	345	137
Chad	50.6	49.3	52.0	209	212	188	124	1,500	3.5	299	207
Comoros	63.2	62.2	64.4	68	76	64	51	400	0.1	44	80
Congo, Dem. Rep.	46.1	44.8	47.5	205	217	192	129	1,100	..	392	224
Congo, Rep.	54.8	53.5	56.1	127	113	103	80	740	3.5	403	78
Côte d'Ivoire	48.1	47.2	49.0	127	225	162	90	810	3.9	420	76
Djibouti	54.5	53.3	55.7	130	131	120	86	650	3.1	809	..
Equatorial Guinea	51.1	49.9	52.4	206	213	195	124	680	3.4	256	152
Eritrea	57.3	55.0	59.8	74	89	75	48	450	1.3	94	74
Ethiopia	52.5	51.2	53.8	123	175	158	78	720	2.1	378	198
Gabon	56.7	56.3	57.2	91	102	80	60	520	5.9	354	80
Gambia, The	59.1	58.2	60.1	113	129	115	84	690	0.9	257	52
Ghana	59.7	59.3	60.1	120	113	111	76	560	1.9	203	70
Guinea	55.5	54.0	57.2	161	160	150	98	910	1.6	265	200
Guinea-Bissau	46.2	44.7	47.8	200	212	194	119	1,100	1.8	219	150
Kenya	53.4	52.4	54.6	121	129	110	79	560	..	385	63
Lesotho	42.9	42.9	42.9	132	87	76	102	960	23.2	635	84
Liberia	45.3	44.4	46.2	235	249	220	157	1,200	1.7	331	201
Madagascar	59.0	57.3	60.8	115	128	117	72	510	0.1	248	184
Malawi	47.6	47.4	47.9	120	179	172	76	1,100	11.9	377	275
Mali	53.8	51.6	56.1	217	230	208	119	970	1.5	280	454
Mauritania	63.7	62.0	65.6	125	134	115	78	820	0.8	316	108
Mauritius	73.2	69.9	76.6	14	17	14	13	15	1.7	23	..
Mozambique	42.5	41.9	43.0	138	154	150	96	520	12.5	443	232
Namibia	52.5	52.0	53.0	61	70	57	45	210	15.3	767	52
Niger	56.4	57.3	55.5	253	256	262	148	1,800	0.8	174	469
Nigeria	46.8	46.3	47.3	191	198	195	99	1,100	3.1	311	141
Rwanda	45.6	44.0	47.3	160	211	195	98	1,300	2.8	397	200
São Tomé and Principe	65.2	63.4	67.1	96	122	114	63	..	..	103	80
Senegal	62.8	60.8	64.8	116	141	132	60	980	1.0	270	72
Seychelles	72.2	68.9	75.7	13	14	13	12	..	..	33	..
Sierra Leone	42.2	40.7	43.9	270	296	269	159	2,100	1.7	517	312
Somalia	47.7	46.5	48.9	146	222	228	90	1,400	0.5	218	81
South Africa	50.7	49.0	52.5	69	72	62	56	400	18.1	940	..
Sudan	58.1	56.7	59.6	89	98	84	61	450	1.4	242	70
Swaziland	40.8	41.6	39.9	164	163	150	112	390	26.1	1,155	..
Tanzania	51.9	50.8	53.0	118	134	117	74	950	6.2	312	130
Togo	58.2	56.5	60.0	108	151	128	69	510	3.3	389	47
Uganda	50.7	50.1	51.4	134	144	132	78	550	5.4	355	152
Zambia	41.7	41.5	41.9	182	190	173	102	830	15.2	553	141
Zimbabwe	42.7	43.3	42.1	105	136	121	68	880	15.3	557	1
NORTH AFRICA	**71.5**	**69.5**	**73.5**	**35**			**30**	**159**		**44**	
Algeria	72.0	70.6	73.4	38	41	39	33	180	0.1	56	..
Egypt, Arab Rep.	71.0	68.8	73.3	35	36	36	29	130	..	24	..
Libya	74.0	71.5	76.6	18	20	19	17	97	..	18	..
Morocco	70.7	68.6	72.9	37	47	38	34	240	..	93	..
Tunisia	73.6	71.7	75.6	23	29	22	19	100	0.1	25	..

a. Diptheria, pertusis, and tetanus toxoid.
b. Data are for most recent year available during the period specified.

Child immunization rate (% of children ages 12–23 months)		Malnutrition (% of children under-five)		Births attended by skilled health staff (% of total)	Contraceptive prevalence rate (% of women ages 15–49)	Children sleeping under insecticide-treated bednets (% of children under age 5)	Tuberculosis cases detected under DOTS (% of estimated cases)	Tuberculosis treatment success rate (% of registered cases)	Children under age 5 with fever receiving any antimalarial drugs within 24 hrs (%)
Measles 2006	DPT[a] 2006	Stunting 2000–06[b]	Underweight 2000–06[b]	2000–06[b]	2000–06[b]	2000–06[b]	2006	2000–06[b]	2000–06[b]
72	**73**								
48	44	50.8	27.5	44.7	6.2	2.3	75.8	72.2	63.0
89	93	39.1	21.5	78.7	17.2	20.1	85.9	86.7	54.0
90	97	29.1	10.7	94.2	44.4	..	80.2	69.9	..
88	95	43.1	35.2	53.5	17.4	9.6	17.2	71.5	48.0
75	74	63.1	38.9	33.6	9.1	8.3	23.5	78.5	30.0
73	81	35.4	15.1	63.0	29.2	13.1	91.2	73.7	57.8
65	72	..	..	..	..	..	33.3	64.4	..
35	40	44.6	21.8	53.4	19.0	15.1	68.6	64.9	57.0
23	20	44.8	33.9	14.4	2.8	0.6	..	69.0	44.0
66	69	46.9	25.0	61.8	25.7	9.3	41.6	91.4	62.7
73	77	44.4	33.6	60.7	31.4	0.7	60.6	84.9	52.0
66	79	31.2	11.8	86.2	44.3	..	51.2	28.1	48.0
73	77	34.0	20.2	56.8	12.9	5.9	37.1	75.0	36.0
67	72	38.8	25.6	92.9	17.8	1.3	39.6	79.6	9.5
51	33	42.6	15.7	64.6	..	0.7	..	51.3	48.6
95	97	43.7	34.5	28.3	8.0	4.2	34.7	88.1	3.6
63	72	50.7	34.6	5.7	14.7	1.5	27.0	78.0	3.0
55	38	26.3	8.8	85.5	32.7	..	57.5	46.4	..
95	95	24.1	15.4	56.8	17.5	49.0	63.9	86.7	62.6
85	84	35.6	18.8	49.7	16.7	21.8	37.6	72.6	60.8
67	71	39.3	22.5	38.1	9.1	0.3	54.6	72.1	43.5
60	77	36.1	21.9	38.8	10.3	39.0	64.3	69.2	45.7
77	80	35.8	16.5	41.6	39.3	4.6	70.0	82.4	26.5
85	83	45.2	16.6	55.4	37.3	..	79.1	72.9	..
94	88	45.3	22.8	50.9	10.0	2.6	55.1	76.0	..
59	61	52.8	36.8	51.3	27.1	0.2	73.2	74.5	34.2
85	99	52.5	18.4	53.6	41.7	23.0	42.0	73.2	23.9
86	85	42.7	30.1	40.6	8.1	8.4	25.5	75.3	38.0
62	68	39.5	30.4	56.9	8.0	2.1	34.5	54.6	33.4
99	97	..	..	99.2	75.9	..	67.1	86.4	..
77	72	47.0	21.2	47.7	16.5	..	46.9	79.4	15.0
63	74	29.5	20.3	75.5	43.7	3.4	82.9	74.6	14.4
47	39	54.8	39.9	17.7	11.2	7.4	49.5	74.0	33.0
62	54	43.0	27.2	36.3	12.6	1.2	20.2	74.9	33.9
95	99	51.7	18.0	38.6	17.4	5.0	27.4	82.9	12.3
85	99	35.2	10.1	80.7	30.3	41.7	..	..	24.7
80	89	20.1	14.5	51.9	11.8	7.1	..	74.4	26.8
99	99	..	..	..	..	..	..	92.3	..
67	64	38.4	24.7	43.2	5.3	5.3	35.0	85.6	51.9
35	35	42.1	32.8	33.0	14.6	9.2	83.0	88.6	7.9
85	99	..	..	92.0	60.3	..	71.2	71.4	..
73	78	47.6	38.4	49.2	7.6	27.6	30.0	82.2	54.2
57	68	36.6	9.1	74.0	48.1	0.1	48.9	42.5	25.5
93	90	44.4	16.7	43.4	26.4	16.0	46.4	82.2	58.2
83	87	..	..	62.4	16.8	38.4	19.4	70.8	47.7
89	80	44.8	19.0	42.1	23.7	9.7	44.3	73.2	61.8
84	80	52.5	23.3	43.4	34.2	22.8	52.5	83.9	57.9
90	90	35.8	14.0	79.7	60.2	2.9	42.4	67.8	4.7
96	**97**					**..**			**..**
91	95	21.6	10.2	95.2	61.4	..	101.6	86.9	..
98	98	23.8	5.4	74.2	59.2	..	59.3	78.5	..
98	98	..	..	..	..	..	156.3	68.6	..
95	97	23.1	9.9	62.6	63.0	..	94.9	81.3	..
98	99	..	..	89.9	62.6	..	81.4	90.0	..

Table 8.2 Health (continued)

	Water and sanitation						Human resources		
	Population with sustainable access to an improved water source (%)			Population with sustainable access to improved sanitation (%)			Health workers (per 1,000 people)		
	Total 2006	Urban 2006	Rural 2006	Total 2006	Urban 2006	Rural 2006	Physicians 2005	Nurses and midwives 2005	Community workers 2005
SUB-SAHARAN AFRICA	**58**	**81**	**46**	**31**	**42**	**24**			
Angola	51	62	39	50	79	16	0.1	1.4	..
Benin	65	78	57	30	59	11	0.0	0.8	0.0
Botswana	96	100	90	47	60	30	0.4	2.7	..
Burkina Faso	72	97	66	13	41	6	0.1	0.5	0.1
Burundi	71	84	70	41	44	41	0.0	0.2	0.1
Cameroon	70	88	47	51	58	42	0.2	1.6	..
Cape Verde	..	..	..	..	..	..	0.5	0.9	0.1
Central African Republic	66	90	51	31	40	25	0.1	0.4	0.1
Chad	48	71	40	9	23	4	0.0	0.3	0.0
Comoros	85	91	81	35	49	26	0.2	0.7	0.1
Congo, Dem. Rep.	46	82	29	31	42	25	0.1	0.5	..
Congo, Rep.	71	95	35	20	19	21	0.2	1.0	0.0
Côte d'Ivoire	81	98	66	24	38	12	0.1	0.6	..
Djibouti	92	98	54	67	76	11	0.2	0.4	0.0
Equatorial Guinea	43	45	42	51	60	46	0.3	0.5	2.5
Eritrea	60	74	57	5	14	3	0.1	0.6	..
Ethiopia	42	96	31	11	27	8	0.0	0.2	0.3
Gabon	87	95	47	36	37	30	0.3	5.0	..
Gambia, The	86	91	81	52	50	55	0.1	1.3	0.7
Ghana	80	90	71	10	15	6	0.2	0.9	..
Guinea	70	91	59	19	33	12	0.1	0.5	0.0
Guinea-Bissau	57	82	47	33	48	26	0.1	0.7	2.9
Kenya	57	85	49	42	19	48	0.1	1.2	..
Lesotho	78	93	74	36	43	34	0.1	0.6	..
Liberia	64	72	52	32	49	7	0.0	0.3	0.0
Madagascar	47	76	36	12	18	10	0.3	0.3	0.0
Malawi	76	96	72	60	51	62	0.0	0.6	..
Mali	60	86	48	45	59	39	0.1	0.6	0.0
Mauritania	60	70	54	24	44	10	0.1	0.6	0.1
Mauritius	100	100	100	94	95	94	1.1	3.7	0.2
Mozambique	42	71	26	31	53	19	0.0	0.3	..
Namibia	93	99	90	35	66	18	0.3	3.1	..
Niger	42	91	32	7	27	3	0.0	0.2	..
Nigeria	47	65	30	30	35	25	0.3	1.7	0.9
Rwanda	65	82	61	23	34	20	0.1	0.4	1.4
São Tomé and Principe	86	88	83	24	29	18	0.5	1.9	2.3
Senegal	77	93	65	28	54	9	0.1	0.3	..
Seychelles	..	100	..	..	..	100	1.5	7.9	..
Sierra Leone	53	83	32	11	20	5	0.0	0.5	0.1
Somalia	29	63	10	23	51	7	..	..	..
South Africa	93	100	82	59	66	49	0.8	4.1	0.2
Sudan	70	78	64	35	50	24	0.3	0.9	0.2
Swaziland	60	87	51	50	64	46	0.2	6.3	4.3
Tanzania	55	81	46	33	31	34	0.0	0.4	..
Togo	59	86	40	12	24	3	0.0	0.4	0.1
Uganda	64	90	60	33	29	34	0.1	0.7	..
Zambia	58	90	41	52	55	51	0.1	2.0	..
Zimbabwe	81	98	72	46	63	37	0.2	0.7	0.0
NORTH AFRICA	**92**	**96**	**87**	**76**	**90**	**60**			
Algeria	85	87	81	94	98	87	1.1	2.2	0.0
Egypt, Arab Rep.	98	99	98	66	85	52	2.4	3.4	..
Libya	..	..	..	97	97	96	1.3	4.8	..
Morocco	83	100	58	72	85	54	0.5	0.8	..
Tunisia	94	99	84	85	96	64	1.3	2.9	..

a. Diptheria, pertusis, and tetanus toxoid.
b. Data are for most recent year available during the period specified.

CAPABLE STATES AND PARTNERSHIP

	Expenditure on health					
	Share of GDP (%)			Share of total health expenditure (%)		Out-of-pocket (% of private expenditure on health)	Health expenditure per capita ($)
Total 2005	Public 2005	Private 2005	Public 2005	Private 2005	2005	2005
6.0	2.6	3.4	43.1	56.8	46.6	49.4
1.8	1.5	0.3	81.5	18.5	100.0	36.0
5.4	3.0	2.4	55.6	44.4	99.9	28.0
8.3	4.5	2.5	78.4	21.6	27.7	431.1
6.7	4.0	2.7	59.5	40.5	94.2	27.0
3.4	1.0	2.4	28.6	71.4	100.0	3.0
5.2	1.5	3.7	28.0	72.0	94.6	49.0
5.6	4.6	1.0	81.8	18.2	99.7	114.0
4.0	1.5	2.5	37.5	62.5	95.3	13.0
3.7	1.5	2.2	39.8	60.2	96.2	22.0
3.0	1.6	1.4	53.3	46.7	100.0	14.0
4.2	1.5	2.7	34.6	65.4	100.0	5.0
1.9	0.9	1.0	47.1	52.9	100.0	31.0
3.9	0.8	3.1	21.5	78.5	87.8	34.0
6.9	4.5	1.7	75.8	24.2	98.4	61.2
1.7	1.3	0.4	78.9	21.1	73.6	211.0
3.7	1.7	2.0	44.9	55.1	100.0	8.0
4.9	3.0	1.9	61.0	39.0	80.6	6.0
4.1	3.0	1.1	74.0	26.0	100.0	276.0
5.2	3.4	1.8	65.4	34.6	70.3	14.8
6.2	2.1	4.1	34.1	65.9	79.1	30.0
5.6	0.7	4.9	11.9	88.1	99.5	21.0
5.2	1.7	3.5	31.9	68.1	85.7	10.0
4.5	2.1	2.4	46.6	53.4	80.0	24.0
5.5	8.5	0.9	56.1	43.9	68.9	40.8
6.4	4.4	2.0	68.2	31.8	98.7	10.0
3.2	2.0	1.2	62.5	37.5	52.6	9.0
12.2	8.7	3.5	71.3	28.7	30.6	19.0
5.8	2.9	2.9	50.6	49.4	99.5	28.0
2.7	1.7	1.0	63.2	36.8	100.0	17.0
4.3	2.2	2.1	51.5	48.5	81.4	218.0
4.3	2.7	1.6	63.6	36.4	40.5	14.0
5.3	3.5	1.8	65.2	34.8	15.5	165.0
3.8	1.9	1.9	50.5	49.5	85.2	9.0
3.9	1.2	2.7	30.9	69.1	90.4	27.0
7.2	4.1	3.1	56.9	43.1	36.9	18.6
9.8	8.3	1.5	84.8	15.2	100.0	49.0
5.4	1.7	3.7	31.7	68.3	90.3	38.0
6.8	4.9	1.9	72.2	27.8	62.5	557.0
3.7	1.9	1.8	51.5	48.5	100.0	8.0
..	..	..	..	..	..	..
8.7	3.6	5.1	41.7	58.3	17.4	437.0
3.8	1.4	2.4	37.6	62.4	98.3	29.0
6.3	4.0	2.3	64.1	35.9	41.7	146.0
5.1	2.9	2.2	56.9	43.1	83.4	17.0
5.3	1.4	3.9	25.5	74.5	84.7	18.0
7.0	2.0	5.0	28.6	71.4	51.8	22.0
5.6	2.7	2.9	49.0	51.0	71.5	36.0
8.1	3.6	4.5	44.8	55.2	52.0	21.0
4.7	2.4	2.4	50.0	50.0	88.7	97.7
3.5	2.6	0.9	75.3	24.7	94.6	108.0
6.1	2.3	3.8	38.0	62.0	94.9	78.0
3.2	2.2	1.0	69.5	30.5	100.0	223.0
5.3	1.9	3.4	36.6	63.4	76.0	89.0
5.5	2.4	3.1	44.3	55.7	82.2	158.5

Table 9.1 Rural development

	Rural population (%)			Rural population below the national poverty line (%)			
	Share of total population 2006	Annual growth 2006	Rural population density (rural population per sq. km of arable land) 2000–06[a]	Surveys 1990–1999		Surveys 2000–2006	
				Year[a]	Percent	Year[a]	Percent
SUB-SAHARAN AFRICA	**64.5**	**1.7**					
Angola	45.1	0.9	224.4	..	..	..	..
Benin	59.6	2.5	185.2	1999	33.0	..	..
Botswana	41.9	−0.6	207.9			..	..
Burkina Faso	81.3	2.5	235.2	1998	61.1	2003	52.4
Burundi	90.2	3.6	732.5	1998	64.6		
Cameroon	44.9	0.3	136.4	1996	59.6	2001	49.9
Cape Verde	41.9	0.5	469.3				
Central African Republic	61.7	1.5	134.4	..	..	..	..
Chad	74.2	2.5	180.4	1996	67.0	..	..
Comoros	72.0	2.1	541.2				
Congo, Dem. Rep.	67.3	2.3	595.3	..	..	..	..
Congo, Rep.	39.4	1.2	290.2	..	..	2005	64.8
Côte d'Ivoire	52.5	0.5	282.5	..	..	..	..
Djibouti	13.5	−1.2	11,178.5	..	..	..	..
Equatorial Guinea	60.9	2.1	227.5				
Eritrea	80.2	3.0	572.8	..	..	..	..
Ethiopia	83.6	2.2	480.9	1996	47.0	2000	45.0
Gabon	15.9	−1.4	65.1	..	..	..	..
Gambia, The	45.3	1.0	213.0	1998	61.0	2003	63.0
Ghana	51.5	0.7	281.1	1997	49.6	2005	39.2
Guinea	66.5	1.2	502.6	..	..	..	..
Guinea-Bissau	70.3	2.9	374.7	..	..	..	..
Kenya	79.0	2.3	536.3	1997	52.9	2005	49.1
Lesotho	76.0	−0.2	460.4	1993	53.9	..	..
Liberia	41.2	2.3	377.5	..	..	..	..
Madagascar	71.2	2.3	451.8	1999	76.7	..	..
Malawi	82.2	2.0	420.7	1998	66.5		
Mali	68.9	2.2	168.1	1998	75.9		
Mauritania	59.4	2.3	353.2	1996	65.5	2000	61.2
Mauritius	57.6	0.7	717.4	..	..	..	..
Mozambique	64.7	0.9	305.7	1996	71.3	2002	55.3
Namibia	64.3	0.4	160.8	..	..	..	..
Niger	83.6	3.4	76.7	1993	66.0	..	..
Nigeria	53.1	1.0	237.7	1992	36.4	2003	63.8
Rwanda	82.2	2.1	634.8	..	..	2000	65.7
São Tomé and Principe	41.1	−0.3	710.5	..	..	..	..
Senegal	58.1	2.1	269.6	1992	40.4	..	..
Seychelles	46.6	1.0	3,904.6	..	..	..	..
Sierra Leone	62.9	2.3	588.4	..	..	2003	78.5
Somalia	64.4	2.3	393.4	..	..	..	..
South Africa	40.2	−0.1	129.4	..	..	..	..
Sudan	58.3	0.7	112.4	..	..	..	..
Swaziland	75.6	0.2	482.3	..	..	2001	75.0
Tanzania	75.4	1.9	317.0	1991	40.8	2001	38.7
Togo	59.4	1.5	150.6	..	..	..	..
Uganda	87.3	3.1	469.1	1999	37.4	2005	34.2
Zambia	64.9	1.7	141.8	1998	83.1	2004	78.0
Zimbabwe	63.6	0.1	261.2	1996	48.0	..	..
NORTH AFRICA	**47.4**	**1.1**					
Algeria	36.1	−0.3	161.8	1995	30.3	..	..
Egypt, Arab Rep.	57.4	1.7	1,393.9	1996	23.3	..	..
Libya	22.8	1.2	77.8	..	..	..	..
Morocco	44.7	0.4	160.0	1999	27.2	..	..
Tunisia	34.3	−0.2	127.5	1995	13.9	..	..

a. Data are for most recent year available during the period specified.

Share of rural population with sustainable access (%)				
To an improved water source 2006[a]	To an improved sanitation facilities 2006[a]	To electricity (%) 2000–06[a]	To transportation (within 2 km of an all-season road) 2000–06[a]	To landline telephone 2000–06[a]
45.6	**24.3**			
39.0	16.0	..	..	..
57.0	11.0	5.6	32.0	1.0
90.0	30.0	..	..	..
66.0	6.0	0.8	25.0	0.3
70.0	41.0	..	..	..
47.0	42.0	16.3	20.0	0.0
73.0	19.0	..	..	..
51.0	25.0	..	..	..
40.0	4.0	0.3	5.0	0.0
81.0	26.0	..	..	..
29.0	25.0	..	26.0	..
35.0	21.0	16.4	..	0.2
66.0	12.0	..	..	..
54.0	11.0	..	..	..
42.0	46.0	..	..	..
57.0	3.0	..	..	..
31.0	8.0	2.0	17.0	0.2
47.0	30.0	31.4	..	1.8
81.0	55.0	..	..	..
71.0	6.0	20.9	..	0.7
59.0	12.0	3.2	..	0.3
47.0	26.0	..	..	..
49.0	48.0	3.6	..	6.0
74.0	34.0	0.8	..	10.6
52.0	7.0	..	..	..
36.0	10.0	9.7	..	3.0
72.0	62.0	2.5	..	2.1
48.0	39.0	2.7	..	0.1
54.0	10.0	2.7	..	0.2
100.0	94.0	..	..	..
26.0	19.0	1.5	..	0.1
90.0	18.0	10.4	..	4.5
32.0	3.0	..	37.0	..
30.0	25.0	34.6	47.0	1.8
61.0	20.0	1.5	..	0.2
83.0	18.0	..	..	..
65.0	9.0	19.0	..	7.5
75.0	100.0	..	..	..
32.0	5.0	..	..	..
10.0	7.0	..	..	..
82.0	49.0	..	..	..
64.0	24.0	..	..	..
51.0	46.0	..	..	..
46.0	34.0	1.8	38.0	3.0
40.0	3.0	..	..	..
60.0	34.0	2.6	..	0.9
41.0	51.0	3.5	..	0.6
72.0	37.0	..	..	..
86.9	**59.5**	..	..	..
81.0	87.0	..	..	..
98.0	52.0	..	..	..
68.0	96.0	..	..	..
58.0	54.0	..	..	..
84.0	64.0	..	..	..

Table 9.2

Agriculture

	Agriculture value added (% of GDP) 2006	Production Index 1999–2001=100			Cereal			Trade Agricultural	
		Crop 2004–06[a]	Food 2004–06[a]	Livestock 2004–06[a]	Production (thousand of metric tons) 2006[a]	Exports (thousand of metric tons) 2005	Imports (thousand of metric tons) 2005	Exports ($ millions) 2005	Imports ($ millions) 2005
SUB-SAHARAN AFRICA	**14.5**								
Angola	8.9	119.2	152.5	100.0	724	1	639	2	1,018
Benin	..	133.9	112.4	116.2	934	15	398	262	262
Botswana	1.7	113.1	103.3	102.4	45	2	33	48	96
Burkina Faso	32.8	130.0	130.0	110.3	3,681	14	288	274	258
Burundi	..	104.2	101.2	100.2	269	..	64	54	34
Cameroon	19.3	104.9	112.2	103.2	1,407	0	767	604	453
Cape Verde	8.8	85.4	91.8	102.1	12	0	76	1	133
Central African Republic	53.4	97.7	108.1	114.7	172	..	38	16	33
Chad	20.9	115.7	122.1	107.6	1,913	..	131	105	90
Comoros	45.2	105.9	98.7	95.9	21	3	49	14	41
Congo, Dem. Rep.	43.3	96.7	95.6	100.4	1,524	0	493	34	406
Congo, Rep.	4	105.5	112.4	121.1	9	2	242	54	285
Côte d'Ivoire	23.1	97.4	105.3	111.0	1,400	21	1,177	3,021	672
Djibouti	3.1	114.6	105.3	108.5	0	1	238	11	151
Equatorial Guinea	2.7	93.8	93.4	101.9	..	..	19	3	57
Eritrea	16	71.5	86.3	99.5	199	1	510	2	139
Ethiopia	44.4	110.5	134.5	115.8	13,393	..	..	1,643	951
Gabon	4.9	102.3	103.3	101.5	32	0	134	43	269
Gambia, The	..	65.6	95.9	103.1	215	0	171	17	168
Ghana	38	121.2	131.5	111.8	1,919	0	927	1,165	1,052
Guinea	12.7	110.4	124.4	115.3	2,445	2	319	74	276
Guinea-Bissau	60.3	109.8	114.6	109.1	225	..	71	87	47
Kenya	24	101.6	128.5	108.7	3,955	20	1,617	1,545	689
Lesotho	14.4	111.2	106.0	100.0	89	0	27	4	64
Liberia	..	99.3	101.8	110.0	107	3	229	105	171
Madagascar	25.1	108.8	114.7	104.4	3,991	0	417	134	255
Malawi	30.5	91.8	91.8	101.9	2,752	3	170	445	142
Mali	34.1	111.2	109.6	117.9	3,693	10	165	240	225
Mauritania	12.1	100.5	108.8	110.0	175	..	403	17	148
Mauritius	4.9	103.5	107.0	113.6	0	42	309	397	417
Mozambique	25.6	107.4	144.3	101.1	2,107	3	919	158	404
Namibia	9.9	110.8	92.9	113.9	139	7	42	156	240
Niger	..	122.1	137.7	104.6	4,030	1	404	69	258
Nigeria	31.7	105.9	130.0	108.8	28,884	20	4,966	655	2,436
Rwanda	41.3	113.1	122.3	109.9	366	0	38	51	60
São Tomé and Principe	..	109.3	110.3	107.7	3	..	11	4	5
Senegal	13.6	76.8	83.9	101.1	988	16	1,313	149	19
Seychelles	3	93.8	104.4	91.1	..	..	18	2	881
Sierra Leone	45.1	115.0	195.0	105.2	1,157	..	123	17	77
Somalia	..	..	..	..	261	0	360	72	104
South Africa	2.4	102.6	107.2	108.6	9,454	2,209	2,279	3,925	254
Sudan	31.3	109.7	116.1	107.2	6,742	3	2,184	504	2,679
Swaziland	6.1	100.8	101.0	111.1	68	14	182	254	798
Tanzania	37.9	106.8	107.4	109.6	5,793	128	596	531	285
Togo	..	110.9	122.7	109.2	889	36	184	95	347
Uganda	28.7	108.7	105.5	110.3	2,557	76	555	416	1,171
Zambia	19.9	108.2	107.0	98.9	1,604	69	177	321	365
Zimbabwe	..	66.1	89.1	99.0	1,849	1	235	449	183
NORTH AFRICA	**10.3**	**118.6**							
Algeria	..	128.4	143.1	104.8	4,018	14	8,263	59	3,922
Egypt, Arab Rep.	13.2	105.5	114.8	122.3	22,991	1,154	10,893	1,169	3,948
Libya	..	99.8	104.7	100.9	210	1	2,457	7	1,267
Morocco	14.0	148.6	142.1	99.8	9,239	93	5,029	1,353	2,303
Tunisia	11.1	101.7	115.9	98.8	1,646	113	2,454	963	85

a. Data are for most recent year available during the period specified.

Trade		Share of land area (%)		Irrigated land (% of cropland) 2002–05[a]	Fertilizer consumption (100 grams per hectare of arable land) 2006[a]	Agricultural machinery Tractors per 100 hectares of arable land 2005	Agricultural employment (% of total employment) 2000–06[a]	Agriculture value added per worker (2000 US$) 2003–05[a]	Cereal yield (kilograms per hectare) 2006
Food									
Exports ($ millions) 2005	Imports ($ millions) 2005	Permanent cropland 2005	Cereal cropland 2006						
					105.7	**13.4**			**1,262**
1	806	0.2	1.2	2.2	22.6	31.2	..	196	485
67	241	2.4	7.5	0.4	-	0.7	..	536	1,125
45	68	0.0	0.1	0.3	122.0	159.2	21.2	367	342
58	189	0.2	12.5	0.5	126.3	4.1	..	179	1,127
1	32	14.2	8.1	1.5	34.9	1.8	..	64	1,330
346	428	2.6	2.3	0.4	78.7	0.8	60.6	666	1,408
0	107	0.7	8.3	6.1	47.8	12.4	..	1,510	355
15	26	0.1	0.3	0.1	3.1	0.2	..	384	1,074
55	73	0.0	2.0	0.8	48.6	0.4	..	225	750
13	38	28.5	8.4	..	37.5	0.6	..	436	1,338
10	370	0.5	0.9	0.1	15.7	3.6	..	149	785
34	244	0.1	0.0	0.4	94.4	14.1	..	..	790
2,452	566	11.3	2.5	1.1	142.2	26.5	..	817	1,777
10	123	..	0.0	..	..	80.0	..	65	1,500
2	23	3.2	..	..	..	16.2	..	1,198	..
1	138	0.0	3.7	3.5	22.0	7.3	..	63	406
681	839	0.8	8.4	2.5	26.0	2.3	80.2	177	1,590
9	221	0.7	0.1	1.4	26.9	28.6	..	1,663	1,540
16	139	0.5	21.0	0.6	25.4	2.9	..	243	1,223
1,101	940	9.7	6.3	0.5	75.4	8.6	..	332	1,335
46	204	2.7	6.9	5.4	28.2	46.3	..	193	1,436
86	34	8.9	4.9	4.5	80.0	0.7	..	246	1,625
400	587	0.8	4.1	1.8	177.9	25.5	..	343	1,675
1	51	0.1	6.1	0.9	343.7	60.6	..	412	654
9	150	2.3	..	0.5	..	8.5	..	..	..
103	216	1.0	2.6	30.6	53.7	1.9	78.0	175	2,511
68	87	1.5	16.4	2.2	352.8	5.5	..	109	1,107
49	187	0.0	2.6	4.9	89.4	5.4	41.5	244	1,068
16	125	0.0	0.2	9.8	59.4	7.6	..	356	782
371	335	3.0	0.0	20.8	2,574.7	53.5	10.0	5,338	7,793
81	347	0.3	2.6	2.6	16.2	14.5	..	157	902
139	167	0.0	0.4	1.0	19.2	38.7	31.1	1,134	434
63	228	0.0	5.3	0.5	3.2	0.1	..	157	605
567	2,249	3.3	21.1	0.8	67.2	9.4	..	..	1,464
0	49	11.1	13.3	0.6	137.1	0.5	..	185	1,118
4	15	49.0	1.1	18.2	..	138.9	27.9	..	2,455
100	797	0.2	5.8	4.8	254.4	2.7	..	227	879
1	67	10.9	..	..	170.0	400.0	..	433	..
14	81	1.1	10.8	4.7	5.6	1.5	..	..	1,485
70	248	0.0	1.1	15.7	4.2	10.2	..	..	589
2,666	1,731	0.8	2.5	9.5	451.4	42.7	10.3	2,636	3,143
295	733	0.1	3.9	10.2	25.8	9.3	..	666	718
225	220	0.8	2.9	26.0	393.3	221.9	..	1,344	547
145	289	1.3	3.9	1.8	103.7	23.4	82.1	306	1,514
50	64	2.6	14.4	0.3	81.8	0.3	..	353	1,135
78	323	11.2	8.5	0.1	10.7	8.7	69.1	235	1,523
158	154	0.0	0.8	2.9	69.2	11.4	..	204	1,837
131	117	0.3	4.3	5.2	338.7	74.5	..	205	714
					1,264.8	**139.3**			**2,906**
50	3,455	0.4	1.1	6.9	144.2	134.5	21.1	2,219	1,503
899	3,355	0.5	3.0	100.4	7,330.7	325.3	29.9	2,128	7,499
1	1,113	0.2	0.2	21.9	671.3	227.1	..	..	611
1,167	1,774	2.1	12.6	15.4	425.7	58.5	44.6	1,657	1,622
782	861	13.9	8.5	7.4	644.2	143.2	..	2,687	1,245

Table 9.3 Environment

	Forests		Renewable internal freshwater resources		Annual freshwater withdrawals	
	Forest area (% of land area)		Total (billion cubic meters)	Per capita (cubic meters)	Total (billions of cubic meters)	Share of internal resources (%)
	1990	2005	2005	2005	2002	2002
SUB-SAHARAN AFRICA						
Angola	48.9	47.4	148	9,195	0.4	0.2
Benin	30.0	21.3	10	1,213	0.1	1.3
Botswana	24.2	21.1	2	1,307	0.2	8.1
Burkina Faso	26.1	24.8	13	897	0.8	6.4
Burundi	11.3	5.9	10	1,285	0.3	2.9
Cameroon	52.7	45.6	273	15,341	1.0	0.4
Cape Verde	14.3	20.7	0	592	0.0	7.3
Central African Republic	37.2	36.5	141	33,640	0.0	0.0
Chad	10.4	9.5	15	1,479	0.2	1.5
Comoros	6.4	3.0	1	1,998	0.0	0.8
Congo, Dem. Rep.	62.0	58.9	900	15,322	0.4	0.0
Congo, Rep.	66.5	65.8	222	61,498	0.0	0.0
Côte d'Ivoire	32.1	32.7	77	4,132	0.9	1.2
Djibouti	0.2	0.2	0	373	0.0	6.3
Equatorial Guinea	66.3	58.2	26	53,708	0.1	0.4
Eritrea	..	15.4	3	619	0.3	10.7
Ethiopia	15.2	13.0	122	1,623	5.6	4.6
Gabon	85.1	84.5	164	127,064	0.1	0.1
Gambia, The	44.2	47.1	3	1,855	0.0	1.0
Ghana	32.7	24.2	30	1,345	1.0	3.2
Guinea	30.1	27.4	226	25,104	1.5	0.7
Guinea-Bissau	78.8	73.7	16	10,019	0.2	1.1
Kenya	6.5	6.2	21	582	1.6	7.6
Lesotho	0.2	0.3	5	2,625	0.1	1.0
Liberia	42.1	32.7	200	58,109	0.1	0.1
Madagascar	23.5	22.1	337	18,077	15.0	4.4
Malawi	41.4	36.2	16	1,217	1.0	6.3
Mali	11.5	10.3	60	5,168	6.5	10.9
Mauritania	0.4	0.3	0	135	1.7	425.0
Mauritius	19.2	18.2	3	2,252	0.6	21.8
Mozambique	25.4	24.5	100	4,885	0.6	0.6
Namibia	10.6	9.3	6	3,070	0.3	4.8
Niger	1.5	1.0	4	264	2.2	62.3
Nigeria	18.9	12.2	221	1,563	8.0	3.6
Rwanda	12.9	19.5	10	1,029	0.2	1.6
São Tomé and Principe	28.5	28.5	2	14,415	..	..
Senegal	48.6	45.0	26	2,192	2.2	8.6
Seychelles	87.0	87.0	..	..	..	..
Sierra Leone	42.5	38.5	160	28,641	0.4	0.2
Somalia	13.2	11.4	6	732	3.3	54.8
South Africa	7.6	7.6	45	955	12.5	27.9
Sudan	32.1	28.4	30	813	37.3	124.4
Swaziland	27.4	31.5	3	2,299	1.0	40.1
Tanzania	46.8	39.8	84	2,183	5.2	6.2
Togo	12.6	7.1	12	1,843	0.2	1.5
Uganda	25.0	18.4	39	1,347	0.3	0.8
Zambia	66.1	57.1	80	6,987	1.7	2.2
Zimbabwe	57.5	45.3	12	938	4.2	34.2
NORTH AFRICA						
Algeria	0.8	1.0	11	341	6.1	54.2
Egypt, Arab Rep.	0.0	0.1	2	25	68.3	3794.4
Libya	0.1	0.1	1	101	4.3	711.3
Morocco	9.6	9.8	29	962	12.6	43.4
Tunisia	4.1	6.8	4	419	2.6	62.9

a. Data are for most recent year available during the period specified.

Water productivity (2000 $ per cubic meter of freshwater withdrawal)			Energy							
			Emissions of organic water pollutants (kilograms per day)		Energy production (kilotons of oil equivalent)		Energy use (kilotons of oil equivalent)		Combustible renewables and waste (% of total energy use)	
Total 2001–04ᵃ	Agriculture 2001–04ᵃ	Industry 2001–04ᵃ	1990	2000–04ᵃ	1990	2005	1990	2005	1990	2005
30.8	3.3	130.8	..	..	28,652	70,700	6,285	9,898	68.8	63.8
19.0	15.4	12.1	..	..	1,774	1,672	1,678	2,584	93.2	64.7
35.4	1.8	105.9	4,509	3,299	910	1,051	1,272	1,895	33.1	24.1
3.6	1.2	105.3	..	..	..	..	..	..	..	..
2.6	1.2	6.1	1,570	..	..	..	..	..	..	..
11.1	3.0	44.9	13,989	10,032	12,090	11,942	5,032	6,978	75.9	78.6
26.2	3.0	269.6	103	..	..	..	..	..	..	..
38.3	502.7	35.3	998	..	..	..	..	..	..	..
7.3	3.3	..	..	..	..	..	..	..	..	..
21.7	23.2	50.4	..	..	..	..	..	..	..	..
12.1	18.7	15.2	..	..	12,019	17,391	11,903	16,967	84.0	92.5
76.1	..	..	..	..	9,005	13,677	1,056	1,199	69.4	56.3
11.0	4.1	21.8	..	..	3,382	8,196	4,408	7,843	72.1	58.3
30.4	6.0	..	..	..	..	..	..	..	..	..
22.7	131.9	129.8	61	..	..	..	..	..	..	..
2.3	0.3	..	..	..	..	..	..	..	..	..
1.6	0.8	51.2	18,593	22,085	14,158	19,855	15,151	21,633	92.8	90.6
43.0	6.2	291.3	..	..	14,630	12,116	1,243	1,721	59.8	58.7
14.1	5.2	15.7	..	..	..	..	..	..	..	..
5.5	2.9	14.9	..	..	4,392	6,356	5,337	8,937	73.1	66.0
2.2	0.5	35.0	..	..	..	..	..	..	..	..
1.1	0.8	3.9	..	..	..	..	..	..	..	..
8.4	3.9	20.5	42,588	56,102	10,272	13,888	12,479	17,246	78.4	74.6
17.9	11.8	17.6	2,958	..	..	..	..	..	..	..
5.4	..	..	..	..	..	..	..	..	..	..
0.2	0.1	1.9	..	67,154	..	..	..	..	..	..
1.6	0.7	4.5	10,024	..	..	..	..	..	..	..
0.4	0.2	11.8	..	..	..	..	..	..	..	..
0.7	0.2	5.8	..	..	..	..	..	..	..	..
7.9	..	..	17,813	..	..	..	..	..	..	..
8.2	2.0	120.3	20,414	10,231	6,846	11,742	7,203	10,207	94.4	85.4
12.4	1.6	69.7	..	..	..	328	..	1,379	..	13.5
0.9	0.4	33.7	..	386	..	..	..	..	..	..
6.0	..	..	..	..	150,453	231,775	70,905	103,785	79.8	78.0
13.9	7.9	23.3	..	..	..	..	..	..	..	..
..	..	..	..	..	..	..	..	..	..	..
2.2	0.3	18.4	10,309	6,603	1,363	1,265	2,238	3,041	60.6	39.2
..	..	..	..	..	..	..	..	..	..	..
2.5	..	..	..	..	..	..	..	..	..	..
..	..	..	..	..	..	..	..	..	..	..
11.3	0.5	53.1	261,618	181,691	114,534	158,590	91,229	127,637	11.4	10.5
0.4	0.2	10.5	..	38,583	8,775	31,127	10,642	18,398	81.7	79.5
1.3	0.1	34.5	6,586	..	..	..	..	..	..	..
2.0	0.9	61.7	31,125	..	9,063	19,099	9,808	20,404	91.0	92.1
8.2	6.5	63.8	..	..	1,203	1,591	1,447	1,995	82.6	79.4
22.1	18.3	25.2	..	..	..	..	..	..	..	..
2.0	0.5	6.7	15,880	..	4,923	6,513	5,470	7,124	73.4	78.7
1.6	0.3	4.3	37,149	..	8,550	8,860	9,384	9,723	50.4	61.9
9.7	1.3	39.5	106,978	..	104,439	175,070	23,858	34,768	0.1	0.2
1.6	0.3	8.2	211,531	186,059	54,869	76,039	31,895	61,301	3.3	2.3
8.7	..	..	..	..	73,173	94,966	11,541	19,047	1.1	0.8
3.3	0.6	28.7	41,710	90,990	773	983	6,725	13,813	4.7	3.3
7.9	1.0	54.7	..	55,775	6,127	6,681	5,536	8,451	18.7	13.3

Table 9.3 Environment (continued)

	Greenhouse gas emissions							
	Carbon dioxide emissions, industrial (thousands of metric tons)		Methane emissions (kt of CO_2 equivalent)		Agricultural methane emissions (% of total)		Industrial methane emissions (% of total)	
	1990	2004	1990	2005	1990	2005	1990	2005
SUB-SAHARAN AFRICA								
Angola	4,645	7,890	13,630	37,020	65.7	39.1	21.6	..
Benin	714	2,385	2,730	4,840	60.1	47.5	16.1	..
Botswana	2,169	4,297	130	4,480	84.6	71.9	7.7	..
Burkina Faso	993	1,095	..	..	..	..	..	..
Burundi	194	220	..	..	..	..	..	..
Cameroon	1,604	3,835	10,500	15,110	57.0	56.0	20.2	890
Cape Verde	88	275	..	..	..	..	..	..
Central African Republic	198	253	..	..	..	..	..	..
Chad	143	125	..	..	..	..	..	..
Comoros	66	88	..	..	..	..	..	..
Congo, Dem. Rep.	3,971	2,103	2,670	5,750	20.2	11.8	47.9	..
Congo, Rep.	1,172	3,539	27,720	50,320	42.9	26.3	10.4	..
Côte d'Ivoire	5,385	5,158	5,410	15,320	49.9	20.6	18.9	..
Djibouti	352	366	..	..	..	..	..	..
Equatorial Guinea	117	5,421	..	..	..	..	..	..
Eritrea	..	755	2,090	2,410	75.6	77.6	11.0	..
Ethiopia	2,963	7,974	39,110	47,740	78.4	77.2	9.3	..
Gabon	5,989	1,370	3,120	2,040	6.7	4.4	46.5	..
Gambia, The	191	286	..	..	..	..	..	..
Ghana	3,766	7,183	5,310	8,630	42.7	49.6	13.7	170
Guinea	1,011	1,337	..	..	..	..	..	..
Guinea-Bissau	209	271	..	..	..	..	..	..
Kenya	5,821	10,579	19,410	20,310	71.4	65.0	15.7	..
Lesotho	..	..	..	..	..	..	..	..
Liberia	465	469	..	..	..	..	..	..
Madagascar	941	2,729	..	..	..	..	..	..
Malawi	601	1,044	..	..	..	..	..	..
Mali	421	564	..	..	..	..	..	..
Mauritania	2,634	2,553	..	..	..	..	..	..
Mauritius	1,462	3,194	..	..	..	..	..	..
Mozambique	996	2,165	9,430	11,680	61.9	64.3	17.5	..
Namibia	7	2,469	4,320	4,260	90.7	89.9	3.7	..
Niger	1,048	1,213	..	..	..	..	..	..
Nigeria	45,326	113,923	59,690	78,290	33.9	33.7	47.3	80
Rwanda	528	571	..	..	..	..	..	..
São Tomé and Principe	66	92	..	..	..	..	..	..
Senegal	3,132	4,989	5,550	6,340	76.2	75.9	4.5	10
Seychelles	114	546	..	..	..	..	..	..
Sierra Leone	333	993	..	..	..	..	..	..
Somalia	18	..	..	..	..	..	..	..
South Africa	331,743	436,641	52,260	59,200	31.2	23.8	52.4	2,600
Sudan	5,381	10,363	39,760	67,310	69.1	73.3	21.4	..
Swaziland	425	956	..	..	..	..	..	..
Tanzania	2,333	4,348	26,860	39,460	66.4	63.5	21.3	..
Togo	751	2,308	1,790	2,840	56.4	48.6	18.4	..
Uganda	813	1,824	..	..	..	..	..	..
Zambia	2,443	2,286	9,820	16,770	72.5	68.6	8.1	..
Zimbabwe	16,641	10,549	10,850	10,400	65.4	60.4	22.2	20
NORTH AFRICA								
Algeria	76,971	193,828	18,570	24,310	19.3	15.3	61.2	110
Egypt, Arab Rep.	75,414	158,095	23,250	32,960	39.0	44.2	33.4	1,820
Libya	37,762	59,861	8,750	8,540	11.8	8.9	79.1	290
Morocco	23,480	41,132	9,070	13,240	57.6	41.6	6.2	..
Tunisia	13,256	22,864	3,740	4,390	42.2	34.2	26.2	30

a. Data are for most recent year available during the period specified.

| Greenhouse gas emissions | | | | | | | | ODA gross aid disbursement for forestry ($ millions) | ODA gross aid disbursement for general environment protection ($ millions) |
| Nitrous oxide emissions (metric tons of CO_2 equivalent) | | Agricultural nitrous oxide emissions (% of total) | | Industrial nitrous oxide emissions (% of total) | | Other greenhouse gas emissions, HFC, PFC and SF6 (thousand metric tons of CO_2 equivalent) | | | |
1990	2005	1990	2005	1990	2005	1990	2005	2006	2006
5,110	28,350	80.4	35.9	..	..	..	..	71	328
2,120	4,660	90.6	68.0	..	..	..	..	0	0
..	2,460	..	96.3	..	..	..	..	0	7
..	..	..	..	..	..	..	..	0	4
..	..	..	..	..	..	..	..	2	10
8,290	14,540	85.5	85.0	..	..	810	890	0	4
..	..	..	..	..	..	..	..	5	12
..	..	..	..	..	..	..	..	0	9
..	..	..	..	..	..	..	..	20	2
..	..	..	..	..	..	..	..	1	2
820	2,250	23.2	15.6	..	..	..	..	..	0
19,390	38,680	43.7	23.2	..	..	..	..	..	2
2,460	12,350	82.1	25.0	..	..	..	..	2	6
..	..	..	..	..	..	..	..	0	13
1,340	2,350	97.0	99.1	..	..	..	..	..	..
50,730	63,130	97.9	98.6	..	..	..	..	0	0
1,850	420	13.0	57.1	..	..	..	..	2	8
..	..	..	..	..	..	..	..	1	5
4,540	10,520	84.1	88.6	..	..	190	170	0	0
..	..	..	..	..	..	..	..	6	6
..	..	..	..	..	..	..	..	2	7
21,830	19,060	97.6	96.4	..	..	..	..	..	1
..	..	..	..	..	..	..	..	1	13
..	..	..	..	..	..	..	..	0	0
..	..	..	..	..	..	..	..	1	0
..	..	..	..	..	..	..	..	0	19
..	..	..	..	..	..	..	..	2	2
..	..	..	..	..	..	..	..	0	8
..	..	..	..	..	..	..	..	0	4
2,950	9,930	72.5	99.7	..	..	..	..	..	0
4,240	4,620	97.2	99.1	..	..	..	..	0	15
..	..	..	..	..	..	..	..	1	2
28,050	39,030	87.9	87.1	..	..	120	80	0	8
..	..	..	..	..	..	..	..	..	1
..	..	..	..	..	..	..	..	0	1
6,220	10,250	95.8	99.0	..	..	..	10	0	0
..	..	..	..	..	..	..	..	4	46
..	..	..	..	..	..	..	..	..	0
..	..	..	..	..	..	..	..	..	0
26,460	29,250	88.0	82.7	3.6	7.3	1,450	2,600	..	..
39,400	59,750	94.1	96.2	..	..	..	..	0	23
..	..	..	..	..	..	..	..	0	0
23,300	31,690	91.3	84.3	..	..	..	..	..	..
1,990	5,470	93.5	88.8	..	..	..	..	4	20
..	..	..	..	..	..	..	..	..	0
4,800	11,410	72.5	65.1	..	3.7	..	..	5	4
8,970	10,160	89.4	97.1	5.9	..	..	20	0	6
8,780	10,330	90.9	89.1	4.4	7.2	230	110	6	65
16,980	27,810	88.6	85.6	8.2	11.5	2,250	1,820	0	3
2,860	2,050	96.5	91.7	..	..	100	290	0	35
14,380	15,510	98.5	75.2	..	..	..	..	..	0
4,260	7,230	87.1	94.2	10.6	4.1	..	30	1	10

Table 9.4 Climate change*

	Temperature (degrees Celsius)			Precipitation (mm)						
	Annual average 2000	Minimum monthly avearge 2000	Maximum monthly average 2000	Annual precipitation 2000	Minimum monthly avearge 2000	Maximum monthly average 2000	Dec. – Feb. (DJF) 2000	Mar. – May (MAM) 2000	Jun. – Aug. (JJA) 2000	Sept. – Nov. (SON) 2000
SUB-SAHARAN AFRICA										
Angola	21.87	18.57	24.11	1,003.83	0.67	176.69	484.29	303.44	5.08	211.02
Benin	27.58	25.31	30.67	931.83	0.21	186.97	3.20	169.36	503.62	255.64
Botswana	21.41	14.18	25.72	543.07	0.17	141.36	313.99	126.04	5.14	97.90
Burkina Faso	28.57	25.35	33.42	705.71	0.03	198.55	1.71	116.90	438.76	148.35
Burundi	21.03	19.82	21.74	833.58	1.65	182.50	284.17	240.15	22.05	287.21
Cameroon	24.85	23.40	27.25	1,724.76	12.20	380.35	73.16	363.75	733.58	554.26
Cape Verde	22.86	20.76	25.25	383.49	11.59	84.49	50.42	42.04	138.75	152.29
Central African Republic	25.07	23.79	27.66	1,256.66	3.05	223.09	23.51	241.70	605.51	385.95
Chad	26.67	21.08	31.12	313.39	0.15	96.83	1.88	40.66	231.87	38.98
Comoros	25.38	23.07	26.70	1,729.80	24.77	308.57	632.10	485.70	437.90	174.10
Congo, Dem. Rep.	24.19	22.98	25.17	1,374.39	62.90	183.98	369.11	368.92	226.87	409.49
Congo, Rep.	24.70	23.04	25.82	1,691.66	33.24	202.17	507.46	421.73	197.19	565.28
Cote d'Ivoire	26.37	24.46	28.74	1,443.77	11.48	275.53	50.22	420.53	627.43	345.59
Djibouti	28.55	23.76	33.54	201.06	2.24	41.22	11.30	56.31	73.10	60.34
Equatorial Guinea	24.76	23.43	25.74	2,426.82	12.83	364.66	426.51	634.94	444.61	920.77
Eritrea	27.47	23.05	30.90	212.60	0.50	52.10	12.20	35.45	103.38	61.58
Ethiopia	23.19	21.40	25.32	734.32	1.35	118.39	13.67	193.86	289.64	237.15
Gabon	25.20	23.12	26.38	1,990.99	4.17	290.09	641.25	535.92	96.49	717.33
Gambia, The	27.98	24.87	31.05	1,043.04	0.00	317.32	0.32	0.52	655.49	386.71
Ghana	27.29	25.16	29.61	1,120.16	5.76	158.05	21.87	431.96	412.06	254.28
Guinea	26.10	24.06	29.51	1,757.30	2.01	459.68	12.38	151.67	1,067.13	526.12
Guinea-Bissau	27.23	24.56	31.01	1,826.07	-	506.87	0.39	10.80	1,144.95	669.92
Kenya	24.62	23.28	26.67	509.03	1.95	109.19	63.80	181.68	77.86	185.69
Lesotho	12.84	6.40	18.13	886.46	1.40	158.46	398.99	264.83	13.04	209.61
Liberia	25.60	24.01	26.95	2,270.66	21.85	383.20	127.69	492.16	922.71	728.11
Madagascar	23.00	19.79	25.10	1,407.48	21.96	271.10	742.48	254.61	154.09	256.30
Malawi	22.20	18.26	24.98	1,150.51	1.05	259.78	705.13	276.92	17.05	151.42
Mali	28.99	22.64	34.57	313.95	0.04	99.90	0.40	25.70	222.98	64.87
Mauritania	28.23	20.47	33.54	89.89	0.26	35.84	1.54	0.96	67.23	20.16
Mauritius	22.91	20.15	25.40	1,643.20	36.80	434.40	758.00	434.35	267.50	183.35
Mozambique	23.87	19.61	26.05	1,171.68	3.82	241.48	660.05	318.57	51.52	141.55
Namibia	20.07	15.07	23.90	331.96	1.05	81.81	187.77	98.16	3.68	42.35
Niger	27.42	19.26	33.47	147.28	0.00	51.24	0.80	4.81	118.99	22.68
Nigeria	26.85	24.12	30.48	1,090.92	0.78	311.58	7.15	152.39	608.80	322.58
Rwanda	19.29	18.16	20.03	797.58	7.89	154.79	190.73	230.49	60.35	316.01
Sao Tome & Principe	23.30	21.70	24.55	2,163.70	24.00	386.75	411.70	486.65	508.50	756.85
Senegal	28.38	25.15	31.58	791.21	0.00	243.25	0.43	2.39	520.17	268.21
Seychelles	..	..	..	..	..	..	..	..	..	..
Sierra Leone	26.46	24.70	28.80	2,518.66	4.76	605.49	30.35	274.17	1,366.26	847.88
Somalia	27.03	24.85	28.94	267.18	3.28	50.21	16.30	109.54	46.56	94.78
South Africa	17.81	11.36	22.92	616.87	6.91	110.03	283.73	175.94	27.19	130.00
Sudan	27.47	22.96	31.08	434.54	0.54	110.13	2.60	74.90	251.63	105.42
Swaziland	20.01	15.23	23.90	1,273.77	4.63	293.91	693.30	325.09	18.72	236.66
Tanzania	22.87	20.95	24.08	887.45	6.34	200.06	354.18	336.43	29.59	167.25
Togo	27.27	24.94	29.92	1,028.10	0.13	167.40	7.83	302.59	443.79	273.88
Uganda	23.25	22.36	24.45	732.87	10.25	108.31	54.72	153.74	208.44	315.97
Zambia	21.91	17.37	25.60	1,105.30	0.12	249.46	708.99	250.64	2.80	142.87
Zimbabwe	21.07	15.29	24.66	1,034.10	0.37	254.31	650.34	231.18	35.94	116.64
NORTH AFRICA										
Algeria	..	..	..	..	..	..	..	..	..	..
Egypt, Arab Rep.	..	..	..	..	..	..	..	..	..	..
Libya	..	..	..	..	..	..	..	..	..	..
Morocco	..	..	..	..	..	..	..	..	..	..
Tunisia	..	..	..	..	..	..	..	..	..	..

a. Data are for the most recent year available during the specified period.
* For a discussion about climate change, see Box 8 in the technical notes.

| CO₂ emissions per capita (metric tons of carbon dioxide per capita) 2002 | Emissions | | Agriculture value added (% of GDP) 2006 | Irrigated land (% of crop land) 2002–03[a] | Total aggregate affected population by disaster | | Malaria | |
	Total greenhouse gas emissions (includes land use change) million metric tons CO₂ 2000	Emissions from land use change & forestry as percentage of greenhouse gas emissions 2000			Drought 2000–07	Flood 2000–07	Number of clinical malaria cases reported 1999–01[a]	Reported malaria deaths 1999–01[a]
1.00	30.8	57.8	8.9	2.2	25,000	563,328	1,385,597	9,255
0.25	37.8	95.8	..	0.4	0	10,000	779,041	670
2.31	23.9	82.4	1.7	0.3	0	111,736	28,221	14
0.09	1.8	33.3	32.8	0.5	0	108,580	880,014	3,479
0.04	7.5	97.3	..	1.5	2,800,000	17,695	2,855,868	1,289
0.42	84.1	91.7	19.3	0.4	0	500	..	..
0.31	0.2	..	8.8	6.1	..	..	29	..
0.07	9.2	97.8	53.4	0.1	..	..	127,964	484
0.02	3.6	97.2	20.9	0.8	800,000	348,763	386,197	1,001
0.11	0.1	..	45.2	..	..	..	3,718	16
0.03	319.4	99.3	43.3	0.1	..	..	46138*	218*
..	12.9	76.7	4.0	0.4	0	25,000	..	
0.33	98.0	93.0	23.1	1.1	..	..	400,402	432
0.48	0.4	0.0	3.1	..	292,750	98,500	..	
3.07	6.5	67.7	2.7	..	..	..	..	
0.17	0.6	..	16.0	3.5	2,300,000	7,000	125,746	129
0.07	12.1	69.4	44.4	2.5	19,700,000	1,105,354	150,715	
3.14	8.2	45.1	4.9	1.4	..	..	..	
0.20	..	..	..	0.6	..	..	127,899	..
0.37	34.4	81.1	38.0	0.5	0	473,800	3,383,025	3,726
0.17	11.9	88.2	12.7	5.4	0	241,885	899,089	441
0.19	1.4	78.6	60.3	4.5	...	..	202,379	631
0.25	22.4	53.1	24.0	1.8	28,802,000	1,129,050	132,590	..
0.13	0.2	0.0	14.4	0.9	975,000	0	..	
0.14	39.8	99.0	..	0.5	0	17,000	..	
0.14	62.5	96.3	25.1	30.6	845,290	111,488	..	
0.07	27.8	96.0	30.5	2.2	8,449,435	1,142,896	2,955,627	59,414
0.05	8.6	93.0	34.1	4.9	1,025,000	68,681	86,512	182
1.12	2.5	..	12.1	9.8	1,000,000	89,120	243,942	337
2.57	2.8	..	4.9	20.8	..	..	..	
0.08	10.7	86.9	25.6	2.6	2,739,500	6,288,151	3,172,106	4,700
1.18	4.1	56.1	9.9	1.0	345,000	89,300	733,509	99
0.10	1.9	36.8	..	0.5	6,584,558	111,420	606,802	987
0.72	270.2	72.1	31.7	0.8	0	382,865	31,685	58
0.07	8.1	91.4	41.3	0.6	1,894,545	27,500	915,916	2,678
0.63	0.1	0.0	..	18.2	...	..	..	
0.39	7.8	46.2	13.6	4.8	284,000	235,577	1,120,094	1,337
..	..	..	3.0	..	..	..	..	
0.14	13.9	95.7	45.1	4.7	0	19,500	..	
..	..	..	..	15.7	1,400,000	659,800	..	
7.82	362.6	0.5	2.4	9.5	15,000,000	97,816	26,506	119
0.27	36.4	83.8	31.3	10.2	2,000,000	1,204,000	..	
0.94	..	..	6.1	26.0	1,380,000	274,500	12,296	..
0.10	17.3	83.8	37.9	1.8	..	..	673,366	..
0.27	10.1	85.1	..	0.3	0	129,880	431,826	791
0.07	41.0	95.9	28.7	0.1	1,955,000	455,710	5,622,934	..
0.19	237.4	99.2	19.9	2.9	1,200,000	2,383,816	2,010,185	5,763
0.93	60.8	78.0	..	5.2	8,100,000	265,000	680,900	412
..	..	..	..	..	..	..	..	..
..	..	..	..	..	..	..	..	..
..	..	..	..	..	..	..	..	..
..	..	..	..	..	..	..	..	..
..	..	..	..	..	..	..	..	..

Table 10.1 Labor force participation

	Total (in thousands)		Labor force ages 15 and older			
			Male (% of total labor force)		Female (% of total labor force)	
	2000	2006	2000	2006	2000	2006
SUB-SAHARAN AFRICA	**276,539**	**323,324**	**57.5**	**57.8**	**42.5**	**42.2**
Angola	6,135	7,329	54.1	54.2	45.9	45.8
Benin	2,810	3,431	60.7	61.7	39.3	38.3
Botswana	628	695	57.2	59.7	42.8	40.3
Burkina Faso	5,268	6,468	52.6	52.9	47.4	47.1
Burundi	3,207	4,188	47.2	48.6	52.8	51.4
Cameroon	6,145	6,989	60.3	60.4	39.7	39.6
Cape Verde	144	169	65.4	66.2	34.6	33.8
Central African Republic	1,760	1,953	53.6	54.0	46.4	46.0
Chad	3,318	4,031	54.1	53.2	45.9	46.8
Comoros	222	259	59.5	60.0	40.5	40.0
Congo, Dem. Rep.	20,234	24,213	58.6	58.7	41.4	41.3
Congo, Rep.	1,423	1,544	59.4	59.9	40.6	40.1
Côte d'Ivoire	6,289	7,139	70.8	70.7	29.2	29.3
Djibouti	294	345	60.1	60.8	39.9	39.2
Equatorial Guinea	175	202	63.6	63.1	36.4	36.9
Eritrea	1,490	1,972	58.6	59.0	41.4	41.0
Ethiopia	28,989	34,427	55.1	55.1	44.9	44.9
Gabon	526	614	56.8	57.3	43.2	42.7
Gambia, The	586	711	58.7	59.2	41.3	40.8
Ghana	8,806	10,285	51.6	52.2	48.4	47.8
Guinea	3,883	4,356	52.7	52.5	47.3	47.5
Guinea-Bissau	556	660	59.2	59.2	40.8	40.8
Kenya	13,959	16,650	55.6	55.8	44.4	44.2
Lesotho	674	697	55.3	56.5	44.7	43.5
Liberia	1,136	1,307	60.5	60.3	39.5	39.7
Madagascar	7,337	8,921	51.4	51.7	48.6	48.3
Malawi	5,450	6,289	50.3	50.0	49.7	50.0
Mali	4,097	4,820	52.3	50.8	47.7	49.2
Mauritania	1,035	1,264	60.3	60.8	39.7	39.2
Mauritius	529	577	65.9	64.3	34.1	35.7
Mozambique	8,797	9,787	46.5	46.6	53.5	53.4
Namibia	613	687	55.3	56.2	44.7	43.8
Niger	4,842	5,931	57.6	57.6	42.4	42.4
Nigeria	45,013	52,668	64.1	64.7	35.9	35.3
Rwanda	3,625	4,385	47.3	48.6	52.7	51.4
São Tomé and Principe	42	47	70.7	70.9	29.3	29.1
Senegal	4,149	4,775	59.3	58.8	40.7	41.2
Seychelles	..	..	..	..	..	..
Sierra Leone	1,939	2,452	61.5	61.5	38.5	38.5
Somalia	3,033	3,612	60.7	60.8	39.3	39.2
South Africa	18,695	19,996	61.2	62.1	38.8	37.9
Sudan	9,076	10,664	74.9	75.1	25.1	24.9
Swaziland	318	360	66.2	67.7	33.8	32.3
Tanzania	16,744	19,317	50.2	50.3	49.8	49.7
Togo	2,130	2,549	62.9	63.3	37.1	36.7
Uganda	10,492	12,609	51.9	51.6	48.1	48.4
Zambia	4,478	4,985	57.0	57.4	43.0	42.6
Zimbabwe	5,447	5,995	55.2	56.4	44.8	43.6
NORTH AFRICA	**46,221**	**54,750**	**75.6**	**74.3**	**24.4**	**25.7**
Algeria	11,101	13,887	72.1	69.0	27.9	31.0
Egypt, Arab Rep.	19,780	23,111	78.2	78.3	21.8	21.7
Libya	1,980	2,498	76.5	72.2	23.5	27.8
Morocco	10,049	11,315	74.2	73.9	25.8	26.1
Tunisia	3,311	3,939	74.6	72.1	25.4	27.9

| Participation rate (%) 15–24 | | | | | | Participation rate (%) 15–64 years | | | | | |
| Total | | Male | | Female | | Total | | Male | | Female | |
2000	2006	2000	2006	2000	2006	2000	2006	2000	2006	2000	2006
73.6	**72.9**	**86.2**	**85.4**	**73.6**	**72.9**	**75.0**	**74.3**	**87.1**	**86.4**	**63.2**	**62.5**
82.9	82.4	92.0	91.5	74.3	73.7	84.3	83.7	92.7	92.2	76.2	75.6
71.4	69.9	87.6	86.1	55.5	53.6	72.1	70.7	87.9	86.4	56.6	54.7
58.9	57.6	69.0	69.6	49.3	45.9	60.1	59.0	69.6	70.5	50.9	47.5
83.9	83.4	90.4	89.4	77.8	77.6	85.6	85.0	91.2	90.2	80.1	79.8
92.4	92.7	92.6	93.3	92.2	92.0	93.1	93.3	93.0	93.7	93.2	93.0
67.9	65.7	82.7	79.9	53.4	51.8	69.6	67.5	83.9	81.0	55.6	54.0
55.8	53.5	79.6	75.9	35.7	34.0	58.3	56.0	81.4	77.6	38.3	36.5
79.7	79.6	89.3	89.4	70.8	70.5	80.1	80.1	89.6	89.7	71.3	71.0
72.8	71.6	80.3	77.5	65.7	65.9	73.0	71.7	80.0	77.2	66.2	66.3
72.2	72.4	86.3	87.3	58.2	57.6	73.1	73.4	86.4	87.4	59.8	59.4
75.3	75.7	90.5	90.6	60.9	61.4	76.7	77.1	91.1	91.3	62.7	63.2
76.7	72.0	93.2	87.7	61.0	56.8	77.0	71.9	93.5	87.6	61.1	56.6
64.9	64.4	88.5	88.7	39.5	38.8	65.8	65.3	89.2	89.3	40.6	40.1
68.5	67.9	83.1	83.0	54.2	53.0	69.9	69.3	84.0	83.9	55.9	54.8
70.3	70.6	91.5	91.0	50.1	51.1	72.6	72.9	94.2	93.7	51.7	52.6
73.9	73.6	90.4	90.3	58.7	58.2	75.2	74.8	90.9	90.7	60.5	59.9
80.9	79.9	90.5	89.2	71.6	70.9	82.9	82.0	91.8	90.6	74.2	73.5
72.6	72.5	83.6	83.3	62.0	61.8	75.0	74.6	85.3	84.8	64.8	64.4
72.9	72.5	86.0	86.1	60.0	59.0	73.7	73.4	86.6	86.7	60.9	60.2
74.3	72.8	76.3	75.3	72.3	70.3	75.3	73.9	76.9	76.0	73.7	71.8
84.5	83.6	88.9	87.4	80.0	79.7	86.4	85.5	89.8	88.3	83.0	82.7
76.0	76.5	92.0	92.6	60.7	61.1	77.5	77.9	92.7	93.1	62.9	63.1
79.6	79.4	89.5	89.5	69.8	69.6	80.9	80.7	90.1	90.0	71.9	71.6
61.6	58.4	77.1	73.5	49.4	46.1	63.9	60.7	78.5	74.9	52.2	49.0
69.4	68.9	84.4	83.4	54.5	54.5	70.2	69.8	84.8	83.8	55.8	55.7
81.9	82.5	85.1	86.2	78.9	78.9	82.6	83.1	85.4	86.4	79.8	79.9
86.9	87.5	89.5	89.5	84.4	85.6	87.6	88.1	89.8	89.8	85.4	86.4
79.4	76.9	87.7	82.3	72.1	72.0	81.8	79.3	89.1	84.0	75.2	74.9
69.2	69.3	84.1	84.2	54.6	54.4	71.0	71.1	85.3	85.4	56.8	56.7
60.0	60.6	79.9	78.8	40.6	42.8	64.6	65.5	84.6	83.7	44.4	47.2
85.8	83.8	85.8	83.0	85.9	84.6	85.9	83.9	85.5	82.8	86.3	84.9
56.6	54.4	64.7	62.8	49.1	46.5	58.4	56.2	66.5	64.4	50.8	48.2
83.2	83.0	95.3	95.1	71.0	70.9	84.5	84.4	96.0	95.8	73.0	73.1
66.0	65.1	85.8	85.2	46.8	45.5	67.0	66.2	86.6	85.9	47.9	46.7
84.7	81.4	86.4	83.6	83.3	79.5	86.2	83.0	87.4	84.5	85.3	81.6
51.5	51.5	74.5	74.7	29.6	29.3	53.9	53.9	77.0	77.2	31.7	31.4
71.2	68.1	84.8	81.0	57.8	55.6	73.5	70.7	86.7	83.4	60.4	58.3
..	..	..	..	..	..	..	..	..	..	..	..
74.7	74.7	94.1	94.2	56.2	56.1	76.2	76.2	94.5	94.6	58.6	58.5
76.8	76.6	94.9	94.8	59.4	59.1	78.0	77.8	95.2	95.1	61.3	61.0
63.6	62.0	80.1	79.2	48.1	45.8	66.7	65.5	82.8	82.2	51.2	49.3
47.0	47.4	70.6	71.2	23.6	23.6	47.5	48.0	70.9	71.8	24.0	24.1
53.4	52.1	75.8	74.8	33.8	31.9	55.2	54.0	77.7	76.8	35.4	33.5
89.1	88.0	91.1	90.1	87.2	86.1	90.5	89.5	91.7	90.7	89.3	88.4
70.9	69.8	90.7	89.9	51.7	50.3	71.9	70.8	91.3	90.5	53.1	51.6
84.3	83.1	88.6	86.3	80.1	80.0	85.7	84.3	89.5	87.1	81.9	81.5
78.5	78.4	91.2	91.0	66.3	66.0	80.0	80.0	92.0	91.8	68.4	68.3
74.0	74.3	83.5	84.7	65.0	64.1	74.9	75.2	84.8	85.9	65.4	64.7
50.3	**51.4**	**76.3**	**76.8**	**50.3**	**51.3**	**52.8**	**54.2**	**79.5**	**80.3**	**26.1**	**28.2**
55.2	58.6	79.3	80.4	30.9	36.6	57.9	61.6	82.6	83.7	32.8	38.9
46.4	46.5	73.0	73.4	20.1	20.1	48.9	49.4	76.2	77.2	21.5	21.6
54.6	59.3	79.4	82.0	27.1	34.5	56.2	61.4	81.3	84.3	28.3	36.3
53.2	52.8	80.9	80.3	26.9	26.8	55.7	55.4	84.0	83.5	28.6	28.7
49.7	52.1	74.2	75.0	25.3	29.2	52.6	55.2	77.7	78.3	27.4	31.9

Table 10.2 Labor force composition

	Sector[a]					
	Agriculture		Industry		Services	
	Male (% of male employment) 2000–06[b]	Female (% of female employment) 2000–06[b]	Male (% of male employment) 2000–06[b]	Female (% of female employment) 2000–06[b]	Male (% of male employment) 2000–06[b]	Female (% of female employment) 2000–06[b]
SUB-SAHARAN AFRICA[c]						
Angola	..	..	..	..	..	..
Benin	..	..	..	..	..	..
Botswana	28.6	12.9	28	16.5	43.3	70.6
Burkina Faso	..	..	..	..	..	..
Burundi	..	..	..	..	..	..
Cameroon	53.1	68.4	14.1	3.9	25.5	22.5
Cape Verde	..	..	..	..	..	..
Central African Republic	..	..	..	..	..	..
Chad	..	..	..	..	..	..
Comoros	..	..	..	..	..	..
Congo, Dem. Rep.	..	..	..	..	..	..
Congo, Rep.	..	..	..	..	..	..
Côte d'Ivoire	..	..	..	..	..	..
Djibouti	..	..	..	..	..	..
Equatorial Guinea	..	..	..	..	..	..
Eritrea	..	..	..	..	..	..
Ethiopia	84.3	75.5	5.2	8.4	10.3	16
Gabon	..	..	..	..	..	..
Gambia, The	..	..	..	..	..	..
Ghana	..	..	..	..	..	..
Guinea	..	..	..	..	..	..
Guinea-Bissau	..	..	..	..	..	..
Kenya	..	..	..	..	..	..
Lesotho	..	..	..	..	..	..
Liberia	..	..	..	..	..	..
Madagascar	76.7	79.3	7.4	6	16	14.6
Malawi	..	..	..	..	..	..
Mali	49.8	29.9	17.8	14.7	32.4	55.3
Mauritania	..	..	..	..	..	..
Mauritius	10.5	8.9	34.2	28.8	55.1	62.2
Mozambique	..	..	..	..	..	..
Namibia	32.8	29.1	17.2	6.7	49.4	63.3
Niger	..	..	..	..	..	..
Nigeria	..	..	..	..	..	..
Rwanda	..	..	..	..	..	..
São Tomé and Principe	30.6	22.8	26.3	5.9	42.6	70.7
Senegal	..	..	..	..	..	..
Seychelles	..	..	..	..	..	..
Sierra Leone	..	..	..	..	..	..
Somalia	..	..	..	..	..	..
South Africa	12.6	7.4	33.3	13.6	53.9	78.9
Sudan	..	..	..	..	..	..
Swaziland	..	..	..	..	..	..
Tanzania	80.2	84	4	1.2	15.7	14.8
Togo	..	..	..	..	..	..
Uganda	60.1	77.3	10.7	4.8	28.8	17.8
Zambia	..	..	..	..	..	..
Zimbabwe	..	..	..	..	..	..
NORTH AFRICA						
Algeria	22.8	11	23.8	25.2	53.4	63.7
Egypt, Arab Rep.	27.7	39	22.9	6.2	49.3	54.7
Libya	..	..	..	..	..	..
Morocco	37.6	62.7	22.1	14	40.2	23.2
Tunisia	..	..	..	..	..	..

a. Components may not sum up to 100 percent because of unclassified data.
b. Data are for most recent year available during the period specified.

| Status[a] | | | | | | | | |
| Wage and salaried workers | | | Self-employed workers | | | Contributing family workers | | |
Total (% of total employed) 2000–06[b]	Male (% of males employed) 2000–06[b]	Female (% of females employed) 2000–06[b]	Total (% of total employed) 2000–06[b]	Male (% of males employed) 2000–06[b]	Female (% of females employed) 2000–06[b]	Total (% of total employed) 2000–06[b]	Male (% of males employed) 2000–06[b]	Female (% of females employed) 2000–06[b]
..	..	..	..	..	..	..	..	..
73.2	74.4	72	12.2	8.1	16.8	2.2	2.3	2.2
..	..	..	..	..	..	..	..	..
19.2	29.3	8.7	59.3	57	61.7	18.2	9.5	27.2
..	..	..	..	..	..	..	..	..
..	..	..	..	..	..	..	..	..
..	..	..	..	..	..	..	..	..
..	..	..	..	..	..	..	..	..
..	..	..	..	..	..	..	..	..
7.9	9.3	6.2	41.5	55.8	25.1	50.3	34.6	68.5
..	..	..	..	..	..	..	..	..
..	..	..	..	..	..	..	..	..
..	..	..	..	..	..	..	..	..
..	..	..	..	..	..	..	..	..
15	17.8	12	43.7	51.6	35.4	40.6	29.7	51.9
13.6	15.2	11.4	71.4	66.4	78.4	15	18.4	10.2
80.4	78.6	84.1	17.3	20.4	11.1	2.1	0.9	4.7
61.5	66.7	54.9	16	15	17.2	16.9	12.8	22
..	..	..	..	..	..	..	..	..
..	..	..	..	..	..	..	..	..
..	..	..	..	..	..	..	..	..
..	..	..	..	..	..	..	..	..
80.9	80.2	80	18.3	17.9	18.8	0.7	0.4	1.1
..	..	..	..	..	..	..	..	..
6.9	..	..	8.4	..	..	3.8	..	..
14.5	22.2	7.5	59.4	67.5	52.1	26.1	10.3	40.5
18.7	..	..	59.7	..	..	19.6	..	..
37.7	51	23.1	50.4	38.6	63.2	11.9	10.4	13.6
64.8	64.6	65.8	27.8	27.9	26.6	7.2	7.2	7.2
56.5	58.3	49.3	29.5	32.3	18.6	14	9.4	32.2
..	..	..	..	..	..	..	..	..
37.4	39.5	31.6	30.9	37.6	12.5	31.7	22.8	55.7
64.3	..	..	26.8	..	..	8.7	..	..

Table 10.3   Unemployment*

	Unemployment (15 and above)			Youth unemployment (15–24 years)			Long term unemployment		
	Total 2000–06[b]	Male 2000–06[b]	Female 2000–06[b]	Total 2000–06[b]	Male 2000–06[b]	Female 2000–06[b]	Total 2000–06[b]	Male 2000–06[b]	Female 2000–06[b]
SUB-SAHARAN AFRICA									
Angola	..	..	..	..	..	..	..	..	..
Benin	..	..	..	..	..	..	..	..	..
Botswana	23.8	21.4	26.3	39.6	33.9	46.1	..	..	..
Burkina Faso	..	..	..	..	..	..	..	..	..
Burundi	..	..	..	..	..	..	..	..	..
Cameroon	7.5	8.2	6.7	..	..	..	..	..	..
Cape Verde	..	..	..	..	..	..	..	..	..
Central African Republic	..	..	..	..	..	..	..	..	..
Chad	..	..	..	..	..	..	..	..	..
Comoros	..	..	..	..	..	..	..	..	..
Congo, Dem. Rep.	..	..	..	..	..	..	..	..	..
Congo, Rep.	..	..	..	..	..	..	..	..	..
Côte d'Ivoire	..	..	..	..	..	..	..	..	..
Djibouti	..	..	..	..	..	..	..	..	..
Equatorial Guinea	..	..	..	..	..	..	..	..	..
Eritrea	..	..	..	..	..	..	..	..	..
Ethiopia	5.4	2.7	8.2	7.7	4.1	11.2	24.4	24.3	24.4
Gabon	..	..	..	..	..	..	..	..	..
Gambia, The	..	..	..	..	..	..	..	..	..
Ghana	..	..	..	..	..	..	..	..	..
Guinea	..	..	..	..	..	..	..	..	..
Guinea-Bissau	..	..	..	..	..	..	..	..	..
Kenya	..	..	..	..	..	..	..	..	..
Lesotho	..	..	..	..	..	..	..	..	..
Liberia	..	..	..	..	..	..	..	..	..
Madagascar	5	3.8	6.2	7.07	6.7	7.3	..	..	..
Malawi	..	..	..	..	..	..	..	..	..
Mali	8.8	7.2	10.9	..	..	..	..	..	..
Mauritania	..	..	..	..	..	..	..	..	..
Mauritius	9.6	5.8	16.5	25.9	20.5	34.3	..	..	..
Mozambique	..	..	..	..	..	..	..	..	..
Namibia	31.1	26.8	35.9	44.8	40.4	49.3	..	..	..
Niger	..	..	..	..	..	..	..	..	..
Nigeria	..	..	..	..	..	..	..	..	..
Rwanda	..	..	..	..	..	..	..	..	..
São Tomé and Principe	14.4	12.5	17.8	..	..	..	..	..	..
Senegal	..	..	..	..	..	..	..	..	..
Seychelles	..	..	..	..	..	..	..	..	..
Sierra Leone	..	..	..	..	..	..	..	..	..
Somalia	..	..	..	..	..	..	..	..	..
South Africa	26.7	26.8	26.6	60.1	55.8	64.7	..	..	..
Sudan	..	..	..	..	..	..	..	..	..
Swaziland	..	..	..	..	..	..	..	..	..
Tanzania	5.1	4.4	5.8	..	..	..	..	..	..
Togo	..	..	..	..	..	..	..	..	..
Uganda	3.2	2.5	3.9	..	..	..	..	..	..
Zambia	..	..	..	..	..	..	..	..	..
Zimbabwe	8.2	10.4	6.1	24.9	28.2	21.4	..	..	..
NORTH AFRICA									
Algeria	15.3	14.9	17.5	43.4	42.8	46.3	..	..	..
Egypt, Arab Rep.	10.7	6.8	24.4	27.1	21.4	40.0	..	..	..
Libya	..	..	..	..	..	..	..	..	..
Morocco	9.7	9.7	9.7	16.6	17.5	14.1	..	..	..
Tunisia	14.2	13.1	17.3	30.7	31.4	29.3	..	..	..

a. Components may not sum up to 100 percent because of unclassified data.

b. Data are for most recent year available during the period specified.

* For a discussion on umemployment inn Africa, see Box 9 in technical notes.

			Unemployment by education level					
Primary			Secodnary			Tertiary		
Total 2000–06[b]	Male 2000–06[b]	Female 2000–06[b]	Total 2000–06[b]	Male 2000–06[b]	Female 2000–06[b]	Total 2000–06[b]	Male 2000–06[b]	Female 2000–06[b]
..	..	..	..	..	..	..	..	..
..	..	..	..	..	..	..	..	..
65.5	64.4	66.3	27.3	23.9	30.2	..	..	..
46.8	44.5	56.9	19.3	16.3	32.4	5.6	5	..
..	..	..	..	..	..	..	..	..
..	..	..	..	..	..	..	..	..
..	..	..	..	..	..	..	..	..
..	..	..	..	..	..	..	..	..
..	..	..	..	..	..	..	..	..
..	..	..	..	..	..	..	..	..
..	..	..	..	..	..	..	..	..
..	..	..	..	..	..	..	..	..
35.9	50.6	30.8	13.3	19	11.3	3.2	5.7	..
..	..	..	..	..	..	..	..	..
..	..	..	..	..	..	..	..	..
..	..	..	..	..	..	..	..	..
..	..	..	..	..	..	..	..	..
..	..	..	..	..	..	..	..	..
61.5	65.6	58.9	18.8	19.9	18.1	6.1	7.8	..
..	..	..	..	..	..	..	..	..
..	..	..	..	..	..	..	..	..
48.6	49.3	48.1	44.9	44.3	45.3	5.4	5.9	..
..	..	..	..	..	..	..	..	..
..	..	..	..	..	..	..	..	..
..	..	..	..	..	..	..	..	..
60.7	62.8	59.4	24.1	23	24.9	5.9	0.5	..
..	..	..	..	..	..	..	..	..
..	..	..	..	..	..	..	..	..
..	..	..	..	..	..	..	..	..
..	..	..	..	..	..	..	..	..
50.2	53.2	47.4	41	38.5	43.3	5.1	4.2	..
..	..	..	..	..	..	..	..	..
..	..	..	..	..	..	..	..	..
..	..	..	..	..	..	..	..	..
..	..	..	..	..	..	..	..	..
..	..	..	..	..	..	..	..	..
59.3	65.2	32.5	23	21.4	30.4	11.4	6.6	..
..	..	..	..	..	..	..	..	..
..	..	..	..	..	..	..	..	..
51.1	57.7	36.6	22.4	21.7	23.9	21.6	16.2	..
79.1	83.3	70.4	..	..	..	13.6	9	..

Table 10.4 Migration and population*

	International migration				Population				
	Stock				Population dynamics				
	Share of population (%) 2006	Total 2006	Net migration 2006	Workers remittances, received ($ millions) 2006	Total (millions) 2006	Male (% of total) 2006	Female (% of total) 2006	Annual growth rate (%) 2006	Fertility rate (births per woman) 2006
SUB-SAHARAN AFRICA	**2.1**	**15,726,612**	**–1,070,433**		**782.5**	**49.8**	**50.2**	**2.5**	**5.2**
Angola	0.4	56,351	175,000	..	16.6	49.3	50.7	2.9	6.5
Benin	2.1	174,726	98,831	..	8.8	50.4	49.6	3.2	5.5
Botswana	4.4	80,064	20,000	78.7	1.9	49.7	50.3	1.2	3.0
Burkina Faso	5.5	772,817	100,000	..	14.4	50.1	49.9	3.1	6.1
Burundi	1.3	100,189	191,600	0.0	8.2	48.9	51.1	4.0	6.8
Cameroon	0.8	136,909	6,254	..	18.2	50.0	50.0	2.1	4.4
Cape Verde	2.2	11,183	–5,000	135.8	0.5	48.1	51.9	2.3	3.4
Central African Republic	1.8	76,484	–45,000	..	4.3	48.8	51.2	1.8	4.7
Chad	4.3	437,049	218,966	..	10.5	49.7	50.3	3.2	6.3
Comoros	11.2	67,185	–10,000	..	0.6	50.2	49.8	2.2	4.0
Congo, Dem. Rep.	0.9	538,838	–236,676	..	60.6	49.5	50.5	3.2	6.3
Congo, Rep.	8	287,603	–10,000	..	3.7	49.6	50.4	2.2	4.6
Côte d'Ivoire	12.8	2,371,277	–338,732	2.1	18.9	50.8	49.2	1.8	4.6
Djibouti	2.5	20,272	..	3.7	0.8	50.0	50.0	1.8	4.1
Equatorial Guinea	1.2	5,800	..	..	0.5	49.5	50.5	2.4	5.4
Eritrea	0.3	14,612	229,376	..	4.7	49.1	50.9	3.7	5.1
Ethiopia	0.7	555,054	–140,460	169.2	77.2	49.8	50.2	2.6	5.3
Gabon	18.9	244,550	9,566	..	1.3	50.1	49.9	1.6	3.1
Gambia, The	14.3	231,739	31,127	62.9	1.7	50.2	49.8	2.8	4.8
Ghana	7.4	1,669,267	11,690	105.3	23.0	50.7	49.3	2.1	3.9
Guinea	4.5	405,772	–425,000	..	9.2	50.5	49.5	2.0	5.5
Guinea-Bissau	1.2	19,171	1,181	..	1.6	49.5	50.5	3.0	7.1
Kenya	1	344,857	25,144	570.5	36.6	49.9	50.1	2.7	5.0
Lesotho	0.3	5,886	–36,000	4.5	2.0	47.1	52.9	0.7	3.5
Liberia	1.5	50,172	–118,767	685.0	3.6	50.0	50.0	4.0	6.8
Madagascar	0.3	62,787	–5,000	..	19.2	49.8	50.2	2.8	4.9
Malawi	2.1	278,793	–30,000	..	13.6	49.7	50.3	2.6	5.7
Mali	0.4	46,318	–134,204	192.7	12.0	48.8	51.2	3.1	6.6
Mauritania	2.2	65,889	30,000	..	3.0	50.7	49.3	2.7	4.5
Mauritius	1.7	20,725	..	..	1.3	49.8	50.2	0.8	2.0
Mozambique	2	405,904	–20,000	15.8	21.0	48.5	51.5	2.1	5.2
Namibia	7.1	143,275	–1,000	6.5	2.1	49.4	50.6	1.3	3.3
Niger	0.9	123,687	–28,497	..	13.7	50.8	49.2	3.6	7.0
Nigeria	0.7	971,450	–170,000	..	144.7	50.0	50.0	2.4	5.4
Rwanda	1.3	121,183	42,943	17.2	9.5	48.2	51.8	2.5	5.9
São Tomé and Principe	4.9	7,499	–7,000	1.6	0.2	49.6	50.4	1.6	4.0
Senegal	2.8	325,940	–100,000	..	12.1	50.0	50.0	2.6	5.3
Seychelles	5.9	4,932	..	13.8	0.1	..	..	2.1	2.0
Sierra Leone	2.1	119,162	472,289	29.6	5.7	49.3	50.7	2.8	6.5
Somalia	3.4	281,702	100,000	..	8.4	49.7	50.3	3.0	6.1
South Africa	2.4	1,106,214	75,000	..	47.4	49.2	50.8	1.1	2.7
Sudan	1.7	638,596	–531,781	1,154.5	37.7	50.4	49.6	2.2	4.3
Swaziland	4	45,459	–6,000	1.3	1.1	48.4	51.6	0.6	3.5
Tanzania	2.1	792,328	–345,000	8.5	39.5	49.8	50.2	2.5	5.3
Togo	2.9	183,304	–3,570	..	6.4	49.5	50.5	2.8	4.9
Uganda	1.8	518,158	–5,000	665.2	29.9	50.1	49.9	3.3	6.7
Zambia	2.4	274,842	–81,713	57.7	11.7	49.9	50.1	1.9	5.3
Zimbabwe	3.9	510,637	–75,000	..	13.2	49.8	50.2	0.8	3.8
NORTH AFRICA	**0.8**	**1,195,541**	**–1,234,000**		**154.2**	**50.2**	**49.8**	**1.6**	**2.6**
Algeria	0.7	242,446	–140,000	..	33.4	50.6	49.4	1.5	2.4
Egypt, Arab Rep.	0.2	166,047	–525,000	5,329.5	74.2	50.2	49.8	1.8	2.9
Libya	10.4	617,536	10,000	6.0	6.0	51.9	48.1	2.0	2.8
Morocco	0.4	131,654	–550,000	5,454.3	30.5	49.3	50.7	1.2	2.4
Tunisia	0.4	37,858	–29,000	1,510.0	10.1	50.5	49.5	1.0	2.0

* For a discussion on demographic transition, see Box 10 in the technical notes.

	Population													
	Age composition (% of total)										Geographic distribution (%)			
	Ages 0–14			Ages 15–64			Ages 65 and older				Share of total population		Annual growth	
	Total	Male	Female	Total	Male	Female	Total	Male	Female	Dependency ratio	Rural population	Urban population	Rural population	Urban population
	2006	2006	2006	2006	2006	2006	2006	2006	2006	2006	2006	2006	2006	2006
43.3	**21.8**	**21.4**	**53.6**	**26.6**	**27.0**	**3.1**	**1.4**	**1.7**	**0.90**	**64.5**	**35.5**	**1.7**	**3.9**
46.3	23.1	23.2	51.3	25.2	26.1	2.4	1.1	1.4	0.90	45.1	54.9	0.9	4.5
44.0	22.4	21.6	53.3	26.9	26.4	2.7	1.1	1.6	0.90	59.6	40.4	2.5	4.1
35.1	17.7	17.4	61.5	30.7	30.8	3.4	1.3	2.1	0.60	41.9	58.1	−0.6	2.5
46.0	23.5	22.5	51.0	25.4	25.6	3.1	1.3	1.8	1.00	81.3	18.7	2.5	5.3
44.7	22.5	22.4	52.7	25.4	27.1	2.6	1.0	1.6	0.90	90.2	9.8	3.6	7.0
41.5	20.9	20.5	55.0	27.5	27.5	3.5	1.6	1.9	0.80	44.9	55.1	0.3	3.6
39.0	19.6	19.4	56.8	27.0	29.7	4.2	1.5	2.7	0.80	41.9	58.1	0.5	3.6
42.5	21.1	21.3	53.7	26.1	27.6	3.9	1.6	2.3	0.90	61.7	38.3	1.5	2.2
46.2	23.2	22.9	50.9	25.2	25.7	2.9	1.3	1.6	1.00	74.2	25.8	2.5	4.9
41.8	21.2	20.5	55.5	27.8	27.7	2.7	1.2	1.5	0.80	72.0	28.0	2.1	2.4
47.3	23.7	23.6	50.1	24.8	25.4	2.6	1.1	1.5	1.00	67.3	32.7	2.3	5.1
41.9	21.0	20.8	54.9	27.3	27.7	3.2	1.4	1.8	0.80	39.4	60.6	1.2	2.8
41.4	20.7	20.7	55.4	28.5	26.9	3.2	1.6	1.6	0.80	52.5	47.5	0.5	3.2
37.9	19.1	18.8	59.1	29.5	29.5	3.0	1.4	1.7	0.70	13.5	86.5	−1.2	2.2
42.3	21.2	21.0	53.6	26.5	27.2	4.1	1.8	2.3	0.90	60.9	39.1	2.1	2.8
42.9	21.7	21.3	54.8	26.5	28.1	2.3	0.9	1.4	0.80	80.2	19.8	3.0	5.8
44.2	22.2	21.9	52.9	26.3	26.7	2.9	1.3	1.6	0.90	83.6	16.4	2.2	4.4
35.4	17.9	17.5	60.0	30.1	29.8	4.6	2.1	2.6	0.70	15.9	84.1	−1.4	2.1
41.0	20.7	20.2	55.2	27.6	27.6	3.8	1.8	2.0	0.80	45.3	54.7	1.0	4.4
38.6	19.8	18.8	57.7	29.2	28.5	3.7	1.7	1.9	0.70	51.5	48.5	0.7	3.6
43.3	22.0	21.2	53.7	27.1	26.5	3.1	1.3	1.7	0.90	66.5	33.5	1.2	3.4
47.6	23.8	23.7	49.4	24.3	25.1	3.0	1.3	1.7	1.00	70.3	29.7	2.9	3.3
42.6	21.5	21.2	54.7	27.2	27.5	2.7	1.2	1.5	0.80	79.0	21.0	2.3	4.1
40.1	20.2	19.9	55.1	25.0	30.2	4.7	1.9	2.8	0.80	76.0	24.0	−0.2	3.8
47.0	23.6	23.4	50.8	25.4	25.4	2.2	1.0	1.2	1.00	41.2	58.8	2.3	5.1
43.6	21.8	21.7	53.3	26.5	26.8	3.2	1.4	1.7	0.90	71.2	28.8	2.3	3.9
47.0	23.7	23.2	49.9	24.7	25.4	3.0	1.3	1.7	1.00	82.2	17.8	2.0	5.4
47.6	24.0	23.7	48.8	23.3	25.5	3.6	1.5	2.0	1.00	68.9	31.1	2.2	4.9
40.1	20.6	19.4	56.3	28.4	27.9	3.6	1.6	2.0	0.80	59.4	40.6	2.3	3.2
24.0	12.2	11.7	69.3	34.8	34.5	6.7	2.8	3.9	0.40	57.6	42.4	0.7	1.0
44.3	22.2	22.0	52.5	25.0	27.6	3.2	1.3	1.9	0.90	64.7	35.3	0.9	4.4
38.3	19.3	19.1	58.2	28.6	29.5	3.5	1.5	2.0	0.70	64.3	35.7	0.4	3.0
48.0	24.6	23.3	48.8	24.5	24.4	3.2	1.7	1.4	1.00	83.6	16.4	3.4	4.0
44.1	22.3	21.7	53.0	26.4	26.6	2.9	1.3	1.6	0.90	53.1	46.9	1.0	3.9
43.1	21.5	21.8	54.5	25.7	28.5	2.5	1.0	1.5	0.80	82.2	17.8	2.1	4.1
41.4	20.9	20.4	54.3	26.8	27.6	4.3	1.9	2.3	0.80	41.1	58.9	−0.3	3.0
41.9	21.2	20.7	53.8	26.7	27.2	4.3	2.1	2.2	0.90	58.1	41.9	2.1	3.2
..	..	..	..	..	..	..	..	..	..	46.6	53.4	1.0	2.9
42.8	21.4	21.4	53.9	26.4	27.4	3.3	1.5	1.9	0.90	62.9	37.1	2.3	3.6
44.2	22.2	21.9	53.2	26.3	27.0	2.6	1.2	1.4	0.90	64.4	35.6	2.3	4.2
31.9	16.1	15.8	63.7	31.4	32.3	4.4	1.7	2.7	0.60	40.2	59.8	−0.1	1.9
40.3	20.5	19.7	56.1	28.2	27.9	3.6	1.6	1.9	0.80	58.3	41.7	0.7	4.3
39.2	19.8	19.6	57.5	27.2	30.2	3.3	1.4	1.9	0.70	75.6	24.4	0.2	1.8
44.4	22.3	22.0	52.6	26.1	26.6	3.0	1.3	1.7	0.90	75.4	24.6	1.9	4.3
43.0	21.5	21.5	53.9	26.7	27.3	3.1	1.3	1.7	0.90	59.4	40.6	1.5	4.5
49.3	24.8	24.4	48.3	24.1	24.2	2.5	1.1	1.4	1.10	87.3	12.7	3.1	4.5
45.6	22.9	22.6	51.4	25.7	25.8	2.9	1.2	1.7	0.90	64.9	35.1	1.7	2.3
39.0	19.6	19.4	57.5	28.7	28.8	3.5	1.5	2.0	0.70	63.6	36.4	0.1	2.2
30.9	**15.8**	**15.1**	**64.2**	**32.1**	**32.0**	**4.9**	**2.2**	**2.7**	**0.60**	**47.4**	**52.6**	**1.1**	**2.0**
28.9	14.9	14.2	66.5	33.6	32.7	4.6	2.1	2.5	0.50	36.1	63.9	−0.3	2.5
33.0	16.9	16.2	62.1	31.1	31.0	4.9	2.2	2.7	0.60	57.4	42.6	1.7	1.9
30.2	15.5	14.8	65.9	34.4	31.4	3.9	1.9	2.0	0.50	22.8	77.2	1.2	2.2
29.7	15.2	14.6	65.0	31.7	33.2	5.3	2.4	2.9	0.50	44.7	55.3	0.4	1.8
25.4	13.2	12.3	68.3	34.4	33.8	6.3	2.9	3.4	0.50	34.3	65.7	−0.2	1.6

Table 11.1 HIV/AIDS*

| | Estimated number of people living with HIV/AIDS (thousands) | | | | Estimated prevalence rate (%) | | |
| | Total 2007 | Adults (ages 15 and older) 2007 | Women (ages 15 and older) 2007 | Children (ages 0–14) 2007 | Adults (ages 15–49) | | |
					Point estimate 2007	Low estimate 2007	High estimate 2007
SUB-SAHARAN AFRICA	**22,000**	**20,300**	**12,000**	**1,800**	**5.0**	**4.6**	**5.4**
Angola	190	180	110	17	2.1	1.7	2.5
Benin	64	59	37	5	1.2	1.1	1.4
Botswana	300	280	170	15	23.9	22.5	24.9
Burkina Faso	130	120	61	10	1.6	1.4	1.9
Burundi	110	90	53	15	2.0	1.3	2.5
Cameroon	540	500	300	45	5.1	3.9	6.2
Cape Verde	..	..	..	..	..	..	..
Central African Republic	160	140	91	14	6.3	5.9	6.7
Chad	200	180	110	19	3.5	2.4	4.3
Comoros	<0.2	<0.2	<0.1	..	<0.1	0.1	0.1
Congo, Dem. Rep.	..	..	..	..	..	1.2	1.5
Congo, Rep.	79	73	43	7	3.5	2.8	4.2
Côte d'Ivoire	480	420	250	52	3.9	3.2	4.5
Djibouti	16	15	9	1	3.1	2.3	3.8
Equatorial Guinea	11	10	6	<1	3.4	2.6	4.6
Eritrea	38	35	21	3	1.3	0.8	2.0
Ethiopia	980	890	530	92	2.1	1.8	2.2
Gabon	49	46	27	2	5.9	4.4	8.3
Gambia, The	8	8	5	<1	0.9	0.4	1.3
Ghana	260	250	150	17	1.9	1.7	2.2
Guinea	87	81	48	6	1.6	1.3	2.2
Guinea-Bissau	16	15	9	2	1.8	1.3	2.6
Kenya	..	..	..	..	..	7.1	8.5
Lesotho	270	260	150	12	23.2	21.9	24.5
Liberia	35	32	19	3	1.7	1.4	2.0
Madagascar	14	13	3	<0.5	0.1	<0.1	0.2
Malawi	930	840	490	91	11.9	11.0	12.9
Mali	100	93	56	9	1.5	1.2	1.8
Mauritania	14	14	4	<0.5	0.8	0.5	1.5
Mauritius	13	13	4	<0.1	1.7	1.0	3.6
Mozambique	1,500	1,400	810	100	12.5	10.9	14.7
Namibia	200	180	110	14	15.3	12.4	18.1
Niger	60	56	17	3	0.8	0.6	1.1
Nigeria	2,600	2,400	1,400	220	3.1	2.3	3.8
Rwanda	150	130	78	19	2.8	2.4	3.2
São Tomé and Principe	..	..	..	..	..	..	..
Senegal	67	64	38	3	1.0	0.7	1.4
Seychelles	..	..	..	..	..	..	..
Sierra Leone	55	51	30	4	1.7	1.3	2.4
Somalia	24	24	7	<1	0.5	0.3	1.0
South Africa	5,700	5,400	3,200	280	18.1	15.4	20.9
Sudan	320	290	170	25	1.4	1.0	2.0
Swaziland	190	170	100	15	26.1	25.1	27.1
Tanzania	1,400	1,300	760	140	6.2	5.8	6.6
Togo	130	120	69	10	3.3	2.7	4.1
Uganda	940	810	480	130	5.4	5.0	6.1
Zambia	1,100	980	560	95	15.2	14.3	16.4
Zimbabwe	1,300	1,200	680	120	15.3	14.6	16.1
NORTH AFRICA							
Algeria	21	21	6	..	0.1	<0.1	0.2
Egypt, Arab Rep.	9	9	3	..	..	<0.1	<0.1
Libya	..	..	..	..	..	<0.2	<0.2
Morocco	21	21	6	..	0.1	<0.1	0.2
Tunisia	4	4	1	..	0.1	<0.1	0.2

* For a discussion on HIV prevalance and incidence, see Box 11 in the technical notes.

| Estimated prevalence rate (%) | | | | | | Deaths of adults and children due to HIV/AIDS (thousands) 2007 | AIDS orphans (ages 0–17, thousands) 2007 |
| Young men (ages 15–24) | | | Young women (ages 15–24) | | | | |
Point estimate 2007	Low estimate 2007	High estimate 2007	Point estimate 2007	Low estimate 2007	High estimate 2007		
1.1	0.8	1.4	3.2	2.6	3.8	1,500	11,600
0.2	0.1	0.4	0.3	0.1	0.5	11	50
0.3	0.1	0.5	0.9	0.6	1.2	3	29
5.1	2.1	7.9	15.3	10.0	20.8	11	95
0.5	0.2	0.8	0.9	0.5	1.3	9	100
0.4	0.2	0.7	1.3	0.6	2.0	11	120
1.2	0.5	2.2	4.3	1.0	5.9	39	300
..	..	..	..	..	..	..	..
1.1	0.5	1.5	5.5	4.1	7.0	11	72
2.0	0.9	2.9	2.8	1.3	4.1	14	85
0.1	<0.1	0.2	<0.1	0.1	0.1	..	<0.1
..	0.1	0.4	..	0.7	1.2	..	..
0.8	0.3	1.1	2.3	1.3	3.3	6	69
0.8	0.3	1.3	2.4	1.0	3.4	38	420
0.7	0.3	1.1	2.1	1.4	3.0	1	5
0.8	0.4	1.4	2.5	1.7	3.7	..	5
0.3	0.1	0.6	0.9	0.4	1.6	3	18
0.5	0.2	0.7	1.5	1.1	1.9	67.0	650.0
1.3	0.6	2.4	3.9	2.0	6.3	2	18
0.2	0.1	0.4	0.6	0.3	1.0	<1	3
0.4	0.2	0.6	1.3	0.9	1.7	21	160
0.4	0.2	0.6	1.2	0.9	1.8	5	25
0.4	0.2	0.8	1.2	0.3	2.5	1	6
..	0.8	2.5	..	4.6	8.4	..	..
5.9	2.5	9.6	14.9	10.6	18.4	18	110
0.4	0.2	0.6	1.3	0.8	1.7	2.3	15.0
0.2	0.1	0.3	0.1	<0.1	0.2	<1	3
2.4	0.9	3.8	8.4	6.7	10.4	68	550
0.4	0.2	0.5	1.1	0.7	1.5	6	44
0.9	0.4	1.9	0.5	0.2	1.0	<1	3
1.8	0.8	4.5	1.0	0.5	2.2	<0.5	<0.5
2.9	1.2	4.2	8.5	5.9	11.1	81	400
3.4	1.4	5.3	10.3	6.2	14.5	5	66
0.9	0.4	1.5	1.5	0.5	0.8	4	25
0.8	0.3	1.2	2.3	1.2	3.3	170	1,200
0.5	0.3	0.7	1.4	0.9	1.9	8	220
..	..	..	..	..	..	..	..
0.3	0.1	0.5	0.8	0.5	1.2	2	8
..	..	..	..	..	..	..	..
0.4	0.2	0.7	1.3	0.7	1.9	3	16
0.6	0.3	1.4	0.3	0.1	0.6	2	9
4.0	1.7	6.0	12.7	9.1	17.0	350	1,400
0.3	0.2	0.5	1.0	0.6	1.5	25	..
5.8	2.2	9.3	22.6	17.7	27.2	10	56
0.5	0.4	0.7	0.9	0.5	1.3	96	970
0.8	0.4	1.2	2.4	1.4	3.3	9	68
1.3	0.6	1.9	3.9	2.7	5.2	77	1,200
3.6	1.6	5.2	11.3	8.5	14.2	56	600
2.9	1.2	4.4	7.7	3.8	11.7	140	1,000
0.1	<0.1	0.3	0.1	<0.1	0.2	<1	..
..	<0.1	<0.1	..	<0.1	<0.1	<1	..
..	..	..	..	..	..	..	..
0.1	<0.1	0.2	0.1	<0.1	0.2	<1	..
0.1	<0.1	0.2	<0.1	0.1	0.1	<0.2	..

Table 12.1 Malaria

	Population (millions) 2006	Risk of malaria (% of population)			Deaths due to malaria (per 100,000 population) 2000–2006[a]
		Endemic 2000–2006[a]	Epidemic 2000–2006[a]	Negligible 2000–2006[a]	
SUB-SAHARAN AFRICA	**782.5**				
Angola	16.6	90.5	8.4	1.2	354
Benin	8.8	100.0	..	..	177
Botswana	1.9	..	31.5	68.5	15
Burkina Faso	14.4	100.0	..	..	292
Burundi	8.2	67.6	17.3	15.2	143
Cameroon	18.2	93.6	4.4	2.0	108
Cape Verde	0.5	..	..	..	22
Central African Republic	4.3	100.0	..	..	137
Chad	10.5	96.5	3.5	0.0	207
Comoros	0.6	..	100.0	..	80
Congo, Dem. Rep.	60.6	91.6	2.6	5.8	224
Congo, Rep.	3.7	100.0	..	..	78
Côte d'Ivoire	18.9	100.0	..	0.0	76
Djibouti	0.8	1.7	98.3	..	..
Equatorial Guinea	0.5	98.0	1.5	0.5	152
Eritrea	4.7	92.2	6.9	1.0	74
Ethiopia	77.2	39.7	23.9	36.4	198
Gabon	1.3	96.5	..	3.5	80
Gambia, The	1.7	100.0	..	..	52
Ghana	23.0	100.0	..	..	70
Guinea	9.2	100.0	0.0	..	200
Guinea-Bissau	1.6	99.5	..	0.5	150
Kenya	36.6	53.4	24.4	22.2	63
Lesotho	2.0	..	..	..	84
Liberia	3.6	100.0	..	..	201
Madagascar	19.2	89.1	7.1	3.8	184
Malawi	13.6	96.7	2.5	0.7	275
Mali	12.0	99.1	0.9	0.0	454
Mauritania	3.0	65.3	34.5	0.2	108
Mauritius	1.3	..	..	..	..
Mozambique	21.0	99.5	0.3	0.2	232
Namibia	2.0	..	40.8	59.2	52
Niger	13.7	97.1	2.8	0.1	469
Nigeria	144.7	100.0	0.0	0.0	141
Rwanda	9.5	53.0	13.6	33.4	200
São Tomé and Principe	0.2	..	100.0	..	80
Senegal	12.1	100.0	..	..	72
Seychelles	0.1	..	..	..	..
Sierra Leone	5.7	100.0	0.0	0.0	312
Somalia	8.4	19.9	79.1	1.1	81
South Africa	47.4	..	19.8	80.2	..
Sudan	37.7	74.1	24.7	1.3	70
Swaziland	1.1	..	76.6	23.4	..
Tanzania	39.5	93.1	3.0	3.9	130
Togo	6.4	100.0	..	..	47
Uganda	29.9	90.2	2.9	6.9	152
Zambia	11.7	96.1	3.0	0.9	141
Zimbabwe	13.2	..	84.2	15.8	1
NORTH AFRICA	**154.2**	**..**	**..**	**..**	**..**
Algeria	33.4	..	..	..	..
Egypt, Arab Rep.	74.2	..	..	..	..
Libya	6.0	..	..	..	..
Morocco	30.5	..	..	..	..
Tunisia	10.1	..	..	..	..

a. Data are for the most recent year available during the period specified.

Under-five mortality rate (per 1,000) 2000–2006[a]	Children sleeping under insecticide-treated bednets (% of chidlren under age 5) 2000–2006[a]	Children with fever receiving antimalarial treatment within 24 hrs (% of children under 5 with fever)		Malaria treatment (% of children <5 with fever being treated with anti-malarial drugs) 2000–2006[a]	Pregnant women receiving two doses of intermittent preventive treatment (%) 2000–2006[a]
		Effective antimalarial treatment 2000–2006[a]	Any antimalarial treatment 2000–2006[a]		
157					
260	2.3	20.0	..	63.0	..
148	20.1	18.5	24.7	54.0	2.5
124	..	..	..	..	..
204	9.6	44.9	41.0	48.0	1.3
181	8.3	..	19.1	30.0	..
149	13.1	26.7	38.2	57.8	5.8
34	..	..	..	..	..
175	15.1	..	41.6	57.0	8.7
209	0.6	..	..	44.0	..
68	9.3	..	..	62.7	..
205	0.7	..	..	52.0	..
127	..	8.6	22.1	48.0	..
127	5.9	..	25.9	36.0	8.3
130	1.3	2.9	9.5	9.5	..
206	0.7	..	..	48.6	..
74	4.2	7.5	1.8	3.6	..
123	1.5	0.7	0.7	3.0	..
91	..	..	..	..	..
113	49.0	..	52.4	62.6	32.5
120	21.8	44.2	48.3	60.8	27.3
161	0.3	13.9	13.9	43.5	2.9
200	39.0	..	27.2	45.7	7.4
121	4.6	10.8	11.1	26.5	3.9
132	..	..	..	..	..
235	2.6	..	..	..	..
115	0.2	..	..	34.2	..
120	23.0	22.7	19.9	23.9	44.5
217	8.4	..	..	38.0	..
125	2.1	11.8	11.8	33.4	..
14	..	..	..	..	..
138	..	8.3	8.3	15.0	..
61	3.4	..	..	14.4	..
253	7.4	24.9	24.9	33.0	0.3
191	1.2	24.9	24.6	33.9	0.8
160	5.0	..	2.5	12.3	0.3
96	41.7	..	17.0	24.7	..
116	7.1	12.2	12.2	26.8	9.2
13	..	..	..	..	..
270	5.3	45.0	45.0	51.9	1.8
146	9.2	..	2.9	7.9	0.9
69	..	..	..	..	..
89	27.6	..	..	54.2	..
164	0.1	..	..	25.5	..
118	16.0	49.3	51.0	58.2	21.7
108	38.4	..	37.5	47.7	18.1
134	9.7	28.9	29.0	61.8	16.6
182	22.8	8.7	37.0	57.9	61.2
105	2.9	3.4	3.4	4.7	6.3
35	..	..	..	..	..
38	..	..	..	..	..
35	..	..	..	..	..
18	..	..	..	..	..
37	..	..	..	..	..
23	..	..	..	..	..

Table **13.1** Aid and debt relief

	Net ODA aid (2005 $ millions)				Net private aid (millions)		
	From all donors 2006	From DAC donors 2006	From non-DAC donors 2006	From multilateral donors 2006	From all donors 2006	From DAC donors 2006	From non-DAC donors 2006
SUB-SAHARAN AFRICA	**37,975**	**27,476**	**312**	**10,187**	**523**	**347**	**176**
Angola	171	−55	102	124	−5	−5	0
Benin	375	228	−0	147	−4	−10	7
Botswana	65	36	−2	30	11	11	..
Burkina Faso	871	386	10	475	99	99	..
Burundi	415	222	0	192	−12	−12	..
Cameroon	1,684	1,505	6	173	84	84	..
Cape Verde	138	99	2	38	57	57	..
Central African Republic	134	65	..	69	3	3	..
Chad	284	153	3	128	25	25	..
Comoros	30	20	1	10	0	0	..
Congo, Dem. Rep.	2,056	1,500	−1	556	−189	−189	..
Congo, Rep.	254	169	1	84	396	396	..
Côte d'Ivoire	251	199	0	52	316	315	1
Djibouti	117	89	2	26	53	53	..
Equatorial Guinea	27	19	−0	8	914	914	..
Eritrea	129	63	−2	67	7	7	..
Ethiopia	1,947	1,024	25	898	24	20	4
Gabon	31	32	1	−1	227	227	..
Gambia, The	74	25	6	43	−2	−2	..
Ghana	1,176	595	1	580	554	553	1
Guinea	164	103	3	58	19	19	..
Guinea-Bissau	82	39	0	43	−1	−1	..
Kenya	943	761	16	166	−177	−177	0
Lesotho	72	38	−1	34	−3	−3	..
Liberia	269	187	0	81	43	43	..
Madagascar	754	266	4	485	142	113	30
Malawi	669	398	12	259	33	33	..
Mali	825	398	9	418	14	14	..
Mauritania	188	94	1	93	−9	−9	..
Mauritius	19	9	−2	12	784	784	..
Mozambique	1,611	938	3	669	−6	−6	..
Namibia	145	106	2	38	53	53	..
Niger	401	235	0	166	−924	−924	..
Nigeria	11,434	10,820	2	613	−8,433	−8,557	123
Rwanda	585	321	0	263	−62	−62	..
São Tomé and Principe	22	18	0	3	4	4	..
Senegal	825	509	12	304	11	11	..
Seychelles	14	7	−1	7	−33	−33	..
Sierra Leone	364	199	0	164	91	91	..
Somalia	392	263	3	125	8	8	..
South Africa	718	561	1	157	7,598	7,592	6
Sudan	2,058	1,518	87	453	62	59	3
Swaziland	35	12	−1	23	−6	−6	..
Tanzania	1,825	992	1	832	127	127	0
Togo	79	55	0	24	88	88	..
Uganda	1,551	938	3	609	23	23	..
Zambia	1,425	1,115	2	308	−81	−81	0
Zimbabwe	280	200	0	80	−202	−202	..
NORTH AFRICA	**2,596**	**1,628**	**196**	**803**	**5,930**	**5,889**	**41**
Algeria	209	205	7	−4	297	291	6
Egypt, Arab Rep.	873	537	50	287	4,174	4,176	−2
Libya	37	33	1	3	761	724	37
Morocco	1,046	567	116	362	323	323	..
Tunisia	432	287	21	154	−65	−65	..

| | Net ODA aid | | | | | Heavily indebted Poor Country (HIPC) Debt Initiative | | |
Share of GDP (%) 2006	Per capita ($) 2006	Share of gross capital formation (%) 2006	Share of imports of goods and services (%) 2006	Share of central government expenditures (%) 2006	Cereal food aid shipments (thousand of tonnes) 2006	Decision point 2006	Completion point 2006	Debt service relief committed ($ millions) 2006
5.1	**48.5**	**27.0**	**7.0**	**28.3**	**2,204**			**52,315**
0.4	10.3	2.8	0.3	..	7	..	..	..
8.1	42.8	..	..	..	6	Jul. 2000	Mar. 2003	460
0.6	35	2.0	0.7	3.1	..	..	..	..
15.1	60.6	83.3	39.4	68.6	24	Jul. 2000	Apr. 2002	930
45.9	50.8	275.7	78.3	157.0	38	Oct. 2000	..	1,472
9.4	92.7	55.8	21.3	97.7	5	Oct.2000	Apr. 2006	4,917
11.7	266.6	30.7	16.2	56.5	16	Sep. 2008	..	..
9.1	31.4	101.3	25.2	85.4	8	..	..	..
4.5	27.1	20.2	4.5	76.8	61	May 2001	..	260
7.5	49.5	76.7	16.0	59.9	..	..	..	..
24.1	33.9	148.8	34.2	331.1	80	Jul. 2003	Floating	10,389
3.3	69	14.4	2.5	24.9	5	Mar. 2006	Floating	2,881
1.5	13.3	14.7	1.5	17.3	13	Mar. 1998	..	..
15.2	143.2	51.6	15.7	54.5	8	..	..	..
0.3	54.1	0.8	0.2	10.9	..	..	..	..
11.9	27.5	63.6	20.5	28.1	10	..	..	..
12.8	25.2	53.0	25.5	106.2	504	Nov. 2001	Apr. 2004	3,275
0.3	23.7	1.4	0.4	3.9	..	..	..	..
14.5	44.5	59.7	..	..	6	Dec. 2000	Dec. 2008	90
9.2	51.1	28.1	8.8	68.9	21	Feb. 2002	Jul. 2004	3,500
5.1	17.8	38.3	7.3	90.7	19	Dec. 2000	Floating	800
26.8	50	155.6	28.3	151.6	7	Dec. 2000	Floating	790
4.1	25.8	19.0	6.6	25.5	245	..	..	..
4.8	36	14.5	3.2	26.6	7	..	..	..
43.8	75.1	..	42.7	..	42	..	..	..
13.7	39.4	55.3	19.4	155.7	37	Dec. 2000	Oct. 2004	1,900
21.1	49.3	89.1	45.5	179.6	52	Dec. 2000	Aug.2006	1,000
14.1	69	61.5	19.5	141.7	49	Sep. 2000	Mar.2003	895
7	61.6	30.3	6.2	35.4	38	Feb. 2000	Jun. 2002	1,100
0.3	14.8	1.2	0.2	2.0	..	..	..	..
23.6	76.8	122.0	26.5	212.4	81	Apr. 2000	Sep. 2001	4,300
2.2	71	7.5	2.0	9.3	0	..	..	..
11.2	29.2	..	..	..	93	Dec. 2000	Apr. 2004	1,190
7.8	79	..	10.9	..	..	..	..	..
20.4	61.8	100.4	54.0	173.8	19	Dec. 2000	Apr. 2005	1,316
17.5	138.9	..	..	..	0	Dec. 2000	Mar. 2008	200
8.9	68.3	30.8	12.9	92.6	12	Jun. 2000	Apr. 2004	850
1.8	164.9	5.5	0.7	7.3	..	..	..	..
25.6	63.4	165.5	42.2	196.1	19	Mar. 2002	Dec. 2006	950
..	46.4	..	..	..	115	..	..	..
0.3	15.1	1.4	0.4	1.4	..	..	..	..
5.7	54.6	22.3	12.9	33.8	425	..	..	..
1.2	30.3	7.8	0.9	6.3	4	..	..	..
12.9	46.3	77.0	25.9	78.8	7	Apr. 2000	Nov. 2001	3,000
3.5	12.3	..	..	..	0	..	..	..
16.3	51.9	69.9	36.4	111.1	36	Feb. 2000	May. 2000	1,950
13.1	121.8	57.9	19.4	130.5	19	Dec. 2000	Apr. 2005	3,900
..	21.2	..	..	..	68	..	..	..
0.7	**16.8**	**..**	**1.6**	**8.0**	**35**			**..**
0.2	6.3	..	..	..	10	..	..	..
0.8	11.8	4.3	1.3	6.6	24	..	..	..
0.1	6.2	..	..	..	..	..	..	..
1.6	34.3	5.1	2.2	8.7	..	..	..	..
1.4	42.7	5.9	1.3	10.4	..	..	..	..

	Viewed by firms as a major contraint (% of firms)		Enforcing contracts		
	Court system is fair, impartial and uncorrupted 2006–07[c]	Crime, theft and disorder 2006–07[c]	Number of procedures 2008	Time required (days) 2008	Cost (% of debt) 2008
SUB-SAHARAN AFRICA			**39**	**673**	**48.6**
Angola	36.1	31.9	46	1,011	44.4
Benin	..	..	42	825	64.7
Botswana	22.6	69.6	29	987	28.1
Burkina Faso	54.0	39.1	37	446	107.4
Burundi	19.7	40.7	44	558	38.6
Cameroon	52.1	25.6	43	800	46.6
Cape Verde	16.3	61.8	37	425	21.8
Central African Republic	..	..	43	660	82.0
Chad	..	..	41	743	77.4
Comoros	..	..	43	506	89.4
Congo, Dem. Rep.	20.0	19.8	43	685	151.8
Congo, Rep.	..	..	44	560	53.2
Côte d'Ivoire	..	..	33	770	41.7
Djibouti	..	..	40	1,225	34.0
Equatorial Guinea	..	..	40	553	18.5
Eritrea	..	..	39	405	22.6
Ethiopia	23.1	24.2	39	690	15.2
Gabon	..	..	38	1,070	34.3
Gambia, The	9.8	62.8	32	434	37.9
Ghana	9.9	59.8	36	487	23.0
Guinea	47.7	25.7	50	276	45.0
Guinea-Bissau	44.0	12.1	41	1,140	25.0
Kenya	..	..	44	465	26.7
Lesotho	..	..	41	695	19.5
Liberia	..	..	41	1,280	35.0
Madagascar	..	..	38	871	42.4
Malawi	46.8	59.2	42	432	142.4
Mali	15.7	49.6	39	860	52.0
Mauritania	17.1	48.5	46	400	23.2
Mauritius	..	..	37	750	17.4
Mozambique	..	..	31	1,010	142.5
Namibia	19.1	66.1	33	270	29.9
Niger	58.5	35.7	39	545	59.6
Nigeria	..	..	39	457	32.0
Rwanda	4.4	67.1	24	310	78.7
São Tomé and Principe	..	..	43	1,185	34.8
Senegal	23.8	55.4	44	780	26.5
Seychelles	..	..	38	720	14.3
Sierra Leone	..	..	40	515	149.5
Somalia	..	..	..	..	..
South Africa	..	..	30	600	33.2
Sudan	..	..	53	810	19.8
Swaziland	24.9	40.3	40	972	23.1
Tanzania	19.7	46.7	38	462	14.3
Togo	..	..	41	588	47.5
Uganda	23.6	43.5	38	535	44.9
Zambia	12.6	54.7	35	471	38.7
Zimbabwe	..	..	38	410	32.0
NORTH AFRICA			**42**	**705**	**23.8**
Algeria	64.3	..	47	630	21.9
Egypt, Arab Rep.	..	..	42	1,010	26.2
Libya	..	..	..	..	..
Morocco	27.3	43.5	40	615	25.2
Tunisia	..	..	39	565	21.8

a. Indexes run from 0 (least desirable) to 10 (most desirable).
b. Average of the disclosure, director liability and shareholder suits indexes.
c. Data are for the most recent year available during the period specified.

Protecting investors[a]				Regulation and tax administration			Extractive Industries Transparency Initiative	
Disclosure index 2008	Director Liability Index 2008	Shareholder Suits Index 2008	Investor Protection Index[b] 2008	Number of tax payments 2008	Time to prepare, file, and pay taxes (hours) 2008	Total tax rate (% of profit) 2008	Endorsed 2007	Report produced 2007
5	3	5	4.2	38	320	66.6		
5	6	6	5.7	31	272	53.2	No	No
6	1	3	3.3	55	270	73.3	No	No
8	2	3	4.3	19	140	17.2	No	No
6	1	4	3.7	45	270	47.6	No	No
4	1	5	3.3	32	140	278.7	No	No
6	1	6	4.3	41	1400	51.9	Yes	Yes
1	5	6	4.0	57	100	54.0	No	No
6	1	5	4.0	54	504	203.8	No	No
6	1	5	4.0	54	122	63.7	Yes	No
6	1	5	4.0	20	100	48.8	No	No
3	3	4	3.3	32	308	229.8	Yes	No
6	1	3	3.3	61	606	65.4	Yes	No
6	1	3	3.3	66	270	45.4	Yes	No
5	2	0	2.3	35	114	38.7	..	..
6	1	4	3.7	46	296	59.5	Yes	No
4	5	5	4.7	18	216	84.5	No	No
4	4	5	4.3	20	198	31.1	No	No
6	1	3	3.3	26	272	44.7	Yes	Yes
2	1	5	2.7	50	376	292.4	No	No
7	5	6	6.0	33	304	32.9	Yes	Yes
6	1	1	2.7	56	416	49.9	Yes	Yes
6	1	5	4.0	46	208	45.9	No	No
3	2	10	5.0	41	432	50.9	No	No
2	1	8	3.7	21	342	20.4	No	No
4	1	6	3.7	32	158	35.8	Yes	No
5	6	6	5.7	26	238	46.5	Yes	No
4	7	5	5.3	19	370	32.2	No	No
6	1	3	3.3	58	270	51.4	Yes	No
5	3	3	3.7	38	696	107.5	Yes	No
6	8	9	7.7	7	161	21.7	No	No
5	4	9	6.0	37	230	34.3	No	No
5	5	6	5.3	37	375	26.5	No	No
6	1	3	3.3	42	270	42.4	Yes	No
5	7	5	5.7	35	1120	32.2	Yes	Yes
2	5	1	2.7	34	168	33.8	No	No
3	1	6	3.3	42	424	48.7	Yes	No
6	1	2	3.0	59	696	46.0	No	No
4	8	5	5.7	16	76	48.4	No	No
3	6	8	5.7	28	399	233.5	Yes	No
..	..	..	..	..	..	..	No	No
8	8	8	8.0	11	350	37.1	No	No
0	6	4	3.3	42	180	31.6	No	No
0	1	5	2.0	33	104	36.6	No	No
3	4	8	5.0	48	172	44.3	No	No
6	1	4	3.7	53	270	48.2	No	No
2	5	5	4.0	33	237	37.4	No	No
3	6	7	5.3	37	132	16.1	No	No
8	1	4	4.3	52	256	53.0	No	No
5	4	4	4.2	30	447	56.9		
6	6	4	5.3	34	451	74.2	..	..
7	3	5	5.0	36	711	47.9	..	..
..	..	..	..	..	..	..	..	..
6	2	1	3.0	28	358	44.6	..	..
0	4	6	3.3	22	268	61.0	..	..

Table 13.3 Governance and anticorruption indicators

	Voice and accountability			Political stability and absence of violence			Government effectiveness		
	1996	2006	2007	1996	2006	2007	1996	2006	2007
SUB-SAHARAN AFRICA									
Angola	−1.5	−1.2	−1.1	−2.3	−0.4	−0.5	−1.4	−1.3	−1.2
Benin	0.7	0.3	0.3	1.1	0.4	0.4	0.0	−0.5	−0.6
Botswana	0.8	0.5	0.5	0.7	1.0	0.8	0.2	0.6	0.7
Burkina Faso	−0.2	−0.3	−0.3	0.0	−0.1	0.1	−0.7	−0.8	−0.8
Burundi	−1.5	−1.1	−0.8	−2.0	−1.4	−1.4	−1.0	−1.3	−1.3
Cameroon	−1.2	−1.0	−0.9	−1.4	−0.3	−0.4	−1.2	−0.8	−0.9
Cape Verde	0.8	0.8	0.9	1.1	1.0	1.0	−0.1	0.2	0.4
Central African Republic	−0.5	−1.0	−0.9	−0.2	−1.8	−1.8	−0.9	−1.4	−1.4
Chad	−0.9	−1.4	−1.4	−0.7	−1.9	−2.0	−0.7	−1.3	−1.5
Comoros	0.0	−0.2	−0.5	1.1	−0.2	−0.4	−0.7	−1.7	−1.8
Congo, Dem. Rep.	−1.6	−1.6	−1.5	−1.9	−2.4	−2.3	−1.7	−1.7	−1.7
Congo, Rep.	−0.5	−1.1	−1.1	−0.8	−1.0	−0.8	−1.2	−1.3	−1.3
Côte d'Ivoire	−0.8	−1.3	−1.3	−0.1	−2.2	−2.1	0.1	−1.4	−1.4
Djibouti	−0.7	−1.0	−1.1	0.2	−0.2	−0.1	−1.0	−1.0	−1.0
Equatorial Guinea	−1.6	−1.8	−1.9	−0.4	−0.1	−0.2	−1.5	−1.3	−1.4
Eritrea	−1.1	−2.0	−2.2	0.3	−0.9	−1.0	−0.4	−1.3	−1.3
Ethiopia	−0.9	−1.2	−1.2	−1.2	−1.7	−1.7	−1.0	−0.6	−0.5
Gabon	−0.4	−0.8	−0.8	−0.3	0.1	0.2	−1.0	−0.7	−0.7
Gambia, The	−1.3	−0.9	−1.0	0.1	0.0	−0.1	−0.4	−0.8	−0.7
Ghana	−0.3	0.5	0.5	−0.2	0.3	0.2	−0.4	0.0	0.0
Guinea	−1.1	−1.2	−1.2	−1.4	−1.8	−2.0	−1.1	−1.4	−1.5
Guinea-Bissau	−0.3	−0.4	−0.5	−0.6	−0.4	−0.4	−0.6	−1.2	−1.2
Kenya	−0.8	−0.1	−0.1	−0.7	−1.0	−1.1	−0.3	−0.7	−0.6
Lesotho	−0.2	0.2	0.1	0.6	0.2	0.0	0.1	−0.4	−0.4
Liberia	−1.4	−0.6	−0.4	−2.6	−1.3	−1.2	−1.8	−1.2	−1.2
Madagascar	0.4	−0.1	0.0	0.1	0.1	−0.1	−1.0	−0.3	−0.3
Malawi	0.0	−0.3	−0.3	−0.3	..	0.0	−0.7	−0.9	−0.6
Mali	0.7	0.3	0.3	0.6	0.0	−0.1	−0.7	−0.5	−0.6
Mauritania	−1.0	−0.8	−0.8	0.6	−0.1	−0.3	0.2	−0.8	−0.7
Mauritius	0.9	0.8	0.9	0.7	0.7	0.8	0.5	0.6	0.6
Mozambique	0.1	−0.1	−0.1	−0.8	0.5	0.4	−0.3	−0.4	−0.4
Namibia	0.6	0.5	0.6	0.5	0.8	0.9	0.5	0.2	0.2
Niger	−1.0	−0.3	−0.4	0.0	−0.3	−0.6	−1.1	−0.9	−0.9
Nigeria	−1.8	−0.5	−0.5	−1.6	−2.1	−2.1	−1.4	−0.9	−0.9
Rwanda	−1.3	−1.2	−1.2	−2.0	−0.5	−0.2	−1.2	−0.4	−0.4
São Tomé and Principe	0.5	0.4	0.4	1.1	0.4	0.3	−0.7	−0.9	−0.8
Senegal	−0.1	0.1	0.0	−0.3	−0.3	−0.2	−0.2	−0.2	−0.3
Seychelles	0.0	0.0	−0.1	1.1	1.1	1.0	−0.6	0.0	0.0
Sierra Leone	−0.9	−0.4	−0.3	−2.3	−0.5	−0.3	−0.6	−1.1	−1.1
Somalia	−1.9	−1.8	−1.9	−2.3	−2.8	−3.0	−1.8	−2.2	−2.4
South Africa	0.8	0.8	0.7	−1.2	0.1	0.2	0.4	0.8	0.7
Sudan	−2.0	−1.7	−1.7	−2.6	−2.1	−2.3	−1.5	−1.1	−1.2
Swaziland	−1.1	−1.1	−1.1	0.0	−0.1	0.1	−0.3	−0.7	−0.7
Tanzania	−0.6	−0.2	−0.2	−0.3	−0.1	−0.1	−0.8	−0.4	−0.4
Togo	−1.0	−1.3	−1.2	−0.5	−0.7	−0.5	−0.7	−1.6	−1.5
Uganda	−0.5	−0.5	−0.5	−1.3	−1.3	−1.2	−0.6	−0.4	−0.4
Zambia	−0.6	−0.3	−0.3	−0.5	0.3	0.2	−0.6	−0.7	−0.6
Zimbabwe	−0.6	−1.5	−1.5	−0.6	−1.1	−1.3	−0.4	−1.4	−1.5
NORTH AFRICA									
Algeria	−1.4	−0.9	−1.0	−2.4	−1.0	−1.2	−0.4	−0.4	−0.5
Egypt, Arab Rep.	−1.0	−1.3	−1.2	−1.1	−0.9	−0.8	0.0	−0.5	−0.4
Libya	−1.8	−2.0	−1.9	−1.8	0.3	0.5	−1.0	−0.8	−1.1
Morocco	−0.6	−0.6	−0.6	−0.6	−0.3	−0.5	−0.1	−0.1	−0.1
Tunisia	−0.9	−1.2	−1.2	0.2	0.3	0.1	0.5	0.5	0.5

Note: The rating scale for each criterion varies from −2.5 (weak performance) to 2.5 (high performance).

Regulatory quality			Rule of law			Control of corruption			Corruption Perceptions Index (mean score, 0 low to 10 high)	
1996	2006	2007	1996	2006	2007	1996	2006	2007	2006	2007
−1.4	−1.1	−1.0	−1.5	−1.3	−1.4	−1.1	−1.2	−1.1	2.2	2.2
0.2	−0.4	−0.4	−0.3	−0.6	−0.6	..	−0.6	−0.5	2.5	2.7
0.7	0.5	0.5	0.6	0.6	0.7	0.4	0.9	0.9	5.6	5.4
−0.1	−0.4	−0.3	−0.3	−0.5	−0.5	−0.3	−0.4	−0.4	3.2	2.9
−1.6	−1.2	−1.2	−0.9	−1.0	−1.2	..	−1.1	−1.1	2.4	2.5
−0.8	−0.7	−0.7	−1.5	−1.0	−1.1	−1.2	−1.0	−0.9	2.3	2.4
−0.8	−0.2	−0.2	0.5	0.6	0.6	..	0.6	0.8	..	4.9
−0.3	−1.3	−1.2	−0.3	−1.5	−1.5	..	−1.0	−0.9	2.4	2.0
−0.9	−1.1	−1.2	−0.9	−1.4	−1.4	..	−1.2	−1.2	2.0	1.8
−0.8	−1.5	−1.4	..	−0.9	−0.9	..	−0.7	−0.7	..	2.6
−2.6	−1.4	−1.4	−2.1	−1.7	−1.7	−2.1	−1.4	−1.3	2.0	1.9
−0.9	−1.1	−1.2	−1.4	−1.2	−1.3	−0.9	−1.1	−1.0	2.2	2.1
0.0	−0.9	−1.0	−0.7	−1.5	−1.5	0.4	−1.2	−1.1	2.1	2.1
0.2	−0.9	−0.8	−0.2	−0.6	−0.5	..	−0.6	−0.5	..	..
−1.0	−1.3	−1.4	−1.2	−1.2	−1.2	−1.1	−1.5	−1.4	2.1	1.9
..	−1.9	−2.0	−0.3	−1.0	−1.1	..	−0.3	−0.6	2.9	2.8
−1.8	−0.9	−0.9	−0.9	−0.6	−0.5	−1.1	−0.7	−0.7	2.4	2.4
0.0	−0.5	−0.5	−0.9	−0.6	−0.6	−1.3	−0.9	−0.9	3.0	3.3
−1.8	−0.4	−0.4	0.4	−0.3	−0.2	0.4	−0.7	−0.8	2.5	2.3
0.1	0.0	..	−0.4	−0.1	−0.1	−0.5	−0.1	−0.2	3.3	3.7
0.2	−1.0	−1.1	−1.4	−1.4	−1.5	0.4	−1.0	−1.3	1.9	1.9
0.1	−1.0	−1.1	−1.7	−1.3	−1.4	−1.0	−1.0	−1.1	..	2.2
−0.4	−0.3	−0.2	−1.1	−0.9	−1.0	−1.1	−0.9	−0.9	2.2	2.1
−0.6	−0.6	−0.7	−0.3	−0.3	−0.4	..	−0.1	−0.2	3.2	3.3
−3.1	−1.4	−1.2	−2.3	−1.0	−1.1	−1.7	−0.7	−0.4	..	2.1
−0.5	−0.2	−0.2	−1.0	−0.4	−0.4	0.4	−0.2	−0.2	3.1	3.2
−0.2	−0.7	−0.5	−0.6	−0.4	−0.4	−0.5	−0.7	−0.7	2.7	2.7
0.0	−0.4	−0.3	−0.6	−0.4	−0.4	−0.3	−0.4	−0.4	2.8	2.7
−0.9	−0.3	−0.4	−0.9	−0.6	−0.6	..	−0.6	−0.5	3.1	2.6
0.1	0.5	0.6	0.8	0.7	0.8	0.5	0.4	0.4	5.1	4.7
−1.0	−0.5	−0.5	−0.9	−0.6	−0.7	−0.4	−0.7	−0.6	2.8	2.8
0.1	0.1	0.0	0.3	0.2	0.1	0.7	0.1	0.2	4.1	4.5
−1.2	−0.6	−0.6	−0.9	−0.8	−0.9	−0.3	−1.0	−0.9	2.3	2.6
−1.1	−1.0	−0.9	−1.4	−1.2	−1.2	−1.3	−1.1	−1.0	2.2	2.2
−1.8	−0.5	−0.6	−1.5	−0.7	−0.7	..	−0.1	−0.1	2.5	2.8
−0.3	−0.7	−0.8	..	−0.5	−0.4	..	−0.5	−0.5	..	2.7
−0.4	−0.3	−0.4	−0.4	−0.4	−0.4	−0.4	−0.5	−0.5	3.3	3.6
−1.4	−0.6	−0.6	..	0.2	0.2	..	0.1	0.0	3.6	4.5
−0.9	−1.1	−1.0	−1.3	−1.2	−1.1	−1.7	−1.1	−1.0	2.2	2.1
−2.9	−2.7	−2.7	−2.1	−2.6	−2.6	−1.7	−1.8	−1.9	..	1.4
0.0	0.6	0.5	0.3	0.2	0.2	0.6	0.4	0.3	4.6	5.1
−1.9	−1.2	−1.3	−1.6	−1.3	−1.5	−1.1	−1.2	−1.3	2.0	1.8
0.1	−0.6	−0.7	0.8	−0.7	−0.8	..	−0.4	−0.5	2.5	3.3
−0.1	−0.4	−0.4	−0.4	−0.5	−0.5	−1.1	−0.4	−0.5	2.9	3.2
0.6	−1.0	−1.0	−1.4	−1.0	−0.9	−1.0	−1.1	−1.0	2.4	2.3
0.3	−0.2	−0.2	−0.6	−0.5	−0.5	−0.6	−0.7	−0.8	2.7	2.8
0.3	−0.6	−0.5	−0.6	−0.7	−0.6	−1.0	−0.7	−0.6	2.6	2.6
−0.8	−2.1	−2.2	−0.7	−1.6	−1.7	−0.2	−1.3	−1.3	2.4	2.1
−0.9	−0.7	−0.7	−1.2	−0.6	−0.7	−0.4	−0.5	−0.5	..	..
0.2	−0.5	−0.3	0.1	−0.1	−0.1	0.1	−0.5	−0.6	..	..
−2.1	−1.3	−1.0	−1.3	−0.7	−0.6	−1.0	−0.9	−0.8	..	..
0.2	−0.2	−0.1	0.1	−0.1	−0.2	0.2	−0.3	−0.2	..	..
0.6	0.1	0.2	−0.2	0.3	0.3	−0.1	0.0	0.1	..	..

Table 13.4 Country policy and institutional assessment ratings

	CPIA Overall rating (IDA resource allocation index)[a]		Economic Management				Structural Policies			
	2006	2007	Average[b] 2007	Macro-economic management 2007	Fiscal policy 2007	Debt policy 2007	Average[b] 2007	Trade 2007	Financial sector 2007	Business regulatory environment 2007
SUB-SAHARAN AFRICA										
Angola	2.7	2.7	3.0	3.0	3.0	3.0	2.8	4.0	2.5	2.0
Benin	3.6	3.6	4.0	4.5	4.0	3.5	3.7	4.0	3.5	3.5
Botswana[c]	..	..	..	..	..	..	..	..	..	..
Burkina Faso	3.7	3.7	4.3	4.5	4.5	4.0	3.3	4.0	3.0	3.0
Burundi	3.0	3.0	3.2	3.5	3.5	2.5	3.0	3.5	3.0	2.5
Cameroon	3.2	3.2	3.7	4.0	4.0	3.0	3.2	3.5	3.0	3.0
Cape Verde	4.1	4.2	4.5	4.5	4.5	4.5	3.8	4.0	4.0	3.5
Central African Republic	2.4	2.5	2.8	3.5	3.0	2.0	2.7	3.5	2.5	2.0
Chad	2.8	2.6	2.7	3.0	2.5	2.5	2.8	3.0	3.0	2.5
Comoros	2.4	2.4	2.0	2.5	1.5	2.0	2.7	3.0	2.5	2.5
Congo, Dem. Rep.	2.8	2.8	3.2	3.5	3.5	2.5	3.0	4.0	2.0	3.0
Congo, Rep.	2.8	2.7	2.5	3.0	2.0	2.5	2.8	3.5	2.5	2.5
Côte d'Ivoire	2.5	2.6	2.3	3.0	2.5	1.5	3.2	3.5	3.0	3.0
Djibouti	3.1	3.1	2.8	3.5	2.5	2.5	3.7	4.0	3.5	3.5
Equatorial Guinea[c]	..	..	..	..	..	..	..	..	..	..
Eritrea	2.5	2.4	2.2	2.0	2.0	2.5	1.8	1.5	2.0	2.0
Ethiopia	3.4	3.4	3.5	3.0	4.0	3.5	3.2	3.0	3.0	3.5
Gabon[c]	..	..	..	..	..	..	..	..	..	..
Gambia, The	3.1	3.2	3.3	4.0	3.5	2.5	3.5	4.0	3.0	3.5
Ghana	3.9	4.0	4.0	4.0	4.0	4.0	4.0	4.0	4.0	4.0
Guinea	2.9	3.0	3.0	3.0	3.5	2.5	3.3	4.0	3.0	3.0
Guinea-Bissau	2.6	2.6	2.0	2.0	2.5	1.5	3.2	4.0	3.0	2.5
Kenya	3.7	3.6	4.2	4.5	4.0	4.0	3.8	4.0	3.5	4.0
Lesotho	3.5	3.5	4.0	4.0	4.0	4.0	3.3	3.5	3.5	3.0
Liberia[d]	..	..	..	..	..	..	..	..	..	..
Madagascar	3.6	3.7	3.7	4.0	3.0	4.0	3.8	4.0	3.5	4.0
Malawi	3.4	3.4	3.3	3.5	3.5	3.0	3.5	4.0	3.0	3.5
Mali	3.7	3.7	4.3	4.5	4.0	4.5	3.5	4.0	3.0	3.5
Mauritania	3.3	3.4	3.5	3.5	3.0	4.0	3.5	4.5	2.5	3.5
Mauritius[c]	..	..	..	..	..	..	..	..	..	..
Mozambique	3.5	3.6	4.2	4.0	4.0	4.5	3.7	4.5	3.5	3.0
Namibia[c]	..	..	..	..	..	..	..	..	..	..
Niger	3.3	3.3	3.7	4.0	3.5	3.5	3.3	4.0	3.0	3.0
Nigeria	3.2	3.4	4.3	4.0	4.5	4.5	3.2	3.0	3.5	3.0
Rwanda	3.6	3.7	3.8	4.0	4.0	3.5	3.5	3.5	3.5	3.5
São Tomé and Principe	3.0	3.0	2.8	3.0	3.0	2.5	3.2	4.0	2.5	3.0
Senegal	3.7	3.7	4.2	4.5	4.0	4.0	3.8	4.0	3.5	4.0
Seychelles	..	..	..	..	..	..	..	..	..	..
Sierra Leone	3.1	3.1	3.7	4.0	3.5	3.5	3.0	3.5	3.0	2.5
Somalia[d]	..	..	..	..	..	..	..	..	..	..
South Africa[c]	..	..	..	..	..	..	..	..	..	..
Sudan	2.5	2.5	2.7	3.5	3.0	1.5	2.7	2.5	2.5	3.0
Swaziland[c]	..	..	..	..	..	..	..	..	..	..
Tanzania	3.9	3.9	4.3	4.5	4.5	4.0	3.7	4.0	3.5	3.5
Togo	2.5	2.5	2.2	2.5	2.5	1.5	3.2	4.0	2.5	3.0
Uganda	3.9	3.9	4.5	4.5	4.5	4.5	3.8	4.0	3.5	4.0
Zambia	3.4	3.5	3.7	4.0	3.5	3.5	3.7	4.0	3.5	3.5
Zimbabwe	1.8	1.7	1.0	1.0	1.0	1.0	2.0	2.0	2.5	1.5
NORTH AFRICA										
Algeria[c]	..	..	..	..	..	..	..	..	..	..
Egypt, Arab Rep.[c]	..	..	..	..	..	..	..	..	..	..
Libya[c]	..	..	..	..	..	..	..	..	..	..
Morocco[c]	..	..	..	..	..	..	..	..	..	..
Tunisia[c]	..	..	..	..	..	..	..	..	..	..

Note: The rating scale for each indicator ranges from 1 (low) to 6 (high).

a. Calculated as the average of the average ratings of each cluster.

b. All criteria are weighted equally.

c. Not an IDA member.

d. Not rated in the International Development Association (IDA) resource allocation index.

| | Policies for Social Inclusion/Equity | | | | | | Public Sector Management and Institutions | | | | | |
Average[b] 2007	Gender equality 2007	Equity of public resource use 2007	Building human resources 2007	Social protection and labor 2007	Policies & institutions for environmental sustainability 2007		Average[b] 2007	Property rights & rule-based governance 2007	Quality of budgetary & financial management 2007	Efficiency of revenue mobilization 2007	Quality of public administration 2007	Transparency, accountability & corruption in public sector 2007
2.7	3.0	2.5	2.5	2.5	3.0		2.4	2.0	2.5	2.5	2.5	2.5
3.3	3.5	3.0	3.5	3.0	3.5		3.3	3.0	3.5	3.5	3.0	3.5
..	..	..	..	..	..		..	..	..			..
3.6	3.5	4.0	3.5	3.5	3.5		3.5	3.5	4.0	3.5	3.5	3.0
3.3	4.0	3.5	3.0	3.0	3.0		2.6	2.5	3.0	3.0	2.5	2.0
3.1	3.0	3.0	3.5	3.0	3.0		3.0	2.5	3.5	3.5	3.0	2.5
4.3	4.5	4.5	4.5	4.5	3.5		4.0	4.0	4.0	3.5	4.0	4.5
2.2	2.5	2.0	2.0	2.0	2.5		2.3	2.0	2.0	2.5	2.0	2.5
2.6	2.5	3.0	2.5	2.5	2.5		2.2	2.0	2.0	2.5	3.0	2.0
2.7	3.0	3.0	3.0	2.5	2.0		2.2	2.5	1.5	2.5	2.0	2.5
2.9	3.0	3.0	3.0	3.0	2.5		2.3	2.0	2.5	2.5	2.5	2.0
2.7	3.0	2.5	3.0	2.5	2.5		2.6	2.5	2.5	3.0	2.5	2.5
2.3	2.5	1.5	2.5	2.5	2.5		2.4	2.0	2.0	4.0	2.0	2.0
3.0	2.5	3.0	3.5	3.0	3.0		2.8	2.5	3.0	3.5	2.5	2.5
..	..	..	..	..	..		..	..	..			..
3.0	3.5	3.0	3.5	3.0	2.0		2.7	2.5	2.5	3.5	3.0	2.0
3.7	3.0	4.5	4.0	3.5	3.5		3.3	3.0	4.0	4.0	3.0	2.5
..	..	..	..	..	..		..	..	..			..
3.1	3.5	3.0	3.5	2.5	3.0		3.0	3.5	3.0	3.5	3.0	2.0
3.9	4.0	4.0	4.5	3.5	3.5		3.9	3.5	4.0	4.5	3.5	4.0
3.0	3.5	3.0	3.0	3.0	2.5		2.7	2.0	3.0	3.0	3.0	2.5
2.6	2.5	3.0	2.5	2.5	2.5		2.6	2.5	2.5	3.0	2.5	2.5
3.2	3.0	3.0	3.5	3.0	3.5		3.3	2.5	3.5	4.0	3.5	3.0
3.4	4.0	3.0	3.5	3.0	3.5		3.4	3.5	3.0	4.0	3.0	3.5
..	..	..	..	..	..		..	..	..			..
3.7	3.5	4.0	3.5	3.5	4.0		3.5	3.5	3.5	3.5	3.5	3.5
3.4	3.5	3.5	3.0	3.5	3.5		3.4	3.5	3.0	4.0	3.5	3.0
3.5	3.5	3.5	3.5	3.5	3.5		3.5	3.5	3.5	4.0	3.0	3.5
3.5	4.0	3.5	3.5	3.0	3.5		3.0	3.0	2.5	3.5	3.0	3.0
..	..	..	..	..	..		..	..	..			..
3.3	3.5	3.5	3.5	3.0	3.0		3.3	3.0	3.5	4.0	2.5	3.0
..	..	..	..	..	..		..	..	..			..
3.0	2.5	3.5	3.0	3.0	3.0		3.2	3.0	3.5	3.5	3.0	3.0
3.2	3.0	3.5	3.0	3.5	3.0		2.9	2.5	3.0	3.0	2.5	3.0
3.8	3.5	4.5	4.5	3.5	3.0		3.5	3.0	4.0	3.5	3.5	3.5
2.8	3.0	3.0	3.0	2.5	2.5		3.1	2.5	3.0	3.5	3.0	3.5
3.4	3.5	3.5	3.5	3.0	3.5		3.5	3.5	3.5	4.0	3.5	3.0
..	..	..	..	..	..		..	..	..			..
2.9	3.0	3.0	3.5	3.0	2.0		2.8	2.5	3.5	2.5	3.0	2.5
..	..	..	..	..	..		..	..	..			..
2.4	2.0	2.5	2.5	2.5	2.5		2.3	2.0	2.0	3.0	2.5	2.0
..	..	..	..	..	..		..	..	..			..
3.8	4.0	4.0	4.0	3.5	3.5		3.7	3.5	4.0	4.0	3.5	3.5
2.6	3.0	2.0	3.0	2.5	2.5		2.2	2.5	2.0	2.5	2.0	2.0
3.9	3.5	4.5	4.0	3.5	4.0		3.3	3.5	4.0	3.0	3.0	3.0
3.4	3.5	3.5	3.5	3.0	3.5		3.2	3.0	3.5	3.5	3.0	3.0
1.8	2.5	1.5	1.5	1.0	2.5		1.8	1.0	2.0	3.5	2.0	1.0
							..	..	..	..	..	..
..	..	..	..	..	..		..	..	..	..	..	..
..	..	..	..	..	..		..	..	..	..	..	..
..	..	..	..	..	..		..	..	..	..	..	..
..	..	..	..	..	..		..	..	..	..	..	..
..	..	..	..	..	..		..	..	..	..	..	..

Table 13.5 Polity indicators

	Polity score[a]			Institutionalized democracy[b]			Institutionalized autocracy[b]		
	1995	2000	2006	1995	2000	2006	1995	2000	2006
SUB-SAHARAN AFRICA									
Angola	..	−3.0	−2.0	..	1.0	2.0	..	4.0	4.0
Benin	6.0	6.0	7.0	6.0	6.0	7.0	..	..	..
Botswana	8.0	9.0	9.0	8.0	9.0	9.0	..	..	..
Burkina Faso	−5.0	−3.0	..	..	..	2.0	5.0	3.0	2.0
Burundi	..	−1.0	6.0	..	1.0	7.0	..	2.0	1.0
Cameroon	−4.0	−4.0	−4.0	1.0	1.0	1.0	5.0	5.0	5.0
Cape Verde	..	..	..	..	..	..	..	..	..
Central African Republic	5.0	5.0	−1.0	5.0	5.0	1.0	..	..	2.0
Chad	−4.0	−2.0	−2.0	..	1.0	1.0	4.0	3.0	3.0
Comoros	..	−1.0	9.0	..	1.0	9.0	..	2.0	..
Congo, Dem. Rep.	..	..	5.0	..	..	6.0	..	..	1.0
Congo, Rep.	5.0	−6.0	−4.0	6.0	..	..	1.0	6.0	4.0
Côte d'Ivoire	−6.0	4.0	..	..	5.0	..	6.0	1.0	..
Djibouti	−7.0	2.0	2.0	..	3.0	3.0	7.0	1.0	1.0
Equatorial Guinea	−5.0	−5.0	−5.0	..	..	..	5.0	5.0	5.0
Eritrea	−6.0	−6.0	−7.0	..	..	..	6.0	6.0	7.0
Ethiopia	1.0	1.0	1.0	3.0	3.0	3.0	2.0	2.0	2.0
Gabon	−4.0	−4.0	−4.0	..	..	..	4.0	4.0	4.0
Gambia, The	−7.0	−5.0	−5.0	..	..	..	7.0	5.0	5.0
Ghana	−1.0	2.0	8.0	1.0	3.0	8.0	2.0	1.0	..
Guinea	−1.0	−1.0	−1.0	1.0	1.0	1.0	2.0	2.0	2.0
Guinea-Bissau	5.0	5.0	6.0	5.0	5.0	6.0	..	..	..
Kenya	−5.0	−2.0	8.0	..	2.0	8.0	5.0	4.0	..
Lesotho	8.0	..	8.0	8.0	..	8.0	..	..	..
Liberia	..	..	6.0	..	3.0	7.0	..	3.0	1.0
Madagascar	9.0	7.0	7.0	9.0	7.0	7.0	..	..	..
Malawi	6.0	6.0	6.0	6.0	6.0	6.0	..	..	..
Mali	7.0	6.0	6.0	7.0	6.0	6.0	..	..	..
Mauritania	−6.0	−6.0	−3.0	..	..	..	6.0	6.0	3.0
Mauritius	10.0	10.0	10.0	10.0	10.0	10.0	..	..	..
Mozambique	6.0	6.0	6.0	6.0	6.0	6.0	..	..	..
Namibia	6.0	6.0	6.0	6.0	6.0	6.0	..	..	..
Niger	8.0	5.0	6.0	8.0	6.0	7.0	..	1.0	1.0
Nigeria	−6.0	4.0	4.0	..	4.0	4.0	6.0	..	..
Rwanda	−6.0	−4.0	−3.0	..	..	..	6.0	4.0	3.0
São Tomé and Principe	..	..	..	..	..	..	..	..	..
Senegal	−1.0	8.0	8.0	2.0	8.0	8.0	3.0	..	..
Seychelles	..	..	..	..	..	..	..	..	..
Sierra Leone	−7.0	..	5.0	..	..	5.0	7.0	..	..
Somalia	..	..	..	..	..	..	..	..	..
South Africa	9.0	9.0	9.0	9.0	9.0	9.0	..	..	..
Sudan	−7.0	−7.0	−4.0	..	..	..	7.0	7.0	4.0
Swaziland	−9.0	−9.0	−9.0	..	..	..	9.0	9.0	9.0
Tanzania	−1.0	1.0	1.0	2.0	3.0	3.0	3.0	2.0	2.0
Togo	−2.0	−2.0	−4.0	1.0	1.0	1.0	3.0	3.0	5.0
Uganda	−4.0	−4.0	−1.0	..	..	1.0	4.0	4.0	2.0
Zambia	6.0	1.0	5.0	6.0	3.0	5.0	..	2.0	..
Zimbabwe	−6.0	−3.0	−4.0	..	1.0	1.0	6.0	4.0	5.0
NORTH AFRICA									
Algeria	−3.0	−3.0	2.0	1.0	1.0	3.0	4.0	4.0	1.0
Egypt, Arab Rep.	−6.0	−6.0	−3.0	..	..	1.0	6.0	6.0	4.0
Libya	−7.0	−7.0	−7.0	..	..	..	7.0	7.0	7.0
Morocco	−7.0	−6.0	−6.0	..	..	..	7.0	6.0	6.0
Tunisia	−3.0	−3.0	−4.0	1.0	1.0	1.0	4.0	4.0	5.0

a The polity rating scale ranges from +10 (strongly democratic) to −10 (strongly autocratic).

b. The institutionalized democracy and autocracy indicator are each an additive eleven-point scale (0–10).

* For a discussion on conflict, fragility and democracy, see Box 12 in the technical notes.

Table 14.1

Burkina Faso household survey, 2003

Indicator	National total	Rural						Urban					
		All	Q1	Q2	Q3	Q4	Q5	All	Q1	Q2	Q3	Q4	Q5
Demographic Indicators													
Sample size (households)	8,494	5,894	618	853	1,020	1,278	2,125	2,600	253	326	387	573	1,061
Total Population (thousands)	11,385	9,317	1,387	1,672	1,804	1,947	2,506	2,068	319	349	390	458	554
Age dependency ratio	1.0	1.1	1.3	1.2	1.2	1.1	0.8	0.6	0.9	0.8	0.7	0.6	0.5
Average household size	6.4	6.6	9.8	8.4	7.5	6.5	4.7	5.6	8.4	7.4	6.8	5.5	3.9
Marital Status of head of household (%)													
Monogamous male	4	3	0	1	1	2	5	10	1	3	4	5	21
Polygamous male	60	59	44	50	57	60	68	63	60	59	67	68	62
Single male	29	33	53	44	37	33	21	13	24	25	18	12	5
De facto female	0	0	0	0	..	..	0	0	..	..	..	..	0
De jure female	7	5	3	4	4	5	6	13	14	13	12	14	12
MDG 1: eradicate extreme poverty and hunger													
Mean monthly expenditure (CFA francs)	75,614	65,140	36,960	46,013	58,598	71,470	112,679	129,090	55,311	81,398	106,453	146,524	256,278
Mean monthly share on food (%)	58	65	72	70	69	65	57	42	54	51	48	44	34
Mean monthly share on health (%)	5	5	2	3	3	3	9	6	3	2	6	7	8
Mean monthly share on education (%)	3	1	2	1	2	1	1	8	4	8	8	7	8
MDGs 2 and 3: education and literacy; gender equality													
Primary school within 30 minutes (% of households)	63	55	56	58	58	54	53	91	87	86	89	93	93
Net primary enrollment rate (% of relevant age group)													
Total	93	91	87	90	92	91	93	96	95	95	94	97	97
Male	93	91	88	90	94	90	93	96	95	93	96	96	98
Female	92	91	84	90	90	92	94	95	94	97	93	97	95
Net secondary enrollment rate (% of relevant age group)													
Total	34	21	16	20	17	23	27	48	24	36	42	52	68
Male	32	21	19	18	14	26	29	47	26	34	41	51	70
Female	36	21	9	24	24	19	23	48	23	38	43	53	66
Tertiary enrollment rate (per 10,000)	..	..	..	..	..	..	..	..	..	..	..	..	..
Total													
Adult literacy rate (%)													
Total	22	13	9	11	10	12	17	56	34	43	49	57	76
Male	29	19	14	18	17	17	23	66	44	54	58	67	83
Female	15	7	4	5	5	7	11	47	25	33	39	49	69
Youth literacy rate (% ages 15–24)													
Total	31	19	15	20	19	18	20	71	53	70	70	74	80
Male	38	26	22	26	26	24	28	78	58	76	75	83	90
Female	25	13	8	13	12	13	14	65	47	62	63	67	72
MDGs 4 and 5: child mortality; maternal health													
Health Center less than 5 km away (% of population)	65	65	64	66	59	66	67	98	94	97	99	99	99
Morbidity (% of population)	6	6	3	4	6	6	8	7	5	4	6	7	10
Health care provider consulted when sick (%)	64	62	44	49	56	65	71	71	55	54	72	77	77
Type of health care provider consulted (% of total)													
Public	70	72	57	62	67	70	79	62	66	67	57	64	61
Private, modern medicine	7	2	1	4	2	2	2	25	8	13	27	25	31
Private, traditional healers	17	20	39	28	25	18	14	8	22	14	12	6	3
Missionary or nongovernmental organization													
Other	..	..	..	..	..	..	..	..	..	..	..	..	..
Child survival and malnutrition (%)													
Birth assisted by trained staff	52	43	32	42	43	46	50	94	86	94	93	96	98
Immunization coverage, 1-year-olds	..	..	..	..	..	..	..	..	..	..	..	..	..
Measles immunization coverage, 1-year-olds	..	..	..	..	..	..	..	..	..	..	..	..	..
Stunting (6–59 months)	43	46	45	46	47	44	47	33	34	29	36	36	31
Wasting (6–59 months)	31	32	35	32	33	32	30	28	24	33	33	28	24
Underweight (6–59 months)	47	50	52	51	51	49	48	35	31	38	43	38	28
MDG 7: environmental sustainability													
Access to sanitation facilities (% of population)	35	20	12	16	18	20	25	91	70	85	92	95	97
Water source less than 5 km away (% of population)	90	88	88	90	90	88	85	98	98	97	97	97	98
Market less than 5 km away (% of population)	83	80	80	80	80	81	79	97	94	96	96	96	98
Access to improved water source (% of population)													
Total[a]	27	15	14	16	15	15	16	72	52	63	75	76	77
Own tap	19	5	4	5	4	5	6	70	44	59	71	74	76
Other piped	..	..	..	..	..	..	..	..	..	..	..	..	..
Well, protected	9	10	10	11	11	11	10	3	8	4	5	2	1
Traditional fuel use (%)													
Total[a]	95	98	99	99	99	99	96	85	99	99	98	93	67
Firewood	91	96	97	98	98	97	94	73	99	94	93	82	47
Charcoal	4	2	2	1	1	2	3	12	1	5	5	11	21

a. Components may not sum to total because of rounding

Table 14.2

Cameroon household survey, 2001

Indicator	National total	Rural						Urban					
		All	Q1	Q2	Q3	Q4	Q5	All	Q1	Q2	Q3	Q4	Q5
Demographic Indicators													
Sample size (households)	10,992	6,017	646	764	1,026	1,217	2,364	4,975	759	786	886	1,061	1,483
Total Population (thousands)	15,473	10,089	2,019	2,016	2,019	2,018	2,018	5,383	1,077	1,076	1,076	1,076	1,078
Age dependency ratio	0.9	1.0	1.4	1.3	1.1	0.9	0.6	0.7	1.0	0.8	0.7	0.5	0.4
Average household size	5.0	5.0	7.2	6.8	5.5	5.0	3.0	4.9	7.3	6.3	5.7	4.5	3.1
Marital Status of head of household (%)													
Monogamous male	44	46	50	50	50	48	40	40	47	49	46	38	32
Polygamous male	14	16	22	22	16	17	11	9	16	11	10	9	6
Single male	18	15	5	6	11	11	26	25	15	15	17	26	38
De facto female	4	4	5	5	5	4	3	4	5	4	5	4	4
De jure female	19	19	18	17	18	20	20	21	17	20	22	23	21
MDG 1: eradicate extreme poverty and hunger													
Mean monthly expenditure (CFA francs)	30,619	22,063	6,609	10,217	13,705	18,951	40,025	46,540	11,847	18,846	25,889	37,099	93,334
Mean monthly share on food (%)	59	69	68	71	70	69	68	42	48	45	44	42	36
Mean monthly share on health (%)	7	7	7	6	7	7	8	7	6	6	7	7	8
Mean monthly share on education (%)	4	3	3	3	3	3	3	6	6	7	7	6	5
MDGs 2 and 3: education and literacy; gender equality													
Primary school within 30 minutes (% of households)	85	79	75	77	79	77	83	96	96	96	96	95	96
Net primary enrollment rate (% of relevant age group)													
Total	93	92	92	91	93	93	92	94	94	95	95	93	89
Male	93	93	93	92	94	93	90	94	94	95	95	94	91
Female	92	92	90	90	93	93	93	93	94	96	95	92	87
Net secondary enrollment rate (% of relevant age group)													
Total	40	29	14	22	28	33	48	57	38	53	59	64	72
Male	39	29	15	22	28	33	49	55	35	49	59	64	73
Female	41	28	12	21	27	33	47	58	40	57	59	64	71
Tertiary enrollment rate (per 10,000)	89	..	..	..	..	..	..	..	..	..	..	..	..
Total													
Adult literacy rate (%)													
Total	68	56	50	50	55	58	62	88	76	85	89	92	94
Male	77	67	61	60	66	69	72	92	83	91	94	96	96
Female	60	47	42	42	46	49	51	83	70	80	84	88	92
Youth literacy rate (% ages 15–24)													
Total	82	73	69	69	76	74	78	94	89	93	95	96	97
Male	88	82	76	78	85	84	85	96	90	95	97	97	98
Female	77	66	62	61	69	67	71	93	87	91	93	95	95
MDGs 4 and 5: child mortality; maternal health													
Health Center less than 5 km away (% of population)	90	84	77	83	84	84	88	100	99	100	100	100	100
Morbidity (% of population)	31	31	28	29	31	33	35	31	30	31	31	30	33
Health care provider consulted when sick (%)	..	..	..	..	..	..	..	..	..	..	..	..	..
Type of health care provider consulted (% of total)													
Public	53	55	53	53	53	59	58	48	44	49	51	49	48
Private, modern medicine	13	7	6	5	7	8	9	23	19	20	20	24	31
Private, traditional healers	15	18	18	21	21	15	14	11	18	12	9	7	6
Missionary or nongovernmental organization													
Other	2	3	2	3	4	3	4	1	1	0	1	1	1
Child survival and malnutrition (%)													
Birth assisted by trained staff	..	..	..	..	..	..	..	..	..	..	..	..	..
Immunization coverage, 1-year-olds	..	..	..	..	..	..	..	..	..	..	..	..	..
Measles immunization coverage, 1-year-olds	..	..	..	..	..	..	..	..	..	..	..	..	..
Stunting (6–59 months)	..	..	..	..	..	..	..	..	..	..	..	..	..
Wasting (6–59 months)	..	..	..	..	..	..	..	..	..	..	..	..	..
Underweight (6–59 months)	..	..	..	..	..	..	..	..	..	..	..	..	..
MDG 7: environmental sustainability													
Access to sanitation facilities (% of population)	43	25	13	15	21	29	35	75	58	68	75	79	84
Water source less than 5 km away (% of population)	68	75	71	80	73	74	76	56	56	59	61	57	50
Market less than 5 km away (% of population)	90	85	82	85	84	86	88	99	99	99	99	100	99
Access to improved water source (% of population)													
Total[a]	66	50	47	44	47	48	58	96	88	94	97	97	98
Own tap	15	6	3	4	4	5	10	32	11	17	24	35	49
Other piped	27	14	12	11	11	13	17	52	58	62	59	51	41
Well, protected	24	31	32	30	32	30	31	12	19	15	14	10	8
Traditional fuel use (%)													
Total[a]	75	94	99	99	97	96	86	41	75	58	51	34	17
Firewood	75	93	99	99	96	96	85	40	75	58	49	33	16
Charcoal	0	0	..	..	0	0	0	1	0	1	2	1	1

a. Components may not sum to total because of rounding

Table 14.3

Ethiopia household survey, 1999/00

Indicator	National total	Rural						Urban					
		All	Q1	Q2	Q3	Q4	Q5	All	Q1	Q2	Q3	Q4	Q5
Demographic Indicators													
Sample size (households)	16,672	8,459	1,469	1,382	1,519	1,678	2,411	8,213	1,118	1,358	1,506	1,883	2,348
Total Population (thousands)	54,756	47,531	9,502	9,513	9,504	9,507	9,505	7,225	1,446	1,443	1,446	1,445	1,445
Age dependency ratio	1.0	1.1	1.3	1.2	1.1	1.0	0.8	0.7	1.0	0.9	0.8	0.6	0.5
Average household size	4.9	4.9	5.9	5.4	5.2	4.8	3.8	4.5	5.6	5.1	4.7	4.3	3.5
Marital Status of head of household (%)													
Monogamous male	68	71	75	72	74	74	64	48	53	50	50	49	41
Polygamous male	1	1	1	1	1	0	1	0	0	0	0	0	0
Single male	6	5	3	4	3	4	8	11	6	4	7	10	23
De facto female	1	1	1	1	1	0	1	3	2	4	4	3	2
De jure female	25	23	20	22	21	22	27	38	39	42	39	38	34
MDG 1: eradicate extreme poverty and hunger													
Mean monthly expenditure (birr)	103	93	42	60	75	95	161	162	49	76	103	147	346
Mean monthly share on food (%)	66	68	72	71	69	68	62	55	66	62	59	53	43
Mean monthly share on health (%)	1	1	1	1	1	1	1	1	1	1	1	1	1
Mean monthly share on education (%)	1	0	0	0	0	0	0	2	2	1	2	2	2
MDGs 2 and 3: education and literacy; gender equality													
Primary school within 30 minutes (% of households)	..	..	..	..	..	..	..	..	..	..	..	..	..
Net primary enrollment rate (% of relevant age group)													
Total	30	25	19	23	29	25	32	75	66	70	76	84	85
Male	32	27	20	25	30	27	35	75	68	68	75	85	86
Female	29	22	18	20	28	21	29	75	64	71	77	82	84
Net secondary enrollment rate (% of relevant age group)													
Total	9	3	2	3	3	3	5	40	30	36	41	50	47
Male	10	4	4	3	3	5	7	43	29	38	47	54	54
Female	8	2	1	2	2	2	3	38	30	35	36	46	42
Tertiary enrollment rate (per 10,000)													
Total	..	..	..	..	..	..	..	..	..	..	..	..	..
Adult literacy rate (%)													
Total	28	21	15	19	20	23	25	67	54	59	66	71	79
Male	41	34	26	32	33	39	39	81	70	75	80	86	91
Female	17	9	6	8	8	9	11	56	43	47	56	61	69
Youth literacy rate (% ages 15–24)													
Total	39	29	24	32	29	30	31	84	80	81	86	87	86
Male	50	43	35	47	43	45	42	90	84	86	91	95	95
Female	28	17	12	17	16	16	20	80	76	78	82	81	81
MDGs 4 and 5: child mortality; maternal health													
Health Center less than 5 km away (% of population)	..	..	..	..	..	..	..	..	..	..	..	..	..
Morbidity (% of population)	26	27	27	27	27	26	31	20	20	20	20	19	20
Health care provider consulted when sick (%)	41	39	30	36	40	41	46	67	60	65	68	70	71
Type of health care provider consulted (% of total)													
Public	45	44	44	49	45	42	41	52	56	59	52	49	43
Private, modern medicine	45	45	46	40	46	46	48	42	36	36	41	43	51
Private, traditional healers	1	1	0	0	1	1	1	1	0	0	1	2	1
Missionary or nongovernmental organization	..	..	..	..	..	..	..	..	..	..	..	..	..
Other	6	7	6	7	5	9	7	4	4	3	4	3	4
Child survival and malnutrition (%)													
Birth assisted by trained staff	..	..	..	..	..	..	..	..	..	..	..	..	..
Immunization coverage, 1-year-olds	45	41	35	48	42	38	45	85	81	81	84	96	88
Measles immunization coverage, 1-year-olds	51	47	44	50	47	49	46	90	84	88	90	98	94
Stunting (6–59 months)	59	61	64	60	61	61	55	47	56	51	49	43	29
Wasting (6–59 months)	11	11	12	11	11	9	11	7	8	9	6	4	7
Underweight (6–59 months)	45	46	53	46	48	41	43	27	36	30	27	22	14
MDG 7: environmental sustainability													
Access to sanitation facilities (% of population)	17	9	7	8	7	9	11	71	48	63	72	78	86
Water source less than 5 km away (% of population)	..	..	..	..	..	..	..	..	..	..	..	..	..
Market less than 5 km away (% of population)	..	..	..	..	..	..	..	..	..	..	..	..	..
Access to improved water source (% of population)													
Total[a]	29	19	15	18	18	19	21	92	83	91	93	92	96
Own tap	0	0	0	0	0	0	0	1	1	1	1	2	2
Other piped	17	7	7	7	6	6	8	82	74	79	84	83	88
Well, protected	11	12	8	11	12	13	13	8	9	11	8	7	6
Traditional fuel use (%)													
Total[a]	77	78	82	78	77	78	77	66	80	74	70	65	51
Firewood	75	78	82	78	77	78	77	58	75	67	61	57	40
Charcoal	1	0	0	..	..	..	0	8	5	7	9	8	11

a. Components may not sum to total because of rounding

Table 14.4 Liberia household survey, 2007

Indicator	National total	Rural All	Rural Q1	Rural Q2	Rural Q3	Rural Q4	Rural Q5	Urban All	Urban Q1	Urban Q2	Urban Q3	Urban Q4	Urban Q5
Demographic Indicators													
Sample size (households)	3,595	2,204	382	386	439	462	535	1,391	283	260	251	270	327
Total Population (thousands)	2,736	1,900	380	379	379	380	379	836	167	167	166	167	167
Age dependency ratio	0.8	0.9	0.9	1.0	0.8	0.8	0.7	0.7	0.9	0.7	0.8	0.6	0.5
Average household size	5	6	6	6	6	5	5	5	6	6	6	5	4
Marital Status of head of household (%)													
Monogamous male	51	55	60	59	54	57	49	43	45	46	46	47	34
Polygamous male	4	6	8	5	6	5	5	1	2	2	1	1	1
Single male	18	14	11	10	13	12	21	26	20	22	23	21	37
De facto female	9	9	6	12	12	8	9	9	13	9	8	8	7
De jure female	18	16	16	14	16	17	16	21	20	21	22	23	21
MDG 1: eradicate extreme poverty and hunger													
Mean monthly expenditure (Liberian dollar)	10,571	10,062	4,128	6,731	8,270	10,224	18,120	11,688	4,774	8,354	10,488	13,340	17,493
Mean monthly share on food (%)	59	59	54	61	61	60	59	59	62	61	61	57	55
Mean monthly share on health (%)	3	3	3	3	3	3	3	2	2	2	2	2	2
Mean monthly share on education (%)	4	3	4	4	3	3	2	5	5	5	5	5	4
MDGs 2 and 3: education and literacy; gender equality													
Primary school within 30 minutes (% of households)	..	..	..	..	..	..	..	..	..	..	..		..
Net primary enrollment rate (% of relevant age group)													
Total	36	30	25	25	36	28	37	51	27	39	51	58	79
Male	37	31	31	32	33	21	40	51	32	38	42	66	80
Female	36	29	19	18	40	35	34	51	23	39	59	51	79
Net secondary enrollment rate (% of relevant age group)													
Total	15	8	6	6	7	7	15	27	16	25	25	36	33
Male	18	10	9	6	10	10	16	30	18	26	27	41	36
Female	13	6	4	6	5	3	14	24	13	24	23	31	29
Tertiary enrollment rate (per 10,000)													
Total	..	..	..	..	..	..	..	..	..	..	..	..	..
Adult literacy rate (%)													
Total	59	50	43	47	50	54	57	76	61	72	77	86	84
Male	72	65	56	60	67	71	71	86	73	84	86	94	90
Female	45	35	30	33	34	38	42	66	48	59	68	77	78
Youth literacy rate (% ages 15–24)													
Total	78	73	63	76	72	78	75	89	82	86	90	94	93
Male	86	83	73	82	86	86	87	92	88	92	92	96	94
Female	71	63	54	70	57	69	64	86	76	79	87	92	92
MDGs 4 and 5: child mortality; maternal health													
Health Center less than 5 km away (% of population)	..	..	..	..	..	..	..	..	..	..	..	..	..
Morbidity (% of population)	43	46	41	46	46	48	49	36	33	36	38	38	36
Health care provider consulted when sick (%)	92	92	89	91	90	93	94	92	86	89	93	93	96
Type of health care provider consulted (% of total)													
Public	55	58	66	59	56	59	50	48	71	54	44	39	40
Private, modern medicine	29	22	16	20	22	24	27	48	23	44	50	58	58
Private, traditional healers	7	8	9	9	7	6	9	2	5	1	2	1	1
Missionary or nongovernmental organization	9	12	9	12	14	12	13	2	1	1	4	2	1
Other	..	..	..	..	..	..	..	..	..	..	..	..	..
Child survival and malnutrition (%)													
Birth assisted by trained staff	63	54	48	53	54	56	60	83	76	81	80	93	99
Immunization coverage, 1-year-olds	68	66	65	65	65	67	68	73	68	72	74	75	84
Measles immunization coverage, 1-year-olds	79	77	77	75	75	79	81	83	78	84	85	84	94
Stunting (6–59 months)	..	..	..	..	..	..	..	..	..	..	..	..	..
Wasting (6–59 months)	..	..	..	..	..	..	..	..	..	..	..	..	..
Underweight (6–59 months)	..	..	..	..	..	..	..	..	..	..	..	..	..
MDG 7: environmental sustainability													
Access to sanitation facilities (% of population)	40	32	21	33	36	30	38	60	46	54	61	73	68
Water source less than 5 km away (% of population)	98	98	96	99	98	99	99	99	99	99	99	99	99
Market less than 5 km away (% of population)	55	39	33	35	37	42	47	92	89	93	94	90	92
Access to improved water source (% of population)													
Total[a]	51	49	54	50	49	52	39	57	62	61	56	54	51
Own tap	4	3	1	5	3	2	3	6	4	6	4	6	7
Other piped	31	29	27	28	34	34	25	33	31	32	37	34	33
Well, protected	17	17	26	17	12	16	11	18	27	23	15	13	10
Traditional fuel use (%)													
Total[a]	99	99	96	99	100	99	100	100	100	100	100	100	99
Firewood	67	90	94	95	91	86	82	15	34	17	11	10	4
Charcoal	32	9	2	4	9	13	17	84	66	83	89	90	94

a. Components may not sum to total because of rounding

Table 14.5

Malawi household survey, 2003/04

	National total	Rural						Urban					
Indicator		All	Q1	Q2	Q3	Q4	Q5	All	Q1	Q2	Q3	Q4	Q5
Demographic Indicators													
Sample size (households)	11,280	9,840	1,495	1,747	1,924	2,106	2,568	1,440	249	246	283	335	327
Total Population (thousands)	12,505	11,075	2,187	2,186	2,200	2,219	2,282	1,429	279	281	280	287	299
Age dependency ratio	1.0	1.0	1.4	1.2	1.1	1.0	0.7	0.7	1.1	0.9	0.8	0.6	0.4
Average household size	4.5	4.6	5.9	5.2	4.7	4.2	3.5	4.3	5.3	4.9	4.5	3.7	3.5
Marital Status of head of household (%)													
Monogamous male	63	62	62	63	63	64	58	69	69	81	76	68	57
Polygamous male	8	9	9	11	10	8	8	3	6	3	2	2	2
Single male	6	5	1	1	2	5	13	13	1	4	8	17	27
De facto female	2	2	3	3	2	2	2	1	3	1	2	0	1
De jure female	21	22	25	21	22	21	19	14	20	11	12	12	14
MDG 1: eradicate extreme poverty and hunger													
Mean monthly expenditure (kwacha)	6,835	5,909	2,721	3,823	4,723	6,086	9,829	13,064	4,238	6,547	8,760	11,133	27,244
Mean monthly share on food (%)	73	75	76	77	77	75	73	61	70	66	63	59	52
Mean monthly share on health (%)	3	3	3	3	3	3	3	2	2	2	2	2	3
Mean monthly share on education (%)	1	1	1	1	1	1	1	2	1	1	1	2	3
MDGs 2 and 3: education and literacy; gender equality													
Primary school within 30 minutes (% of households)	..	..	..	..	..	..	..	..	..	..	..	..	..
Net primary enrollment rate (% of relevant age group)													
Total	65	64	57	60	64	69	73	78	71	78	86	79	81
Male	64	63	57	59	63	68	72	78	71	78	86	75	79
Female	66	65	58	61	65	70	74	79	71	78	86	83	83
Net secondary enrollment rate (% of relevant age group)													
Total	7	5	2	3	3	6	10	20	4	12	16	30	37
Male	7	5	2	3	3	6	10	20	3	14	16	33	35
Female	6	5	2	2	3	6	10	20	4	10	15	28	39
Tertiary enrollment rate (per 10,000)													
Total													
Adult literacy rate (%)													
Total	63	60	50	56	57	63	69	83	69	80	85	90	89
Male	74	72	64	69	71	75	77	89	82	86	92	91	90
Female	52	49	39	44	45	52	60	77	56	73	76	89	88
Youth literacy rate (% ages 15–24)													
Total	75	73	68	72	71	75	76	86	83	86	87	90	85
Male	79	77	74	76	77	80	77	87	87	86	91	87	86
Female	71	69	62	68	66	70	75	85	78	86	84	92	85
MDGs 4 and 5: child mortality; maternal health													
Health Center less than 5 km away (% of population)	..	..	..	..	..	..	..	..	..	..	..	..	..
Morbidity (% of population)	28	29	22	27	29	32	33	17	18	16	18	17	16
Health care provider consulted when sick (%)	87	87	83	86	86	89	88	90	84	90	93	92	89
Type of health care provider consulted (% of total)													
Public	36	35	39	38	35	32	32	44	41	51	44	50	31
Private, modern medicine	52	52	48	51	53	54	54	51	51	45	48	45	66
Private, traditional healers	5	5	6	4	5	6	3	3	5	2	3	2	1
Missionary or nongovernmental organization	4	4	3	3	3	4	7	2	1	2	4	1	1
Other	4	4	4	3	4	4	3	1	2		1	1	2
Child survival and malnutrition (%)													
Birth assisted by trained staff	..	..	..	..	..	..	..	..	..	..	..	..	..
Immunization coverage, 1-year-olds	..	..	..	..	..	..	..	..	..	..	..	..	..
Measles immunization coverage, 1-year-olds	..	..	..	..	..	..	..	..	..	..	..	..	..
Stunting (6–59 months)	39	39	39	39	41	39	36	35	43	36	30	39	19
Wasting (6–59 months)	2	2	3	3	2	2	2	2	2	4	2	0	2
Underweight (6–59 months)	16	16	18	17	15	14	16	15	19	18	12	11	14
MDG 7: environmental sustainability													
Access to sanitation facilities (% of population)	18	9	6	7	9	9	11	66	57	68	68	73	65
Water source less than 5 km away (% of population)	..	..	..	..	..	..	..	..	..	..	..	..	..
Market less than 5 km away (% of population)	..	..	..	..	..	..	..	..	..	..	..	..	..
Access to improved water source (% of population)													
Total[a]	67	64	64	63	64	62	67	88	69	86	86	92	97
Own tap	5	2	1	1	1	2	4	28	6	13	16	30	61
Other piped	15	11	10	10	11	9	13	49	42	55	60	56	33
Well, protected	47	51	53	53	52	51	50	11	21	18	10	7	3
Traditional fuel use (%)													
Total[a]	97	98	99	99	99	98	98	87	99	95	96	89	62
Firewood	90	97	99	98	98	97	94	38	71	50	40	29	16
Charcoal	7	1	..	0	0	1	3	49	28	45	56	61	47

a. Components may not sum to total because of rounding

Table 14.6

Niger household survey, 2005

Indicator	National total	Rural All	Rural Q1	Rural Q2	Rural Q3	Rural Q4	Rural Q5	Urban All	Urban Q1	Urban Q2	Urban Q3	Urban Q4	Urban Q5
Demographic Indicators													
Sample size (households)	6,690	4,670	670	787	863	1,024	1,326	2,020	273	308	381	449	609
Total Population (thousands)	12,627	10,510	2,100	2,106	2,099	2,103	2,100	2,116	423	422	423	423	423
Age dependency ratio	1.1	1.2	1.4	1.3	1.3	1.1	0.9	0.9	1.2	1.1	0.9	0.8	0.7
Average household size	6.4	6.4	8.4	7.4	6.8	6.0	4.7	6.3	7.8	7.2	6.9	6.1	4.5
Marital Status of head of household (%)													
Monogamous male	68	69	62	68	69	72	70	64	60	63	59	66	67
Polygamous male	22	22	32	26	23	20	16	18	22	19	24	18	12
Single male	3	3	1	2	2	2	6	4	1	2	2	3	9
De facto female	1	0	0	0	0	1	1	1	2	1	..	1	1
De jure female	7	5	4	4	6	5	7	13	15	14	15	12	11
MUG 1: eradicate extreme poverty and hunger													
Mean monthly expenditure (CFA franc)	61,173	53,499	20,610	31,335	40,516	50,124	97,417	98,719	34,161	55,544	76,782	100,276	176,847
Mean monthly share on food (%)	81	83	78	82	83	84	85	71	76	76	75	69	62
Mean monthly share on health (%)	3	3	3	2	2	3	3	3	2	2	3	4	5
Mean monthly share on education (%)	0	0	0	0	0	0	0	1	1	1	1	2	2
Mugs 2 and 3: education and literacy; gender equality													
Primary school within 30 minutes (% of households)	..	..	..	..	..	..	..	..	..	..	..	..	..
Net primary enrollment rate (% of relevant age group)													
Total	32	28	26	26	29	30	30	54	40	47	63	63	67
Male	35	32	29	30	33	35	33	55	40	49	67	63	62
Female	29	24	21	20	25	25	27	54	40	46	58	63	71
Net secondary enrollment rate (% of relevant age group)													
Total	7	3	3	2	4	4	3	22	9	16	21	32	34
Male	9	5	5	3	7	7	4	22	8	12	24	33	39
Female	6	1	0	2	2	1	2	22	10	20	19	31	30
Tertiary enrolment rate (per 10,000)													
Total	..	..	..	..	..	..	..	..	..	..	..	..	..
Adult literacy rate (%)													
Total	29	24	20	22	23	25	27	52	35	43	49	63	66
Male	43	38	34	37	37	39	43	64	47	53	61	76	76
Female	15	9	6	8	8	11	12	41	22	33	37	50	56
Youth literacy rate (% ages 15–24)													
Total	38	31	26	29	32	31	36	66	48	58	68	78	73
Male	52	47	41	44	50	46	53	72	56	62	75	86	81
Female	23	15	10	13	15	16	19	59	40	54	60	69	65
Mugs 4 and 5: child mortality; maternal health													
Health Center less than 5 km away (% of population)	..	..	..	..	..	..	..	..	..	..	..	..	..
Morbidity (% of population)	10	10	9	10	9	10	12	7	6	7	8	7	10
Health care provider consulted when sick (%)	8	8	7	8	7	8	10	6	4	6	7	6	9
Type of health care provider consulted (% of total)													
Public	64	63	58	63	69	67	61	67	65	72	69	68	62
Private, modern medicine	21	20	24	23	14	16	23	27	28	17	25	26	34
Private, traditional healers	15	16	18	14	16	17	16	6	7	10	6	5	4
Missionary or nongovernmental organization	..	..	..	..	..	..	..	..	..	..	..	..	..
Other	..	..	..	..	..	..	..	..	..	..	..	..	..
Child survival and malnutrition (%)													
Birth assisted by trained staff	..	..	..	..	..	..	..	..	..	..	..	..	..
Immunization coverage, 1-year-olds	..	..	..	..	..	..	..	..	..	..	..	..	..
Measles immunization coverage, 1-year-olds	..	..	..	..	..	..	..	..	..	..	..	..	..
Stunting (6–59 months)	..	..	..	..	..	..	..	..	..	..	..	..	..
Wasting (6–59 months)	..	..	..	..	..	..	..	..	..	..	..	..	..
Underweight (6–59 months)	..	..	..	..	..	..	..	..	..	..	..	..	..
MUG 7: environmental sustainability													
Access to sanitation facilities (% of population)	21	10	8	8	11	12	12	75	56	71	75	83	92
Water source less than 5 km away (% of population)	86	83	83	83	82	84	85	99	99	99	98	99	99
Market less than 5 km away (% of population)	51	42	39	37	46	46	43	97	96	97	98	96	99
Access to improved water source (% of population)													
Total[a]	51	44	42	40	48	45	45	84	86	87	79	84	86
Own tap	8	3	4	3	3	3	4	32	13	17	28	44	55
Other piped	26	21	22	21	22	22	19	51	70	68	49	38	28
Well, protected	17	19	16	16	23	20	23	2	3	2	2	2	2
Traditional fuel use (%)													
Total[a]	97	97	96	96	97	97	98	96	95	99	98	94	95
Firewood	96	96	95	96	97	97	97	95	95	98	96	93	92
Charcoal	1	1	1	0	1	0	1	1	0	1	2	1	3

a. Components may not sum to total because of rounding

14.7 Nigeria household survey, 2003/04

Indicator	National total	Rural						Urban					
		All	Q1	Q2	Q3	Q4	Q5	All	Q1	Q2	Q3	Q4	Q5
Demographic Indicators													
Sample size (households)	19,158	14,512	2,321	2,446	2,717	3,120	3,908	4,646	783	779	834	988	1,265
Total Population (thousands)	126,305	70,599	14,115	14,127	14,116	14,122	14,118	55,706	11,144	11,138	11,140	11,131	11,153
Age dependency ratio	0.8	0.9	1.1	1.0	0.9	0.8	0.6	0.8	0.8	0.9	0.8	0.7	0.5
Average household size	4.7	4.8	6.5	6.0	5.2	4.5	3.4	4.6	5.6	5.7	5.1	4.4	3.3
Marital Status of head of household (%)													
Monogamous male	58	58	54	63	65	62	51	57	56	61	59	59	51
Polygamous male	15	18	32	26	20	14	8	12	16	17	15	10	7
Single male	11	9	4	3	5	8	19	14	10	7	8	13	25
De facto female	3	2	2	2	2	2	3	3	4	3	4	3	3
De jure female	13	12	8	7	9	14	19	14	13	12	14	16	14
MDG 1: eradicate extreme poverty and hunger													
Mean monthly expenditure (Nigeria naira)	11,635	9,924	3,922	6,391	8,008	9,939	16,272	13,705	4,548	8,809	11,580	14,279	22,892
Mean monthly share on food (%)	54	61	57	65	65	64	54	45	36	51	51	50	41
Mean monthly share on health (%)	8	8	3	4	5	7	16	7	4	5	6	6	13
Mean monthly share on education (%)	5	3	4	3	3	3	3	8	11	7	8	7	7
MDGs 2 and 3: education and literacy; gender equality													
Primary school within 30 minutes (% of households)	..	..	..	..	..	..	..	..	..	..	..	..	..
Net primary enrollment rate (% of relevant age group)													
Total	..	..	..	..	..	..	..	..	..	..	..	..	..
Male	..	..	..	..	..	..	..	..	..	..	..	..	..
Female	..	..	..	..	..	..	..	..	..	..	..	..	..
Net secondary enrollment rate (% of relevant age group)													
Total	..	..	..	..	..	..	..	..	..	..	..	..	..
Male	..	..	..	..	..	..	..	..	..	..	..	..	..
Female	..	..	..	..	..	..	..	..	..	..	..	..	..
Tertiary enrolment rate (per 10,000)													
Total	..	..	..	..	..	..	..	..	..	..	..	..	..
Adult literacy rate (%)													
Total	62	50	38	42	48	55	63	75	71	68	73	80	83
Male	69	57	44	49	55	62	71	83	78	77	81	86	89
Female	54	43	31	36	41	49	54	68	65	59	65	73	75
Youth literacy rate (% ages 15–24)													
Total	78	68	55	60	66	72	81	88	84	86	89	93	89
Male	82	74	60	67	75	81	86	90	85	88	92	96	92
Female	73	62	50	53	58	65	77	86	82	84	85	90	87
MDGs 4 and 5: child mortality; maternal health													
Health Center less than 5 km away (% of population)	..	..	..	..	..	..	..	..	..	..	..	..	..
Morbidity (% of population)	12	12	8	10	11	14	21	11	7	9	10	11	17
Health care provider consulted when sick (%)	57	57	31	41	50	62	74	57	30	50	56	58	71
Type of health care provider consulted (% of total)													
Public	38	37	27	26	31	32	47	40	36	41	41	39	40
Private, modern medicine	57	58	69	69	63	64	49	55	58	54	56	56	53
Private, traditional healers	2	2	1	1	2	1	2	1	..	2	0	1	2
Missionary or nongovernmental organization	..	..	..	..	..	..	..	..	..	..	..	..	..
Other	3	3	3	4	4	3	3	4	6	4	3	4	4
Child survival and malnutrition (%)													
Birth assisted by trained staff	..	..	..	..	..	..	..	..	..	..	..	..	..
Immunization coverage, 1-year-olds	..	..	..	..	..	..	..	..	..	..	..	..	..
Measles immunization coverage, 1-year-olds	..	..	..	..	..	..	..	..	..	..	..	..	..
Stunting (6–59 months)	..	..	..	..	..	..	..	..	..	..	..	..	..
Wasting (6–59 months)	..	..	..	..	..	..	..	..	..	..	..	..	..
Underweight (6–59 months)	..	..	..	..	..	..	..	..	..	..	..	..	..
MDG 7: environmental sustainability													
Access to sanitation facilities (% of population)	60	50	47	48	50	50	52	72	73	71	71	72	75
Water source less than 5 km away (% of population)	..	..	..	..	..	..	..	..	..	..	..	..	..
Market less than 5 km away (% of population)	..	..	..	..	..	..	..	..	..	..	..	..	..
Access to improved water source (% of population)													
Total[a]	61	42	41	41	43	41	43	83	81	82	82	86	84
Own tap	13	4	3	3	4	3	5	23	18	21	23	24	28
Other piped	11	4	3	4	5	4	5	18	24	18	17	17	16
Well, protected	38	34	35	35	35	34	33	42	39	43	42	45	40
Traditional fuel use (%)													
Total[a]	65	88	92	93	91	89	79	38	44	52	43	36	24
Firewood	64	87	92	93	90	89	79	37	42	51	42	35	23
Charcoal	1	0	0	0	1	0	1	1	2	1	1	1	2

a. Components may not sum to total because of rounding

Table 14.8

São Tomé and Principe household survey, 2000/01

Indicator	National total	Rural						Urban					
		All	Q1	Q2	Q3	Q4	Q5	All	Q1	Q2	Q3	Q4	Q5
Demographic Indicators													
Sample size (households)	2,416	1,173	179	197	215	244	338	1,243	187	202	242	264	348
Total Population (thousands)	128	57	11	11	11	11	11	71	14	14	14	14	14
Age dependency ratio	0.9	1.0	1.3	1.1	1.0	1.0	0.6	0.8	1.1	1.0	0.8	0.8	0.6
Average household size	4.6	4.5	6.3	5.7	4.9	4.2	3.0	4.6	6.2	5.5	4.9	4.4	3.3
Marital Status of head of household (%)													
Monogamous male	51	53	62	66	66	48	37	50	51	50	46	56	46
Polygamous male	..	..	..	..	..	..	..	..	..	..	..	..	..
Single male	16	18	9	5	10	16	36	15	4	9	12	14	26
De facto female	7	6	5	5	5	8	7	8	7	11	12	5	8
De jure female	25	23	25	24	19	27	20	27	37	29	30	25	20
MDG 1: eradicate extreme poverty and hunger													
Mean monthly expenditure (dobras)	451,490	318,313	80,362	128,371	175,196	243,054	679,373	560,829	108,471	179,366	252,850	359,041	1,403,366
Mean monthly share on food (%)	72	75	78	77	78	76	71	69	76	74	69	68	62
Mean monthly share on health (%)	3	3	3	3	2	3	3	4	3	3	4	3	5
Mean monthly share on education (%)	2	2	2	2	2	2	1	3	2	3	3	3	2
MDGs 2 and 3: education and literacy; gender equality													
Primary school within 30 minutes (% of households)	34	33	46	44	37	35	16	35	51	39	35	38	23
Net primary enrollment rate (% of relevant age group)													
Total	70	67	68	68	63	68	67	73	71	73	78	73	74
Male	71	70	67	75	62	71	70	73	72	71	75	80	66
Female	69	64	68	60	63	64	63	73	69	75	81	65	79
Net secondary enrollment rate (% of relevant age group)													
Total	43	29	13	26	23	34	50	52	32	39	64	62	64
Male	43	29	15	24	24	42	47	52	30	41	65	66	66
Female	42	28	11	28	22	25	51	52	35	37	62	59	63
Tertiary enrollment rate (per 10,000)													
Total	..	..	..	..	..	..	..	..	..	..	..	..	..
Adult literacy rate (%)													
Total	83	80	76	82	79	77	85	86	78	83	85	89	91
Male	92	89	87	89	89	87	92	94	90	92	92	95	97
Female	76	72	67	76	70	69	77	79	68	75	80	84	84
Youth literacy rate (% ages 15–24)													
Total	94	92	90	92	91	91	95	96	91	94	98	98	96
Male	95	93	95	91	90	94	96	96	94	96	97	98	98
Female	93	91	86	92	92	88	95	95	88	92	98	98	95
MDGs 4 and 5: child mortality; maternal health													
Health Center less than 5 km away (% of population)	84	81	77	74	81	82	85	87	86	90	85	89	87
Morbidity (% of population)	18	15	12	14	14	17	20	19	12	19	19	22	24
Health care provider consulted when sick (%)	48	45	41	45	40	50	47	50	38	44	50	56	57
Type of health care provider consulted (% of total)													
Public	70	81	94	88	78	83	68	64	80	78	68	62	53
Private, modern medicine	25	14	4	9	16	10	27	31	15	18	29	32	43
Private, traditional healers	3	2	..	3	..	3	4	4	5	1	3	6	2
Missionary or nongovernmental organization	..	..	..	..	..	..	..	..	..	..	..	..	..
Other	1	2	2	..	6	3	1	1	..	3	..	..	2
Child survival and malnutrition (%)													
Birth assisted by trained staff	..	..	..	..	..	..	..	..	..	..	..	..	..
Immunization coverage, 1-year-olds	..	..	..	..	..	..	..	..	..	..	..	..	..
Measles immunization coverage, 1-year-olds	..	..	..	..	..	..	..	..	..	..	..	..	..
Stunting (6–59 months)	..	..	..	..	..	..	..	..	..	..	..	..	..
Wasting (6–59 months)	..	..	..	..	..	..	..	..	..	..	..	..	..
Underweight (6–59 months)	..	..	..	..	..	..	..	..	..	..	..	..	..
MDG 7: environmental sustainability													
Access to sanitation facilities (% of population)	28	21	18	12	20	20	27	35	14	26	36	41	46
Water source less than 5 km away (% of population)	88	93	93	94	93	95	92	84	82	80	87	86	85
Market less than 5 km away (% of population)	87	81	74	73	80	86	86	92	90	88	91	93	94
Access to improved water source (% of population)													
Total[a]	77	67	74	70	64	70	63	84	82	79	81	89	88
Own tap	20	10	7	9	7	13	12	27	12	20	26	29	40
Other piped	8	13	19	15	15	11	10	4	4	3	5	5	4
Well, protected	49	44	48	46	42	46	41	53	65	56	49	56	43
Traditional fuel use (%)													
Total[a]	84	95	100	98	99	94	88	75	96	83	81	72	57
Firewood	73	91	98	96	97	90	82	59	88	74	63	50	36
Charcoal	11	4	1	2	2	4	6	16	8	9	18	22	20

a. Components may not sum to total because of rounding

Table 14.9

Sierra Leone household survey, 2002/03

Indicator	National total	Rural						Urban					
		All	Q1	Q2	Q3	Q4	Q5	All	Q1	Q2	Q3	Q4	Q5
Demographic Indicators													
Sample size (households)	3,713	2,396	412	451	453	511	569	1,317	223	246	277	276	295
Total Population (thousands)	5,337	3,440	688	689	688	688	688	1,897	379	379	380	379	380
Age dependency ratio	0.9	1.0	1.1	1.0	1.0	0.9	0.9	0.8	1.0	1.0	0.8	0.7	0.6
Average household size	7.4	7.3	8.2	7.6	7.5	6.8	6.3	7.5	8.4	7.6	7.1	7.2	7.4
Marital Status of head of household (%)													
Monogamous male	61	60	52	56	61	65	64	63	56	62	66	67	64
Polygamous male	19	23	31	28	26	19	15	10	13	13	13	8	6
Single male	4	3	2	2	3	3	4	6	2	3	3	7	14
De facto female	2	2	3	1	1	2	2	2	1	3	2	2	1
De jure female	14	12	12	13	10	11	15	19	27	19	16	16	16
MDG 1: eradicate extreme poverty and hunger													
Mean monthly expenditure (leones)	294,515	239,364	103,175	150,703	197,851	237,999	438,780	378,978	154,151	242,246	322,612	385,918	685,453
Mean monthly share on food (%)	52	59	60	61	62	61	53	42	49	46	45	43	32
Mean monthly share on health (%)	10	2	6	9	7	10	14	13	8	10	12	12	19
Mean monthly share on education (%)	4	2	3	2	2	2	2	6	5	6	6	6	5
MDGs 2 and 3: education and literacy; gender equality													
Primary school within 30 minutes (% of households)													
Net primary enrollment rate (% of relevant age group)													
Total	73	67	62	64	67	69	75	86	78	85	89	87	91
Male	72	66	58	65	66	70	72	85	78	83	88	88	93
Female	74	68	66	63	68	67	77	86	78	87	90	87	89
Net secondary enrollment rate (% of relevant age group)													
Total	19	10	7	7	11	10	18	33	27	23	24	37	51
Male	22	13	9	10	12	13	22	36	31	28	24	47	48
Female	17	7	4	3	9	7	13	30	23	18	24	27	54
Tertiary enrollment rate (per 10,000)													
Total	..	..	..	..	..	..	..	..	..	..	..	..	..
Adult literacy rate (%)													
Total	27	13	11	10	11	14	20	49	32	37	41	52	75
Male	35	20	17	17	17	21	27	58	43	50	49	59	81
Female	19	8	6	5	6	8	14	40	24	26	33	46	68
Youth literacy rate (% ages 15–24)													
Total	40	23	18	17	17	28	35	62	49	51	56	62	81
Male	47	31	26	24	25	36	42	68	59	62	64	65	85
Female	33	16	12	11	11	20	27	55	39	42	48	60	78
MDGs 4 and 5: child mortality; maternal health													
Health Center less than 5 km away (% of population)													
Morbidity (% of population)	44	42	34	40	42	42	49	45	37	44	45	45	54
Health care provider consulted when sick (%)	59	65	49	64	67	68	75	56	41	50	49	58	75
Type of health care provider consulted (% of total)													
Public	53	55	50	39	53	51	61	51	51	52	49	55	51
Private, modern medicine	30	27	16	31	27	33	25	36	18	32	28	31	48
Private, traditional healers	9	11	23	16	12	8	9	4	6	5	12	5	..
Missionary or nongovernmental organization	8	7	11	14	8	9	5	8	25	11	12	10	2
Other	..	..	..	..	..	..	..	..	..	..	..	..	..
Child survival and malnutrition (%)													
Birth assisted by trained staff	..	..	..	..	..	..	..	..	..	..	..	..	..
Immunization coverage, 1-year-olds	72	72	74	57	64	71	96	73	70	75	71	63	87
Measles immunization coverage, 1-year-olds	16	16	16	24	15	13	8	18	19	17	21	21	9
Stunting (6–59 months)	..	..	..	..	..	..	..	..	..	..	..	..	..
Wasting (6–59 months)	..	..	..	..	..	..	..	..	..	..	..	..	..
Underweight (6–59 months)	..	..	..	..	..	..	..	..	..	..	..	..	..
MDG 7: environmental sustainability													
Access to sanitation facilities (% of population)	4	2	2	2	1	2	4	7	1	2	4	5	23
Water source less than 5 km away (% of population)	..	..	..	..	..	..	..	..	..	..	..	..	..
Market less than 5 km away (% of population)	..	..	..	..	..	..	..	..	..	..	..	..	..
Access to improved water source (% of population)													
Total[a]	37	25	24	25	23	22	31	59	40	51	52	67	79
Own tap	7	1	0	1	1	0	4	18	0	3	10	20	49
Other piped	12	5	6	8	5	3	5	24	19	23	19	33	23
Well, protected	18	19	18	17	17	20	22	17	21	24	22	15	7
Traditional fuel use (%)													
Total[a]	97	99	99	99	99	99	98	95	99	98	98	95	86
Firewood	93	98	98	98	98	98	97	83	98	96	91	83	55
Charcoal	5	1	1	1	1	0	1	12	1	2	7	12	32

a. Components may not sum to total because of rounding.

Table 14.10

Tanzania household survey, 2000/01

Indicator	National total	Rural All	Rural Q1	Rural Q2	Rural Q3	Rural Q4	Rural Q5	Urban All	Urban Q1	Urban Q2	Urban Q3	Urban Q4	Urban Q5
Demographic Indicators													
Sample size (households)	22,178	7,627	2,022	1,436	1,378	1,390	1,401	14,551	4,797	3,063	2,528	2,137	2,026
Total Population (thousands)	31,897	25,723	5,146	5,142	5,144	5,151	5,148	6,168	1,233	1,234	1,234	1,236	1,234
Age dependency ratio	0.9	1.0	1.3	1.1	1.0	0.9	0.7	0.7	1.0	0.9	0.7	0.6	0.4
Average household size	4.9	5.1	6.7	5.9	5.5	4.9	3.6	4.4	6.1	5.5	4.7	4.1	3.1
Marital Status of head of household (%)													
Monogamous male	65	66	69	70	69	68	60	62	60	68	67	64	54
Polygamous male	3	4	3	5	4	5	3	1	3	2	1	1	0
Single male	8	8	4	6	3	5	15	12	6	5	7	9	23
De facto female	7	7	7	6	8	9	7	6	7	6	7	5	5
De jure female	16	15	16	14	16	14	15	20	23	19	18	21	18
MUG 1: eradicate extreme poverty and hunger													
Mean monthly expenditure (Tanzania Shilling)	52,827	42,975	20,255	29,886	37,024	44,600	64,738	88,541	34,912	55,335	69,467	87,064	145,942
Mean monthly share on food (%)	76	79	78	80	81	79	76	68	76	74	71	67	60
Mean monthly share on health (%)	2	2	2	2	2	2	3	3	3	2	3	3	2
Mean monthly share on education (%)	2	1	2	1	1	1	1	2	2	2	2	2	3
Mugs 2 and 3: education and literacy; gender equality													
Primary school within 30 minutes (% of households)													
Net primary enrollment rate (% of relevant age group)													
Total	60	58	50	53	58	62	70	71	60	73	78	77	69
Male	59	56	46	51	60	59	66	72	60	72	79	79	76
Female	62	60	53	55	56	65	76	71	61	75	77	75	63
Net secondary enrollment rate (% of relevant age group)													
Total	5	2	0	2	2	2	5	14	6	9	17	16	19
Male	4	2	0	2	1	2	5	14	5	10	16	19	21
Female	5	3	0	3	3	2	5	14	7	9	18	13	18
Tertiary enrolment rate (per 10,000)													
Total	..	..	..	..	..	..	..	..	..	..	..	..	..
Adult literacy rate (%)													
Total	71	67	56	63	66	69	76	88	77	84	87	91	96
Male	80	76	66	71	76	79	83	93	87	91	91	95	97
Female	64	59	48	56	57	60	70	83	70	78	84	88	94
Youth literacy rate (% ages 15–24)													
Total	82	78	73	72	78	82	85	94	88	92	96	96	97
Male	84	81	74	75	82	84	87	95	89	93	97	97	97
Female	80	76	71	70	74	80	84	94	88	92	96	95	97
Mugs 4 and 5: child mortality; maternal health													
Health Center less than 5 km away (% of population)													
Morbidity (% of population)	27	28	27	28	28	28	31	22	24	23	22	24	20
Health care provider consulted when sick (%)	100	100	100	100	100	100	100	100	100	100	100	100	100
Type of health care provider consulted (% of total)													
Public	56	57	54	50	62	59	61	49	54	55	52	44	43
Private, modern medicine	26	23	21	28	23	20	25	36	31	29	33	42	47
Private, traditional healers	14	16	20	20	13	16	12	4	7	5	2	4	2
Missionary or nongovernmental organization	3	2	1	1	1	3	2	9	8	9	12	10	9
Other	2	2	4	2	1	2	1	1	1	1	1	1	0
Child survival and malnutrition (%)													
Birth assisted by trained staff	..	..	..	..	..	..	..	..	..	..	..	..	..
Immunization coverage, 1-year-olds	..	..	..	..	..	..	..	..	..	..	..	..	..
Measles immunization coverage, 1-year-olds	..	..	..	..	..	..	..	..	..	..	..	..	..
Stunting (6–59 months)	..	..	..	..	..	..	..	..	..	..	..	..	..
Wasting (6–59 months)	..	..	..	..	..	..	..	..	..	..	..	..	..
Underweight (6–59 months)	..	..	..	..	..	..	..	..	..	..	..	..	..
MUG 7: environmental sustainability													
Access to sanitation facilities (% of population)	96	93	89	93	93	95	97	98	97	98	98	98	98
Water source less than 5 km away (% of population)	92	91	91	91	92	90	90	97	95	98	98	99	98
Market less than 5 km away (% of population)	80	76	74	72	73	77	84	99	97	99	99	99	100
Access to improved water source (% of population)													
Total[a]	54	46	44	49	43	43	51	88	79	85	91	93	93
Own tap	4	1	1	0	0	1	2	16	7	11	15	16	32
Other piped	34	28	23	30	26	27	32	61	55	61	65	69	56
Well, protected	16	17	19	19	17	15	17	11	17	12	10	8	6
Traditional fuel use (%)													
Total[a]	95	98	98	98	97	98	97	82	96	92	87	76	60
Firewood	82	94	97	97	96	94	87	30	60	40	27	15	7
Charcoal	13	3	1	2	1	3	10	52	36	52	60	61	53

a. Components may not sum to total because of rounding

Table 14.11

Uganda household survey, 2005/06

Indicators	National total	Rural						Urban					
		All	Q1	Q2	Q3	Q4	Q5	All	Q1	Q2	Q3	Q4	Q5
Demographic Indicators													
Sample size (households)	7420	5722	984	1039	1104	1189	1406	1698	310	324	329	311	424
Total Population (thousands)	27,157	22,987	4,597	4,595	4,599	4,597	4,597	4,169	833	834	828	840	832
Age dependency ratio	1.2	1.2	1.6	1.4	1.3	1.2	0.8	0.8	1.3	1.0	1.0	0.7	0.5
Average household size	5	5	6	6	6	5	4	5	6	5	5	4	3
Marital Status of head of household (%)													
Monogamous male	3	4	1	2	3	4	6	3	0	1	2	6	3
Polygamous male	5	4	0	1	1	2	10	9	0	3	6	11	17
Single male	74	76	78	82	80	77	67	65	78	76	68	63	52
De facto female	8	7	6	6	6	8	9	13	7	8	12	10	20
De jure female	10	10	15	9	10	8	8	11	14	13	11	11	7
MDG 1: eradicate extreme poverty and hunger													
Mean monthly expenditure (Uganda shillings)	210,511	81,422	81,422	121,094	149,974	196,944	321,952	319,608	119,278	173,209	237,305	322,609	573,926
Mean monthly share on food (%)	56	58	60	60	61	59	52	46	53	50	47	45	38
Mean monthly share on health (%)	6	7	4	6	6	7	9	5	4	4	6	4	5
Mean monthly share on education (%)	5	4	2	3	3	4	7	8	5	6	7	8	12
MDGs 2 and 3: education and literacy; gender equality													
Primary school within 30 minutes (% of households)	..	..	..	..	..	..	..	..	..	..	..	..	..
Net primary enrollment rate (% of relevant age group)	..												
Total	..	..	..	..	..	..	..	..	..	..	..	..	..
Male	..	..	..	..	..	..	..	..	..	..	..	..	..
Female	..	..	..	..	..	..	..	..	..	..	..	..	..
Net secondary enrollment rate (% of relevant age group)	..												
Total	..	..	..	..	..	..	..	..	..	..	..	..	..
Male	..	..	..	..	..	..	..	..	..	..	..	..	..
Female	..	..	..	..	..	..	..	..	..	..	..	..	..
Tertiary enrollment rate (per 10,000)													
Total	..	..	..	..	..	..	..	..	..	..	..	..	..
Adult literacy rate (%)													
Total	60	58	47	52	59	60	66	69	58	71	71	70	73
Male	62	60	51	53	62	62	70	72	61	72	75	74	75
Female	51	48	37	49	48	53	53	61	52	67	61	58	64
Youth literacy rate (% ages 15–24)													
Total	58	58	57	53	62	61	59	55	57	63	61	50	50
Male	59	59	59	51	61	61	61	57	58	63	64	53	50
Female	56	57	53	63	63	59	50	52	53	61	53	44	50
MDGs 4 and 5: child mortality; maternal health													
Health Center less than I hour away (% of population)	..	..	..	..	..	..	..	..	..	..	..	..	..
Morbidity (% of population)	40	42	39	40	44	44	42	33	36	32	37	30	30
Health care provider consulted when sick (%)	88	87	83	86	86	90	91	89	84	90	90	90	92
Type of health care provider consulted (% of total)													
Public	28	29	40	31	27	26	24	23	35	29	21	13	14
Private, modern Medicine	59	58	45	54	61	62	64	66	51	62	71	75	74
Private, traditional Healers	1	1	1	1	1	1	1	1	2	2	1	1	1
Missionary or nongovernmental organization	6	6	8	7	5	6	6	7	7	5	5	8	8
Other	5	5	5	6	5	5	4	3	5	3	2	4	3
Child survival and malnutrition (%)													
Birth assisted by trained staff	..	..	..	..	..	..	..	..	..	..	..	..	..
Immunization coverage, 1-year-olds	..	..	..	..	..	..	..	..	..	..	..	..	..
Measles immunization coverage, 1-year-olds	..	..	..	..	..	..	..	..	..	..	..	..	..
Stunting (6-59 months)	..	..	..	..	..	..	..	..	..	..	..	..	..
Wasting (6-59 months)	..	..	..	..	..	..	..	..	..	..	..	..	..
Underweight (6-59 months)	..	..	..	..	..	..	..	..	..	..	..	..	..
MDG 7: environmental sustainability													
Access to sanitation facilities (% of population)	78	76	61	69	76	83	90	94	82	93	96	99	99
Water source less than I hour away (% of population)	..	..	..	..	..	..	..	..	..	..	..	..	..
Market less than 1 hour away (% of population)	..	..	..	..	..	..	..	..	..	..	..	..	..
Access to improved water source (% of population)													
Total[a]	99	99	100	99	99	98	97	99	100	100	100	98	100
Own tap	6	2	1	1	1	1	7	19	3	3	9	30	46
Other piped	14	7	5	5	6	9	12	43	28	51	60	40	38
Well, protected	79	89	93	93	92	88	79	38	69	45	31	28	16
Traditional fuel use (%)													
Total[a]	99	99	99	100	99	99	98	96	100	100	98	96	86
Firewood	83	93	98	98	94	94	81	29	56	34	24	22	11
Charcoal	15	6	1	2	5	6	17	66	44	65	74	74	75

Note: Data are provisional.
Mean monthly expenditure is deflated by regional price deflators and not by Consumer Price Index.
Consumer Price Index allows for time period comparison.
a. Components may not sum to total because of rounding.

Users Guide

Tables

The tables are numbered by section and display the identifying icon of the section. Countries are listed alphabetically. Indicators are shown for the most recent year or period for which data are available and, in most tables, for an earlier year or period (usually 1980 or 1990 or 1995 in this edition). Time-series data are available on the *Africa Development Indictors* CD-ROM and *ADI online*. Known deviations from standard definitions or breaks in comparability over time or across countries are footnoted in the tables. When available data are deemed to be too weak to provide reliable measures of levels and trends or do not adequately adhere to international standards, the data are not shown.

Aggregate measure for region and sub-classifications

The aggregate measures cover only low- and middle-income economies.

Statistics

Data are shown for economies as they were constituted in 2006, and historical data are revised to reflect current political arrangements. Exceptions are noted throughout the tables. Data will, however, be provided for some macro indicators as well as doing business, investment climate, governance and anticorruption indicators, and Country Policy and Institutional Assessment ratings (CPIA) for later years (2007–08).

Data consistency, reliability and comparability

Considerable effort has been made to harmonize the data, but full comparability cannot be assured, and care must be taken in interpreting indicators. Many factors affect data availability, comparability, and reliability. Data coverage may not be complete because of special circumstances affecting the collection and reporting of data, such as conflicts. Except where otherwise stated, growth rates are in real terms.

Classification of economies

For operational and analytical purposes the World Bank's main criterion for classifying economies is gross national income (GNI) per capita (calculated by the *World Bank Atlas* method. See Box 1). Every economy is classified as low income, middle income (subdivided into lower middle and upper middle) or high income. Low- and middle-income economies are sometimes referred to as developing economies. The term is used for convenience; it is not intended to imply that all economies in the group are experiencing similar development or that other economies have reached a preferred or final stage of development. Note the classification by income does not necessarily reflect development status. Because GNI per capita changes over time, the country composition of income groups may change from one edition of the *Africa Development Indicators* to the next. Once the classification is fixed for an edition, based on GNI per capita in the most recent year for which data are available (2006 in this edition), all historical data presented are based on the same country grouping.

Low-income economies are those with a GNI per capita of $905 or less in 2006. Middle-income economies are those with a GNI per capita of more than $905 but less than $11,116. Lower middle-income and up-

Classification of Economies

Low income	Lower middle income	Upper middle income
Benin	Algeria	Botswana
Burkina Faso	Angola	Equatorial Guinea Gabon
Burundi	Cameroon	Libya
Central Africa Republic	Cape Verde	Mauritius
Chad	Congo, Rep.	Seychelles
Comoros	Djibouti	South Africa
Congo, Dem. Rep.	Egypt, Arab Rep.	
Côte d'Ivoire	Lesotho	
Eritrea	Morocco	
Ethiopia	Namibia	
Gambia, The	Swaziland	
Ghana	Tunisia	
Guinea		
Guinea-Bissau		
Kenya		
Liberia		
Madagascar		
Malawi		
Mali		
Mauritania		
Mozambique		
Niger		
Nigeria		
Rwanda		
São Tomé and Principe		
Senegal		
Sierra Leone		
Somalia		
Sudan		
Tanzania		
Togo		
Uganda		
Zambia		
Zimbabwe		

Source: World Bank.

per middle-income economies are separated at a GNI per capita of $3,595. High-income economies are those with a GNI per capita of $11,116 or more.

Alternative conversion factors

The World Bank systematically assesses the appropriateness of official exchange rates as conversion factors. An alternative conversion factor is used when the official exchange rate is judged to diverge by an exceptionally large margin from the rate effectively applied to domestic transactions of foreign currencies and traded products. This applies to only a small number of countries. Alternative conversion factors are used in the *Atlas* methodology and elsewhere in *Africa Development Indicators* as single-year conversion factors.

Symbols

.. means that data are not available or that aggregates cannot be calculated because of missing data in the years shown

$ means U.S. dollars

0 or 0.0 means zero or small enough that the number would round to zero at the displayed number of decimal places.

Dash or hyphen in dates, as in 2004–06, means that the period of time straddles between those years.

Data presentation conventions

A blank means not applicable or, for an aggregate, not analytically meaningful.

A billion is 1,000 million.

In calculating GNI and GNI per capita in U.S. dollars for certain operational purposes, the *World Bank uses the Atlas conversion factor*. The purpose of the *Atlas* conversion factor is to reduce the impact of exchange rate fluctuations in the cross-country comparison of national incomes. The *Atlas* conversion factor for any year is the average of the official exchange rate or alternative conversion factor for that year and for the two preceding years, adjusted for difference between the rate of inflation in the country and that in Japan, the United Kingdom, the United States, and the euro area. A country's inflation rate is measured by the change in its GDP deflator.

The inflation rate for Japan, the United Kingdom, the United States, and the euro area, representing international inflation, is measured by the change in the "SDR deflator." The SDR (Specila drawing rights or SDRs are the International Monetary Fund's unit of account) is calculated as a weighted average of these countries GDP deflators in SDR terms, the weights being the amount of each country's currency in one SDR unit. Weights vary over time because both the composition of the SDR and the relative exchange rates for each currency change. The SDR deflator is calculated in SDR terms first and then converted to U.S. dollars using the SDR to dollar *Atlas* conversion factor. The *Atlas* conversion factor is then applied to a country's GNI. The resulting GNI in U.S. dollars is divided by the midyear population for the latest of the three years to derive GNI per capita.

When official exchange rate are deemed to be unreliable or unrepresentative of the effective exchange rate during a period, an alternative estimate of the exchange rate is used in the *Atlas* formula below.

The following formulas describe the procedures for computing the conversion factor for year *t*:

$$e_t^* = \frac{1}{3}\left[e_{t-2}\left(\frac{p_t}{p_{t-2}} / \frac{p_t^{S\$}}{p_{t-2}^{S\$}} \right) + e_{t-1}\left(\frac{p_t}{p_{t-1}} / \frac{p_t^{S\$}}{p_{t-1}^{S\$}} \right) + e_t \right]$$

and for calculating per capita GNI in U.S. dollars for year *t*:

$$Y_t^\$ = \left(\frac{Y_t}{N_t} \right) / e_t^*$$

where e_t^* is the *Atlas* conversion factor (national currency to the U.S. dollar) for year *t*, e_t is the average annual exchange rate (national currency to the U.S. dollar) for year *t*, p_t is the GDP deflator for year *t*, $p_t^{S\$}$ is the SDR deflator in U.S. dollar terms for year *t*, $Y_t^\$$ is current GNI per capita in U.S. dollars in year t, Yt is current GNI (local currency) for year *t*, N_t is midyear population for year *t*.

Technical notes

1. Basic indicators

TABLE 1.1. BASIC INDICATORS

Population is total population is based on the de facto definition of population, which counts all residents regardless of legal status or citizenship, except for refugees not permanently settled in the country of asylum, who are generally considered part of the population of their country of origin. The values shown are midyear estimates.

Land area is the land surface area of a country, excluding inland waters, national claims to continental shelf, and exclusive economic zones.

Gross domestic product (GDP) per capita is gross domestic product divided by midyear population. GDP is the sum of gross value added by all resident producers in the economy plus any product taxes and minus any subsidies not included in the value of the products. It is calculated without making deductions for depreciation of fabricated assets or for depletion and degradation of natural resources. Data are in constant U.S. dollars. Growth rates are shown in real terms. They have been calculated by the least-squares method using constant 2000 (See Box 2).

Life expectancy at birth is the number of years a newborn infant would live if prevailing patterns of mortality at the time of its birth were to remain the same throughout its life. Data are World Bank estimates based on data from the United Nations Population Division, the United Nations Statistics Division, and national statistical offices.

Under-five mortality rate is the probability that a newborn baby will die before reaching age 5, if subject to current age-specific mortality rates. The probability is expressed as a rate per 1,000.

Gini index is the most commonly used measure of inequality. The coefficient ranges from 0, which reflects complete equality, to 100, which indicates complete inequality (one person has all the income or consumption, all others have none). Graphically, the Gini index can be easily represented by the area between the Lorenz curve and the line of equality.

Adult literacy rate is the percentage of adults ages 15 and older who can, with understanding, read and write a short, simple statement on their everyday life.

Net ODA aid per capita is calculated by dividing the nominal total net aid (net disbursements of loans and grants from all official sources on concessional financial terms) by midyear population. These ratios offer some indication of the importance of aid flows in sustaining per capita income and consumption levels, although exchange rate fluctuations, the actual rise of aid flows, and other factors vary across countries and over time.

Regional aggregates for GNI per capita, life expectancy at birth, and adult literacy rates are weighted by population.

Source: Data on population, land area, GDP per capita, life expectancy at birth, under-five mortality, Gini coefficient, and adult literacy are from the World Bank's World Development Indicators database. Data on aid flows are from the Organization for Economic Co-operation and Development's Geographic Distribution of Aid Flows to Developing Countries database.

2. National accounts

TABLE 2.1. GROSS DOMESTIC PRODUCT, NOMINAL

Gross domestic product (GDP), nominal, is the sum of gross value added by all resident producers in the economy plus any product taxes and minus any subsidies not included in the value of the products. It is calculated without making deductions for depreciation of fabricated assets or for depletion and degradation of natural resources. GDP figures are shown at market prices (also known as purchaser values) and converted from domestic currencies using single year official exchange rates. For a few countries where the official exchange rate does not reflect the rate effectively applied to actual foreign exchange transactions, an alternative conversion factor is used.

The sum of the components of GDP by industrial origin (presented here as value added) will not normally equal total GDP for several reasons. First, components of GDP by expenditure are individually rescaled and summed to provide a partially rebased series for total GDP. Second, total GDP is shown at purchaser value, while value added components are conventionally reported at producer prices. As explained above, purchaser values exclude net indirect taxes, while producer prices include indirect taxes. Third, certain items, such as imputed bank charges, are added in total GDP. Growth rates have been calculated by the least-squares growth rate formula (See Box 2).

Source: World Bank country desk data.

TABLE 2.2. GROSS DOMESTIC PRODUCT, REAL

Gross domestic product (GDP), real, is obtained by converting national currency GDP series to U.S. dollars using constant (2000) exchange rates. For countries where the official exchange rate does not effectively reflect the rate applied to actual foreign exchange transactions, an alternative currency conversion factor has been used. Growth rates are shown in real terms. They have been calculated by the least-squares method using constant 2000 (See Box 2).

Source: World Bank country desk data.

TABLE 2.3. GROSS DOMESTIC PRODUCT GROWTH

Gross domestic product (GDP) growth is the average annual growth rate of real GDP (Table 2.2) at market prices based on constant local currency. Aggregates are based on constant 2000 U.S. dollars.

Source: World Bank country desk data.

Box 2	Growth rates

Growth rates are calculated as annual averages and represented as percentages. Except where noted, growth rates of values are computed from constant price series. Rates of change from one period to the next are calculated as proportional changes from the earlier period. **Least-squares growth rate**. Least squares growth rates are used wherever there is a sufficiently long time series to permit a reliable calculation. No growth rate is calculated if more than half the observations in a period are missing. The least squares growth rate, r, is estimated by fitting a linear regression trend line to the logarithmic annual values of the variable in the relevant period. The regression equation takes the form

$$\ln X_t = a + bt$$

which is equivalent to the logarithmic transformation of the compound growth equation,

$$X_t = Xo(1 + r)^2$$

In this equation X is the variable, t is time, and $a = \ln Xo$ and $b = \ln(1 + r)$ are parameters to be estimated. If b* is the least squares estimate of b, then the average annual growth rate, r, is obtained as [exp(b*) − 1] and is multiplied by 100 for expression as a percentage. The calculated growth rate is an average rate that is representative of the available observations over the entire period. It does not necessarily match the actual growth rate between any two periods.

TABLE 2.4. GROSS DOMESTIC PRODUCT PER CAPITA, REAL

Gross domestic product (GDP) per capita, real, is calculated by dividing real GDP (Table 2.2) by corresponding midyear population.

Source: World Bank country desk data.

TABLE 2.5. GROSS DOMESTIC PRODUCT PER CAPITA GROWTH

Gross domestic product (GDP) per capita growth is the average annual growth rate of real GDP per capita (Table 2.4).

Source: World Bank country desk data.

TABLE 2.6. GROSS NATIONAL INCOME, NOMINAL

Gross national income, nominal, is the sum of value added by all resident producers plus any product taxes (less subsidies) not included in the valuation of output plus net receipts of primary income (compensation of employees and property income) from abroad. Data are converted from national currency in current prices to U.S. dollars at official annual exchange rates. Growth rates are calculated by the least-squares method growth rate formula (See Box 2).

Source: World Bank and Organisation for Economic Co-operation and Development (OECD) national accounts data.

TABLE 2.7. GROSS NATIONAL INCOME, REAL

Gross national income, real, is obtained by converting national currency gross national income series to U.S. dollars using constant (2000) exchange rates. Growth rates are shown in real terms. They have been calculated by the least-squares method using constant 2000 (See Box 2).

Source: World Bank and OECD national accounts data.

TABLE 2.8. GROSS NATIONAL INCOME PER CAPITA

Gross national income (GNI) per capita is calculated using the *World Bank Atlas* method (See Box 1). It is similar in concept to GNI per capita in current prices, except that

the use of three-year averages of exchange rates smoothes out sharp fluctuations from year to year.

Source: World Bank country desk data.

TABLE 2.9. GROSS DOMESTIC PRODUCT DEFLATOR (LOCAL CURRENCY SERIES)

Gross domestic product (GDP) deflator (local currency series) is nominal GDP in current local currency divided by real GDP in constant 2000 local currency, expressed as an index with base year 2000. It is the total domestic and foreign value added claimed by residents, which comprises gross domestic product plus net factor income from abroad (the income residents receive from abroad for factor services including labor and capital) less similar payments made to nonresidents who contribute to the domestic economy, divided by midyear population. It is calculated using the *World Bank Atlas* method (See Box 1) with constant 2000 exchange rates.

Source: World Bank country desk data.

TABLE 2.10. GROSS DOMESTIC PRODUCT DEFLATOR (U.S. DOLLAR SERIES)

Gross domestic product (GDP) deflator (U.S. dollar series) is nominal GDP in current U.S. dollars (Table 2.1) divided by real GDP in constant 2000 U.S. dollars (Table 2.2), expressed as an index with base year 2000. The series shows the effects of domestic price changes and exchange rate variations.

Source: World Bank country desk data.

TABLE 2.11. INFLATION, CONSUMER PRICE INDEX

Inflation as measured by the consumer price index reflects the annual percentage change in the cost to the average consumer of acquiring a basket of goods and services that may be fixed or changed at specified intervals, such as yearly. The Laspeyres formula is generally used.

Source: International Monetary Fund, International Financial Statistics and data files.

What do higher food prices mean for poverty in Africa? A series of recent papers — based for the most part on recent household survey data — finds that rising food prices generate higher poverty because the adverse impact on households that are net food consumers outweighs benefits to net food producers. The series also uses the survey data to examine common policy responses in order to determine which are likely to have the largest benefit for the poor.

Data from a dozen countries are used to simulate the poverty impact of higher food prices. The measurements obtained when considering only the effect on consumers are considered as upper-range estimates. Those also factoring in producer gains are considered as lower-range estimates, because producers may not reap the full benefit of price increases (market intermediaries may keep part of the higher food prices to boost their margins or pay for higher transport costs, while producers face higher operating costs that limit their profits). With a 50% increase in selected food prices, upper-range increases in poverty measures range from 1.8 percentage points in Ghana to 9.6 points in Senegal. The average impact, considering both upper- and lower-range estimates, is around 3.5 percentage points. For Africa as a whole, this would mean 30 million more poor people. Poverty mapping techniques show that the degree of impact varies within countries. This poses a dilemma in focusing policy responses, since the hardest-hit areas in a country often are not the poorest.

As a first step in dealing with the crisis, governments have reduced food taxes. But such tax cuts have large fiscal costs and are poorly targeted. For example, the share of rice consumed by the poorest 40% of the population ranges from 11% in Mali to 32% in Sierra Leone. Therefore, on average only about 20 cents out of every dollar of tax cut might benefit this group. In addition, if markets are dominated by a few traders, tax cuts may not be fully passed on to consumers. And lowering import tariffs may hurt domestic producers if prices of locally produced foods adjust to international prices.

Expanding social protection programs shows more promise. In Burundi and Liberia household survey data suggest that the poor are roughly as likely as the non-poor to benefit from food aid. This does not constitute good targeting, but it is better than tax cuts. Simulations suggest that geographic targeting is required to avoid high leakage in labor-intensive public programs since most countries have large populations working without pay or at very low pay. Thus, even among the non-poor, participation in public programs could be high even if wages are low. In addition, part of the wages paid through public works may not reduce poverty because of substitution effects (participants typically have to give up some sources of income to enroll in the programs).

The most promising interventions are those boosting agricultural productivity. Mali's rice initiative aims to increase production by 50%. Using a dynamic computable general equilibrium model for Mali, analysis shows that a 15% increase in productivity could generate a large increase in rice production that would ultimately reduce poverty despite the increase in international rice prices. By contrast, the model suggests that import tax cuts would not reduce poverty by much. Another finding is that the general equilibrium effect of the increase in international rice prices is about half the impact predicted using household surveys. This suggests that without policy interventions, behavioral changes following price increases could help offset part, but certainly not all, of the adverse impact on the poor.

Another general equilibrium finding relates to the relative way in which households are affected by oil and food price increases. Using social accounting matrices, analysis shows that in some countries the indirect multiplier effect of higher oil prices may be more severe than that of higher food prices. This suggests that even though the food price crisis has recently attracted more attention, the effects of the oil price crisis must also be dealt with.

Source: Wodon (2008).

TABLE 2.12. PRICE INDICIES
Inflation, GDP deflator is measured by the annual growth rate of the GDP implicit deflator and shows the rate of price change in the economy as a whole.

Consumer price index is a change in the cost to the average consumer of acquiring a basket of goods and services that may be fixed or changed at specified intervals, such as yearly.

Exports price index is derived by dividing the national accounts exports of goods and services in current U.S. dollars by exports of goods and services in constant 2000 U.S. dollars, with 2000 equaling 100.

Imports price index is derived by dividing the national accounts exports of goods and services in current U.S. dollars by imports of goods and services in constant 2000 U.S. dollars, with 2000 equaling 100.

Source: World Bank national accounts data, and OECD National Accounts data files.

TABLE 2.13. GROSS DOMESTIC SAVINGS
Gross domestic savings is calculated by deducting total consumption (Table 2.17) from nominal gross domestic product (Table 2.1).

Source: World Bank country desk data.

There is general consensus in Ethiopia that the country is experiencing high inflation, though there is considerable confusion about the inflation number itself. Such a problem however is not unique to Ethiopia since inflation numbers tend to be scrutinized more closely during episodes of high inflation. This technical box identifies some of the underlying reasons why the public perception about inflation may be different from the government reported inflation number.

I. Variations in the Consumption Basket

Inflation is defined as the change in the general price level. The latter, technically captured by the Consumer Price Index (CPI), is measured by tracking the prices of a fixed basket of goods and services that is consumed by the representative consumer (household) in the country. The CPI is usually based on household expenditure weights of the goods and services in the basket and their current market prices. In case of Ethiopia, the weights used for computing the CPI are shown in Figure 1.

The consumption basket (i.e., the goods and services consumed by the household) is likely to vary considerably across households. A relatively poor household is likely to spend a much larger share of its expenditure on food than a relatively rich household and vice-versa for luxury goods and services, for example, recreation and entertainment. As shown in Figure 2, the inflation rate facing different households could vary considerably. In Ethiopia, since a large part of the general inflation is due to food price inflation and the poor households spend a larger share of their expenditure on food, they have experienced a twelve month inflation rate of 66% at the end of June 2008. The corresponding number for the rich households is found to be 33%—almost half the rate facing the poorer households. The government, based on the consumption basket of the representative household, reported the national inflation rate to be 55%. It is therefore easy to see why the inflation experienced by one household may vary considerably from its neighbors.

II. Regional Variation in Inflation

Inflation rates could also vary substantially across regions, especially in large countries and/or if the regional markets are not well integrated with one another. For example, in Ethiopia the difference in inflation between the highest and lowest inflation region is found to be as high as 29 percentage points—households in Afar experienced an inflation rate of 36% compared to 66% for households in SNNP.

III. Average vs. End of Period Inflation

In some cases, the difference between perception and reality could be explained by the method the government uses to estimate and report the annual inflation rate. For example, in Ethiopia, the twelve month *end of period* inflation rate was 55% in June 2008 (i.e., the CPI increased by 55% between June 2007 and June 2008). On the other hand, the twelve month annual *average* inflation rate was only 25%, which is calculated by averaging the *end of period* inflation rate of the past twelve months. Since inflation rate has accelerated in recent months, the difference between the two estimates has widened by as much as 30 percentage points.

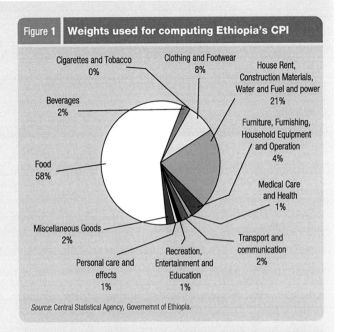

Figure 1 | Weights used for computing Ethiopia's CPI

Cigarettes and Tobacco 0%
Clothing and Footwear 8%
House Rent, Construction Materials, Water and Fuel and power 21%
Beverages 2%
Furniture, Furnishing, Household Equipment and Operation 4%
Food 58%
Medical Care and Health 1%
Miscellaneous Goods 2%
Transport and communication 2%
Personal care and effects 1%
Recreation, Entertainment and Education 1%

Source: Central Statistical Agency, Governemnt of Ethiopia.

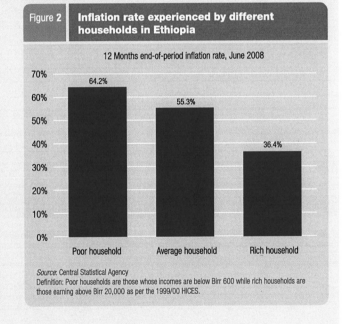

Figure 2 | Inflation rate experienced by different households in Ethiopia

12 Months end-of-period inflation rate, June 2008

Poor household: 64.2%
Average household: 55.3%
Rich household: 36.4%

Source: Central Statistical Agency
Definition: Poor households are those whose incomes are below Birr 600 while rich households are those earning above Birr 20,000 as per the 1999/00 HICES.

(continued on next page)

In Ethiopia the newspaper articles tend to quote the *end of period* inflation (55%), while the Government of Ethiopia uses the *average* inflation rate (25%). Understandably, most citizens feel confused. It is, however, important to note that despite the huge variation between the above two inflation estimates, they are both correct and they capture different aspects of the inflation rate. In periods of rising inflation, the *end of period* inflation rate tends to exceed the *average* inflation rate and vice versa in periods of falling inflation rate.

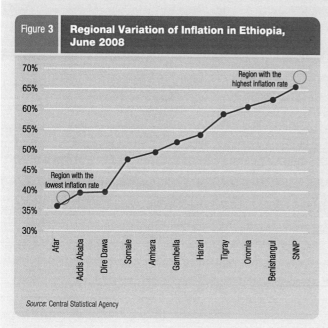

Figure 3 Regional Variation of Inflation in Ethiopia, June 2008

Source: Central Statistical Agency

Table 1 Average vs. End of period Inflation, in percent

	2005/06	2006/07	2007/08
Overall inflation			
Average	11%	17%	25%
End of period	12%	15%	55%
Difference	−1%	1%	−30%
Food inflation			
Average	13%	18%	35%
End of period	11%	18%	78%
Difference	1%	0%−	43%

Source: CSA

TABLE 2.14. GROSS NATIONAL SAVINGS
Gross national savings is the sum of gross domestic savings (Table 2.13), net factor income from abroad, and net private transfers from abroad. The estimate here also includes net public transfers from abroad.

Source: World Bank country desk data.

TABLE 2.15. GENERAL GOVERNMENT FINAL CONSUMPTION EXPENDITURE
General government consumption is all current expenditure for purchases of goods and services by all levels of government, including capital expenditure on national defense and security. Other capital expenditure by government is included in capital formation.

Source: World Bank country desk data.

TABLE 2.16. HOUSEHOLD FINAL CONSUMPTION EXPENDITURE
Household final consumption expenditure (formerly private consumption) is the market value of all goods and services, including durable products (such as cars, washing machines, and home computers), purchased by households. It excludes purchases of dwellings but includes imputed rent for owner-occupied dwellings. It also includes payments and fees to governments to obtain permits and licenses. Here, household consumption expenditure includes the expenditures of nonprofit institutions serving households, even when reported separately by the country

Source: World Bank national accounts data, and OECD National Accounts data files

TABLE 2.17. FINAL CONSUMPTION EXPENDITURE PLUS DISCREPANCY
Final consumption expenditure (formerly total consumption) is the sum of household final consumption expenditure (Table 2.16) and general government final consumption expenditure (Table 2.15) shown as a share of gross domestic product. This estimate includes any statistical discrepancy in the

use of resources relative to the supply of resources. Private consumption, not separately shown here, is the value of all goods and services purchased or received as income in kind by households and nonprofit institutions. It excludes purchases of dwellings, but includes imputed rent for owner-occupied dwellings. In practice, it includes any statistical discrepancy in the use of resources.

Source: World Bank country desk data.

TABLE 2.18. FINAL CONSUMPTION EXPENDITURE PLUS DISCREPANCY PER CAPITA
Final consumption expenditure per capita is final consumption expenditure in current U.S. dollars (Table 2.17) divided by midyear population.

Source: World Bank country desk data.

TABLE 2.19. AGRICULTURE VALUE ADDED
Agriculture corresponds to ISIC divisions 1–5 and includes forestry, hunting, and fishing, as well as cultivation of crops and livestock production. Value added is the net output of a sector after adding up all outputs and subtracting intermediate inputs. It is calculated without making deductions for depreciation of fabricated assets or depletion and degradation of natural resources. The origin of value added is determined by the International Standard Industrial Classification (ISIC), revision 3. Note: For VAB countries, gross value added at factor cost is used as the denominator.

Source: World Bank national accounts data, and OECD National Accounts data files.

TABLE 2.20. INDUSTRY VALUE ADDED
Industry corresponds to ISIC divisions 10–45 and includes manufacturing (ISIC divisions 15–37). It comprises value added in mining, manufacturing (also reported as a separate subgroup), construction, electricity, water, and gas. Value added is the net output of a sector after adding up all outputs and subtracting intermediate inputs. It is calculated without making deductions for depreciation of fabricated assets or depletion and degradation of natural resources. The origin

of value added is determined by the International Standard Industrial Classification (ISIC), revision 3. Note: For VAB countries, gross value added at factor cost is used as the denominator.

Source: World Bank national accounts data, and OECD National Accounts data files.

TABLE 2.21. SERVICES PLUS DISCREPANCY VALUE ADDED
Services correspond to ISIC divisions 50–99 and include value added in wholesale and retail trade (including hotels and restaurants), transport, and government, financial, professional, and personal services such as education, health care, and real estate services. Also included are imputed bank service charges, import duties, and any statistical discrepancies noted by national compilers as well as discrepancies arising from rescaling. Value added is the net output of a sector after adding up all outputs and subtracting intermediate inputs. It is calculated without making deductions for depreciation of fabricated assets or depletion and degradation of natural resources. The industrial origin of value added is determined by the International Standard Industrial Classification (ISIC), revision 3. Note: For VAB countries, gross value added at factor cost is used as the denominator.

Source: World Bank national accounts data, and OECD National Accounts data files.

TABLE 2.22. GROSS FIXED CAPITAL FORMATION
Gross fixed capital formation consists of gross domestic fixed capital formation plus net changes in the level of inventories. Gross capital formation consists of outlays by the public sector (Table 2.23) and the private sector (Table 2.24). Examples include improvements in land, dwellings, machinery, and other equipment. For some countries the sum of gross private investment and gross public investment does not total gross domestic investment due to statistical discrepancies.

Source: World Bank country desk data.

TABLE 2.23. GENERAL GOVERNMENT FIXED CAPITAL FORMATION

General government fixed capital formation is gross domestic fixed capital formation (see Table 2.22) for the public sector.

Source: World Bank country desk data.

TABLE 2.24. PRIVATE SECTOR FIXED CAPITAL FORMATION

Private sector fixed capital formation is gross domestic fixed capital formation (see Table 2.22) for the private sector.

Source: World Bank country desk data.

TABLE 2.25. RESOURCE BALANCE (EXPORTS MINUS IMPORTS)

Resource balance is the difference between free on board exports (Table 2.26) and cost, insurance, and freight imports (Table 2.27) of goods and services (or the difference between gross domestic savings and gross capital formation). The resource balance is shown as a share of nominal gross domestic product (Table 2.1).

Source: World Bank country desk data.

TABLES 2.26 AND 2.27. EXPORTS AND IMPORTS OF GOODS AND SERVICES, NOMINAL

Exports and *imports of goods and services, nominal,* comprise all transactions between residents of an economy and the rest of the world involving a change in ownership of general merchandise, goods sent for processing and repairs, nonmonetary gold, and services expressed in current U.S dollars.

Source: World Bank country desk data.

TABLES 2.28 AND 2.29. EXPORTS AND IMPORTS OF GOODS AND SERVICES (% OF GDP)

Exports and *imports of goods and services* are defined as in Tables 2.24 and 2.25, but expressed as a proportion of GDP.

Source: World Bank country desk data.

TABLE 2.30. BALANCE OF PAYMENT AND CURRENT ACCOUNT

Exports of goods and services is the value of all goods and other market services provided to the rest of the world.

Imports of goods and services is the value of all goods and other market services received from the rest of the world.

Net income is the receipts and payments of employee compensation paid to nonresident workers and investment income (receipts and payments on direct investment, portfolio investment, other investments, and receipts on reserve assets).

Net current transfers are recorded in the balance of payments whenever an economy provides or receives goods, services, income, or financial items without a quid pro quo.

Current account balance is the sum of net exports of goods, services, net income, and net current transfers.

Total reserves is the holdings of monetary gold, special drawing rights, reserves of IMF members held by the IMF, and holdings of foreign exchange under the control of monetary authorities.

Source: Data on current account balance, net income, net transfers and total reserves are from the International Monetary Fund, International Financial Statistics and data files. Data on exports and imports of goods and services are from the World Bank national accounts data, and OECD National Accounts data files

TABLE 2.31. STRUCTURE OF DEMAND

Household final consumption expenditure (formerly private consumption) is the market value of all goods and services, including durable products (such as cars, washing machines, and home computers), purchased by households.

General government final consumption expenditure (formerly general government consumption) is all government current expenditures for purchases of goods and services.

Gross capital formation (formerly gross domestic investment) consists of outlays on additions to the fixed assets of the economy plus net changes in the level of inventories.

Exports of goods and services is the value of all goods and other market services provided to the rest of the world.

Imports of goods and services is the value of all goods and other market services received from the rest of the world.

| Box 5 | Africa at Purchasing Power Parity |

The International Comparison Project (ICP) round of 2005 marks a significant departure from the previous one in 1993—for Sub Saharan Africa (SSA) in particular—for two major reasons. The first one is the increased coverage of SSA countries. While in 1993 only 19 countries actually participated through their statistical offices to the ICP round, there were 44 participants out of a potential 53 in 2005, covering 98% of the region's population. The second one is the likely improvement in data quality. Statistical capacity in participating countries greatly improved since 1993, notably when it comes to data collection, validation and processing. Furthermore, the ICP 2005 put particular efforts in linking regions across the globe in order to minimize the inherent tension between comparability and representativeness. Goods and services should have similar characteristics (comparable) and be consumed everywhere (representative). To compensate for non comparability of representative products, the ICP conducted for the first time in 2005 two parallel programs: selecting items at the regional level, where consumption patterns are broadly similar across countries, and selecting items for global comparison among a few countries from each region. The results of this second program were used to link the results of the first into a single set of global Purchasing Power Parities (PPPs).[1]

Thus, the new ICP round provides a more accurate view of the Africa Region in 2005, and unsurprisingly, a different picture of its relative size and structure. Measured at PPPs, in 2005 the SSA region represented 2.3% of World GDP, against 1.4% measured at market exchange rates. The difference from previous estimates is minimal, as the SSA region was believed to represent 2.4% of GDP based on ICP 1993 data. But this comparison conceals great revisions in countries' GDP at PPP between the two ICP rounds. Indeed, SSA countries' GDP were on average revised upwards or downwards by 35%. Largest revisions concern the Republic of Congo and Gabon, which see their GDP at PPP revised upwards by 133% and 96% respectively. But many countries record lower GDP at PPP than previously estimated. Among the largest 20 revisions (Figure 1) 16 countries did not participate to the ICP round of 1993.

With new PPPs, poverty in SSA is being revised upwards. Revised PPPs in SSA entail—as for most other developing countries, a downward revision of GDP levels, since prices in these countries are now generally believed to be higher than previously thought. In turn, poverty lines and rates were revised upwards accordingly. While the number of poor at US$1 a day was estimated at 298 millions in 2004 using old PPPs, it is now estimated at 299 millions in 2005 using new PPPs, an insignificant change overall.[2] But the availability of new PPPs also prompted the revision of poverty lines to reflect the average poverty lines of the poorest countries as of 2005.[3] Accordingly, the international poverty line for extreme poverty is now

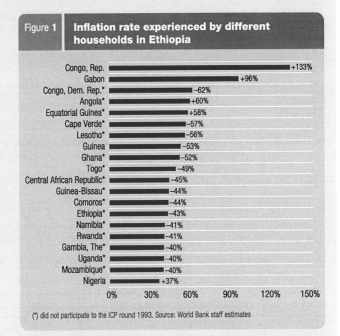

Figure 1 | **Inflation rate experienced by different households in Ethiopia**

(*) did not participate to the ICP round 1993. Source: World Bank staff estimates

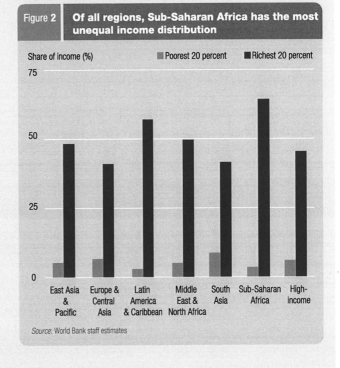

Figure 2 | **Of all regions, Sub-Saharan Africa has the most unequal income distribution**

Source: World Bank staff estimates

(continued on next page)

---

[1] For more details see World Bank (2008A).
[2] Poverty figures at the country level might be more affected given the significant PPP revisions at the country level and the use of more recent household surveys.
[3] See Chen and Ravallion (2008).

| Box 5 | **Africa at Purchasing Power Parity** (*continued*) |

set at US$1.25 a day. Using this figure, the number of poor in SSA was close to 384 millions in 2005, or 50% of the population. But if higher today than previously thought, past figures of poverty were also revised upwards. This leaves basically unchanged the recent evolution of poverty rates, a five-percentage-point decline since 1990, from 55% to 50%. Thus akin to conclusions reached using old PPPs, the SSA region is at current trends off-track to meet the Millennium Development Goal of halving poverty between 1990 and 2015.

High inequalities make the goal of halving poverty in SSA particularly challenging. One important reason behind the slow decline in poverty rates is the high degree of inequality in SSA, compared with other regions (Figure 2). Using PPPs, inequalities within and between countries can be combined to create regional income distributions, gathering all individuals from the same region. Such calculations reveal that inequalities between individuals are particularly high in Sub-Saharan Africa. Besides, half of Sub-Saharan Africa's inequalities can be attributed to differences in average per capita incomes across countries, reflecting the region's low economic integration (Figure 3). Its average per capita income is the lowest of all regions, but there are large differences across countries. In the last decade, inequalities between African countries did not narrow. Indeed, there is no evidence of income convergence, and countries with lowest initial per capita incomes did not grow significantly faster than richer ones. This confirms previous in-depth analysis on the distribution of incomes and growth across Sub-Saharan countries based on PPPs derived from the ICP round 1993.[4]

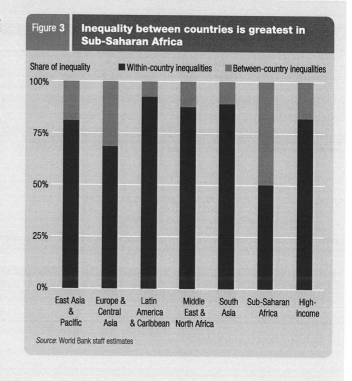

Figure 3 | **Inequality between countries is greatest in Sub-Saharan Africa**

Source: World Bank staff estimates

Gross National Savings, growth is the gross national income less total consumption, plus net transfers.

Source: World Bank national accounts data, and OECD National Accounts data files.

TABLE 2.32. EXCHANGE RATES AND PURCHASING POWER PARITY

Official exchange rate is the exchange rate determined by national authorities or to the rate determined in the legally sanctioned exchange market.

Purchasing power parity (PPP) conversion factor is the number of units of a country's currency required to buy the same amount of goods and services in the domestic market as a U.S. dollar would buy in the United States.

Ratio of PPP conversion factor to market exchange rate is the a national price level, making it possible to compare the cost of the bundle of goods that make up gross domestic product (GDP) across countries.

Real effective exchange rate is the nominal effective exchange rate (a measure of the value of a currency against a weighted average of several foreign currencies) divided by a price deflator or index of costs.

GDP, PPP is gross domestic product converted to international dollars using purchasing power parity rates. An international dollar has the same purchasing power over GDP as the U.S. dollar has in the United States. GDP is the sum of gross value added by all resident producers in the economy plus any product taxes and minus any subsidies not included in the value of the products. It is calculated without making deductions for

---

[4] See Arbache and Page (2007).

Box 6   **The Franc Zone**

One of the most important economic and monetary unions in sub-Saharan Africa is the franc zone. Consisting of two separate regional groupings in Central and West Africa, the CFA zone consists of fourteen Francophone countries – six in Central Africa (Congo, Chad, Central African Republic, Gabon, Cameroon, and Equatorial Guinea) and eight in West Africa (Benin, Burkina Faso, Ivory Coast, Guinea-Bissau, Mali, Niger, Senegal and Togo). Created in March, 1994, the *Communauté Economique et Monétaire d Afrique Centrale* (CEMAC), previously known as UDEAC (Union Douanière et Economique de l'Afrique Centrale), is a customs and monetary union among the former French Central African countries, while the *Union Economique et Monétaire Ouest-africaine* (UEMOA) is the equivalent organization in West Africa.

Since the mid-1990s, in both Francophone West and Central Africa, macroeconomic policy convergence, trade liberalization and a resulting common external tariff, and fiscal reforms have led to greater economic integration. The overall goal of the two unions, modeled in many ways on the European Union, has been to strengthen regional integration and cooperation and improve economic space through reduced barriers to trade and the flow of goods and services between these countries. Moreover, the zone is based on the premise that through economic union, these countries can be locked into policy reform.

A product of French colonial history, the groups consist of two customs and monetary unions united by a common currency and a fixed exchange rate regime pegged to the euro (the French franc before 1999). The rationale for the fixed exchange rate regime was to introduce greater stability to the economies of the zone and prevent risks that result from a more volatile flexible exchange rate. Furthermore, since under the prevailing institutional arrangement, the goal of monetary policy is to support the fixed exchange peg, the exchange rate arrangement is meant to lead to greater fiscal discipline. Countries relinquish their monetary policy to a regional central bank in exchange for price stability, and there is a clear output-inflation tradeoff as the desire for stability can offset policies which are growth-enhancing. Reserves are deposited in an Operations Account with the French Treasury, and the fixed parity has helped guarantee the convertibility of the CFA franc.

However, this arrangement has had costs, especially from the perspective of the poor economies in the zone. The predominance of agricultural products and natural resource exports makes these economies especially vulnerable to terms of trade shocks. As a result, the adjustment to these shocks has been difficult, leading to balance of payments difficulties and 50% devaluation in 1994. Nevertheless, in a world of increasingly floating exchange rates, the CFA fixed regime has been one of the few exchange rate arrangements which have not been altered over the years.

However, the recent sustained appreciation of the dollar against the euro, especially since 2001, has put some pressure on the exchange rate arrangement and led to an appreciation of the trade-weighted real effective exchange rate of both CFA zones.[5] From May, 2000 to May, 2008, there has been an appreciation in real terms of more than twenty percent in CEMAC and fifteen percent in UEMOA, as the dollar has slid against the euro by more than 30 percent. The REER is the geometric product of the bilateral effective exchange rates that are adjusted for inflationary differences between countries.

Although there has been an appreciation, different methodologies yield diverse estimates of overvaluation. The PPP exchange rate, which is defined as that rate which equalizes the cost of a market basket of goods between two countries, is useful as a first approximation although it does not hold in the long-run. Under PPP, there should be no changes in REERs over time if the currencies are in equilibrium. A single-equation estimation is potentially very fruitful, as it assesses an exchange rate's departure from a vector of fundamentals, although there are various estimates depending on methodology and econometric technique. While some work finds an overvaluation, others find no major deviation between the current REER and its long-run fundamentals in the franc zone. Overall, the peg to the rising euro has led to a loss in competitiveness for the franc zone's exports, although the impact has been felt asymmetrically.

Moreover, the precise nature of the impact depends on each country's economic structure and on the policy regime in place. For many CFA countries, especially cotton producers in West Africa such as Burkina, Benin, and Niger, the appreciation of the euro has translated into an increase in production costs; since world-prices for most of these commodities are dollar-based and farmers are paid in CFA, the recent dollar decline has hindered these countries' competitiveness. As a result, the cotton sector in these countries is facing financial difficulties and questions are emerging about their long-term future. For other CFA countries whose exports are petroleum, such as Republic of Congo and Equatorial Guinea, the effect on the REERs have been significant, although other factors have offset the loss of competitiveness. Although the oil windfalls have contributed to an increase in domestic inflation rates, a percentage of oil production costs are dollar-based and off-shore, and the high oil prices have allowed these countries to reap significant windfalls.

Finally, the current accounts of each of the CFA nations differ depending on economic structure, terms of trade shocks, and debt and aid flows and hence, measurements of underlying "sustainable" current accounts vary. As a result, the changes in exchange rates that are needed to yield a more balanced current account are difficult to determine for the region as a whole. Overall, the rise in the euro/dollar exchange has raised concerns about the efficacy and the sustainability of the CFA fixed parity to the euro and led to increasing concerns of loss of competitiveness. A persistently overvalued REER will hinder the export diversification of the franc zone.

---

[5] See Zafar (2005).

depreciation of fabricated assets or for depletion and degradation of natural resources. Data are in current international dollars.

GDP per capita, PPP is GDP per capita based on purchasing power parity (PPP). PPP GDP is gross domestic product converted to international dollars using purchasing power parity rates. An international dollar has the same purchasing power over GDP as the U.S. dollar has in the United States. GDP at purchaser's prices is the sum of gross value added by all resident producers in the economy plus any product taxes and minus any subsidies not included in the value of the products. It is calculated without making deductions for depreciation of fabricated assets or for depletion and degradation of natural resources. Data are in current international dollars.

Source: International Monetary Fund, International Financial Statistics

3. Millennium Development Goals

TABLE 3.1. MILLENNIUM DEVELOPMENT GOAL 1: ERADICATE EXTREME POVERTY AND HUNGER

Share of population below national poverty line (poverty headcount ratio) is the percentage of the population living below the national poverty line. National estimates are based on population-weighted subgroup estimates from household surveys.

Share of poorest quintile in national consumption or income is the share of consumption, or in some cases income, that accrues to the poorest 20 percent of the population.

Prevalence of child malnutrition, underweight, is the percentage of children under age 5 whose weight for age is more than two standard deviations below the median for the international reference population ages 0–59 months. The reference population, adopted by the World Health Organization in 1983, is based on children from the United States, who are assumed to be well nourished.

Population below minimum dietary energy consumption (also referred to as prevalence of undernourishment) is the population whose food intake is insufficient to meet dietary energy requirements continuously.

Source: Data on poverty measures are prepared by the World Bank's Development Research Group. The national poverty lines are based on the World Bank's country poverty assessments. Data have been compiled by World Bank staff from primary and secondary sources. Efforts have been made to harmonize these data series with those published on the United Nations Millennium Development Goals website (www.un.org/ millenniumgoals), but some differences in timing, sources, and definitions remain.

Data on child malnutrition and population below minimum dietary energy consumption are from the Food and Agriculture Organization (see *www.fao.org/faostat/foodsecurity/index_en.htm*).

TABLE 3.2. MILLENNIUM DEVELOPMENT GOAL 2: ACHIEVE UNIVERSAL PRIMARY EDUCATION

Primary education provides children with basic reading, writing, and mathematics skills along with an elementary understanding of such subjects as history, geography, natural science, social science, art, and music.

Net primary enrollment ratio is the ratio of children of official primary school age based on the International Standard Classification of Education 1997 who are enrolled in primary school to the population of the corresponding official primary school age.

Primary completion rate is the percentage of students completing the last year of primary school. It is calculated as the total number of students in the last grade of primary school minus the number of repeaters in that grade divided by the total number of children of official graduation age.

Share of cohort reaching grade 5 is the percentage of children enrolled in grade 1 of primary school who eventually reach grade 5. The estimate is based on the reconstructed cohort method. The estimate is based on the constructed cohort method. Editor's note: is the estimate based on the reconstructed cohort method or the constructed cohort method. Please choose one and eliminate the extra sentence.

Youth literacy rate is the percentage of people ages 15–24 who can, with understanding, both read and write a short, simple statement about their everyday life.

It is often argued that faith-inspired organizations (FIOs) provide a substantial share of education, health and other social services in African countries, and that the services provided by FIOs tend to be better targeted to the poor and possibly more cost effective than is the case for other private service providers and even for public providers. These assertions, if correct, could have implications for policy, since donors (and possibly governments) might then be more inclined to support FIOs in their service delivery activities. It is also important to consider the substantial and growing service delivery partnerships that do exist between governments, donors, and FIOs. In addition, governments might expand their efforts to benefit from the expertise acquired by FIOs in reaching the poor, so that government agencies might learn from FIOs (and vice versa).

Unfortunately, good data necessary to document such assertions and hypotheses about the role of FIOs in service delivery are often missing. At least two different types of data can be used to assess the role played by FIOs in service delivery. Administrative data kept by FIOs as well as government agencies could provide information on the market share of FIOs in terms of students served, patients received in health care facilities and the like. In addition, household surveys (as well as other types of surveys dealing with the beneficiaries of social services) may also provide useful data, to the extent that the surveys include questions on the types of service providers used by households and assuming that the users of services know whether the service provider they use is faith-based or not. If household survey data were available to document the role of FIOs, they would have an advantage over administrative data because of the ability to link the uptake of services to many other household and individual characteristics, including the poverty status of the household and the degree of satisfaction of the household with the services received. It is therefore useful to assess to what extent information can be extracted from household surveys on the role of FIOs.

Table 1 provides preliminary estimates of the market share of FIOs in the delivery of health and education services in twenty West and Central African countries according to the data available in the main multi-purpose household surveys implemented in the various countries. Two main observations can be made. First, for half of the countries in the case of health, and for one fourth of the countries in the case of education, the survey questionnaires do not include any information on whether the education and health service providers are faith-based or not. Second, when data are available, the market shares of FIOs appear to be low, with the exception of Sierra Leone in the case of

Table 1	Preliminary Data on service delivery by faith-inspireded organizations in African household surveys			
	Identification of FIOs in survey questionnaire		Preliminary estimate of market share of FIOs	
Country and household survey	Education	Health	Education	Health
Benin (QUIBB 2003)	Yes	No	<5%	NA
Burkina Faso (QUIBB 2003)	Yes	No	5%–10%	NA
Burundi (QUIBB 2006)	Yes	Yes	<5%	10%–20%
Cameroon (ECAM 2007)	Yes	Yes	10%–20%	<5%
Cape Verde (CWIQ 2007)	No	No	<5%	NA
Chad (ECOSIT2 2003/04)	No	Yes	NA	10%–20%
Cote d'Ivoire (ENV 2002)	No	No	NA	NA
DRC (Enquête 1–2–3 2004/05)	No	No	NA	NA
Gabon (CWIQ 2005)	Yes	No	5%–10%	NA
Ghana (GLSS 2005/2006)	Yes	Yes	5%–10%	5–10%
Guinea (ELEP 2007)	Yes	No	<5%	NA
Liberia (CWIQ 2007)	Yes	No	<5%	NA
Mali (CWIQ 2006)	Yes	Yes	<5%	5%–10%
Niger (ENBC 2007)	Yes	Yes	<5%	<5%
Nigeria (LMS 2003/2004)	Yes	Yes	<5%	<5%
ROC (ECOM–CWIQ 2005)	Yes	Yes	<5%	<5%
Rwanda (EICV 1997/1998)	No	No	NA	NA
Senegal (ESPS 2005)	Yes	Yes	5%–10%	<5%
Sierra Leone (QUIBB 2003)	Yes	Yes	>50%	<5%
Togo (QUIBB 2006)	Yes	No	5%–10%	NA

Source: Wodon et al. (2008). NA means not applicable.

(continued on next page)

education, as well as Burundi and Chad for health. In a large majority of cases, less than 5% of the students enrolled in school (all levels included) or patients seeking health care would do so through faith-based service providers according to those data.

These data are preliminary, but they do suggest a lower market share of FIOs than commonly assumed, at least as measured through the household surveys. At the same time, it is likely that in many countries, household surveys underestimate the market share of FIOs in service delivery. Consider Ghana for which the GLSS5 household survey suggests that 44% of health care visits are made to public organizations, versus 7% to private religious organizations and 49% to private non-religious facilities. The market share for religious organizations appears low, given that it is often argued that CHAG (the Christian Health Association of Ghana) provides about a third of health services in Ghana, and that administrative data available from the District Health Information System on the number of facilities operated by CHAG in comparisons to other private and public providers also suggests a higher market share than 7%.

Various factors could lead household surveys to underestimate the market share of FIOs in service delivery when the survey questionnaire does include questions as to whether the providers are public, private religious, or private non-religious. One possibility is that some households may simply not know that their service provider is faith-based. Another possibility could be that the way the questions on service providers are asked in the surveys is too generic and not adapted enough to the particularities of the education and health systems in various countries, so that specific faith-based groups that may operate large networks of providers such as CHAG are not well identified in the questionnaires. In contrast to evidence here derived from household surveys, alternative methods like community-level participatory mapping, employed by the African Religious Health Assets Program (ARHAP) and the World Health Organization (WHO) to measure FIO service delivery in Lesotho and Zambia, suggest that as high as 70% of health services are provided by faith organizations. The magnitude of the discrepancy in findings from household surveys and the recent ARHAP/WHO study further suggest that more efforts are needed to better capture the scope of FIO service delivery on the ground and to reconcile findings from various sources of data.

Changes that would need to be made to household survey questionnaires to better identify FIOs as service providers are relatively minor and probably not too difficult or costly to implement. In the case of health for example, many surveys today only seek information as to whether households seek care in hospitals, clinics, or other health facilities, without information on who runs the facilities. It should be feasible to provide additional modalities for the responses that households can provide to the questions asked in those surveys. This was done for example in Burundi's 2006 QUIBB survey. That survey identified ten different types of providers, namely hospitals, missionary hospitals, private hospitals, public health centers, missionary health centers, private health centers, pharmacies, private doctors, private "sage-femme," and traditional healers. With these additional options provided in the questionnaire, it is feasible not only to compare the market shares of FIOs and other service providers, but also to analyze which segments of the population the various providers are reaching and to what extent the population groups served by the various providers are satisfied with the services provided to them. This type of analysis can provide useful information for the policy dialogue on alternative service provision schemes.

Source: Data are from the United Nations Educational, Scientific, and Cultural Organization Institute for Statistics. Data have been compiled by World Bank staff from primary and secondary sources. Efforts have been made to harmonize these data series with those published on the United Nations Millennium Development Goals website (www.un.org/millenniumgoals), but some differences in timing, sources, and definitions remain.

TABLE 3.3. MILLENNIUM DEVELOPMENT GOAL 3: PROMOTE GENDER EQUITY AND EMPOWER WOMEN
Ratio of girls to boys in primary and secondary school is the ratio of female to male gross enrollment rate in primary and secondary school.

Ratio of young literate women to men is the ratio of the female to male youth literacy rate.

Women in national parliament are the percentage of parliamentary seats in a single or lower chamber occupied by women.

Share of women employed in the nonagricultural sector is women wage employees in the nonagricultural sector as a share of total nonagricultural employment.

Source: Data on net enrollment and literacy are from the United Nations Educational, Scientific, and Cultural Organization Institute for Statistics. Data on women in national parliaments are from the Inter-Parliamentary Union. Data on women's employment are from the International Labor Organization's *Key Indicators of the Labor Market,* fourth edition.

TABLE 3.4. MILLENNIUM DEVELOPMENT
GOAL 4: REDUCE CHILD MORTALITY

Under-five mortality rate is the probability that a newborn baby will die before reaching age 5, if subject to current age-specific mortality rates. The probability is expressed as a rate per 1,000.

Infant mortality rate is the number of infants dying before reaching one year of age, per 1,000 live births.

Child immunization rate, measles, is the percentage of children ages 12–23 months who received vaccinations for measles before 12 months or at any time before the survey. A child is considered adequately immunized against measles after receiving one dose of vaccine.

Source: Data on under-five and infant mortality are the harmonized estimates of the World Health Organization, United Nations Children's Fund (UNICEF), and the World Bank, based mainly on household surveys, censuses, and vital registration, supplemented by the World Bank's estimates based on household surveys and vital registration. Other estimates are compiled and produced by the World Bank's Human Development Network and Development Data Group in consultation with its operational staff and country offices. Data on child immunization are from the World Health Organization and UNICEF estimates of national immunization coverage.

TABLE 3.5. MILLENNIUM DEVELOPMENT
GOAL 5: IMPROVE MATERNAL HEALTH

Maternal mortality ratio, modeled estimate is the number of women who die from pregnancy-related causes during pregnancy and childbirth, per 100,000 live births. The data are estimated with a regression model using information on fertility, birth attendants, and HIV prevalence.

Maternal mortality ratio, national estimate is the number of women who die during pregnancy and childbirth, per 100,000 live births.

Births attended by skilled health staff is the percentage of deliveries attended by personnel who are trained to give the necessary supervision, care, and advice to women during pregnancy, labor, and the postpartum period; conduct deliveries on their own; and care for newborns.

Source: Data on maternal mortality are from AbouZahr and Wardlaw (2003). Data on births attended by skilled health staff are from the United Nations Children's Fund's *State of the World's Children 2006* and Childinfo, and Demographic and Health Surveys by Macro International.

TABLE 3.6. MILLENNIUM DEVELOPMENT
GOAL 6: COMBAT HIV/AIDS, MALARIA, AND
OTHER DISEASES

Prevalence of HIV is the percentage of people ages 15–49 who are infected with HIV.

Contraceptive prevalence rate is the percentage of women who are practicing, or whose sexual partners are practicing, any form of contraception. It is usually measured for married women ages 15–49 only.

Deaths due to malaria is the number of malaria deaths per 100,000 people.

Children sleeping under insecticide-treated bednets is the percentage of children under age 5 with access to an insecticide-treated bednet to prevent malaria.

Incidence of tuberculosis is the estimated number of new tuberculosis cases (pulmonary, smear positive, and extrapulmonary), per 100,000 people.

Tuberculosis cases detected under DOTS is the percentage of estimated new infectious tuberculosis cases detected under DOTS, the internationally recommended tuberculosis control strategy.

Source: Data on HIV prevalence are from the Joint United Nations Programme on HIV/AIDS and the World Health Organization's (WHO) *2006 Report on the Global AIDS Epidemic.* Data on contraceptive prevalence are from household surveys, including Demographic and Health Surveys by Macro International and Multiple Indicator Cluster Surveys by the United Nations Children's Fund (UNICEF). Data on deaths due to malaria are from the WHO. Data on insecticide-treated bednet use are from UNICEF's *State of the World's Children 2006* and Childinfo, and Demographic and Health Surveys by Macro International. Data on tuberculosis are from the WHO's *Global Tuberculosis Control Report 2006.*

Table 3.7. Millennium Development Goal 7: Ensure Environmental Sustainability

Forest area is land under natural or planted stands of trees, whether productive or not.

Nationally protected areas are totally or partially protected areas of at least 1,000 hectares that are designated as scientific reserves with limited public access, national parks, natural monuments, nature reserves or wildlife sanctuaries, and protected landscapes. Marine areas, unclassified areas, and litoral (intertidal) areas are not included. The data also do not include sites protected under local or provincial law.

Gross domestic product (GDP) per unit of energy use is the GDP in purchasing power parity (PPP) U.S. dollars per kilogram of oil equivalent of energy use. PPP GDP is gross domestic product converted to 2000 constant international dollars using purchasing power parity rates. An international dollar has the same purchasing power over GDP as a U.S. dollar has in the United States.

Carbon dioxide emissions are those stemming from the burning of fossil fuels and the manufacture of cement. They include carbon dioxide produced during consumption of solid, liquid and gas fuels, and gas flaring.

Solid fuels use is the percentage of the population using solid fuels as opposed to modern fuels. Solid fuels are defined to include fuel wood, straw, dung, coal, and charcoal. Modern fuels are defined to include electricity, liquefied petroleum gas, natural gas, kerosene, and gasoline.

Population with sustainable access to improved water source is the percentage of the population with reasonable access to an adequate amount of water from an improved source, such as a household connection, public standpipe, borehole, protected well or spring, or rainwater collection. Unimproved sources include vendors, tanker trucks, and unprotected wells and springs. Reasonable access is defined as the availability of at least 20 liters a person a day from a source within 1 kilometer of the dwelling.

Population with sustainable access to improved sanitation is the percentage of the population with at least adequate access to excreta disposal facilities that can effectively prevent human, animal, and insect contact with excreta. Improved facilities range from simple but protected pit latrines to flush toilets with a sewerage connection. The excreta disposal system is considered adequate if it is private or shared (but not public) and if it hygienically separates human excreta from human contact. To be effective, facilities must be correctly constructed and properly maintained.

Source: Data on forest area are from the Food and Agricultural Organization's Global Forest Resources Assessment. Data on nationally protected areas are from the United Nations Environment Programme and the World Conservation Monitoring Centre. Data on energy use are from electronic files of the International Energy Agency. Data on carbon dioxide emissions are from the Carbon Dioxide Information Analysis Center, Environmental Sciences Division, Oak Ridge National Laboratory, in the U.S. state of Tennessee. Data on solid fuel use are from household survey data, supplemented by World Bank estimates. Data on access to water and sanitation are from the World Health Organization and United Nations Children's Fund's *Meeting the MDG Drinking Water and Sanitation Target* (www.unicef.org/wes/mdgreport).

Table 3.8. Millennium Development Goal 8: Develop a Global Partnership for Development

Heavily Indebted Poor Country (HIPC) Debt Initiative decision point is the date at which a HIPC with an established track record of good performance under adjustment programs supported by the International Monetary Fund (IMF) and the World Bank commits to undertake additional reforms and to develop and implement a poverty reduction strategy.

HIPC completion point is the date at which the country successfully completes the key structural reforms agreed on at the decision point, including developing and implementing its poverty reduction strategy. The country then receives the bulk of debt relief under the HIPC Initiative without further policy conditions.

Debt service relief committed is the amount of debt service relief, calculated at the *Enhanced HIPC Initiative* decision point that will allow the country to achieve debt sustainability at the completion point.

Public and publicly guaranteed debt service is the sum of principal repayments and interest actually paid on total long-term debt (public and publicly guaranteed and private nonguaranteed), use of IMF credit, and interest on short-term debt.

Youth unemployment rate is the percentage of the labor force ages 15–24 without work but available for and seeking employment. Definitions of labor force and unemployment may differ by country.

Fixed-line and mobile phone subscribers are subscribers to a fixed-line telephone service, which connects a customer's equipment to the public switched telephone network, or to a public mobile telephone service, which uses cellular technology.

Personal computers are self-contained computers designed for use by a single individual.

Internet users are people with access to the worldwide web.

Source: Data on HIPC countries are from the IMF's March 2006 "HIPC Status Reports." Data on external debt are mainly from reports to the World Bank through its Debtor Reporting System from member countries that have received International Bank for Reconstruction and Development loans or International Development Association credits, as well as World Bank and IMF files. Data on youth unemployment are from the International Labor Organization's *Key Indicators of the Labor Market,* fourth edition. Data on phone subscribers, personal computers, and Internet users are from the International Telecommunication Union's (ITU) World Telecommunication Development Report database and World Bank estimates.

4. Paris Declaration indicators

TABLE 4.1. STATUS OF PARIS DECLARATION INDICATORS
The Paris Declaration is the outcome of the 2005 Paris High-Level Forum on Aid Effectiveness. In the Declaration, 60 partner countries, 30 donor countries, and 30 development agencies committed to specific actions to further country ownership, harmonization, alignment, managing for development results, and mutual accountability for the use of aid. Participants agreed on 12 indicators. These indicators include good national development strategies, reliable country systems for procurement and public financial management, the development and use of results frameworks, and mutual assessment of progress. Qualitative desk reviews by the Organization for Economic Co-operation and Development's Development Assistance Committee and the World Bank and a survey questionnaire for governments and donors are used to calculate the indicators. Table 4.1 includes these indicators.

PDI-1 Operational national development strategies are the degree to the extent to which a country has an operational development strategy to guide the aid coordination effort and the country's overall development. The score is based on the World Bank's 2005 Comprehensive Development Framework Progress Report. An operational strategy calls for a coherent long-term strategy derived from it; specific targets serving a holistic, balanced and well sequenced development strategy; and capacity and resources for its implementation.

PDI-2a Reliable public financial management is the World Bank's annual Country Policy and Institutional Assessment rating for the quality of public financial management. Measured on a scale of 1 (worst) to 5 (best), its focus is on how much existing systems adhere to broadly accepted good practices and whether a reform program is in place to promote improved practices.

PDI-2b Reliable country procurement systems. Donors use national procurement procedures when the funds they provide for the implementation of projects and programs are managed according to the national procurement procedures as they were established in the general legislation and implemented by government. The use of national procurement procedures means that donors do not make additional, or special, requirements on governments for the procurement of works, goods and services. (Where weaknesses in national procurement systems have been identified, donors may work with partner countries in order to improve the efficiency, economy, and transparency of their implementation). The objective of this indicator is to measure and encourage improvements in developing countries' procurement systems.

PDI-3 Government budget estimates comprehensive and realistic. The objective of this indicator is to improve transparency and accountability by encouraging partner countries and donors to accurately record aid as much as possible in the national budget, thereby allowing scrutiny by parliaments.

PDI-4 Technical assistance aligned and coordinated with country programs. Coordinated technical co-operation means free standing and embedded technical co-operation that respects the following principles: (i) *Ownership* – partner countries exercise effective leadership over their capacity development programs; (ii) *Alignment* – technical co-operation in support of capacity development is aligned with countries' development objectives and strategies; and (iii) *Harmonization* – where more than one donor is involved in supporting partner-led capacity development, donors co-ordinate their activities and contributions.

PDI-5a and 5b Aid for government sectors uses of country public financial management and procurement systems. The objective is to encourage donors to increasingly use country, rather than donor, systems for managing.

PDI-6 Parallel project implementation units (PIUs) is the number of parallel project implementation units. "Parallel" indicates that the units were created outside existing country institutional structures. The survey guidance distinguishes between PIUs and executing agencies and describes three typical features of parallel PIUs: they are accountable to external funding agencies rather than to country implementing agencies (ministries, departments, agencies, and the like), most of the professional staff is appointed by the donor, and the personnel salaries often exceed those of civil service personnel. Interpretation of the Paris Declaration survey question on this subject was controversial in a number of countries. It is unclear whether within countries all donors applied the same criteria with the same degree of rigor or that across countries the same standards were used. In several cases the descriptive part of the survey results indicates that some donors applied a legalistic criterion of accountability to the formal executing agency, whereas the national coordinator and other donors would have preferred greater recognition of the substantive reality of accountability to the donor. Some respondents may have confused the definitional question (Is the unit "parallel?") with the aid management question (Is the parallelism justified in terms of the developmental benefits and costs?).

PDI-7 Aid disbursements on schedule and recorded by government. The objective is twofold. First and foremost, it is to encourage disbursements of funds within the year they are scheduled. Second, it is to encourage accurate recording of disbursements by partner authorities. Both objectives require strong cooperation between donors and partner authorities.

PDI-8 Bilateral Aid that is untied. Tied aid is aid provided on the condition that the recipient uses it to purchase goods and services from suppliers based in the donor country. The target for this indicator is to increase untied aid over time.

PDI-9 Aid provided in the framework of program-based approaches (PBAs) are a way of engaging in development co-operation based on the principles of coordinated support for a locally owned program of development, such as a national development strategy, a sector program, a thematic program or a program of a specific organization. Program-based approaches share the following features: (i) leadership by the host country or organization; (ii) a single comprehensive program and budget framework; (iii) a formalized process for donor co-ordination and harmonization of donor procedures for reporting, budgeting, financial management and procurement; and (iv) efforts to increase the use of local systems for programme design and implementation, financial management, monitoring and evaluation.

PDI-10a Donor co-ordinated missions focuses only on the proportion of (i) missions undertaken jointly by two or more donors, or (ii) missions undertaken by one donor on behalf of another (delegated co-operation).

PDI-10b Country analysis coordinated (i) Country analytic work undertaken by one or more donors jointly; (ii) Country analytic work undertaken by one donor on behalf of another donor (including work undertaken by one and/or used by another when it is co-financed and formally acknowledged in official documentation); (iii) Country analytic work undertaken with substantive involvement from government.

PDI-11 Existence of a monitorable performance assessment frameworks measure the extent to which the country has realized its commitment to establishing performance frameworks. The indicator relies on the scorings of the 2005 CDF Progress Report and considers three criteria: the quality of development information, stakeholder access to development information, and coordinated country-level monitoring and evaluation. The assessments therefore reflect both the extent to which sound data on development outputs, outcomes and impacts are collected, and various aspects of the way information is used, disseminated among stakeholders, and fed back into policy.

PDI-12 Existence of a mutual accountability indicates whether there is a mechanism for mutual review of progress on aid effectiveness commitments. This is an important innovation of the Paris Declaration because it develops the idea that aid is more effective when both donors and partner governments are accountable to their constituents for the use of resources to achieve development results and when they are accountable to each other. The specific focus is mutual accountability for the implementation of the partnership commitments included in the Paris Declaration and any local agreements on enhancing aid effectiveness.

Source: Overview of the Results 2007 Survey on Monitoring the Paris Declaration and World Bank data.

5. Private sector development

Number of startup procedures to register a business is the number of procedures required to start a business, including interactions to obtain necessary permits and licenses and to complete all inscriptions, verifications, and notifications to start operations.

Time to start a business is the number of calendar days needed to complete the procedures to legally operate a business. If a procedure can be speeded up at additional cost, the fastest procedure, independent of cost, is chosen.

Cost to start a business is normalized by presenting it as a percentage of gross national income (GNI) per capita.

Minimum capital (% of income per capita) is paid-in minimum capital requirement and reflects the amount that the entrepreneur needs to deposit in a bank or with a notary before registration and up to 3 months following incorporation and is recorded as a percentage of the country's income per capita.

Number of procedures to register property is the number of procedures required for a business to secure rights to property.

Time to register property is the number of calendar days needed for a business to secure rights to property.

Cost (% of property value) is recorded as a percentage of the property value, assumed to be equivalent to 50 times income per capita. Only official costs required by law are recorded, including fees, transfer taxes, stamp duties and any other payment to the property registry, notaries, public agencies or lawyers. Other taxes, such as capital gains tax or value added tax, are excluded from the cost measure. Both costs borne by the buyer and those borne by the seller are included. If cost estimates differ among sources, the median reported value is used.

Number of procedures to enforce a contract is the number of independent actions, mandated by law or courts that demand interaction between the parties of a contract or between them and the judge or court officer.

Time required to enforce a contract is the number of calendar days from the filing of the lawsuit in court until the final determination and, in appropriate cases, payment.

Cost to enforce a contract is court and attorney fees, where the use of attorneys is mandatory or common, or the cost of an administrative debt recovery procedure, expressed as a percentage of the debt value.

Number of procedures dealing with construction permits is the number of procedures required to obtain construction-related permits.

Time to deal with construction permits is the average wait, in days, experienced to obtain construction-related permit from the day the establishment applied for it to the day it was granted.

Cost (% of income per capita) is recorded as a percentage of the country's income per capita. Only official costs are recorded. All the fees associated with completing the procedures to legally build a warehouse are recorded, including those associated with obtaining land use approvals and preconstruction design clearances; receiving inspections before, during and after construction; getting utility connections; and registering the warehouse property. Nonrecurring taxes required for the completion of the warehouse project also are recorded. The building code, information from local experts and specific regulations and fee schedules are used as sources for costs. If several local partners provide different estimates, the median reported value is used.

Protecting investors disclosure index measures the degree to which investors are protected through disclosure of ownership and financial information.

Director liability index measures a plaintiff's ability to hold directors of firms liable for damages to the company).

Shareholder suits index measures shareholders' ability to sue officers and directors for misconduct.

Investor protection index measures the degree to which investors are protected through disclosure of ownership and financial information regulations.

Rigidity of hours index has 5 components: (i) whether night work is unrestricted; (ii) whether weekend work is unrestricted; (iii) whether the work week can consist of 5.5 days; (iv) whether the workweek can extend to 50 hours or more (including overtime) for 2 months a year to respond to a seasonal increase in production; and (v) whether paid annual vacation is 21 working days or fewer. For each of these questions, if the answer is no, the economy is assigned a score of 1; otherwise a score of 0 is assigned.

Difficulty of hiring index is the applicability and maximum duration of fixed-term contracts and minimum wage for trainee or first-time employee. It measures (i) whether fixed term contracts are prohibited for permanent tasks; (ii) the maximum cumulative duration of fixed term contracts; and (iii) the ratio of the minimum wage for a trainee or first time employee to the average value added per worker.

Difficulty of firing index is the notification and approval requirements for termi-

nation of a redundant worker or a group of redundant workers, obligation to reassign or retrain and priority rules for redundancy and reemployment. It has 8 components: (i) whether redundancy is disallowed as a basis for terminating workers; (ii) whether the employer needs to notify a third party (such as a government agency) to terminate 1 redundant worker; (iii) whether the employer needs to notify a third party to terminate a group of 25 redundant workers; (iv) whether the employer needs approval from a third party to terminate 1 redundant worker; (v) whether the employer needs approval from a third party to terminate a group of 25 redundant workers; (vi) whether the law requires the employer to reassign or retrain a worker before making the worker redundant; (vii) whether priority rules apply for redundancies; and (viii) whether priority rules apply for reemployment. For the first question an answer of yes for workers of any income level gives a score of 10 and means that the rest of the questions do not apply. An answer of yes to question (iv) gives a score of 2. For every other question, if the answer is yes, a score of 1 is assigned; otherwise a score of 0 is given. Questions (i) and (iv), as the most restrictive regulations, have greater weight in the construction of the index.

Firing cost is the notice requirements, severance payments and penalties due when terminating a redundant worker, expressed in weeks of salary.

Rigidity of employment index measures the regulation of employment, specifically the hiring and firing of workers and the rigidity of working hours. This index is the average of three subindexes: a difficulty of hiring index, a rigidity of hours index, and a difficulty of firing index.

Source: Data are from the World Bank's Doing Business project (http://rru.worldbank.org/DoingBusiness/).

Table 5.2. Investment Climate
Private investment is private sector fixed capital formation (Table 2.24) divided by nominal gross domestic product (Table 2.1).

Net foreign direct investment is investment by residents of the Organization for Economic Co-operation and Development's (OECD) Development Assistance Committee (DAC) member countries to acquire a lasting management interest (at least 10 percent of voting stock) in an enterprise operating in the recipient country. The data reflect changes in the net worth of subsidiaries in recipient countries whose parent company is in the DAC source country.

Domestic credit to private sector is financial resources provided to the private sector, such as through loans, purchases of non-equity securities, and trade credits and other accounts receivable that establish a claim for repayment. For some countries these claims include credit to public enterprises.

Corruption, is the percentage of firms identifying corruption as a major constraint. The computation of the indicator is based on the rating of the obstacle as a potential constraint to the current operations of the establishment.

Court system is fair, impartial and uncorrupted, is the percentage of firms believing the court system is fair, impartial and uncorrupted as a major constraint. The computation of the indicator is based on the rating of the obstacle as a potential constraint to the current operations of the establishment.

Crime, theft and disorder is *the percentage of firms* who ranked crime, theft, and disorder as a major constraint. The computation of the indicator is based on the rating of the obstacle as a potential constraint to the current operations of the establishment.

Tax rates are the percentage of firms who ranked tax rates as a major constraint. The computation of the indicator is based on the rating of the obstacle as a potential constraint to the current operations of the establishment.

Finance is the percentage of firms who ranked access to finance or cost of finance as a major constraint. The computation of the indicator is based on the rating of the obstacle as a potential constraint to the current operations of the establishment.

Electricity is the percentage of firms who ranked electricity as a major constraint. The computation of the indicator is based on the rating of the obstacle as a potential constraint to the current operations of the establishment.

Labor regulations is the percentage of firms who ranked labor regulations as a major constraint. The computation of the indicator is

based on the rating of the obstacle as a potential constraint to the current operations of the establishment.

Labor skills are the percentage of firms who ranked skills of available workers as a major constraint. The computation of the indicator is based on the rating of the obstacle as a potential constraint to the current operations of the establishment.

Transportation is the percentage of firms who ranked transportation as a major constraint. The computation of the indicator is based on the rating of the obstacle as a potential constraint to the current operations of the establishment.

Trade identifying customs & trade regulations is the percentage of firms who ranked trade identifying customs and trade regulations as a major constraint. The computation of the indicator is based on the rating of the obstacle as a potential constraint to the current operations of the establishment.

Number of tax payments is the number of taxes paid by businesses, including electronic filing. The tax is counted as paid once a year even if payments are more frequent.

Time to prepare, file, and pay taxes is the number of hours it takes to prepare, file, and pay (or withhold) three major types of taxes: the corporate income tax, the value added or sales tax, and labor taxes, including payroll taxes and social security contributions.

Total tax rate is the total amount of taxes payable by the business (except for labor taxes) after accounting for deductions and exemptions as a percentage of profit.

Highest marginal tax rate, corporate, is the highest rate shown on the schedule of tax rates applied to the taxable income of corporations.

Time dealing with officials is the average percentage of senior management's time that is spent in a typical week dealing with requirements imposed by government regulations (for example, taxes, customs, labor regulations, licensing, and registration), including dealings with officials, completing forms, and the like.

Average time to clear direct exports through customs is the number of days to clear direct exports through customs.

Average time to clear imports through customs (days) is the average number of days to clear imports through customs. For survey data collected in 2006 and 2007, this indicator is computed for the manufacturing module only.

Interest rate spread is the interest rate charged by banks on loans to prime customers minus the interest rate paid by commercial or similar banks for demand, time, or savings deposits.

Listed domestic companies are domestically incorporated companies listed on a country's stock exchanges at the end of the year. They exclude investment companies, mutual funds, and other collective investment vehicles.

Market capitalization of listed companies, also known as market value, is the share price of a listed domestic company's stock times the number of shares outstanding.

Turnover ratio for traded stocks is the total value of shares traded during the period divided by the average market capitalization for the period. Average market capitalization is calculated as the average of the end-of-period values for the current period and the previous period.

Source: Data on private investment are from the World Bank's World Development Indicators database. Data on net foreign direct investment are from the World Bank's World Development Indicators database. Data on domestic credit to the private sector are from the International Monetary Fund's International Financial Statistics database and data files, World Bank and OECD gross domestic product (GDP) estimates, and the World Bank's World Development Indicators database. Data on investment climate constraints to firms are based on enterprise surveys conducted by the World Bank and its partners during 2001–07 (http://rru. worldbank.org/EnterpriseSurveys). Data on regulation and tax administration and highest marginal corporate tax rates are from the World Bank's Doing Business project (http:// rru.worldbank.org/DoingBusiness). Data on time dealing with officials and average time to clear customs are from World Bank Enterprise Surveys (http://rru.worldbank.org/ EnterpriseSurveys/). Data on interest rate spreads are from the IMF's International Financial Statistics database and data files and the World Bank's World Development Indicators database. Data on listed domestic companies and turnover ratios for traded stocks are from Standard & Poor's *Emerging Stock Markets Factbook* and supplemental data and the World Bank's World Development Indicators database. Data on market capitalization of listed companies are from Standard & Poor's *Emerging Stock Markets Factbook* and supplemental data, World Bank and OECD estimates of GDP, and the World Bank's World Development Indicators database.

6. Trade

TABLE 6.1. INTERNATIONAL TRADE AND TARIFF BARRIERS

Merchandise trade is the sum of imports and exports of divided by nominal gross domestic product.

Exports and *imports* comprise all transactions between residents of an economy and the rest of the world involving a change in ownership of general merchandise, goods sent for processing and repairs, and nonmonetary gold. Data are shown in current U.S. dollars. Exports and imports as a share of gross domestic product (GDP) are calculated as merchandise exports and imports divided by nominal GDP. Annual growth of exports and imports is calculated using the real imports and exports.

Terms of trade index measures the relative movement of export and import prices. This series is calculated as the ratio of a country's export unit values or prices to its import unit values or prices shows changes over a base year (2000) in the level of export unit values as a percentage of import unit values.

Structure of merchandise exports and *imports* components may not sum to 100 percent because of unclassified trade.

Food comprises the commodities in Standard International Trade Classification (SITC) sections 0 (food and live animals), 1 (beverages and tobacco), and 4 (animal and vegetable oils and fats) and SITC division 22 (oil seeds, oil nuts, and oil kernels).

Agricultural raw materials comprise the commodities in SITC section 2 (crude materials except fuels), excluding divisions 22, 27 (crude fertilizers and minerals excluding coal, petroleum, and precious stones), and 28 (metalliferous ores and scrap).

Fuel comprise SITC section 3 (mineral fuels).

Ores and metals comprise the commodities in SITC sections 27, 28, and 68 (nonferrous metals).

Manufactures comprise the commodities in SITC sections 5 (chemicals), 6 (basic manufactures), 7 (machinery and transport equipment), and 8 (miscellaneous manufactured goods), excluding division 68.

Export diversification index measures the extent to which exports are diversified. It is constructed as the inverse of a Herfindahl index, using disaggregated exports at four digits (following the SITC3). A higher index indicates more export diversification.

Competitiveness Indicator has two aspects: *Sectoral effect* and *Global competitiveness effect*. To calculate both indicators, growth of exports is decomposed into three components: the growth rate of total international trade over the reference period (2002–2006); *the sectoral effect*, which measures the contribution to a country's export growth of the dynamics of the sectoral markets where the country sells its products, assuming that sectoral market shares are constant; and the *competitiveness effect*, which measures the contribution of changes in sectoral market shares to a country's export growth.

Tariff barriers are a form of duty based on the value of the import.

Binding coverage is the percentage of product lines with an agreed bound rate.

Simple mean bound rate is the unweighted average of all the lines in the tariff schedule in which bound rates have been set.

Simple mean tariff is the unweighted average of effectively applied rates or most favored nation rates for all products subject to tariffs calculated for all traded goods.

Weighted mean tariff is the average of effectively applied rates or most favored nation rates weighted by the product import shares corresponding to each partner country.

Share of lines with international peaks is the share of lines in the tariff schedule with tariff rates that exceed 15 percent.

Share of lines with specific rates is the share of lines in the tariff schedule that are set on a per unit basis or that combine ad valorem and per unit rates.

Primary products are commodities classified in SITC revision 2 sections 0–4 plus division 68.

Manufactured products are commodities classified in SITC revision 2 sections 5–8 excluding division 68.

Average cost to ship 20 ft container from port to destination is the cost of all operations associated with moving a container from onboard a ship to the considered economic center, weighted based on container traffic for each corridor.

Average time to clear direct exports through customs is the number of days to clear direct exports through customs.

Average time to clear imports through customs (days) is the average number of days to clear imports through customs. For survey data collected in 2006 and 2007, this indicator is computed for the manufacturing module only.

Source: All indicators in the table were calculated by World Bank staff using the World Integrated Trade Solution system. Data on the export diversification index and the competitiveness indicator are from the Organization for Economic Co-operation and Development. Data on tariffs are from the United Nations Conference on Trade and Development and the World Trade Organization. Data on global imports are from the United Nations Statistics Division's COMTRADE database. Data on merchandise exports and imports are from World Bank country desks. Data on shipping costs are from the World Bank's Sub-Saharan Africa Transport Policy Program (SSATP). Data on average time to clear customs are from World Bank Enterprise Surveys (*http://rru.worldbank.org/EnterpriseSurveys/*).

TABLE 6.2 TOP THREE EXPORTS AND SHARE IN TOTAL EXPORTS, 2006
Top exports and share of total exports are based on exports disaggregated at the four-digit level (following the Standard International Trade Classification Revision 3*).*

Number of exports accounting for 75 percent of total exports is number of exports in a country that account for 75 percent of the country's exports.

Source: All indicators in the table are from the Organisation for Economic Co-operation and Development.

TABLE 6.3 REGIONAL INTEGRATION, TRADE BLOCS

Merchandise exports within bloc are the sum of merchandise exports by members of a trade bloc to other members of the bloc. They are shown both in U.S. dollars and as a percentage of total merchandise exports by the bloc.

Source: Data on merchandise trade flows are published in the International Monetary Fund's (IMF) *Direction of Trade Statistics Yearbook* and *Direction of Trade Statistics Quarterly*. The data in the table were calculated using the IMF's Direction of Trade database. The United Nations Conference on Trade and Development publishes data on intraregional trade in its *Handbook of International Trade and Development Statistics*. The information on trade bloc membership is from World Bank.

7. Infrastructure

TABLE 7.1. WATER AND SANITATION

Internal fresh water resources per capita is the sum of total renewable resources, which include internal flows of rivers and groundwater from rainfall in the country, and river flows from other countries.

Population with sustainable access to an improved water source is the percentage of population with reasonable access to an adequate amount of water from an improved source, such as a household connection, public standpipe, borehole, protected well or spring, or rainwater collection. Unimproved sources include vendors, tanker trucks, and unprotected wells and springs. Reasonable access is defined as the availability of at least 20 liters a person a day from a source within 1 kilometer of the user's dwelling.

Population with sustainable access to improved sanitation is the percentage of the population with at least adequate access to excreta disposal facilities that can effectively prevent human, animal, and insect contact with excreta. Improved facilities range from simple but protected pit latrines to flush toilets with a sewerage connection. The excreta disposal system is considered adequate if it is private or shared (but not public) and if it hygienically separates human excreta from human contact. To be effective, facilities must be correctly constructed and properly maintained.

Water supply failure for firms receiving water is the average number of days per year that firms experienced insufficient water supply for production.

Committed nominal investment in water projects with private participation is annual committed investment in water projects with private investment, including projects for potable water generation and distribution and sewerage collection and treatment projects.

Official development assistance (ODA) gross aid disbursements for water supply and sanitation are disbursements for water supply and sanitation by bilateral, multilateral, and other donors. The release of funds to, or the purchase of goods or services for a recipient; by extension, the amount thus spent. Disbursements record the actual international transfer of financial resources, or of goods or services valued at the cost of the donor.

Source: Data on fresh water resources are from the World Bank's World Development Indicators database. Data on access to water and sanitation are from the World Health Organization and United Nations Children's Fund's Meeting the MDG Drinking Water and Sanitation Target (www.unicef.org/wes/mdgreport). Data on water supply failure are from World Bank Investment Climate Surveys. Data on committed nominal investment in potable water projects with private participation are from the World Bank's Private Participation in Infrastructure database. Data on ODA disbursements are from the Organization for Economic Co-operation and Development.

TABLE 7.2. TRANSPORTATION

Road network is the length of motorways, highways, main or national roads, secondary or regional roads, and other roads.

Rail lines are the length of railway route available for train service, irrespective of the number of parallel tracks.

Road density, ratio to arable land is the total length of national road network per 1,000 square kilometers of arable land area. The use of arable land area in the denominator focuses on inhabited sectors of total land area by excluding wilderness areas.

Road density, ratio to total land is the total length of national road network per 1,000 square kilometers of total land area.

Rural access is the percentage of the rural population who live within 2 kilometers of an all-season passable road as a share of the total rural population.

Vehicle fleet is motor vehicles, including cars, buses, and freight vehicles but not two-wheelers.

Commercial vehicles are the number of commercial vehicles that use at least 24 liters of diesel fuel per 100 kilometers.

Passenger vehicles are road motor vehicles, other than two-wheelers, intended for the carriage of passengers and designed to seat no more than nine people (including the driver).

Road network in good or fair condition is the length of the national road network, including the interurban classified network without the urban and rural network, that is in good or fair condition, as defined by each country's road agency.

Ratio of paved to total roads is the length of paved roads—which are those surfaced with crushed stone (macadam) and hydrocarbon binder or bituminized agents, with concrete, or with cobblestones—as a percentage of all the country's roads.

Price of diesel fuel and gasoline is the price as posted at filling stations in a country's capital city. When several fuel prices for major cities were available, the unweighted average is used. Since super gasoline (95 octane/A95/premium) is not available everywhere, it is sometime replaced by regular gasoline (92 octane/A92), premium plus gasoline (98 octane/A98), or an average of the two.

Committed nominal investment in transport projects with private participation is annual committed investment in transport projects with private investment, including projects for airport runways and terminals, railways (including fixed assets, freight, intercity passenger, and local passenger), toll roads, bridges, and tunnels.

Official development assistance (ODA) gross aid disbursements for transportation and storage are disbursements for transportation and storage by bilateral, multilateral, and other donors. The release of funds to, or the purchase of goods or services for a recipient; by extension, the amount thus spent. Dis-bursements record the actual international transfer of financial resources, or of goods or services valued at the cost of the donor.

Source: Data on length of road network and size of vehicle fleet are from the International Road Federation's *World Road Statistics*. Data on rail lines and ratio of paved to total roads are from the World Bank's World Development Indicators database. Data on road density and rural access to roads are from the World Bank's Sub-Saharan Africa Transport Policy Program (SSATP) and World Development Indicators database. Data on length of national network in good or fair condition and average time and costs are from the World Bank's SSATP. Data on fuel and gasoline prices are from the German Agency for Technical Cooperation (GTZ). Data on committed nominal investment in transport projects with private participation are from the World Bank's Private Participation in Infrastructure database. Data on ODA disbursements are from the Organization for Economic Co-operation and Development.

TABLE 7.3. INFORMATION AND COMMUNICATION TECHNOLOGY

Telephone subscribers are subscribers to a main telephone line service, which connects a customer's equipment to the public switched telephone network, or to a cellular telephone service, which uses cellular technology.

Households with own telephone is the percentage of households possessing a telephone.

Average delay for firm in obtaining a telephone connection is the average actual delay in days that firms experience when obtaining a telephone connection, measured from the day the establishment applied to the day it received the service or approval.

Internet users are people with access to the worldwide network.

Duration of telephone outages is the average duration in hours of instances of telephone unavailability related to production.

Telephone faults are the total number of reported faults for the year divided by the total number of mainlines in operation multiplied by 100. The definition of fault can vary. Some countries include faulty customer equipment; others distinguish between reported and actual found faults. There is also sometimes a distinction between residential and business lines. Another consideration is the time period: some countries report this indicator on a monthly basis; in these cases data are converted to yearly estimates.

Price basket for Internet is calculated based on the cheapest available tariff for accessing the Internet 20 hours a month (10 hours peak and 10 hours off-peak). The basket does not include telephone line rental but does include telephone usage charges if applicable. Data are compiled in the national currency and converted to U.S. dollars using the annual average exchange rate.

Cost of 3 minute local phone call during peak hours is the cost of a three-minute local call during peak hours. Local call refers to a call within the same exchange area using the subscriber's own terminal (that is, not from a public telephone).

Cost of 3 minute cellular local call during off-peak hours is the cost of a three-minute cellular local call during off-peak hours.

Cost of 3 minute phone call to the U.S, during peak hours is the cost of a three-minute call to the United States during peak hours.

Residential telephone connection charge refers to the one time charge involved in applying for basic telephone service for business purposes. Where there are different charges for different exchange areas, the charge is generally for the largest urban area unless otherwise noted. This indicator is expressed in US dollars.

Mobile cellular connection charge is the initial, one-time charge for a new subscription. Refundable deposits are not counted. The price of the SIM card is included in the connection charge. A note indicates whether taxes are included (preferred) or not. It is also noted if free minutes are included in the plan. This indicator is expressed in US dollars.

Annual investment in telephone service is the annual investment in equipment for fixed telephone service.

Annual investment in mobile communication is the capital investment on equipment for mobile communication networks.

Annual investment in telecommunications is the expenditure associated with acquiring the ownership of telecommunication equipment infrastructure (including sup-porting land and buildings and intellectual and non-tangible property such as computer software). It includes expenditure on initial installations and on additions to existing installations.

Committed nominal investment in telecommunication projects with private participation is annual committed investment in telecommunication projects with private investment, including projects for fixed or mobile local telephony, domestic long-distance telephony, and international long-distance telephony.

Official development assistance (ODA) gross aid disbursements for communication are disbursements for communication by bilateral, multilateral, and other donors. The release of funds to, or the purchase of goods or services for a recipient; by extension, the amount thus spent. Disbursements record the actual international transfer of financial resources, or of goods or services valued at the cost of the donor.

Source: Data on telephone subscribers, reported phone faults, and cost of local and cellular calls are from the International Telecommunications Union. Data on households with own telephone are from Demographic and Health Surveys. Data on delays for firms in obtaining a telephone connection and duration of telephone outages are from World Bank Investment Climate Assessments. Data on Internet users and pricing are from the *International Telecommunication Union, World Telecommunication Development Report and database, and World Bank estimates.* Data on cost of a call to the United States are from the World Bank's Global Development Finance and World Development Indicator databases. Data on committed nominal investment are from the World Bank's Private Participation in Infrastructure database. Data on ODA disbursements are from the Organization for Economic Co-operation and Development.

TABLE 7.4. ENERGY

Electric power consumption is the production of power plants and combined heat and power plants, less distribution losses and own use by heat and power plants.

GDP per unit of energy use is nominal GDP in purchasing power parity (PPP) U.S. dollars divided by apparent consumption, which is equal to indigenous production plus imports and stock changes minus exports and fuels supplied to ships and aircraft engaged in international transport.

Access to electricity is the percentage of the population living in households with access to electricity.

Solid fuels use is the percentage of the population using solid fuels as opposed to modern fuels. Solid fuels include fuel wood, straw, dung, coal, and charcoal. Modern fuels include electricity, liquefied petroleum gas, natural gas, kerosene, and gasoline.

Average delay for firm in obtaining electrical connection is the average actual delay in days that firms experience when obtaining an electrical connection, measured from the day the establishment applied to the day it received the service or approval.

Electric power transmission and distribution losses are technical and nontechnical losses, including electricity losses due to operation of the system and the delivery of electricity as well as those caused by unmetered supply. This comprises all losses due to transport and distribution of electrical energy and heat.

Electrical outages of firms are the average number of days per year that establishments experienced power outages or surges from the public grid.

Firms that share or own their own generator is the percentage of firms that responded "Yes" to the following question: "Does your establishment own or share a generator?"

Firms identifying electricity as major or very severe obstacle to business operation and growth is the percentage of firms that responded "major" or "very severe" obstacle to the following question: "Please tell us if any of the following issues are a problem for the operation and growth of your business. If an issue (infrastructure, regulation, and permits) poses a problem, please judge its severity as an obstacle on a five-point scale that ranges from 0 = no obstacle to 5 = very severe obstacle."

Committed nominal investment in energy projects with private participation is annual committed investment in energy projects with private investment, including projects for electricity generation, transmission, and distribution as well as natural gas transmission and distribution.

Official development assistance (ODA) gross aid disbursements for energy are disbursements for energy by bilateral, multilateral, and other donors. The release of funds to, or the purchase of goods or services for a recipient; by extension, the amount thus spent. Disbursements record the actual international transfer of financial resources, or of goods or services valued at the cost of the donor.

Source: Data on electric power consumption and PPP GDP per unit of energy use are from the World Bank's World Development Indicators database. Data on access to electricity and solid fuels use are from household survey data, supplemented by World Bank Project Appraisal Documents. Data on delays for firms in obtaining an electrical connection, electrical outages of firms, firms that share or own their own generator, and firms identifying electricity as a major or very severe obstacle to business operation and growth are from World Bank Investment Climate Assessments. Data on transmission and distribution losses are from the World Bank's World Development Indicators database, supplemented by World Bank Project Appraisal Documents. Data on committed nominal investment are from the World Bank's Private Participation in Infrastructure database. Data on ODA disbursements are from the Organization for Economic Cooperation and Development.

TABLE 7.5. FINANCIAL SECTOR INFRASTRUCTURE

Sovereign ratings are long- and short-term foreign currency ratings.

International Long-Term Credit Ratings (LTCR) may also be referred to as Long-Term Ratings. When assigned to most issuers, it is used as a benchmark measure of probability of default and is formally described as an Issuer Default Rating (IDR). The major exception is within Public Finance, where IDRs will not be assigned as market convention has always focused on timeliness and does not draw analytical distinctions between issuers and their underlying obligations. When applied to issues or securities, the LTCR may be higher or lower than the issuer rating (IDR) to reflect relative differences in recovery expectations.

A *Short-term rating* has a time horizon of less than 13 months for mostobligations, or up to three years for US public finance, in line with industrystandards, to reflect unique risk characteristics of bond, tax, and revenueanticipation notes that are commonly issued with terms up to three years.Short-term ratings thus place greater emphasis on the liquidity necessary to meet financial commitments in a timely manner.

Gross national savings are the sum of gross domestic savings (Table 2.13) and net factor income and net private transfers from abroad. The estimate here also includes net public transfers from abroad.

Money and quasi money (M2) are the sum of currency outside banks, demand deposits other than those of the central government, and the time, savings, and foreign currency deposits of resident sectors other than the central government. This definition of money supply is frequently called M2 and corresponds to lines 34 and 35 in the IMF's *International Financial Statistics*.

Real interest rate is the lending interest rate adjusted for inflation as measured by the gross domestic product (GDP) deflator.

Domestic credit to private sector is financial resources provided to the private sector, such as through loans, purchases of non-equity securities, and trade credits and other accounts receivable, that establish a claim for repayment. For some countries these claims include credit to public enterprises.

Interest rate spread is the interest rate charged by banks on loans to prime customers minus the interest rate paid by commercial or similar banks for demand, time, or savings deposits.

Ratio of bank nonperforming loans to total gross loans is the value of nonperforming loans divided by the total value of the loan portfolio (including nonperforming loans before the deduction of specific loan-loss provisions). The loan amount recorded as nonperforming should be the gross value of the loan as recorded on the balance sheet, not just the amount that is overdue.

Listed domestic companies are domestically incorporated companies listed on a country's stock exchanges at the end of the year. They exclude investment companies, mutual funds, and other collective investment vehicles.

Market capitalization of listed companies, also known as market value, is the share price of a listed domestic company's stock times the number of shares outstanding.

Turnover ratio for traded stocks is the total value of shares traded during the period divided by the average market capitalization for the period. Average market capitalization is calculated as the average of the end-of-period values for the current period and the previous period.

Source: Data on sovereign ratings are from Fitch Ratings. Data on gross national savings are from World Bank country desks. Data on money and quasi money and domestic credit to the private sector are from the IMF's International Financial Statistics database and data files, World Bank and OECD estimates of GDP, and the World Bank's World Development Indicators database. Data on real interest rates are from the IMF's International Financial Statistics database and data files using World Bank data on the GDP deflator and the World Bank's *World Development Indicators* database. Data on interest rate spreads are from the IMF's International Financial Statistics database and data files and the World Bank's World Development Indicators database. Data on ratios of bank nonperforming loans to total are from the IMF's *Global Financial Stability Report* and the World Bank's World Development Indicators database. Data on bank branches are from surveys of banking and regulatory institutions by the World Bank's Research Department and Financial Sector and Operations Policy Department and the World Development Indicators database. Data on listed domestic companies and turnover ratios for traded stocks are from Standard & Poor's *Emerging Stock Markets Factbook* and supplemental data and the World Bank's World Development Indicators database. Data on market capitalization of listed companies are from Standard & Poor's *Emerging Stock Markets Factbook* and supplemental data, World Bank and OECD estimates of GDP, and the World Bank's World Development Indicators database.

8. Human development

TABLE 8.1. EDUCATION

Youth literacy rate is the percentage of people ages 15–24 who can, with understanding, both read and write a short, simple statement about their everyday life.

Adult literacy rate is the proportion of adults ages 15 and older who can, with understanding, read and write a short, simple statement on their everyday life.

Primary education provides children with basic reading, writing, and mathematics skills along with an elementary understanding of such subjects as history, geography, natural science, social science, art, and music.

Secondary education completes the provision of basic education that began at the primary level and aims to lay the foundations for lifelong learning and human development by offering more subject- or skill-oriented instruction using more specialized teachers.

Tertiary education, whether or not at an advanced research qualification, normally requires, as a minimum condition of admission, the successful completion of education at the secondary level.

Gross enrollment ratio is the ratio of total enrollment, regardless of age, to the population of the age group that officially corresponds to the level of education shown.

Net enrollment ratio is the ratio of children of official school age based on the International Standard Classification of Education 1997 who are enrolled in school to the population of the corresponding official school age.

Student-teacher ratio is the number of students enrolled in school divided by the number of teachers, regardless of their teaching assignment.

Public spending on education is current and capital public expenditure on education plus subsidies to private education at the primary, secondary, and tertiary levels by local, regional, and national government, including municipalities. It excludes household contributions.

Source: United Nations Educational, Scientific, and Cultural Organization Institute for Statistics.

TABLE 8.2. HEALTH

Life expectancy at birth is the number of years a newborn infant would live if prevailing patterns of mortality at the time of its birth were to remain the same throughout its life. Data are World Bank estimates based on data from the United Nations Population Division, the United Nations Statistics Division, and national statistical offices.

Under-five mortality rate is the probability that a newborn baby will die before reaching age 5, if subject to current age-specific mortality rates. The probability is expressed as a rate per 1,000.

Infant mortality rate is the number of infants dying before reaching one year of age, per 1,000 live births.

Maternal mortality ratio, modeled estimate is the number of women who die from pregnancy-related causes during pregnancy and childbirth, per 100,000 live births. The data are estimated with a regression model using information on fertility, birth attendants, and HIV prevalence.

Prevalence of HIV is the percentage of people ages 15–49 who are infected with HIV.

Incidence of tuberculosis is the number of tuberculosis cases (pulmonary, smear positive, and extrapulmonary) in a population at a given point in time, per 100,000 people. This indicator is sometimes referred to as "point prevalence." Estimates include cases of tuberculosis among people with HIV.

Deaths due to malaria is the number of malaria deaths per 100,000 people.

Child immunization rate is the percentage of children ages 12–23 months who received vaccinations before 12 months or at any time before the survey for four diseases—measles and diphtheria, pertussis (whooping cough), and tetanus (DPT). A child is considered adequately immunized against measles after receiving one dose of vaccine and against DPT after receiving three doses.

Stunting (height for age) is the percentage of children under 5 whose height for age is more than two standard deviations below the median for the international reference population ages 0 to 59 months. For children up to two years of age, height is measured by recumbent length. For older children, height is measured by stature while standing. The reference population adopted by the WHO in 1983 is based on children from the United States, who are assumed to be well-nourished.

Underweight (weight for age) is the percentage of children under 5 whose weight for age is more than two standard deviations below the median reference standard for their age as established by the World Health Organization, the U.S. Centers for Disease Control and Prevention, and the U.S. National Center for Health Statistics. Figures are based on children under age 3, 4, and 5 years of age, depending on the country.

Births attended by skilled health staff are the percentage of deliveries attended by personnel trained to give the necessary supervision, care, and advice to women during pregnancy, labor, and the postpartum period; to conduct deliveries on their own; and to care for newborns.

Contraceptive prevalence rate is the percentage of women who are practicing, or whose sexual partners are practicing, any form of contraception. It is usually measured for married women ages 15–49 only.

Children sleeping under insecticide-treated bednets is the percentage of the children under 5 with access to an insecticide-treated bednets to prevent malaria.

Tuberculosis cases detected under DOTS is the percentage of estimated new infectious tuberculosis cases detected under DOTS, the internationally recommended tuberculosis control strategy.

Tuberculosis treatment success rate is the percentage of new smear-positive tuberculosis cases registered under DOTS in a given year that successfully completed treatment, whether with bacteriologic evidence of success ("cured") or without ("treatment completed").

Children under age 5 with fever receiving antimalarial drugs within 24 hrs are the percentage of children under age 5 in malaria-risk areas with fever being treated with any antimalarial drugs.

Population with sustainable access to an improved water source is the percentage of the population with reasonable access to an adequate amount of water from an improved source, such as a household connection, public standpipe, borehole, protected well or spring, or rainwater collection. Unimproved sources include vendors, tanker trucks, and unprotected wells and springs. Reasonable access is defined as the availability of at least 20 liters a person a day from a source within 1 kilometer of the dwelling.

Population with sustainable access to improved sanitation is the percentage of the pop-

ulation with at least adequate access to excreta disposal facilities that can effectively prevent human, animal, and insect contact with excreta. Improved facilities range from simple but protected pit latrines to flush toilets with a sewerage connection. The excreta disposal system is considered adequate if it is private or shared (but not public) and if it hygienically separates human excreta from human contact. To be effective, facilities must be correctly constructed and properly maintained.

Physicians are the number of physicians, including generalists and specialists.

Nurses and midwives are professional nurses, auxiliary nurses, enrolled nurses, and other nurses, such as dental nurses and primary care nurses, and professional midwives, auxiliary midwives, and enrolled midwives.

Total health expenditure is the sum of public and private health expenditure. It covers the provision of health services (preventive and curative), family planning activities, nutrition activities, and emergency aid designated for health but does not include provision of water and sanitation. This is expressed as a proportion of GDP.

Public health expenditure consists of recurrent and capital spending from government (central and local) budgets, external borrowings and grants (including donations from international agencies and nongovernmental organizations), and social (or compulsory) health insurance funds. This is expressed as a proportion of GDP.

Private health expenditure includes direct household (out-of-pocket) spending, private insurance, charitable donations, and direct service payments by private corporations. This is expressed as a proportion of GDP.

Public health expenditure consists of recurrent and capital spending from government (central and local) budgets, external borrowings and grants (including donations from international agencies and nongovernmental organizations), and social (or compulsory) health insurance funds. This is expressed as a proportion of total health expenditure

Private health expenditure includes direct household (out-of-pocket) spending, private insurance, charitable donations, and direct service payments by private corporations. This is expressed as a proportion of total health expenditure.

Out-of-pocket expenditure is any direct outlay by households, including gratuities and in-kind payments, to health practitioners and suppliers of pharmaceuticals, therapeutic appliances, and other goods and services whose primary intent is to contribute to the restoration or enhancement of the health status of individuals or population groups. It is a part of private health expenditure.

Total government expenditure includes consolidated direct outlays and indirect outlays, including capital of all levels of government, social security institutions, autonomous bodies, and other extrabudgetary funds.

Health expenditure per capita is the total health expenditure. It is the sum of public and private health expenditures as a ratio of total population. It covers the provision of health services (preventive and curative), family planning activities, nutrition activities, and emergency aid designated for health but does not include provision of water and sanitation. Data are in current U.S. dollars.

Source: Data are from the latest Core Health Indicators from World Health Organization sources, including *World Health Statistics 2006 and World Health Report 2006* (*http://www3.who.int/whosis/core/core_select.cfm?path=whosis,core&language=english*). Data on health expenditure are from the World Health Organization's *World Health Report* and updates and from the OECD for its member countries, supplemented by World Bank poverty assessments and country and sector studies, and household surveys conducted by governments or by statistical or international organizations.

9. Agriculture, rural development, and environment

TABLE 9.1. RURAL DEVELOPMENT
Rural population is the difference between the total population and the urban population.

Rural population density is the rural population divided by the arable land area. Arable land includes land defined by the Food and Agriculture Organization (FAO) as land under temporary crops (double-cropped areas are counted once), temporary meadows for mowing or for pasture, land under market or kitchen gardens, and land temporarily fal-

low. Land abandoned as a result of shifting cultivation is excluded.

Rural population below the national poverty line is the percentage of the rural population living below the national poverty line.

Share of rural population with sustainable access to an improved water source is the percentage of the rural population with reasonable access to an adequate amount of water from an improved source, such as a household connection, public standpipe, borehole, protected well or spring, or rainwater collection. Unimproved sources include vendors, tanker trucks, and unprotected wells and springs. Reasonable access is defined as the availability of at least 20 liters a person a day from a source within 1 kilometer of the dwelling.

Share of rural population with sustainable access to improved sanitation facilities is the percentage of the rural population with at least adequate access to excreta disposal facilities that can effectively prevent human, animal, and insect contact with excreta. Improved facilities range from simple but protected pit latrines to flush toilets with a sewerage connection. The excreta disposal system is considered adequate if it is private or shared (but not public) and if it hygienically separates human excreta from human contact. To be effective, facilities must be correctly constructed and properly maintained.

Share of rural population with access to electricity is the percentage of the rural population living in households with access to electricity.

Share of rural population with access to transportation is the percentage of the rural population who live within 2 kilometers of an all-season passable road as a share of the total rural population.

Share of rural households with access to a landline telephone is the percentage of rural households possessing a telephone.

Source: Data on rural population are calculated from urban population shares from the United Nations Population Division's *World Urbanization Prospects* and from total population figures from the World Bank. Data on rural population density are from the FAO and World Bank population estimates. Data on rural population below the poverty line are national estimates based on population-weighted subgroup estimates from household surveys. Data on rural population with access to water and rural population with access to sanitation are from World Health Organization and United Nations Children's Fund's *Meeting the MDG Water and Sanitation Target* (www.unicef.org/wes/mdgreport). Data on rural population with access to electricity are from household survey data, supplemented by World Bank Project Appraisal Documents. Data on rural population with access to transport are from the World Bank's Sub-Saharan Africa Transport Policy Program (SSATP). Data on rural households with own telephone are from Demographic and Health Surveys.

TABLE 9.2. AGRICULTURE

Agriculture value added is shown at factor cost in current U.S. dollars divided by nominal gross domestic product. Agriculture corresponds to ISIC divisions 1–5 and includes forestry, hunting, and fishing, as well as cultivation of crops and livestock production. Value added is the net output of a sector after adding up all outputs and subtracting intermediate inputs. It is calculated without making deductions for depreciation of fabricated assets or depletion and degradation of natural resources. The origin of value added is determined by the International Standard Industrial Classification (ISIC), revision 3. Note: For VAB countries, gross value added at factor cost is used as the denominator.

Crop production index shows agricultural production for each year relative to the base period 1999–2001. It includes all crops except fodder crops. Regional and income group aggregates for the Food and Agriculture Organization's (FAO) production indexes are calculated from the underlying values in international dollars, normalized to the base period 1999–2001.

Food production index covers food crops that are considered edible and that contain nutrients. Coffee and tea are excluded because, although edible, they have no nutritive value.

Livestock production index includes meat and milk from all sources, dairy products such as cheese, and eggs, honey, raw silk, wool, and hides and skins.

Cereal production is crops harvested for dry grain only. Cereals include wheat, rice, maize, barley, oats, rye, millet, sorghum, buckwheat, and mixed grains. Cereal crops harvested for hay or harvested green for food, feed, or silage and those used for grazing are excluded.

Cereals (exports and imports) quantities and include wheat, rice, maize, barley, oats, rye, millet, sorghum, buckwheat, and mixed grains.

Agricultural exports and *imports* are expressed in current U.S. dollars at free on board (fob) prices for exports and cost-insurance freight (cif) prices for imports. The term agriculture in trade refers to both food and agriculture and does not include forestry and fishery products.

Food exports and *imports* are expressed in current U.S. dollars at free on board prices (fob) prices for exports and cost-insurance freight (cif) prices for imports.

Permanent cropland is land cultivated with crops that occupy the land for long periods and need not be replanted after each harvest, such as cocoa, coffee, and rubber. It includes land under flowering shrubs, fruit trees, nut trees, and vines, but excludes land under trees grown for wood or timber.

Cereal cropland refers to harvested area, although some countries report only sown or cultivated area.

Irrigated land is areas equipped to provide water to the crops, including areas equipped for full and partial control irrigation, spate irrigation areas, and equipped wetland or inland valley bottoms.

Fertilizer consumption is the aggregate of nitrogenous, phosphate, and potash fertilizers.

Agricultural machinery refers to the number of wheel and crawler tractors (excluding garden tractors) in use in agriculture at the end of the calendar year specified or during the first quarter of the following year. Arable land includes land defined by the FAO as land under temporary crops (double-cropped areas are counted once), temporary meadows for mowing or for pasture, land under market or kitchen gardens, and land temporarily fallow. Land abandoned as a result of shifting cultivation is excluded.

Agricultural employment includes people who work for a public or private employer and who receive remuneration in wages, salary, commission, tips, piece rates, or pay in kind. Agriculture corresponds to division 1

(International Standard Industrial Classification, ISIC, revision 2) or tabulation categories A and B (ISIC revision 3) and includes hunting, forestry, and fishing.

Agriculture value added per worker is the output of the agricultural sector (ISIC divisions 1–5) less the value of intermediate inputs. Agriculture comprises value added from forestry, hunting, and fishing as well as cultivation of crops and livestock production. Data are in constant 2000 U.S. dollars.

Cereal yield is dry grain only and includes wheat, rice, maize, barley, oats, rye, millet, sorghum, buckwheat, and mixed grains. Production data on cereals relate to crops harvested for dry grain only. Cereal crops harvested for hay or harvested green for food, feed, or silage and those used for grazing are excluded.

Source: Data on agriculture value added are from World Bank country desks. Data on crop, food, livestock, and cereal production, cereal exports and imports, agricultural exports and imports, permanent cropland, cereal cropland, and agricultural machinery are from the FAO. Data on irrigated land are from the FAO's *Production Yearbook* and data files. Data on fertilizer consumption are from the FAO database for the *Fertilizer Yearbook*. Data on agricultural employment are from the International Labor Organization. Data on incidence of drought are from the Southern Africa Flood and Drought Network and East Africa Drought (CE). Data on agriculture value added per worker are from World Bank national accounts files and the FAO's *Production Yearbook* and data files.

TABLE 9.3. ENVIRONMENT
Forest area is land under natural or planted stands of trees, whether productive or not.

Renewable internal freshwater resources refer to internal renewable resources (internal river flows and groundwater from rainfall) in the country.

Annual freshwater withdrawals refer to total water withdrawals, not counting evaporation losses from storage basins. Withdrawals also include water from desalination plants in countries where they are a significant source. Withdrawals can exceed 100 percent of total renewable resources where extraction from nonrenewable aquifers or desalination plants is considerable or where there is significant water reuse. Withdrawals for agriculture and industry are total withdrawals for irrigation and livestock production and for direct industrial use (including withdrawals for cooling thermoelectric plants). Withdrawals for domestic uses include drinking water, municipal use or supply, and use for public services, commercial establishments, and homes.

Water productivity is calculated as gross domestic product in constant prices divided by annual total water withdrawal. Sectoral water productivity is calculated as annual value added in agriculture or industry divided by water withdrawal in each sector.

Emissions of organic water pollutants are measured in terms of biochemical oxygen demand, which refers to the amount of oxygen that bacteria in water will consume in breaking down waste. This is a standard water-treatment test for the presence of organic pollutants.

Energy production refers to forms of primary energy—petroleum (crude oil, natural gas liquids, and oil from nonconventional sources), natural gas, solid fuels (coal, lignite, and other derived fuels), and combustible renewables and waste—and primary electricity, all converted into oil equivalents.

Energy use refers to use of primary energy before transformation to other end-use fuels, which is equal to indigenous production plus imports and stock changes, minus exports and fuels supplied to ships and aircraft engaged in international transport.

Combustible renewables and waste comprise solid biomass, liquid biomass, biogas, industrial waste, and municipal waste, measured as a percentage of total energy use.

Carbon dioxide emissions are those stemming from the burning of fossil fuels and the manufacture of cement. They include carbon dioxide produced during consumption of solid, liquid, and gas fuels and gas flaring.

Industrial methane emissions (% of total) are emissions from the handling, transmission, and combustion of fossil fuels and biofuels.

Agricultural methane emissions (% of total) are emissions from animals, animal waste, rice production, agricultural waste burning (nonenergy, on-site), and savannah burning..

Agricultural nitrous oxide emissions (% of total) are emissions produced through fertilizer use (synthetic and animal manure), animal waste management, agricultural waste burning (nonenergy, on-site), and savannah burning.

Industrial nitrous oxide emissions (% of total) are emissions produced during the manufacturing of adipic acid and nitric acid.

Nitrous oxide emissions (metric tons of CO_2 equivalent) are emissions from agricultural biomass burning, industrial activities, and livestock management

Other greenhouse gas emissions, HFC, PFC and SF6 (thousand metric tons of CO_2 equivalent) are by-product emissions of hydrofluorocarbons, perfluorocarbons, and sulfur hexafluoride.

Methane emissions (kt of CO_2 equivalent) are those stemming from human activities such as agriculture and from industrial methane production.

Official development assistance (ODA) disbursements for forestry are disbursements for forestry by bilateral, multilateral, and other donors. The release of funds to, or the purchase of goods or services for a recipient; by extension, the amount thus spent. Disbursements record the actual international transfer of financial resources, or of goods or services valued at the cost of the donor.

Official development assistance (ODA) disbursements for general environment protection are disbursements for general environment protection by bilateral, multilateral, and other donors. The release of funds to or the purchase of goods or services for a recipient; by extension, the amount thus spent. Disbursements record the actual international transfer of financial resources, or of goods or services valued at the cost of the donor.

Source: Data on forest area and deforestation are from the Food and Agriculture Organization's (FAO) Global Forest Resources Assessment 2005. Data on freshwater resources and withdrawals are from the World Resources Institute, supplemented by the FAO's AQUASTAT data. Data on emissions of organic water pollutants are from the World Bank. Data on energy production and use and combustible renewables and waste are from the International Energy Agency.

Data on carbon dioxide emissions are from Carbon Dioxide Information Analysis Center, Environmental Sciences Division, Oak Ridge National Laboratory, in the U.S. state of Tennessee. Data on disbursements are from the Organization for Economic Cooperation and Development (OECD)

TABLE 9.4. CLIMATE CHANGE
Annual average is the average annual of temperature (degree Celsius).

Minimum monthly average is the minimum of the monthly averages of temperature (degree Celsius).

Maximum monthly average is the maximum of the monthly averages of temperature (degree Celsius).

Annual precipitation is the average annual of precipitation (millimeters).

Minimum monthly average is the minimum of the monthly averages of precipitation in year 2000 (millimeters).

Maximum monthly average is the maximum of the monthly averages of precipitation in year 2000 (millimeters).

DJF is the sum of the precipitation in the quarter: December, January, February (millimeters).

MAM is the sum of the precipitation in the quarter: March, April, May (millimeters).

JJA is the sum of the precipitation in the quarter: June, July, August (millimeters).

SON is the sum of the precipitation in the quarter: September, October, November (millimeters).

Carbon dioxide emissions per capita are those stemming from the burning of fossil fuels and the manufacture of cement. They include carbon dioxide produced during consumption of solid, liquid, and gas fuels and gas flaring.

Total greenhouse gas emissions is the combination of atmospheric gases, primarily carbon dioxide, methane, and nitrous oxide, restricting some heat energy from escaping from the earth's atmosphere directly back into space.

Emissions from land-use change and forestry include the following types of land-use change and management activities: (a) clearing of natural ecosystems for permanent croplands (cultivation) (b) clearing of natural ecosystems for permanent pastures (no cultivation) (c) abandonment of croplands and pastures with subsequent recovery of carbon stocks to those of the original ecosystem (d) shifting cultivation (swidden agriculture, repeated clearing, abandonment, and reclearing of forests in many tropical regions) (d) wood harvest (industrial wood as well as fuel wood). It is important to note that these estimates include the emissions of carbon from wood products (burned, stored in longterm pools, decayed over time).

Agriculture value added is shown at factor cost in current U.S. dollars divided by nominal gross domestic product. Agriculture corresponds to ISIC divisions 1–5 and includes forestry, hunting, and fishing, as well as cultivation of crops and livestock production. Value added is the net output of a sector after adding up all outputs and subtracting intermediate inputs. It is calculated without making deductions for depreciation of fabricated assets or depletion and degradation of natural resources. The origin of value added is determined by the International Standard Industrial Classification (ISIC), revision 3. Note: For VAB countries, gross value added at factor cost is used as the denominator.

Irrigated land refers to areas purposely provided with water, including land irrigated by controlled flooding. Cropland refers to arable land and permanent cropland.

Flood is a significant rise of water level a stream, lake, reservoir or coastal region

Drought is a long lasting event; triggered by lack of precipitation. Drought is an extended period of time characteristics by a deficiency in a region's water supply that is the supply that is the result of constantly below average precipitation. Drought can lead to losses to agriculture, affect inland navigation and hydropower plants, and cause lack of drinking water and famine.

Number of clinical malaria cases reported are the sum of cases confirmed by slide examination or RDT and probable and unconfirmed cases (cases that were not tested but treated as malaria). NMCPs often collect data on the number of suspected cases, those tested, and those confirmed. Probable or unconfirmed cases are calculated by subtracting the number tested from the number suspected. Not all cases reported as malaria are true malaria cases since most health facilities lack appropriate diagnostic services. The misdiagnosis may have led to under- or over-reporting malaria cases and missing diagnosis of other treatable diseases.

Reported malaria deaths include all deaths in health facilities that are attributed to malaria, whether or not confirmed by microscopy or by RDT.

Source: Data on temperatures and rainfall are from IRI (2008) based on CRU datasets. Data on carbon dioxide emissions are from Carbon Dioxide Information Analysis Center, Environmental Sciences Division, Oak Ridge National Laboratory, in the U.S. state of Tennessee. Data on Agriculture value added are from the World Bank country desks. Data on irrigated land are from the Food and Agriculture Organization, Production Yearbook and data files. Data on malaria are from World Health Organization Global Malaria Programme. Data on drought and floods are from The International Emergency Disasters Database or *www.em-dat.net*. Data on greenhouse gas emissions are from World Resources Institute and International Energy Agency

10. Labor, migration, and population

TABLE 10.1. LABOR FORCE PARTICIPATION
Labor force is people ages 15 and older who meet the International Labor Organization (ILO) definition of the economically active population. It includes both the employed and the unemployed. While national practices vary in the treatment of such groups as the armed forces and seasonal or part-time workers, the labor force generally includes the armed forces, the unemployed, and first-time job seekers, but excludes homemakers and other unpaid caregivers and workers in the informal sector.

Participation rate is the percentage of the population ages 15–64 that is economically active, that is, all people who supply labor for the production of goods and services during a specified period.

Source: International Labor Organization, Global Employment Trends Model 2006, Employment Trends Team.

Box 8 | **Climate Variability and Change in Sub-Saharan Africa**

In Africa, the number of weather-related disasters, droughts, and floods, has doubled over the last 25 years, and Africa has higher mortality rates from droughts than any other region. According to the IPCC (TAR 2001a, b, c and FAR 2007a, b, c, d), temperatures are rising and rainfall is becoming more unpredictable in Africa. Potential future climate changes in Africa include: an increase in global mean temperatures between 1.4°C and 5.8°C by 2100; temperature warming across the continent ranging from 0.2°C per decade to more than 0.5°C per decade, with warming expected to be greatest over semi-arid regions of the Sahara and central and South Africa; varying precipitation (southern Africa will become hotter and drier, while central Africa is expected to become hotter and wetter; some of the drylands may get higher rainfall, but in the form of heavier torrential rains); an increasing probability of the occurrence of extreme weather events: droughts, floods, and typhoons; and a projected rise in sea levels of 15–95 cm by 2100, with projections suggesting that the number of people at risk from coastal flooding could increase from 1 million in 1990 to 70 million in 2080, forcing major population movements.

Along with rising temperatures, there is also likely to be an increase in rainfall variability, leading to more extreme precipitations and growing water stress. Crop-growing seasons will be affected. There are likely to be more intense and unpredictable weather events in countries such as Kenya, Ethiopia, Malawi, Mozambique, and Madagascar.

Despite the fact that Africa accounts for only 4% of global CO_2 emissions (two-thirds of which are from land-use changes), Africa's vulnerability to climate change is compounded by the fact that two-thirds of the continent is fragile desert or dryland. Agriculture, which contributes some 30% of GDP and employs 70% of the population, is mainly rainfed and highly sensitive to droughts and floods. Water storage capacity is the lowest in the world; only one in four people have access to electricity; and malaria, which is already the biggest killer in Africa, is spreading to higher elevations. Moreover, Africa's rapidly urbanizing population are vulnerable due to poorly defined property rights, weak land use planning, and informal settlements, frequently on land subject to erosion or flood plains. Finally, armed conflict, terms of trade shocks, and aid dependence add to the continent's vulnerability to climate change.

Countries Most Affected by Climate-Related Threats

Droughts	Floods	Storms	Sea Level rise (1m)	Agriculture
Malawi	Bangladesh	Philippines	All low-lying Island States	Sudan
Ethiopia	China	Bangladesh	Vietnam	Senegal
Zimbabwe	India	Madagascar	Egypt	Zimbabwe
India	Cambodia	Vietnam	Tunisia	Mali
Mozambique	Mozambique	Moldova	Indonesia	Zambia
Niger	Laos	Mongolia	Mauritania	Morocco
Mauritania	Pakistan	Haiti	China	Niger
Eritrea	Sri Lanka	Samoa	Mexico	India
Sudan	Thailand	Tonga	Myanmar	Malawi
Chad	Vietnam	China	Bangladesh	Algeria
Kenya	Benin	Honduras	Senegal	Ethiopia
Iran	Rwanda	Fiji	Libya	Pakistan

Note: The typology is based on both absolute effects (i.e., total number of people affected) and relative effects (i.e., number affected as a share of GDP) – *Source:* World Bank 2008b.

TABLE 10.2. LABOR FORCE COMPOSITION
Agriculture corresponds to division 1 (International Standard Industrial Classification, ISIC, revision 2) or tabulation categories A and B (ISIC revision 3) and includes hunting, forestry, and fishing.

Industry corresponds to divisions 2–5 (ISIC revision 2) or tabulation categories C–F (ISIC revision 3) and includes mining and quarrying (including oil production), manufacturing, construction, and public utilities (electricity, gas, and water).

Services correspond to divisions 6–9 (ISIC revision 2) or tabulation categories G–P (ISIC revision 3) and include wholesale and retail trade and restaurants and hotels; transport, storage, and communications; financing, insurance, real estate, and business services; and community, social, and personal services.

Wage and salaried workers are workers who hold the type of jobs defined as paid employment jobs, where incumbents hold explicit (written or oral) or implicit employment contracts that give them a basic remuneration that is not directly dependent on the revenue of the unit for which they work.

Self-employed workers are self-employed workers with employees (employers), self-employed workers with without employees (own-account workers), and members of producer cooperatives. Although the contributing family workers category is technically part of the self-employed according to the classification used by the International Labor Organization (ILO), and could therefore be combined with the other self-employed categories to derive the total self-employed, they are reported here as a separate category in order to emphasize the difference between the two statuses, since the socioeconomic implications associated with each status can be significantly varied. This practice follows that of the ILO's *Key Indicators of the Labor Market*.

Contributing family workers (unpaid workers) are workers who hold self-employment jobs as own-account workers in a market-oriented establishment operated by a related person living in the same household.

Source: Data are from the ILO's *Key Indicators of the Labor Market*, fourth edition.

Table 10.3. Unemployment

Unemployment, total (% of total labor force ages 15 and over) is the share of the labor force ages 15 and over without work but available for and seeking employment.

Unemployment, male (% of male labor force ages 15 and over) is the share of the labor force ages 15 and over without work but available for and seeking employment.

Unemployment, female (% of female labor force ages 15 and over) is the share of the labor force ages 15 and over without work but available for and seeking employment.

Unemployment, youth male (% of male labor force ages 15–24) is the share of the labor force ages 15–24 without work but available for and seeking employment.

Unemployment, youth total (% of total labor force ages 15–24) is the share of the labor force ages 15–24 without work but available for and seeking employment.

Unemployment, youth female (% of female labor force ages 15–24) is the share of the labor force ages 15–24 without work but available for and seeking employment.

Long-term unemployment (% of total unemployment) is the number of people with continuous periods of unemployment extending for a year or longer, expressed as a percentage of the total unemployed.

Long-term unemployment, female (% of female unemployment) is the number of people with continuous periods of unemployment extending for a year or longer, expressed as a percentage of the total unemployed.

Long-term unemployment, male (% of male unemployment) is the number of people with continuous periods of unemployment extending for a year or longer, expressed as a percentage of the total unemployed.

Unemployment with primary education, female (% of female unemployment) is the unemployed by level of educational attainment, as a percentage of the unemployed.

Unemployment with primary education, male (% of male unemployment) is the unemployed by level of educational attainment, as a percentage of the unemployed.

Unemployment with primary education (% of total unemployment) is the unemployed by level of educational attainment, as a percentage of the unemployed.

Unemployment with secondary education, female (% of female unemployment) is the unemployed by level of educational attainment, as a percentage of the unemployed..

Unemployment with secondary education, male (% of male unemployment) is the unemployed by level of educational attainment, as a percentage of the unemployed.

Unemployment with secondary education (% of total unemployment) is the unemployed by level of educational attainment, as a percentage of the unemployed

Unemployment with tertiary education, female (% of female unemployment) is the unemployed by level of educational attainment, as a percentage of the unemployed.

Unemployment with tertiary education, male (% of male unemployment) is the unemployed by level of educational attainment, as a percentage of the unemployed.

Unemployment with tertiary education (% of total unemployment) is the unemployed by level of educational attainment, as a percentage of the unemployed.

Source: International Labor Organization, Key Indicators of the Labour Market database.

| Box 9 | **Unemployment and the Process of Development** |

Growing unemployment is a major concern for policy makers as it is often seen as a symptom of poor economic performance. This view reflects the experience of the developed world where growing unemployment is mostly associated with poor GDP performance and higher poverty incidence. However, the relationship appears to be reversed in the developing world, where richer countries experience comparatively higher unemployment rates. This is evident in the figure below, which plots unemployment and GDP per capita for 64 developing countries for all available years. The positive long-run relationship—with an elasticity of 0.46—can be explained by the occurrence of two related phenomena: urbanization and rising incomes.[7]

During the initial stages of development, economic growth accelerates the pace at which the rural population is drawn into urban areas in search of waged work. But employment is frequently hard to come by in an often demand-constrained, rationed waged sector. Nevertheless, in low income settings with scarce safety nets, unemployment is a luxury that few urban labor workers can afford, so that most are forced to earn a meager living in low-productivity, self-employment activities. As growth raises incomes and wealth, unemployment becomes a viable option for a larger proportion of the labor force, informality decreases and unemployment rises.

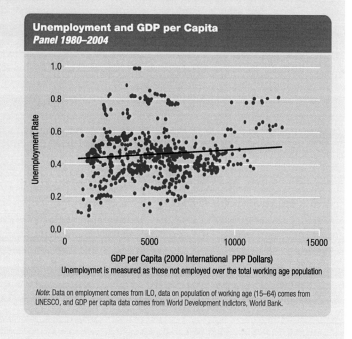

Unemployment and GDP per Capita
Panel 1980–2004

GDP per Capita (2000 International PPP Dollars)
Unemploymet is measured as those not employed over the total working age population

Note: Data on employment comes from ILO, data on population of working age (15–64) comes from UNESCO, and GDP per capita data comes from World Development Indictors, World Bank.

Therefore, using unemployment as an indicator of poor economic performance in poor developing countries is often misleading. The main concern of policy makers in developing countries should be with the low productivity/earnings of existing jobs rather than with the number of unemployed. This is not to say that the growing unemployment that is associated with urbanization should not be also addressed. However, in doing so it is essential to remember that the priority of policies should lie with creating better employment opportunities for the working poor.

TABLE 10.4. MIGRATION AND POPULATION
Stock is the number of people born in a country other than that in which they live. It includes refugees.

Net migration is the net average annual number of migrants during the period, that is, the annual number of immigrants less the annual number of emigrants, including both citizens and noncitizens. Data are five-year estimates.

Workers remittances received comprise current transfers by migrant workers and wages and salaries by nonresident workers.

Population is World Bank estimates, usually projected from the most recent population censuses or surveys (mostly from 1980–2004). Refugees not permanently settled in the country of asylum are generally considered to be part of the population of their country of origin.

Fertility rate is the number of children that would be born to a woman if she were to live to the end of her childbearing years and bear children in accordance with current age-specific fertility rates.

Age composition refers to the percentage of the total population that is in specific age groups.

Dependency ratio is the ratio of dependents—people younger than 15 or older than 64—to the working-age population—those ages 15–64.

Rural area population is calculated as the difference between the total population and the urban population.

Urban area population is midyear population of areas defined as urban in each country.

Source: World Bank's World Development Indicators database.

---

[6] The relation is statistically significant, and holds for different samples of countries. This relationship holds in the long run (several years). In the short and medium-run within countries, unemployment is countercyclical: it shrinks during economic booms and increases during recession.

Box 10 | The Demographic Transition in Sub-Saharan Africa

The demographic transition, which is also referred to as the demographic revolution, is defined as the shift from a traditional demographic regime with a high semi-equilibrium (high mortality and high fertility) to a modern regime with a low semi-equilibrium (low mortality and low fertility). This shift, which is accompanied by transformations in the socio-economic context and by increasing urbanization, results in profound changes. The most important is the decline of mortality (the initial phase of the demographic transition), which usually occurs first because of improvements in survival conditions, especially during early childhood. These improvements are most often exogenous, as exemplified by immunization campaigns and programs to control diarrhea and malaria. The ensuing reduction in mortality triggers rapid and currently accelerating rates of population growth. The onset of fertility decline, which often occurs with a time lag, marks the second phase of the demographic transition.

Most regions of the world have undergone the demographic transition. This process started in Britain and France at the beginning of the eighteenth century, and then spread to the rest of Europe and the territories of European settlement and, finally, to the other parts of the world. In the 1960s and 1970s, population programs were implemented in Asia and Latin America, with the specific purpose of accelerating the fertility decline. Along with other socio-economic changes, the rate of population growth fell in these two regions from about 2.5% per year in the 1960s to less than 1.5% today.

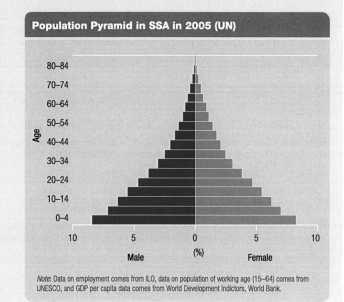

By contrast, the population growth rate in sub-Saharan Africa has remained at 2.5% per year over the past half century, except in southern Africa. The second phase of the demographic transition has started in the region, but it appears to be slower than in other parts of the world. The large number of young Africans (almost 2 out of 3 people are under 25), and the current high fertility levels (above 5 children per woman on average) imply that population growth will continue despite the HIV/AIDS epidemic. In mid-2008, Sub-Saharan Africa had an estimated 800 million people – 12.1% of the world's population. This share will increase to 18.2% in 2050, or about 1.8 billion people. This assumes an average of 2.5 children per African woman by 2050, according to the medium variant of the United Nations 2006 population projections. The medium variant implies a sharp reduction in fertility, but also substantial improvements in the expectancy of life at birth. However, this rapid decline in fertility levels has not yet occurred, except in southern Africa. As such, higher 2050 population figures, potentially reaching 2 billion or more, are plausible if fertility declines more slowly.

The sustained population growth of the past 50 years in Sub-Saharan Africa has resulted in a very young age structure, as illustrated by the population pyramid (UN 2006 medium variant). Slower population growth in the region, thereby reducing the youth bulge, may help improve Africa's human capital formation (e.g., education and health), enhance youth employment opportunities, and ease poverty reduction efforts. As the East Asia experience has shown, a slower rate of population growth leads to more favorable dependency ratios — limiting the number of child dependents on a comparatively larger, productive workforce. A slower population growth would also help reduce the pressures countries face regarding food security, land tenure, and environmental degradation. However, the question of how to accelerate fertility decline in sub-Saharan Africa, particularly in rural areas, remains difficult in a context of low education attainments, gender inequality, and logistical difficulties to set up effective programs.

11. HIV/AIDS

TABLE 11.1. HIV/AIDS
Estimated number of people living with HIV/AIDS is the number of people in the relevant age group living with HIV.

Estimated prevalence rate is the percentage of the population of the relevant age group who are infected with HIV. Depending on the reliability of the data available, there may be more or less uncertainty surrounding each estimate. Therefore, plausible bounds have been presented for each age-range rate (low and high estimate).

Deaths due to HIV/AIDS are the estimated number of adults and children that have died in a specific year based in the modeling of HIV surveillance data using standard and appropriate tools.

AIDS orphans are the estimated number of children who have lost their mother or both parents to AIDS before age 17 since

| Box 11 | HIV Prevalence and Incidence |

In order to understand reductions in HIV prevalence, it is important to distinguish between HIV prevalence and HIV incidence. HIV prevalence includes all HIV infections, new and old. HIV incidence is limited to new HIV infections, acquired in the last year. Because of the long duration between HIV infection and death, HIV prevalence trends lag HIV incidence trends by several years, as shown below:

U.S. Bureau of the Census models suggest that HIV incidence began to fall in several countries in Eastern and Southern Africa in the late 1980s and early 1990s, as shown below:

Incidence is a better measure of HIV trends and program effectiveness, because it measures new infections. However, it is much harder to measure. There are three major approaches, each with limitations:

First, we can establish a cohort, follow HIV-negative people over time and as they seroconvert, establish the HIV incidence. However, cohorts are expensive to establish and usually require a major research study. Moreover, the results are limited to the specific cohort in question.

Second, we can use techniques to identify recent infections in cross-sectional data, such as the detuned elisa or the BED test. However, these are not considered accurate enough to establish incidence rates.

Third, we can model incidence from several years of prevalence data. If we have comprehensive, regular prevalence data, this is an attractive option.

In summary, incidence is scientifically a better measure, but is rarely available.

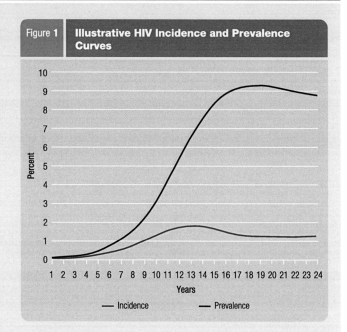

Figure 1 | Illustrative HIV Incidence and Prevalence Curves

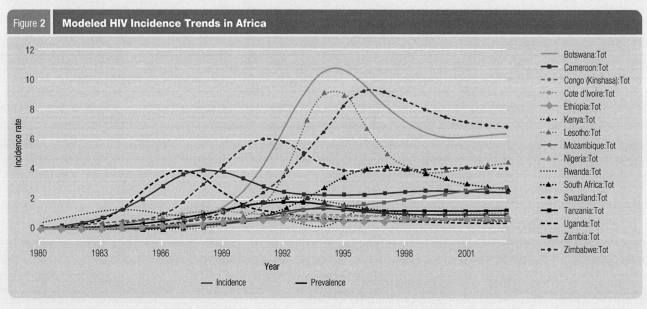

Figure 2 | Modeled HIV Incidence Trends in Africa

Data Source: US Bureau of Census.

the epidemic began in 1990. Some of the orphaned children included in this cumulative total are no longer alive; others are no longer under age 17.

Source: The Joint United Nations Programme on HIV/AIDS and the World Health Organization's *2008 Report on the Global AIDS Epidemic.*

12. Malaria

TABLE 12.1. MALARIA
Population is the total population based on the de facto definition of population, which counts all residents regardless of legal status or citizenship, except for refugees not permanently settled in the country of asylum, who are generally considered part of the population of their country of origin. The values shown are midyear estimates.

Endemic risk of malaria is the percentage of the population living in areas with significant annual transmission of malaria, be it seasonal or perennial.

Epidemic risk of malaria is the percentage of the population living in areas prone to distinct interannual variation, with no transmission taking place at all in some years.

Negligible risk of malaria is the percentage of the population living in areas where malaria is ordinarily not present and where the risk of malaria outbreaks is negligible.

Deaths due to malaria are the number of malaria deaths per 100,000 people.

Under-five mortality rate is the probability that a newborn baby will die before reaching age 5, if subject to current age-specific mortality rates. The probability is expressed as a rate per 1,000.

Children sleeping under insecticide-treated bednets is the percentage of the children under 5 with access to an insecticide-treated bednet to prevent malaria.

Children with fever receiving any antimalarial drugs are the percentage of children under age 5 in malaria-risk areas with fever being treated with antimalarial drugs.

Children with fever receiving effective antimalarial drugs are the percentage of children under age 5 in malaria-risk areas with fever being treated with effective antimalarial drugs.

Pregnant women receiving two doses of intermittent preventive treatment are the number of pregnant women who receive at least two preventive treatment doses of an effective antimalarial drug during routine antenatal clinic visits. This approach has been shown to be safe, inexpensive, and effective.

Source: Data on population are from the World Bank's World Development Indicators database. Data on risk of malaria, children with fever receiving antimalarial drugs, and pregnant women receiving two doses of intermittent preventive treatment are from Demographic Health Surveys, Multiple Indicator Cluster Surveys, and national statistical offices. Data on deaths due to malaria are from the United Nations Statistics Division based on World Health Organization (WHO) estimates. Data on under-five mortality are harmonized estimates of the WHO, United Nations Children's Fund, and the World Bank, based mainly on household surveys, censuses, and vital registration, supplemented by World Bank estimates based on household surveys and vital registration. Data on insecticide-treated bednet use are from Demographic and Health Surveys and Multiple Indicator Cluster Surveys.

13. Capable states and partnership

TABLE 13.1. AID AND DEBT RELIEF
Net aid from all donors is net aid from the Organization for Economic Co-operation and Development's (OECD), Development Assistance Committee (DAC), non-DAC bilateral (Organization of Petroleum Exporting Countries [OPEC], the former Council for Mutual Economic Assistance [CMEA] countries, and China [OECD data]), and multilateral donors. OPEC countries are Algeria, Iran, Iraq, Kuwait, Libya, Nigeria, Qatar, Saudi Arabia, the United Arab Emirates, and Venezuela. The former CMEA countries are Bulgaria, Czechoslovakia, the former German Democratic Republic, Hungary, Poland, Romania, and the former Soviet Union).

Net aid from DAC donors is net aid from OECD's DAC donors, which include Australia, Austria, Belgium, Canada, Denmark, Finland, France, Germany, Greece, Ireland, Italy, Japan, Luxembourg, the Netherlands, New Zealand, Norway, Portugal, Spain, Sweden, Switzerland, the United Kingdom, and United States.

Net aid from non-DAC donors is net aid from OECD's non-DAC donors, which include Czech Republic, Hungary, Iceland, Israel, Korea Republic, Kuwait, Poland, Saudi Arabia, Slovak Republic, Taiwan China, Thailand, Turkey and United Arab Emirates and other donors.

Net aid from multilateral donors is net aid from multilateral sources, such as the African Development Fund, the European Development Fund for the Commission of the European Communities, the International Development Association, the International Fund for Agricultural Development, Arab and OPEC financed multilateral agencies, and UN programs and agencies. Aid flows from the International Monetary Fund's (IMF) Trust Fund and Structural Adjustment Facility are also included. UN programs and agencies include the United Nations Technical Assistance Programme, the United Nations Development Programme, the United Nations Office of the High Commissioner for Refugees, the United Nations Children's Fund, and the World Food Programme. Arab and OPEC financed multilateral agencies include the Arab Bank for Economic Development in Africa, the Arab Fund for Economic and Social Development, the Islamic Development Bank, the OPEC Fund for International Development, the Arab Authority for Agricultural Investment and Development, the Arab Fund for Technical Assistance to African and Arab Countries, and the Islamic Solidarity Fund.

Net private aid is private transactions broken down into direct investment, portfolio investment and export credits (net). Private transactions are those undertaken by firms and individuals resident in the reporting country. Portfolio investment corresponds to bonds and equities. Inflows into emerging countries' stocks markets, are, however, heavily understated. Accordingly, the coverage of portfolio investment differs in these regards from the coverage of bank claims, which include indistinguishably export credit lending by banks. The bank claims data represent the net change in banks' claims after adjustment to eliminate the effect of changes in exchange rates. They are therefore a proxy for net flow data, but are not themselves a net flow figure. They differ in two further regards from other OECD data.

First, they relate to oans by banks resident in countries which report quarterly to the Bank for International Settlements (BIS). Secondly, no adjustment has been made to exclude short-term claims.

Net aid as a share of gross domestic product (GDP) is calculated by dividing the nominal total net aid from all donors by nominal GDP. For a given level of aid flows, devaluation of a recipient's currency may inflate the ratios shown in the table. Thus, trends for a given country and comparisons across countries that have implemented different exchange rate policies should be interpreted carefully.

Net ODA aid per capita is calculated by dividing the nominal total net aid (net disbursements of loans and grants from all official sources on concessional financial terms) by midyear population. These ratios offer some indication of the importance of aid flows in sustaining per capita income and consumption levels, although exchange rate fluctuations, the actual rise of aid flows, and other factors vary across countries and over time.

Net aid as a share of gross capital formation is calculated by dividing the nominal total net aid by gross capital formation. These data highlight the relative importance of the indicated aid flows in maintaining and increasing investment in these economies. The same caveats mentioned above apply to their interpretation. Furthermore, aid flows do not exclusively finance investment (for example, food aid finances consumption), and the share of aid going to investment varies across countries.

Net aid as a share of imports of goods and services is calculated by dividing nominal total net aid by imports of goods and services.

Net aid as a share of central government expenditure is calculated by dividing nominal total net aid by central government expenditure.

Heavily Indebted Poor Country (HIPC) Debt Initiative decision point is the date at which a HIPC with an established track record of good performance under adjustment programs supported by the International Monetary Fund and the World Bank commits to undertake additional reforms and to develop and implement a poverty reduction strategy.

Cereal food aid shipments represent a transfer of food commodities from donor to recipient countries on a total-grant basis. Processed and blended cereals are converted into their grain equivalent by applying the conversion factors included in the Rule of Procedures under the 1999 Food Aid Convention to facilitate comparisons between deliveries of different commodities. For cereals, the period refers to July/June, beginning in the year shown.

HIPC Debt Initiative completion point is the date at which the country successfully completes the key structural reforms agreed on at the decision point, including developing and implementing its poverty reduction strategy. The country then receives the bulk of debt relief under the HIPC Initiative without further policy conditions.

Debt service relief committed is the amount of debt service relief, calculated at the decision point, that will allow the country to achieve debt sustainability at the completion point.

Source: Net ODA data are OECD and World Bank data. Data on food aid shipments from 1970/71 to 1990/91 was compiled by FAO from the information provided by donor countries, and complemented by data provided by the FAO Consultative Sub-Committee on Surplus Disposal, the World Food Programme (WFP), the International Wheat Council, OECD, and other international organizations. From 1990/91 to date, the information on food aid shipments has been provided to FAO exclusively by WFP.

TABLE 13.2. CAPABLE STATES
Court system is the percentage of firms believing the court system is fair, impartial and uncorrupted as a major constraint. The computation of the indicator is based on the rating of the obstacle as a potential constraint to the current operations of the establishment.

Crime is the percentage of firms who ranked crime, theft, and disorder as a major constraint. The computation of the indicator is based on the rating of the obstacle as a potential constraint to the current operations of the establishment.

Number of procedures to enforce a contract is the number of independent actions, mandated by law or courts that demand interaction between the parties of a contract or between them and the judge or court officer.

Time required to enforce a contract is the number of calendar days from the filing of the lawsuit in court until the final determination and, in appropriate cases, payment.

Cost to enforce a contract is court and attorney fees, where the use of attorneys is mandatory or common, or the cost of an administrative debt recovery procedure, expressed as a percentage of the debt value.

Protecting investors disclosure index measures the degree to which investors are protected through disclosure of ownership and financial information.

Director liability index measures a plaintiff's ability to hold directors of firms liable for damages to the company).

Shareholder suits index measures shareholders' ability to sue officers and directors for misconduct.

Investor protection index measures the degree to which investors are protected through disclosure of ownership and financial information regulations.

Number of tax payments is the number of taxes paid by businesses, including electronic filing. The tax is counted as paid once a year even if payments are more frequent.

Time to prepare, file, and pay taxes is the number of hours it takes to prepare, file, and pay (or withhold) three major types of taxes: the corporate income tax, the value added or sales tax, and labor taxes, including payroll taxes and social security contributions.

Total tax payable is the total amount of taxes payable by the business (except for labor taxes) after accounting for deductions and exemptions as a percentage of gross profit. For further details on the method used for assessing the total tax payable, see the World Bank's *Doing Business 2006*.

Extractive Industries Transparency Initiative (EITI) Endorsed indicates whether a country has implemented or endorsed the EITI, a multi-stakeholder approach to increasing governance and transparency in extractive industries. It includes civil society, the private sector, and government and requires a work plan with timeline and budget to ensure sustainability, independent audit of payments and disclosure of revenues, publication of results in a publicly accessible manner, and an approach that covers all companies and government agencies. EITI *supports improved governance in resource-rich countries through the verification and full publication of company payments and government revenues from oil, gas, and mining. EITI is a global initiative and the EITI Secretariat has developed an EITI Source Book that provides guidance for countries and companies wishing to implement the initiative (http://www.eitransparency.org/ section/abouteiti).*

EITI report produced indicates which the country has publicly released an EITI report. This appears only for those in which a public report is released. Generally, the production of a report is subsequent to the adoption of the EITI principles.

Source: Data on investment climate constraints to firms are based on enterprise surveys conducted by the World Bank and its partners during 2001–05 (http://rru.worldbank.org/EnterpriseSurveys). Data on enforcing contracts, protecting investors, and regulation and tax administration are from the World Bank's Doing Business project (http://rru.worldbank.org/DoingBusiness/). Data on the EITI are from the EITI website, www.eitransparency.org. Data on corruption perceptions index are from Transparency International (www.transparency.org/policy_ research/surveys_indices/cpi).

TABLE 13.3. GOVERNANCE AND ANTICORRUPTION INDICATORS

Voice and accountability measures the extent to which a country's citizens are able to participate in selecting their government and to enjoy freedom of expression, freedom of association, and a free media.

Political stability and absence of violence measures the perceptions of the likelihood that the government will be destabilized or overthrown by unconstitutional or violent means, including domestic violence or terrorism.

Government effectiveness measures the quality of public services, the quality and degree of independence from political pressures of the civil service, the quality of policy formulation and implementation, and the credibility of the government's commitment to such policies.

Regulatory quality measures the ability of the government to formulate and implement sound policies and regulations that permit and promote private sector development.

Rule of law measures the extent to which agents have confidence in and abide by the rules of society, in particular the quality of contract enforcement, the police, and the courts, as well as the likelihood of crime and violence.

Control of corruption measures the extent to which public power is exercised for private gain, including petty and grand forms of corruption, as well as "capture" of the state by elites and private interests.

Corruption Perceptions Index transparency index is the annual Transparency International corruption perceptions index, which ranks more than 150 countries in terms of perceived levels of corruption, as determined by expert assessments and opinion surveys.

Source: Data are from the World Bank Institute's Worldwide Governance Indicators database, which relies on 33 sources, including surveys of enterprises and citizens, and expert polls, gathered from 30 organizations around the world.

TABLE 13.4. COUNTRY POLICY AND INSTITUTIONAL ASSESSMENT RATINGS

The Country Policy and Institutional Assessment (CPIA) assess the quality of a country's present policy and institutional framework. "Quality" means how conducive that framework is to fostering sustainable, poverty-reducing growth and the effective use of development assistance. The CPIA is conducted annually for all International Bank for Reconstruction and Development and International Development Association borrowers and has evolved into a set of criteria grouped into four clusters with 16 criteria that reflect a balance between ensuring that all key factors that foster pro-poor growth and poverty alleviation are captured, without overly burdening the evaluation process.

- Economic management
  - *Macroeconomic management* assesses the quality of the monetary, exchange rate, and aggregate demand policy framework.
  - *Fiscal policy* assesses the short- and medium-term sustainability of fis-

cal policy (taking into account monetary and exchange rate policy and the sustainability of the public debt) and its impact on growth.

- *Debt policy* assesses whether the debt management strategy is conducive to the minimization of budgetary risks and ensures long-term debt sustainability

- Structural policies
  - *Trade* assesses how the policy framework fosters trade in goods. It covers two areas: trade regime restrictiveness—which focuses on the height of tariffs barriers, the extent to which nontariff barriers are used, and the transparency and predictability of the trade regime; and customs and trade facilitation—which includes the extent to which the customs service is free of corruption, relies on risk management, processes duty collections and refunds promptly, and operates transparently.
  - *Financial sector* assesses the structure of the financial sector and the policies and regulations that affect it. It covers three dimensions: financial stability; the sector's efficiency, depth, and resource mobilization strength; and access to financial services.
  - *Business regulatory environment* assesses the extent to which the legal, regulatory, and policy environment helps or hinders private business in investing, creating jobs, and becoming more productive. The emphasis is on direct regulations of business activity and regulation of goods and factor markets. It measures three subcomponents: regulations affecting entry, exit, and competition; regulations of ongoing business operations; and regulations of factor markets (labor and land).

- Policies for social inclusion and equity
  - *Gender equality* assesses the extent to which the country has enacted and put in place institutions and programs to enforce laws and policies that promote equal access for men and women to human capital development, and to productive and economic resources and that give men and women equal status and protection under the law.
  - *Equity of public resource use* assesses the extent to which the pattern of public expenditures and revenue collection affects the poor and is consistent with national poverty reduction priorities. The assessment of the consistency of government spending with the poverty reduction priorities takes into account the extent to which individuals, groups, or localities that are poor, vulnerable, or have unequal access to services and opportunities are identified; a national development strategy with explicit interventions to assist those individuals, groups, and localities has been adopted; and the composition and incidence of public expenditures are tracked systematically and their results fed back into subsequent resource allocation decisions. The assessment of the revenue collection dimension takes into account the incidence of major taxes—for example, whether they are progressive or regressive—and their alignment with the poverty reduction priorities. When relevant, expenditure and revenue collection trends at the national and sub-national levels should be considered. The expenditure component receives two-thirds of the weight in computing the overall rating.
  - *Building human resources* assesses the national policies and public and private sector service delivery that affect access to and quality of health and nutrition services, including: population and reproductive health; education, early childhood development, and training and literacy programs; and prevention and treatment of HIV/AIDS, tuberculosis, and malaria.
  - *Social protection and labor* assess government policies in the area of social protection and labor market

regulation, which reduce the risk of becoming poor, assist those who are poor to better manage further risks, and ensure a minimal level of welfare to all people. Interventions include social safety net programs, pension and old age savings programs, protection of basic labor standards, regulations to reduce segmentation and inequity in labor markets, active labor market programs (such as public works or job training), and community driven initiatives. In interpreting the guidelines it is important to take into account the size of the economy and its level of development.

- *Policies and institutions for environmental sustainability* assess the extent to which environmental policies foster the protection and sustainable use of natural resources and the management of pollution. Assessment of environmental sustainability requires multidimensional criteria (that is, for air, water, waste, conservation management, coastal zones management, and natural resources management).

- Public sector management and institutions
  - *Property rights and rule-based governance* assess the extent to which private economic activity is facilitated by an effective legal system and rule-based governance structure in which property and contract rights are reliably respected and enforced. Three dimensions are rated separately: legal basis for secure property and contract rights; predictability, transparency, and impartiality of laws and regulations affecting economic activity, and their enforcement by the legal and judicial system; and crime and violence as an impediment to economic activity.
  - *Quality of budgetary and financial management* assesses the extent to which there is a comprehensive and credible budget, linked to policy priorities; effective financial

management systems to ensure that the budget is implemented as intended in a controlled and predictable way; and timely and accurate accounting and fiscal reporting, including timely and audited public accounts and effective arrangements for follow-up.
- *Quality of public administration* assesses the extent to which civilian central government staffs (including teachers, health workers, and police) are structured to design and implement government policy and deliver services effectively. Civilian central government staffs include the central executive together with all other ministries and administrative departments, including autonomous agencies. It excludes the armed forces, state-owned enterprises, and sub national government.
- *Efficiency of revenue mobilization* assesses the overall pattern of revenue mobilization—not only the tax structure as it exists on paper, but revenue from all sources as they are actually collected.
- *Transparency, accountability, and corruption in the public sector* assess the extent to which the executive branch can be held accountable for its use of funds and the results of its actions by the electorate and by the legislature and judiciary, and the extent to which public employees within the executive are required to account for the use of resources, administrative decisions, and results obtained. Both levels of accountability are enhanced by transparency in decision-making, public audit institutions, access to relevant and timely information, and public and media scrutiny.

Source: World Bank's Country Policy and Institutional Assessment 2005.

TABLE 13.5. POLITY INDICATORS
Polity score is computed by subtracting the *Institutionalized autocracy* score from the *In-*

stitutionalized democracy score; the resulting unified polity scale ranges from +10 (strongly democratic) to –10 (strongly autocratic).

Institutionalized democracy is conceived as three essential, interdependent elements. One is the presence of institutions and procedures through which citizens can express effective preferences about alternative policies and leaders. Second is the existence of institutionalized constraints on the exercise of power by the executive. Third is the guarantee of civil liberties to all citizens in their daily lives and in acts of political participation. Other aspects of plural democracy, such as the rule of law, systems of checks and balances, freedom of the press, and so on are means to, or specific manifestations of, these general principles. We do not include coded data on civil liberties. This is an additive eleven-point scale (0–10). The operational indicator of democracy is derived from codings of the competitiveness of political participation using some weights.

Institutionalized autocracy is a pejorative term for some very diverse kinds of political systems whose common properties are a lack of regularized political competition and concern for political freedoms. The term Autocracy is used and defined operationally in terms of the presence of a distinctive set of political characteristics. In mature form, autocracies sharply restrict or suppress competitive political participation. Their chief executives are chosen in a regularized process of selection within the political elite, and once in office they exercise power with few institutional constraints. Most modern autocracies also exercise a high degree of directiveness over social and economic activity, but we regard this as a function of political ideology and choice, not a defining property of autocracy. Social democracies also exercise relatively high degrees of directiveness. We prefer to leave open for empirical investigation the question of how Autocracy, Democracy, and directiveness (performance) have covaried over time.

Source: Polity IV Project Political Regime Charateristics and Transitions, 1800–2006, Center for Systemic Peace *www.systemic-peace.org/polity*

14. Household welfare

The questions asked in household surveys vary by country. Quintiles are derived by ranking weighted sample population by area of residence (rural and urban) and per capita expenditure. Two sets of quintiles are calculated, one for rural and one for urban. Each quintile contains an equal number of people rather than households. The definitions of rural and urban also vary by country.

Sample size is the number of households surveyed in the country.

Total population is the weighted estimate of all the surveyed population in the country based on the survey—that is, it is the weighted sample population.

Age dependency ratio is the ratio of dependents—people younger than 15 or older than 64—to the working-age population—those ages 15–64.

Average household size is the average number of people in a household.

Monogamous male is a household headed by man who has no more than one spouse (wife).

Polygamous male is a household headed by a man who has more than one spouse (wife).

Single male is a household headed by a man who is widowed or divorced or who has never married.

De facto female refers to a household without a resident male head or where the male head is not present and the wife is the head by default and serves as the main decision maker in his absence or a household where the resident male head has lost most of his functions as the economic provider due to infirmity, inability to work, or the like.

De jure female refers to a household headed by a woman who is widowed, separated, or divorced or who has never been married.

Mean monthly expenditure is the average monthly expenditure on both food and non-food items.

Mean monthly share on food is total monthly food expenditure and food own consumption as a share of total household expenditure.

Mean monthly share on health is total health expenditure (consultation, medical procedure, among other) as a share of total household expenditure. Health expenditure excludes hospitalization.

| Box 12 | Conflict, Fragility and Democracy |

Countries that have experienced conflict or have weak institutions face unique challenges to development. Conflicts often result in tremendous loss of life, destroyed infrastructure, and losses in human capital due to interrupted education and displacement that can slow or reverse the progress of developing countries. Such setbacks may increase the likelihood of conflict relapse, resulting in a "conflict trap" wherein violence begets poverty and visa versa, perpetuating a cycle of conflict. Likewise, the effects of conflict can weaken or destroy institutions and contribute to what could be called a "fragility trap." While it is difficult to separate out the causes of conflict and fragility as they reflect systemic collapses of governments and social order, analysis demonstrates that these afflictions are related. It is also possible that one way out of these traps may be through representative government reflected by democracy.

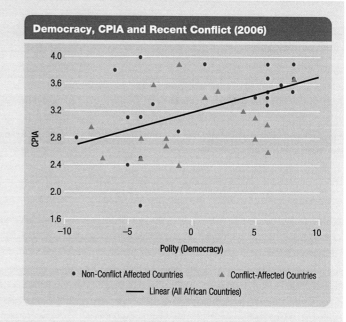

Democracy, CPIA and Recent Conflict (2006)

Conflict While definitions of conflict may vary, measures of conflict usually involve the number of casualties or battle deaths resulting from violence. The common academic definition of a major conflict is violence between at least two organized groups that results in more than 1000 battle deaths in a calendar year, with more than 5% of the battle deaths from each side. Minor conflict is defined as violence with more than 25 battle deaths per annum. Persistent minor conflict is violence with more than 25 battle deaths per annum and more than 1000 battle deaths over the length of the conflict. Generally, countries are defined as "conflict-affected" if they have had a major or persistent minor conflict in the last ten years.

Fragility The term "fragile state" is intended to capture both the instability and the delicate nature of the limited capacity, unstable governance, and fledgling institutions often found in these environments. Measures of fragility reflect the quality of institutions in these states; therefore the World Bank defines low-income countries as "fragile" if they have a Country Policy and Institutional Assessment (CPIA) score of 3.2 or below. Although a threshold is used to define fragility, it should be noted that the CPIA is an index, an average of twenty different subjective measures and therefore an imperfect measure of state capacity. Thus the term "fragile" is intended only as a guideline for identifying those countries that may have special needs due to particularly low institutional capacity and a low IDA allocation out of the entire spectrum of developing countries that are the Bank's clients.

Democracy Researchers of political systems use many sources to measure the level and quality of democratic institutions. The Polity Index measures the constraints on the executive branch of government and the quality of competition for elected positions yielding a score on a scale of -10 to 10. A score of –10 on the Polity Index suggests a very autocratic state and a score of 10 on the Polity index reflects a very democratic state. Typically, countries with a Polity score over 3 are considered "democratic" while those with a polity score under -3 are considered "autocratic."

The relationship between institutional capacity (measured by CPIA) and democracy is strong. Countries with highly representative and freely and fairly elected governments reflected by high Polity scores often have better quality institutions and improved capacity for service delivery reflected by higher CPIA scores. This relationship is demonstrated by the trendline in the figure below for African states. Additionally, the figure demonstrates the interrelationship between conflict and fragility traps that can contribute to persistent poverty. Of the 22 low-income African states with a CPIA score 3.2 or below in 2006, 14 (64%) were conflict-affected.[8] Additionally, of these same 22 countries, only seven (32%) had democratized (had a Polity Score>3). All six low-income countries with low CPIA and Polity greater than 3: (Burundi, DRC, Guinea-Bissau, Liberia (not shown in the figure), Sierra Leone and Nigeria) were conflict-affected in the last decade.

Source: World Bank and Polity IV Project Political Regime.

Mean monthly share on education is total education expenditure (tuition, transport, and the like) as a share of total household expenditure

Primary school within 30 minutes is the share of households that live within 30 minutes of a primary school.

Net primary enrollment rate is the ratio of children of a country's official primary school age who are enrolled in primary school to

[7] Four countries are not shown in the figure because they are missing CPIA or Polity data or both (Somalia, Cote d'Ivoire, Liberia, São Tomé and Principe).

the total population of the corresponding official primary school age. Primary education provides children with basic reading, writing, and mathematics skills along with an elementary understanding of such subjects as history, geography, natural science, social science, art, and music.

Net secondary enrollment rate is the ratio of children of a country's official secondary school age who are enrolled in secondary school to the total population of the corresponding official secondary school age. Secondary education completes the provision of basic education that began at the primary level and aims to lay the foundations for lifelong learning and human development by offering more subject- or skill-oriented instruction using more specialized teachers.

Tertiary enrolment rate is the number of students currently in tertiary education per 10,000 people. Tertiary education, whether or not to an advanced research qualification, normally requires, as a minimum condition of admission, the successful completion of education at the secondary level.

Adult literacy rate is the percentage of adults ages 15 and older who can both read and write a simple sentence in any language.

Youth literacy rate is the percentage of youth ages 15–24 who can both read and write a simple sentence in any language.

Health center less than 1 hour away is the percentage of the population living less than 1 hour away from a health center.

Health center less than 5 km away is the percentage of the population living less than 5 kilometers away from a health center

Morbidity is the percentage of the population who were sick or injured within a given number of weeks before the survey.

Health care provider consulted when sick is the percentage of sick people who took any remedial action when sick.

Type of health care provider consulted is the type of facility visited by a sick household member. *Public* includes fully government-owned as well as semi-public health facilities.

Private, modern medicine, is facilities set up with profit as their main focus and includes private doctors. *Private, traditional healers* refer to health care providers whose knowledge, skills, and practices are based on the experiences indigenous to different cultures and whose services are directed toward the maintenance of health, as well as the prevention, diagnosis, and improvement of physical and mental illness.

Missionary is one managed and supported by a religious organization. A *Non-Governmental Organization (NGO)* includes a wide range of local organizations in countries that are recipients of local and foreign assistance. It is a voluntary non-profit grouping of individuals with a purpose of enhancing the legitimate economic, social and/or cultural development organization.

Other is other types of health providers that cannot be classified by the categories described above.

Birth assisted by trained staff are the percentage of deliveries attended by personnel trained to give the necessary supervision, care, and advice to women during pregnancy, labor, and the postpartum period; to conduct deliveries on their own; and to care for newborns.

Immunization coverage, 1-year-olds, is the percentage of children ages 12–23 months at the time of survey who received one dose of Bacille Calmette Guerin vaccine, three doses of polio vaccine, three doses of diphtheria, pertussis, and tetanus vaccine, and one does of measles vaccine.

Measles immunization coverage, 1-year-olds, is the percentage of children ages 12–23 months at the time of survey who received a dose of measles vaccine. A child is considered adequately immunized against measles after receiving one dose of vaccine.

Stunting is the percentage of children under age 5 whose height for age is more than two standard deviations below the median for the international reference population ages 6–59 months. The reference population, adopted by the World Health Organization in 1983, is based on children from the United States, who are assumed to be well nourished.

Wasting is the percentage of children under age 5 whose weight for height is more than two standard deviations below the median for the international reference population ages 6–59 months. The reference population, adopted by the World Health Organization in 1983, is based on children from the United States, who are assumed to be well nourished.

Underweight is the percentage of children under age 5 whose weight for age is more than two standard deviations below the median for the international reference population ages 6–59 months. The reference population, adopted by the World Health Organization in 1983, is based on children from the United States, who are assumed to be well nourished.

Access to sanitation facilities is the percentage of the population with at least adequate access to excreta disposal facilities that can effectively prevent human, animal, and insect contact with excreta. Improved facilities range from simple but protected pit latrines to flush toilets with a sewerage connection. The excreta disposal system is considered adequate if it is private or shared (but not public) and if it hygienically separates human excreta from human contact. To be effective, facilities must be correctly constructed and properly maintained.

Water source less than 5 km away is the percentage of the population living less than 5 kilometers away from a water source.

Market less than 5 km away is the percentage of the population living less than 5 kilometers away from a market.

Access to improved water source refers to the percentage of the population with reasonable access to an adequate amount of water from an improved source, such as a household connection, public standpipe, borehole, protected well or spring, or rainwater collection. Unimproved sources include vendors, tanker trucks, and unprotected wells and springs. *Own tap* is a household water connection. *Other piped* is a public water connection. *Well, protected,* is a ground water source.

Traditional fuel use is the percentage of the population using traditional fuels such as firewood and charcoal as the main source of cooking fuel.

TABLE 14.1. BURKINA FASO HOUSEHOLD SURVEY, 2003

Household is the basic socioeconomic unit in which the different members—related or living in the same house or property—put together their resources and jointly meet their basic needs, including food, under the authority of one person who is recognized as the head.

Source: Burkina Faso's Institut National de la Statistique et de la Démographie carried out the Enquête Prioritaire II sur les Conditions de Vie des Ménages au Burkina. Data were collected in 2003. The project was funded by the government of Burkina Faso, the World Bank, the African Development Bank, and the United Nations through the United Nations Development Program. Sample size selected about 8,500 households.

TABLE 14.2. CAMEROON HOUSEHOLD SURVEY, 2001

Household is people who live under the same roof, take their meals together or in little groups, and put some or all of their incomes together for the group's spending purposes, at the head of household's discretion.

Source: Cameroon's Bureau Central des Recensements et des Enquêtes of the Direction de la Statistique et de la Comptabilité carried out the Enquête Camerounaise auprès des Ménages in 2001. Data collection between October 2001 and December 2001. Sample size selected about 12,000 households.

TABLE 14.3. ETHIOPIA HOUSEHOLD SURVEY, 1999/00

Household is a person or a group of people who live under the same roof, share the same meals, and recognize one person as the head.

Source: The 1999/2000 Household Income, Consumption, and Expenditure Survey was carried out by the Central Statistical Office. The data collection process was carried out from June 1999 to February 2000. Sample size selected was about 26,000 for the Income and Expenditure survey.

TABLE 14.4. LIBERIA HOUSEHOLD SURVEY, 2007

Household is a person living alone or a group of people, either related or unrelated, who live together as a single unit in the sense that they have common housekeeping arrangements (that is, share or are supported by a common budget). Someone who did not live with the household during the survey period was not counted as a current member of the household.

Source: Liberia Core Welfare Indicators Questionnaire (CWIQ) Survey. Sample size selected about 3,600 households.

TABLE 14.5. MALAWI HOUSEHOLD SURVEY, 2003/04

Household is a person living alone or a group of people, either related or unrelated, who live together as a single unit in the sense that they have common housekeeping arrangements (that is, share or are supported by a common budget). Someone who did not live with the household during the survey period was not counted as a current member of the household.

Literacy measures the ability to read and write a simple sentence for those who had not attended school in the past two months and was defined based on education attainment for those who had attended school in the past two months.

Source: The Malawi National Statistics Office carried out the Integrated Household Survey in 2004/5. Sample size selected about 11,280 households.

TABLE 14.6. NIGER HOUSEHOLD SURVEY, 2005

Household is the set of people who partly or totally shared their expenditures, had not been absent for more than 6 of the 12 months preceding the survey, and were not domestic help. In the case of polygamous households, each wife and her children were considered to be a separate household.

Literacy measures the number of people with ability to read and write in Portuguese.

Source: Direction de la Statistique et des comptes nationaux carried out the Enquete Nationale sur les Conditions de vie des Menages from April 14 to July 11, 2005. Sample size selected about 6,690 households.

TABLE 14.7. NIGERIA HOUSEHOLD SURVEY, 2003/4

Household is a group of persons who normally cook, eat, and live together. Number of months sharing in these activities was another criterion used to qualify as a household member (minimum of three months). However, all heads of households irrespec-

tive of number of months living elsewhere were included as household members. These people may or may not be related by blood, but make common provision for food or other essentials for living, and they have one person whom they all regard as the head of the household.

Literacy measures the number of people with the ability to read and write either in English or any of the local languages.

Source: The Federal Office of Statistics, Abuja, of Nigeria carried out the Nigeria Living Standards Survey, an integrated survey. Data were collected between September 2003 and August 2004. Sample size selected was about 22,000 households.

TABLE 14.8. SÃO TOMÉ AND PRINCIPE HOUSEHOLD SURVEY, 2000/01

Household is the set of people, related or not, who live together under the same roof, put their resources together, and address as a unit their primary needs, under the authority of one person whom they recognize as the head of the household.

Literacy measures the number of people with the ability to read and write a simple sentence.

Source: The Instituto Nacional de Estatistica of the Ministério de Planomento, Finanças e Cooperaçao carried out the Enquête sur les Conditions de Vie des Ménages in 2000. The project was financed by the government of São Tomé and Principe with assistance from the African Development Bank and the United Nations Development Programme. Technical assistance was provided by the International Labour Organization. Data collected between November 2000 and February 2001 and sample size selected about 5,200 households.

TABLE 14.9. SIERRA LEONE HOUSEHOLD SURVEY, 2002/03

Household is a group of people who normally cook, eat, and live together. Number of months sharing in these activities was another criterion used to qualify as a household member (minimum three months). However, all heads of households irrespective of number of months living elsewhere were included as household members. These people may or may not be related by blood, but make common provision for food or other essentials for living, and they have one person whom they all regarded as the head of the household.

Literacy measures the number of people with the ability to read and write a simple sentence in either English or the local languages.

Source: The Sierra Leone Central Statistical Office carried out the Living Conditions Monitoring Survey. Data were collected between November 2002 and January 2003. Sample size selected was about 3,720 households.

Table 14.10. Tanzania Household Survey, 2000/01

Household is a group of people who normally cook, eat, and live together. Number of months sharing in these activities was another criterion used to qualify as a household member (minimum three months). However, all heads of households irrespective of number of months living elsewhere were included as household members. These people may or may not be related by blood, but make common provision for food or other essentials for living, and they have one person whom they all regarded as the head of the household.

Source: Tanzania Bureau of Statistics. The Tanzanian Household Budget Survey (HBS), conducted in 2000/01 by the National Bureau of Statistics (NBS), is the largest-ever household budget survey in Tanzania. Data collection between May 2000 and June 2001. Sample size selected covered 22,178 households.

Table 14.11. Uganda Household Survey, 2005/06

Household is individuals who normally eat and live together.

Literacy measures the number of people who responded that they could both read and write. The level of education was also used to determine literacy.

Source: The Uganda Bureau of Statistics carried out the National Household Survey. Data collection occurred between May 2005 and April 2006. Sample size selected covered about 7,400 households.

Technical notes references

AbouZahr, Carla and Tessa Wardlaw (2003), "Maternal Mortality in 2000. Estimates Developed by WHO, UNICEF, and UN-FPA" World Health Organization, Geneva.

Arbache, Jorge Saba and John Page (2007), "Patterns of Long Term Growth in Sub-Saharan Africa". Policy Research Working Paper No. 4398, The World Bank , Washington D.C.

Central Statistical Agency, Government of Ethiopia

Chen, Shaohua, and Martin Ravallion (2008), "The Developing World Is Poorer Than We Thought, But no Less Successful in The Fight Against Poverty". Policy Research Working Paper No. 4703, The World Bank, Washington D.C.

ILO (International Labor Organization) Various years. *Key Indicators of the Labor Market*. Geneva.

IPCC (Intergovernmental Panel on Climate Change) (2001a): Climate Change 2001: The Scientific Basis. Contribution of Working Group I to the Third Assessment Report of the Intergovernmental Panel on Climate Change, J.T. Houghton, Y. Ding, D.J. Griggs, M. Noguer, P.J. van der Linden, X. Dai, K. Maskell and C.A. Johnson, Eds., Cambridge University Press, Cambridge.

IPCC (Intergovernmental Panel on Climate Change) (2001b): Climate Change 2001: Impacts, Adaptation, and Vulnerability. Contribution of Working Group II to the Third Assessment Report of the Intergovernmental Panel on Climate Change, J.J. McCarthy, O.F. Canziani, N.A. Leary, D.J. Dokken and K.S. White, Eds., Cambridge University Press, Cambridge.

IPCC (Intergovernmental Panel on Climate Change) (2001c): Climate Change 2001: Mitigation. Contribution of Working Group III to the Third Assessment Report of the Intergovernmental Panel on Climate Change, B. Metz, O. Davidson, R. Swart and J. Pan, Eds., Cambridge University Press, Cambridge.

IPCC (Intergovernmental Panel on Climate Change) (2007a): Climate Change 2007: The Physical Science Basis. Contribution of Working Group I to the Fourth Assessment Report of the Intergovernmental Panel on Climate Change, S. Solomon, D. Qin, M. Manning, Z. Chen, M. Marquis, K. B. Averyt, M. Tignor and H. L. Miller, Eds., Cambridge University Press, Cambridge.

IPCC (Intergovernmental Panel on Climate Change) (2007b): Climate Change 2007: Impacts, Adaptation and Vulnerability. Contribution of Working Group II to the Fourth Assessment Report of the Intergovernmental Panel on Climate Change, M.L. Parry, O.F. Canziani, J.P. Palutikof, P.J. van der Linden and C.E. Hanson, Eds., Cambridge University Press, Cambridge.

IPCC (Intergovernmental Panel on Climate Change) (2007c): Climate Change 2007: Mitigation. Contribution of Working Group III to the Fourth Assessment Report of the Intergovernmental Panel on Climate Change, B. Metz, O. Davidson, P.Bosch, R. Dave and L. Meyer, Eds., Cambridge University Press, Cambridge.

IPCC (Intergovernmental Panel on Climate Change) (2007d): Climate Change 2007: Synthesis Report. Contribution of Working Groups I, II and III to the Fourth Assessment Report of the Intergovernmental Panel on Climate Change, Core Writing Team, R.K Pachauri and A. Reisinger, Eds., IPCC, Geneva.

U.S. Census Bureau. HIV/AIDS surveillance data base. September, 2004: http://www.census.gov/ipc/www/hivaidsd.html (accessed March 23, 2006).

World Bank. 2008a. *Global Purchasing Power Parities and Real Expenditures: 2005 International Comparison Program*. Washington D.C.

World Bank 2008b. IDA 15 Background Paper. *Toward a Strategic Framework on Climate Change and Development for the World Bank Group*. Washington D.C.

World Bank. 2000. *Trade Blocs*. New York: Oxford University Press.

World Bank. Various years. "World Development Indicators". Washington, D.C.

Wodon, Q. (2008), Using Data to Inform Policy: Impact of the Food Price Crisis in Africa and Policy Responses, Development Dialogue on Values and Ethics Note, World Bank, Washington, DC.

Wodon, Q., P. Backiny-Yetna and C. Tsimpo (2008), The Role of Faith-Based Organizations in Service Delivery for Education and Health: Estimates from Household Surveys in West and Central Africa, Development Dialogue on Values and Ethics Note, World Bank, Washington, DC.

Zafar, Ali (2005) "The Impact of the Strong Euro on the Real Effective Exchange Rates of the Two Francophone African Zones". World Bank Policy Research Working Paper Series No.3751.

User's Guide

Africa Development Indicators 2008/09 CD-ROM

Introduction

This CD-ROM is part of the Africa Development Indicators suite of products. It was produced by the Office of the Chief Economist for the Africa Region and the Operational Quality and Knowledge Services Group in collaboration with the Development Data Group of the Development Economics Vice Presidency. It uses the latest version of the World Bank's *STARS* data retrieval system, Win*STARS version 5.0.

The CD-ROM contains about 1,400 macroeconomic, sectoral, and social indicators, covering 53 African countries. Time series include data from 1965 to 2006. A few macro indicators have provisional data for 2007 while others indicators have data for 2007-2008. Win*STARS 5.0 features mapping and charting and several data export formats (Access™, ASCII, dBASE™, Excel™, and SAS™). We invite you to explore it.

A note about the data

Users should note that the data for the Africa Development Indicators suite of products are drawn from the same database. The general cutoff date for data is September 2008.

Help

This guide explains how to use the main functions of the CD-ROM. For details about additional features, click *Help* on the menu bar or the *Help* icon; or call one of the hotline numbers listed in the *Help* menu and on the copyright page of this booklet.

Installation

As is usual for Windows™ products, you should make sure that other applications are closed while you install the CD-ROM. *To install the single-user version:* Insert the CD-ROM into your CD drive.

2. Click on *Start* and select *Run.* Type D:\SETUP.EXE (where D: is your CD-ROM drive letter), click *OK* and follow the instructions. For Windows Vista™, click the Computer icon on your desktop, navigate to your CD-ROM drive, and launch the Setup application.

3. Win*STARS 5.0 requires Microsoft Internet Explorer™ 4.0 or higher. If you do not have Internet Explorer, it may be downloaded at no charge from www.microsoft.com. It does not need to be your default browser. If you do not wish to use Internet Explorer, you have the option to install Win*STARS 4.2.

4. You can delete this program at any time by clicking on *Start, Settings, Control Panel, Add/Remove Programs.* To reinstall it, reboot your computer first.

Operation

To start the CD-ROM, go to the *WB Development Data* program group and click on the *Africa Development Indicators 2008/09* icon.

Note that standard Windows™ controls are used for most functions. For detailed instructions, refer to the on-screen *Help* menu or tool tips (on-screen explanations of buttons that are displayed when the cursor rolls over them).

Features and instructions

Win*STARS has four main functions— *Home, Query, Result,* and *Map.* Move among them at any time by clicking on the respective tabs.

Home

On the *Home* screen you can access each element of the Africa Development Indicators 2008/09 CD-ROM. Use the browser controls to link to the Africa Development Indicators tables, *The Little Data Book on Africa 2008/09,* time series database, maps, and other related information.

Query

1. Click on the *Query* button to start your time series selection.
2. Click on each of the *Country, Series,* and *Periods* buttons and make your selections on each screen. There are many ways to make a selection—see below, or use the *Help* menu.
3. Highlight the items you want.
4. Click on the *Select* button to move them into the *Selected* box.
5. Deselect items at any time by highlighting them and clicking on the *Remove* icon.
6. When selection is complete, click on *OK* to return to the main *Query* screen.
7. If you want to, you can display information on data availability by clicking on the *Availability* icon. You can choose to count time series or total observations.
8. Click on *View Data* to see the data on the *Result* screen.

Making selections. Countries: You can select countries from an alphabetical list, by *Classification* (region, income group, or lending category), by *Criteria* (up to two can be specified), or by *Group* (aggregates have been calculated only when there were adequate data). *Series:* You can choose from an alphabetical list or by *Category.* When selecting series by category, the subcategory buttons change with each category. *Periods:* Select time periods from the *Periods* list box.

Creating your own country or indicator list. You can create your own group of countries, series, or periods by saving your query on the appropriate screen. You can also save all elements of the query on the *Query* screen. You can reload a saved query in a future session.

To save a query:
1. Highlight items on any of the *Countries, Series,* or *Periods* (or any two or all three) selection screens and click on *Select* to place them in the *Selected* box.
2. Click on the *Save Query* icon and follow the naming prompts.

To load a query:
1. Go to the selection screen in which your query is saved. For example, if you have saved a set of countries, go to the *Countries* selection screen.
2. Click on the *Load Query* icon, select the query you want, and click on *OK.*

To modify a saved query:
1. Load the query.
2. In the *Selected* box, highlight the items to be removed and click on the *Remove* icon.
3. Add new items if necessary.
4. Resave the query.

Result

On the *Result* screen, data are presented in a three-dimensional spreadsheet and, initially, in scientific notation. Data for the third dimension are presented on separate screens. You can change the selection displayed by clicking on the third dimension scroll box. You can also change the scale and the number of digits after the decimal. If the column is too narrow to present all the digits, they will appear as a series of ######. Double click on the column's guideline to widen it, or choose a larger scale (millions, for example). To scale series individually, click *Options* and check *Enable Series-Level Scaling.* Click the far right scroll box to view the percentage change over each selected period or to index the data.

Changing the orientation. You can view the result in six different orientations (countries down/periods across, series down/countries across, etc.). To change the orientation, click on the *Orientation* scroll box.

Charting and mapping data. On the *Result* screen, you can chart or map the data displayed. Highlight a set of cells for charting or a particular cell for mapping. Click on the *Chart* or *Map* icon on the toolbar accordingly. The charting function has many features. After you have displayed a chart, right click on the chart to open the *Chart Wizard* for more options. Mapping is described on page 8. From this screen you can choose to map all countries or only your selected countries.

Cutting, pasting, printing, and saving. You can cut, paste, and print the result, or you can save the spreadsheet in another format. Click on the appropriate icon on the toolbar and follow the prompts. Click on Help for more details.

Map

On the *Map* screen, you can select a country and view a set of tables describing it, or you can map a series for all countries. In the upper left corner of the screen, the country name will appear as the cursor rolls slowly over the map. To zoom in for a closer look at the map, click on the *Zoom* icon.

Selecting a country or viewing country tables. To highlight a country and view any of its tables, click on the country on the map or select it in the *Locate a Country* scroll box in the upper right corner.

Mapping a series. On the *Map* screen, click on the *Series* icon. A list of key indicators will be displayed. (To show all available indicators, click on the box by *Show default series* to remove the *X*.) Highlight a series, select a period from the *Available Periods* list box (the default is the latest available) and click on *Paint Map*. The map will be colored according to the legend settings, any of which you can change. Note that as the cursor moves across the map, the series value is now also displayed in the upper left corner.

Changing the map legend and colors. The default interval range is an equal number of countries. To set an equal interval range or to map multiple periods, click on the *Recalculate* icon. Set your own intervals by editing the legend. To change map colors, double click on the legend color boxes. Press the *Remap* icon to see your changes.

Printing and saving. Click on the appropriate icon to print the map or save it as a bitmap or metafile.

License agreement

You must read and agree to the terms of this License Agreement prior to using this CDROM product. Use of the software and data contained on the CD-ROM is governed by the terms of this License Agreement. If you do not agree with these terms, you may return the product unused to the World Bank for a full refund of the purchase price.

1. **LICENSE.** In consideration of your payment of the required license fee, the WORLD BANK (the "Bank") hereby grants you a nonexclusive license to use the enclosed data and Win*STARS retrieval program (collectively, the "Program") subject to the terms and conditions set forth in this license agreement.

2. **OWNERSHIP.** As a licensee you own the physical media on which the Program is originally or subsequently recorded. The Bank, however, retains the title and ownership of the program recorded on the original CD-ROMs and all subsequent copies of the Program. This license is not considered to be a sale of the Program or any copy thereof.

3. **COPY RESTRICTIONS.** The Program and accompanying written materials are copyrighted. You may make one copy of the Program solely for backup purposes. Unauthorized copying of the Program or of the written materials is expressly forbidden.

4. **USE.** You may not modify, adapt, translate, reverse-engineer, decompile, or disassemble the Program. You may not modify, adapt, translate, or create derivative works based on any written materials without the prior written consent of the Bank. If you have purchased the single-user version of this product, you may use the Program only on a single laptop/desktop computer. You may not distribute copies of the Program or accompanying written materials to others. You may not use the Program on any network, including an Intranet or the Internet, without obtaining prior written permission from the Bank. If you have purchased the multiple-user version of this product, your license is valid only up to 15 users. Should you need to add additional users, please send a request, indicating the number of users you would like to add, to: World Bank Publications, Rights and Permission, 1818 H Street, N.W., Washington, D.C. 20433, fax: 202-522-2422, email: pubrights@worldbank.org.

5. **TRANSFER RESTRICTIONS.** This Program is licensed only to you, the licensee, and may not be transferred to anyone without prior written consent of the Bank.

6. **LIMITED WARRANTY AND LIMITATIONS OF REMEDIES.** The Bank warrants that under normal use the CDROMs on which the Program is furnished are free from defects in materials and workmanship for a period of ninety (90) days from delivery to you, as evidenced by a copy of your receipt. The Bank's entire liability and your exclusive remedy shall be the replacement of any CD-ROMs that do not meet the Bank's limited warranty. Defective CD-ROMs should be returned within the warranty period, with a copy of your receipt, to the address specified in section 9 below. EXCEPT AS SPECIFIED ABOVE, THE PRODUCT IS PROVIDED "AS IS" WITHOUT WARRANTY OF ANY KIND, EITHER EXPRESSED OR IMPLIED, INCLUDING, BUT NOT LIMITED TO, THE IMPLIED WARRANTIES OF MERCHANTABILITY AND FITNESS FOR A PARTICULAR PURPOSE. THE BANK DOES NOT WARRANT THAT THE FUNCTIONS CONTAINED IN THE PROGRAM WILL MEET YOUR REQUIREMENTS OR THAT THE OPERATION OF THE PROGRAM WILL BE UNINTERRUPTED OR ERROR-FREE. IN NO EVENT WILL THE BANK BE LIABLE TO YOU FOR ANY DAMAGES ARISING OUT OF THE USE OF OR THE INABILITY TO USE THE PROGRAM. THE ABOVE WARRANTY GIVES YOU SPECIFIC LEGAL RIGHTS IN THE UNITED STATES THAT MAY VARY FROM STATE TO STATE. BECAUSE SOME STATES DO NOT ALLOW THE EXCLUSION OF IMPLIED WARRANTIES OR LIMITATION OF EXCLUSION OF LIABILITY FOR INCIDENTAL OR CONSEQUENTIAL DAMAGES, PARTS OF THE ABOVE LIMITATIONS AND EXCLUSIONS MAY NOT APPLY TO YOU.

7. **TERMINATION.** This license is effective from the date you open the package until the license is terminated. You may terminate it by destroying the Program and its documentation and any backup copy thereof or by returning these materials to the Bank. If any of the terms or conditions of this license are broken, the Bank may terminate the license and demand that you return the Program.

8. **GOVERNING LAW.** This license shall be governed by the laws of the District of Columbia, without reference to conflicts of law thereof.

9. **GENERAL.** If you have any questions concerning this product, you may contact the Bank by writing to World Bank Publications, CD-ROM Inquiries, The World Bank, 1818 H Street, N.W., Washington, D.C. 20433, email: data@worldbank.org. All queries on rights and licenses should be addressed to World Bank Publications, Rights and Permission, 1818 H Street, N.W., Washington, D.C. 20433, fax: 202-522-2422, email: pubrights@worldbank.org.